Lion *of the* Valley

Lion *of the* Valley

St. Louis, Missouri, 1764–1980

Third Edition

James Neal Primm

Missouri Historical Society Press
Saint Louis

Distributed by University of Missouri Press

Published in the United States of America by the
Missouri Historical Society Press
P.O. Box 11940, St. Louis, Missouri 63112-0040
13 12 11 10   2 3 4 5

Third Edition, 2010 reprint

Library of Congress Cataloging-in-Publication Data

Primm, James Neal, 1918–
    Lion of the valley : St. Louis, Missouri, 1764–1980 / James Neal Primm. –
3rd ed.
        p.   cm.
    Includes bibliographical references (p.   ) and index.
    ISBN 1-883982-24-3 (cloth : alk. paper). – ISBN 1-883982-25-1 (pbk. :
alk. paper)
    1. Saint Louis (Mo.) – History.   I. Title
F474.S257P75   1998
977.8'66 – dc21   98-20315
                                                                                       CIP

Distributed by University of Missouri Press

Design by Robyn Morgan
Index by Sara Davis
Printed and bound in the United States by Sheridan Books

∞ The paper used in this publication meets the minimum requirements of the ANSI/NISO,
Z39.48-1992 (R 1997) (Permanence of Paper).

Cover illustration:
View of Front Street, by J. C. Wild, 1840. MHS-PP.

To Christopher, Tony, and Jackie

Contents

Foreword, by Robert R. Archibald. ix
Preface xi
Acknowledgments xiii

Prologue 1
1.   Borderland Capital 7
2.   Colony in Transition. 37
3.   The Frontier Town 72
4.   The Gateway City. 110
5.   Growing Pains 149
6.   Rails and Mills 188
7.   For the Union 227
8.   The Fourth City? 272
9.   Meet Me in St. Louis 327
10. The Decline of the Inner City. 396
11. The New Spirit of St. Louis 452
12. Urban Renaissance 497

List of Abbreviations. 553
Notes on Sources 555
Index 575

Foreword

When James Neal Primm finished *Lion of the Valley* in 1981, he had written the first comprehensive history of our city and region to be published in nearly a century. That fact alone would have gained the book a place of note on numerous bookshelves, but the author was not only a "local historian," but also a historian with a broad and deep knowledge and perspective, an indefatigable and exacting researcher, and a teacher of some renown at the University of Missouri–St. Louis.

In 1990, Primm updated his book with a chapter on urban renaissance. By the time this second edition had nearly sold out, the Missouri History Museum had established its publishing program, and Primm, who had been a member of our Board of Trustees for several years, offered the remaining books and future publishing rights to our institution. With gratitude and pride, we accepted this generous gift.

In and out of the classroom, Primm was a storyteller. His stories of St. Louis were always entertaining and impressive, but they have become essential to our well-being. A healthy and enduring community will respect its past and encourage the examination of both the burdens and the legacies of its history. Our stories help define and explain relationships with places, landscapes, events, and one another, because a shared narrative of a mutual past imparts a sense of continuity and provides context and perspective.

On several mornings in the spring of 2009, James Neal Primm made his way to my office at the Missouri History Museum. Even at ninety-one years of age, when he began to speak his voice was strong and assured, just as it had been in the classrooms and at the podiums he had frequented for so many decades. Neal died that summer. I was immensely saddened but so grateful for those conversations and for the legacy his *Lion* had left us.

Read and absorb and savor *Lion of the Valley*, for a consciousness of the past is an excellent antidote for a stultifying preoccupation with the present and an essential ingredient for the choices and decisions that will very much influence our future.

ROBERT R. ARCHIBALD
PRESIDENT, MISSOURI HISTORY MUSEUM
2010

Preface

I feel privileged that the Missouri Historical Society Press is publishing this edition of *Lion of the Valley*. The text has not been extended, but the press has revised and improved the illustrations.

There are several reasons why there is no Chapter 13, covering the 1990s. The best reason is that current events and prophecy are dangerous areas for historians. This point, which I was reminded of long ago, was brought home to me again as I revisited the latter pages of Chapter 12. Because the 1980s were promising and exciting, with an aggressive and charismatic mayor and a flurry of downtown projects completed or under way, I called the chapter the "Urban Renaissance."

From the present perspective, that title seems extravagant. Yet, with the exception of the St. Louis Centre, the downtown initiatives of the 1980s have met or exceeded expectations. The major commercial buildings and the Union Station are assets to the community, and the MetroLink system is a winner. The downtown football stadium has been controversial from its beginning, but it is there and professional teams play to capacity crowds. The humiliations involved in the acquisition of the team aside, the downtown powers were determined to have a team at all costs, and they achieved their goal.

On the positive side during the decade, the voters have elected successive African American mayors, and the institutions of the Zoo-Museum District are thriving and expanding their physical spaces and their missions, with aggressive leadership and remarkable private as well as public support. The universities have also prospered, and Saint Louis University in particular appears to have been transformed.

On the negative side, the St. Louis public school system has failed many of its students, and people still leave the city by the thousands for the ever more distant suburbs. In 1990, the Federal Census reported that the population had passed four hundred thousand in the wrong direction, to levels of more than a century ago. Kansas City, which has partly contained its urban sprawl by expanding its boundaries, is now the largest city in Missouri—a deceptive statistic, to be sure.

Sadly, many of those who have left the city appear to despise it, even though they fill the seats for baseball, football, and hockey games and claim to be St. Louisans when they are away from home. Perhaps this love-hate relationship can be resolved into a fruitful partnership. Various groups and committees are working to that end, some of them inspired by the Peirce Report, the result of an investigation sponsored by the *Post-Dispatch* and published in 1997. In this construct, all elements of the metropolitan community must come together to diminish racism and particularism and bring people back to the city to live and to fill the downtown streets, which will be attractive, colorful, open, and friendly. If this happens, and one devoutly hopes that it will, things will be better than they were in 1904.

JAMES NEAL PRIMM, 1998

Acknowledgments

I am most indebted to Lyle Dorsett of the University of Denver, who first suggested that I include my projected history of St. Louis in the Western Urban America series and has given the manuscript keen critical analysis and its author unflagging moral support. A. Theodore Brown of the University of Wisconsin–Milwaukee has also read the manuscript. Glen Holt, my neighbor at Washington University, has lent me items from his personal collection, offered useful suggestions about the last two chapters, and above all, made contributions to St. Louis historiography that have enriched my perceptions of the city's past. I am also grateful for the pioneering work of John F. McDermott, Louis Houck, and the students of Ralph Bieber at Washington University.

James Laue, director of the University of Missouri–St. Louis's Center for Metropolitan Studies, has made substantial material and clerical support available to me, and I am proud to have written this book as a fellow of the center. The university granted me sabbatical leave in 1978–79, and History Department Chairman Louis Gerteis and Dean Robert Bader of the College of Arts and Sciences arranged my schedule in 1979–80 in a way which expedited the completion of the manuscript. My departmental colleagues have endured my tendency to tell them more than they want to know about St. Louis, and I am especially grateful to Howard S. Miller, Louis Gerteis, and Walter Ehrlich for their insights into special aspects of the city's history. Irene Cortinovis and Jean Tucker, both fellows of UMSL's Metropolitan Studies Center, have put me in their debt by sharing their knowledge of St. Louis's cultural history. Joy Whitener, dean of UMSL's Evening College, lent me valuable documents from the Louisiana Purchase Exposition, and I am indebted to the history department of the University of Missouri–Columbia and to Chairman Edward McGuire of the history department at Saint Louis University for the loan of theses and dissertations.

Staff members of the libraries at Washington University; the Missouri Historical Society, Frances Hurd Stadler and Judy Ciampoli in particular; the University of Missouri–St. Louis; and Saint Louis University have been unfailingly kind and helpful, as have their counterparts at the Mercantile Library, the St. Louis Public Library, the St. Louis County Library, and the Municipal Reference Library. Jewell Ballman of the Land Clearance for Redevelopment Authority and Wayne Weidemann of the Metropolitan Port

Authority were receptive and cooperative, as were the staffs of the St. Louis Zoo, the Art Museum, the Bi-State Development Agency, the Terminal Railroad Association, the St. Louis Housing Authority, the Jefferson National Expansion Memorial, Marie Portell of the Alfonso J. Cervantes Convention Center, the St. Louis Airport Authority, the MacArthur Bridge, a host of agencies and businesses, and Robert Broeg of the *St. Louis Post-Dispatch*.

For diligent and painstaking typing assistance (and words of encouragement), I am indebted to my daughter Jacqueline Termine, Richalyn Martin, and Patricia Minute. For their patience and understanding, I thank my wife Marian Primm, and Jerry Keenan of Pruett Publishers.

I am indebted to Dean E. Terrence Jones of the University of Missouri–St. Louis for valuable suggestions and corrections to the manuscript of Chapter 12, and to Jeanne Mongold, who compiled the index for Chapter 12 and integrated it into the existing index.

No one mentioned above is responsible for any errors of fact or interpretation in this book, which are my own responsibility. If there are no such errors, new ground has been broken.

Lion *of the* Valley

Prologue

Before the Americans came to the valley west of the confluence of the great rivers, the French and the Spanish were there, following the Siouan-speaking Missouris and Osages, who in turn had followed the disintegrated Mississippi culture. Thousands of years before the Mississippians, perhaps as early as 20,000 B.C., the first humans had drifted into the lower Missouri River valley. Of these earlier visitations, the most imposing remains encountered by those seventeenth-century Frenchmen who first sampled the humid air at the site of "the future great city of the world" were the enormous Mississippian temple and burial mounds which clustered in the area. Until they were flattened in the name of progress, more than two dozen of these monuments, dominated by one the Creoles called *La Grange de Terre* (the barn of earth), loomed over St. Louis's north side, giving the town its nineteenth-century nickname, "the Mound City." These mound builders, having developed intensive agriculture, art forms, and scientific techniques, were destroyed at their peak and their remnants scattered in the thirteenth and fourteenth centuries, probably by a long period of severe drought. It has been estimated that as many as forty thousand people lived an orderly, sophisticated urbanized existence in the area centering on Cahokia, just across the Mississippi from St. Louis.

Less than two centuries before St. Louis became the commercial metropolis of the lower Missouri basin, the Osages and Missouris and their Siouan kinfolk—the Kansas, the Otoes, the Iowas, and the Omahas—under pressures generated by the activities of the French in Canada, left their homes in the Great Lakes region to live in the valley of the Missouri. These tribes lived in villages and cultivated corn, squash, beans, and sometimes tobacco. They gathered nuts, berries, and acorns, and hunted bear, deer, and buffalo. Their clothing was made from the skins of these animals and was usually ornamented with quills (or beads after the traders came).

The Osages ranged in hunting and war from their principal village on the Missouri River tributary which bears their name east to the Mississippi and southwest to the Arkansas River valley. Their numbers, truculence, and prowess made them a force to be reckoned with by the agents of French and Spanish colonial policy. The

Missouri tribe, closely related in language and appearance to the
Osages and allied with them against the encroachment of the Sauks
and Foxes from the northeast, gave their name to the great river. The
French captain, Étienne de Bourgmont, who lived with one of a
succession of Indian wives at the Missouri village 240 miles up the
Missouri River for a year or more (1712–13), in his *Exacte
Description de la Louisiane,* described the Missouris as great hunters
and boatmen, who were "not very numerous they are of very good
blood and are more alert than any other tribe." They were somewhat
more dependent upon planting and gathering than the Osages, but war
and trade brought them frequently to the Mississippi and beyond. De
Bourgmont had first become acquainted with the Missouris when they
helped the French defend Detroit against the Foxes in 1712.

When the first Europeans arrived, both the Osages and Missouris
were thriving, but the latter, decimated by smallpox and the repeated
onslaughts of the Sauks and Foxes, were by the early nineteenth
century destroyed as a tribe, their straggling remnants living with the
Osages, Otoes, and Kansas. The powerful Osages, less exposed to the
Sauks and Foxes and early white soldiers, resisted the white man's
ways more doggedly, refusing to "exchange their pursuits" for the
white man's lest they become slaves as he was, as one of their chiefs
put it. They survived in strength in the lower Missouri basin well into
the nineteenth century and never lost their tribal identity.

Despite the sixteenth-century expeditions to the continental
interior by the Spanish explorers Francisco Coronado and Hernando
de Soto, the French were the first Europeans in the area that became
Missouri. Fur traders and missionaries from Quebec, where Samuel de
Champlain had planted the French flag in 1608, explored the Great
Lakes and upper Missouri country, reaching the Fox River
(Wisconsin) in 1634 and the south shore of Lake Superior in 1659. In
the later year Louis Jolliet proved it was possible with one minor
portage to travel by water from the St. Lawrence to Lake Michigan.
Excited by Indian accounts of a great river to the west, Jean Talon, the
French intendant at Quebec, ordered Jolliet to find out whether this
"Mesippi" river emptied into the Pacific—the coveted passage to
India, which fired imperial imaginations for centuries.

Accompanied by a Jesuit passenger, Father Jacques Marquette,
and a few *voyageurs* (boatmen), Jolliet reached the Mississippi in June
1673. In the only journal that survived the trip, Marquette reported
that on their voyage downriver the explorers had encountered
monstrous fish (catfish) that threatened to tear their canoes apart, and
that they had seen herds of buffalo and a gigantic painting of two
monsters (the Piasa bird) on the rock cliffs a few miles above the

Pekitanoui (muddy waters in Algonquian), the river of the "ou-missouries." The name Missouri, meaning "people of the wooden canoes," was applied by the Algonquian tribes east of the Mississippi to the magnificent boatmen who rode the churning waters of their river in hollowed-out logs. After failing to get their own people to call it the St. Philip, the French recognized common usage in naming the river after the tribe.

Of the meeting of the two great rivers Marquette wrote, "I never saw anything more terrific; a tangle of entire trees, of branches, of floating islands, issued from the mouth of the Pekitanoui with such impetuosity that one could not attempt to cross it without great danger. . . ." They did cross, however, and continued downstream to the mouth of the Arkansas, where Jolliet, certain that the Mississippi would not veer westward to the Pacific and fearing an encounter with the Spanish, decided to return to the Great Lakes. Nine years later Robert Cavelier, Sieur de LaSalle, led an expedition down the Illinois and Mississippi Rivers to the Gulf of Mexico, whereupon he claimed the entire Mississippi basin for France, naming it Louisiana for his king, Louis XIV.

Determined to make good their imperial claims and to profit from them, the French strung a chain of forts between their St. Lawrence bases and the Mississippi valley. After their powerful Iroquois enemies and trading rivals had destroyed a French trading village on the Illinois River, LaSalle, on his return trip from the gulf in 1682, built Fort St. Louis farther upstream at Starved Rock. Ten years later this post was moved to a site near Lake Peoria, and with the arrival of French settlers, it became the first permanent settlement in the Illinois country. War with the Iroquois disrupted organized trading in the West until a peace treaty was signed in 1700, although missionaries and *coureurs-de-bois* continued their activities.

In 1699 and 1700 French villages were founded at Cahokia and Kaskaskia on the east bank of the Mississippi. Also in 1700, the Kaskaskia Indians, who had moved to the west and south under pressure from the Iroquois, established themselves at the mouth of a small river within the present limits of St. Louis. The Jesuit Fathers Gabriel Marest and François Pinet, who accompanied them, established a mission at the site (*Le Riviére des Peres*—River of the Fathers). After some construction had been completed and a few Tamaroas and Frenchmen from Cahokia had joined them, the Kaskaskias, presumably having learned of the Iroquois treaty, moved farther downstream to the east bank (Kaskaskia). By 1703, the site was totally abandoned. Other Frenchmen, seeking gold, trade with the Spanish in New Mexico, or furs, worked their way up the Missouri and its tributaries, but coordinated efforts to develop Louisiana were abandoned for more than a decade after LaSalle's death in Texas in 1685.

In 1698–1700, under orders from Louis XIV to forestall English and Spanish efforts to enter the Mississippi, Pierre Le Moyne, Sieur d'Iberville, fortified the Gulf Coast at Biloxi, Mobile Bay, and the mouth of the Mississippi. Organized commercial activity began in 1712 when, in a classic example of Colbertism (mercantilism), the French Crown entered into a partnership with the wealthy merchant-banker Antoine Crozat, granting him a monopoly of the mines and trade of Louisiana for fifteen years. According to the charter, Louisiana included the valleys of the St. Louis (the Mississippi), the St. Philip (Missouri), and the Ouabache (lower Ohio and Wabash) Rivers and their tributaries. Politically, the province was to be dependent to Quebec, and Crozat was not to diminish Canadian profits. Governor Antoine de la Mothe Cadillac and the principal royal officers were to receive their salaries from Crozat, and they in turn were to support his enterprises. Precious stones, gold, and silver found were to be shared with the king. Crozat expected large profits from trade with the Spanish gulf ports and the interior of Mexico, but the inhospitable Spaniards turned Crozat's ships away and strengthened their barriers against internal penetration. Precious stones and minerals eluded him too, and in 1717, depleted in purse and defeated in spirit, Crozat surrendered his charter to the Crown.

Crozat's failure opened a golden door for John Law, a Scottish financier-promoter who convinced the French Crown that what Louisiana needed was a vast infusion of capital. Law's "Company of the West," a joint-stock enterprise, was granted a monopoly of Louisiana's external trade for twenty-five years, ownership of all mines in the area, other economic concessions, and virtually unchecked military and judicial authority. In its turn, the company was to build churches, supply clergymen, and settle six thousand whites and three thousand black slaves in the colony. In 1719, Law combined this company and several others to form the Royal Company of the Indies. Portraying the Mississippi valley as a vast treasure-house of precious metals and furs, Law sold stock to the *bourgeoisie,* the nobility, the Church, the peasants—to everyone who wanted to own part of Eldorado. In a frenzy of speculation, eager buyers drove the price of the company's shares to nearly seventy times their nominal value, far beyond any conceivable return. In 1720, the "Mississippi Bubble" burst, ruining tens of thousands of investors, and dampening Gallic enthusiasm for Louisiana, though the company of the Indies continued.

During its glory days, flush with funds, the Company of the Indies moved to harvest its assets in Louisiana. In 1718, New Orleans was founded, and in 1720, Fort de Chartres, the Illinois country (upper Louisiana) capital, was completed on the east bank of the Mississippi fifteen miles north of the French-Indian village of Kaskaskia. In 1723 Philippe François Renault began mining operations west of the Mississippi near the Meramec River. Rumors of silver and copper deposits in the area proved to be unfounded, but within two years Renault's French miners and black slaves were producing fifteen hundred pounds of lead a day. Renault's base remained at Fort de Chartres, even after settlers and traders from the east side began to cluster at Ste. Genevieve, directly across the Mississippi from Kaskaskia (about 1732). Ste. Genevieve, the first permanent settlement in Missouri, was a convenient shipping point for ore, but its first residents were primarily *habitants,* who farmed and worked the salt springs in the area.

These French outposts in the Illinois country quickly became western-oriented. Situated at the point of contact between the French thrusts from Canada and the Gulf of Mexico, traders followed the line of least resistance and greatest opportunity, the Missouri River highway to the western fur bonanza. Coureurs-de-bois roamed the lower Missouri basin before 1700, and reports of trading contacts with Indians several hundred miles up the Missouri reached French officials as early as 1702. In 1719, after war broke out between France and Spain, an agent of the Company of the Indies, Charles Claude Du Tisné, traveled and traded among the Osages and the Pawnees, seeking the friendship of those tribes which stood between upper Louisiana and New Mexico. His efforts to contact the Padoucas (Comanches), who stood at the gates of the Spanish empire, were blocked by his Indian hosts. Du Tisné verified rumors of Indian unrest caused by unauthorized traders—"thieves," as the colonial authorities called them—who were bribing the tribes to raid each other for horses and slaves, which the traders then sold in Illinois or to the English in Carolina for shipment to the West Indian sugar plantations.

Determined to control the renegade traders, pacify the Indians, and trade with New Mexico if possible or defend against the Spanish if necessary, company officials in Paris ordered Étienne de Bourgmont, an experienced frontiersman who had lived with the Missouris, to the Missouri as commandant with instructions to build a fort. De Bourgmont completed Fort Orleans on the north bank of the river near the principal village of the Missouris in 1723. During the next year the commandant, with a few soldiers and a large party of Missouris and Osages, took a mountain of trade goods to the Kansas,

Otoes, and other Siouan tribes near the great bend of the Missouri River (the present site of Kansas City). After winning their hearts with gifts and promises, de Bourgmont followed the Kansas River westward to a village of the Padoucas, who responded to his prodigality by allying themselves with the French and agreeing not to make war against France's other Indian allies. After this master stroke, de Bourgmont returned as a hero to Paris, bringing with him a delegation of Missouri and Osage chiefs. The Indians were lionized in Paris and were impressed by French power, but the advantages gained were soon lost, as the financial straits of the Company of the Indies forced a general retrenchment. Fort Orleans was abandoned before 1730, and in 1731 the company retroceded its Louisiana grant to the Crown.

For the next two decades, French efforts in the Illinois country were directed toward New Mexico. At first hoping that the Missouri River would be the golden highway to the Santa Fe market, traders learned that beyond its great bend, the river stretched relentlessly to the north and became reconciled to an overland route. In 1739, the long-sought goal was reached when the brothers Pierre and Paul Mallet arrived in Santa Fe with a stock of manufactured goods. They were greeted with tolling bells by the Spanish frontiersmen and became honored guests of the governor, but the imperial authorities in Mexico City rudely ordered them deported with a reminder that the empire was closed to foreign traders. It was a long way to Mexico City, however, and the New Mexicans assured the Mallets that anyone bringing them cloth and implements would always be welcome. Thereafter, several French traders traveled between the Mississippi valley and New Mexico, exchanging manufactured goods for gold, silver, and furs. With the completion of Fort Cavagnolle near the great bend of the Missouri in the mid-1740s, the French expanded their influence with the Plains Indians and strengthened the bond between New Mexico and the Illinois country.

This flow of wealth from the Southwest, though interrupted for several decades, eventually became an important factor in the growth of St. Louis. The French policy of accommodating to Indian ways and supplying them with brandy and weapons was far more effective among the Indians of the Missouri valley than the Spanish missions-and-villages approach. This advantage, which might have made New Mexico a French province, was quickly lost as events in Europe led France into a disastrous world war which cost the French nation its North American empire.

1.
Borderland Capital

On February 14, 1764, a working party of thirty employees of Maxent, Laclède and Company of New Orleans, headed by Auguste Chouteau, an extraordinary young man of fourteen years, stepped ashore from a *bateau* to the west bank of the Mississippi River, eighteen miles below its confluence with the Missouri and more than twelve hundred miles by water above New Orleans. On the next day they began to build St. Louis, according to the directions of Pierre de Laclède, who had selected the site for his village trading post three months earlier.

This step in the creation of a commercial village, which became a colonial capital, the center of mid-continental river traffic, the terminus of western trade, and one of the great cities of America, was

Founding of St. Louis, 1764. *Chromolithograph after E. J. Cameron, 1902. In this turn-of-the-century Sunday supplement insert published by the* St. Louis Globe-Democrat, *a young Auguste Chouteau directs clearing of the new settlement. MHS-PP.*

not merely one of fortune's whimsies but the result of a series of deliberate and rational decisions. At the end of France's disastrous Seven Years' War with England (the French and Indian War in the American colonies), both its treasury and its appetite for colonial investment were depleted. Wartime restraints on trade had ruined many New Orleans merchants, created shortages, and led to a raging inflation. In the summer of 1763, the new (and last) French governor of Louisiana, Jean Jacques D'Abbadie, granted trading monopolies in certain areas to several merchants, hoping to stimulate trade and restore prosperity.

One of the recipients of these exclusive privileges was Gilbert Antoine Maxent, one of New Orleans's leading merchants, who was awarded the trade with the Indian tribes on the Missouri and the west bank of the upper Mississippi for six years. Maxent then entered into partnership with Jean François Le Dée and Pierre de Laclède, the latter agreeing to establish and manage a trading post in the Illinois country (upper Louisiana). It became known in New Orleans just before Laclède headed upriver that France had relinquished Canada and the Illinois country east of the Mississippi to the English (Treaty of Paris, 1763). Thus, Laclède's post would not only be the spearhead of France's western trade but a defensive bastion against the English to the north and east. That Laclède understood the significance of his task and that "town-booming" boosterism had its eighteenth-century Gallic antecedents is clear. According to Auguste Chouteau, in his "Narrative of the Founding of St. Louis," Laclède told Captain Neyon de Villiers, the commandant of the Illinois country, and his officers at Fort de Chartres that the site he had chosen for his fur post "might become, hereafter, one of the finest cities" of the continent, so many advantages did it have "by its locality and central position."

Laclède had moved fast after the formation of the company. On August 10, 1763, or thereabouts, accompanied by his young clerk-assistant Chouteau and twenty or so boatmen, he started upriver from New Orleans with a large cargo of merchandise. On November 3, the expedition arrived in Ste. Genevieve, Laclède having expected to store his goods there for the winter. Since that village was too far from the mouth of the Missouri and insalubrious (vulnerable to flooding and disease), he never considered it as a possible location for his enterprise. There were no buildings in Ste. Genevieve large enough to hold Laclède's merchandise, but de Villiers furnished temporary storage space at Fort de Chartres.

In December Laclède and his assistant Chouteau scouted the west bank of the Mississippi from the mouth of the Missouri southward until Laclède found what he sought. A gently sloping plateau terminating in a rocky bluff safely above the river's flood presented an ideal site for his headquarters. A break in the bluff afforded easy access to the river; and there was plenty of timber for firewood and lumber, outcroppings of stone for building, flowing springs, good drainage, and no deep ravines to hinder the laying out of streets. After marking some trees at the site, the two men returned to Fort de Chartres, the younger to return in the spring to clear away the timber and begin construction.

Laclède spent the rest of the winter recruiting workers and buying tools and supplies in Kaskaskia, Cahokia, and the other Creole villages in Illinois. He was in a hurry, since he did not care to be on hand with his merchandise when the English came to take possession at Fort de Chartres. Having no doubts about his assistant's ability to supervise the initial construction of the fur post, Laclède was busy with planning and general company business when Chouteau and his mechanics (craftsmen) headed upriver to the construction site in February 1764.

Upon arrival Chouteau and his crew built cabins for themselves and "a large shed" for their tools and supplies, and began the task of clearing the village site. In April, Laclède inspected the work in

Laclède House. *Ink on paper by Clarence Hoblitzelle, 1898. Hoblitzelle created a series of views of early St. Louis buildings for Pierre Chouteau, a fifth-generation descendant of Madame Chouteau, for a proposed re-creation of the original colonial village on the riverfront. MHS-Art.*

progress, named the village St. Louis in honor of the reigning French King Louis XV (whose patron saint was Louis IX), and gave Chouteau detailed plans for laying out streets and the construction of his home and headquarters. He then returned to Fort de Chartres to make final preparations for moving his merchandise and part of the Creole population from the older Illinois villages to St. Louis. After Laclède's departure several hundred Missouri Indians, including 150 warriors, descended upon Chouteau and his workmen, declaring that they intended to be permanent residents. A few Creole families from Cahokia who had been attracted to the new village promptly fled across the river. Feeling that the Indian presence would strangle the village in its infancy, Chouteau sent for Laclède, in the meantime making the best of the situation by distributing "vermilion, awls, and verdigris" to the Missouri women and children in payment for their digging the cellar for Laclède's large stone house.

Laclède returned immediately, to be told by their chief that the Missouris were "like the ducks and the geese, who sought open water in order to rest, and procure an easy subsistence. . . . No place was more suitable," they believed, than the place where they were. On the next day, Laclède told them that the ducks and geese were bad guides, or they would not put themselves in open water "so that the eagles and birds of prey could discover them easily. . . ." He then informed the Missouris that six or seven hundred warriors from the north country were at Fort de Chartres, intending to prevent the English takeover. "If they learn you are here," he warned, "beyond the least doubt, they will come to destroy you." The Missouris saw the wisdom of this advice, and after accepting presents of guns, ammunition, corn, and cloth, they returned to their village up the Missouri. Normally Indians were welcome at French outposts but in smaller numbers and at more auspicious times. The thriving commercial center that Laclède had in mind would need a stable and unterrified supporting population.

As soon as the Missouris left, the Cahokians returned and began building their cabins on lots Laclède assigned them. During the summer of 1764 Laclède completed his commercial and domestic arrangements by transferring his merchandise and Madame Marie Thérèse Chouteau and their four young children from Fort de Chartres. In recruiting settlers he had to compete with Captain de Villiers, who urged the Creoles to accompany him to New Orleans. Eighty of the villagers did so, frightened by de Villiers' horror stories about the English infidels; but the majority, some of them persuaded by Laclède's assurances that the English were not devils and others by his offer of lots in St. Louis, decided to stay in Illinois. When the English troops finally arrived more than a year later, some forty families had moved to St. Louis from Fort de Chartres and Cahokia. A number of Kaskaskians crossed the river to Ste. Genevieve, but a good many others chose to take their chances with the conquerors.

In October 1765 Captain Louis St. Ange de Bellerive, who had been left in command at Fort de Chartres, formally transferred the eastern Illinois country to the English and moved with a few troops to St. Louis, bringing with him additional habitants, artisans, and traders. A trusted veteran of the French frontier service and a skilled Indian diplomatist, St. Ange had been second in command to de Bourgmont at Fort Orleans forty years earlier, and for the past twenty-five years he had commanded the French post at Vincennes. His standing with the Indians and the affection and respect he commanded among the Creoles was a great source of strength to St. Louis in its formative years. Upon his arrival he became the chief civil and military authority in upper Louisiana (the Illinois country west of the Mississippi). Now free of governmental responsibility, Laclède was soon to lose his trade monopoly. In 1769, protests in New Orleans forced the cancellation of D'Abbadie's grants, causing Laclède's partners to lose interest and sell their shares in the company's assets in St. Louis to Laclède. The founder then settled in as the leading trader and private citizen of the village. He had prospered greatly, and continued to, until he suffered financial reverses in the 1770s. In August 1766, Captain Harry Gordon, a British officer from Fort de Chartres, described Laclède's operation in his journal:

> The village of Paint Court [*Pain Court*—short of bread—a derisive nickname applied to St. Louis because it occasionally had to import food] is pleasantly situated on a high Ground which forms the W. Bank of the Mississippi, it . . . has already fifty Families . . . & seems to flourish very quick.
>
> At This place Mr. LeClef [Laclède] the principal Indian trader resides, who takes so good Measures, that the whole Trade of the Missouri That of the Mississippi Northwards, and that of the Nations near La Baye, Lake Michigan, and St. Josephs, by the Illinois River, is entirely brought to Him. He appears to be sensible, clever, and has been very well educated; is very active, and will give us some trouble before we get the Parts of this trade that belongs to us out of His hands.

The accomplished and energetic subject of Captain Gordon's rueful admiration was the second son of prominent lawyer and landholder of the province of Béarn in the southwest corner of France. Members of his family for many generations had been officeholders and his older brother Jean, a lawyer, public official, and scholar, enjoyed the favor of Louis XV and the friendship of Voltaire. Laclède himself read widely and brought with him to his frontier village more than two hundred books, including English and French grammars, more than two dozen volumes of ancient and modern histories, books on finance and double-entry bookkeeping, the *Code Militaire*, geographies, Spanish and French dictionaries, volumes on the natural sciences, Bacon's *Essays*, the works of Descartes, Locke's *Essay on Human Understanding*, and Rousseau's *Contrat Social* and *La Nouvelle Heloise*. Laclède was impressive; his firmness, self-assurance, and informed good judgment commanded respect from British officer, habitant, and Indian alike.

Like other second sons of propertied gentlemen, whether French, Spanish, or English, Laclède had come to America to improve his purse. After landing in New Orleans in 1755 at the age of twenty-six,

Marie Thérèse Bourgeois Chouteau *(Mme. René Auguste Chouteau). Oil on board by François Guyol de Guiran, ca. 1812. MHS-Art.*

he became a militia officer and wholesale trader. Owing to his background or his success in business, or both, Laclède moved in the upper echelon of New Orleans merchants and officials. Details are unavailable, but it is probable that he was a heavy loser in New Orleans's economic crash in the early 1760s. The timely opportunity to share in a trade monopoly in the vast reaches of the Missouri and upper Mississippi valleys promised him far greater riches within a few years.

Soon after he came to New Orleans, Laclède met Marie Thérèse Chouteau, the estranged wife of René Auguste Chouteau and the mother of a seven-year-old son, Auguste. Their lives were linked thereafter until Laclède's death, though they could not be legally married in Catholic Louisiana, given the inconvenient fact that René Chouteau was alive until 1776. Despite the contrary evidence of the official records, Laclède was the father of Marie Thérèse's four younger children, Pierre, Pelagie, Marie Louise, and Victoire, born between 1758 and 1764. Each was baptized as the child of René Chouteau, following the usual pattern in countries where divorce was impossible. According to family legend, Laclède and Madame Chouteau were married in a civil ceremony, which if true could have been little more than a symbolic act. Until his death in 1778 Laclède maintained the facade, never formally acknowledging his children. But in 1768 he gave the Chouteau family a residence lot with a stone house, a farm lot, and two African and two Indian slaves. Madame Chouteau was to have the use of this property during her lifetime, with the right to sell and purchase other property. According to the deed, these gifts were made in consideration of the services performed by Auguste Chouteau and as a demonstration of Laclède's affection for all of Madame Chouteau's children.

In laying out his village, Laclède followed a gridiron pattern similar to that of New Orleans, featuring a public *place* (market) centered on the riverfront at the most accessible landing for boats. Thus, from its beginning St. Louis differed from the early Ste. Genevieve and most other Creole villages, which were random collections of cabins and crooked streets. The *Place d'Armes* (*la Place*) and the company headquarters and church blocks in line behind it were each three hundred French feet square, the first separated from the river by limestone ledges. At the foot of the bluff was a towpath for bateaux and other boats, which was under water at high-river stages. Parallel to the river, and therefore with a northeast to southwest tilt, were three long streets thirty-six French feet (38.37 feet) wide: *La Rue Royale* or *Le Grande Rue* (Main or First Street), *La Rue d'Eglise* (Church or

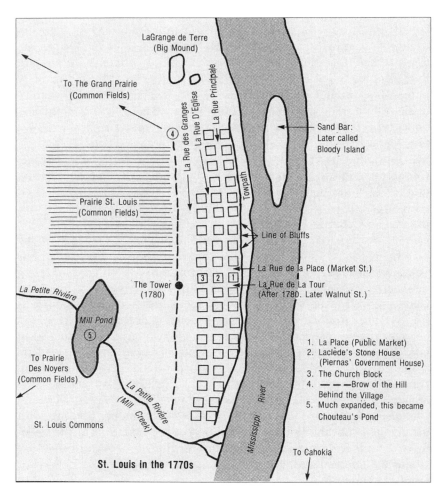

St. Louis in the 1770s. *Map by James Neal Primm, 1980.*

Second Street), and *La Rue des Granges* (Barn or Third Street). Crossing these streets at regular intervals were short streets thirty feet wide, including *La Rue de la Place* or *La Rue Bonhomme* (Market Street), *La Rue de la Tour* (now Walnut Street), and *La Rue Missouri* (Chestnut Street). Except for the three dedicated to public use, blocks were 240 by 300 feet, usually divided into four 120-by-150-foot lots, which were granted without charge to individuals for their homes and businesses. Laclède awarded these lots by verbal agreement until St. Ange's arrival; thereafter, they were the responsibility of the senior public official. After 1765, grants were recorded in *Livres Terriens*, or land books, which included both village lots and farm lands. For example, in May 1766 François Bissonet received two town lots and strips of land in the St. Louis and Grand prairies. Usually the deeds contained performance clauses providing that the property be forfeited unless improved within a year and a day. In some cases a special use was indicated—the erection of barns, mills, or other useful structures. A total of forty-nine blocks were contained in the village; fifteen between the river bluffs and La Rue Royale, nineteen between La Rue Royale and La Rue d'Eglise, and fifteen between La Rue d'Eglise and La Rue des Granges. Between 1766 and 1770, St. Ange awarded eighty-one lots, which, added to Laclède's previous verbal grants, absorbed most of the lots available.

Once allotted, real estate could be transferred or mortgaged freely, and such transactions were frequent. For security reasons the village was kept compact by granting lots contiguously, with the owners expected to enclose their property with *pieux debout* (upright stakes of rot-resistant cedar or mulberry about seven feet high and sharpened to a point at the top). Thus, in the event of an Indian attack, a continuous enclosure could be provided simply by barricading the ends of the streets. These stockades also kept out marauding domestic or wild animals and discouraged surprise visits by wandering Indians. Some of the more affluent residents enclosed their lots with stone walls instead of stakes. In addition to the houses, these private lots contained sheds or barns for domestic animals and poultry, vehicle and tool storage, a courtyard, a vegetable garden, and a few fruit trees. Root cellars provided storage for vegetables and fruit.

These individual dwellings dominated Creole St. Louis. There was no private retail district nor industrial center. Business was transacted in homes or on the streets. Houses varied in size from the one-room huts (ten to twelve feet square) of boatmen to that of the notary, Joseph Labusciere, which was sixty-six feet long. Laclède's stone house, which measured twenty-three by sixty feet originally, after serving as the government house for several years during the Spanish regime, was acquired by Auguste Chouteau, who added to it as his fortune grew. John F. Darby, who first saw the house in 1818, described it as an "elegant domicile," which, with servant's quarters, occupied the entire square bounded by Main, Market, Walnut, and Second Streets. "The whole square was encased by a stone wall two feet thick and ten feet high. . . . The walls of Colonel Chouteau's mansion were two and a half feet thick, of solid stone work, two stories high and surrounded by a portico about fourteen feet wide. . . . The house was elegantly furnished . . . (with) floors made of black walnut, and polished so finely that they reflected like a mirror."

Several of the larger houses in the village were built of stone, but the usual dwelling was made of cedar or mulberry logs set vertically in the ground. Limestone plaster filled the cracks between the logs and whitewash covered the entire exterior. Most of these houses were square, or nearly so, with two doors and four glass casement windows. Under the long overhang of the roofs, on two, three, or all sides, galleries eight or nine feet wide protected the plaster from rain and the house from the blistering heat of the St. Louis summers. Steep, two-planed hip roofs, designed to shed water quickly from thatch, continued to typify Creole architecture, even though the thatch had been replaced by oak shingles. Interiors had walnut floors, in contrast to the bare earth of the habitant's home. Fireplaces provided heating and some cooking facilities, though outside kitchens were common.

In addition to their home vegetable gardens and orchards, most of the residents of early St. Louis depended upon a controlled agricultural system outside the village. In the pattern of medieval French, English, and German agriculture, followed in early New England as well as in Cahokia, Kaskaskia, and other Creole villages, Laclède's plan called for a village commons and common fields. The commons, which was a source of firewood, nuts, berries, and game, was chiefly a foraging area for the villagers' cows, pigs, and horses. At its greatest extent the commons stretched from the back of the village, with *Le Petite Riviere* (Mill Creek) as its northern boundary, for nearly three miles westward, and south along the Mississippi for several miles. In 1771 it was reduced by an alienation of land for the new village of Prairie à Catalan or Louisbourg, renamed Carondelet in the 1790s, and known familiarly as *Vide Poche* (empty pockets). Individual grants and other intrusions gradually reduced the area of the commons after the mid-1780s. The only section of the original commons never alienated is the present Lafayette Park, on the near south side.

Bordering the commons on the rolling plateau behind the village, the common fields provided the staples which supported the dominant trading economy. Strips of land one arpent (180 French or 192.5 English feet) wide and forty arpents long (1.46 miles) running generally east to west were assigned to each village lot-holder. The common fields of St. Louis, all in use by 1769, began with the *Prairie St. Louis*, which stretched from the village fence at the back of the Third Street lots westward along the Petite Riviere for nearly a mile and a half (to the present Jefferson Avenue) and north for about two miles to a small stream called *Ruisseau des Pierres*. In 1766 fields were laid out on the *Grand Prairie*, which lay about a mile northwest of the St. Louis Prairie and separated from the latter by a cluster of

Mississippi mounds, dominated by *La Grange de Terre* (the barn of earth). Somewhat larger than the St. Louis Prairie, the Grand Prairie was so far from the village that huts for shelter or overnight stays were built on it. Some of these "shelters" were actually country homes, such as that of Pierre Laclède, which was eighty feet long, with slave cabins, barns, orchards, and a garden. The next of the fields to be opened was *La Petite Prairie* (1766) located about one mile south of the village near a settlement of the Peoria Indians, newly arrived from across the Mississippi. Thus the Petite Prairie's second name, *Prairie du Village Sauvages*. Immediately south of the Grand Prairie was the small Cul de Sac field, and beyond it the *Prairie des Noyers*. A continuous cultivated area six miles long and one and one-half miles wide (about 5,760 acres) stretched from the north end of the Grand Prairie to the southern extremity of the Carondelet common fields.

In the spring of each year the habitants and the slaves of the more affluent traders and artisans rumbled into the fields with their plows, *charettes* (two-wheeled carts), and tools to begin their planting. Once the earth was turned and the seeds in the ground, the Creole, like his Indian neighbors, usually did not bother to combat the weeds, but let nature take its course until harvest time. Despite this practice, the fields produced abundantly. The principal crops grown were corn and wheat, followed usually by tobacco, rye, buckwheat, flax, cotton, oats, barley, and beans. In ordinary years the fields produced enough for the village and the Indian fur trade, but at times extraordinary demands required additional supplies from Cahokia, Ste. Genevieve, or New Madrid. Although a majority of the villagers were at least part-time farmers, the fur trade and its supporting enterprises were their major interests.

In March 1766 the other shoe dropped in Louisiana. A Spanish ship arrived in New Orleans carrying the grim Don Antonio Ulloa to take over as the territory's first Spanish governor. Louisianans had learned in September 1764 that France had ceded the province to Spain nearly two years earlier, and they had been outraged by what seemed to them a senseless and callous action. They did not know that French diplomats had offered Louisiana to Spain in return for the latter's agreement to British peace terms, which were as costly to their Spanish allies as to themselves. Any delay in signing, the French foreign office had feared, might cause the British to raise the ante by demanding the rich French West Indian sugar islands. Privately, the foreign minister, Duc Étienne de Choiseul, regarded France's North

American losses as temporary, pending an opportune moment to strike
back at the British. The Spanish made no move to claim the territory
for more than three years, and they sent no supply vessels to New
Orleans. French local officials still governed, and French ships
brought in French goods as much as before. In Laclède's village,
where St. Ange had assumed command in 1765, they were busy with
the beaver trade. The world would end, and the Spanish would
come—some day.

Ulloa did not take charge immediately in New Orleans. Having
brought only two companies of infantry (ninety men) with him, he
preferred to wait until reinforcements arrived. Reluctantly, the acting
French commandant, Captain Charles Philippe Aubry, agreed to keep
his administration in place and issue orders as Ulloa's agent, with
Spain assuming the expenses of administration. Faced with an
antagonistic population, Ulloa nurtured their hostility by impolitic
public speeches and efforts to limit trade between Louisiana and
France. The situation worsened in October 1768 when the Crown
placed Louisiana within the rigid Spanish mercantile system. Only
Spanish ships from Spanish ports with Spanish crews could enter
Louisiana ports. Since no Spanish merchant ships had ever come to
New Orleans, the decree seemed to promise total isolation for the
colony.

At that point, the New Orleans French declared Ulloa a usurper
and chased him out of the colony. The uneasy Aubry was still
commandant, but he was not sure whom he represented. The Superior
Council of Louisiana (mostly New Orleans merchants) then petitioned
Louis XV for restoration to France, arguing that Spain would be
unable to protect the colony against the British. Choiseul evidently
considered rescinding the Louisiana cession, but, despite their
previous slowness, the Spanish saw the province as a buffer against
any British threat to New Mexico, and were determined to hold it.
Since his strategy against the British depended upon the Spanish
alliance, Choiseul could not afford to offend Madrid. So the pleas
from New Orleans went unanswered.

Despite his troubles in New Orleans, Ulloa had decided that he
must move quickly to stop the British fur traders in upper Louisiana.
Though the actual traders were French Canadians, they had adjusted
readily to British rule, and were fanning out in all directions from
Quebec and the Illinois posts. Knowing that the Missouri River was
the key to the western fur trade, Ulloa ordered Captain Don Francisco
Riú to the mouth of the Missouri in 1767 to build forts there, one on
each side of the river. According to Ulloa's secret instructions, the
forts were "to keep the savages in friendship and alliance with the

colony . . . [and] to prevent the neighboring English from entering the territories and domains of his majesty." To give the military post and surrounding settlement a Spanish character, Ulloa brought workmen from Havana, and assigned soldiers from his New Orleans command to the fort. Only the superintendent of construction, Captain Guy de Fossat, and an interpreter were French. Ulloa intended the post to be headquarters for a new district of the Missouri River, separate from "Ylinneses" (Spanish Illinois). Riú's secret instructions in no way diminished St. Ange's authority as commandant of Spanish Illinois, defined by the Spanish at the time as stretching along the west bank of the Mississippi from the mouth of the Ohio to *Pencur* (Pain Court—St. Louis).

When they examined the proposed construction site, de Fossat and Riú learned what Laclède or St. Ange could have told them—no permanent construction was possible on the north bank of the Missouri near its mouth because the site was regularly eight or nine feet under water at flood stage. Accordingly, they built a small movable blockhouse on the north side and began construction of Fort Don Carlos on the south bank. Riú, who was disliked by his men, perhaps because he denied them liquor rations, required attendance at Mass, and otherwise enforced the strict regimen prescribed by Ulloa, lost control of the situation; and when the storekeeper and twenty men deserted, Ulloa removed him. As ordered by Ulloa, he had reserved the Missouri River fur trade to himself and the members of the Spanish garrison at Fort Don Carlos. This policy threatened to ruin the St. Louis traders and infuriated the Indians, especially since Riú had brought insufficient merchandise and no brandy with him, and received none from New Orleans. The presence of two six-pounder and three four-pounder cannons at Fort Don Carlos detoured the irate tribes to St. Louis, where they harassed and threatened the villagers.

According to Laclède, Amable Guion, Dr. André Condé (the post surgeon), René Kiercereau, and other "principal habitants and merchants of Ylinneses," they had been "compelled to abandon our labors and the cultivation of our fields in order to shut ourselves up in our villages, destitute of all fortification . . . and in danger of seeing our wives and children murdered. . . ." Knowing that Spanish interests required that the Indians be pacified, Riú granted the St. Louisans' petition to reopen the Missouri River trade. When Lieutenant Don Pedro Piernas appeared in March 1769 to relieve Riú, St. Ange, Laclède, and others sent testimonials to Ulloa supporting the deposed commander, attesting to his good judgment, character, and ability. The worthy Ulloa, of course, was by then safe in Havana.

At that point, perhaps to impress upon the Spanish the key role of St. Louis in the fur trade, St. Ange reported that twenty-three Indian tribes regularly and four occasionally received presents at the village. There were four Illinois tribes; the Miamis and four other tribes from the Wabash River area; three from the St. Joseph (Michigan) and upper Illinois Rivers; five from the upper Mississippi, including the (Santee) Sioux, the Sauks, and the Panimahas from the Missouri valley; and others. Four tribes from the Straits of Mackinac dropped in now and then. During the period of its monopoly Laclède's company was responsible for annual gifts of blankets, mirrors, vermilion, awls, knives, guns, powder and ball, corn, tobacco, cloth, and other commodities, including brandy at times, to the tribes. As French traders had done for decades, Laclède ceremoniously gave elaborate large and small medals, fancy plumed military hats, and even uniform jackets to the chiefs—usually distributed according to rank. Any lesser chief who could wangle a medal or a high hat stood a good chance of elevation in status in his tribe. After Laclède's monopoly was rescinded, St. Ange was responsible for distributing presents, although traders licensed by him were expected to assist. Indian, trader, and commandant alike knew the rules of the game. No presents—no trade, no peace.

On August 17, 1769, Spain's intentions in Louisiana became crystal clear. The new governor, Lieutenant General Count Alejandro O'Reilly, one of Spain's top military trouble-shooters, arrived before New Orleans with a squadron of twenty-one ships, many tons of supplies, and more than two thousand first-line troops. Enough, considering that New Orleans's free population was eighteen hundred. Within a few days the hard-boiled Irishman, armed with extraordinary powers, had arrested the leaders of the insurrection and forced the residents to swear an oath of allegiance to King Charles III of Spain. Five of the rebels were executed and six were imprisoned. With his authority thus established, O'Reilly proceeded to reorganize the colony. Spain's trade regulations were strictly enforced, the Superior Council abolished, and "undesirable" (Jewish and Protestant) merchants expelled. With plenty of funds and supplies, in contrast to the unfortunate Ulloa, O'Reilly paid the government's debts to the merchants, clamped down on price-gougers by regulating food prices, and gave the territory a market by establishing free trade with Havana and Spanish home ports.

To tighten the territorial administration, O'Reilly created the offices of lieutenant governor for the districts of Natchitoches and Illinois, the latter having been expanded in one of Ulloa's last acts to include all of upper Louisiana. Don Pedro Piernas, Riú's successor at Fort Don Carlos, was named to the Illinois post, headquartered at

St. Louis. Two weeks after having relieved Riú in March 1769, Lieutenant Piernas had received orders from Ulloa to turn Fort Don Carlos over to St. Ange and return with his command to New Orleans. On his return trip Piernas stopped at St. Louis, where to his discomfiture, certain merchants, backed by the council, attempted to seize his goods as compensation for debts incurred by Riú's absconding storekeeper. Upon Piernas's appeal, St. Ange disallowed the claims, but the Spanish officer had acquired a distaste for Creole ideas of government. He reported to O'Reilly that a council of six, with St. Ange presiding, actually governed the village and district.

Piernas portrayed St. Ange as an ineffectual commandant who allowed the council to use his "respectable old age" as a cover for advancing their own interests at the expense of the common welfare. The council itself he characterized as "four useless habitants and one attorney, a notorious drunkard called La Bussiere" [Joseph Labusciere], the dominant member whom he compared to one of the leaders of the rebellion in New Orleans. Obviously smarting from his quick removal from a post of honor and profit at Fort Don Carlos, Piernas made a strong case for change in St. Louis, one which he must have hoped would work to his own advantage. On a more favorable note, he emphasized the "high and pleasant" location of the village, improved by a higher plain behind it suitable for a fort. The citizens were more numerous than those of *Misera* (Ste. Genevieve) and more industrious, according to Piernas. The total population of Ste. Genevieve was greater, however, because more citizens of the older village could afford slaves. (In 1772, St. Louis's population, including slaves, was reported as 577, Ste. Genevieve's, 691.) Except for the bad example of the selfish and wilful major fur traders, the St. Louisans seemed amenable to discipline; they applied themselves vigorously to their vast fields, producing much wheat. Like the citizens of Misera, however, they emphasized the fur trade above all, lacked respect for religion, and were addicted to vice. In both villages there were unattached wandering hunters who worked hard for four to six months, then spent the rest of the year corrupting the village youth by their example of "reveling and chambering." Obviously, Piernas thought "Ylinneses" needed a firm Spanish hand.

O'Reilly reacted as Piernas hoped he would. He promoted Piernas to captain, appointed him lieutenant governor of Spanish Illinois, and directed him to create love and respect for the government, protect and increase commerce, and prosecute troublemakers and faithless debtors. He was to keep the peace with the English while keeping them on their side of the river, prevent the Indians from attacking the English or each other, and see that his licensees did not trade with the

English or invade their territory. Trade goods were to be purchased only in New Orleans, and all furs shipped there. No "honest man" should be refused a trading license, and no monopolies were to be granted. Indians must be treated kindly, just prices paid for their furs; and their chiefs assured of annual presents. Despite O'Reilly's profession of friendship for the English, Indians from the *Belle Riviére* (Ohio River) would be encouraged to trade and receive presents in Spanish Illinois (provided they could get past the English). As final evidence of His Majesty's affection and good intentions, the inhumane and trouble-making practices of buying, holding, or selling Indian slaves was outlawed.

For the military protection of the district, O'Reilly authorized garrisons of one lieutenant, one corporal and six regular soldiers at Ste. Genevieve and one sergeant and six soldiers at Fort Don Carlos "to examine all the boats which go out and enter by the [Missouri] river." Those not licensed by the lieutenant governor were to be seized and their crews prosecuted. At St. Louis, the regular detachment was to consist of two sergeants, five corporals, one drummer, and twenty-five soldiers. To augment the regular troops, militia companies were established in St. Louis and Ste. Genevieve, consisting of all men between fifteen and fifty capable of bearing arms. As captain of the St. Louis militia, O'Reilly named Jean Baptiste Martigny, a French-Canadian fur trader who had come to St. Louis from Cahokia in 1764. The merchant-trader François Vallé, a French-Canadian, former Kaskaskian, and reputedly the wealthiest man in the Mississippi Valley, was named militia captain and civil commandant at Ste. Genevieve.

Having set affairs in order in Louisiana, O'Reilly, as the king's special commissioner, installed Don Luis de Unzaga as his successor in March 1770, and departed for Havana. Upon his recommendation, Louisiana lost its special status under the Ministry of State to become a dependency of the captaincy-general of Cuba. Now the territory was to be administered exactly as Spain's other American colonies, under the Ministry of the Indies. As ordered by O'Reilly, St. Ange formally transferred to Piernas his authority over the Illinois district on May 20, 1770. In deference to the villagers' and the old commandant's feelings, St. Ange was appointed assistant to Piernas and special adviser on Indian affairs.

The French were naturally apprehensive about their prospects under direct Spanish rule, especially in view of their earlier difficulties with Piernas, but they were quickly reassured. In one of his first official acts, the lieutenant governor confirmed the grants of lots and land made by St. Ange. Since the latter had recognized Laclède's oral assignment of lots, real property holdings were now secure. Despite his earlier reservations about them, Piernas was amiable and fair with the people. The Spanish soldiers were kept well in hand to minimize friction; legal disputes were quickly settled; and there was no interference with the day-to-day lives of individuals. Neither Piernas nor his successors attempted to replace French with Spanish as the language of commerce, requiring it only as the language of record in formal legal proceedings. The district council was abolished, but Piernas was an attentive listener. Whether or not Laclède had been among those traders previously denounced by Piernas, the two men quickly established an amicable relationship; and the lieutenant governor rented Laclède's company block and large stone house for his headquarters for 350 pesos a year.

Piernas's tolerance for his new charges was severely tested during his first weeks at his post. Despite his having published O'Reilly's decree abolishing Indian slavery in May, various residents in June bought fourteen Indians. Stunned by this flagrant violation, Piernas referred the matter to Governor Unzaga, who also ducked the issue by ruling that the slaves could be retained pending a decision by the Crown. Meanwhile, Piernas ordered a census of Indian slaves, as he had been directed to do by O'Reilly. In July he reported that sixty-nine Indians were held in bondage in St. Louis, including twenty-eight males and forty-one females, averaging eighteen years of age and worth 62,744 livres ($12,544). In Ste. Genevieve, Commandant François Vallé reported twenty-nine Indian slaves, including his own. There were a few more black than Indian slaves in St. Louis, and nearly two hundred in Ste. Genevieve, but Spain's humane concerns were not extended to them. Black slavery posed no threat to commerce or good order.

To Piernas, the situation was especially trying because the thirty-six Indian slaveowners included the most prominent residents of the village. St. Ange and Laclède led the list with six each; Madame Chouteau owned two, the notary Joseph Labusciere one, the miller Joseph Taillon four, militia captain Jean Baptiste Martigny five, the merchant Pierre Montardy two, and Eugene Pouré (Beausoliel), merchant and militia sublieutenant, four. Most of the other owners were in the Indian fur trade. Piernas's summary report provides an interesting glimpse of the village's caste structure. The military officers, the notary, and most of the merchants and major traders were designated by polite titles, the rest by name and occupation only. Marie Thérèse Chouteau, an active trader on her own account, was "Dame Choutaud," the other women owners, "the widow Dodier" and

Veronique Desnoyers. St. Ange, Laclède, and the former French officer Pierre de Volsay were "Monsieur"; six merchants, the notary, and the militia captain were "sieur." All of those given titles affirmed the report with their signature; fourteen of the other twenty-four made an "X". Since slave-owning was a mark of status in the village, it is probable that most of its adult residents could not write. Perhaps it is more remarkable that at least twenty-two of them could.

The Spanish Crown's position on Indian slavery matched that of its colonial agents in ambiguity. O'Reilly's decree was neither rescinded nor fully implemented. By outlawing further purchases and sales, and at times by ransoming captives held by Indians, Piernas and his successors virtually halted the Indian slave trade; but slaveowners retained Indians already held and any children born to them. As a percentage of the total of unfree persons, the number of Indians in bondage in St. Louis declined as more Africans became available. The latter were generally preferred as better workers and less likely to escape, rebel, or be rescued by relatives. Indians could be troublesome property indeed. On one occasion eight of them made off with horses, guns, and ammunition stolen from their masters, freed several black slaves and hid in the forest near the Meramec River. From this base they raided the fields and the village, seemingly intent upon stamping out slavery. After having slipped inside the palisade one evening to free some black women, two of the raiders were seen in Madame Chouteau's barn by her black slave and factotum Baptiste, who informed Joseph Papin and then held the Indians' attention with a bottle of rum while Papin went for help. After enlisting Silvestre Labbadie and some militia and regulars, Papin returned to the scene with guns blazing. The Indians, one wounded, were taken to jail; but a militia bullet had killed Baptiste, who died as Papin put it, "without the satisfaction of witnessing the end of the glorious action." Madame Chouteau, in outrage, sued her son-in-law Papin, his brother-in-law Labbadie, and the other owners of the escapees. Upon the recommendation of a local panel of three, Governor Miro at New Orleans ordered the defendants to pay Veuve Chouteau six hundred pesos in silver.

In addition to those who ran to freedom, a good many Indians, as well as black slaves, were manumitted; often, as in the case of St. Ange, by provisions in the master's will. A few Indians were still enslaved at St. Louis at the end of the Spanish period, the last one to be freed by a state court in 1834. In this case (*Marguerite v. Chouteau*) the point at issue was whether Marguerite was legally Indian or African.

Piernas's handling of Indian slavery was approved by the villagers. He had cemented his popularity when he reinforced his confirmation of St. Ange's grants by appointing a local merchant, a Spaniard named Martin Miloney Duralde, as district surveyor. Duralde's work gave permanence and definition to existing holdings and laid the groundwork for orderly future development. The lieutenant governor also encouraged and kept a close eye on the fur business and agriculture. In 1772 he reported that 950 packs of furs and hides (one pack weighed 100 livres—108 pounds), 1,200 quintals of flour (one quintal was 100 Spanish libras—101.4 pounds), and 600 quintals of lead were shipped by bateaux from St. Louis and Ste. Genevieve to New Orleans. Some of the flour went to the Spanish fort at Arkansas Post. Most of the 5,898 quintals of flour produced that year was consumed locally. In this and subsequent years the volume of furs was deceptively low, since it did not include the illegal trade with Cahokia, Prairie du Chien, Kaskaskia, and other British posts. In the following year fur shipments declined slightly because of troubles with the Osages, but they tripled in 1774. Indian harassment and low prices reduced lead production and halted shipments entirely for the next several years. By December 1773 St. Louis's population had increased to 444 whites (285 males and 159 females) and 193 slaves. Indian slaves, being illegal, were not reported in the census.

The pugnacious Osage Indians were a major problem for the administration and the fur traders. Almost constantly at war with their neighbors, the Osages had decades earlier won a nasty reputation with the Spaniards because of their raids near the New Mexican frontier. Since they regularly received presents at St. Louis, the Great Osages seldom caused trouble there; but the Caddoes and other tribes along the Arkansas River and in the Natchitoches district, and the licensed traders as well, were harassed, robbed, and killed with monotonous frequency. From their villages on the Missouri River, the Little Osages and the Missouris visited the British, who gave them more and better presents than the Spanish could afford. As a result, according to Piernas, these two small tribes were unmatched in insolence and evil intentions. During 1771 and 1772 they repeatedly stole horses from St. Louis and Ste. Genevieve; and worse, they levied heavy tribute upon St. Louisans headed upriver to trade with the Pawnees, Otoes, Poncas, and Mahas. The merchandise thus acquired was incidental to their main purpose—to deprive the upriver tribes of weapons.

Piernas, who was reluctant to do more than remonstrate with the Big Osages because they kept their depredations outside of his jurisdiction, had no reservations about the right medicine for the Little Osages and Missouris. They should be made an example of because they had dealt dishonestly with their Spanish father; that is, they were playing the British against the Spanish in the same manner that the imperial powers played one tribe against the other. The Spanish goals were profit, protection of their posts, and preservation of their empire. The Little Osages and their Missouri allies, having learned their lesson well, had in mind survival and profits. They had fought for their French father for three generations as far from home as Detroit and the Ohio valley; now he was gone. They did not like the aloof, unfriendly seeming Piernas; and the British, with their profusion of handsome gifts, seemed to be winners. The more the lieutenant governor understood this, the less he liked it. On July 4, 1772, he suggested to Governor Unzaga that since the two tribes were "the least numerous of all," they would be "the easiest to reduce by means of extermination."

With Unzaga's approval, Piernas forbade all trade with the Missouris and Little Osages until they gave evidence of "peacefulness and submission." Apparently the Indians were about to submit when they learned that help was at hand. An alert Prairie du Chien trader under English license, Jean Marie Ducharme, had seen Piernas's interdict as a golden opportunity and had slipped past Fort Don Carlos at night with two bateaux loaded with a large supply of trade goods, including plenty of guns and ammunition. For four months during the winter and spring of 1772–73 Ducharme traded at the Little Osage village 240 miles up the Missouri before he was surprised by Pierre Laclède and forty well-armed St. Louisans.

These avenging volunteers were financed by the merchants Benito Vasquez and Joseph Motard upon Piernas's promise of one-half of any furs seized from Ducharme, the other half to be shared by the volunteers. This expedient was necessary because Governor Unzaga could spare no funds for catching Ducharme. Laclède's acceptance of the command, Piernas believed, gave the expedition credibility with the residents; and his ability and sense of honor assured its success. Despite Ducharme's escape at the first sound of firing, the venture succeeded in its major purposes. The volunteers captured the invader's entire crew and all of his furs and remaining merchandise; the show of force alarmed the Little Osages and Missouris, discredited Ducharme, and to some extent, the British; and the Missouris returned some stolen horses and promised peace and submission. Piernas's triumph was completed when the Big Osages, though not involved with Ducharme, delivered to St. Louis the chief of the band responsible for most of the troubles on the Arkansas River.

For the Missouris, the Ducharme incident and its aftermath was a fatal blow. Repeated assaults from other tribes, particularly their ancient enemies the Sauks and Foxes, who had been encouraged by Piernas and who sought further favors, nearly wiped them out. In 1777 the Little Osages abandoned their Missouri River village to return to their former home on the Osage River 150 miles to the south. Piernas's extermination policy had worked well enough. His local popularity was enhanced, as well as his standing with his superiors, who admired subordinates who got things done at no cost to the Crown. In 1775, his administration a success, Piernas left St. Louis to become lieutenant colonel of the stationary regiment at New Orleans.

Lieutenant Colonel Francisco Cruzat, Piernas's successor, continued the policy of accommodation to the interests and lifestyles of the French. That is, he was genial, gregarious, and lax in enforcing mercantile regulations. Smuggling merchandise from British Illinois, fairly common under Piernas, increased during Cruzat's regime. So popular was the lieutenant governor that residents later recalled his administration as a time of perfect contentment. St. Louis's population had stabilized at just under seven hundred; the Indians were temporarily more tractable; and agricultural production increased (St. Louis shipped several hundred quintals of flour to New Orleans in 1775—Ste. Genevieve more than ten thousand). The lucrative beaver trade was declining as the supply diminished in the lower Missouri basin, but deerskins were plentiful, supplied largely by the wide-ranging Big Osages.

Lieutenant Colonel Francisco Cruzat. *Lithograph by Goupil and Sons, 1904, from Alceé Fortier,* A History of Louisiana. *MHS-Library.*

These deerskins provided the village with its principal circulating medium. Except in precious-metal or sugar colonies, specie shortages were chronic in the outposts of mercantilist empires. Prevented by Spanish policy from trading with foreigners, and having an unfavorable trade balance with Spain, New Orleans merchants were squeezed for cash. They were reluctant to let silver escape upriver, to the distress of large shippers such as François Vallé in Ste. Genevieve and Benito Vasquez in St. Louis. Even the illicit trade with the British posts produced little specie, and no matter how large the St. Louis merchants' profits, fortunes expressed only as credit balances in New Orleans seemed insubstantial. In 1777 Vasquez, Joseph Motard, and others petitioned Cruzat for relief, but having no real remedy to offer, the lieutenant governor decreed that peltry currency must be of good quality.

In a desperate effort to reduce their losses in Louisiana, Spain tried to stimulate the production of tobacco and hemp, valuable commodities which would improve the empire's balance-of-payments position. Tobacco production was substantial in St. Louis, but most of it was consumed in the district. Not until the American period would it become an important export item. In 1775 Pierre Laclède shipped fifteen quintals of hemp to New Orleans, which delighted the Spanish because of their huge annual outlays of specie for Russian hemp (required by all naval and merchant vessels). Great Britain's American colonies were beginning to produce hemp in quantity, which had no doubt encouraged Laclède to try his hand. In June 1777, as instructed by the Crown, Governor Bernardo Gálvez ordered Cruzat to encourage the Indians to cultivate hemp, with the inducement of duty-free passage to the Spanish market. Since hemp production is even more labor-intensive than cotton or sugar cane it required precisely what "Ylinneses" did not have, a substantial labor supply.

Cruzat knew, as Gálvez should have, that the Plains Indians of his district, free or slave, would not break their backs in hemp fields. With more than a dozen slaves, Laclède had produced only a modest amount. Clearly, even though several residents were eager to cultivate hemp, its production in quantity would require a large infusion of black slaves. The Crown attempted to meet the need by permitting Louisianans to exchange their products for slaves brought from the West Indies by the French; but war with England made this concession impracticable. Few additional slaves came to St. Louis, and hemp production languished.

Spain's trade imbalances and the specie shortage were of little concern to most of the Creoles, who were accustomed to deerskin currency. Their only steady sources of specie were the expenditures of the Spanish administration and military garrison, only a small part of the village's annual income. But food was plentiful; their land had cost nothing; their debts were few—except to the doctor—and their peltries and foodstuffs bought them the rest of their material and ornamental needs from New Orleans. The bateaux that labored up the Mississippi at ten miles a day brought them their "tafia" (ratafia), the bitter, half-distilled New Orleans rum that was the Creole's answer to the "Bostonese's" red-eye whisky. Their merchants sold them all their fabrics, cloth-making being forbidden, and their silver, iron and copper ware, mirrors, clothing, blankets, and Iberian wines. Furniture was made by local artisans. Prices in peltry currency were high; but so were wages; and few who were not slaves felt poor.

Despite its appearance of easygoing democracy—a reality in religious and most social life—there were wide differences in living standards in St. Louis. At all levels the people ate sparingly by choice, their diets featuring vegetables, cereals, and fruits, supplemented by poultry and eggs, milk for the young, and fish. One notable dish for which the Creole cooks were famous was a West Indian Gumbo, a spicy concoction of fricasseed chicken, crayfish, okra, tomatoes, and lima beans, with variations according to taste or availability. Once or twice a week they served meat, usually venison, possum, or other wild game, and cured pork in winter. Though they abounded in the village, cattle were seldom slaughtered. The more affluent drank Madeira in addition to the local brandies and claret-type wine, and they occasionally served sumptuous banquets, especially when outside visitors were present. Their light eating, one visitor wrote, explained their good health and long lives. Once past childhood, their chances of living to the eighties or nineties were excellent, providing they kept their scalps.

The merchants, successful artisans, and professional elite bought the fine wines; the silks, linens, and lace; the fancy bonnets and shoes; the silverware; the velvet coats; the dresses of fine woolen and cotton cloth; the large ornamental mirrors. Habitants and boatmen and their families made do with cheap muslins and rough cloth, tafia and the home-made claret, blue or red handkerchiefs to cover their heads, and moccasins or *sabots* in bitter weather. Men, women, and children of this class went barefooted most of the time, but it was not unusual for the well-to-do to doff their shoes in the hot months. Men of all classes wore the capote, or hooded cloth coat, which was available in various weights and quality. In October 1771, Denau Detailly, a hunter and interpreter for the Indian traders, with "an Indian wife legally married," died leaving her "an old feather bed covered with skin, another with ticking, four delf plates, an earthen pan, 7 pewter spoons,

4 iron forks, an axe, a saw, a tin pan, a shovel, an oven, a table, four old chairs, two sheets, two pair old cotton breeches, ragged and holy, shirt worn and torn, an old blanket coat, a straw hat, and mittens." In contrast, William Bissette, merchant, in 1772 willed one thousand livres (about two hundred dollars) to the Church, twenty-three hundred livres to relatives, and "peltries, silverware, slaves, animals, houses, building, lands, and debts due him" to his brother Charles as executor.

The land and commercial policies established by Laclède and St. Ange and continued by Piernas and his successors—though far more generous than was customary with the French—tended to perpetuate class distinctions. Laclède had given one lot and a strip in the common fields to those with little property and two or more to those he believed to have the material or personal resources to develop them. Joseph Labusciere was awarded a 300-by-150-foot lot (2.5 ordinary lots) in April 1766 and another half-lot in August. Laclède had six village lots, Pierre de Volsay six, Eugene Pouré two, Dr. Condé four, Louis Lambert four, and so on. When the company monopoly was in force, *voyageurs* and small traders worked for Laclède in the fur trade for a small percentage. When it was cancelled, a few others who could obtain capital and a license from St. Ange competed with Laclède. The actual upriver trading, however, was often managed by *engagés* who worked for the licensees. Under the Spanish, the Indian trade was theoretically open to all, but in practice the lieutenant governors assigned the Missouris, Osages, Kansas, and other tribes to a small group of established traders on an alternating basis. Until the 1790s a percentage of the profits from the Big Osage trade was reserved to the lieutenant governors. The small trader had little chance to gain enough capital or influence to break into this tightly knit group unless, like ex-Private Benito Vasquez, he enjoyed the special favor of the lieutenant governor. Some merchants who shipped peltries to and brought merchandise from New Orleans were also licensed traders, but more often they were not.

With few exceptions, those of the bourgeois establishment in the 1770s and 1780s were natives of France or Canada, had some education, and, most of them, personal libraries. Only a few members of this class lived in stone houses. Among them, in addition to Laclède, were Pierre de Volsay, Joseph Labusciere, Silvestre Labbadie, Louis Perrault, Dr. André Condé, Antoine Hubert, and a few others, all French natives. Canadian members of the elite included Jean Baptiste Martigny and Eugene Pouré (Beausoliel). Auguste Chouteau from New Orleans and the Spaniards Benito Vasquez and Miloney Duralde also became insiders; Chouteau was eventually acknowledged as the leading member of the elite group.

Below the elite were the artisans and small traders of whom Amable Guion, Joseph Taillon, and Louis Bissonette were examples. Guion, a stone mason from Fort de Chartres, could read and write, but the other two could not. Taillon, a Canadian from Cahokia, dammed Le Petite Riviere and built the village's first water mill. He prospered, and lived so long (ninety-two years) that he became a most revered citizen, though he was never really an insider. Bissonette, an Illinois Creole, was a small trader whose diligence finally earned him a share of the Little Osage trade (in 1777 when the tribe was on the move). Finally, at the bottom of the free population were the boatmen and laborers, hunters and trappers, and the few farmers who were not otherwise employed. Most of these men were uneducated natives of the eastern Illinois country.

In their religious lives, the St. Louisans of the 1770s and 1780s were as one. They were Catholics, many of whom had come from the villages across the Mississippi primarily because they preferred His Catholic Majesty of Spain to the heretical British, whose recent brutal treatment of the Acadians was well remembered. When Don Pedro Piernas first saw the villagers, however, he hardly recognized them as Catholics. He had lived in New Orleans and his wife was French, but Piernas had never known such light-hearted, careless Catholics. After five years they had not built a church; and their everlasting parties and other amusements, to the seeming exclusion of everything save trade, bespoke a moral laxity and irreligion. The lieutenant governor to be, in his report to O'Reilly in 1769, attributed this regrettable state of affairs to the absence of laws enforcing the faith and the lack of a regular priest.

In 1766 and 1767, Father Sebastian Meurin, pastor at Ste. Genevieve, had baptized eight children at St. Louis, "in a tent for want of a church." Within a month after Piernas took up his duties, the residents at his urging had built a small log chapel on the church block. Father Pierre Gibault from Kaskaskia, pastor to the two thousand Catholics of British Illinois, dedicated this first church in St. Louis on June 24, 1770. During the next two years Gibault officiated there at regular intervals, even though he was under the ecclesiastical authority of the French bishop at Quebec and was a British subject. If this bothered Don Pedro, he gave little evidence of it. To the contrary, Piernas probably attended at least some of the masses and sixty-four baptisms performed by Father Gibault in St. Louis from 1770 to 1772. The lieutenant governor apparently believed that strengthening the faith in the village was more important than technicalities.

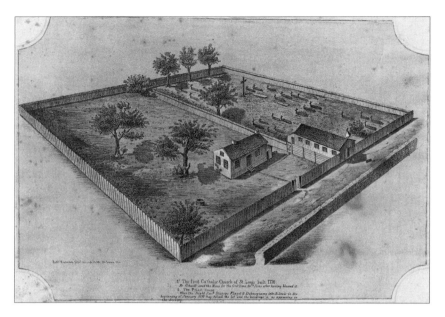

First Catholic Church in St. Louis. *Lithograph by Julius Hutawa, ca. 1850. This rendering shows the original church and the priest house as they appeared in 1819. MHS-PP.*

In May 1772, Father Valentine, a Capuchin priest with proper Spanish credentials, but technically chaplain to the Spanish garrison rather than village pastor, became the first resident priest in St. Louis. During the next three years he baptized sixty-four French, twenty-four blacks, and nineteen Indians, and officiated at seventy-two funerals and four weddings. In 1774, the priest, the lieutenant governor, and leading residents planned a new church thirty by sixty feet, to be constructed of white oak timber, with the majority of the funding from St. Ange's estate. Piernas assessed the residents for the additional funds needed, and the carpenter Pierre Baron was employed to build the church. Unfortunately, within a few months Baron died and Piernas and Valentine returned to New Orleans. Nothing was done until January 1776 when the new lieutenant governor ordered the project resumed. Just before the building was completed, a German-born Capuchin, Father Bernard de Limpach, arrived to become the first pastor of the St. Louis parish. As the king's agent, and therefore the church's, Cruzat installed Father Bernard on May 19, 1776. He selected leading members of the village elite to witness and certify the installation, including Laclède, Labusciere, Antoine Berard, and Vasquez.

With the installation of Father Bernard, the completion of the new church, and the strong support of the Spanish administration, a pattern of regular church-going was established. Attendance was not compulsory; but it was expected; and it became customary for all. Religion in St. Louis was never to be the solemn affair that they were accustomed to, but the local Spanish officials wisely adjusted to these external differences. At this time, the Catholic Church in Spain, as well as in France, was a national, rather than international institution and was becoming more so as Charles III of Spain tightened the royal reins. The Jesuits had been expelled from France and Spain for resisting royal absolutism, and the papal authority was severely limited. In Louisiana, church and state were so intertwined that parishes were also political units; and the pastor served the state, as the military or civil officer intervened at times in ecclesiastical matters. This caused no problems in St. Louis, since it did not conflict with the *Coutumes de Paris*, which had been adapted by the French to Canada and the Illinois country.

Under this customary law, local residents were permitted a wide latitude in their personal lives, and males over fourteen could select minor civil and church officials. No direct taxes or tithes were levied in Louisiana, a happy condition which reinforced the Creole tendency to accept designated authority without question. Other than the notary-attorney Labusciere, who was a custodian and certifier of documents rather than a prosecutor, there were no lawyers in the area in the 1770s and none were wanted. Complaints or civil suits for slander or boundary disputes were either decided quickly by the lieutenant governor or referred by him to a panel of leading residents for their advice. Violent crimes and theft were rare and punishment severe. Peace disturbance and other minor infractions were handled with paternal indulgence, but the benevolent despotism did not tolerate threats to the system. When Amable Letourneau spoke contemptuously of a decree published by Piernas, the merchant Louis Lambert and Labusciere reported him. The lieutenant governor promptly convicted Letourneau of sedition and banished him for ten years from Spanish territory.

Despite the presence of volumes by the French philosophers and other proscribed literature in their libraries, the expression of dangerous opinions in public were no more tolerable to the district's elite than to the government, as the Letourneau case demonstrated. In the prosecution of smuggling, where merchants were the culprits, Piernas and Cruzat were less efficient. Of course merchants made no speeches against His Majesty's trade regulations; they merely broke them. In manners and morals, where behavioral standards were deeply

Festivities of the Early French of Illinois. *Wood engraving by N. Sanford from Henry Howe,* Historical Collections of the Great West, *1854. MHS-Library.*

ingrained by tradition, officials were well advised not to interfere, whatever their private views. Piernas and Cruzat had directed the strengthening of religion in St. Louis as a matter of public policy, but they had to live with the Creole Sunday.

The weekly ball after Mass; the singing of profane songs; the horse racing, billiards, and card playing for money; the gaiety and excitement of Sundays and Feast days were parts of a pattern that served the community well. Just as the drunken sprees of the returning voyageurs relieved their tensions after a hard and dangerous winter's trading, so did the shared good times of merchants, farmers, artisans, and laborers and their families bond the community. The appearance of carefree disorder supported the larger order, as the merchants and eventually the Spaniards understood. The Creoles were reported to believe that their Sunday fun contained a "true and undefiled religion" which pleased their Creator as themselves. They distrusted the gloomy and stiff Sunday worshipper as one who was planning to cheat his neighbor the rest of the week.

This feeling of general contentment at the border capital was seriously disturbed in 1778. The popular Cruzat was replaced and Pierre Laclède died at the age of forty-eight. The new governor at New Orleans, the twenty-two-year-old Bernardo Gálvez, son of the viceroy of Mexico and nephew of Spain's secretary of state, first reprimanded and then removed Cruzat because of British complaints that Spanish agents had violated their territory in Illinois. Gálvez, who had his own anti-British agenda, wanted no premature excursions by his subordinates. Laclède, on a return trip from New Orleans, died "of a fever" at Arkansas Post. His grave marker, if any, soon disappeared, and the grave's location remains unknown.

Before the demise of his partnership's monopoly, Laclède had estimated his net worth at more than 200,000 livres ($37,000); but in 1769 he pledged his sizeable though illiquid fortune to his partner, Gilbert Antoine Maxent, as payment for the company's St. Louis properties, boats, and equipment. After 1766 Laclède diversified, becoming a major producer, shipper, and processor of grains. In 1767, he bought Joseph Taillon's water mill on Le Petite Riviere for four hundred livres, raised the height of the dam, and obtained from St. Ange a 240-arpent land grant to accommodate the resulting larger lake (later called Chouteau's Pond). In 1770, when he rented his block and buildings to Piernas for government headquarters, the latter awarded Laclède the flour and meal concession for the Indian trade. This arrangement assured the founder substantial annual income in addition to the revenues from farming, rentals, and his mercantile business. Laclède should have died rich, but he did not, apparently because his liberal extensions of credit filled his accounts with worthless personal notes. Shortly before his death, and seemingly aware of its imminence, Laclède deeded the former company block and buildings back to Maxent.

In 1779, with Maxent's and the governor's approval, Auguste Chouteau sold Laclède's remaining property at public auction, the proceeds to go to Maxent. Madame Chouteau bought the 480-arpent farm with its large farmhouse, barn, slave cabins, and equipment for 750 livres. Auguste Chouteau acquired the gristmill, dam, lake, and surrounding land for two thousand livres. Slaves are not mentioned in the records; either Laclède had disposed of them, which seems unlikely, or they were included with the farm and mill. Presumably there were no competing bids. Maxent's acquiescence to this procedure and the modest sums involved suggest the possibility that Laclède had arranged this convenient method of transferring his property to his heirs without so designating them. Maxent was one of the wealthiest and most powerful merchants in Louisiana, a strong supporter of the Spanish regime, and the father-in-law of successive Louisiana governors, Unzaga and Gálvez. No arrangement damaging to his interests made without his approval could have succeeded. At this time, the stone house and surrounding buildings were in bad repair, and in 1783 the government headquarters were moved to Jean Baptiste Martigny's house. The Laclède house stood vacant thereafter until 1789 when Maxent sold it to Auguste Chouteau for three thousand dollars. Chouteau gradually transformed it into a showplace.

The village by the river had survived its birthing and its founder. Superficially, like its neighbors to the south and the east, it was much more. It was imperial Spain's borderland capital, the hub of the Missouri River trade, the place of contact with the powerful and capricious Plains tribes, and a key location in the competition with Great Britain. Its opportunities and its promise had attracted to it a number of men of superior education, talent, and ambition. In the next few years, the revolution to the east would spill into the upper Mississippi valley, with difficult and trying consequences for St. Louis and its people.

Auguste Chouteau. *Oil on canvas, ca. 1810. MHS-Art.*

2.
Colony in Transition

Francisco Cruzat's successor, Captain Fernando de Leyba, was welcomed warmly by St. Louisans, who hoped that he would continue Cruzat's benign administration. Events then unforeseen, however, were to make the unlucky Leyba's tenure a stormy one. From the beginning of the American rebellion, Spanish officials had kept in close touch with Virginia and the Continental government, staying alert to developments that might be turned to advantage. Although Spain was technically neutral until 1779, its sympathies were with the Americans, or more accurately, against the British. If the Americans did well, Spain might find an opportunity to even old scores. From 1776 onward the governors at New Orleans aided the Virginians. Unzaga sent five tons of gunpowder to Virginia forts in 1776, and during the next two years Gálvez furnished munitions to Fort Pitt, spied on British defenses in Florida, and gave sanctuary to American raiders. "Volunteers" from New Orleans captured British vessels on the Mississippi and turned them over to Americans. Gálvez even allowed American Captain James Willing to sell captured British slaves in New Orleans.

Gálvez knew early in 1778 that the Virginians planned to attack the British posts in Illinois. Accordingly, on March 9 he instructed Leyba, who was headed upriver to assume command in St. Louis, to recruit Catholics from British territory by offering them free land, tools, and rations. If Leyba should happen to contact "any American chief" in the Illinois country, he should "observe the greatest secrecy and report the same to me." In effect, the new lieutenant governor was to go to the brink of war without getting caught. Leyba wasted little time. On July 8, less than a month after his arrival in St. Louis and four days after George Rogers Clark, an American colonel, had captured Kaskaskia, Leyba invited Clark to St. Louis. Shortly thereafter Clark arrived to the booming guns of full military honors. During his two-day visit the colonel was feted at receptions, balls, and banquets at Leyba's house. Clark repeated these visits frequently enough to form a mutual attachment with Leyba's beautiful younger sister Teresa. Cooperation between the two commanders continued thereafter. Clark kept the Spaniard informed about British activities, and Leyba persuaded his merchants to supply the American troops on credit. When some refused because they did not like their chances of being paid, Leyba personally guaranteed Clark's notes.

After France declared war on Great Britain in 1778, it was clear to Gálvez and Leyba that Spain would soon be drawn in. Gálvez perfected plans to seize Natchez, Mobile, and other British posts in West Florida, and Leyba studied the defenses of Spanish Illinois. In November 1778 he proposed to the governor that Fort Don Carlos be abandoned as useless, and it be replaced by a new fort five miles upstream, where a rocky bluff more than sixty feet high overlooked the Missouri near Coldwater Creek (later the site of Fort Bellefontaine). Leyba suggested further that a fort be built 240 miles up the Mississippi at the mouth of the Mua (Des Moines) River, to block that stream to British traders who annually took fifteen to twenty thousand dollars in furs from its valley. Two hundred Spanish soldiers would be required to garrison these forts and strengthen the defenses of St. Louis and Ste. Genevieve. Unfortunately for this well-reasoned plan, Gálvez could supply neither construction funds nor men. He ordered Leyba to keep the Indians happy, protect Spain's interests against British traders, and repel invaders with his existing resources.

Danger signals began to fly early in 1779. Henry Hamilton, the British commandant at Detroit, informed Gálvez that he and his Indian allies resented Louisiana's assistance to the Americans. Hamilton had just taken Vincennes from the Virginians, and he was coming soon to Illinois. No doubt the Americans upon his approach would flee to Spanish territory. If they did, the British colonel warned, he would come after them; and their protectors would suffer the consequences. Leyba was aware that Hamilton knew everything about St. Louis: the number of houses, the size of the garrison, and the lack of fortifications. If the British and Indians came to the Mississippi, Leyba reasoned, they would strike first at St. Louis because it was not fortified as Cahokia was. Hamilton's letter moved Gálvez to offer Leyba, not soldiers nor money, but advice to "preserve the honor of our arms." Fortunately, Clark recaptured Vincennes and the arrogant Hamilton as well. Instead of chasing rebels through the Grand Prairie, the British colonel spent the spring as a guest of the Commonwealth of Virginia.

Clark's victory had removed the immediate danger, but the little Spanish capital was a continuing irritant to the British. With its traders swarming up the rivers, the post was the eyes and ears for Clark's western flank. It controlled the rich trade of the Missouri, which the British coveted, and it was a supply base for the rebels. In June 1779, when Spain officially entered the war, the British colonial office

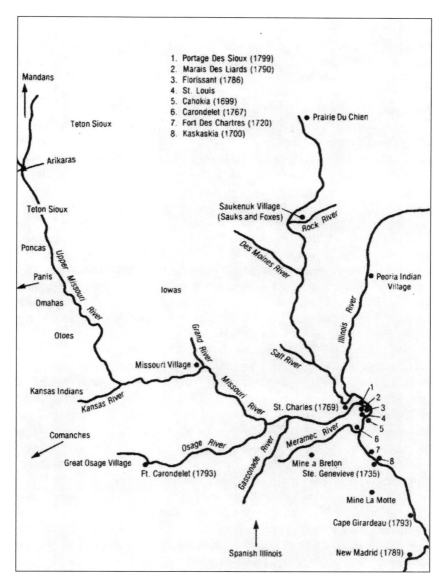

1. Portage Des Sioux (1799)
2. Marais Des Liards (1790)
3. Florissant (1786)
4. St. Louis
5. Cahokia (1699)
6. Carondelet (1767)
7. Fort Des Chartres (1720)
8. Kaskaskia (1700)

Mandans

Teton Sioux

Arikaras

Teton Sioux

Poncas

Panis

Omahas

Otoes

Kansas Indians

Comanches

Upper Missouri River

Kansas River

Great Osage Village

Ft. Carondelet (1793)

Osage River

Missouri Village

Grand River

Missouri River

Iowas

Prairie Du Chien

Saukenuk Village
(Sauks and Foxes)

Rock River

Des Moines River

Peoria Indian Village

Illinois River

Salt River

St. Charles (1769)

Gasconade River

Meramec River

Mine a Breton
Ste. Genevieve (1735)

Mine La Motte

Cape Girardeau (1793)

New Madrid (1789)

Spanish Illinois

Spanish Illinois. *Map by James Neal Primm, 1980.*

ordered General Frederick Haldimand in Canada to reduce the Mississippi posts. Patrick Sinclair, commandant at Michilimackinac, charged with planning the operation, picked Emanuel Hesse, a fur trader and former British officer, to lead the expedition. Hesse and other Canadian traders were promised the "rich fur trade of the Missouri," vengeance for old injuries inflicted by St. Louis traders, and large stores of furs and other loot from the captured posts. Indians from the Wisconsin River and western Great Lakes regions, already partisans because of Britain's relatively generous trade policy, were loaded down with presents to induce them to form the main body of the invading force.

On May 2, 1780, Hesse left Prairie du Chien with two dozen traders and their servants, Chief Wabasha and two hundred Santee Sioux warriors, Chief Matchekewis and a party of Chippewas, large contingents of Winnebagoes and Menominees, and a few warriors from a half-dozen other tribes. Wabasha and Matchekewis, with general's commissions and uniforms to match, were probably the most zealous British officers anywhere. According to Sinclair's plan, after an easy victory at St. Louis, Hesse was to remain in command there while Wabasha went on to Ste. Genevieve and Kaskaskia.

At the end of March, an American trader came downriver with word that an attack on St. Louis was in preparation. To defend his post, Leyba had thirty-four regulars, including the Fort Don Carlos and Ste. Genevieve garrisons, and the militia. The local militia was organized into an infantry company of 168 men commanded by Jean Baptiste Martigny, with the Spaniard Benito Vasquez as lieutenant and a former French soldier, Pierre Montardy, as sublieutenant; and a cavalry company of fifty men (most of them without horses), with Eugene Pouré (Beausoliel) as captain, Louis Chancelier as lieutenant, and Charles Taillon as sublieutenant. On the militia roster were eighty-five boatmen, forty-six farmers, thirty-eight merchants and traders, twenty-four hunters, twenty-three artisans, one constable, and one musician. With the exception of the officers, only Joseph Hortez and two or three others had any military experience, and their occasional Sunday formations had not supplied even the rudiments of discipline and drill. An attack in the early spring, moreover, would find no more than one-third of the men present; the rest would be up the Missouri or down the Mississippi.

Shortly after learning that the British were coming, Leyba began to fortify the village. Four circular stone towers around the perimeter were central to his plan. When completed these towers, with cannons in each, would make the village impregnable to Indian attacks, Leyba believed. Since he had no Spanish funds except for the military payroll, he had to ask the villagers for voluntary contributions to pay for the materials and masonry work. Leyba gave four hundred *piastres* (dollars) and asked the residents for another six hundred. They met their quota, at great sacrifice to some, and also volunteered four hundred days of labor without pay. Since that side of the village was the most exposed, work began first on the west tower, situated on the hill above the village (now Fourth and Walnut Streets). As it neared completion Leyba ran out of funds. Some of the merchants could have afforded more, but many of them had not been paid for supplies furnished to George Rogers Clark. They had been forced to donate for Indian presents, and they felt put upon. With no show of support from New Orleans, the people felt abandoned by their government in the face of great danger. As the most visible symbol of that government, Leyba was in a delicate position. He did not request further donations, and none were offered.

The west tower, about thirty feet in diameter and perhaps thirty-five feet in height, was completed in late May except for the roof. As a makeshift replacement for the other three towers, the defenders had to settle for entrenchments. Lieutenant Picote de Belestre, one of St. Ange's officers who had transferred to the Spanish service, supervised the digging of more than a mile of trenches around the village.

Leyba had ordered the ramshackle Missouri River fort abandoned and its armament and garrison moved to St. Louis in April. When hunters warned that Hesse's flotilla was at the mouth of the Des Moines, Leyba ordered Lieutenant Francisco de Cartabona at Ste. Genevieve to bring his regulars and sixty militiamen to St. Louis immediately. Cartabona responded quickly, as did many hunters and traders nearby. Within four or five days, according to Leyba, he had been reinforced by "about 150 men, all good shots," who were housed and fed by the residents. The three four-pounder and two six-pounder cannons from Fort Don Carlos were mounted in the tower, and other cannons were emplaced at each end of the line of trenches.

Hesse's force consisted of more than one thousand men as it neared the village, having been augmented en route by some 250 Sauk and Fox warriors. Despite their having regularly received presents at St. Louis, these Indians had been cajoled to join Hesse by the trader Joseph Calvé. On the night of May 24 the attackers camped on the east bank of the Mississippi a few miles above the village. The next morning, scouts slipped across the river to spy out the defenses. As it happened, May 25 was the Feast of Corpus Christi, and many men, women, and children were in the fields picking wild strawberries and flowers. Their presence outside the trenches was extremely risky under the circumstances; and it is difficult to explain, but it prevented the Indians from getting close enough to see that the village was fortified. Even from several miles away they must have seen the tower, but if so they did not understand its purpose.

The next day Hesse divided his command, sending the trader Ducharme (Laclède's former quarry) with about three hundred Indians to seize Cahokia, which they believed was undefended. About 1:00 P.M., the main body crossed the river for the assault on St. Louis. As soon as they came into view, the tower guard fired the signal gun sending the militia into the trenches, Cartabona and twenty men to guard the governor's house where the women and children were gathered, and Leyba and his gunners to the tower where he directed the artillery fire. Secure in their belief that the village was unfortified, the Sioux and the Winnebagoes poured down from the north, as Leyba described it, "like madmen, with an unbelievable boldness and fury, making terrible cries and a terrible firing." Behind them, in less of a hurry, were the Sauks and Foxes. Hesse and the Canadians were safely at the rear.

To the amazement of the attackers, as they neared the village the tower began to spit flame and grapeshot, and the clatter of musketry greeted them from the trenches. At the first volley the Sauks and Foxes backed off giving the vanguard, as Patrick Sinclair reported, "the but too well grounded suspicions that they were between two fires." The Canadians never came forward, to the disgust of the Sioux and Winnebagoes who apparently wanted to storm the trenches. Frontal assaults against strong defenses were most un-Indian, and these attackers' furious zeal reflected their fidelity to their British Father, as well as their well-founded hatred and fear of the "long knives" (Americans) and any friends of the Americans. For two hours after the first exchange, Wabasha directed a series of feints toward the trenches, hoping to draw the defenders into the open. Failing in that, the Indians nearly succeeded by disembowelling the corpses of the unfortunates they had caught in the fields. This so enraged the militia that they asked Leyba to lead or permit a sortie against their tormentors. Knowing that this was precisely what the enemy wanted, the lieutenant governor prudently refused.

Frustrated by the stiff defense, the apparent cowardice of the Canadian traders, and the "treachery" of the Sauks and Foxes, the Sioux and Winnebagoes swept through the fields, destroying crops and buildings and killing cattle, horses, and pigs. Additional habitants and slaves were flushed out of hiding places and killed or captured. By late afternoon the invaders were gone, leaving fourteen whites and seven slaves dead, six whites and one slave wounded, and twelve whites and thirteen slaves carried off as prisoners. Farther up the Mississippi, forty-six whites, some of them from St. Louis, were captured. According to British reports, only four Indians had been killed and four wounded. Across the river at Cahokia, Ducharme's assault had been quickly beaten off by Clark and his Americans, whose timely arrival had been another unwelcome surprise. On both sides of the river it had been the presence and sound of the cannons, rather than their effectiveness, that had intimidated the Indians. Very few of them had come close enough to be hit by musket fire, which was not effective much beyond one hundred yards. Some defenders had been wounded at the northwest corner of the trenches, where the high mounds had enabled the Indians to fire down at them, but most of the casualties occurred, and all the prisoners were taken, outside the lines. Among those killed was Amable Guion, one of the first settlers. A few berrypickers had reached the village gates, including some women who had dashed through the attackers in a horse-drawn cart. One black slave, running for his life, wrested a musket from an Indian pursuer, shot him, and burst through the lines waving the gun as a trophy.

The actions at St. Louis and Cahokia ruined the British plan for the Mississippi. If they had succeeded, despite their final defeat in Virginia, they would have had a strong claim to the Illinois country at the peace conference in 1783; and the western boundary of the United States might well have been the Appalachians instead of the Mississippi River. Ironically, the Sauks and Foxes, who were nearly annihilated by the Americans a half-century later, had by their refusal to attack virtually handed the victory to the Spanish and French defenders and ultimately to the Americans. In his report of the battle, Patrick Sinclair blamed the defeat on treachery by Calvé, Ducharme, and the Sauks and Foxes. For St. Louisans, their personal losses made the victory a hollow one. Their friends and relatives had been butchered before their eyes, their crops ruined, and their livestock killed. Leyba did not explain the presence of villagers in the fields; and unless they were there without his knowledge, it must be attributed to poor judgement on his part. The oral tradition and eventually the written accounts of *L 'Année du Grand Coup* falsely charged Leyba with lack of planning, treachery, and cowardice. This jaundiced version can be attributed to the financial losses of the merchants during two stressful years, the death and destruction of the battle, and the seeming indifference of the Spanish government which Leyba represented. These St. Louisans were neither the first nor the last people to attribute their misfortunes to a demonic individual.

Leyba's personal affairs at this time were a disaster. In December 1779, his young wife, despondent over their finances and aching to return to Spain, had died after a brief illness. He had been ill himself for several months and was barely able to walk at the time of the battle. He had two small daughters, whose futures were clouded by his illness and the mountain of debt which hung over him. The notes Clark had given him for supplies were worthless unless redeemed by the American or the Spanish government, and the latter denied responsibility. New Orleans had given Leyba only the same amount of Indian presents and rations that had been furnished to Piernas, even though the Indians "left only their dogs in their villages" when they came to St. Louis during the war. Supplies had been furnished by the St. Louis merchants upon his guarantee; and he could not deliver; yet cutting off rations and presents completely would have ruined the Indian trade. As it was, the skimpy allowances were resented, and the angry Kansas killed nine St. Louis voyageurs at their village. Leyba had profited from a trading partnership with a local merchant, as his predecessors had done, to supplement his military pay, but these profits had vanished; and he had worked under pressures they had never dreamed of. Everything considered, Leyba had done well—for Spain, for St. Louis, for the Americans, for everyone but himself and his family. Three weeks after the battle, his illness growing worse each day, Leyba handed over his command to Cartabona. On June 28, he died and was buried at the parish church. Unaware of his death, King Charles III promoted Leyba to lieutenant colonel, "as proof of his sovereign gratitude."

Victory had not quieted the fears of the people. Leyba had retained the "foreign" troops and kept guards in the trenches at all times, finally agreeing after fifteen days to cooperate with the Americans in a retaliatory strike. In the middle of June, Picote de Belestre and one hundred St. Louis militiamen joined Captain John Montgomery and more than two hundred Virginians and Creole volunteers to punish the Sauks and Foxes. Since the Indians did not stay to greet them, the invaders burned the Saukenuk village and crops and left a message promising to return. The tribes immediately made peace overtures to St. Louis and returned three habitants and three slaves they said they had taken from the Winnebagoes.

Upon the news of Leyba's death Gálvez reappointed Francisco Cruzat as lieutenant governor of the Illinois district. Cruzat broke all records for the upriver trip, bringing with him the governor's explanation that his Pensacola campaign had prevented his sending assistance. More important, Cruzat brought plenty of gunpowder, ammunition, and Indian presents. His most pressing task, Cruzat believed, was to bolster the defenses at St. Louis. The people were still agitated, knowing that the British were bribing the northern chiefs to mount another attack on the Illinois posts. After examining the existing fortifications, he decided that Leyba's four-tower plan would be expensive and ineffectual against night attacks. Trenches eroded rapidly, and a fort outside the village would not protect its people. Completed under Auguste Chouteau's supervision in 1781, Cruzat's fortifications featured a small stone *demi-lune* on the bluff at the north end of the village and a wooden stockade nine feet high and six inches thick from the demi-lune around the village back to the river. The tower, Fort San Carlos, would still be artillery headquarters.

A fort on the St. Joseph River near Lake Michigan was known to be the major supply depot for the second British thrust. When he learned that a raiding party of Cahokians had been repulsed with heavy losses there, Cruzat decided on a preemptive strike from St. Louis. A victory would discourage the pro-British Indians and win over the undecided. To lead the mission, Cruzat selected the intrepid Eugene Pouré, his captain of militia, "skilled in war and accustomed to waging it." With Louis Honoré (Tesson), Joseph Labusciere, Charles Taillon, and sixty volunteers, "Beausoliel" was to be joined by sixty Sauk, Fox, and Pottawatomie warriors enroute. On February 12, 1781, after a six-hundred-mile march carrying heavy packs in the dead of winter, the small army surprised and captured the Canadians at St. Joseph. Pouré planted the Spanish flag in the middle of the square and claimed the St. Joseph River and the area south of Lake Michigan in the name of "His Most Catholic Majesty the King of Spain."

Pouré and his volunteers stayed at St. Joseph long enough to divide the British loot among their Indian allies; then he burned the fort and returned to St. Louis. The raid created a sensation in Spain, where the ministry and the press credited the St. Louis militiamen with scotching the British threat to Louisiana. Later, during the peace negotiations between Great Britain and the allies in 1783, Spain laid claim to the Illinois River valley on the strength of Pouré's conquest.

Farther south in Illinois, George Rogers Clark's Virginians had created tensions with the French villagers and the Illinois Indians. Although Clark allayed Creole fears by not interfering in religious matters, his soldiers often treated the villagers and their Indian neighbors with contempt. The Illinois Creole was soft-spoken, polite, usually slow-moving, while the frontier Virginian was strident and quarrelsome. The frontier bully-boy democrats openly despised losers;

the paternal order of the French villages, which the British had not disturbed, had room for all. A number of the eastside French were half-castes, which was obnoxious to the Americans. When Clark assumed no responsibility for routine civil administration, a kind of frontier lawlessness existed during the American occupation. Since there was always a possibility that the British would return, farmers, merchants, and Indians alike could never be sure when they would be cast as traitors to one side or the other. The farmer and laborer hated the Americans' arrogance and rough ways; the merchant felt insecure in his property and privileges. The Indians could get no presents nor rations from the Americans, and the British were gone, so they looked to their Spanish Father. For the ordinary Creole, the certainty of familiar paternal justice was west of the river; for the merchant, Spanish St. Louis meant privilege protected.

By 1781 it was obvious that the Americans were in Illinois to stay. St. Louisans began to refer to the strip of lowlands between the river and the bluffs on the east bank of the Mississippi as the American Bottoms, and the villagers there resumed their emigration to Spanish Illinois. Chaotic conditions under American rule and Spanish inducements combined to bring about an increase of 19 percent in St. Louis's population between 1780 and 1783, to about nine hundred excluding Indian slaves. Since there was virtually no natural increase, owing to low birth or infant survival rates and wartime casualties, immigration accounted for this modest but steady growth.

At the end of the Revolutionary War in 1783 anarchy reigned on the American side of the Mississippi. Virginia, which had established the county of Illinois in 1778, allowed county government there to lapse in 1782, leaving each village to govern itself. Longstanding land titles were now in danger, and the future seemed clouded to many Creole families. In 1784 the United States accepted Virginia's western land, with a guarantee that the Creole land titles would be confirmed. The Land Ordinance of 1785 then provided an orderly though expensive public land policy for the American territory north of the Ohio. Some pressure for emigration was relieved by these measures, and between 1784 and 1787 St. Louis grew slowly. Then in 1787 Congress passed the Northwest Ordinance, organizing the territory politically; providing for its division eventually into states; guaranteeing freedom of religion, trial by jury, and public support of education; and prohibiting slavery. The prospect of a flood of Americans and their taxes to the American Bottoms may have spurred the growth of the St. Louis district between 1787 and 1791; but the antislavery provision of the Northwest Ordinance, the usual explanation, was not a major factor. The population of the district increased by 34 percent, from 1,028 to 1,378, and the number of slaves rose as well; but the owners of these slaves in 1791, with few exceptions, had come to St. Louis before 1787. Most of them had lived in the village for ten years or more.

Since 1765 the British had complained that the more substantial and talented French families were leaving their territories. This continued to be so under the Virginian and American regimes. The wealthier the merchant the more vulnerable he was and the more he sought stability and order. Among these individuals were the principal merchants of Kaskaskia and Cahokia, Gabriel Cerré and Charles Gratiot. Cerré, the older of the two, was a native of Montreal, who had come to Kaskaskia as a merchant in 1755 at the age of twenty-two. For the next twenty-four years his caravans traversed the

Gabriel Cerré. *Photograph of painting. MHS-PP.*

Ohio-Wabash-Maumee Portage route to Montreal, carrying furs and hides to their best market and returning to Illinois laden with merchandise and cash. This round trip of more than three thousand miles was even more difficult and dangerous than the routes to New Orleans (closed to him as a British subject) or Prairie du Chien; but the daring and resourceful Cerré, who personally led his caravans, preferred his family connections and the higher prices and better merchandise available at Montreal.

Cerré was a close friend of Laclède, who had witnessed his wedding in 1764; and despite Spanish restrictions, he did a lot of business in Spanish Illinois long before he moved to St. Louis. His Catholic Majesty's writ did not run everywhere in his territories; and Cerré's engagés operated not only in Illinois and Tennessee, where he built a post on the later site of Nashville, but on the west side of the Mississippi south of Ste. Geneviève. Despite his dislike of the British, Cerré was a successful merchant desiring to remain so, and he adjusted quickly to their rule at both ends of his business. By the 1770s he was a valued friend of the highest British officials in Canada and Detroit. When George Rogers Clark took Kaskaskia in 1778 he was warned that Cerré was pro-British, but the Virginian needed this man whom he described as "one of the most eminent men in the country, of great influence among the people." Clark guessed correctly that Cerré's interests would determine his politics. Accordingly, the colonel accepted the merchant's promise of loyalty to Virginia and watched with approval as Cerré won a hot contest for judge of the Kaskaskia District Court.

After a few months as a magistrate, sickened by the slashing politics and often lawless conduct of Virginia's frontier officials, Cerré bought the Labusciere block on La Rue Royale in St. Louis from Louis Perrault with its large stone house and stone warehouse. Having lost no time in moving his family and business, Cerré sought and was granted a large share of the Missouri River fur trade in October 1779. As soon as he arrived in St. Louis, Cerré was its wealthiest and leading merchant. Even under the Spanish flag he continued to trade at Montreal, but he did enough business in New Orleans to win the friendship of two Spanish governors. As his business prospered in St. Louis, Cerré amassed property around the edges of the village amounting to more than 1,000 arpents, in addition to 7,056 arpents (about 6,000 acres) on the Meramec River. The census of 1791 showed Cerré to be the largest slaveholder in upper Louisiana, with forty-three slaves in a household of sixty-one. He also owned Indian slaves but their number was not recorded.

Gabriel Cerré's influence was felt in many ways in St. Louis. His opinion was valued by the Spanish authorities, and his presence affected the conduct of their offices. In 1796, at the height of their concern about disloyalty, the governor advised a military commander to seek Cerré's counsel and trust his word. In 1782 he was elected a syndic (trustee), and he was a father figure to many residents throughout his career. He gave legal advice, acted as guardian to many village children, and assumed responsibility for a number of orphans. Perhaps his most lasting influence, however, was through his family. His oldest daughter Marie Anne married a Canadian, Pierre Panét, in 1781. Their home at Montreal was open to relatives and other St. Louisans seeking business and educational opportunities. Pascal Cerré, the only son, married Marie Thérèse Lamy of a merchant family in 1797 and was active in the fur trade and business until 1849. As was usually the case among affluent St. Louisans, marriages were arranged in heaven with a good deal of help from the parents below. Cerré's second daughter Thérèse married Auguste Chouteau in 1786

Antoine Soulard. *Photograph of painting. MHS-PP.*

when she was seventeen and he thirty-six. This was the most advantageous match possible for both parties. Chouteau's extraordinary talents and the Laclède heritage had already made him a powerful man; his marriage added substantially to his prestige and property. Julia, Gabriel and Catherine Cerré's youngest child, delighted her parents too. In 1795 she married Antoine P. Soulard, a former French naval lieutenant who was the king's surveyor for upper Louisiana. Soulard's brilliance, engineering training, and military skills made him a favorite with Spanish officials; and his office gave him opportunities to enhance Julia's substantial dowry and inheritance. The lasting significance of Cerré's and Soulard's property accumulations were demonstrated in the nineteenth century by the numerous Soulard additions to the city.

When Catherine Cerré died in 1800 the family fortune was assessed at twenty-six thousand dollars, with little value assigned to the thousands of acres of land. Under the Spanish (and French) law, 50 percent of the estate went to Gabriel and 50 percent was divided equally among the children. The inheritance law did not discriminate against women, and, in fact as well as in theory, the wives in St. Louis's French and Creole families were the partners rather than the property of their husbands. After his wife's death, Cerré continued his annual trips to Montreal, motivated now not only by business, but the presence there of his grandchildren, including Auguste Chouteau's oldest son who was attending school there. In April 1805 Gabriel Cerré died, only a few months after returning from Montreal with two boatloads of merchandise.

Charles Gratiot, a native of Switzerland, whose family had mercantile connections in London and Montreal, established a trading house in Cahokia in 1777 after several years learning the Indian trade in Canada. As a well-educated man with capital, knowledgeable about agriculture and the fur business, and adept in both the French and English languages, Gratiot naturally cut a figure in British Illinois. After George Rogers Clark drove out the British, Gratiot became a partisan of the Americans and worked closely with Clark, serving as a link between the Virginian and the residents, as Cerré did in Kaskaskia. His relationship with Clark kept Gratiot on the east side for more than three years, but eventually he sought the relative safety and stability of Spanish territory. Early in 1781 he moved to St. Louis and a few weeks later was married to Victoire Chouteau, eldest daughter of Laclède and Madame Chouteau. Though no formal partnership existed, Gratiot thereafter frequently participated in joint trading ventures with Auguste and Pierre Chouteau. For the next dozen years, envisioning himself as an international merchant,

Gratiot travelled widely—to London, Paris, Philadelphia, New York, Montreal, seeking contacts and trading alliances. Generally, he made more friends than money on these junkets, but in St. Louis his business prospered. After 1795, when Kentuckians, Pennsylvanians, and other Americans began to come to the area in significant numbers, much of their business went to Gratiot, whose cosmopolitan manners, friendliness, and proficiency in English impressed them.

In addition to his fur trading and retail business, Gratiot operated a mill and distillery on his farm four miles from the village and a tannery and salt works on the Meramec. First awarded by Cruzat in 1785 and finally confirmed by Governor Gayoso de Lemos in 1798, Gratiot's "farm" was nearly three miles square (5,712 acres), the largest grant ever made by the Spanish near the village. It was bounded on the east by the Prairie Des Noyers common field (Kingshighway Boulevard) and on the west it extended well beyond the present city limits to Big Bend Boulevard. Including much of the Forest Park on the north, it reached to the vicinity of Chippewa Avenue on the south. Through this and other grants and purchases near and in St. Louis, Gratiot eventually accumulated a fortune through land speculation. He needed it, since he and Victoire had thirteen children, nine of whom grew to maturity. When the Americans took over Louisiana in 1804, Gratiot was among the half-dozen most powerful men in the district. Until his death in 1817, Gratiot and Auguste Chouteau were officeholders and major figures in the area's dominant political faction.

The marriages and careers of Gratiot's children illustrate the nature and complex interrelationships of St. Louis's ruling elite, who, according to Amos Stoddard, had built fortunes on "the labor of nine-tenths of the population on the distant lakes and rivers." Though basically the same group in 1800 as in the 1770s, death and misfortune had removed some familiar names and immigration had added others. French or Canadian bourgeois origins, with a dash of emigre nobility, characterized the newcomers. Property and education mattered, but the pervasive feature of the dominant families was their connection with Madame Chouteau. During the Spanish regime, they supported and were favored by the Spanish officials. Lieutenant governors Piernas and Cruzat and several governors had Creole wives, Unzaga and Gálvez having married daughters of Laclède's partner Maxent. The last two lieutenant governors, Zenon Trudeau and Charles de Hault de Lassus, were of French origin, the latter from the Ste. Genevieve area. Maintenance of this elite depended upon intermarriage and the absorption of qualified outsiders, preferably from France. Charles Gratiot's own excellent credentials were enhanced by his timely union with Victoire Chouteau, and their children dutifully followed the formula. In 1799, their daughter Julia married Jean P. Cabanné, a recent arrival from Laclède's home district of Béarn, France. Another daughter, Victoire, married her mother's nephew, Sylvestre Labbadie, Jr.; Marie Thérèse married a Frenchman; and Emilie Anne married her first cousin Pierre Chouteau, Jr. Henri Gratiot chose Susan Hempstead, of a substantial Connecticut family which became prominent in St. Louis; and his beautiful sister Isabella carried off the prize, the Vicomte without portfolio, Jules De Mun, born in Santo Domingo of French emigre parents. His father's pride and joy, Charles Gratiot, Jr., a graduate of West Point who became a general and engineer of distinction (he built Fortress Monroe and other military installations), married well in Philadelphia.

In the same pattern, the Labbadies, Papins, and Cerrés united and reunited among themselves and with the Chouteaus, Kiercereaus, Dubreuils, Prattes, Cabannés, Sarpys, and other leading Creole families. In 1814, when the revered *grande dame*, Madame Chouteau, died in her eighty-second year, most of the many mourners at her funeral had familial reasons for weeping, some of them several times over. By this time, Pierre Laclède was a distant memory for a few older St. Louisans, his name seldom mentioned.

The successful outcome of the Revolutionary War, by which Spain regained the Floridas and acquired new neighbors on the east bank of the Mississippi, did little to solve its imperial problems. To the west the Osages despoiled the Arkansas River area killing traders and Indians and stealing livestock and merchandise. To the east, the Americans too were difficult neighbors. Their relentless extermination and dispossession of the Indians in and below the Ohio Valley created pressures on the Spanish frontier—from desperate Indians alternately seeking sanctuary and presents and raiding in Louisiana. American farmers pouring down the Ohio and into Kentucky posed a dilemma for the Spanish ministry. Should traditional Spanish imperial restrictions be imposed, antagonizing the American settlers and inviting border warfare, or should Spain relax further the relatively generous trade policies it had recently practiced in Louisiana? To the north, the British, unchastened by defeat and citing the failure of the United States to honor its commitments under the Treaty of Paris, clung to Detroit, Michilimackinac, and other Northwest posts from which their Scots and Creole traders moved aggressively into the upper Mississippi, Des Moines, and upper Missouri River beaver bonanzas.

For the merchants the British were both a problem and a solution. British traders had enormous advantages over their competitors. They had the best and cheapest goods, the world's premier fur market in London, and strong backing by British capitalists and their government. They gave the Indians a better bargain than the Creoles could, and their illegal presence on the Des Moines and upper Missouri effectively barred those regions to their rightful owners. On the other hand, the British would buy and sell wherever and whenever it was to their advantage, and they welcomed not only Gabriel Cerré and Auguste Chouteau but anyone else who brought furs to their markets. As a further inducement, furs transported over the cool northern waters did not lose value from spoilage as they often did on the steamy lower Mississippi. Though never endorsed by official policy, this illegal traffic was known about, understood, and usually winked at in New Orleans, Havana, and even Madrid, except when Spain and Great Britain were at war. Without this market and source of merchandise and capital the Spanish outpost at St. Louis would have required much greater expenditures by the Crown to survive, and its survival was still essential for the protection of New Spain (Mexico).

In 1784 Spain decided to stifle the American threat by closing the lower Mississippi to all foreign nations. This was intended to stem the flood of Americans across the Appalachians by depriving them of the major outlet for their flour and tobacco, but its major effects on Louisiana were negative. Lower Louisiana, already committed to a plantation economy producing sugar, cotton, and rice for export, was continually short of flour, which if not obtainable from the upper valley had to be bought at ruinous prices, chiefly from the French West Indies. In upper Louisiana this restriction simply increased the illegal trade with British Canada. Since 1777 Spain had been trying to entice Catholics from British territory to St. Louis and Ste. Genevieve, both for defensive purposes and to increase agricultural production, and had ordered the lieutenant governors to encourage the residents to grow more foodstuffs for export. Despite the generous terms offered to new settlers, they had not come in large numbers and the efforts to stimulate production had been ineffective. People had come to St. Louis to be in the fur business, it was their way of life; and for the merchants, whose influence was paramount, there was no reason to change. As Leyba stated to Governor Gálvez in 1778: "These people are interested in commerce and not in farming because the latter gives them little or no gain, while the former supports them and even makes them rich."

The common field system of farming, while far less productive than the Americans' individual farms, also required less time and effort; and the concentration of homes in the village protected the farmers from marauding Indians. Not until after Americans had arrived in significant numbers, in the late 1790s, was the system abandoned by St. Louisans. Not laziness but perceived economic interest kept them, in the words of U.S. Captain Amos Stoddard, "ever engaged in the pursuit of phantoms."

To Stoddard, who handled the transfer of upper Louisiana to the United States in 1804, and to the Spanish governors at New Orleans who wanted cheap flour, the Creoles were a misguided lot. But from the local point of view, the community they had built was a congenial and successful place; and if it showed no signs of becoming a vast agricultural entrepôt, why should they shed tears? Ironically, the Americans, even to the severest critics, were the best witnesses to the quality of life in St. Louis. Brigadier General Joseph Harmar wrote in 1787 that "St. Louis is the handsomest and genteelest village I have seen on the Mississippi. . . . The inhabitants are the same sort as before described [French and Creoles] except they are more wealthy. . . ." Arthur St. Clair, governor of the Illinois Territory, observed in 1790 that "at present . . . St. Louis, is the most flourishing village of the Spaniards on the upper part of the Mississippi and it has been greatly advanced by the people who have abandoned the American side." The Virginian Moses Austin thought in 1797 that it was "better built than any Town on the Mississippi, and has a Number of wealthy Mercht. and an extensive trade. . . . Its fast improving and will soon be a large place. . . . The large Settlements making on the Missouri by the Americans will be of great advantage to St. Louis the wealth of which is so much greater than any other town on the Missisipi." Even Amos Stoddard, despite his official criticisms, wrote to his sister on June 16, 1804: "The compact part of St. Louis contains upwards of 200 houses, mostly very large, and built of stone; it is elevated and healthy, and the people are rich and hospitable. They live in a style equal to the large seaboard towns, and I find no want of education among them."

In 1788 the Spanish eased their restrictions to allow Americans to ship produce to New Orleans upon payment of a 15 percent tariff. General James Wilkinson, a conniving Kentucky trader-politician, had advised this as a means of luring Kentuckians into the Spanish fold. He had also wanted a monopoly of this trade in return for his help in the projected separation. The Spanish refused him the monopoly, but they did put him on their payroll as a secret agent at four thousand pesos a year and gave him and his friends a special 6 percent tariff rate. Governor Estevan Miró believed that detaching Kentucky from the United States would save Spanish Louisiana, but his immediate purpose was to forestall an attack reportedly being organized by George Rogers Clark. Under the new policy, thousands of barrels of flour, tobacco, and salt pork moved from the Ohio valley to New Orleans each year. Ironically, it also sharply reduced separatist sentiment in the American West.

Miró clung to his separatist goal, but he also developed another strategy to strengthen Spanish defenses. Only three years earlier Bernardo de Gálvez had called the few Americans living in Spanish territory "enemies within," but now his successor Miró offered free land to Americans who came to Louisiana or Florida. Protestants were required only to swear allegiance to the Spanish Crown and refrain from holding public church services. They were assured that there would be no interference with their private beliefs and practices. Hundreds of Americans accepted the invitation to West Florida and lower Louisiana, where the government tobacco market at New Orleans was an attraction; and in 1789 they began to arrive in numbers near the mouth of the Ohio (New Madrid). St. Louis was too far from the downriver markets to share in this influx, however; and Philip Fine, John Coons, and Ann Camp, who had come to the village between 1781 and 1787, remained its only native Americans.

Meanwhile, merchants looked for solutions to their problems with the Osages and the invading British fur traders. Though the Osages were still peaceable in the St. Louis district, since 1783 they had accelerated their attacks along the Arkansas, at Natchitoches and into Texas. The Spaniards had tried withholding presents from and prohibiting trade with the Osages and had urged other tribes to wage war on them, but these tactics failed. When the Osages were under the ban, they denied traders access to other tribes and took their own business to the British on the Des Moines River. When other Indians attacked the Osages they invited destruction. While St. Louis traders were seldom direct targets of Osage raiders, they suffered from the loss of their most lucrative business while the Osages were under interdiction. In 1793, Governor Baron de Carondelet ordered a general war on the Osages. Under his campaign plan the Sauks and Foxes wiped out a few remaining Missouris and killed three or four wandering Osages, but they never approached the Osage villages.

The remainder of Carondelet's strategy was cancelled by a new threat. Edmond Genét, the French minister to the United States, believed that American sympathy for the French Revolution was so overwhelming and the United States so weak that he could use it as a staging area for attacks on France's enemies. George Rogers Clark,

St. Louis's former great friend, in a move which could have landed him in prison, accepted a major-general's commission from Genét and called for volunteers to invade Louisiana. With this grim prospect in view, Carondelet needed peace with the Osages whose fighting force of more than fifteen hundred warriors would threaten the rear of the Spanish defenders against Clark. At this point Auguste Chouteau proposed an audacious plan which pleased the Osages and astonished and gratified the governor. In return for a monopoly of the Osage trade for six years, Chouteau contracted to build a stone fort at his own expense at the Big Osage village 350 miles southwest of St. Louis. Pierre Chouteau was to command the fort's garrison of twenty militiamen, each of whom would be paid one hundred pesos a year by the Crown. After six years the fort would become Spanish property.

The beauty of Chouteau's scheme was that it worked. The Osages viewed the fort primarily as a trading post despite its cannons, and so it was. If the Indians had not wanted it, they could have prevented its construction; and once it was built, they could have destroyed it at will, but they did not. A trading post run by the Chouteaus and located in their village would add to their prestige and affluence. The Osages trusted and respected the brothers, both of whom, but especially Pierre, had lived with them periodically for nearly twenty years. The Chouteaus understood the Osages—could think as they thought, speak as they spoke, and live as they lived. The Spaniards, accustomed to authoritarian structures—their own and the great Indian civilizations of Mexico and Peru—never understood the limits of chiefly authority among the Osages. As the Chouteaus knew, the killings of lone hunters, traders, and other Indians were often neither for plunder nor vengeance but to complete a religious ritual known as the mourning-war ceremony by lifting a scalp to place at the bier of a departed relative or person of importance. Once this ritual was under way, neither chief nor treaty nor prince could stop it. Thus the repeated laments of the Spanish that the Osage chiefs had broken their word.

As soon as the plan was agreed upon, the delighted Carondelet reported to his superiors: "All the risk falls on Don Renato Augusto Chouteau, a man of incorruptible integrity and friendliness to the government, . . . the great authority that he possesses over these savages, furnish him with facilities for succeeding in an enterprise so arduous that no other man could attain it." As Carondelet saw it, the Chouteaus would control the Osages by persuasion when possible, by force when necessary. If the young warriors started after scalps, Pierre Chouteau could stop them. In practice, the Chouteaus "controlled" the Osages by flattering attentions, well-timed presents to cooperative chiefs or warriors, personal fearlessness, and by sitting in council with the elders and chiefs. Meetings of the elders were usually held in the fort, with the hosts providing refreshments and thereby gaining prestige with each meeting. With all this, the "control" was not perfect. Pierre Chouteau usually prevailed in council, but when mourning-war rituals reached the scalp-seeking stage, he and the elders got out of the way. Fewer scalping parties headed for the Spanish posts than before; and the governor was pleased; but the Pawnees and Padoucas paid the bill.

Fort Carondelet, as the Chouteaus shrewdly named it, was completed in 1795 though not to specifications. Chouteau apparently erected a large log trading house atop a rocky bluff with a wall of stone and stakes around it. There was little point in a stone fort which would have required an army to defend it, and what Carondelet did not know would not hurt him. Despite occasional incidents on the Arkansas River, the relationship thrived. The Osages grew more affluent, and so did the Chouteaus. During the better years of the monopoly, the brothers took out twenty-four thousand pesos in furs of which a third or more was profit. Earlier, when the Indians were less sophisticated, traders had netted up to 300 percent in the lower Missouri trade. In 1798 Zenon Trudeau noted that Auguste Chouteau had "accredited ascendancy" in the Big and Little Osage tribes, apparently meaning that the brothers had been adopted into the hereditary chieftainship clans.

In 1792, in response to complaints by excluded traders, Carondelet had opened the Missouri trade, except for the Osages, to all Spanish subjects. The resulting cut-throat competition, confusion, and brawling was more advantageous to the Indians than to the traders, and the trade was closed in 1793. At the same time a Board of Trade was founded in St. Louis, headed by a syndic elected by all merchants. Carondelet prescribed, and the board expanded, a set of regulations for the fur trade restricting eligibility to residents of Spanish Illinois who had a trading connection with a New Orleans merchant. The board also set prices for furs and merchandise. On May 5, 1794, the board drew up articles of incorporation for "The Company of Explorers of the Upper Missouri," which was authorized to carry the St. Louis trade to the Arikaras, Mandans, and other tribes above the Poncas. In addition, the Missouri Company would "make expeditions against foreigners who . . . attract the trade of our savages, and . . . confiscate their furs or goods." The "foreigners" were the Scots and French Canadians of the British Northwest and Hudson's Bay Companies who had built trading posts on the upper Missouri.

The syndic and leading spirit of the Missouri Company was Jacques Clamorgan, a West Indian native of Welsh descent who had come to St. Louis a dozen years earlier. Clamorgan apparently had some legal training and was a flamboyant wheeler-dealer the likes of which the village had never seen. His fluency and imperial imagination impressed the Spaniards and nearly everyone else who heard him. He lived openly with several mulatto concubines, which barred him from the social but not the commercial elite. Clamorgan sold his brainchild to Carondelet and Trudeau not only as a means of expanding St. Louis's trade territory and driving out the British, but as an exploration which would give Spain a route through the northern Rockies to the Pacific—a vantage point from which the Spaniards could keep an eye on Russian activity in northern California. Carondelet was so overwhelmed by the proposal that he sweetened his endorsement with an offer of three thousand pesos to the first Spanish subject who reached the Pacific via the Missouri River.

Despite the great expectations of its promoter and the authorities, the Missouri Company did not attract St. Louis's wealthiest and most respected merchants. Gabriel Cerré, the Chouteaus, Charles Gratiot, Sylvestre Labbadie, and Joseph Papin declined to participate. Each of them had taken great risks in the past and would in the future, but they did not care to entrust their capital to Jacques Clamorgan. The members of the company, with one or two exceptions, were ambitious fringe members of the St. Louis merchant elite. In addition to Clamorgan, they were: Antoine Reilhe, a Canadian who had come to St. Louis in 1786; Joseph Motard, a major St. Louis fur merchant for twenty years; Laurent Durocher, a minor trader who had explored on the western plains; Benito Vasquez; Joseph Robidoux, a shoemaker and merchant; Charles Sanguinet, a Canadian who had gained status by marrying Marie Condé; Hyacinthe St. Grasse, whose wife signed for him; and Louis Dubreuil, a young merchant from a leading family.

To head the company's first expedition, its directors chose Jean Baptiste Truteau, an occasional trader who had conducted the village's private school for boys for two decades. Apparently chosen for his powers of observation and intelligence rather than his experience, Truteau was given absolute power on the upper Missouri, including the fixing of prices of furs and merchandise, subject only to the company's general guidelines. He was instructed to gather information about the geography and Indians of the upper country with special emphasis upon the country beyond the Rockies—the Shoshone and the Flathead Indians and the rivers to the Pacific. Truteau was to seize without compensation the furs and merchandise of anyone, Spanish or foreigner, who was found trading north of the Ponca villages—with the Arikaras, Mandans, Cheyennes, Sioux, Shoshones, and Gros Ventres (Big Bellies), among other tribes. The Indians were to be kept simple in their habits, active in reproduction, diligent in finding and curing furs, and friendly to Spain. A "very high price" was to be charged for goods and the Indians were to be encouraged to place a high value on "bagatelles." Truteau was also advised by the directors not to send those of his men who owed large sums to the company on dangerous missions.

With eight men and a large pirogue full of trade goods, Truteau left St. Louis on June 7, 1794, bound for the Mandan villages twelve hundred miles up the winding Missouri. He slipped past the familiar tribes which might have detained him only to be surprised by a band of Teton Sioux, who promptly relieved him of half his goods. The demoralized party then went into camp near the Ponca village and spent the winter trading with that nation, the Omahas, and the Sioux. A few dozen packs of furs were obtained during this period; but the brilliant and imperious Omaha chieftain Blackbird, after chiding Truteau for avoiding him on the upstream journey, demanded and received gunpowder and goods on credit. In the spring, the company party went on to the Arikaras, where they contacted the Mandans, the Cheyennes, the Gros Ventres, and a Canadian named Menard, who had lived with the Mandans for sixteen years. From these sources Truteau recorded much valuable data about the Missouri River almost to its source and its tributaries including the Yellowstone. The Cheyennes told him of the Snake Indians and a great river (the Snake-Columbia) which flowed to the western sea; and Menard explained the idiosyncracies of the various tribes. Others told him of the bighorn sheep and other unique animals of the high mountains. By the summer of 1796 Truteau was back in St. Louis laden with information but not with furs.

Only a few months after Truteau's departure, the company had dispatched a second and larger party after him which was plundered by the Poncas and disbanded—almost a total loss. Undaunted, Clamorgan, whose colleagues were now financially ruined, found another backer in New Orleans, Regis Loisel, and hired James Mackay, a Scot who had come to St. Louis in 1793, to lead a new expedition. Mackay had been to the Mandan villages with one of the British fur companies; he knew the upper Missouri region; and he knew his business. In August 1795 Mackay set out from St. Louis with thirty-three men and fifty thousand pesos worth of merchandise. By acceding to Blackbird's usual extortionate demands, Mackay proceeded to the Arikara villages in good order; and in 1796 one of his lieutenants seized the British post at the Mandan village and ordered the British to vacate the area. The Hudson's Bay Company complied, but the Northwest Company belligerently responded that it would yield only to superior force. When Mackay returned to St. Louis in 1797, he had gathered enough information to draw an accurate map of the entire upper Missouri valley. In less than three years, despite a good many blunders and some bad luck, the Missouri Company had traversed much of the route later followed by Lewis and Clark. If Napoleonic diplomacy had not cost them Louisiana, the Spaniards would undoubtedly have extended and secured their Northwest empire to the Pacific within a few years.

Financially, the Missouri Company was a disaster. Its ventures had returned only a fraction of the 250,000 pesos expended. Several members of the company charged Clamorgan with duplicity and bad management, and Clamorgan railed at Mackay for his generosity to Blackbird. With funds from Loisel, Clamorgan bought out at a discount or traded for all of the shares except those of Joseph Robidoux, who was still hoping to profit from his interest in the company, though he was Clamorgan's most persistent detractor. From 1797 on, the company, now essentially a partnership between Clamorgan and Loisel, concentrated on profits rather than exploration.

Even without the bitterness caused by the Missouri Company's losses, the St. Louis mercantile community had lost its cohesiveness by the mid-1790s. The abstention of Cerré, the Chouteaus, Gratiot, and their in-laws from the company carried the seeds of factionalism, and tensions mounted as more aspiring traders clamored for licenses. Free trade had failed disastrously in 1792 and few really wanted it resumed. The petitions against the existing monopolies in the 1790s were promoted chiefly by Manuel de Lisa, Charles Sanguinet, and Joseph Robidoux, who were less opposed to the principle than they were in favor of themselves as the monopolists. Chouteau's Osage venture had shut off the most profitable trade to others, but its success in taming these tribes muted the criticisms. With all of its promise, the Missouri Company had not immediately expanded St. Louis's trade territory, and the hard-pressed lieutenant governor was in the position of having less to give to more qualified applicants. Despite his financial setback, Clamorgan was judged to have served the Crown well and thus deserving of further special consideration. Under pressure from New Orleans, Trudeau in 1796 awarded the Oto, Ponca, and Omaha trade to Clamorgan and Loisel.

By 1798, however, Trudeau had had enough of Clamorgan, who

had requested a ten-thousand-peso annual subsidy to support further explorations. The lieutenant governor, having decided that the Welshman was either "a daring knave or a complete madman," removed all of his exclusive privileges. But the ebullient Clamorgan did not squelch easily; and in 1802 he persuaded a new governor, Don Manuel de Salcedo, to give his firm the entire Missouri River trade north of the Kansas River. Now, the entire trade was in the hands of Clamorgan and a partnership headed by Manuel de Lisa.

Lisa, a Spaniard born in New Orleans in 1771, had come to St. Louis in the late 1790s. A match for Clamorgan in ambition, imagination, and energy, he had wrested the Osage monopoly from the Chouteaus in 1802 through the influence of relatives in the New Orleans bureaucracy and by pleading the poverty and large hungry families of his partners Charles Sanguinet, Gregoire Sarpy, and Francois Benoist. Salcedo, whose weaknesses nearly matched those of his royal master Charles IV, had granted Lisa the concession over the opposition of Lieutenant Governor Charles DeLassus. The triumph over Chouteau proved to be a hollow one. With DeLassus's help Chouteau collected fifteen hundred pesos from the Lisa firm for the loss of his monopoly, which had been renewed in 1801. A greater blow came when Chief White Hair moved half of the Osages to the Arkansas River where they resumed trading with Pierre Chouteau. After quarreling with his senior partner, Sanguinet withdrew from the firm; and when Lisa accused DeLassus of favoring his fellow Frenchmen against Spanish traders, the lieutenant governor jailed him for sedition. After apologizing, the audacious Spaniard was released.

The spiteful quarrels of the merchants were only surface manifestations of the winds of change that were blowing in St. Louis. Superficially the little village seemed much the same. The fur trade was still dominant; the social life and amusements continued with the benevolent participation of the leading families; and though more stone houses had been built, the village was still under the hill. The population, having reached 1,168 in 1791, had actually declined to 1,039 in 1800. But these figures are somewhat misleading. By 1800, St. Louis had spawned several satellite villages, most of whose residents had come from St. Louis.

The first of these, Carondelet, was nearly as old as St. Louis. First called Delor's Village and then Louisbourg, but popularly known as *Vide Poche*, this little settlement developed slowly after 1767 around the home of an ex-naval officer named Clement Delor de Treget, near the mouth of the River des Peres. In 1796,

Carondelet, renamed for the Spanish governor, had 181 residents, including only three slaves. The village had a common field of six thousand arpents, to which its married men devoted their working hours. Single men usually worked for St. Louis traders as boatmen. Carondelet produced a large surplus and occasionally shipped flour to New Orleans, but most of its produce was peddled in St. Louis. The clattering Vide Poche charettes laden with produce and wood were a familiar sight (and sound) in St. Louis for decades after the transfer to the United States. The villagers, following Delor's example, were content with the simple medieval agricultural lifestyle; and after a generation, even the aristocratic founder's descendants could not read and write.

Twenty-one miles northwest of St. Louis, on the north bank of the Missouri, stood the village of *San Carlos de Misuri* (St. Charles), known originally as *Les Petites Cotes*. Founded by Louis Blanchette and a group of Creole hunters in 1768, the location had attracted hunters and farmers from St. Louis because of its nearness to game and the fertility of the nearby bottom lands. Charles Taillon, a veteran militia officer who had been Pouré's lieutenant in the capture of Fort St. Joseph in 1781, was commandant at St. Charles from 1792 to 1804. The village's population in 1800 was 614, including 39 slaves. Its residents considered themselves hunters and voyageurs, but in 1796, St. Charles grew more than one-fourth of the wheat and one-fifth of the tobacco produced in Spanish Illinois.

Near the south bank of the Missouri, about fifteen miles north and slightly west of St. Louis, in the vicinity of Coldwater Creek, was the village of St. Ferdinand (Florissant). By 1785 Jacques, Nicholas, Antoine, and Francois Marechal, and a half-dozen other Creole farmers from St. Louis, Kaskaskia, and Cahokia, had built a cluster of homes and were working a common field there. In 1796 Florissant had 185 residents, including seven slaves. Zenon Trudeau's opinion that its residents were exceptional workers was supported by their production. Despite its small population, only Ste. Genevieve and St. Charles surpassed Florissant in wheat-growing, and the prairie settlement produced 10,670 pounds of tobacco, more than 43 percent of the total in Spanish Illinois. Its two-mile-wide prairie and rich bottom lands attracted a good many Americans during the next few years, and by 1800 the population of the village and nearby farms was nearly three hundred.

Other settlements in the St. Louis district included *Village à Robért*, or *Marais des Liards*, founded in 1794 by Robert Owens about five miles west of Florissant. Its 208 residents in 1800 were primarily hunters, although most of the families cultivated some corn and tobacco. The village and the nearby river bottoms attracted a number of Americans, and by 1804 the latter outnumbered the French. Deplorably, the Americans changed its name to Owens' Station and later to Bridgeton. After his return from the upper Missouri in 1797, James Mackay founded the settlement of St. Andrews on the Bonhomme bottoms of the Missouri, twenty-four miles west of St. Louis. By 1800, 380 persons, mostly Americans, were living in the vicinity of Mackay's gristmill. A few years later, this promising settlement was destroyed by a shift in the river's channel.

Eighty-five percent of the district's residents (St. Charles not included) had lived in the village in 1791. Five years later the ratio had shrunk to 64 percent, and by 1800 only 1,039 of the district's 2,447 people lived in St. Louis (42.5 percent). This trend signalled a significant change in the capital's social and economic structure. The more affluent merchants, no longer needing to grow their own food, had abandoned subsistence farming. Artisans tended to spend more time at their crafts, and most of the 269 slaves and 67 free mulattoes and blacks were withdrawn from agriculture into domestic service, warehouse, mill and dock labor, and certain crafts. This occupational specialization might have led to expansion of the village limits to accommodate additional farmers, but the need for compact defense kept St. Louis below the hill. There was no master plan for satellite agricultural villages, but their growth was in part a response to the capital's needs. As merchants and traders dropped strip farming, some of them had increased their common field holdings as speculations, leaving arriving farmers no choice but to go farther afield.

As an occupation, farming had lost its already modest status in St. Louis. The village needed flour, but it no longer needed its own farmers. Residents with capital and ambition, whatever the pressure from officials, had little reason to attempt commercial farming. The New Orleans market was too far away to make the shipment of bulky agricultural products competitive with the economic and psychic rewards of the fur business. On the other hand, poor farmers, many of them part Indian or with Indian wives and with no prospects of betterment in St. Louis, could sell their homes and outlots to the Cerrés, Chouteaus, Soulards, or Labbadies and move to Florissant or St. Charles, where the land was rich and free, and their neighbors simple farmers too. By 1796 St. Louis grew only half as much grain as its neighbors, and two years later Lieutenant Governor Trudeau lamented that there were few farmers left in the capital. Despite its common fields, St. Louis had never been just an agricultural village, and now it had lost even the appearance of one. By 1800 the common field fences were a shambles, and most of the land was enclosed in individual farms in the efficient but dangerous American fashion. Agricultural processing was still centered at the capital, however. All of the wheat in the district, including the scattered settlements on the Meramec River, and St. Charles as well, was ground into flour at Auguste Chouteau's mill.

External defense was still a major problem during the last decade of the Spanish regime. The Citizen Genét–George Rogers Clark threat had been removed in 1794 by Genét's removal as the French Minister at the insistence of President Washington. Only Clark's war record and his friendship with prominent Virginians had saved him from worse than the chilling reprimand he received from Washington. Chouteau's deft handling of the Osages and the Mackay expedition to the Mandan villages were reassuring, but Governor Carondelet still had the invasion jitters. He had been committed to the Miró-Wilkinson plan to separate Kentucky from the United States; but the French army's victories in northern Spain forced the Spanish ministry to drop its British alliance and make peace with the Jacobins, which in turn raised the specter of a British attack on Louisiana through American territory. To appease the United States, Foreign Minister Manuel Godoy in 1795 conceded to the Americans free navigation of the Mississippi, the right of deposit and transshipment of goods at New Orleans, and their claim to the thirty-first parallel as the boundary between the United States and West Florida. This Treaty of San Lorenzo, when implemented, ended any possibility that Kentucky would leave the United States and forced Spain to abandon its forts at Natchez, Chickasaw Bluffs (Memphis), and others built to protect the Chickasaws, Creeks, and Choctaws from the Americans. Carondelet protested the treaty as disastrous for Louisiana, for its Indian allies, and ultimately for Mexico, but to no avail.

Now the British were the chief external threat, but rumors of American plots against the Floridas and Louisiana (the Blount Conspiracy) and fears of revolutionary activity continued to agitate Carondelet. The resurgence of French power in Europe had awakened latent French patriotism in New Orleans; and the governor was especially concerned about St. Louis, the key to the safety of New Mexico and fifteen hundred miles and four months away from New Orleans at low water. In November 1795 Manuel Gayoso de Lemos, governor of the Natchez district and Carondelet's second in command, went to St. Louis in the galiot *La Vigilante* (a small galley with a bank of sixteen oars). Gayoso's mission was to examine its

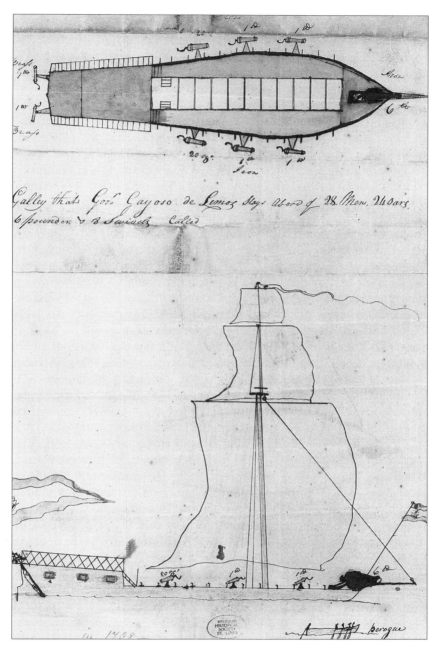

Galley of Spanish Governor Gayoso de Lemos. *Ink and wash on paper by George Rogers Clark, 1798. A fleet of three galleys like this put an end to Jacobin agitation in St. Louis and gave 1797 the name* L' Année des Galerés. *MHS-Archives, Clark Papers.*

defenses and cement Creole and Indian loyalty to the Crown. Zenon Trudeau had given assurances that St. Louisans were trustworthy; and Gayoso, somewhat to his surprise, was able to confirm this. He reported that "all show the greatest affection for the King." At a "magnificent assembly" at the home of Auguste Chouteau, Gayoso "saw neither a tricolored ribbon nor an adornment that could cause suspicion; . . . only the wife of Mr. Robidou had a dress of three colors, but I attribute it to bad taste; besides, it was older than the French Revolution, and her husband and she herself are persons of good character." The only "ungovernable person" in St. Louis was Jean Marie Pepin, but "his relatives and a large family restrain him."

In contrast to his good news about the loyalties of its citizens, Gayoso reported that the capital's fortifications were inadequate. Manuel Perez, when he became lieutenant governor in 1787, had found Cruzat's wooden stockade rotted away leaving only the Fort San Carlos tower and the demi-lune usable. Perez's answer to territorial defense problems had been to invite Shawnee and Delaware bands from east of the Mississippi to settle along its west bank as a buffer against the Osages and to rebuild the crumpled north bastion in stone. His successor Zenon Trudeau in 1792 built a plank stockade around Leyba's tower, with a wooden bastion at each of its four corners. Outside of the stockade an earthen parapet descended to a shallow moat. Within the enclosure Trudeau built stone barracks and a powder magazine. The San Carlos tower with its eight cannons still dominated the defensive structure. At the time of Gayoso's visit the garrison had fifty soldiers. Victor Collot, a French general who visited St. Louis in 1796, characterized its defenses as worthless. He recommended construction of a large earthen redoubt on the north and west with a deep moat in front of it capable of being flooded from Chouteau's Pond. To man these defenses, fifteen hundred soldiers would be needed. Collot felt that the village's strategic importance justified an expensive defense system. Since the entire Louisiana regiment would have been required to carry out this plan, Carondelet had to develop an alternative. After war with Great Britain resumed in 1797, the governor hired Louis Vandenbenden, a Flemish engineer, to strengthen St. Louis's fortifications. Vandenbenden added four stone towers thirty-nine feet in diameter by nineteen feet in height and a large wooden blockhouse. The governor hoped that these structures and the north bastion, with the help of the river fleet, would withstand any British attack, unless the invaders performed the virtually impossible by dragging heavy artillery across the long portages from Canada to the Mississippi. The defenses would be manned by one hundred or so regulars, mostly cannoneers, supported by six hundred militiamen from St. Louis, Carondelet, and St. Charles. In addition, the British would have five hundred Osage warriors harassing their flanks and rear, courtesy of Pierre Chouteau.

The most effective deterrent to a British invasion was probably the freshwater navy. Upon Gayoso's recommendation, Carondelet in 1792 had built a fleet of galleys to protect the river villages and keep an eye on the Americans. By 1795 five large galleys, each with sails and thirty-two or thirty-four oars, one large and two small cannons, and eight swivel guns; four galiots, each with eight swivel guns; and a gunboat with one cannon were available for duty above New Orleans. They were soon to be required in St. Louis.

Inspired by revolutionary pamphlets sent from Philadelphia and further stimulated by General Collot's visit, restless spirits in St. Louis in 1796 formed a society of *Sans Culottes* to promote the ideas of the French Revolution. Led by Louis Coignard and Jean Marie Pepin, artisans, they staged a noisy celebration on September 22, New Year's Day by the Revolutionary calendar. By songs, toasts, and parades they denounced royal tyranny and saluted the imminent return of Louisiana to France, this time to an egalitarian France. The Jacobin songs and shouts were loudest under the windows of the merchant elite who were not amused. Lieutenant Governor Trudeau was not especially alarmed, but he reported the incident to Carondelet, who never took bad news lightly. Seditious behavior at the exposed nerve-end of the Spanish empire demanded a firm response. Accordingly, the governor sent Lieutenant Colonel Don Carlos Howard upriver with a fleet of three galleys, two galiots, and one gunboat; cannons; military supplies; and 110 of His Catholic Majesty's regular soldiers. Howard was to supervise the completion of Vandenbenden's fortifications, ferret out seditious inhabitants, and hamper the activities of British fur traders. While in St. Louis he was to seek the advice and support of the brothers Chouteau, Antoine Soulard, Gabriel Cerré, Charles Gratiot, and Jacques Ceran St. Vrain, the lieutenant governor's brother.

The squadron's arrival on April 27, 1797, created a sensation, most of the people having never seen war vessels of such size in such numbers. In the Creole fashion, the year was named *L'Année des Galerés,* taking its place with the memorable *L'Année du Grand Coup* of 1780 and *L'Année des Grandes Eaux* of 1785. During Howard's stay he detached two galiots to block the Des Moines River to British traders, finished the defense works, and sent spies to Prairie du Chien, the upper Illinois River, Canada, and Philadelphia. Apparently convinced that the revolutionary threat was overrated and an immediate attack unlikely, Howard returned to New Orleans in July,

leaving the two galiots for the village's defense and the Des Moines
patrol. In 1799, when Spain asked "patriotic citizens" for voluntary
donations for defense, the "Jacobin" Louis Coignard contributed ten
pesos, as did the Americans Mackey Wherry and Patrick Lee. The
flood of Americans across the Appalachians after the opening of the
Mississippi, the filibustering activities of some Americans as far as
Texas, and news of a plot by Alexander Hamilton to grab Florida and
Louisiana kept St. Louis apprehensive until 1800.

As early as 1795 the Spanish foreign office had been willing to
sell Louisiana to France. At the time the French thought the price too
high, but the staggering cost of maintaining the province kept the idea
alive in Madrid. Spain's expenditures in Louisiana in 1797 were
$795,662; its customs revenue only $68,143. Mexico, for which
Louisiana was a buffer, provided a subsidy of $453,964, leaving a net
Louisiana deficit of $257,793. There was no prospect that the situation
would improve nor that American pressures at the Mississippi frontier
would lessen. To pleas for additional funds for defense, Foreign
Minister Godoy cracked, "you cannot lock up an empty field."

As much as Spain wanted to be rid of Louisiana, abandoning it to
the rambunctious Americans was unthinkable. They would soon be
pounding at the gates of Mexico, hot after its silver mines. But if
France took over Louisiana, Mexico and California would be
protected at the expense of the French Treasury. So in June 1800 the
Spanish foreign office made an offer which led to the Treaty of San
Ildefonso (October 1, 1800), by which Napoleon promised to carve
out a kingdom in Italy for Charles IV's son-in-law in return for
Louisiana. Two years later, after Napoleon had promised not to sell
Louisiana without giving Spain first refusal, the Crown ordered
Governor Salcedo to deliver the province to the French whenever they
presented themselves.

Rumors of the impending retrocession had circulated in the
United States for years, and when the Spanish Intendant Juan Morales
revoked the right of deposit at New Orleans in October 1802 the
furious Americans assumed that Napoleon had ordered it. President
Thomas Jefferson had learned of the transfer several months earlier,
and Morales's action only confirmed his opinion that Napoleon would
be a bad neighbor. Americans shared the traditional English contempt
for Spain, and they believed that Louisiana would eventually fall to
the United States. With Spain in New Orleans and St. Louis there had
been no hurry, but Bonaparte was a different story. Jefferson
instructed his Minister in Paris, Robert R. Livingston, to seek
permanent guarantees of free navigation and deposit on the

Mississippi, and then sent James Monroe, a Virginian with speculative interests in the West, to Paris with instructions to buy New Orleans and adjacent territory in West Florida. Napoleon had planned a North American empire, but rebellion in Haiti and the imminence of a new war with Great Britain changed his mind; and he offered all of Louisiana to the surprised Americans. In spite of having no authority to do so, the delighted envoys signed a treaty dated April 30, 1803, purchasing Louisiana and assuming France's debts to American citizens for a total of $15 million.

Western Americans were elated, a majority of Southerners pleased, and New England Federalists outraged by the Louisiana Purchase. Federalists feared western domination, and they pointed out that the Constitution did not authorize the purchase of territory (a strict construction that was Jefferson's dogma, not theirs). Further, they argued that Napoleon had no right to sell Louisiana because he had not given Spain first refusal as promised. Therefore, the treaty was illegal and immoral as well as unconstitutional. The constitutional argument worried Jefferson but the moral one did not. With most Americans, he believed that Spain had no rights that he was bound to observe. The Spanish were furious, but powerless to do anything about it. The Senate confirmed the treaty, and on December 20, 1803, William C. C. Claiborne and General James Wilkinson (the former Spanish agent) took formal possession of Louisiana at New Orleans, three weeks after France had finally taken over from Spain. According to the American view, the Purchase territory extended to the Rockies thus doubling the size of the United States. The Spanish held that the new boundary was the Missouri River, but they lost that argument in the Adams-Onis Treaty of 1819.

At St. Louis on March 9, 1804, Lieutenant Governor de Lassus surrendered upper Louisiana to Amos Stoddard, acting as France's representative. Charles Gratiot served as interpreter during the signing and translated Stoddard's remarks for the assembled crowd. When the ceremony was over, the Spanish garrison fired a salute and then turned over Fort San Carlos to the American troops. According to local tradition, the flag of the French Republic flew over the fort for the next twenty-four hours. Perhaps it did. On March 10, Stoddard signed the documents transferring upper Louisiana from France to the United States.

While there was no great outcry at St. Louis against the transfer, neither was there much enthusiasm from the French or American subjects of the King of Spain. Especially since 1796 Americans had come to the district between the Missouri and the Meramec in substantial numbers, and they were in the majority in the areas outside of St. Louis and Carondelet. They had come at Spain's invitation; they had been given good land (usually eight hundred arpents), which most of them could not have afforded in the United States; and they paid no taxes.

Charles Gratiot noted that many tears were shed in St. Louis because of the transfer—tears for the departing Spanish and a way of life, it should be noted, not for a French government the people had never known. The landowners would now pay direct taxes, and many of them feared with reason that the change from despotic to republican government would cost them some of their liberties. At best they would be infected with a plague of lawyers. As for the affluent merchants, any regrets were tempered by the near-certainty that their large land grants would bring them speculative profits under the Americans.

Perhaps the chief mourners were the Spanish officials. In St. Louis the lieutenant governors had performed their duties ably and honestly—more than the latest Spanish King deserved. They had served without compensation except for their army pay, supplemented by modest shares of the fur trade. The interests of the Crown and the welfare of the people had been their major concerns. Even the Indians had been protected from the land raids and the wholesale slaughter the Americans practiced. Under their generous land policies and loose enforcement of trade regulations some families had become rich, and even the poor had it better than many Americans. Even after he knew of the retrocession to France, Charles DeLassus had done his best. To hold off British traders, he sent his brother, St. Vrain, to the Des Moines and Prairie du Chien in a war galiot. Without support from his government DeLassus could not stem the tide, and by 1804 the British controlled the Missouri River as far south as the Omahas. Even after Stoddard had taken over, DeLassus begged his superiors to reclaim Louisiana, correctly pointing out that the Americans were plotting to grab New Mexico. Fittingly, the last entry in his fur-trade journal for 1804 read, "The Devil may take all."

Transfer of Upper Louisiana at St. Louis, 1804.

Transfer of Upper Louisiana at St. Louis, 1804. *Pastel on paper by F. L. Stoddard, ca. 1904. This depiction of the transfer was one of many made between the Louisiana Purchase Exposition and the Pageant and Masque of 1914. MHS-Art.*

3.
The Frontier Town

Captain Amos Stoddard was a busy man in St. Louis. Not only did he represent both France and the United States in the transfer of upper Louisiana, he was to act as civil commandant of the territory until Congress made other arrangements. He had to move carefully to allay the doubts and fears of the people. Fortunately, he had the support of the merchant elite whose property interests favored an orderly transition and welcomed the rise in land values that was sure to follow from the American policy of selling rather than giving away the public domain. While Charles Gratiot was the most openly pro-American among them, his Chouteau brothers-in-law and their Cerré, Papin, Sarpy, Labbadie, Dubreuil, and Soulard connections also had a stake in the success of the new regime.

In his first address to the people, Stoddard stressed the advantages of republicanism and assured them that their customs would be respected and their land titles confirmed. These assurances were quickly put to the test. The district's slaves, comprising about 25 percent of the population, had become unruly in the expectation that the Americans would free them as they had their brethren in the Northwest Territory. A citizens' committee headed by Auguste Chouteau warned the commandant that there was "amongst the blacks a fermentation—which may become dangerous," and urged a "Watchfull policy" which would prevent slave assemblies and contacts with white troublemakers, and "put them again under the Subordination which they were heretofore." At Stoddard's suggestion, this committee drew up a set of regulations for slave control, which he agreed to enforce.

Stoddard's attitude was reassuring, but the favorable mood was soon dispelled by shocking news from Washington. After hearing several vitriolic speeches about the land-grabbing venality of the Creoles, Congress had separated upper and lower Louisiana at the thirty-third parallel, the latter to be called the Territory of Orleans. The former Spanish Illinois and Arkansas were lumped together in a new District of Louisiana, to be governed by the officers of the Territory of Indiana. The district was divided into the subdistricts of St. Charles, St. Louis, Ste. Genevieve, Cape Girardeau, and New Madrid, the last to include Arkansas. Courts of Quarter Sessions and the appointive offices of commandant, sheriff, and recorder were established in each subdistrict. The act outlawed the foreign slave trade, authorized the settlement of eastern Indians in the district, and nullified Spanish land grants awarded after October 1, 1800, except for those of 640 acres or less that had been cultivated before the Louisiana Purchase in 1803. All of this was obnoxious to St. Louisans. Despite the Louisiana Treaty, which had guaranteed them "all the rights, advantages, and immunities of the citizens of the United States" and Stoddard's fine words about republicanism, they were not to have a trace of self-government. The strictures against the slave trade rekindled their fears about the future of slavery, and settling eastern Indians in the district would increase pressures on the white population and enrage the Missouri River tribes, with consequent damage to the fur trade. Subordination to the insignificant Indiana capital at Vincennes wounded local pride, as did the reduction of St. Louis to equality with other subdistrict capitals.

In October 1804 Governor William Henry Harrison and the three Indiana judges arrived in St. Louis with a set of laws for the district and a list of local appointments. Judiciously, Harrison named Charles Gratiot presiding judge and Auguste Chouteau, Jacques Clamorgan, David Delaunay, and James Mackay justices of the Court of Quarter Sessions. Samuel Hammond, a Virginian, was appointed civil commandant; and Edward Hempstead, an ambitious young Connecticut lawyer, was named acting attorney general. Harrison's effort to appease the French was backed by Jefferson, who appointed Auguste P. Chouteau, Jr., Charles Gratiot, Jr., and Pascal Vincent Bouis to West Point.

These appointments did not quiet the outcry against the new government. A convention representing all parts of Louisiana met in St. Louis on September 30, with Gratiot presiding. The delegates petitioned Congress for relief, protesting that the act did not provide for self-government, failed to protect slavery, and would settle unwanted Indians at their doorstep. At the heart of their protest was the invalidation of post-1800 land grants, which they charged was a violation of the Louisiana Treaty guarantees. It certainly violated the sensibilities of the delegates, all of whom held large Spanish claims. Some of them had even discussed the possibility of Napoleonic intervention. Half of the eighteen signers were Americans, some of whom were more extreme than the French. Gratiot and Auguste Chouteau, who counseled moderation, persuaded Amos Stoddard to prune the petition of some of its biting sarcasm.

Some late arrivals who had no large claims opposed the petition. Rufus Easton, St. Louis's first postmaster, a confidant of the president, described the petitioners to Jefferson as greedy monopolists who had called the Indiana officials "foreign bashaws and proconsuls" in their original draft. Easton's attitude exemplified the hostility between two groups of speculators that underlay political factionalism in St. Louis for two decades. He had come to Louisiana to make his fortune, and the French and American holders of large Spanish claims were in his way. The Creole leaders, their handful of American sons-in-law, and Americans who held large Spanish claims stubbornly held their ground.

Governor Harrison exerted himself to be agreeable. He wrote to congressmen in support of the petition, excusing its bristling language as a natural reaction to the insulting attitudes expressed during the congressional debates. Harrison also reassured the citizens by including a slave code among the district's laws. Modeled on those of his native Virginia, these regulations were elaborate enough for ten times Louisiana's thirteen hundred slaves. Slaves were defined as personal property and mulattoes as persons with "one-fourth or more of negro blood." They could not leave their homes without permission, assemble in large gatherings, buy or sell goods, own guns or real property, administer medicine, strike a white person, conspire to rebel, or testify in court against a white person. Whipping was an acceptable punishment for insubordination, and mutilation was not forbidden. Slaves could be emancipated by their masters but they could be re-enslaved for failure to pay taxes.

Harrison made further concessions to St. Louis interests in his infamous Sauk and Fox Treaty of 1804. Under presidential instructions to arrange a limited cession of lands along the Illinois River, the governor initiated discussions with five Sauk and Fox chiefs who had come to St. Louis to ransom an imprisoned Saukee brave. Assisting in the negotiations were Pierre Chouteau (the United States Indian agent for Louisiana), Auguste Chouteau, David Delaunay, and Amos Stoddard. At the outset, the Chouteaus gave two thousand dollars in presents and plenty of whiskey to the chiefs on Harrison's behalf. At the end, the Indians had received an annuity of one thousand dollars a year, the government's promise to establish fur factories (trading posts) among them, and guarantees of peace with the Osages, whom the Sauks and Foxes jealously regarded as under the special protection of the United States (because of the Chouteaus). In return, these chiefs, without tribal sanction, had surrendered fifty million acres in northern Illinois, southern Wisconsin, and the St. Charles district of Louisiana. The Louisiana lands included most of ten present Missouri counties and the "Spanish Mines" lead district of eastern Iowa. Auguste Chouteau had just acquired half of the Spanish

Pierre Chouteau. *Engraving, ca. 1898. MHS-PP.*

Mines claim (61,500 acres) from Julien Dubuque and had other claims in the treaty lands totaling more than 25,000 acres. Pierre Chouteau claimed 7,900 acres in the affected district, and Delaunay and Gratiot had smaller grants there. For their protection, the treaty provided that the cession would not invalidate such grants.

In response to the Louisiana petition, Harrison's recommendations, and many individual complaints, Congress took up the question of territorial status. Those favoring change argued that the Louisiana Treaty had been violated and that republican government did not exist in the district. Vigorously opposed to higher status for Louisiana, ironically, were two congressmen of French descent, Benjamin Huger of South Carolina and John B. C. Lucas of Pennsylvania, who argued that the Creoles did not understand republican principles and could not manage their own affairs. Lucas thought they should have only the rights and liberties that they had enjoyed as Spanish subjects. He pointed out that they had cried when the American flag was raised, and he argued that they were not as friendly to the United States as they claimed.

Pierre Chouteau had given Lucas plenty of ammunition. While in Washington with a delegation of Osage chiefs, Chouteau told Secretary of the Treasury Albert Gallatin that his friends in St. Louis would prefer military government to civil administrators, civil courts, grasping lawyers, and popular elections. As a leading member of a favored elite under Spain's paternal despotism, Chouteau's attitude was not surprising. He felt that merit had been rewarded and justice easily obtained under the Dons. By almost any standards, and certainly by Spanish standards, he and his brother had earned their preferment. Gallatin reported that Chouteau believed that as Indian agent he was entitled to monopolize Louisiana's fur trade. The concept of conflict of interest was foreign to one accustomed to a government-business partnership, with those who served the state rewarded by mercantile privileges. Chouteau had not learned that when Americans used their offices to gain commercial advantages, as they often did, they were expected to feel guilty about it.

In the last analysis, its inconsistency with republicanism persuaded Congress to repeal the district arrangement. In July 1805 Louisiana became a territory of the first (lowest) grade, with a resident governor at St. Louis appointed by the president for three years. The governor was also to command the militia and supervise Indian affairs. A territorial secretary would record governmental proceedings and report them to Washington. Three judges comprised the superior court, and with the governor, the territorial legislature was empowered to establish inferior courts and pass laws. All criminal cases were to be tried by jury, as well as civil cases involving more than one hundred dollars. The provision for jury trial, in civil suits especially, was distasteful to the French merchants. They had observed that in Kaskaskia and Cahokia after the Americans came, the prolonged trials before juries enriched the lawyers whether justice triumphed or not.

In another respect as well, the Creole leaders were still disappointed. The hated law invalidating post-1800 land grants was repealed, but continuing rumors of widespread fraud in land titles convinced Congress to oppose blanket confirmation of Spanish grants. Furthermore, President Jefferson believed that land sales were a desirable source of public revenue. If there was to be any good land left to sell, dubious claims must be disallowed. Jacques Clamorgan, for example, claimed five hundred thousand arpents, an area more than half the size of Rhode Island. If all of his grants were approved, the federal treasury would feel the sting.

Accordingly, in March 1805 Congress established guidelines for approving titles and created a board of land commissioners to make the decisions. A recorder of titles and two other members constituted the board, which was expected to approve small occupied claims but to subject large grants to close scrutiny. Once again, claimants argued that Congress had violated the Louisiana Treaty provision that "the inhabitants shall be maintained in the full enjoyment of their property." Since many claims had been purchased by American speculators after the treaty, these complaints at times had a hollow ring. John Rice Jones and Rufus Easton had rushed over from Kaskaskia to sweep up smaller claims for a few pennies an acre from the unsophisticated. Knowing Jefferson, Easton knew that federal policy would favor small claimants, so he became a small claimant many times over. He acquired fifteen parcels averaging eight hundred acres each and made himself the champion of the small farmer. The French could play that game too. Jacques St. Vrain bought twenty-two titles totalling nearly twelve thousand acres within a few months after the Louisiana Purchase.

To the delight of the Creoles, President Jefferson selected General James Wilkinson to be the first governor of the Louisiana Territory. Auguste Chouteau, Charles Gratiot, and Antoine Soulard wrote to Wilkinson, "The political wishes of the citizens of St. Louis are accomplished." Wilkinson was well briefed by Amos Stoddard on the land-claims question, and he was advised by Governor Harrison to ally himself with the stable element (the French elite) in St. Louis. The new governor lost no time in doing so. In Washington, Secretary Gallatin had opposed combining military and civil authority in the Louisiana executive, and he had "no very exalted opinion" of

Governor James Wilkinson. *Lithograph by Goupil and Sons, 1904, from Alceé Fortier,*
A History of Louisiana. *MHS-Library.*

Wilkinson; but he could not deny that the general knew the territory,
its people, and its former government.

For the other territorial offices, Jefferson chose Joseph Browne
(Aaron Burr's brother-in-law) as secretary, and John Coburn, Rufus
Easton, and J. B. C. Lucas as judges of the Superior Court. Browne
and Coburn were transients, but Easton and Lucas were to be key
figures in St. Louis for many years. Jean Baptiste Charles Lucas, born
in 1758 in Normandy, was a graduate of the School of Law in Caen
and had emigrated to the United States in 1784. On the advice of his
friend Albert Gallatin, he had settled near Pittsburgh, where he
practiced law, traded in furs, speculated in land and town lots, and
served in the Pennsylvania legislature. He represented the Pittsburgh
district in Congress from 1803 to 1805, when he resigned to accept the
dual appointments of superior judge and land commissioner in
Louisiana.

Judge Lucas was a man of great personal charm when it suited
him, but he was also given to violent passions. It was easy to become
his friend, but difficult to remain so. Territorial Secretary Frederick
Bates, who admired Lucas's towering intellect, characterized him as
"a man of superior order, but so completely a child of passion . . . as
to run every hour into the grossest and most palpable inconsistencies.
He has absolutely no attachments and his animosities are immortal."
On one occasion Bates called Lucas "a designing old Ruffian . . .
(and) a crafty old Cerberus," yet in 1810 Bates supported Lucas's

J. B. C. Lucas. *Engraving by H. B. Hall and Sons, 1883. MHS-PP.*

reappointment. Wilson Price Hunt, who later married Lucas's daughter, opposed his land policy and lobbied strenuously in Congress against the reappointment. Bates attributed Lucas's periodic verbal assaults against him to jealousy of his connections in Washington.

James L. Donaldson of Maryland and Clement Biddle Penrose of the Philadelphia Biddles (Wilkinson's nephew), joined Lucas on the Board of Land Commissioners. To assist the board, Wilkinson appointed Antoine Soulard as surveyor general, the post he had held under Trudeau and DeLassus. The land question had united former merchant-trader rivals against certain American officeholder-speculators and residents of other Louisiana districts who resented the St. Louis elite's domination over the territory. Clamorgan, James Mackay, Manuel Lisa, the Chouteaus, Gratiot, Soulard, St. Vrain, and a lead-mine claimant named John Smith T. joined Secretary Browne and Commissioners Penrose and Donaldson in the Wilkinson faction. Leading the opposition were Judges Lucas and Easton, Major James Bruff, Samuel Hammond, and William C. Carr, the United States land agent for the territory. Edward Hempstead and several other young lawyers were also anti-Wilkinson, as was Smith T.'s major rival in the lead district, Moses Austin.

Commissioner Lucas held that all land claims, except those exempted under the Territorial Act, should meet the requirements of Spanish law to the letter. Grants signed by Trudeau and DeLassus with size and location to be filled in later by the grantees were obviously irregular, as were predated or altered documents. Lucas insisted that large grants made after 1798 conform to "the rules of Morales" requiring validation by the intendant at New Orleans. Claimants argued that the lieutenant governors had never recognized the intendant's authority over land grants; that most residents had never heard of Morales's rules; and that few of them could have afforded to validate their claims at New Orleans. The large grants, which were exceptions to Spanish policy, had been awarded for important services to Spain. However repugnant to American practice, these instruments of Spanish colonial policy should not be reversed by Americans after the fact.

At first the land board was lenient, Lucas being in the minority and not always told when and where meetings were to be held. After Bates replaced Donaldson, approval became more difficult. For example, in 1792 Pierre Chouteau had been given 30,000 arpents (25,500 acres) in their territory by the Great Osages. Lieutenant Governor DeLassus confirmed this "Lamine Grant" in 1799, for services to Spain. Under the rules of Morales, the claim was not valid and was rejected (reversed in 1833). In 1800 Auguste Chouteau had applied for 1,281 arpents of forest land to supply firewood for his distillery. DeLassus had approved the grant promptly, on the grounds that the distillery would reduce imports of a valuable commodity and thereby serve the Crown. This grant had been supported by Governor Gayoso de Lemos, but it was rejected by the commissioners because it lacked Morales's signature. Chouteau took his case to court, and this decision too was reversed in the 1830s. Another notable case was that of Daniel Boone, who had come to the Femme Osage settlement in 1798 at Trudeau's invitation. In 1799 DeLassus appointed Boone syndic at Femme Osage and granted him land there. Boone testified that he had never cultivated his land, as required by Spanish law, because the lieutenant governor had assured him that for syndics it was not necessary. The claim was ruled invalid. By special act, Congress later regranted the land to Boone, who promptly lost it to his Kentucky creditors.

Wilkinson's interference in the land-claims process and his refusal to convene the legislature generated strong pressures for his removal. In addition, his friendship with Aaron Burr and association with the latter's famous trip to the Mississippi sparked rumors that the governor planned either to start a western rebellion or invade Mexico. Burr's intentions were never fully revealed, but they were definitely not in the interests of the United States. It is equally certain that Wilkinson, Joseph Browne, and John Smith T. were involved in Burr's plan, at least in the early stages; and it is possible that Wilkinson instigated it. In May 1806 Wilkinson was ordered to New Orleans, where he was to take charge of the defenses in anticipation of war with Spain over the Louisiana boundary. While in the Orleans Territory, Wilkinson reported to Jefferson that Burr was engaged in treasonous activities.

Wilkinson's new assignment conveniently removed him from the governorship. For a few months Secretary Browne was acting governor until his son-in-law's arrest for conspiracy convinced Auguste Chouteau to join a move for his ouster. Early in 1807 Frederick Bates was appointed secretary and recorder of titles and Meriwether Lewis was named governor of the Louisiana Territory. At Lewis's insistence, William Clark replaced Pierre Chouteau as Indian agent for all of the Louisiana tribes except for the Osages. Lewis and Clark had returned to St. Louis in 1806 from their expedition to the Pacific, bringing information of great importance to the fur traders and to the future of St. Louis. Since Lewis did not take up his duties until March 1808, Bates was acting governor for nearly a year.

Wilkinson's departure encouraged a political realignment in St. Louis. Despite their alliance with the ex-governor, the French leaders had no taste for rebellion or filibustering expeditions against Spain. The land claimants did not intend to reduce their pressure for confirmation of their titles, but they needed American allies who did not have a Burrite tinge. Their need coincided with the ambitions of the young anti-Wilkinson lawyers, who now saw the land claims as an inexhaustible gold mine. Politically, the lawyer-hating Creoles were becoming Americanized. They saw that it was useless to fight the lawyers in the United States; they filled the legislatures, wrote the laws, and, as judges, made the final decisions. Accordingly, a new and powerful political faction emerged—the French elite and their American attorneys. Edward Hempstead, an anti-Wilkinson firebrand who became the territorial attorney general, became an avid student of Spanish law, language, and imperial practice and a determined advocate of a liberal land-claims policy. As an example of the new order, Hempstead married Clarissa Dubreuil, a sister-in-law of Jacques St. Vrain and the cousin or niece of half the members of St. Louis's dominant French families. Hempstead's sister Susan married Charles Gratiot's son Henry; her children were thus direct descendants of Pierre Laclède.

As opportunities for advancement attracted well-educated young men from the East to St. Louis, the charms of the poised and graceful daughters of the French merchants, as well as their own economic and political interest, drew many of them into the orbit of the old families. The rather priggish Frederick Bates found the "french ladies" lovely in appearance, and "inimitably graceful" dancers, "but rather too much in the style of actresses" for his taste; but his reservations were not widely shared. Christian Schultz, who visited St. Louis in 1807, wrote that the ladies there were noted for their beauty, modesty, and agreeable manners, as well as for "the taste and splendor of their dress." Observers who reported as early as 1817 that French influence was no longer significant did not understand the web of family, economic, and political connections between the Creoles and Americans such as Hempstead, Alexander McNair, and Thomas Hart Benton.

Despite the influx of lawyers, speculators, and office seekers, St. Louis grew slowly after the transfer of Louisiana. Amos Stoddard observed that the complexities and uncertainties of the American legal system had a stifling effect on commerce for several years after 1804. In addition, the land-claims struggle and factional infighting absorbed the energies of the major merchant-traders. Indian problems also erupted. The Sauks and Foxes, jealous of the favored Osages and furious about the trimming they had taken in the Harrison Treaty, raged through the St. Charles district harassing isolated families and inhibiting immigration. The tribes of the upper Mississippi and Missouri valleys, disillusioned by the government's failure to deliver promised presents, turned again to the British traders. The fur trade at St. Louis, having averaged $203,000 a year between 1789 and 1804, languished in 1805 and 1806.

Although farmers from Kentucky, Tennessee, and North Carolina doubled the St. Louis district's population between 1804 and 1810, the capital itself increased only from twelve hundred to fourteen hundred. By the latter date, a few buildings were scattered north of Laclède's original village boundary, but the town was still under "Chouteau's Hill." On this rise to the west, stretching for a mile and a half, were the holdings of Auguste Chouteau and John B. C. Lucas. By additional grants and timely purchases, Chouteau had extended his pond and mill-tract property to the Market Street line on the north and to within a block of the village limits on the east. Through purchases of common-field lots and the holdings of Antoine Soulard, Lucas had acquired the corresponding land north of Market Street in the line of probable expansion. Unlike his enemies, who it seems were invariably greedy speculators, Judge Lucas presented himself as a wise investor who believed in the future of St. Louis. As proof of his faith, Lucas built a large stone home on the hill in 1811, which was still the only house there in 1816.

Despite the town's limited growth, significant changes occurred during the decade after 1804. Visitors still noted the prevalence of fragrant gardens, the liberal use of whitewash, and narrow streets, but Christian Schultz, John Bradbury, Henry Brackenridge, and other observers spoke of a decidedly American tone developing during the period. Of sixty-eight families who came to St. Louis between 1804 and 1816, nineteen were from Virginia, ten from Pennsylvania, five each from Maryland, France, Santo Domingo, and Ireland, four from Connecticut, three each from Massachusetts and New Jersey, two from North Carolina, and one each from Scotland, Wales, Italy, Ohio, Tennessee, Kentucky, and the Indiana Territory. Of this sample, 80 percent were Americans; and since most Americans disliked Creole architecture, frame homes and a few horizontal log cabins replaced many houses of posts. In 1812 brick homes and stores began to appear, both because they were handsome and durable and because timber suitable for building had been stripped for more than ten miles in every direction. Cedar logs were floated down the Missouri from the Gasconade River more than one hundred miles away, but transportation charges reduced the advantages of wood construction. Stone and brick were readily available, although brick construction was slowed by a scarcity of artisans until a brickyard opened in 1813.

In 1812 Bartholomew Berthold built a two-story brick store and dwelling, as did William Smith. Christian Wilt, Manuel Lisa, Thomas McKnight and Thomas Brady, William C. Carr, Sylvestre Papin, William Clark, and William Rector had all completed combination brick homes and business buildings by 1816. In 1804, 33 of the 180 homes in St. Louis had been built of stone. During the next twelve years, a few Americans and some rising French families built twenty-six stone houses or stores, most of them replacing houses of posts. Another small but significant change of style was apparent by 1810, when signs identifying shop and office locations appeared on French as well as American establishments.

The most obvious result of Americanization in St. Louis was deplorable public behavior. The celebrations of returning voyageurs, episodes involving irate or drunken Indians, occasional slave belligerence, and the merrymaking of feast days and Sundays featured the Spanish regime; but in general, life had been peaceable and serene. Gabriel Cerré and the unlettered boatmen alike were as courteous and considerate of others on the streets and in the market place as in their homes. Disagreements there were, but they were not settled in violence. Except for one Indian, killed by another Indian, there had been no murders in St. Louis for forty years. Fighting was rare, and crimes against property few. Individuals who could not negotiate their differences took them to the lieutenant governor, who settled them firmly, fairly, and finally.

In contrast, after 1804 brawling and eye-gouging fights, cursing and shouting, political arguments, and generally churlish behavior became commonplace on the streets; and good manners found shaky refuge behind private entry gates. Friendly Indians living near the town for protection, such as the remnant of the Peoria tribe, found their villages invaded, their horses stolen, and their families terrorized by bullying bad men. Drunkenness as a day-after-day habit was virtually unknown to the Creoles until they encountered the American frontiersman's prodigious appetite for alcohol. Nor were the prominent Americans above violence. In 1806 Rufus Easton burst into a meeting of the land board and gave Commissioner Donaldson a merciless clubbing. Acting Governor Frederick Bates, a few months after his arrival in St. Louis in 1807, wrote to his brother in Virginia that especially in the lead district, "Speculators of the most desperate and dangerous cast . . . are making continual intrusions. . . .

Manuel Lisa Residence, Second and Plum Streets. *Photograph by H. Hazenstab, ca. 1900, of daguerreotype, ca. 1855. MHS-PP.*

Contending parties are always armed for *attack* as well as *defense* with Pistols & Durks and sometimes with Rifles also. . . . At the last Court, the Jury gave a countryman the sum of 120 dols, in damages, against a Bravo-Erratic, who had gouged both his Eyes out. . . ." Bates noted that public behavior had acquired "an astonishing degree of ferocity," most of it influenced by the example of "John Smith, lately of Tennessee, the brother-in-law of Mr. Early, a member of Congress," who usually carried "two durks, two pairs of pistols and a Rifle." Once, when federal officers tried to arrest him, Smith had "refused" arrest, backing his refusal with a pistol. When Bates discharged him as a judge, Smith issued a challenge, which the acting governor wisely declined. By the end of his career this well-educated and wealthy Smith T. had killed at least fourteen men in his "duels."

Thomas Ashe, an Englishman who visited St. Louis in 1806, wrote that its standards had decayed since the dilution of its French stock by Americans who pursued drinking and fighting "with as much zeal as they are (practiced) in the Virginian and Kentuckyan States." As he was close to the mark in this instance, he erred badly in others. Most visiting writers made superficial judgments or preferred their preconceptions to the facts. Visiting Americans attributed vigorous commercial activity to a burst of energy provided by Americans. In his account of the American Fur Company's overland expedition to the Pacific, *Astoria*, written in 1836, Washington Irving described St. Louis in 1810:

> Here were to be seen about the river banks, the hectoring, extravagant, bragging, boatmen of the Mississippi, with the gay, grimacing, singing, good-humored Canadian voyageurs. Vagrant Indians, of various tribes, loitered about the streets. Now and then, a stark Kentucky hunter, in Leathren hunting-dress, with rifle on shoulder and knife in belt, strode along. Here and there were new brick houses [sic] and shops, just set up by bustling, driving, and eager men of traffic from the Atlantic states, while on the other hand, the old French mansions, with open casements, still retained the easy indolent air of the original colonists.

Wilson Price Hunt, who had commanded the Astoria expedition, wrote to John Jacob Astor that Irving should have had someone who knew St. Louis check his facts, "St. Louis was always remarkable since I have known it for a degree of gentility among the better sort of its inhabitants and the correctness with which they spoke French. One would suppose . . . that it had never contained such men as Charles Gratiot, Auguste Chouteau, and many others who were gentlemen in any country." Hunt might have added that a half-dozen of these "indolent" original settlers had controlled most of the commerce at the Louisiana capital in 1810, and that the indefatigable oarsmen, who had pulled his expedition up the long reaches of the Missouri, were of the same relaxed breed.

After 1808 "slanders" against the town were rebutted in print. Joseph Charless, an Irish printer who had escaped from the English after the Irish Rebellion of 1795, had practiced his trade in Philadelphia and then Louisville before he printed the first issue of the first newspaper west of the Mississippi, the *Missouri Gazette and Louisiana Advertiser*, on July 12, 1808. A year's subscription to Charless's weekly was three dollars in cash, or four dollars in "Country Produce." Advertisements cost one dollar for the first insertion (one column inch), and fifty cents a week thereafter. In 1809, when Charless changed its name to the *Louisiana Gazette*, the newspaper consisted of four pages, seventeen by twelve inches, each page four columns wide. During its first year, the *Gazette* had 174 subscribers. Through Charless's efforts and those of his agents in St. Charles, Kaskaskia, Ste. Genevieve, and other river towns, the *Gazette* had more than five hundred subscribers by 1815, and one thousand in 1819.

As did all frontier editors, Charless had collection problems. In 1810 he reminded subscribers who had been "in arrears *almost two years*, that he [Charless] is made of flesh and blood, that . . . he does not live on air, but endeavers [sic] to subsist like other folks. . . ." After four years of publication, delinquencies amounted to more than one thousand dollars, despite Charless's willingness to accept flour, pork, sarsaparilla, and snakeroot in payment. After his assistant left him in 1808, Charless worked alone until twelve-year-old Nathaniel Paschall joined him as an apprentice in 1814.

Most of the news columns of the *Gazette* were filled with reports of Indian activity and national and international articles reprinted verbatim from eastern papers such as the *Boston Mirror* and the *Virginia Patriot*. Mail from the East was irregular and the contract carriers irresponsible, much to Charless's disgust. Usually his eastern papers reached St. Louis in four or five weeks, occasionally in three months; and a few times, when the carrier felt overloaded, not at all. Since European news took several weeks to reach eastern cities, it was well-aged by the time St. Louisans read it. At times subscribers complained about the dull details of Prussian campaigns on the Oder, but without effect, because the editor considered it his duty to

Missouri Gazette.

VOL. I.   TUESDAY, JULY 26, 1808.   No 3.

ST. LOUIS, LOUISIANA,
PRINTED BY JOSEPH CHARLESS,
Printer to the Territory.

—o—

Terms of Subscription for the

MISSOURI GAZETTE.

Three Dollars paid in advance.

Advertisements not exceeding a square, will be inserted one week for one dollar, and Fifty cents for every continuance, those of a greater length in proportion.

Advertisements sent to this Office, without specifying the time they are to be inserted, will be continued until forbid, and charged accordingly.

—o—

LONDON, April 22.

Upon the subject of Sir John Duckworth's late cruise, we have been favored with the following extract of a letter from an officer belonging to the squadron, dated

"Casand Bay, April 18.

"Having run down the Bay of Biscay, and called off Capes Ortugal and Finisterre, and Lisbon, we arrived off Madeira, and found Sir Samuel Hood, laying in Funschall roads, where we remained for two days. On the morning of the 3d of February, his majesty's ship Comus, gave us intelligence of her having been chased two days before to the N. W. of Madeira, and it then became obvious that the destination of the French squadron was the West Indies, for which we proceeded with all the expedition & made the islands of St. Lucia and Martinique in twenty one days. Off the east end of Martinique we saw six sail of the line; we cleared for action, but, on exchanging signals we found instead of enemies; it was Sir Alexander Cochrane, with his squadron, who was waiting to give that enemy a reception which we were in chase of, conceiving that he would take refuge in that port. Finding that his fleet was sufficient to cope with them in those seas, we passed all the Windward Island, and anchored on the 16th of February in Bassaterre Roads, St. Kitts, where we remained only 18 hours, just long enough to take in water, but no provisions, nor even linen washed. We then proceeded to Saint Domingo,

where it was supposed the enemy had proceeded for the purpose of landing troops; but on our arrival there we found no ships. After cruising in the Mono Passage for seven or eight days, we made all dispatch for the coast of America, and arrived off the Chesepeake on the 11th March. We communicated with the Statira frigate, and found that our Ambassador, Mr. Rose, was at Washington for the last time, to determine whether it should be peace or war with England. *We* should have gone in, but the Yankies would not let us have a pilot, nor supply us with water and provisions, which forced us to be content to live upon half our usual allowance; they would not give us a single pint of water or a cabbage stock. We left the Eurydice, to bring us any intelligence that might occur as to peace or war with America, and quitted the inhospitable shores of America for the Western Islands, where we procured all we wanted, after a long and very anxious cruise. The Governor of Flores [a Portuguese,] came off to us, but not being able to give us any information, the Admiral thought it most expedient to proceed for England, where we arrived this morning, after having been three months at sea, and made a complete circuit of the Westesn and Atlantic Ocean, a journey of upwards of thirteen thousand miles."

We learn by other letters, that our squadron remained several days off the Chesepeake, and that the treatment it experienced was such as by no means to encourage the hopes of late entertained by many, of an amicably termination of our present negotiation with the United States. It is certain, that no article whatever of supply could be obtained by our admiral from the inhospitable and hostile Amerians; and it follows of course, that the reparation offered by our government for the affair of the Chesepeake frigate was made in vain; although that circumstance alone, since so amply atoned for, was assigned by the President's proclamation as the motive for prohibiting all intercourse between the inhabitants and such British ships of war as might arrive in the American waters. Such conduct ar-

gues so hostile a determination in the government of the United States, that the general opinion expressed by the officers of our squadron, "that a war with America is inevitable," cannot be considered as founded upon weak or trivial, grounds. We should have expected that Mr. Rose's mission would at least have procured for our squadron the rights of hospitality, if it did not effect a complete re-establishment of the former good understanding between the two countries; but we fear the Frenchified government of the United States has so far resigned itself to the baseful influence of the cabinet of the Thuilleries, that nothing but salutary chastisement will bring it to a due sense of the pernicious error into which its unnatural propensities have permitted it to be led. If America will have war with Great Britain, she will have herself only to blame for the consequences. It is our sincere wish to remain at peace with her, and our ministers, it is well known, have adopted every expedient short of comprising the honor, the dignity of the nation to avoid the extremity of warfare; but we are certainly not prepared to lay the honor and essential interests of the empire at the feet of any junto upon earth. The blustering American demagogues may perhaps have founded some portion of their confidence upon the support of a certain party in this country; some of them, as we lately took occasion to remark, may derive hope from the confiscation of property and the non-payment of debts; they may conceal from themselves their comparative impotence, by throwing their weight into the aggregate of the enemies of G. Britain; but a few short months of war would convince these politicons of the folly of measuring their puny strength with the colossal power of the British empire. We do not ourselves wish to be understood, as stating positively that a war with the United States is become inevitable; the door for amicable adjustment still remains open, and while it continues so, hopes of adjustment may not irrationally be indulged. But in whatever manner the negotiation may terminate, we shall have the consolation to re-

(*See 4th Page.*)

First page of the Missouri Gazette, *26 July 1808, published by Joseph Charless. MHS-Library.*

enlighten them. The proceedings of Congress, the Louisiana legislature, and the St. Louis Board of Trustees were printed regularly, but there was usually only one or two columns of local news. There were no editorials identified as such, but Charless freely expressed his opinions of local officials, individuals, or "combinations"; at least two of which were answered by physical assaults.

The editor was generous with suggestions for local improvements, irate in his responses to external criticism of St. Louis, and unremitting in his castigation of the Indians and the English, whom he hated with equal ferocity. He favored eliminating the Indians and called George III "the Modern Nero." Notices of births and deaths, bankruptcies, and marital desertions appeared regularly, but Charless would not give details of "affairs of honor" (duels), which he frequently lambasted as barbaric. Some duels may have had an assist from the *Gazette*, however, which in nearly every issue carried letters from readers commenting on current issues. Customarily these letters were signed "Veritas," "Brutus," "Friend of the People," "An Old Farmer," or some other pseudonym presumably expressive of the author's theme. When a letter struck home, it was answered by "Anthony," charging Brutus with ignorance or deceit. Then Brutus would retaliate; the editor would be required to reveal identities; and personal confrontation would follow.

On the first and last pages of the *Gazette* local merchants, artisans, doctors, lawyers, and occasionally Cincinnati, New Orleans, and Pittsburgh firms advertised their wares or services. Usually these were of two to four lines without illustrations; although Christian Wilt, who operated a general store and soap factory, frequently took an entire column. On one occasion, Doctor Robert Simpson used the entire first and fourth pages to advertise his patent medicine (mostly testimonials from survivors). A few notices and advertisements appeared in French, but the *Gazette*'s readers were primarily Americans; and Charless made no concessions in his news to French readers. He twice announced plans to begin a French newspaper, but the response was negative, perhaps because the Creoles disliked his views on local issues.

In pursuit of his mission to elevate his clientele, Charless published instructive feature articles, such as Brackenridge's *Views of Louisiana* and essays such as "The True Ambition of an Honest Mind," "The Nature of Laws, both Physical and Moral," and "Are the Planets Inhabited or not?" Uplifting poems and songs appeared frequently, most of them composed by local bards. "The Music of Life" was submitted by "Alexis of Bellefontaine," and "The Dying Daughter to Her Mother" and "Money" (as the root of evil) by anonymous correspondents. Atrocious anecdotes, particularly if they derogated the British, were welcomed by the editor: "Sir David *Beard* must have thought it *close shaving* when his army was taken off by the French and the more so, as the operation was performed before they had *lathered* him and his troops."

In addition to his newspaper, Charless published the first book produced in the territory, *The Laws of the Territory of Louisiana*, and subsequently the acts of each session of the territorial legislature. The editor also ran a boarding house to supplement his income and sold books of fiction and nonfiction. Certain merchants also retailed books, few of which sold well. Christian Wilt complained in 1813 that his stock of *Love's Labours Lost* would last him for fifty years.

Those with a taste for good literature did not rely upon Charless and Wilt to supply them. There were several substantial private libraries in the community, and their owners lent them freely. Dr. Antoine Saugrain, one of the founders of the ill-fated French emigré colony at Gallipolis, Ohio, in 1790, who was St. Louis's only physician from 1800 to 1806, had more than three hundred books on a wide variety of topics. Auguste Chouteau, who had acquired several books from Laclède's estate, had added six hundred more by the 1820s. He bought them at estate auctions and through his trading connections in Montreal, New Orleans, and London. The noted historian and jurist, Henry M. Brackenridge, spent many delightful hours in Chouteau's library in 1810, describing it as one of the largest and finest he had ever seen. It included Bacon's *Essays*, biographies and campaign histories of the French Revolution, *Don Quixote, Robinson Crusoe, Tom Jones*, the thirty-five volumes of Diderot's *Encyclopedie*, sixty volumes of Voltaire's writings, books of travel and exploration, and agricultural, medical, and scientific works. Smaller, but of good quality, were the libraries of the Dubreuil, Labbadie, Gratiot, Cerré, and other leading Creole families. Among the Americans, Frederick and Edward Bates, J. B. C. Lucas, Rufus Easton, Joseph Charless, John Mullanphy, and other officials and professional men had sizeable book collections. Book auctions were frequent, and requests for the return of borrowed volumes appearing in the *Gazette* attested that these private libraries were a community resource.

Not everyone could use this resource, however. In 1819 when Catholic families of St. Louis agreed to erect a combination clerical quarters and school building, 52 of the 117 heads of families who pledged their support signed with an "X". Given the probability that a few who signed their names had thereby exhausted their supply of literacy, it would seem that a majority of adults had received no schooling, formal or informal. To put this in perspective, about half of the children of grammar school age in New York City in 1820 were not and had never been in school.

Elementary schooling had been available in St. Louis since 1774, when Jean Baptiste Truteau opened a fee school for the sons of leading families. With time off for occasional trading expeditions, Truteau taught elementary subjects and possibly beginning Latin and Greek. Pierre Chouteau, who at sixteen was too old for Truteau's school, claimed that his only school was the "Osage Academy," and yet his contemporaries reported that he could recite *Cicero's Orations* in the original. If so, it is possible that Truteau gave individual instruction to older students (or that Laclède, Dr. Condé, or Father Bernard was Chouteau's mentor). Truteau's school continued until the 1820s, although in later years he was given to drink and tended to fall asleep during recitations. In 1797 Madame Marie Rigauche began a school for girls which survived for a few years. Those who began their education in these private schools could continue it in the private libraries, and many young persons did so. The more ambitious scholars, such as Sylvestre Labbadie, Jr., Auguste Chouteau, Jr., and others completed their studies in Paris, Montreal, or after 1804, in Lexington or Bardstown, Kentucky.

An English school was opened in St. Louis in 1804 by a Professor Rotchford, but it soon expired for want of scholars. In 1809 Frederich Schewe started a French and English grammar school, offering both languages, mathematics, drawing, and geography. Schewe also taught evening classes for adults and made and sold candles. Pierre St. Martin taught fencing, the use of the broadsword, and dancing, with emphasis upon the waltz; and François Guyol advertised courses that would prepare young gentlemen for the Army Corps of Engineers. Beginning in 1813, Veuve Pescay's Young Ladies' Academy presented reading, writing, ancient history, French grammar, sewing, and embroidering. Tuition was $36 a year for day students and $140 for boarders. The most substantial school before 1818 was James Sawyer's Lancastrian Seminary, which offered reading and writing, modern languages, mathematics, Latin, Greek, and philosophy.

In all of these schools, classes were held in homes or rented rooms, and enrollment was small. Those teachers who survived had to supplement their income however they could. In November 1818 the Catholic Church began a more substantial educational venture. Bishop Louis William DuBourg, newly installed in the vast diocese which included the entire Louisiana Purchase, opened the St. Louis Academy to be conducted by Father François Niel and three other young priests. In conjunction with the academy,

Father Felix de Andreis, the vicar-general of the diocese, directed young seminarians in their studies of divinity, philosophy, and Oriental languages. By 1820 the academy, then called St. Louis College, had its own two-story brick building and sixty-five students. One of its major assets was the bishop's eight-thousand-volume library, one of the finest in the United States. Day students paid twelve dollars a quarter, and, most unusual for the time, admission was open to students of all faiths. The curriculum included Greek, Latin, French, English, Spanish, and Italian; arithmetic, mathematics, drawing, and geography. Boarding facilities were available, and evening classes in French were offered to adults. In 1822, when the St. Mary's of the Barrens Seminary was chartered at Perryville, seminary instruction at St. Louis was discontinued.

The Catholic Church had suffered severely with the transfer of Louisiana to the United States. Since the Spanish government had paid all the Church's operating expenses, the parishioners were unaccustomed to tithing and liked it that way. With no guarantee of future support, Father Pierre Janin in 1804 had accepted DeLassus's invitation to leave with his party. Father James Maxwell of Ste. Genevieve visited St. Louis periodically until 1814; and Father Thomas Flynn, a free-lancing Capuchin, was resident pastor in 1807; but for the next six years, Catholics were fortunate if they saw a priest six times a year. Father Marie Joseph Dunand, a Trappist visitor in 1808 found Catholicism "in a pitiful state." He blamed the prevailing irreligion and licentiousness on "the incursion of foreigners" and persecution of priests by the Americans. Between 1813 and 1818 Father Francis Savine of Cahokia said Mass in St. Louis every third Sunday, but when Bishop Flaget of Kentucky visited the parish in 1814, he was virtually ignored by the elite and described Catholics in the town as "in a state of extreme indifference."

Non-Catholics too were struck by the apathy of the communicants. Frederick Bates remarked that the priests who visited St. Louis were very indulgent, "and when they cease . . . to be so, the People withhold those contributions which are necessary for their support." John Mason Peck, a Baptist minister, was astonished in 1818 to discover that the Creoles were not religious; that Mass was attended only by "females and illiterate Frenchmen." The French leadership, according to Peck, under the influence of Voltaire and other liberal thinkers, thought of religion as "priestcraft" relevant only to the ignorant and superstitious. The clerics were irritated by the paltry collections and the lack of deference shown to them by important men, and Bates and Peck were unfriendly witnesses; but

Bishop Louis W. V. DuBourg. *Oil on canvas by Louis Schultze, ca. 1885. MHS-Art.*

clearly the Church was in trouble. The external forms were preserved, however. Between 1804 and 1816, 397 whites, 100 blacks, and 5 Indians were baptized in the Catholic Church in St. Louis.

What the parish needed was a stronger commitment from the Church, a resumption of the authority they had known during the Spanish regime. Further, the literate and well-to-do leading families would respond only to a religious leader of high abilities and intellectual force. They had known such a priest, Father Marie Joseph Didier, their pastor from 1793 to 1799. Like Dr. Saugrain, Father Didier had been a leader of the genteel Gallipolis emigré community, and his superior qualities made him hard to follow.

Napoleon's final defeat and a decision made in Rome were destined to strengthen Catholicism in St. Louis. Louis William DuBourg, born in Santo Domingo in 1766 and educated as a Sulpician priest in Paris, had fled from the Reign of Terror to Spain, and then in 1794 to Baltimore. He served as president of Georgetown College, founded St. Mary's College in Baltimore, and in 1812 became apostolic administrator (not quite a bishop) at New Orleans. DuBourg was soon at odds with the New Orleans clergy, who were insubordinate, and the local people whom he thought to be both dissolute and Bonapartists. Accordingly, in 1815, when the diocese of Louisiana and the Floridas was created and DuBourg made bishop, he decided to establish his residency at St. Louis. In preparation for his new assignment, DuBourg spent several months in Italy and France collecting funds, books, and works of art from wealthy friends and patrons of the Church to further his work in Louisiana. Through persuasion and pressure, he was also able to recruit several outstanding young missionary priests for his diocese, including the Vincentian Fathers Felix de Andreis and Joseph Rosati. In another master stroke, he persuaded the Superior General of the Order of the Sacred Heart in Paris to allow Mother Rose Philippine Duchesne and four nuns to join him. The priests were to establish a seminary and Mother Duchesne a school for girls, but their enthusiasm for the assignment chiefly reflected their eagerness to work with the western Indians.

Early in January 1818 Bishop DuBourg and his party arrived in St. Louis to an enthusiastic welcome from most of the town's twenty-five hundred residents. According to de Andreis, DuBourg's response was eloquent and masterful. "Kindness, dignity and suavity of manner . . . dissipated in a great measure every prejudice, and captivated all hearts." A few days later the bishop wrote:

> Here I am in St. Louis, and it is no dream. The dream would be most delightful, but the reality is even more so. . . . My home is not magnificent, but it will be comfortable. . . . I will have a parlor, a sleeping room, a very nice study, besides a dining room, and four rooms for the ecclesiastics, and an immense garden. My cathedral, which looks like a poor stable, is falling in ruins, so that a new church is an absolute necessity. . . . Its construction will take time, especially in a place where everything is just beginning. The country, the most beautiful in the world, is healthy and fertile, and emigrants pour in. But everything is dear.

The old log church of Laclède, Vasquez, Cruzat, and Father Bernard, in a state of decay for many years, was torn down and a brick structure, 135 by 40 feet, was begun immediately on Laclède's church square between Second and Third Streets, just west of Auguste Chouteau's home. Substantial pledges for its construction were made by the Creole leaders Auguste and Pierre Chouteau, Bernard Pratte, Marie P. Leduc, Manuel Lisa, and the Sarpy, Robidoux, Gratiot, Papin, Soulard, and Cabanne families; the well-to-do Irish businessmen Jeremiah Connor, Thomas Brady, Thomas Maguire, and John Mullanphy; and the Anglo-Americans Alexander McNair, Thomas Hart Benton, William C. Carr, William Clark, Frederick Bates, and Theodore Hunt. Civic duty, their marital and political alliances, and perhaps political ambition moved this last group.

Construction expenses reached twenty-four thousand dollars, higher than expected; and collections of pledges and sales of pews were disappointing. The interior of the cathedral was never completed, but the first Mass was celebrated there on Christmas Day 1819. Civic boosters had a field day. The *St. Louis Directory* in 1821 claimed that the church was unmatched in the United States for magnificence, "and indeed few churches in Europe possess anything superior to it." Decorated with "elegant sacred vases, ancient and precious gold embroideries, . . . (and) the original paintings of Rubens, Raphael, Guido, Paul Veronese," and other masters of the Flemish, Italian, and French schools contributed by Louis XVIII and other ranking dignitaries of France and Italy, it was a delight to an "American of taste." The author's soaring imagination had outstripped the facts: no one else ever noticed a Rubens or a Raphael in the cathedral; but as it was, the collection was a spectacular addition to the civic assets of the frontier capital.

In November 1820 the pressure of logic and the New Orleans clergy inclined Bishop DuBourg toward New Orleans. For two years thereafter he shared his time between the two cities, and in 1822 he left St. Louis permanently except for short visits. Certain of his decisions had caused difficulties in the district, but he and the recruited priests and nuns had put the Catholic Church on a solid foundation. In addition to the academy and seminary, DuBourg organized an orchestra and a choir composed of Catholics and Protestants, men and women, black and white. He received an Osage delegation and sent a missionary priest to their village; he brought in a group of Belgian Jesuits who established an Indian school at Florissant; he encouraged the French-Americans to maintain their traditions and feast days; and he had wisely insisted that his Italian and French priests become proficient in English. Father de Andreis had died in 1820, but under the leadership of Father Niel at St. Louis, Rosati at Perryville, and Mother Duchesne at St. Charles and Florissant, the Church thrived in the area. In 1826 a separate St. Louis diocese was created, and Joseph Rosati was named its first bishop in 1827.

During the latter years of the Spanish regime, the lieutenant governors had pretended not to notice the itinerant preachers who made quick forays across the river to lead worship in Protestant homes. When forced to acknowledge an evangelist's presence, Trudeau would allow him to complete his mission before threatening him with jail if he did not depart within three days. Everyone concerned understood the game and obeyed its rules. The Baptists, who organized a congregation on Fee Fee Creek in 1807 and built a log church in 1815, were first in the district after the transfer of

Louisiana. St. Louis itself was slender pickings for the evangelists who preached "as if they were fighting bees," however. Not until 1818, with the help of the missionaries John Mason Peck and James E. Welch, was the First Baptist Church of St. Louis organized with eleven members. The Methodists, whose local ministers, like those of the Baptists, were usually uneducated, made only a few abortive efforts to assail "the citadel of Romanism," until 1821, when they organized a small congregation in the town.

Although it had little appeal for the Kentuckians and Tennesseans who swarmed into the farming regions, Presbyterianism had an initial advantage in St. Louis. Its educated ministry and rational religion, combined with an influential nucleus of easterners who had been reared in the Calvinist faith, were the basis for a solid beginning. Stephen Hempstead, Edward's father, who moved his family to St. Louis in 1811, organized a Presbyterian Bible Society with the assistance of William C. Carr, Clement Penrose, and Charles Gratiot, the last still a confirmed Calvinist after thirty-three years in Louisiana. At Hempstead's request, the Connecticut Missionary Society sent Salmon Giddings and Timothy Flint to the district in 1816. Giddings preached in the combination theatre-courthouse-legislative hall for more than a year before the First Presbyterian Church was founded. There were only nine original members, but they were all community leaders or connected with them. Flint had been fairly successful in St. Charles, as had both missionaries in other towns, and by December 1817, there was enough interest to organize the Missouri Presbytery in St. Louis.

Unlike other Protestants in Missouri at that time, the Presbyterians wanted to Anglicize the Indians and save their souls. With the assistance of the government and the Congregationalists, they established Harmony Mission near the Great Osage village in southwest Missouri. There, missionaries preached; and, with their wives, taught the Bible, reading and writing, and "useful arts" like spinning and weaving to Osage children from 1821 to 1835. The school was successful, but the preaching was less so, perhaps because of a bad start. Against the advice of William S. (Old Bill) Williams, who had an Osage wife and acted as interpreter, one of the preachers delivered a sermon on Jonah and the Whale, to which an outraged chief responded: "We have heard . . . white people talk and lie; we know they will lie, but that is the biggest lie we have ever heard."

A fourth Protestant denomination was solidly established in St. Louis by 1825, when Thomas Horrell became rector of the Christ Church Episcopalian parish. The principal founding member, Thomas Fiveash Riddick, was a banker and political leader. Like the Presbyterians, the Episcopalians appealed to a small but powerful group, primarily merchants and professionals of Virginian and Carolinian origins, including Wilson Price Hunt, Robert Wash, William Rector, Henry Von Phul, James Kennerly, Samuel Hammond, and Theodore Hunt. The late start and initially slow growth of the Protestant congregations reflected not only Creole numerical predominance but a lack of interest. Many of the ambitious and energetic men who sought wealth and power at the frontier capital had some religious affiliation, but few were disturbed by the absence of Protestant churches. They were too busy buying and selling, looking for clients, or holding and running for office (or all of these at once). According to the Baptist evangelist John Mason Peck, one source of irreligion was the Fort Bellefontaine officer corps made up of Universalists and agnostics. Even worse, in Peck's view, was the lower half of the Anglo-American population (rivermen, petty artisans, laborers), consisting of "infidels of a low and indecent grade," who despised religion, were "vulgarly profane," and "poured out scoffings and contempt on the few Christians." The taunts of these "drunken scoffers" and the good-natured jibes of the French kept many good men away from his sermons.

Opportunities for public office, a powerful attraction for many emigrants, naturally expanded as the territory grew. In 1809, after a similar effort had failed the year before because of procedural errors, the District Court of Common Pleas approved a petition from the citizens of St. Louis for incorporation as a town. On November 27, Auguste Chouteau, William C. Carr, Jean Cabanne, Edward Hempstead, and William Christy were elected to the Board of Trustees, which in turn elected Chouteau chairman. The court had authorized greatly expanded boundaries for the town, including more than six miles of riverfront, but the board defined much smaller taxable limits. An ordinance of 1811 described the boundaries as beginning at the low-water mark of the Mississippi, "near the windmill of Antoine Roy, then due west to the east line of the 40 arpens lot of the hill back of St. Louis, then along the line of said lots to Mill Creek, then down said creek to its mouth, thence up the River Mississippi, along the low-water mark, to the place of beginning." Roy's windmill was a half-block north of the original north boundary (the present Martin Luther King Drive), and the new limits were one block farther west to the brow of the hill (Fourth Street). The southern extension below the original boundary (Poplar Street) to Mill Creek added several blocks of river frontage and a small wedge of land to the town.

Except for a ban on horse racing on the streets, the first board devoted itself to slave control. The municipal slave regulations, more specific than the territorial code, forbade slaves to be drunk in public, assemble at night or in groups larger than four during the day without the board's permission, attend parties or balls given by free blacks or mulattoes without permission, or ride a horse without its owner's permission. Any person giving or selling liquor to a slave was fined ten dollars. Owners of slave transgressors were to give ten lashes on the bare back to the offender. If the owner refused, he was to be fined up to ten dollars. Violators of the horse-riding provision received twenty lashes, and free blacks or mulattoes who gave balls or parties were fined ten dollars for each unauthorized slave attending.

To enforce the ordinances, an armed patrol (the constabulary) was established, consisting of four men appointed by the board and serving without pay. Except for invalids, paupers, and preachers, each male inhabitant over eighteen was subject to patrol duty. Personnel were rotated each day, and the constabulary served willingly, even proudly, according to the *Gazette*. Their chief duty was to return slaves found on the streets after 9:00 P.M. to their masters and Indians to the Indian agent. Drunkenness and riotous behavior by whites usually went unchecked during the town's early years. The district jail, located in the Fort San Carlos tower after Fort Bellefontaine was established in 1806, was managed by Sheriff Jeremiah Connor until 1809, when Secretary Bates removed him for neglect of duty. He was replaced by Alexander McNair who had married into the Creole elite. The jail housed town as well as district (county) prisoners. Crimes of sufficient gravity to be reported in the *Gazette* included the absconding of Charless's pressman Joseph Hinkle, who left town owing $600, the theft of $282 from Daniel Freeman's house, and the bilking of certain citizens by a man "of polished manners, gentlemanly exterior, and of a superior education." None of these three offenders were apprehended.

Killing of white persons, except in duels, was rare. In 1806 Samuel Hammond, Jr., son of the district commandant, killed a Kickapoo Indian, but a jury found that he had acted in the defense of two prominent citizens. Governor Wilkinson thought otherwise, or Hammond would never have been arrested (another reason for Wilkinson's unpopularity). A riverman was killed in a brothel brawl in 1812, but no one was brought to trial. The first execution in St. Louis took place in 1809, when John Long of Bonhomme was hanged for murdering his stepfather. Other murders occurred in the district, but none in the town before 1817.

The citizen's patrol sufficed until 1818, when Mackey Wherry was appointed police captain at four hundred dollars a year. Two men were added to the patrol, and an assistant chief and constable were hired for night duty. Police and patrol were now empowered to "enforce order and silence of all persons after 9 o'clock in the evening on all streets," and anyone found "in Gardens or lots not their own" were to be fined five dollars.

Originally, the town's only provision for fire protection required the patrol to warn occupants of a building on fire and alarm the town by ringing the church bell. In 1810 an ordinance enrolled all male inhabitants over eighteen in two fire companies. Pierre Didier was named fire captain, Edward Hempstead first lieutenant, and Gregoire Sarpy second lieutenant. Householders and storekeepers were required to have two leather or other buckets on hand for use in fires and to clean their chimneys once a month, with delinquents subject to a five dollar fine. For using chimneys of other than brick or stone or placing a stovepipe within six inches of wood, the fine was from five to fifty dollars. Only three large fires were reported between 1808 and 1816: Louis Labeaume lost five horses and five hundred bushels of corn and Pierre Chouteau five hundred tons of hay in barn fires, and Jacques St. Vrain's brewery and several hundred bushels of grain were destroyed.

To protect the public health and safety, the board ordained that dead animals must be removed from town immediately by their owners, and that no person could erect "a necessary house or privy" facing the street. Violators of the latter provision were to be fined twenty dollars, and the town collector could draft citizens to assist him in pulling down the privy. Slaughterhouses could be operated only by board permission, and must be kept "clean and in good order to the end that the health of the inhabitants shall not be injured." Dog owners were required to pay one dollar a year for each dog in excess of one, and all dogs were to have collars with the collector's stamp on them (those without collars could be killed). The owner of a dog or pig running at large was subject to a fine of two dollars.

Clement Penrose, who had long been disturbed by the gaiety and impieties of the St. Louis Sunday, attempted to bring the town up to the moral standards of his native Philadelphia when he was elected to the board in 1811. He proposed an ordinance prohibiting buying, selling, working, gambling, or card playing on Sunday, and setting a fine for anyone who lost more than seven dollars gambling during any twenty-four-hour period. This sumptuary legislation had little appeal for Creole board members Auguste Chouteau and Bernard Pratte, and only the section prohibiting the selling of merchandise between 8:00 A.M. and sundown on Sundays was passed. In a further concession to Penrose, the board later set a license fee of fifty dollars annually for operating billiard tables, gambling tables, or wheels of fortune. This nuisance tax was increased to one hundred dollars in 1816.

For the construction and maintenance of streets and bridges, an ordinance in 1811 created the office of overseer of roads and two property assessors to determine liability for service. Each able-bodied male over twenty-one was required to work from two to thirty days on the streets depending upon the value of his property, substitutes permitted. Owners were also directed to remove any timber, stone, or carts from the streets in front of their houses or lots.

At the market house on the public square (La Place), completed in 1812, the board set the rent of its twelve public stalls at ten to thirty dollars a year. A clerk was appointed to supervise the market and inspect the produce, and those who sold spoiled produce or gave false measure were to be fined. No produce could be sold anywhere else in town between daybreak and 10:00 A.M.. on Wednesdays and Saturdays. The constant and annoying presence of hordes of yapping dogs at the market house underlined the futility of the board's concerns. Few citizens paid dog taxes or fines, live pigs and cattle roamed and dead ones littered the streets; and the streets themselves were bottomless mudholes or piles of choking dust, depending upon the season. As late as 1822, a local wag cracked that Main Street was "the only navigable water course through the city for craft of the larger size, though there are several which answer for scows and dugouts." In 1819, after one year, the police chief and his night assistant were discharged as too expensive. There had been problems with waste disposal and roaming animals throughout St. Louis's existence, especially after the Spanish departed, but they reached epic proportions after 1815 as dozens of new businesses and thousands of people crowded into the town. The restrictive ordinances were unenforceable—the floating population was too large, the municipal treasury too small, and, to many residents, such laws were alien and unnatural.

Various other local taxes and licenses eked out the town's meager revenues. An ordinance of 1810 exempted peltries, lead, and other products of the Louisiana Territory from municipal taxation, and established a tax schedule as follows: taverns, public houses, or liquor retailers, fifteen dollars annually; retailers of non-Louisiana products, fifteen dollars; ferries, fifteen dollars; four-wheel pleasure carriages, two dollars; two-wheel pleasure carriages, one dollar; real property, .25 percent of assessed valuation. Auguste Chouteau, as treasurer, reported collections in 1810 of $350 from licenses, $163.68 from property taxes, and $16 in fines, for a total of $529.68.

Expenditures that year were $116 to Joseph Garnier, clerk of the board for services and expenses, $33 to David Delaunay as road overseer, $114 to Joseph Charless for printing the laws; and $53 to the collector, representing 10 percent of his collections, leaving a balance of more than $130. Eight years later, though its population and volume of business had multiplied, St. Louis's income was still a modest $1,307, the property tax accounting for over half of the total.

The nuisance tax on players, acrobats, and animal acts had not been intended to curtail legitimate drama. In 1814, Christian Wilt, Charles Hempstead, Dr. Robert Simpson, Thomas F. Riddick, and others organized The Thespian Society, purchased a large (forty-by-eighty-foot) frame building on the Rue des Granges (Third Street), erected a stage and installed seats, and named it "the Theatre." For the next several years in that location, the local amateur company presented serious dramas such as *Richard III, Henry IV,* and the Scottish dramatist John Homes's *Douglas; She Stoops to Conquer, The Heir at Law, The Poor Gentleman,* and other comedies; and a persistent diet of farces such as *The Budget of Blunders, Killing No Murder,* and *Who's the Dupe?* Admission was one dollar for adults and fifty cents for children, with the receipts often donated to an indigent or unfortunate person. Beginning in April 1818 a company headed by a Mr. Turner, the first professionals to appear in St. Louis, presented a series of dramas and "Orations" over a period of several months. The original theatre continued in use for several years, still usually featuring amateur talent, before a more ambitious program was undertaken.

In 1812, the territorial government was reorganized. President Jefferson's ex-secretary Meriwether Lewis, the hero of the transcontinental expedition of 1804–5, had become governor in 1808; but his tenure was a short one, disappointing to the people and to himself. Relations were strained between the governor and Secretary Frederick Bates, compounded by the latter's inflated view of his own talents and achievements. Bates expected to guide Lewis in territorial matters, but after the first few weeks, the governor began to seek counsel elsewhere, primarily from the Indian Agent William Clark. Lewis was a moody and unpredictable man who managed to alienate important constituents, as much by his manner as by his deeds. His strict requirements for licensing Indian traders irritated smaller traders, and his effort to force the reluctant Creoles into active militia service was resented. In August 1809 he set out for Washington to straighten out his territorial accounts, a necessary step because some of his expenditures had been disallowed. He died on the way, probably by his own hand, in a cabin on the Natchez Trace in Tennessee.

Lewis's performance as governor had been positive in two respects. He had brought Joseph Charless and the *Gazette* to St. Louis by giving him the territorial printing contract, and he had cooled down the land-claims controversy somewhat by refusing to identify himself with either faction.

Lewis's successor, General Benjamin Howard of Kentucky, distinguished himself primarily by being absent most of the time, leaving affairs in the hands of Frederick Bates. In 1811, agitation began in the territory for advancement to second-class status. The chief impetus for this change was the widespread belief that Congress and the executive were ill-informed about conditions in the territory. Elevation to the second class would entitle Louisiana to elect a nonvoting delegate to Congress, who could expedite solutions to such problems as unconfirmed land titles, inadequate defenses, and unsatisfactory mail service. Defenders of the status quo argued that the additional taxation required for more government would not be offset by increased federal spending in the territory. Especially persistent were the Chouteaus and other "ancient inhabitants" who feared taxation of their large speculative holdings. In addition, elevated status would probably stimulate a horde of immigrants who could reduce Creole political influence.

Opposition was hopeless. The growing population and the established national pattern of territorial advancement toward self-government and eventual statehood mandated a change. On June 4, 1812, President Madison signed the bill establishing Missouri as a second-class territory, the change in name necessary because the Territory of Orleans had been admitted to the Union as the state of Louisiana. Under the new dispensation, the former districts were designated as counties. All tax-paying adult white males were eligible to vote for a congressional delegate and for members of a territorial house of representatives. An upper house, the legislative council, consisted of nine members appointed by the president from a list of eighteen submitted by the lower house. Officeholders were required to be property owners. St. Louis County was entitled to four members in the lower house, Ste. Genevieve three, and St. Charles, Cape Girardeau, and New Madrid two each.

As soon as this new status was confirmed, aspiring politicians began to scramble for office. Edward Hempstead, Rufus Easton, and Samuel Hammond, all of St. Louis, announced their candidacies for congressional delegate. Hempstead was favored by the Creoles, Charless, and the long-established Americans; Easton by the southern counties and most of the newer arrivals; and Hammond by Frederick Bates, a bitter enemy of Hempstead. The results of the balloting showed that the old elite had little to fear from the new government. Hempstead won by a substantial margin over Easton, with Hammond third. Auguste Chouteau was appointed by President Madison to the legislative council; and in 1813 William Clark, Indian agent and partner in the fur business with Manuel Lisa and Silvestre Labbadie, was named governor, with veto power over all territorial legislation. In addition, a coalition of land claimants and fur-trading interests easily controlled the lower house. As territorial delegate, Hempstead was effective. He won commitments from Congress to add to the defenses of the Missouri Territory; to liberalize the law for confirmation of land titles, including those dated after 1800; and to set aside portions of the public lands for the support of public schools.

St. Louis grew only slightly between 1811 and 1815. The threat posed by the powerful Shawnee chief Tecumseh's confederacy in the Indiana territory, the raids on St. Charles County by the embittered Sauks and Foxes, and the fear of a British-Indian attack kept St. Louisans edgy and cautious, and severely limited expansion of population and business. Immigration was also inhibited somewhat by the devastating New Madrid earthquake in 1811, the most severe ever experienced in the United States.

Despite these concerns, the British mounted no major invasions of the territory during the war of 1812. The presence of two hundred or more soldiers at Fort Bellefontaine and the influence of William Clark and the Chouteaus with nearby tribes created unacceptable risks for attackers. The Spanish from Santa Fe were intriguing with the Kansas, Pawnees, and other plains tribes; but the Osages, reconciled after a temporary rupture in 1808, gave protection to the west. Acting Governor Bates asked Pierre Chouteau early in 1813 to seek Osage help in defending St. Louis, and Chouteau complied by bringing 260 warriors to an encampment near the town.

Before 1811, despite threats of imprisonment, it had been impossible to get St. Louis militamen to accept active duty at any distance from their homes. With the onset of war, the moribund territorial militia revived a little, especially after Auguste Chouteau was commissioned a colonel and Pierre Chouteau a major. But in 1813, when Clark, now governor, planned an assault against the British at Prairie du Chien, he obtained 140 sixty-day volunteers only by paying them twenty dollars a month and one and one-half rations a day. With these men and sixty regulars, Clark captured the post. Some Sauks and Foxes sued for peace, but the British had escaped. When Clark went home, the enemy reoccupied Prairie du Chien. At first, St. Louisans thought this a famous victory. At a banquet for Clark in the Missouri Hotel, a toast was drunk to "Prairie du Chien . . . the late

William Clark, Governor of the Missouri Territory, 1813–21. *Oil on canvas by John Wesley Jarvis, ca. 1810. MHS-Art.*

expedition has cleansed it of spies and traitors." But within a few weeks refugees from the upper country began to trickle in with tales of mutilations and other acts of reprisal by the Indians.

Not until they heard of Andrew Jackson's victory at New Orleans did the people breathe easily. They had felt certain that a British victory there would spring a host of Indians and Canadians down the river for a rendezvous at New Orleans, pausing enroute only to annihilate St. Louis. When the British in Canada heard of the peace treaty of December 1814, they stopped fighting; but Indian attacks on remote communities and farms continued until June 1816, when Clark, Auguste Chouteau, and Ninian Edwards of Illinois negotiated a treaty with ten tribes at Portage des Sioux in St. Charles County. Since this agreement left the Indians alive and in possession of some of their lands, it was unpopular with farmers, Joseph Charless, and American merchants such as Christian Wilt, all of whom believed that the Indians should be exterminated all the way to the Rockies. Charless never forgave Clark and hounded him mercilessly thereafter in the columns of the *Gazette.* Any show of consideration for Indians became politically more dangerous as the proportion of Americans in the population increased. Ultimately, this attitude was fatal to Clark's political ambitions, and no doubt reduced Chouteau's influence.

With the end of the war, immigration resumed with a rush. As John Mason Peck put it, "Some families came in the spring of 1815 . . . but in the winter, summer, and autumn of 1816, they came like an avalanche. Caravan after caravan passed over the prairies of Illinois, crossing the 'great river' at St. Louis." The territorial capital's population, about fifteen hundred in January 1815, had grown to more than two thousand a year later, even though most of those ferried across the Mississippi were headed for farms on Salt River or the Boonslick country. By 1818 estimates of St. Louis's population ranged as high as 3,300, and the federal census of 1820 credited the town with 4,598 residents, a gain of 228 percent in ten years. The county had increased from 5,567 to 9,850 people during the decade, up 77 percent. Much of the initial increase in 1815 had resulted from decisions of mustered-out officers and men from Fort Bellefontaine to bring their families to St. Louis.

To take advantage of this influx, Chouteau and J. B. C. Lucas subdivided their land on the hill. The Chouteau-Lucas addition extended from Fourth to Seventh Streets on the east and west, and from St. Charles to Cerré on the north and south, a total of about thirty blocks. Its east-west streets were extensions of the streets of the town, but at just over sixty feet they were twice as wide. Lucas advertised the site as "mostly level and commanding," averaging nearly forty feet higher than the town with "a full view of the Mississippi River for 5 or 6 miles down, and from several parts as far up, offering a horizon nearly as vast as the ocean." In 1822, the promoters donated to the county a block for a courthouse and public square, bounded by Fourth and Fifth, Market and Chestnut Streets. By late 1818 Chouteau had sold fifty-one lots for $15,392, and Lucas twenty-seven for $9,883. Within ten years Lucas had turned a profit of more than 1,200 percent on his entire common-field speculation by selling less than one-fourth of it. Several multiple buyers such as Lucas's son-in-law Theodore Hunt, Dr. Saugrain, Charles Gratiot, William Christy, Thomas Brady, and Thomas F. Riddick also expected a quick profit, and more than half of the lots sold had been reconveyed by 1825.

According to the *Gazette*, more than one hundred houses were built in St. Louis in 1818, and many more were under way. Between 1815 and 1821 the town gained 108 frame and log buildings, to a total of 306; 13 of stone, to 77; 69 of brick, to 75. Material and labor shortages and high costs kept construction behind population growth; from about six persons per building in 1815, occupation density increased to eleven per building in 1821. Pine lumber in 1818 was eight dollars per one hundred board feet, ten times the Pittsburgh price, and twice the local price a year earlier.

During this post-war period, St. Louis was in transition from a barter to a money economy. Peltries, lead, and whiskey had been the principal exchange media, their value negotiable within rough limits. Spanish-milled dollars, which could be broken up into eight "bits," appeared fairly often but quickly disappeared into the money chests of the merchants. The soldiers at Bellefontaine and federal officials were paid in U.S. Treasury warrants until 1817, and thereafter in notes or drafts of the Bank of the United States, providing the area with a sound paper circulation of several thousand dollars a month. The demand for eastern goods constantly exceeded the value of the territory's exports, however, forcing local merchants to remit the difference in specie or acceptable paper notes, keeping the local markets drained of currency.

By 1816, the despised "rag" currency, the notes of chartered banks of Kentucky, Ohio, and western Pennsylvania which passed at a discount, had begun to flow into the territory with immigrants and traders. Prices, always high in St. Louis, climbed to new heights. John Mason Peck called these notes "shinplasters . . . the droppings of that first generation of banks instituted in the far West without any adequate specie basis. Their leaves were scattered over the frontiers like the leaves of trees by an autumn frost, and the price of every article . . . was higher in proportion." The risk involved in accepting these shaky notes was compounded by a flow of counterfeits from Kentucky and Tennessee. Peck paid twelve dollars a month for a single room, thirty-five to fifty cents a pound for butter, thirty to forty cents for sugar, and seventy-five cents for coffee. The *Missouri Gazette* in 1818 reported that common laborers would work for no less than $1.50 a day, and that many of them had earned enough in a year to buy 160 acres of land. Lots below the hill sold for five hundred to three thousand dollars, and some houses rented for fifty dollars a month. Farm land between St. Louis and St. Charles, worth twenty-five to fifty cents an acre ten years earlier, sold in 1818 for eight to twelve dollars an acre.

In December 1816, in an effort to loosen the coils of the barter economy, local capitalists opened the Bank of St. Louis, in the rear of Riddick and Pilcher's store on Main Street. Chartered by the legislature in response to a petition from Auguste Chouteau and other fur merchants, the bank accepted furs and lead as security for loans. It made loans by printing paper notes and issuing them to borrowers, who then put them into circulation. These "beaver bills," so-called because they aptly featured a sketch of a trapped beaver, were to be redeemable in specie (gold or silver) upon demand. Though its promoters intended its issue to be sound, in contrast to other western banks, the Bank of St. Louis promptly got into trouble as its cashier, John B. N. Smith made wildly speculative real estate loans to friends (or accomplices) in Kentucky and large unsecured loans to certain of the bank's directors. Soon it was clear that the bank's circulation was vastly overextended. A minority stockholders' bloc associated with Chouteau, using Joshua Pilcher as its agent and Thomas Hart Benton as its attorney, succeeded in deposing Smith as cashier.

Smith's replacement proving unacceptable, a group of these stockholders, led by Benton, General Daniel Bissell, Jeremiah Connor, and Pilcher, strode into the bank, ejected its officers and directors, and demanded the keys to the vault. When President Samuel Hammond refused, the dissidents padlocked the doors determined to stand their ground until their interests were safeguarded. Claiming they feared for their lives, the directors obtained indictments against the invaders who were forced to post peace bonds and surrender the door keys. After trying for a year to straighten out the mess, the officers reopened the bank only to have it expire in July 1819, caught at the beginning of land-price panic with a drawer full of bad loans. Several of the directors and investors were ruined, including Moses Austin, who was jailed when he could not raise enough money on his vast lead-mining properties to repay his bank loans. The panic was blamed for the bank's demise, but mismanagement and fraud had made the failure inevitable.

Meanwhile, early in 1817, the Bank of Missouri had been chartered to "repel the influx" of the notes of nonspecie-paying banks, which the speculative Bank of St. Louis was not doing. Eighty-three St. Louisans, several of them disgruntled stockholders of the other bank, comprising a broad cross-section of the merchant and professional classes, subscribed $78,500 to the capital stock of the Bank of Missouri. While Creole merchants and traders and their allies predominated, Frederick Bates, J. B. C. Lucas, Joseph Charless, Christian Wilt, and even Charles Dehault DeLassus were among the stockholders. Auguste Chouteau was elected president and furnished quarters for the bank in the basement of his home (the basement dug by Missouri Indian women in 1764).

The new bank was successful at first. Since its notes, in denominations of one, three, five, and twenty dollars, were always redeemed in specie, they were trusted and passed at par. In 1818 the Bank of Missouri became a United States depository, guaranteeing it a minimum federal deposit of $150,000. This permanent fund, augmented by money collected by the public land office, amounted to more than $700,000 in 1819, 90 percent of the bank's total deposits. Despite its relative conservatism, the Bank of Missouri made personal loans to its directors and loans on real estate at the inflated 1818

Old Chouteau Mansion, St. Louis, Mo. *Lithograph by J. C. Wild, 1840, from J. C. Wild and Lewis Thomas,* The Valley of the Mississippi Illustrated. *Wild's rendering shows Auguste Chouteau's reconstruction of Laclède's original house, and was published with a heartfelt plea to save it from demolition. MHS-Library.*

prices. When the Second Bank of the United States reversed itself and began to contract its issue late in 1818, the squeeze was on the state and territorial banks. The collapse of credit punctured the western land boom. Farms in the St. Louis area worth ten thousand dollars in 1818 were going begging at one thousand dollars in 1820. Under pressure to redeem its overextended note issue, the Bank of Missouri was in dire straits by 1821, when Thomas F. Riddick succeeded a weary Auguste Chouteau as president. In August the bank closed, technically not a failure but unable to foreclose on its mortgages because of a Stay Law (debt moratorium) passed by the state legislature.

The inglorious end of both territorial banks, the one primarily because of fraudulent management, the other a result of market forces only dimly understood, helped raise serious doubts about the commercial future of St. Louis. More important in the long run, the debacle contributed to the long life of "hard money" sentiment in Missouri. Thomas Hart Benton, who had been stung by both local banks, blamed the Bank of the United States for the troubles of the Bank of Missouri. Nicknamed "Old Bullion" for his hard-money stance, Benton described the situation in 1821 in these words: "All the flourishing cities of the West are mortgaged to this money power. They may be devoured by it at any moment. They are in the jaws of the Monster. A lump of butter in the mouth of a dog—one gulp, one swallow, and all is gone!"

After 1816, the rapid increase and diversification of business in St. Louis demonstrated its growing importance as a terminal and shipping point for the produce of the Missouri and upper Mississippi River settlements. Outfitting and supplying farmers on their way west and provisioning the western army posts were important sources of income, though the Indian fur trade still dominated St. Louis's commerce. As a harbinger of the future on August 2, 1817, the *Zebulon M. Pike*, the first steamboat to pass the mouth of the Ohio, docked at the foot of Market Street to the cheers of the entire able-bodied population. It was smaller than some keelboats, and pole men lined its sides to assist its chuffing steam engine; but it brought St. Louis closer to eastern markets. By 1819 steamboat arrivals and departures were commonplace, and one had even braved the treacherous currents of the Missouri River.

In 1821, John Paxton's *St. Louis Directory* listed forty-six mercantile houses, "carrying on an extensive trade with the most distant parts of the republic, in merchandise, produce, furs and peltry." There were artisans of all kinds, including silversmiths, jewelers, bricklayers, stone-cutters, twenty-eight carpenters, nine blacksmiths, gunsmiths, cabinetmakers, coachmakers, turners and chair-makers, twelve tailors, thirteen boatmakers, sign painters, hatters, coopers, bakers, clock and watchmakers, and saddlers. Fifty-seven "groceries" (primarily saloons), five billiard halls, three large inns (the Missouri Hotel, the Planter's Hotel, and the Mansion House), many smaller taverns and boarding houses, three drugstores, three auctioneers, six livery stables, and three newspapers (the *Missouri Gazette*, the *St. Louis Enquirer,* and the *St. Louis Register*). Twenty-seven attorneys and thirteen physicians provided professional services. A portrait painter, "several musicians," four hairdressers and perfumers, and three midwives also served the public. Light industries included one brewery, which brewed "the first ale, beer, and porter in the West," one tannery, one nail factory, three soap and candle factories, a comb factory, and near St. Louis, several distilleries and potteries.

Most of the merchants operated general stores, offering everything that had a market. John Campbell and White Matlock, who had opened for business in 1804, sold loaf and brown sugar, coffee, Madeira wine, rum, ratafia, rice, salt, salt fish, and Spanish "segars" from New Orleans; hardware, tinware, medicines, dry goods, paints, crockery, and ladies' bonnets from Philadelphia; and flour and whiskey from Pittsburgh and local sources. Whiskey sold for twenty-five cents a gallon, and its consumption on the premises made the stores hangouts for loungers and free-loaders. Some specialization was evident by 1819, especially in hardware, drugs, and "ladies' fineries." Peter Lindell and other "heavy grocers" imported large quantities, sometimes whole boatloads of flour, sugar, coffee, and tea and resold them to retailers.

More than half of the businesses listed in 1821, and many of the artisans and professional men, had come to St. Louis after 1817. Many of these newcomers were single men with only tentative commitments to St. Louis, who kept "bachelor's hall" in their business quarters. The enthusiasm and optimism engendered by rapid growth and impending statehood were dampened by the financial panic and bank failures and severe drop in commodity and land prices that accompanied them. This change in resources and mood was felt by Jeremiah Connor, whose subdivision, opened in 1819 just north of the Chouteau-Lucas addition, attracted few buyers despite its favorable location and its eighty-foot-wide Washington Street. Connor was patient, however; and better times would come.

4.
The Gateway City

Henry Rowe Schoolcraft, a major chronicler of the West, described St. Louis in 1819 as the "future seat of empire for the vast basin of land, situated between the Alleghany [*sic*] and the Rocky Mountains on the east and west, and between the northern Lakes and the Gulph [*sic*] of Mexico on the north and south." It was beautiful, healthful, and convenient, and "no place in the world, situated so far from the ocean, can at all compare with it for commercial advantages." Henry Vest Bingham thought it inevitable that the commerce of all the rich country drained by the Missouri, Illinois, and Des Moines Rivers would center at St. Louis.

This view was the consensus in the town itself—its greatness decreed first by nature and geography, only the efforts of enterprising men and the "fostering care" of government were needed for St. Louis to realize its destiny. By 1819, the leading prophet of that destiny was the editor of the *St. Louis Enquirer*, Thomas Hart Benton, who would persist in this role for more than thirty years. From his talks with Manuel Lisa, Charles Gratiot, Auguste and Pierre Chouteau (senior and junior), Bernard Pratte, William Clark, and ordinary voyageurs, Benton sketched a vision of western development and the town's role in it. A man of monumental ego who once said "Benton and the people, Sir, one and the same!" Benton, in like fashion, equated St. Louis with the West, and the West with the nation. Outraged by Secretary of State John Quincy Adams's "giveaways" of Oregon (the 1818 joint occupation treaty with Britain) and Texas (the Adams-Onis treaty of 1819), Benton wrote, "it is time that western men had some share in the destinies of this Republic."

Editor Benton foresaw a time not far distant when armies of immigrants to the Oregon country would march through Missouri. Once in Oregon they would produce a harvest of "furs and bread." Goods bound for Japan, China, and India would originate in or pass through St. Louis, then up the Missouri, across the Rockies, and down the Columbia to the Pacific. This dream of Oriental trade—the passage to India—had been explicit in the plans of Baron de Carondelet and Jacques Clamorgan in 1795, implicit in those of Thomas Jefferson and Meriwether Lewis in 1804, and the main reason for John Jacob Astor and Wilson Price Hunt's Astoria expedition in 1810; but for Thomas Hart Benton, it was the passion of a lifetime.

The overland route to the Pacific would enable the "small capitalists" of St. Louis and its hinterland to share in the China trade, a privilege previously reserved to the wealthy Eastern merchants who monopolized the ocean traffic. Along the trail to Oregon, a great national fur company, protected by a string of army posts, would "sap at its foundation . . . the solid pillar of British wealth and power" and give to the United States a place among the great nations. This route would pass near the northern provinces of Mexico, and expanded trade along that frontier would supply St. Louis and Missouri with sorely needed gold and silver. If Spain objected to this trade, Americans should help the Mexicans win their independence. All of this was intended to appeal not only to Benton's fur-trading friends, but to the farmers who would have the rough work of getting to Oregon.

"The Enquirer Man," as his dedicated enemy Joseph Charless called him, had come to St. Louis in 1815 after a public brawl with Andrew Jackson in Nashville had damaged his prospects there. As a lawyer and militia colonel under Jackson's command, Benton had been a favorite of the general, but his powder was quick to ignite. He interpreted an action of Jackson's as an insult, and the general's fiery temper had done the rest. Soon after Benton alighted from the ferry at the foot of Market Street in St. Louis with four hundred dollars in his pocket, he met Charles Gratiot and so impressed him that he was invited to live in Gratiot's home indefinitely. Within a few days Benton had met the most powerful men in St. Louis and was soon installed as Edward Hempstead's partner, busily employed as a land claims attorney. His remarkable memory and penchant for detail, his powerful six-foot frame, and his harsh, barking courtroom style (an exact copy of Hempstead's) made him a formidable advocate, soon recognized as a leader of the St. Louis bar.

Benton had landed squarely at the center of the "Little Junto," as Joseph Charless called it, the dominant faction of the landed elite. Its leaders at the time were Auguste Chouteau and Edward Hempstead, and it included Charles Gratiot, John Scott of Ste. Genevieve, Bernard Pratte, Pierre Chouteau, and Dr. Bernard Farrar. Most of these men held large Spanish claims or were in the fur business, or both; or they were their attorneys. Governor William Clark, who supported and was supported by his friends in this group, was more nationally oriented than most of them. Manuel Lisa, since 1804 the leading Missouri River trader, was an ally even before he married Mary Hempstead in 1818, though he kept a low political profile because of his reputation for ruthless double-dealing and long absences from St. Louis. Governor Clark's nephew, Captain John O'Fallon, though still under twenty-one, was a reliable and violent junto partisan. Alexander

McNair, the former sheriff, merchant, and registrar of the federal land office, usually cooperated with his in-laws in the Creole elite and shared their distaste for J. B. C. Lucas, whom he had known and disliked in Pennsylvania. The astute McNair was quicker than others to see that the surge of small farmers to Missouri would eventually upset the traditional power structures and was therefore careful to avoid total identification with a faction. In 1816, when Governor Clark ordered squatters removed from the public lands (pursuant to a federal directive), McNair, as the ranking colonel in the territorial militia, announced that the militia would refuse to carry out the order (technically, he did not himself refuse).

The opposition to the junto was headed by J. B. C. Lucas, Joseph Charless, Rufus Easton, William Russell, and David Barton. All of these men were speculators; Russell, the most audacious land pirate of all, held 309 separate claims ranging from 160 to 640 acres each. J. B. C. Lucas's son Charles, Russell, and several other St. Louisans had gobbled up most of the so-called New Madrid certificates (land warrants authorized by Congress in 1815 as compensation for property destroyed by the New Madrid earthquake) by purchasing ruined property for a few cents an acre before its owners learned about the Act of Congress. (As territorial delegate, Easton had been instrumental in getting the compensation bill passed.) These certificates entitled their holders to claim public land in the territory wherever they chose. Many of the New Madrid claims were located where Spanish claims were still pending or where holders of war veterans' warrants (most of them speculators too) had conflicting claims. Most of the New Madrid certificates had been acquired by fraud, and a majority were eventually disallowed; but substantial holdings in the rich Boonslick region in central Missouri and in the area near St. Louis were thus acquired. One speculator claimed part of the Carondelet commons without success, but Charles Lucas was confirmed in his 640-acre New Madrid claim a few miles northwest of St. Louis, which he called Normandy after his father's ancestral home.

In this struggle for economic and political plums, the Chouteau-Hempstead faction drew strength from the loyalties of the Creole fur traders and from a community of interest with those farmers who had small Spanish claims. The "anti-junto" group profited from Charless's editorial shafts in the *Gazette* and anti-Creole sentiment among the Anglo-Americans. Neither of these lawyer-speculator groups represented the substantial interests of the majority. A good many St. Louisans did not meet the taxpaying requirement for voting, and many other townspeople and farmers voted as suggested by members of the elite factions, either out of respect or because they

Charles Lucas. *Photograph of miniature by William Lucas, ca. 1815. MHS-PP.*

were bribed or intimidated. Editor Charless had some success in pinning the aristocratic label on his opponents with his repeated references to the "junto," "the colonels," "the lawyers' clique," and "Federalists," but it was hard to cast Judge Lucas and William Russell as "plain republicans."

In 1817 the town and the territory suffered three severe shocks. Charles Gratiot, still in his sixties, died of the "numb palsy" (a paralytic stroke), and Edward Hempstead, only thirty-eight, collapsed and died in a courtroom, apparently as a result of a fall from a horse a few weeks earlier. Even their political opponents mourned their deaths. Gratiot had always been a favorite of the Anglo-Americans; and Hempstead, the most popular man in the territory, was just past the threshold of an apparently unlimited political career. Shortly after Hempstead's death, the most notorious of the numerous local duels of the era was fought on an islet in the Mississippi channel off St. Louis between Thomas Hart Benton and Charles Lucas. Both men were self-confident, imperious ex-militia officers; Benton, at thirty-five, was ten years older than Lucas. As lawyers they had often opposed each other, especially in land-claims cases. After a heated exchange during one such trial, Benton challenged Lucas to a duel, but the latter refused to be held accountable personally for remarks made in his professional capacity (correct under the *code duello*). A few weeks later, Lucas rekindled the fire by implying at the polls that Benton had not paid

taxes in St. Louis and was thus ineligible to vote. The colonel told the
election judges that he would answer their proper questions, but he
would not be accountable to "any puppy who may happen to run
across my path!" After a week, Lucas sent a challenge and Benton
accepted. As agreed by their seconds (an Irish lawyer named Luke E.
Lawless for Benton and Joshua Barton, an attorney, for Lucas), they
met on "Bloody Island," as it was called thereafter, at 6:00 A.M. on
August 12, 1817. Their weapons were pistols; the distance thirty feet.
Both men fired on signal, Benton's ball passing through Lucas's
throat, Lucas's glancing off Benton's knee. With blood gushing from
his wound, Lucas indicated that he was satisfied, but Benton
demanded another meeting. A month later, persuaded by friends that
to persist would appear vindictive, Benton withdrew his challenge and
the matter appeared to be settled.

Unfortunately for all concerned, word soon reached the hotheaded colonel that both Lucases had attributed his departure from
Tennessee to a flight from criminal proceedings. He promptly issued a
new challenge, and despite his opponent's denial of the rumor, Benton
would not withdraw it without written assurances. Lucas refused this
demand and agreed to fight again. This time, at the murderous
distance of ten feet, Benton killed his young rival with a shot through
the heart. In all of this sad affair, there was plenty of blame to be
shared: the extreme touchiness and arrogance of both men; Benton's
initial insistence on a second meeting after nearly killing his man the
first time; the town's rumor-mongers; and the stubborn pride and acid
tongue of Judge Lucas, who had fed the flames by prodding his son
and traducing Benton. For the rest of his life, Benton was haunted by
"the pang which went through his heart when he saw the young man
fall." Lucas's family and friends neither forgave nor forgot. The judge
charged that Benton had killed his son to be rid of a promising
political rival; three years later the *Gazette* called the colonel "a man
crimsoned with the blood of one of our most promising young
citizens." To these and other such attacks Benton never responded.
This duel, which created a national sensation, reinforced the view that
St. Louis was a violent and dangerous place, now confirmed in the
"Kentuckyan and Tennesseean" image.

Regardless of factional preferences and ethnic origins,
Missourians had agreed by 1818 that statehood was essential. Unlike
1812, when the Creoles had opposed second-class territorial status,
they now saw further change as beneficial. Even if they had not,
opposition would have been fruitless and likely to rob them of
political allies and their remaining influence. Voting representation

in Congress would give fur traders more impact on federal policy. Specifically, they wanted the government fur factories eliminated. These federal trading posts, at Fort Bellefontaine and Fort Osage and elsewhere, served to some extent as yardsticks for fur prices, especially on the lower Missouri, tending to force private traders farther afield. Congress had hampered the factories by requiring them to sell only American-made goods and forbidding them to extend credit to the Indians as private traders did. As political appointees, the factors were often ignorant of the fur trade and the Indians, and they had to wait for the Indians to come to them, which reduced their competitive impact. The factories' potential for "mischief," however, was alarming to private traders, and they wanted to be rid of them.

Continuing exasperation with the capricious mail service; the desire for completion of a national road from Washington to St. Louis; frustration with the standoff between the locally oriented territorial legislature and the federally appointed governor; the prestigious federal and state offices that would be available to ambitious men; the anticipated flow of immigrants and capital; and the desire for political equality with easterners were all factors in the drive for statehood. Several petitions for admission had been presented to Congress by territorial delegate John Scott before Speaker Henry Clay laid a statehood petition from the Missouri legislature before the House on December 16, 1818. Two months later Congress, and Missouri when the news arrived, was galvanized when Representative James Tallmadge of New York proposed an amendment to the Missouri Bill prohibiting the further introduction of slavery into Missouri and freeing children of slaves born after statehood at the age of twenty-five.

The Missouri question raged in a monumental and nationally divisive debate in Congress for the next two years, but in Missouri it created a consensus. The French elite and the "junto" were strongly proslavery as always but no more so than a majority of the opposition. David Barton, speaker of the Territorial House, and Rufus Easton, both anti-junto leaders, the latter the Creoles' most persistent detractor for fifteen years, united with Benton, Bernard Pratte, and the Chouteaus to preserve slavery in Missouri. Despite the influx of slaveholding settlers from Kentucky and Tennessee to the Boonslick region after 1815, slaves comprised only 15 percent of the territory's population in 1820, and fewer than 10 percent of the white families owned slaves. In St. Louis County there were eighteen hundred slaves (18 percent of the population) and two hundred free blacks. While a good many nonslaveholders undoubtedly hoped to own blacks eventually, the major reason for the overwhelming proslavery sentiment was that the leaders to whom the majority deferred, the well-to-do merchants, traders, professional men, and politicians, were slaveowners almost without exception.

In the *Enquirer* and in mass meetings, Benton, David Barton, and others attacked Tallmadge and the congressional restrictionists as oppressors who would strip Missourians of the Louisiana Purchase treaty's property guarantees and deny them equality with citizens of other states. Such an unconstitutional assumption of power by Congress, roared Benton, would put "lighted torches" in the hands of slaves "to rouse their sleeping masters from their beds amid the flames of their houses and the cries of their slaughtered children." Despite this demagogic passage, Benton usually emphasized equality with older states and freedom of choice for property owners rather than the advantages of slavery itself.

The restriction issue isolated J. B. C. Lucas and Joseph Charless from the rest of the territorial leadership. Both men were slaveowners who stoutly denied abolitionist leanings, but Charless drew fire by publishing antislavery letters in the *Gazette,* and Lucas, though he deplored the Tallmadge Amendment, emphasized the advantages of free over slave labor. When Congress, in accordance with the Missouri Compromise, passed the Enabling Act in March 1820 authorizing Missouri to adopt a state constitution and elect a state government, Lucas, with the *Gazette*'s support, ran for delegate to the constitutional convention as a state restrictionist. He was the leader of a small group which wanted the further introduction of slaves into Missouri forbidden by the state (after slaveowning southerners had been given a few years to move to Missouri). Lucas expressed economic rather than moral objections to slavery, but he was supported by two small abolitionist Baptist congregations near St. Louis. Proslavery delegates were elected overwhelmingly throughout Missouri, Lucas losing in St. Louis County by a two-to-one margin.

The constitutional convention began its work on June 12, 1820, in the Mansion House hotel on Third Street. Forty-one delegates had been elected, including David Barton, Edward Bates, Pierre Chouteau, Jr., Alexander McNair, Bernard Pratte, William Rector, Thomas F. Riddick, and John C. Sullivan from St. Louis. Merchants, large farmers, and lawyers predominated among the delegates, thirty-three of whom had been born in slave states or territories. Twenty-six had received some advanced education, and with the exception of two schoolteachers, all were well-to-do. In short, the delegates were men of property, respected by the electorate, but by no means representative of them. Led by David Barton and Edward Bates, the lawyers dominated the convention. As expected, the framers drew up a conservative document, copied from the constitutions of Kentucky and such recently admitted states as Illinois. The standard provisions for a government of limited powers, a representative system, separation of powers, checks and balances, judicial review of legislation, and a bill of rights were included. All adult white male citizens could vote without restriction, but proof of payment of taxes was required for election to state office. Since there was no provision for ratification of the constitution by the voters, the election machinery was set in motion as soon as it had been adopted by the convention and signed on July 19, 1820.

Of chief interest in the first state election was the contest between Alexander McNair and William Clark for the governorship, a final act in the factional struggle for power. Both candidates had strong ties to the elite, but McNair, originally a Pennsylvania Federalist, had gauged the political breezes more accurately. His pro-squatter attitude as United States land agent, and his opposition at the convention to life tenure for judges and high salaries (two thousand dollars a year) for the governor and judges, had endeared him to many voters. He campaigned vigorously throughout the settlements, as Clark did not, and charges that he had been inactive at the convention backfired on his opponents. Most of the lawyer clique supported Clark, which pinned the elitist tag on him, and his pro-Indian and anti-squatter image was damaging. Charless, who hated Clark more than he disliked McNair, supported the latter in the *Gazette*, and the *Enquirer*, though no longer edited by Benton, backed Clark. McNair won by a landslide, 6,576 to 2,556, beating Clark in St. Louis County by two-to-one.

Among the duties of the First General Assembly, which met at the Missouri Hotel, was the selection of a state capital. The constitution required that it be a town yet to be built on the Missouri River near the mouth of the Osage. The legislature, after considering several locations, selected St. Charles as the temporary capital; two years later the legislature designated a site on the south bank of the Missouri, twelve miles west of the Osage, as the permanent capital, to be known as the "City of Jefferson." In October 1826, the government was established there. With no apparent regrets, since they made so little effort to retain the title, St. Louisans after more than a half century no longer lived at a capital.

Judicious choices for Missouri's first United States senators were crucial for the legislature. Effective representation in Washington was essential for the state and for St. Louis. David Barton was a strong favorite for one of the seats, but the other was hotly contested between Thomas Hart Benton and J. B. C. Lucas. The damage to Benton's reputation caused by the Lucas duel was more than offset by his

Missouri Hotel. *Engraving by Russell, ca. 1909. The State Legislature first met here in 1820. MHS-PP.*

leadership in the fight against slavery restriction and his ebullient vision of western development. As the only Missourian to have proposed a coherent program for federal assistance to local interests, he was a logical choice for senator and was elected on the first ballot by a bare majority over Lucas and several other candidates. He had enjoyed the quiet support of Barton, the active support of John Scott, and the crucial backing of Auguste Chouteau, Bernard Pratte, and other Creole leaders.

Benton, Barton, and Scott, the last having been elected Missouri's first congressman, went to Washington to represent a state which had not been admitted to the Union. This embarrassing *de facto* status, which denied them a vote in Congress, ended on August 10, 1821, when Missouri was finally admitted. Speaker Henry Clay, by various maneuvers, had handled the matter by tricking Congress into accepting a worthless promise from the Missouri legislature that the state would never enforce the clause in its constitution forbidding the further admission of free blacks.

Shortly after this momentous political change, St. Louis was incorporated as a city. Petitions to the legislature had been circulated as early as 1818, but nothing was done until December 1822, when the General Assembly passed a charter that was subject to the approval of the town's qualified voters (adult white males who had paid municipal taxes during the past year). Ironically, St. Louis was less prepared to assume additional expenses in 1823 than it had been three years earlier. The twin scourges of depression and malaria had substantially reduced the city's population since 1820. One hundred twenty-one persons had died of the "virulent fever" in 1821, yet the epidemic was described as less severe than those of the two preceding years. Most of the victims were transients crowded into the riverfront area, a majority recently arrived from the American Bottoms or downriver. Their deaths gave St. Louis an evil reputation as an unhealthful place, speeding the departures of newcomers who had suffered financial reverses.

After the failure of the territorial banks and the drop in real estate and commodity prices, merchants had been unable to collect enough cash to maintain their credit with eastern suppliers. Governor McNair, under pressure from debtors throughout the state, called a special session of the legislature in 1821 to adopt measures "to relieve the financial difficulties of the citizens." In addition to a stay law postponing debt payments, the legislature established a state loan office which was authorized to lend its notes to individuals in amounts of one thousand dollars secured by real estate or two hundred dollars secured by personal property. These certificates, receivable by the state for taxes, were expected to provide an acceptable circulating medium. Unfortunately for the merchants, their customers could pay them in loan office paper, but it could not be remitted to their New Orleans or eastern creditors. Squeezed in this fashion, and with the prices of and demand for furs and lead ruinously low, half of the major firms in St. Louis closed their doors. Only the "groceries," which dispensed liquor, continued to prosper. Among those going out of business were Christian Wilt and Company (Wilt had died, but his successor failed); general merchants Waddle and Blanchard, John Lindell, Nathaniel Payne, S. R. Ober; and the druggist David Tuttle. In all, more than two dozen merchants decamped or went into bankruptcy. Several of them had failed chiefly because of their real estate speculations. In August 1821 alone, the sheriff sold 105 lots in St. Louis and more than fourteen thousand acres in the county for nonpayment of taxes. Wealthy individuals, John Mullanphy in particular, reaped a harvest of bargains.

Depression, business failures, and disease had temporarily squelched the optimism of 1819 and 1820, and the population had dropped by 35 percent to about three thousand at the time the city charter was submitted to the people. Nonpayment of taxes disqualified many, and the decision to become a city was made by a fraction of the electorate, by the small margin of 107 to 90. In April

William Carr Lane. *Oil on canvas by Alban Conant after Chester Harding, 1881. Lane, a newly arrived physician, was elected the first mayor of St. Louis in 1823. MHS-Art.*

1823, William Carr Lane, a physician who had come to St. Louis from Pennsylvania in 1819, was elected the city's first mayor by a vote of 122 to 70 over the seventy-three-year-old Auguste Chouteau. The mayor's salary was three hundred dollars a year, increased to six hundred dollars in 1824. Nine aldermen, all lawyers or merchants, were elected in 1823 to serve without pay. The decline in St. Louis's fortunes, which might have been expected to delay its becoming a city, had actually favored the change. Stronger government was seen by some as a rescue operation, a quick fix for the city's economic and health problems. Commerce had to be facilitated by the municipality and the recurring epidemics halted if the trend was to be reversed. By choosing a doctor of medicine for mayor over its venerable first citizen, the limited electorate expressed its determination in the face of economic stringency to offer improved services, a healthy city, an activist government, and higher taxes.

In recognition of St. Louis's new status, the charter expanded its limits to Seventh Street on the west, to include the Chouteau-Lucas and Jeremiah Connor additions. To the south and north, the boundaries were extended an average of five and three blocks respectively. In all, some fifty blocks were added to the city's area, and the municipal river frontage now extended for nearly two miles, approximating the developed area along the river.

In his inaugural address, Mayor Lane quickly tackled the city's major problems. Improvement of the riverfront and health conditions, closely associated in his view, were most urgent. St. Louis had been charged with turning its back to the river: only Market and Oak Streets gave rough access to the Mississippi, and boats had to load and discharge their cargoes on the sand (mud). Wharves needed to be built, not only to expedite the movement of goods but also to reduce the "pestilential influence" of decaying animal and vegetable matter. Doctor Lane recommended that a Board of Health be appointed to "search out and remove nuisances." St. Louis had of late acquired an unhealthful reputation, "which it did not formerly bear and does not deserve." Mayor Lane had been told that until the recent epidemics high fevers were rarely seen. "To what is the distressing change attributable?" he asked. "May we not say principally to the insufficiency of our police regulations? What is the present condition of your drains, etc.? May we not dread the festering heat of next summer?"

The mayor also emphasized the need to widen, straighten, and pave the streets, urged that a street be built along the riverfront, and recommended that a hospital or asylum be built for the indigent aged and sick. As to education, Lane asserted that "a free school is more needed here than in any town of the same magnitude in the Union." He closed his address with an optimistic portrayal of the future, not for the purpose of eulogy, he said, but to point out that "a suitable system of improvements" would be necessary if the city's mighty potential was to be realized.

In response, the aldermen ordered the gradation of Main Street, necessary on all north-south streets below Fourth Street because of the side-hill slope the old village was built upon. Main Street had been partially graded and paved with stone several years earlier, and within a few years paving was completed for most of its length. Straightening the older streets proved impractical. They had been laid out in line by Laclède, but property owners had encroached on them in an irregular manner, and straightening would have destroyed some of the city's better buildings. In 1824, the board ordered that Main, Second, and Third Streets be extended to the new north boundary and Fifth Street to the south boundary. North-south alleys fifteen feet wide were to be cut through every city block, and the paving of streets and laying of sidewalks, to be financed by assessments against lot owners, was to proceed. Paving ordinances were enacted each year, but, because of meager assessment collections, the work went slowly. A decade after St. Louis became a city, most of its streets still featured their primal mud.

On July 1, 1826, the board renamed the streets. Their French names, still current with older residents, had already been replaced in general usage by numbers for the north-south streets (except for First— usually called Main). With only a few exceptions, the French had not named the east-west streets. After 1815, those in the original village, with Market the point of origin, had been designated North or South *A, B, C,* and so on. Mayor Lane and Aldermen Henry Von Phul and Thomas McKnight, all Pennsylvanians, persuaded the board to adopt the unimaginative Philadelphia system of naming streets for trees. Northward from Market (the only street reflecting its origins), the east-west streets were Chestnut, Pine, Olive, Locust, Vine, Laurel, Prune, Oak, Cherry, Hickory, Pear, and Willow. South of Market were Walnut (Rue de la Tour [Tower]), Elm, Myrtle, Spruce, Almond, Poplar, Plum, Cedar, Mulberry, Lombard, Hazel, and Sycamore. The olive was not even a native tree, and several of the others had never grown near St. Louis. The recently completed street on the river side of Laclède's front lots was named Front; the remaining north-south streets were First (La Rue Principale [Main]), Second (Rue de l'Eglise [Church]), Third (Rue des Granges [Barn]), and so on to the west. No doubt some of the French and older Americans regretted these changes, but the "go-ahead" spirit had little use for the relics of the past.

Despite continuing bankruptcies and tax-sales of real estate, St. Louis was on the road to recovery in 1824 and 1825. It had undergone a thorough shakeout after the national depression had halted immigration, but a powerful countervailing force had been created. Once economic recovery began, Missouri's new status made St. Louis and its hinterland more attractive to immigrants and capital. The bountiful land remained, and statehood would provide a more orderly and safer society, with property better protected, Indians likely soon to be removed, powerful local voices in Congress, and more accessible and responsive local government.

Although the majority of newcomers did not remain in St. Louis, they all enriched the city. By 1823 the East had recovered from the depression, optimism was returning, and soon the wagons began to roll. They trickled onto the Mississippi ferries in 1824, and in the fall of 1825 the *Missouri Republican* (successor to the *Gazette,* published by Joseph Charless's son Edward) announced that ten times as many immigrants had crossed the river as during the previous year. By December 1829, nine hundred thousand acres of public land had been sold in Missouri since 1820, most of it since 1824. Many of these purchasers boarded their families in St. Louis while they searched for choice land to bid on at the federal auctions. They often bought furniture, utensils, and staple foods before moving on. While migrating farmers are usually pictured as moving all their household goods and chattels from their homes in Kentucky, Tennessee, or North Carolina, a substantial number of them found it more practical, despite higher prices in the West, to sell out, travel light, and buy their "necessaries" in the town nearest their destination.

Another factor in the restoration of economic health to St. Louis was the rapid expansion of its trade territory. Between 1805 and 1821, the major fur-trading operations had been the Chouteau family fiefdom among the Osages and Manuel Lisa's Missouri Fur Company. After being squeezed out of the Osage area by the Chouteaus, Lisa, supported by various partners through several reorganizations, had made himself master of the upper Missouri. Brilliant, aggressive, and litigious, "Black Manuel" was an eagle among hawks, always seeking the advantage and pressing hard when he got it. His ascendancy among the Omahas, Poncas, Yankton and Teton Sioux, Mandans, and even the capricious Arikaras was unprecedented. Lisa's formula was simple; he was bold and fearless and kept his brass cannons at the ready until the Indians had sampled his flavor. Once a working relationship was established, he was generous with favors and honest

Manuel Lisa. *Oil on canvas, ca. 1818. MHS-Art.*

in dealing. He took Mitain, a beautiful Omaha woman, as his consort and included their children among his heirs. During the War of 1812, as General Clark's subagent for the upper Missouri, Lisa kept the Santee Sioux and other pro-British tribes in the Minnesota region neutralized by inspiring repeated attacks on their villages by the powerful Tetons.

In explaining his success, Lisa said, "I put into my operations great activity; I go great distances, while some are considering whether to start today or tomorrow. I impose upon myself great privations; ten months in a year I am buried in the forest, at a vast distance from my own house." Henry M. Brackenridge, who accompanied Lisa on an expedition to the Mandans and Arikaras in 1811, described the indefatigable trader as "Ardent, bold, and enterprising . . . no dangers, or sufferings, are sufficient to overcome his mind . . . there are few men so completely master of doing much in a short space of time. . . ." At the end of the War of 1812, a British agent in the Northwest testified that all of his efforts and the money given to the Sioux had been wasted because of Lisa, and Governor William Clark reported his valuable services to Washington. Perhaps because of these wartime exploits, Lisa's reputation in St. Louis improved. He became a close friend of Edward Hempstead, Benton, and other junto figures; he supervised the building of a bridge over Mill Creek; and in 1818, when he married for a second time (not counting Mitain) to Mary Hempstead, Pierre Chouteau was one of his witnesses.

In 1820 the principal fur-trading firms in St. Louis were the Missouri Fur Company, with an invested capital of about $10,000; Robidoux, Papin, Chouteau (Pierre), and Berthold, $12,000; Paul Chouteau and Brothers, $6,000; Pratte and Vasquez, $7,000; Gabriel and Francis Chouteau, $4,000. According to the 1821 *St. Louis Directory*, the fur trade represented $600,000 of the town's annual commerce of $2 million. This figure may be somewhat inflated; in any case, it declined sharply after 1820, not only because of depressed prices, but also because Manuel Lisa died on August 12, 1820. He was succeeded as head of the firm by Joshua Pilcher, an able and energetic man, but the latter's strenuous efforts were unavailing. Once again the Teton Sioux, the Arikaras, and the Mandans became unreliable, ready to pounce at the first sign of weakness. Because of Lisa, the river had been safe for almost its entire length for other St. Louis traders as well as his own company. When the "wild tribes" learned of their friend's death, all bets were off. Respected and even loved by the Indians and his Creole employees, though not by most of his peers, Manuel Lisa had extended St. Louis's commercial outreach to the Yellowstone and the Bighorn, and to many tribes formerly under British influence or simply unfriendly (Mandans, Arikaras, Gros Ventres, Tetons, Cheyennes). Only the Blackfeet had resisted him—they had never forgiven the Americans for murders committed among them by some of Lewis and Clark's men.

It was apparent by 1823 that a new approach to the fur business was required if the richest beaver country was to be tapped. Lisa had relied chiefly on trading posts (Fort Lisa near Omaha, Fort Mandan, Fort Manuel on the Bighorn) where Indians and some white trappers exchanged their furs for merchandise. These posts depended for survival upon the continued good will of the Indians. Despite the renewed hostility of the Arikaras after Lisa's death, William H. Ashley, brigadier general of the Missouri Militia, and Andrew Henry, a lead miner and former partner of Lisa's, formed a partnership in 1822 to exploit the upper Missouri trade. They anticipated large profits, enhanced by the abolition of federal competition in 1822 after impassioned and unfair charges against the fur factories were leveled by Thomas Hart Benton on the Senate floor.

Ashley and Henry's first expedition, eventually consisting of 180 men, left St. Louis for the three forks of the Missouri in April 1822. According to the *Enquirer,* the party was "composed entirely of young

TO Enterprising Young Men.

THE subscriber wishes to engage ONE HUNDRED MEN, to ascend the river Missouri to its source, there to be employed for one, two or three years.—For particulars, enquire of Major Andrew Henry, near the Lead Mines, in the County of Washington, (who will ascend with, and command the party) or to the subscriber at St. Louis.

Wm. H. Ashley.

February 13   ——98 tf

Newspaper advertisement for men for the Ashley-Henry expedition of 1822, published in both the Missouri Gazette *and the new* Missouri Republican. Missouri Republican, *March 27, 1822. MHS-Library.*

men, many of whom have relinquished the most respectable employment and circles of society." Among these young men, employed as salaried trappers, were such soon-to-be-famous "mountain men" as Jim Bridger, Jedediah Smith, Thomas Fitzpatrick, Jim Beckwourth, and Etienne Provost. A few months later James Clyman, William Sublette, and David Jackson joined the enterprise. The legendary riverman Mike Fink murdered a man and then was killed by another boatman on this expedition. The partners planned to establish forts in the Yellowstone and Bighorn region, as Lisa had done, relying less on the capricious Indians and more on white trappers for their fur supply. The forts were built, but they were constantly threatened by the Blackfeet. In the summer of 1823, Ashley had fifteen men killed and ten wounded as he tried to go upstream past the Arikaras. When an army detachment, supported by the Teton Sioux, retaliated feebly against the Arikaras, the Tetons were disgusted and alienated.

Under this pressure, Ashley abandoned the upper Missouri route. Convinced of the advantages of trapping over the Indian trade, Ashley quit his fur posts because they were vulnerable and limited his trappers' mobility. When Jedediah Smith and Tom Fitzpatrick reported in 1824 that the Green River on the western slope of the Rockies was teeming with beaver, Ashley transferred his operation to the central Rockies, safe from the Blackfeet and the Arikaras. Each year, at a previously designated rendezvous point (Jackson's Hole, Pierre's Hole, Cache Valley, or Henry's Fork of the Green River, for example), company trappers, Indians, and free trappers would meet a pack train from St. Louis. It was a grand carousal with much drinking, fighting, contests of skill and strength, and trading of tall tales; but essentially the rendezvous was a business meeting, where the company exchanged the necessities at enormously inflated prices for valuable furs.

By 1830, more than six hundred mountain men were trapping in the central Rockies. Many of them did not return to St. Louis for years, preferring to spend their winters "holed up" in a protected valley, usually with an Indian consort. Except for a dozen or so of the more ambitious, the wild and free life was its own justification, and spending their profits on a week's debauchery at the rendezvous seemed quite natural and logical. It was understood in St. Louis that those who thought the mountain men romantic figures should take care not to stand downwind from them. James Clyman, one of Ashley's lieutenants, was at a loss to describe their recruits, except to say that "Fallstaff's Battalion was genteel by comparison." The Creole keelboat crews he called "St. Louis Gumboes."

Very large profits were made in the Rocky Mountain trade. Andrew Henry left the firm after the 1824 beaver pack was sold, having cleared a tidy sum, and in 1826 General Ashley sold out to Jedediah Smith, David Jackson, and William Sublette. In three years, despite several disasters, General Ashley's 2,000 percent markups paid his debts and made him comfortably wealthy, with a fortune estimated at eighty thousand dollars. If he had won his race against Frederick Bates for the Missouri governorship in 1824, he would have earned one thousand dollars a year.

In October 1825, the *Enquirer* reported that after returning with "the most valuable collection of furs ever brought to this place," Ashley, within twenty-five days, had organized a party of 70 men, 160 mules and horses, $20,000 worth of merchandise, and was ready to depart again for the Green River. The editor pointed out that "the amount of capital vested in this single party, will give some idea of the great importance of the Fur Trade to this State. The money circulated by Gen'l Ashley, for men, mules, horses, traps, among our fellow-citizens will be of the most essential service to them." The *Enquirer* also emphasized that Smith and Fitzpatrick's discovery of South Pass had opened a broad highway to the Pacific from St. Louis to the "river Platte a short distance above its junction with the Missouri, (it) then pursues the waters of the Platte to their sources, and . . . crosses the headwaters of what Gen'l Ashley believes to be, the Rio Colorado of the West, and strikes for the first time, a ridge . . . running from north to south. This, however, presents no difficulty, as a wide gap is found."

The company prospered under Smith, Jackson, and Sublette. When they returned to St. Louis in 1830, after selling their goods to the Rocky Mountain Fur Company (RMFC) (Thomas Fitzpatrick, Jim Bridger, Milton Sublette, Jean Baptiste Gervais, and Henry Fraeb), they came with a caravan of "large and substantial waggons," horses, "50 hardy and sunburned mountaineers," and "furs and mules valued at one hundred and fifty thousand dollars." They were rich and they had made a major contribution to geographical knowledge. Ranging westward from Great Salt Lake in 1826 with a few men to find new sources of beaver, Jedediah Smith had traversed the Great Basin and the High Sierras to reach Mission San Gabriel near Los Angeles. Ordered to leave by the Spanish governor, he had returned to Salt Lake, but in 1827 he was back in California. This time he was jailed for a few weeks, but upon his release, instead of returning to the Rockies, he headed north up the San Joaquin and Sacramento valleys and then to the Hudson's Bay Company post at Fort Vancouver. In 1828 he returned to Pierre's Hole in the Tetons. Smith had lost a dozen men in Indian attacks, but he had discovered two overland routes to California and had noted the magnificent fertility of its inland valleys.

The RMFC's successes attracted a host of competitors to the central Rockies after 1830. Gantt and Blackwell of St. Louis, Antoine Robidoux of St. Louis, Nathaniel Wyeth of Boston, Captain Benjamin Bonneville (backed by New York capital), and William (Ole Bill) Williams of Taos sent hundreds of trappers to the Green, Sweetwater, Hoback, and Snake Rivers; but the powerful RMFC could handle them. More formidable was John Jacob Astor's American Fur Company, which, with its great resources, could bid the price of beaver out of sight. In 1827, Astor had put the experienced fur trader Bernard Pratte of St. Louis in charge of his western operations and then entered the dangerous country vacated by Ashley a few years earlier. By first employing Kenneth McKenzie and other British traders who were friendly with the Blackfeet, and then by sending the steamboat *Yellowstone*, "the Fire Boat that walks on the Waters," to the upper Missouri to impress them, Pratte was able to come to terms with the Indians. McKenzie, now "King of the Upper Missouri," sent brigades of trappers down from his forts to dog the footsteps of the RMFC's men to the richest beaver streams. For more than two years there was unremitting warfare. Traders and trappers fought to the death; the demoralized Indians became more hostile; and the beaver streams were depleted. The out-manned RMFC finally surrendered; Fraeb and Gervais sold their interests to Bridger, Fitzpatrick, and Milton Sublette, who then merged with the American Fur Company.

The western fur business was still centered in St. Louis, however. Astor had sold the Missouri River branch of the American Fur Company to Bernard Pratte and Pierre Chouteau, Jr., in 1834. Pratte and Chouteau operated at a profit for several years, but the diminishing beaver supply and the high prices paid for furs by their Hudson's Bay Company competitors forced them to declare the rendezvous on the Green River in 1840 to be their last. Thereafter, the American fur business in the central Rockies was confined to individuals and to posts on the high plains, such as Fort Laramie. As the supply diminished, demand dropped even faster as beaver gave way to silk hats as the proper headwear for English gentlemen. Buffalo hides and other furs increased in volume, however, and shipments from St. Louis did not decline substantially. Between 1808 and 1847, the annual value of furs exported averaged about $250,000 (higher between 1824 and 1834). According to Indian Agent John Dougherty, between 1815 and 1830 the American Fur Company netted $1.65 million on its Missouri River and Rocky Mountain operations, primarily on buffalo robes and beaver. These profits came at a heavy cost. There are no records of Indian casualties, but 148 American trappers and traders were killed in the region by Indians between 1815 and 1831. Trappers died of everything but disease—grizzlies and drowning took a good many. Few records are available for 1831–40, but the killing continued. (Five trappers were killed by Gros Ventres at the Pierre's Hole rendezvous in 1832, for example.)

Commercial penetration of the Southwest also spurred St. Louis's recovery. As DeLassus had warned the Spanish in 1804, Americans were soon at the gates of New Mexico. Lieutenant Zebulon Pike, a henchman of Governor Wilkinson, who took an exploring party onto Spanish soil in 1806, was arrested, jailed, and charged with spying (he was). William Morrison of Kaskaskia sent Jean Baptiste LaLande to Santa Fe with a shipment of merchandise in that same year. LaLande sold the goods but Morrison made no profit—LaLande did not come back. Thereafter, the Spanish arrested the traders repeatedly, detaining one party for three years and another for eight. Jules De Mun and Auguste P. Chouteau were imprisoned for several weeks in New Mexico in 1817 and forced to surrender furs worth thirty thousand dollars. Chouteau had planned to explore the entire Southwest to California, and it appears that only his family's past services to Spain saved the expedition from longer

The Steamer *Yellowstone. Lithograph by Carl Bodmer, 1848. Bodmer sketched the* Yellowstone *on his travels in 1833 with Prince Maximillian of Wied. MHS-Library.*

detention. These arrests, ostensibly to enforce trade regulations, showed that the jittery Spaniards, who felt their empire slipping away, saw the encroaching Americans as revolutionary agents.

After Mexico won its independence in 1821, Americans could enter New Mexico legally. First was William Becknell of Franklin, whose party of hunters and trappers was invited to Santa Fe by Mexican soldiers who encountered them at Raton Pass. Becknell sold his Indian trade goods there at a good profit and hurried home for more. The inaccessibility of the *Provinces Internas* from Vera Cruz had left unmet a ravenous demand in New Mexico for cotton cloth, silks, hardware, and cutlery, which could be supplied by Missouri merchants over a relatively easy trail, negotiable in forty to fifty days. Becknell returned to Santa Fe in 1822 with a pack train and light wagons and netted a profit of 2,000 percent. This party, overtaken at the Arkansas River by the Osages, escaped with their lives and goods only by the timely intervention of A. P. Chouteau. Thomas James and John McKnight were robbed by Comanches in 1821, but numerous other caravans from St. Louis made large profits in the Santa Fe trade in the 1820s. By 1824, most expeditions were outfitted two hundred miles up the Missouri at Franklin, and the first leg of the journey had been made safer by bribing the Osages. After 1828, Franklin having been destroyed by flood, the eastern terminus of the trade moved west to Independence, and eventually to Westport, on Missouri's western boundary. The Pawnees who stole their horses, and the Comanches who killed the traders (especially after a dozen of the tribe were slaughtered as they approached a caravan making the peace sign), continued to harass the trains; but the risks were reduced by using slow but powerful oxen, unwanted by the Indians, for the outward trip, and by banding together under military-type discipline. Fast mules, pulling the lighter loads of the return journey, reduced the period of exposure and brought high prices in Missouri.

Even after the development of market towns in western Missouri, St. Louis played a major role in the Santa Fe trade. The deadly Hawken rifles and the sturdy Murphy wagons of the caravans were made there; outstate traders bought merchandise in the city; and William Sublette, Robert Campbell, and other local capitalists invested in the enterprises of the new towns. By the 1830s, New Mexican merchants and ranchers kept substantial funds on deposit with the city's private bankers. Ceran St. Vrain, a nephew of Charles DeLassus and a great-grandson of Laclède, joined with Charles and William Bent of St. Louis in 1828 to build Bent's Fort on the Arkansas River, which for many years was the center of the fur trade in the southern Rockies and an outpost of empire in the Southwest.

Senator Benton, ever conscious of the western hinterland, pressed hard in Washington for federal protection of the southwestern commercial lifeline. At the request of Governor McNair and other petitioners, he introduced a bill in 1825 providing for marking the trail through Mexican territory all the way to Santa Fe and appropriating thirty thousand dollars for the purpose. The bill passed, but Benton failed to win approval for a military fort on the Arkansas River. Military escorts accompanied the caravans sporadically, but they were of little value, since they could not enter Mexican territory, where the danger was greatest.

Most important to St. Louis was the favorable balance produced by the Santa Fe trade. The city was to Santa Fe as Philadelphia and New Orleans were to St. Louis, a commercial emporium shipping manufactured goods to a colonial outpost in exchange for raw materials. Since their exports (furs and mules) were of less value than the merchandise received, Mexicans shipped large quantities of silver to Missouri, most of which found its way to St. Louis. In 1824, returns from the trade were estimated at $180,000, mostly in coins and bullion. In 1829, at least $200,000 in specie was hauled up the trail, and the average for the first twenty years has been estimated at $100,000 to $200,000. This figure seems extremely conservative, considering the fact that two parties each brought in more than $200,000 in silver within five weeks in 1839. For the first time, the area had a substantial hard-money supply, reducing its reliance on barter and the uncertain notes of out-of-state banks. This steady supply of specie and the banking disasters of the post-1819 depression strengthened the hard-money bias that characterized "Old Bullion" Benton and his constituency for decades. For St. Louis, Mexican silver was a stimulus to economic activity and renewed growth.

The destruction of the myth that the Southwest was a vast desert impassable for wagons was among the tangential results of the Mexican trade. Traders, in reports that whetted the appetites of American expansionists, revealed the weaknesses of Mexican defenses and the details of its geography and resources. Missouri pack trains reached Chihuahua and roamed the trails of the state of Sonora, close to the sources of Mexican silver. In 1830, Smith, Jackson, and Sublette led an expedition of ten wagons, each pulled by five mules, carrying eighty-one men and thirty thousand dollars in merchandise from St. Louis to southern California, only fifty miles from the Pacific. The party returned within six months, but without Jedediah Smith, who was killed by Comanches while he was scouting for water in the Cimarron Desert. Smith, a national celebrity, was mourned by many, including Captain William Waldo, who called the explorer-entrepreneur the only professing Christian ever known among the early Rocky Mountain trappers.

The economic stirring resulting from the western trade and the renewal of immigration brought a resurgence of construction in 1825, when more buildings were erected than during the previous four years. The assessed valuation of city property, which had declined from $1.21 million in 1818 to $810,000 in 1823, rose to $1.5 million in 1828. Jobs for bricklayers, plasterers, carpenters, and laborers were plentiful, primarily in the construction of brick replacements of Creole houses. There had been 651 dwellings in 1821, and despite the construction flurry, there were only 700 in 1829. In 1826, the County Court let contracts for a brick courthouse, which was completed in 1832 at a cost of fourteen thousand dollars. This building stimulated further construction on the hill, and in 1833, J. B. C. Lucas opened an addition between Seventh and Ninth Streets, Market to St. Charles (ten square blocks). Shortly thereafter, the city built a new market and office building on Front Street. The city jail was located in the basement, market stalls on the ground floor, city offices on the second, and rental offices on the third. Other buildings on Front Street were soon to follow.

After the city paved lower Olive and Chestnut Streets in 1827, Matthew Kerr built a row of two-story brick houses on the north side of Chestnut, between Main and Second (quickly dubbed Quality Row). The new construction created a nasty environmental problem. In 1824, the Board of Aldermen prohibited brickmaking in the city because of the nauseous smoke which poured from the fire clay kilns. Under pressure from citizens who preferred the smoke to higher costs, the board reversed itself. To compound the problem, the cartloads of driftwood from Carondelet and the rafts from upriver no longer met the city's need for fuel. With wood at $1.25 to $1.50 a cord and hard to get, consumers shifted to soft coal from the ridge east of the American Bottoms. Coal was available in 1829 for 12.5¢ a bushel, but frugal citizens could dig it easily from exposed outcroppings at several places in the county. Almost every building in the city contributed to this choking pall of sulphurous smoke. Citizens complained, but only as they did about the weather.

By 1827, St. Louis had recovered to its 1820 population level, and the 1830 census showed 5,852 residents, a modest increase of 27.3 percent during the decade (the state's population had more than doubled, to 140,455 in 1830). The distribution of sexes was more balanced than ever before, 42.8 percent of the population being white males and 32.3 percent white females. Slaves comprised 20 percent and free blacks 4.9 percent of the total. Steady but not spectacular gains for the next few years brought the population to 8,316 in 1835, when it was on the threshold of a long period of very rapid growth. As it had been for two decades, the population was heterogeneous, although the Creole portion had declined relatively. Timothy Flint observed in 1828 that "very few towns in the United States, or the world, have a more mixed population. . . . The American population now predominates over the French; and is made up of immigrants from all of the states. There is also a sprinkling of people from all quarters of the world."

Most visitors to the city were favorably impressed by it during this period. A member of the Marquis de Lafayette's party, impressed by the grand reception given by the Chouteaus, Mayor Lane, and the other dignitaries when the general visited St. Louis in 1825, called the city "the grand storehouse of all of the commerce of the countries west of the Mississippi," the achievement of a few years. The aide did not report Lafayette's reaction when a local matron asked: *"C'est votre premier visite en Amerique, Monsieur le General?"* Charles Sealsfield, an English visitor in 1827, noted that St. Louis received immigrants from many foreign places, though "Kentucky manners" predominated (not a compliment). A New Englander, Senator Caleb Atwater, called the city in 1829 a successful place, "growing fast, and mechanics of all sorts in great demand, wages high, costs moderate." Its professional men, Atwater had found, were "well-bred and well-educated."

The expansion of the U.S. Army's western operations contributed substantially to St. Louis's economic growth in the 1830s. Fort Bellefontaine, on the Missouri River north of the city, had poor access to the river and was too small to handle the volume of military supplies destined for western ports. In July 1826 the garrison moved to Jefferson Barracks, a new federal installation located on the Mississippi ten miles below St. Louis. By 1829, five hundred troops were stationed there, in what had become a training school for infantry recruits scheduled for assignment farther west. Formerly, much of the army's western supply business had been contracted to Pennsylvania, Ohio, and Virginia firms, but by 1830 local merchants could find sufficient supplies of agricultural staples to underbid their rivals. Such firms as Scott and Rule, Hezekiah Simmons, John O'Fallon, and Hill and M'Gunnegle held the supply contracts for Forts Crawford, Snelling, Armstrong, Leavenworth, and Jefferson Barracks for most of this period. Until 1837, when the barracks were completed, the soldiers lived in tents, a rugged and appropriate introduction to the Spartan regimen of the frontier posts.

During the 1830s merchandising in St. Louis was rapidly diversifying. At the beginning of the decade general stores that sold drugs, yard goods, hardware, wine and whiskey, coffee, sugar, crockery, and a wide range of other items dominated the scene. There had been single-line shops before the depression of the early 1820s, but most of them had not survived. A few drug stores, some of them operated by doctors adjacent to their offices, persisted, and in 1825 Laveille and Morton began selling Pittsburgh lumber at their yard. Deaver's clothing store opened in 1828, and Louis Jaccard's jewelry store in 1829. In the latter year, W. A. Lynch, reputed to be the first undertaker west of the Mississippi, offered coffins for sale. By 1835, confectioneries had spun off from bakeries and were offering candies, cakes, cordials, jellies, pies, and tarts to their customers. Bookstores, such as B. L. Turnbull's, which advertised twenty thousand volumes for sale, served the retail and outstate wholesale trade. Carpet stores and dry goods emporiums, where the sharp-dealing "yankee clerk" presided, were proliferating, and music shops sold instruments and tasteful sheet music such as "A Tear Shall Tell him All," and "A Wealthy Old Man A' Wooing did go." Since merchandise of all kinds had become plentiful and reasonably priced, consumer price resistance became a factor, and periodic bargain sales were featured to clear shelves for the new season's goods. In January 1835, Robert Rankin advertised a winter clearance sale with prices of dry goods, shoes, and leghorn hats reduced by 15 to 30 percent.

Merchandise in quantity at competitive prices had become available chiefly because of the steamboat. Early retailers had made eastern buying trips themselves, using pack horses to carry their goods back to St. Louis. The *Zebulon Pike* had barely managed to move against the upstream current, but boats of ample size and power, such as the *Maid of Orleans* and the *Cincinnati*, plied the river to and from New Orleans in the early 1820s. The depression kept traffic down for several years, but in 1826 at least one steamboat docked at St. Louis daily during the warmer months. In 1827, 259 steamboats and 110 keelboats arrived, most of them from New Orleans. Steamers in the 1830s averaged twelve to fourteen days for the trip upriver, depending on the river's stage; keelboats took ninety to one hundred days, and the former reduced downstream time by two-thirds. In 1831, when St. Louis was designated a port of entry for foreign goods, there were 432 steamboat arrivals; two years later, 99 different boats made 573 landings. On a Sunday morning in July 1833, according to the

Missouri Republican, there were 21 steamboats lying in port. In 1836, 144 steamboats delivered 19,477 tons of cargo in 1,355 landings. By 1841, the Mound City was second only to New Orleans in the river traffic, with 186 steamboats, 86 of them owned wholly or partly by local merchants, discharging 262,681 tons in 1,928 landings.

St. Louis had become part of a transportation network that included Philadelphia, New York, and other eastern ports; New Orleans; and Pittsburgh, Louisville, and Cincinnati on the Ohio River. Steamships from Atlantic ports discharged cargo at New Orleans, which was then reloaded on river steamers. Since heavier vessels could not ascend beyond St. Louis, cargoes intended for the upper Mississippi or the Missouri were unloaded there, to be reloaded on smaller vessels. On downriver trips, this procedure was reversed. During the 1830s, St. Louis's principal hinterland ports were Prairie du Chien, Galena, Quincy, and Kaskaskia on the Mississippi; Beardstown and Pekin on the Illinois; and Lexington, Liberty, Independence, and Fort Leavenworth on the Missouri (plus American Fur Company cargoes from as far as the mouth of the Yellowstone). New Orleans was its major downriver trading partner, but the volume of traffic from Pittsburgh, including goods and immigrants headed for central and western Missouri, the Iowa territory, and northern Illinois was even heavier until the 1840s.

Between 1830 and 1840, Missouri's population increased by 173 percent, from 140,455 to 383,702. More than 90 percent of the people were farmers, and, especially in the central part of the state, many of them had progressed beyond the pioneer to the commercial stage of agriculture. Two decades earlier, when they could not find local buyers, farmers had rafted salt pork, tobacco, and other commodities to New Orleans where they sold their produce and rafts before trudging the long trail back. With the advent of steamboats, even bulky items could stand the cost of long-distance transportation, and St. Louis became a major collecting point for agricultural produce. According to the *St. Louis Directory* for 1836–37, the export trade consisted primarily of furs and hides, lead, iron, yellow pine, beef, pork, poultry, whiskey, hemp, tobacco, and corn. The enormous increase in the population of its hinterland had made the city what the Spanish governors had wanted it to be, a thriving agricultural entrepôt. Steamboats had not simply given Missouri farmers parity with their Ohio valley rivals; they now had the advantage because the lower Missouri and its tributaries were navigable at lower water stages. Ironically, booming agriculture had relegated the fur business to a secondary role in the city's commerce at the time of its greatest volume. Just as this process was underway, Auguste Chouteau, the quintessential fur magnate, died in the stone house he had built for Laclède in his seventy-ninth year (February 1829).

While the stream of silver from New Mexico expedited local transactions, it did not solve the problems of those who had to pay bills to eastern creditors. With no local banking facilities, merchants had to carry the money themselves or consign it to others for eastern delivery. The former was time-consuming and the latter risky — as demonstrated by Scott and Rule, who tried to send four thousand dollars to a Pittsburgh firm in 1829 by another merchant, Joseph W. Jones. Jones gave the money to a Wheeling merchant, who entrusted it to a steamboat captain, who delivered it to the wrong address. When it finally reached its intended recipient, the package contained nothing but brown paper. Though he was apparently innocent, Jones committed suicide, which was small comfort to Scott and Rule. Another merchant lost twelve thousand dollars on a similar mission, and lesser losses were frequent. Only a fool would have sent money by mail, given the quality of the postal service and the absence of postal insurance.

Local merchants were delighted with the news in 1828 that a branch of the Bank of the United States was planned for St. Louis. Not only did this demonstrate the city's growing importance as a commercial center, it reflected the large increase in federal activity in the West, especially in public land sales and military expenditures. On April 20, 1829, the branch opened with John O'Fallon as president and William H. Ashley, Thomas Biddle, Pierre Chouteau, Jr., William Clark, James Clemens, Matthew Kerr, Peter Lindell, and John Mullanphy among the directors. By 1831, the branch's discounts (loans — represented by notes in circulation) exceeded $400,000, and by late 1832 they had reached $883,000. This increase in its money supply was a boon to the city as well as to its merchants — it increased the volume of transactions, employment, wages, profits, and property values; and along with Mexican silver it drove the "rag-money" of the Illinois and Ohio banks out of the city. There were few critics of the branch bank until the power struggle between President Andrew Jackson and Nicholas Biddle, president of the parent bank in Philadelphia, made the Bank of the United States a political issue. Passions ran high in St. Louis, peaking in 1831 when branch director Thomas Biddle (Nicholas's brother) charged into the City Hotel bedroom of the sleeping Spencer Pettis, a Jackson-Benton congressman, and beat him with cowhide whip and cane. The resulting duel, fought with pistols on Bloody Island in August 1831 (at a distance of five feet because Biddle was nearsighted) ended two promising careers.

After Jackson's veto of a bill rechartering the Bank of the United States and his reelection in 1832, the local branch, following Nicholas Biddle's lead, curtailed its loans, thereby reducing its note issue. The directors retrenched as slowly as possible and finally closed the bank in 1835 without seriously disrupting the local economy. Western immigration and business were booming, and St. Louis merchants had diversified, expanded, and improved their facilities, both retail and wholesale. The Cincinnati Commercial Agency, one of Jackson's "pet banks," took over the vacated spot and provided fairly acceptable credit facilities; but the drain of its profits and most of its investments to the Cincinnati area built pressures for the establishment of a state bank.

The Missouri constitution authorized the legislature to charter one bank with no more than five branches, but the feverish passions aroused by the Jackson-Biddle Bank War and native hard-money sentiment made its establishment a delicate matter. St. Louis businessmen preferred a bank owned and managed by private interests; some outstate Democrats opposed all banks; and a moderate Democratic group favored an exclusively state-owned and controlled bank. The result was a conservative compromise, the brainchild of Democrat James Bowlin of St. Louis and acceptable even to Benton and his hard-money Boonslick allies, creating a specie-paying state bank, capitalized at $5 million, with half of its stock owned by the state and half by individuals. The president and six directors were elected by the legislature, and six directors were chosen by the private stockholders, thus insuring that the hard-money legislators would control bank policies. Loans were limited to one year and to a maximum of 8 percent interest. Banknotes, issued in denominations of ten dollars or more, would provide a sound circulating medium, their total not to exceed the bank's paid-in capital during the first five years. If the directors violated the charter's restrictions, they were personally liable for resulting losses.

The Bank of the State of Missouri opened at St. Louis in 1837 just as the national financial panic was beginning. The city was heavily represented on its board by William L. Sublette, Edward Walsh, John O'Fallon, George M'Gunnegle, Hugh O'Neil, and others, most of whom were hard-money men and friends of Benton and the legislative majority, as was the president, John Smith. Having inherited the business of the Cincinnati Commercial Agency, and as a depository of both state and federal funds, the state bank had a substantial business at the beginning. As the depression tightened, however, it contracted its note issue, declined after 1839 to accept the notes of nonspecie paying Illinois banks, and built up its silver reserves. This conservative policy was called treachery by elements of the merchant

*Twenty dollar note of the Bank of the State of Missouri, issued November 1, 1838.
MHS Museum Collections.*

community, especially those with substantial debts. In November
1839, Pierre Chouteau, Jr., and eleven other businessmen offered to
indemnify the state bank for any losses incurred if it would reverse its
stand against the Illinois banks, but the board refused. As a result, the
Bank of Missouri's deposits shrank from $1.75 million to $332,000 in
1840. Since Illinois banknotes comprised 60 percent of the city's
circulation in 1839 and nearly all of it by 1841, and since they saw the
alternative as a virtual suspension of business, other institutions took
over most of the city's banking functions.

Private bankers or brokers, such as L. A. Benoist, had operated
in St. Louis since the late territorial period, exchanging banknotes
for silver or other notes at a profit, accepting deposits, and making
loans. To the brokers' and the hard-money Democrats' distress, a
flock of corporations, chartered for other purposes, now entered the
banking business. By 1841, the St. Louis Gas Light Company
(which had yet to light a lamp), the Mutual Insurance Company
(which sold no insurance), the Perpetual Insurance Company, and
seven other insurance companies were in the banking business,
keeping the Illinois notes in circulation. Except for the Mutual,
which had obtained its charter under false pretenses, these firms had
been created primarily to insure steamboats, cargoes, and
warehouses (steamboat disasters from snags and bursting boilers
were commonplace, especially on the Missouri and the "Graveyard"
stretch of the Mississippi between St. Louis and Cairo). Thirty
locally owned boats, one-sixth of St. Louis's tonnage, went down
between 1838 and 1841 (but the insurers prospered by charging
1,518 percent premiums).

William Gilpin, a fiery young Pennsylvanian who tried to outdo Benton as a propagandist for Oregon, the West, and St. Louis's importance as the "hub of the Great Valley," had been made editor of the *Missouri Argus* in 1838 upon the recommendation of Montgomery Blair. In 1840 he charged that the "illegal banking" by the Gas Light and insurance companies had driven specie out of circulation, ruined public respect for the law, inflated prices, and cheated farmers and workingmen by forcing them to accept rag money (Illinois notes passed at par for goods and services, but they were discounted at 7 or 8 percent against specie). A. B. Chambers of the *Missouri Republican* responded that the much-maligned corporations were saving the city from disaster. To compound the muddle, in 1841 the city issued warrants to pay its employees and suppliers, which were immediately discounted heavily by the money brokers. Under the threat of mob action the bankers reversed themselves, and the warrants passed at par for a few weeks before the butchers who supplied the jail refused to accept them. Within four months they were discounted by 43 percent with no takers. By 1842 the Bank of Illinois was sinking, its notes at a 45 percent discount, and L. A. Benoist and the Perpetual had temporarily closed their doors, awash in Illinois paper.

Unauthorized banking had served the merchants well for a few years, but its dependence upon the notes of speculative banks had delayed rather than averted the inevitable liquidation. Perhaps this dubious activity had softened the impact of the depression in St. Louis — it hit harder elsewhere — but the major palliatives were the immigrant stream and Mexican silver. The Bank of Missouri had chosen to survive rather than rescue the overextended merchants, and it earned a reputation as the soundest bank west of the Appalachians. Democrats split between the "Soft" merchants and the "Herds" led by Boonslick planters (the Fayette clique) and a small but influential minority of St. Louis businessmen, the latter motivated by loyalty to Benton or their interests in the mountain and Santa Fe trade or both (William E. Sublette and Robert Campbell, for example). Most of the yeoman farmers (the most numerous class in the state) and the new German and Irish immigrants also supported the state bank's conservatism. In 1842 the legislature passed two "bills of pains and penalties," forbidding corporations other than the state bank to discount notes, make loans, or accept deposits. Brokers were barred from dealing in notes smaller than ten dollars after 1844 (with the return of prosperity, they broke this law freely).

The heat of the "little bank war" led to several violent episodes. In 1840 William Gilpin called the Soft leader William P. Darnes "a jackass," "a toady," and a "half-witted drone" in an *Argus* editorial. Darnes's blood boiled but not enough to challenge Gilpin, who was a tall, tough ex-army officer known to be handy with weapons or fists. Instead, Darnes sought out the *Argus*'s publisher, Andrew Jackson Davis, a smaller man, and broke his skull with an iron cane. Davis died a week later. The internationally famous doctor William P. Beaumont had attempted to relieve the pressure on Davis's brain by boring holes in his skull (trephining); and the wily Whig defense attorney, Henry S. Geyer, obtained three Whig doctors, including William Carr Lane, who attacked Beaumont's judgement and competence and blamed Davis's death on the trephining. Despite their admission under cross-examination that they might not have been able to save Davis, the befuddled jury, having been led away from the major issue, found Darnes guilty of fourth-degree manslaughter. He was fined five hundred dollars. One of his cronies, Thornton Grimsley, himself a recipient of Gilpin's barbs, vowed vengeance too. Whereupon Davis's successor, Abel R. Corbin (notorious later as U. S. Grant's crooked cousin-in-law), announced that he fought only with his pen and that Gilpin would handle all physical matters thereafter. With Gilpin temporarily absent from the city, Grimsley posted an announcement that he would thrash the editor publicly if he dared to return. Gilpin came back promptly and administered the thrashing to Grimsley. Thereafter, the latter was known as a man of peace.

Gilpin left St. Louis late in 1841, finding America's future great city first in Independence and then in Kansas City. He was the booster *par excellence*, a well-educated scion of a prominent Pennsylvania family and a disciple of Alexander von Humboldt, who believed that since the world's great civilizations had developed near the fortieth parallel in the north temperate zone, the Mississippi-Missouri valley, the richest of all such regions, was destined to be the new Tigris-Euphrates, the center of world empire. As a kind of comic sideshow to the Darnes-Davis tragedy, A. B. Chambers of the *Missouri Republican* and Thomas B. Hudson, a Hard who later turned Soft, fought a famous duel on Bloody Island. After having missed each other three times, they gave it up as a bad job.

Throughout this financial-political imbroglio, the merchant community was expanding and changing. Though a few large retailers, such as James and Robert Aull of Lexington, still bought directly from eastern suppliers, St. Louis's share of the western wholesale market was growing rapidly. Before 1832, large local retailers often filled emergency orders for local or upriver merchants or regularly supplied small retailers who could not afford an eastern trip. Scott and Rule, Tracy and Wahrendorff, Deaver and Cromwell, and Henry Shaw, most of whom were also commission agents or forwarders for exporters, were the principal wholesalers of this type. As Missouri and western Illinois filled with people, demand became sufficient to justify concentration on wholesaling. By 1834, J. S. Pease (English and American cutlery and hardware), Piggott and O'Dwyer (drugs and medicine), Shaw and Cross (dry goods, hardware, Queensware, and cutlery), and P. and J. Powell (dry goods, shoes, and hats) were primarily wholesalers, the last having built a four-story warehouse on Front Street. Steamboats had sharply reduced price differentials at St. Louis, but imported and eastern goods were still higher than in the major coastal markets. In 1837, coffee at wholesale averaged eleven cents a pound at New Orleans, twelve cents at New York, fourteen cents at Cincinnati, and fifteen cents at St. Louis. Wrought iron was $100 a ton at New York and New Orleans, $140 at Cincinnati, and $150 at St. Louis. Cotton yarn, averaging twenty-two cents a pound at New York and thirty-two cents at Cincinnati, was thirty-five cents at St. Louis.

Front View of St. Louis. *Lithograph by E. Dupre, 1838.* Atlas of the City and County of St. Louis. *MHS-PP.*

These differentials decreased as steamboats and volume grew larger, and there were advantages to buying in St. Louis that were of overriding importance to many retailers. Risks were reduced (or insurance fees avoided), extensive personal travel was unnecessary, and delivery time was cut by months. Even those retailers who made annual eastern buying trips bought wholesale in St. Louis in emergencies. By 1836 seven local firms were exclusively in wholesaling, dealing chiefly in dry goods, hardware, and leather goods. There was some attrition in 1838–39, but in 1841 twenty wholesale grocers sold sugar, coffee, molasses, salt, and miscellaneous items worth $3.5 million, and ten firms disposed of dry goods worth $1.25 million. In 1842, with local money problems at their peak, imports and exports from the city were valued at $30 million. During the depression, as usual, farm prices dropped faster and farther than imports—wheat from $1.37 a bushel in 1837 to forty-five to fifty cents in 1842—and farmers could not pay their bills at the country stores, which in turn reduced their purchases or asked for extended credit. By 1845, however, the state bank expanded its note issue, farm prices rose, and the volume of trade exploded upward. Further acceleration came in 1846, as St. Louis became a major staging area for the invasion of Mexico, and the farmers of its trade territory sold horses, mules, oxen, corn, and other items to government buyers at spectacular prices.

St. Louis grew so rapidly after 1835 that housing construction fell far behind demand. Free-state merchants, artisans, professional men, and southerners (chiefly nonslaveholders), attracted by high wages, speculative opportunities, and booster literature—some of the last home-grown puffery and some of it travelers' accounts of the "Queen of the West," "Lion of the Valley," or "The Valley Queen"—swarmed to the city. The *Missouri Republican* reported in 1835: "Every steamboat that arrives at our wharves is crowded with passengers. Some of the Louisville boats bringing three hundred at a time . . . many of these remain with us." In 1840 the same newspaper marveled: "One might imagine that the 'world and his family' are coming here. We have never witnessed such crowds of people as now throng our streets. . . . The hotels, boarding houses, etc. are crowded to excess. . . . If a tenth part of the immense throng now pouring into the city stay, our population will be augmented several thousands this season." George Featherstonhaugh, an English visitor, suffered "a sensible chill" to find the old Creole town just another Yankee trading center filled with "Reuben Doolittles and Jeremiah Cushings." Where were the "Canadian cottages, old French physiognomies, and the crowds of Indians walking about"? To his dismay, "the everlasting Jonathan had struck his roots deep in the ground . . . ," the forest-roaming Creoles had given way to "Doolittle and Company." This Yankee-hating traveler could have seen (and probably did see) plenty of Canadian cottages south of Market Street; and French physiognomies abounded there, in old and new mansions both on and below the hill and in the mercantile and counting houses; but apparently the hustling Jonathans clouded his vision.

Between 1835 and 1840 the city's population doubled, from 8,316 to 16,439 and doubled again in five years, to 35,390. By comparison, Pittsburgh, twice St. Louis's size in 1830, had been overtaken in 1845. The seeds of even greater growth had been planted, in the booming western hinterland and in central Europe. In addition to Missouri's 243,247 increase between 1830 and 1840, more than 40,000 people had settled in the Iowa Territory, and Arkansas and western Illinois were growing rapidly. In Germany, tens of thousands of hopeful people were thrilling in response to Gottfried Duden's stirring eulogy to the Missouri valley in his *Report of a Journey to the Western States of North America.*

A few Germans had settled in the St. Louis district during the Spanish period, including John Helderbrand, Abram and David Musick, and John Coons. In the American territorial period, a half-dozen more came, including Christopher Schewe, a teacher; Christian Wilt; Frederick Weber, a tavern keeper; Henry S. Geyer, an attorney and politician; Henry Von Phul, a merchant and civic leader; and Charles Wahrendorff, a wealthy wholesale merchant. But as late as 1833, there were only eighteen German families in the city. Gottfried Duden, a wealthy young lawyer and medical student from the Rhineland, had come to Missouri in 1824 looking for a haven for victims of overcrowding in his native land. Duden bought land fifty miles up the Missouri in the present Warren County, built a house, and farmed it for three years before returning to Germany. He had chosen Missouri because good land was cheap and because it was where the Americans were going. His *Report*, a highly colored, romantic account of Missouri, which he compared to the Rhineland, was published first in 1829. Its several printings had reached every corner of the German states in 1833, when Friedrich Muench and Paul Follenius organized the Gieszen Emigration Society in Hesse and came with seven hundred followers to St. Louis. They wanted farms, as did most of their compatriots who followed, whether they came in organized groups or as individuals; but for various reasons, including exhaustion of their funds, many of them stayed in the city of St. Louis.

By 1837, there were thirty thousand Germans in Missouri, and according to the *Missouri Republican*, more than six thousand of them were living in St. Louis. They had come chiefly to find a better life, to improve their purses, as had the thousands who preceded them, but with a difference. Unlike the American frontiersmen they sought permanence, a place where they could put down roots for generations, as opposed to "buy cheap, mine the soil, sell high, and move on." Material reasons motivated most German immigrants, but their leaders—Muench, Follenius, Hermann Steines, E. K. Angelrodt, J. G. Bruehl, and others—emphasized the advantages of freedom and democracy. Most of these early leaders were rationalists, as much opposed to the strictures of religion as to the autocratic state, but in 1839 a different kind of German came to St. Louis. Several hundred Saxons, dissatisfied with the religiously liberal but autocratically governed established church in Saxony, sought in Missouri a place to practice their own conservative, traditional Lutheranism. Under the leadership of Martin Stephan and Carl F. W. Walther, the main body of Saxons settled in the barren hills of Perry County, some fifty miles south of the city. Otto Walther and a congregation of 120 voting members stayed in St. Louis and founded the Trinity Lutheran Church. Out of these congregations, under the leadership of C. F. W. Walther, grew the Lutheran Church-Missouri Synod, doctrinally the most conservative as well as the most numerous branch of Lutheranism in America. Immediately upon their arrival in Perry County, the Saxons founded the first coeducational college in Missouri. Concordia Seminary, as it became, was moved to St. Louis in 1849.

Beginning with J. B. C. Lucas's extension of his subdivision to Ninth Street in 1833, thirty-one additions to the city were made by 1845; the most important were those of Julia (Cerré) Soulard, from the river to Fourteenth Street between Park and Geyer; John O'Fallon, from Seventh to Twelfth Streets between Franklin and Biddle; E. T. and William Christy, Ninth Street to Jefferson (twenty-four blocks west of Main) between Franklin and Lucas; and Lucas's third addition, Ninth to Eleventh Streets between Market and St. Charles. In 1827, in conjunction with its move to Jefferson Barracks, the army purchased a thirty-seven-acre tract of land three miles south of the city for a close-in location for its Quartermaster Corps. In the next dozen years, in addition to supply headquarters, a small arms armory, a wagon-repair shop, a cartridge-manufacturing plant, and an artillery-wagon shop were constructed. In 1836, twenty-three landowners led by John Withnell, an English builder and speculator, dedicated an addition called South St. Louis just south of the armory, from the river to Carondelet Avenue (Broadway) between Guthrie (President) and Government (Utah). A proposal to construct a railroad to Iron

Mountain was before the legislature, and the developers hoped to build a short rail line to it from the Cahokia Ferry landing, making South St. Louis an industrial and commercial center connecting the Iron Mountain ore with the Illinois coal fields. Because of the depression, the legislature abandoned the railroad project, leaving South St. Louis dependent upon its limestone quarries and employment at the arsenal.

Just north of the military reservation, William Carr Lane had built the Eagle Powder Works on a twenty-acre plot, which was producing six hundred pounds of powder a day when it blew up in April 1836. In an attempt to salvage something from this disaster, Lane dedicated the St. George addition on the site, retaining for himself and his heirs the right to build a railway on any of its streets and the title to any land deposited by the river. He hoped to take advantage of rail construction to the ferry landing and to attract working-class families and industry to his location. The town of St. George was bounded by the river and Carondelet Avenue, Victor and Lynch. In 1844 Bremen, a German enclave, was incorporated about 2.5 miles north of Market, between the river and Broadway from Buchanan to Salisbury. The river curved back sharply to the west of this site, and Bremen's developers, as William Christy had done in "North St. Louis" in 1816, insisted on using the river as a base line instead of building their streets north and south, east and west. The result was a maze of odd little triangles, parallelograms, and dead ends as they encountered the differently angled streets of other subdivisions. Later developers would do the same, and the jumble of streets at subdivision intersections became characteristic of both north and south St. Louis (where the river also curves back to the west). Rare indeed is the St. Louis street that is oriented to the cardinal points of the compass.

Including Bremen, St. George, and South St. Louis, available residential space in 1845 stretched from Salisbury on the north to Guthrie on the south, a distance of seven miles along the river and five and one-half miles along the west line, and from the river to Beaumont Street (2700 west). These additions trended south, northwest, and north of the old village, with long westward arms projecting north and south of Chouteau's Pond, which presented serious problems in providing connective municipal services, such as streets, water mains, sewers, and transportation lines. Few persons before 1845 regretted this barrier to the southwest, because it was the city's grand recreation spot.

Chouteau's Pond was described as "a beautiful fairy lake," in the shape of a half-moon, more than two miles long and averaging a quarter-mile or more in breadth according to the season. James Essex, who reveled in it as a youth, called it "clear and cold" and well-stocked with bass, crappie, catfish, sunfish, and buffalo. It was "a great

Chouteau's Pond. *Daguerreotype by Thomas M. Easterly, 1851. MHS-PP.*

resort for boys, and all the inhabitants for bathing, fishing, boating, and picnicks in summer, and for skating in the winter." Gabriel Chouteau operated the two-story stone flour mill at the dam, furnishing the residents with a "fine quality of flour." Indian delegations, in the city to receive their annuities from the government, camped on its shores in colorful array. Essex had seen the noted black Baptist preacher, John Berry Meachum, immerse candidates for salvation in wholesale lots there and had witnessed John Mason Peck break its ice in order to baptize converts. The pond and dam had remained long after other relics of the past, such as the stone tower and the Laclède-Chouteau mansion. But after the devastating cholera epidemic of 1849, with the pond a stinking sewer full of offal from butcheries, garbage from residences, and nauseous waste from industries near its north banks, there was a clamor led by doctors to get rid of it. In 1851–52 the pond was drained as a menace to public health.

After making a small addition to its southern limits in 1839, the legislature in 1841 expanded St. Louis from .75 to 4.78 square miles (480 to 3,060 acres). The new boundary ran from the southeast corner of St. George west to Second Carondelet Avenue (Thirteenth Street), then north to Eighteenth Street at Chouteau Avenue, then north by northeast to the mouth of Stony Creek just south of Bremen, then east to the main channel of the river. Under the charter of 1835 the legislature, which kept a suspicious eye and a tight rein on the city, divided St. Louis into four wards (increased to five in 1841 and six in 1843). In 1839 the state bestowed the blessings of a bicameral council, designating the Board of Aldermen as the upper house and a Board of Delegates as the lower. Tensions ran high between the Democrats in Jefferson City and the Whig local government, especially in 1841, when the General Assembly removed the taxpaying and reduced the residence requirements for city electors, and made the offices of auditor, marshal, and register elective. These actions, reflecting the legislature's displeasure with local banking heresies, were expected to strengthen the Democratic Party. Thus, at a time of mushrooming growth, heavy debt, and weak municipal services, when coherent planning and administration were sorely needed, outside authority had mandated the long ballot and decentralized government in St. Louis.

After laying out boundaries, the legislators numbered six wards from south to north, each extending from the river to the city's western limits. The First Ward, south of Mill Creek, grew most rapidly in the early 1840s, with many immigrants and working people attracted to its inexpensive lots. The Second Ward included the southern tip of the business district, the Creole enclave in the old village, Chouteau's Pond, and a narrow strip north of the pond. Wards Three and Four encompassed the richer residential areas of the old village, the Lucas, Connor, O'Fallon, and Christy additions on the hill, the main business district, and the raffish population of the levee. The Fifth and Sixth Wards, comprising the city's northern triangle, contained a few outlying mansions; but like the First Ward, they were populated chiefly by immigrant and working-class families. A few old Creole houses were scattered through the central wards, along with other exceptions to the above generalizations, but a definite pattern of distribution by class had developed, dictated primarily by wide variances in the site value of land. In 1848, lots in St. George (First Ward) sold for $1.50 to $4.00 per front foot, while residential lots on Fourth Street in the Third Ward commanded as much as $200 per front foot ($600 in 1854).

The distribution of slaves was also revealing. St. Louis doubled in population between 1845 and 1850 to 77,860, of which 2,636 (3.4 percent) were slaves and 1,398 (1.79 percent) were free blacks. Wards Three and Four, in the affluent central section, had 35.5 percent of the city's people, 67 percent of its slaves, and 58 percent of its free blacks, while the outlying wards (One and Six), with 35.3 percent of the population, had only 10 percent of its slaves and 7 percent of its free blacks. The latter were concentrated in the Second, Third, and Fourth Wards because they had always lived there. Some, such as the Clamorgans, owned houses below the hill; others lived with their employers; and still others clustered on or near Front Street and the warehouses and wharves where they worked.

According to the *Republican*, in 1838 there were no classes in St. Louis; "the great body" of its citizens "do not desire and will not tolerate any attempt to create distinctions in society" (a myth agreed upon by those who expected to manage the affairs of their fellows, or to sell them something). It meant that one could not openly espouse doctrines of superiority, except racial, sexual, or (within limits) ethnic superiority. A rough democracy prevailed on the streets, in the taverns, and at the polling places, and egalitarian doctrines poured from the rostrums and the presses, but gentlemen only fought duels with other gentlemen; they caned their "inferiors" or had them arrested. Senator Benton may have been the voice of the people, as he said, but he did not claim to be one of them, nor was he expected to be.

St. Louis in the 1840s was a city in motion. Always a trader's city, it would remain so, but industry was stirring too. It had been a French village, a mélange as a town, and it was becoming a melting-pot city. Having grown 1,500 percent in population and 550 percent in area in two decades, its sewage was still running in open gutters; its water supply was untreated and its delivery uncertain; its vehicles were denied direct access to its southern section; its fire and police protection was largely voluntary and unprofessional; and its priceless harbor was threatened with extinction by encroaching sand. To counter these liabilities, the city was bursting with vitality; it was a promised land for a diligent, determined, intelligent, and self-disciplined people; it had achieved the commercial supremacy predicted by its early boosters and an industrial future was in the offing. To its residents, to the thousands who came every year, and to most visitors, it was an exciting place of unlimited opportunity. Much energy, skillfully applied, would be required during the next decades if it were to meet its problems and deliver on its promise.

5.
Growing Pains

Since the early 1820s the wayward Mississippi channel had threatened the lifeline of St. Louis commerce. In the first place it was full of snags. The ferry boat *Ozark* sank in the harbor in 1841, and on the night of January 3, 1844, the steamboat *Shepherdess* sank within three miles of the Market Street dock. She had struck a snag which tore open her hull, drowning many of the deck passengers and crew immediately. Some passengers reached the Illinois and Carondelet shores, and some cabin passengers were taken off the floating wreck by rescuers, but at least forty died by drowning and more than twenty from the effects of exposure in the icy waters. Local appeals to Congress produced one snag boat which operated in the "Graveyard" between St. Louis and Cairo for a few months with meager results, and further appeals went unheeded for a time. Snag boats were expensive to operate and could not function at low stages of the river because they drew more water than ordinary steamboats. At high water they could not reach the snags; thus, they were limited to the few weeks each year when the river was at medium stage.

More threatening to St. Louis than the snag problem were the sandbars in its harbor. Duncan's Island, a small bar in the channel near the mouth of Mill Creek in 1815, had begun to close in on the west bank by 1820; and by 1837 it was a two-hundred-acre island covered with cottonwood trees, with a mere trickle of water flowing between it and the shore, denying access to the river for a dozen blocks below Market Street. Worse, a sandbar was growing between Duncan's Island and Bloody Island, a mile upstream near the Illinois shore. In the words of Captain Robert E. Lee, an army engineer assigned by his chief, General Charles Gratiot, to inspect and improve the harbor: "A flat bar projects from the upper end (of Duncan's Island), to the foot of Bloody Island, opposite the town, which at low stage of the river, presents an obstacle to the approach of the city, and gives reason to apprehend that, as some future day, this passage may be closed."

East of Bloody Island, the Illinois shore was rapidly caving in, widening and deepening the chute between it and the island, threatening to make it the main channel leaving St. Louis "high and dry." Local saviors had come forward from time to time; one such worthy, at considerable expense to the city, had dropped tons of sand in wooden boxes at the head of Bloody Island to throw the current toward St. Louis. Unfortunately, the current smashed the boxes and the sand washed down to the flat bar. Captain Lee had better materials. Congress gave him fifty thousand dollars, about one-third of his estimate, with which he built a system of underwater dikes, consisting of wooden piles interspersed with alternate layers of stone and brush, stretching from the Illinois shore to the head of Bloody Island and down the west shore of the island. Insufficient funds kept Lee from completing the task, but he loaned his equipment to his assistant Henry Kayser, a German university graduate who resigned his army position to become St. Louis's first city engineer. Lee's temporary barriers worked well at first; in 1838 the channel was thirteen and one-half feet deep at low water, as opposed to six feet a year earlier, and Duncan's Island was moving downstream. Kayser's efforts to continue were blocked by an Illinois injunction in 1839, and the stubborn river gradually found its way around the dikes to deepen the eastern chute. The harbor filled again, and by 1842 ferry boats had to make a two-mile detour in crossing the river. The *Republican* shamefacedly reported in that year that the steamboat *Louisiana* was stuck on a sandbar a few feet from the dock. Petitions and pleas to Congress and pressure from Senator Benton obtained an appropriation of seventy-five thousand dollars for the St. Louis harbor, but President Polk vetoed the Rivers and Harbors Bill of 1847. Efforts to override the veto were blocked by the strenuous objections of Senator Stephen A. Douglas of Illinois.

At the city's expense Kayser kept the harbor open by temporary stratagems until he was replaced in 1850 by Samuel R. Curtis. In 1851 the controversy with Illinois was finally settled, and Curtis then directed the completion of Lee's plan with some variations, until he was replaced in 1853. In January 1854 the *Republican* reported that the "whole volume of the Mississippi between Bloody Island and the city has been compressed into a channel about 600 yards wide." Large steamboats could now make landings "along the whole front of the city, a distance of nearly five miles, instead of shallows . . . which often caught and detained boats for days within a few rods of the shore. These works cost the city about $250,000."

During his stay in St. Louis, Robert E. Lee formed close friendships with Dr. William Beaumont and other St. Louisans, invested in the city's 10 percent bonds, and developed an especial fondness for Kayser. In response to an agitated letter from the latter about a proposal to make his office elective, Lee teasingly advised his German friend on how a gentleman should behave in a democracy: "I can hardly think that sensible men would make the office of *City Engineer* elective. It would be the means of making it *null & void* as regards the benefits to be derived from it. Still if they do & we good democrats do strange things sometimes, you must lay aside your foreign aristocracy & throw up your hat with the highest and hurra with the loudest. When I left you, you were a good locofoco [Democrat], what has come over you? Evil company I fear has been the spoil of you." Despite Kayser's fears, he did not have to "hurra with the loudest"; and except for 1846, he continued in office until he was removed by Whig Mayor Luther M. Kennett in 1850. When a Benton Democrat, John How, replaced Kennett in 1853, he reinstated Kayser. By 1855 Bloody Island had become a part of Illinoistown (East St. Louis), and Duncan's Island was a memory, though other problems lay ahead as the wharf-line lengthened.

Low taxes and minimal services still prevailed a decade after St. Louis became a city. Except for Mayor Lane's city hall and market and minor street and levee improvements, little had been done to enhance the city's amenities. During the 1827–28 tax year, with real and personal property in the city valued at $1.8 million, receipts from the one-fourth of one percent property tax were $2,108, with $830 in delinquencies. Merchants' and dramshop licenses brought in $5,687, wharfage fees $1,608, and miscellaneous fees $1,984. Total revenues were $11,662 and expenditures $11,190. The major outlays were for paving short sections of Chestnut, Olive, and Second Streets. For the first time, St. Louis went into debt ($13,000 for the city hall–market). Ten years later property valuations had risen to $7.4 million and tax collections (at one-third of one percent) to $22,395. Licenses totalled $21,317, wharfage fees $10,649, other fees $14,803, and income from the municipal waterworks $8,372.

Before 1832 residents had laboriously hauled their water directly up the hill from the Mississippi, at first by hand, and then by sledges after access to the river was improved. There were several springs nearby, and the water in Chouteau's Pond was cleaner and clearer until the 1840s, but the people had always believed that the murky river water had special health-giving properties. Mark Twain once described it as "too thick to drink and too thin to plow," except for the natives, who upon finding mud in the bottom of a glass, would "stir it up, and take the draught as they would gruel." In 1830, J. C. Wilson and Abraham Fox, with a subsidy from the city, purchased the "little Mound" at Ashley and Collins Streets from General Ashley as the site for their reservoir and set up a pumping station on the river bank to supply the reservoir. Six-inch iron pipes were laid for the mains and smaller iron or lead pipes for the branch lines. Wilson and Fox were to furnish free water to the city hydrants (for street washing and fires), to the Sisters of Charity Hospital and General Ashley's private fountain.

Water service began in 1832, but even with frequent city subsidies the operators were suffering annual losses until 1835, when Mayor John F. Darby purchased the plant and distribution system for the city for eighteen thousand dollars. In 1839 rates ranged from eight dollars a year for families and businesses of less than six persons to five hundred dollars for machine shops and distilleries. This schedule produced inadequate revenues, and the plant could not meet the demand. In one year outlays exceeded collections by eighty-seven thousand dollars, hydrants on Fourth Street, the system's western limit, were often dry because of elevation and low pressure. The works were often shut down for cleaning, and the feeble flow contributed to fire damage, especially on the upper streets. A proposal to build a reservoir on top of Big Mound, which would have provided a powerful head of pressure, was rejected as too costly, and nothing was done until 1843, when alterations to the existing unit increased its capacity to four hundred thousand gallons. Since daily consumption often exceeded that figure, sediment could not settle as intended. In 1845 Mayor Bernard Pratte proudly announced the completion of a new reservoir, which would "afford an abundance of water, both for the convenience of the public and their safety from fire." This additional unit, which tripled the system's capacity, was a huge tank of solid oak, built atop the original stone reservoir, adding twelve feet to its elevation and a bit more pressure in the lines.

Mayor Pratte had been overoptimistic. In 1846 an aldermanic committee recommended immediate construction of a new reservoir at a higher elevation, since the existing units would soon be "wholly inadequate, from their want of capacity, . . . [and] frail character." Under this plan, four reservoirs, each with a capacity of four million gallons, were to be built in the North St. Louis addition, at a point forty-three feet above the highest elevation in the center of the city. The first of these was completed in 1849, but accelerating demand quickly swamped the system again, and the plan was abandoned in favor of a forty-million-gallon reservoir on Benton Street at Eleventh. When completed in 1855, this giant towered 40 feet above its base and 140 feet above the city directrix at the foot of Walnut Street. By 1859, more than seventy miles of pipe furnished an "abundant supply" of water to the city, according to the works superintendent. More than six hundred thousand dollars had been spent on reservoirs, pumping engines, and mains by 1851, and nearly three times that amount by 1860, but the quality of water had not improved since the first reservoir was built. Expansion had been accompanied by simultaneous complaints about prodigal expenditures and demands for further extension.

The waterworks and the battle against the sandbars, financed by the sale of 10 percent bonds, largely to eastern investors, were chiefly responsible for elevating the debt to $437,112 in 1839, about $27 per capita. Debt service in that year consumed nearly one-third of the revenue, the rest going for salaries, streets, wharf maintenance, and operations of the municipal offices, jail, and hospital. In the next four years the debt rose to $912,734 ($32 per capita). This increase was attributable to the laying of new water mains, land purchases for public parks, markets, and buildings, an investment of $50,000 in the stock of the St. Louis Gas Light Company, and a constant nagging deficit in the operating budget. The 1843 budget included $67,000 for interest payments, $57,705 for bond retirement, and $103,694 for operating expenses, a total of $228,399. Taxes, fees, and licenses amounted to $193,771, leaving a deficit of $34,628.

Despite its sizeable debt, the city's financial condition was improving. St. Louis bonds had been discounted from 25 to 32 percent during the financial crisis, but in 1843 an improving economy, the retirement of the city warrants, a charter amendment sequestering a share of the property tax for debt retirement, and an increase in that tax to 1 percent of assessed valuation reduced the discount on city bonds to less than 1 percent. By April 1852 the debt had doubled again to $1.74 million, but the population had more than tripled in nine years to 94,819, reducing the per capita debt to $18. Annual operating deficits were still the rule—both a result of the debt load and one of the causes of its expansion. A frustrated comptroller outlined the problem in 1850: "If the faith and credit of the city for the future, is called in question . . . it is because the revenues . . . have, in a large measure been drawn from her coffers to meet engagements which her present representatives did not contract . . . it is not possible to carry on improvements commensurate with the wants of the city, and *provide for the legitimate expenditures*, out of *one-half* of her general revenues (net after debt service)." After current expenses for salaries, hospitals, the workhouse, the waterworks, and other services were paid, only $9,407 remained for street maintenance and improvements. Operating deficits, the Benton Street waterworks, and other new commitments boosted the debt to $2.7 million by December 1853 ($28 per capita).

The new undertakings, some of them long overdue, included $202,000 for sewer construction, $200,000 to enlarge and improve the wharf, and a subscription of $250,000 to the stock of the Pacific Railroad Company. The waterworks and sewer bond issues were essential to the existing city; but the wharf extension, the willingness to expand the debt further, and especially the railroad stock purchase underlined the prevailing optimism and the conviction that the city should use its powers to assure its commercial future. Whigs usually controlled the city administration, but Democratic mayors George Maguire in 1842, Bryan Mullanphy in 1847, and John M. Krum in 1848, despite their party's record of opposition to federal internal improvements, were no less eager than the Whigs John F. Darby and Luther M. Kennett to tax and borrow for local improvements. The Whig *Missouri Republican* in 1842 blasted Mayor Maguire, asking whether a city "already involved in a large debt, which she has not the ability to meet, and in the midst of a monetary crisis and a general prostration of business . . . , should go into expenditures, which . . . will not cost less than half a million dollars." Irrespective of party, the leadership believed that the growing tax base and improved credit rating made additional debt not only feasible but realistic. Assessed at close to market prices, taxable property in St. Louis tripled in value between 1845 and 1855 to $43 million, and more than doubled in the next five years to $102.4 million in 1860. With the retirement of the older 10 percent bonds, the debt had been refunded at an average of 7 percent by 1850.

Drainage had always been a problem in St. Louis. Francisco Cruzat in 1778 had authorized construction of a gutter down a cross street (later Chestnut) to "allow a constant drainage . . . from the gullies and sinkholes" to the Mississippi. Mayor Krum in 1848 alluded to complaints about the lack of sewers in recommending that they be built as soon as "the public mind" would sanction the expenditure. Surface drainage into the sinkholes that yawned between Eighth and Twentieth Streets from Chestnut to Salisbury was blocked as the city grew, and these natural drains were filled with garbage. With their underground outlets choked, they became stagnant ponds covered in summer with slime, their pungent waters believed to be the source of the malaria that gave the city a sickly reputation. Between Eleventh and Twelfth Streets lay "Kayser's Lake," an enormous sinkhole which the city engineer had attempted to use as a drain for the upper city's surplus water. The underground caves in the vicinity had filled with noxious water, draining slowly not to the river but into nearby basements.

After 1849 the need for sewers was no longer debated as Asiatic Cholera struck its most devastating blow at St. Louis. The dreaded disease had made its first appearance in 1832, after having traveled from the Atlantic ports to Pittsburgh and Cincinnati, down the Ohio and up the Mississippi to the Mound City. Between 15 and 30 October, 140 persons died. Two weeks later, according to Doctors William Carr Lane, Samuel Merry, and others, the epidemic had ended, but in May 1833 it returned with a vengeance, killing a dozen or so each week until August. There was no recurrence in 1834, but in 1835 Frederick

Steines wrote to relatives in Germany: "The cholera is again raging in St. Louis. Entire families have been carried away by it."

The outbreak in 1832 was traced to Jefferson Barracks and later ones to steamboats from Pittsburgh and New Orleans. Slaves and levee roustabouts were the first to die, and incidence was highest among them. Before *Vibrio Comma* found St. Louis, a citizens' committee recommended a day of "Fasting, Humiliation, and Prayer, and to implore the Divine Providence to avert from our city the threatened calamity of Asiatic Cholera." A month later, another committee suggested an earthier solution, the prohibition of "watermelon, green corn, cucumbers, cabbages, and any other vegetable . . . prejudiced to health, as also fresh pork; and they further recommend that . . . no tainted or unhealthy animal food be sold. . . ." This committee also requested the aldermen to "prescribe the manner of erecting necessaries, designating the depth of the vaults. . . ." The doctors apparently suspected that the disease might be transmitted through the human feces, though fifty years would pass before Robert Koch would isolate the responsible bacterium.

Those who survived the cholera and its remedies were hardy indeed. Dr. Hardage Lane prescribed two-grain pills of asafoetida, opium, and pulverized black pepper, one to be administered every half or three-quarters of an hour until the patient recovered or died, usually a matter of three or four hours. If there was severe stomach pain, eight to ten grains of calomel were prescribed. Where there was "collapse and great prostration of strength, application of the tourniquet to the arms and legs has been recommended, in order, as it were, to husband the vital power by limiting the extent of the circulation." After recovery was apparent, a dose of castor oil was in order. Other doctors had their own prescriptions, some of them contraindicative, but they were all praised for their unremitting efforts. Ironically, Dr. Hardage Lane himself was to be a victim of the 1849 epidemic.

In 1848 immigrants from Germany and Holland, where cholera was raging, brought it to New Orleans. Most of the Germans were bound for St. Louis and Cincinnati, and the Hollanders for Iowa. They were transferred directly from their cramped and filthy quarters on the ships to the main decks of river steamers under optimum conditions for the spread of disease. By late December cholera deaths were reported in St. Louis. Eight persons died during the first week in January 1849 and the disease idled along until May, when it began to strike with trip-hammer blows, reaching a peak in July, when 145 persons died in one grisly day and 722 in one week. By July 30, 4,547 cholera victims had been buried in the city since the first of the year. Until July 3, when a special Board of Health, which had extraordinary emergency powers, declared a quarantine on incoming northbound steamboats, infected passengers were disembarked on the wharves without hindrance. Thereafter, the boats were stopped at Quarantine (Arsenal) Island, near the city's southern limits, where Dr. Henry Carrow and his staff examined every person on board. Those who appeared to be sick and those just arrived from overseas were sequestered on the steamboat *St. Louis,* which was moored at the island. Permanent barracks and an infirmary were under construction by August 1, by which time seventeen hundred persons had been quarantined. Mayor James Barry then lifted the quarantine, which had been credited with stopping the epidemic, but some observers pointed out that there had been a general exodus, leaving few candidates for the disease. Many of those who left died elsewhere, and the official casualty count was probably much too low.

The *Republican* was alarmed by the ending of the quarantine, pointing out that if cholera reappeared, the city would have "such bills of mortality as will produce almost entire nonintercourse between us and the interior—the fall trade will be destroyed, and our business men severely injured or ruined." From May to August, except for groceries and grogshops, business had been at a standstill, and the merchant R. S. Elliott observed that "real estate will sell but slowly, when no one was sure from day to day whether he would ever need more land than enough to bury him." The custom of tolling church bells for funerals was abandoned, because of the "injurious effect on the imagination of those touched by the disease, as well as of those in sound health." Under pressure from businessmen and doctors, the quarantine was made permanent in 1850, and more than 2,500 persons were detained, but there were 883 cholera deaths in the city in that year and 845 in 1851. A few cases appeared each year through 1855, with no recurrences thereafter until 1866, when another epidemic claimed 3,527 lives.

In proportion to population, seventy thousand in 1849, St. Louis had been hit harder by cholera than any other city in the nation. A majority of the victims were recent immigrants, and about one-third were children of five years and under. As in 1832 many blamed the disease on cabbage and other vegetables, with sauerkraut as an added entry. A minority of doctors disagreed with their fellows about diet, recommending that only vegetables be eaten. This added to the general confusion and sense of helplessness. Despite their shortcomings, St. Louis's medical men knew as much about cholera as their colleagues elsewhere, and they paid dearly for their efforts to control it. In addition to Hardage Lane, Bernard Farrar (the city's senior physician who had attended Benton on Bloody Island),

Marcellus Edwards, James Wishart, and George McCullough succumbed to the disease in 1849. As a melancholy footnote to the general anguish, the epidemic purportedly claimed the life of the brother to the Osage, Pierre Chouteau, Sr., the last of St. Louis's original settlers, in his ninety-first year.

After the cholera onslaught, underground sewers became a high priority. Since it was believed that pollution filled the air with deadly organisms that were ingested in breathing, Chouteau's Pond and the sinkholes had to go. The city council in 1849 appropriated fifty thousand dollars for the construction of a horseshoe-shaped sewer twelve feet in diameter along Biddle Street from Ninth Street to the river, which would drain "Kayser's Lake." In 1850 the council created a general sewerage system and a common sewer fund to be supported by a tax of .5 percent on property in each of thirty-three sewer districts. In 1855 the city engineer reported that thirty-one main sewers had been built at a cost of $525,000, draining more than four hundred acres in the central part of the city. Chouteau's Pond was still a major problem, since it had never fully drained, parts of it being lower than its outlet. For this purpose the Mill Creek sewer was built, beginning at the head of the former pond. This massive sewer, the largest in the city, was rectangular in shape, fifteen feet high by twenty feet wide. By 1861, nearly thirty-two miles of mains and laterals were in place. During the Civil War, construction went slowly, but the recurrence of cholera in 1866 spurred new activity. By December 1868 all parts of the city were served, 101 miles of lines having been built since 1850 at a cost of just under $3 million.

During the 1840s and 1850s the business and population boom kept the heat on the city engineer for street improvements. By 1845 the annual budget for streets had reached ten thousand dollars, but there was never enough to meet the demand. New streets were opened but none were paved outside of the central wards. Some were macadamized, but the broken limestone used as top dressing was so soft that it was soon pulverized and the streets reduced to mud. As late as 1848 carriages and wagons mired down so frequently at Eleventh and Olive that a nearby resident offered to take out a ferry license to carry passengers across the intersection. Jenny Lind, the "Swedish Nightingale," who sang to enraptured audiences in St. Louis in 1851, was impressed by her reception and the quality of local society, but as to externals she described the place as "a huge reservoir devoted to the manufacture of mud on a wholesale scale, by the joint operation of art and nature." The great coloratura soprano only said what the residents were painfully aware of, and during Mayor Kennett's tenure (1850–52) a good deal was done about it.

City Engineer Samuel Curtis reported in 1851 that within the old (pre-1841) city limits there were 14.3 miles of improved (paved or macadamized) streets and 2.1 miles unimproved. In the new section there were 18 miles of improved and 66.4 miles of unimproved streets. In an April referendum, the citizens approved a twenty-five thousand dollar street bond issue and contracts were let for grading, curbing, guttering, and macadamizing a northern extension of Main, Seventh Street, and the remaining dirt streets within the old limits. Later in 1851 some streets were paved as far west as Seventeenth Street. In 1852 landowners were required to build sidewalks whenever their facing streets had been paved or macadamized. In cases of noncompliance, the work was done by the city at the owners' expense. By 1853 there were fifty-three miles of improved streets and one hundred miles of sidewalks in St. Louis.

By the 1840s the condition of the levees was abominable. Travelers often had to walk from the steamboat landings to their hotels. Horses and mules, fetlock deep in mud, strained under the lash to pull heavily loaded drays. In 1845 the center section was paved with stone, but the jumble of vehicles often became entangled, creating a snarl of angry, cursing drivers, screaming animals, and spilled produce. Efforts

St. Louis Levee. *Daguerreotype by Thomas M. Easterly, 1853. MHS-PP.*

by the harbor master to control traffic on the wharf were fruitless. With the proceeds from a two hundred thousand dollar bond issue, the wharf was paved in 1854 for nearly a mile, but the pressure for space was still intense. In 1857, by reclaiming several feet from the river by a buildup of paving stone at the water's edge the city engineer extended the wharf sufficiently to reduce loading time by one-half. A reporter described the levee scene as: "A mile of steamboats. Hundreds of drays, wagons, and carriages rushing along at all speed. Thousands of men jostling each other. . . ." At the time of this description (March 1857) ice still blocked the river above Keokuk and the Missouri River traffic had just begun to move. Another observer claimed that he could walk the length of the wharf over piles of produce.

All sections of St. Louis's trade territory contributed to its explosive commercial expansion in the two decades before the Civil War. John Hogan rhapsodized in 1854 about the city's situation:

> On the mighty Mississippi, below the mouth of the vast extended Missouri, draining a country of unrivalled productiveness . . . capable of sustaining a population as dense as almost any region of the globe. . . . While just above enters the Illinois, draining the very heart of that most productive State—while to the north . . . the states of Iowa and Wisconsin—the northern part of Illinois and Minnesota, each of them destined to sustain millions . . . of agriculturalists and mechanics, will always have their natural markets at St. Louis.

Hogan's superlatives were close to the mark. Missouri's population had grown from 384,000 in 1840 to 682,000 in 1850 and in 1860 would reach 1,118,012, making the state the eighth largest in the Union and first among the fifteen slave states in free population. Its improved farmlands were worth $231 million, ninth in the nation; it was seventh in livestock; third in corn production; seventh in tobacco; fourth each in molasses, honey, and hemp; and tenth in wool. Most of its commercial crops, especially hemp, tobacco, corn, and hogs, were produced in the counties adjacent to the Missouri, Illinois, and upper Mississippi Rivers.

Illinois in 1840 furnished more than one-half of the farm produce shipped to St. Louis, and its people consumed a major share of the city's merchandise exports. For the next two decades it continued to be a large market and supplier, though its relative share of the St. Louis trade declined as the other hinterland regions filled with settlers. Wheat, corn, hogs, cattle, wool, butter, and vegetables poured

onto the wharves from the Illinois River steamboats and the busy
ferries from the American Bottoms. When the Illinois and Michigan
Canal was completed in 1848, linking the Illinois valley with Lake
Michigan and New York via the Erie Canal, St. Louis merchants
feared a serious loss of business, but at first the new canal merely
diverted part of their Atlantic trade from New Orleans to the cheaper
Great Lakes route. Even after rail connections were completed in 1853
between New York and Chicago, St. Louis wholesalers did a
substantial business in Chicago and continued to be the primary
suppliers of merchandise for the Illinois valley as near as eighty miles
from the Windy City.

The rich black loam of the Iowa prairies was a magnet for
farmers, and its population grew from 43,112 in 1840 to 674,913 in
1860 (statehood was granted in 1846). Iowa's farm products and lead
were shipped to St. Louis, both for local consumption or processing
and for transshipment to New Orleans; and St. Louis merchandise and
farm implements were shipped back. Wisconsin, which became a state
in 1848, grew even faster than Iowa, from 30,945 in 1840 to 775,881
in 1860. Wisconsin had an 80 percent share of the upper Mississippi
lead district (the Galena-Dubuque field), much of which had been
developed initially by St. Louis interests. The pull of these historic ties
was strengthened by the lower cost of shipping downriver as opposed
to the overland haul across the state to Lake Michigan. Eastern
Wisconsin was oriented to Chicago and eastern markets, but the older
southwestern section belonged to the Mississippi. Across the river,
Minnesota, organized as a territory in 1849 and granted statehood in
1858, grew to 172,073 by 1860. Huge rafts of Minnesota yellow pine
towed by steamboats reached St. Louis by 1860, and a decade later,
thirteen St. Louis towboats were engaged in the Minnesota and
Wisconsin lumber trade. West of the Missouri border, where pro- and
antislavery partisans struggled for control after 1854, St. Louis
merchants sold their wares without involving themselves in the
political fate of the Kansas Territory.

Frederika Bremer, in *The Homes of the New World* (1853),
thought St. Louis looked "as if it was besieged from the side of the
river by a number of huge Mississippi beasts, resembling a sort of
colossal white sea-bears." And so they were; they were "those large,
three decked white painted steamers, which line the shore, lying
closely side by side to the number of above a hundred." The number
of annual arrivals of these "Mississippi beasts" presents a rough
measure of the accelerating volume of St. Louis commerce. In 1844,
boats averaging about three hundred tons in cargo capacity made
2,105 landings at the levee; in 1857, arrivals increased to 3,443 boats

averaging between five and six hundred tons in capacity. These figures suggest that the volume of goods and produce delivered by steamboats approximately tripled during this thirteen-year period. By comparison, New Orleans and Cincinnati logged 2,570 and 1,922 arrivals respectively in 1844 and 2,745 and 2,703 in 1857.

Between 1845 and 1852, 24.5 percent of the arrivals at St. Louis were from the upper Mississippi, including smaller Missouri ports such as Hannibal; 22.8 percent were from the Illinois River; 16.2 percent were from Cincinnati, Louisville, Pittsburgh, and other Ohio River ports; 12.7 percent came upriver from New Orleans; 11.4 percent arrived from the Missouri; 3.9 percent were from Cairo, Illinois; and 8.5 percent came from other points. By the late 1850s St. Louis had become the commercial metropolis of the entire river basin above New Orleans, sending nearly three times as many boats to New Orleans annually as its closest rival, Cincinnati. In addition, St. Louis was first in steamboat ownership, with 168 vessels operating in 1860. Six boats were built in St. Louis yards in 1860, thirty were repaired, thirty machine shops manufactured boat machinery, and twenty-eight iron foundries served the machine shops. In all, some thirty-five hundred men were employed in steamboat-connected enterprises, not including stevedores, harbor employees, deckhands, and other crewmen.

The glamor and romance of the steamboat era was associated primarily with the passenger traffic. Unlike those on the eastern rivers, western steamboats, with rare exceptions, carried both freight and passengers. Freight traffic was much more important, but few owners could resist the attraction of extra income from the relatively higher (though very low) rates and light weight of the passenger trade. Conversely, even the passenger packets found it profitable to fill available space with freight. Freight rates from St. Louis to New Orleans usually ranged from five to twenty dollars a ton in the 1850s, depending upon the river's stage (higher rates at low water), with upstream rates averaging about one-third higher. Cabin passenger fares for the same trip were twelve to fifteen dollars, though on some luxury boats they were as high as twenty-five dollars, while deck fares were as low as three dollars. The ornate trimmings of the cabins and the passenger saloons on the leading boats made them the marvel of the age, and even the smaller, poorer vessels tried to imitate their betters. More was involved than profit; local and personal pride led owners to compete in luxury as well as speed. "Steamboat gothic" symbolized elegance in an age of gilt, gingerbread, and red plush. Those who could afford a cabin ticket stepped into the world of privilege. Cabin quarters were on the second deck, isolated from the common herd, in airy, comfortable quarters with a promenade gallery surrounding them and a spacious "grand saloon" in the center of the cabin area. By 1850, some new steamboats supplied cabins with water closets, to replace chamber pots or the outdoor-type toilets that were built into the wheelhouses or projected over the sterns. Despite their privileges, cabin travelers could not completely escape the multifarious odors of the main deck, the noise and vibration of the high-pressure engines, or the nerve-racking scraping over sandbars at low water. But these discomforts were minor compared to the miseries of deck passage or the bone-rattling stagecoaches and early railroads.

The cuisine for cabin passengers varied according to the pretensions of the owners, but it was generally noted for abundance if not for dietary balance (most Americans cared little for dietary balance, if they had ever heard of it). A passenger from St. Louis to Louisville in 1833 reported that thirty-two different dishes were served at one meal. Typically, except on the fried-pork and fried-bean boats, breakfast included steak, fowl, chicken fricassee, ragout, cold sliced meat, coffee, and tea; dinner was steak, baked pork or turkey, duck or chicken, cold sliced meat, potatoes, rice, corn, rice or cornmeal pudding, tarts, and watered rum. Supper was like breakfast. Wine and whiskey were available in the bar, at extra cost. By the 1850s the crack steamers between St. Louis and New Orleans served truly elegant meals, matching those of the finest hotels in the country with place cards, printed bills of fare, small oval tables separating the genteel from the ordinary diner, courses served with panache by professional waiters, and after-dinner music. These were the exceptions, however; Charles Dickens and other cosmopolitan observers were thunderstruck by the table manners prevailing on the western steamboats. Many passengers had never heard of the grand dishes set before them and were determined to get their money's worth as quickly as possible. One easterner described the experience (in 1844) as follows: "When the supper bell rang with a rush, one grand race, and woe to the luckless wight who should stop in his course, he might well expect to be crushed to death—and then such a clatter of knives and forks and tableware, such screaming for waiters, such appeals to Bill, Tom, Jack & Pomp and such exhibitions of muscle and nerve as men entered with all their power into the game of knife and fork. It was worse than a second Babel. . . ."

The steamboats brought together western farmers, southern planters, merchants, politicians, artists, theatrical companies, titled Europeans, writers, speculators, preachers, slave traders, gamblers— the rich and not-so-rich (not the poor, they were on the main deck) in a grand social mix. To an extent, social barriers were lowered and horizons broadened. The passengers shared at night the folk music of the black deck crews; they learned something of the art of river piloting (and swallowed a few lies about it); and they shared the thrills of the impromptu races that enlivened the river scene, not only for the passengers and crew, but for the people of the river towns. The risk of a boiler explosion that would "blow them all to Kingdom come" frightened some passengers, but for the majority a hell-for-leather contempt for death seemed to prevail, a western characteristic, according to eastern writers. Gambling was another commonplace diversion on the river steamers, even on those where it was officially banned. Professional gamblers were good customers, lavish tippers, and free spenders at the bar, and captains seldom expelled any except flagrant cheaters. When they were thrown off the boat, usually at the demand of the shorn lambs, they were left on the first convenient sandbar. As many as four to six poker tables would be set up in the saloons at one time, and a lot of money changed hands, though the stories of entire plantations or mercantile houses being lost at a single session were dismissed by one retired Mississippi River gambler, George Devol, as "pure humbug." Devol doubted that as much as two thousand dollars had ever been won or lost on a Mississippi steamboat at one time.

Steamboating was a high-risk, high-profit business. The cost of construction varied according to size, equipment, and furnishings, with an average cost in 1851 of twenty-five to thirty thousand dollars for boats in the 300–350 ton class. Large, elaborately equipped boats could cost sixty thousand dollars or more. In 1850, the natural life span of a Mississippi sidewheeler was considered to be five years, but a Missouri River boat had only a three-year life expectancy because of the greater hazards on that tempestuous stream. A clean, fully laden round trip of a thousand miles could net owners 30 to 40 percent on their original investment, but low-water delays or other misadventures brought staggering losses. Boats could be insured for about two-thirds of their value, but losses traceable to boiler explosions were usually not recoverable, and even snag- or fire-caused claims might be rejected if negligence was involved. Through 1849, 550 steamboats had been destroyed on the Mississippi River system, at an average age of 2.86 years. A boat that survived for three years or more usually returned a substantial profit, comparing favorably with alternative investments. Most owners suffered severely during economic downturns, but some boats made money even then. In the early years, merchants or combinations of merchants were the typical owners, because they had capital and they needed the services. As other investors appeared, merchants tended to withdraw from a high-risk enterprise that they could not directly supervise. By the 1850s boat and engine builders, captains, and others who were exclusively involved in river transportation owned a substantial majority of the steamers.

The element of human risk did not figure much in the boatowners' calculations, but it was constantly present. When the *John Adams* was wrecked on a Mississippi snag in 1851, fewer than half of those on board were saved: eighty-four of one hundred cabin passengers, all of the eleven officers, seven of thirty-two crewmen, and five of eighty-seven deck passengers. Virtually imprisoned by cargo, exposed to the direct blast and scalding steam of the exploding boilers, and riding only a foot or so above the waterline, deck passengers and crew often died within minutes. Cabin passengers could jump into the river, or if in relatively shallow water, they could stay on the cabin deck or climb to the hurricane deck and never get wet. In one instance the cabin simply floated off the wreck, with its passengers safe and sound. This dismal story was repeated time and again; captains often referred to human losses only in terms of cabin passengers and officers.

Most of the wave of immigrants who came to St. Louis after 1846 arrived on the steamboats. The defeat of German Liberalism in the Revolutions of 1848, the Irish potato famine of 1845–46, and the "young Ireland" rebellion of 1848 were the motive forces. A potent group, known as the "Irish Crowd," including Jeremiah Connor, John O'Fallon, Thomas Brady, William Christy, and John Mullanphy, had been prominent in the city's leadership since territorial days, and they had assisted their countrymen who came to and through St. Louis after 1818 through the "Erin Benevolent Society." By 1840 there were several hundred Irish families in the city, enough in combination with the Germans to threaten the Whig stranglehold on the city and arouse anti-foreign sentiment. In that year, the "Native American" Party was formed in St. Louis as in other cities. Locally, it was at first just a pressure group within the Whig Party, anti-Irish, anti-German, anti-Catholic—appalled by the prospect of being dominated by the "dirty" Irish and "Dutch." John F. Daggett, a conventional Whig merchant, was elected mayor over Democrat Hugh O'Neil in 1841, but in the following year the nativists controlled the Whig caucus and nominated one of their own, the second-generation Irish Protestant, Joseph Charless, Jr. Ironically, the *Missouri Republican*, descended from his father's *Gazette*, refused to support Charless, asserting that "the success of the Whig Party would be more jeopardized by the election of a Native American candidate than by the temporary ascendancy of locofocoism." When the young attorney Wilson Primm, of Creole ancestry, offered to run as an anti-nativist Independent Whig, editor A. B. Chambers discouraged him. With the Whigs thus divided, the coalition of Hards, Germans, Workingmen, and Irish elected the city's first Democratic mayor, the Irish native George Maguire.

When the Democrats repeated in 1843, this time with a blacksmith of German descent, John Wimer, the alarmed Whigs reunited behind the Creole fur magnate Bernard Pratte. Excited about their presidential candidate Henry Clay, they staged a determined, well-organized campaign against the Democrat J. I. Reily in 1844. For their part the "Americans" carried out a campaign of intimidation and hatred, beginning with an attack on the Saint Louis University Medical College, which began as a protest against the dissection of human cadavers, but which had some ugly anti-Catholic overtones. Laboratories, specimens, and furniture were destroyed by a mob estimated at more than three thousand. On election day in April, attempts to keep the foreign born from voting resulted in pitched battles at the polls. One brave soul even challenged Senator Benton's right to vote, charging that he was not a resident. This time Benton calmly swore he was a citizen and voted without further comment. Pratte won the election, but he disappointed the nativists by reappointing "foreigners," such as city engineer Kayser. In 1845 the Americans nominated their own candidate, but the Democrats outfoxed them by endorsing Pratte, who was reelected. The next year, the American Party's Peter G. Camden won easily, with the Democrats divided again over banking legislation.

By this time, enough immigrants had been naturalized to give the Democrats a majority in St. Louis, and they elected three mayors in sequence: Bryan Mullanphy in 1847, John M. Krum in 1848, and James G. Barry in 1849. Having nominated the influential Luther M. Kennett, an ex-alderman whose nativism would attract the Americans, the Whigs had felt certain of victory in 1848, but to their discomfiture, they learned that one hundred or more Germans had received their naturalization papers on election day and had voted immediately. Between 1847 and 1850 the city gained thirty thousand people, despite the heavy losses from cholera and the departure of several hundred young men for the gold fields of California. In ten years, St. Louis had grown by 373 percent to 77,860. In 1850 it was nearly twice as large as Pittsburgh, which had doubled in size to 46,601. New Orleans and Cincinnati, both still larger than St. Louis, had grown by 14 and 149 percent respectively between 1840 and 1850. Chicago, a new settlement of 4,470 in 1840, reached 29,963 in 1850. Nearly 43 percent of St. Louis's people were German or Irish natives in 1850

(22,534 and 9,719). Including children of foreign-born parents and second-generation Germans from Pennsylvania and other states, more than half of the population were Germans and Irish.

A majority of the Germans and Irish who came after 1846 reached St. Louis in a destitute condition and with a mixed reception. Officially, they were welcome, as industrialists favored the addition to the labor force, but the nativist element harassed and tried to intimidate them. However, they were given considerable private assistance. Bryan Mullanphy, who died in 1851, left more than a half-million dollars for the relief of immigrants passing through St. Louis on their way west (contested unsuccessfully by the family); the Mullanphy Hospital, established by John Mullanphy in 1827 and operated by the Sisters of Charity, gave free medical care to indigent patients, with some financial support from the city; and there were three Catholic and two Protestant orphanages. The Catholic Church also offered free education to three thousand pupils in ten schools. In the public sector, the county "Poor Farm" housed the indigent aged, the mentally ill and retarded, and orphans, providing some schooling for the latter.

The German and Irish Emigrant Societies gave immediate relief to new arrivals and helped them find work, and the subscription-supported "Committee For the Relief of the Poor" distributed food, clothing, and fuel to their clients. Most able-bodied immigrants could find work as cooks, maids, nurses, valets, gardeners, seamstresses, and laborers, although a few of the Irish and a substantial minority of the Germans were professionals or skilled workers. With the relative decline of the slave population in the 1850s and the increasing number of affluent families, Irish and German women became the major source of domestic labor. In 1850 the German Emigrant Society reported that it had found jobs for 801 immigrants during the year, buried 36, sent 17 to an orphanage and 114 to the city hospital, and recommended 139 to various charities.

From 1849 through the 1850s, nativists and immigrants engaged in a series of bloody brawls and riots. On July 29, 1849, several companies of volunteer firemen were fighting a blaze that had spread to several steamboats, when a heckling comment from an Irish onlooker led first to a fist fight and then to a wild, rock-throwing melee. Badly outnumbered by the firemen, the Irish bystanders retreated along the levee to J. O'Brien's coffeehouse (saloon), where they repelled the firemen by shooting at them. Soon there were two armies of rioters, the smaller made up of Irish boatmen and dock laborers, the other of firemen was augmented by several hundred anti-Irish partisans. Eventually, Mayor Barry and the police dispersed the mobs and led ringleaders from both sides off to jail, leaving the Irish so outnumbered that they could offer no defense. The nativist mob then systematically destroyed the furniture and interiors of O'Brien's, Murphy's Boarding House on Battle Row (on the levee), Shannon's coffeehouse, Gilligan's on Cherry Street, and Terrence Brady's coffeehouse at Fifth and Morgan. After this damage was done, fifty volunteer policemen were added to the force and more arrests were made. All was quiet then until the mob reassembled in the evening, this time with a six-inch howitzer loaded with scrap-iron, with which they proposed to rake and demolish the Battle Row boarding houses. After several futile attempts by the police to seize the gun, the mob moved it to the Missouri Volunteer Fire Company's engine house, where the police finally captured it.

No further major riots occurred until 1852, but mobs of teenage "hose companies" (assistant firemen) and hangers-on periodically harassed prostitutes and destroyed property in the brothels near Third and Almond. Police dispersed these gangs from time to time, usually after the damage was done, but the offenders knew that they had a degree of community sanction for their assaults on the "lower orders"—the free mulattoes, Irish laborers, and drifters of the downtown and levee areas.

In 1850, the Whig-American Luther M. Kennett was elected mayor, partly because of a rift in the Democratic Party created by Senator Benton's reelection campaign, but also because the Democrats had made the mistake of being in office during the twin disasters of cholera and a fire that swept through the downtown area in 1849. This fire, which began on the steamboat *White Cloud*, spread to twenty-three other steamers and then to the huge piles of freight on the levee. Soon a row of Front Street shanties was burning, followed quickly by buildings on Main, Second, Market, Elm, Myrtle, Locust, and Olive. A strong wind blew during the entire night, the water supply failed early, and the only resort was to blow up buildings in advance of the flames. The city assessor estimated the property losses at $6.1 million, including six hundred thousand dollars for the twenty-three steamboats and their cargoes. Thousands were thrown out of work, hundreds were made homeless, and dozens of the city's leading businesses, including the *Missouri Republican*, the *St. Louis Reveille*, L. A. Benoist and Company, Page and Bacon's banking house, Sublette and Campbell, Pierre Chouteau, Jr., Cabanne, Rasin & Company, Henry Chouteau, Adolphus Meier, and Berthold and Ewing, had their business buildings burned or lost heavily in the wharf fire.

On the favorable side, the fire left room for widening the streets and extending the wharf inland. The fire companies had labored hard

The Great Fire at St. Louis, Mo., Thursday Night, May 17, 1849. *Hand-colored lithograph by Nathaniel Currier, 1849. MHS-PP.*

under incredibly adverse conditions, one of their members losing his life by the premature explosion of a keg of black powder, but the magnitude of the disaster pointed up the glaring deficiencies of the water delivery system and the voluntary fire companies. Under the circumstances, it was a miracle that a catastrophic fire had not occurred earlier. Kennett's promises to improve city services, as well as the infighting among Democrats, was sufficient to carry him to victory three times in succession. The agile mayor walked a fine line; he kept the support of the powerful Catholic Whigs (Creoles and some wealthy Irish) by public professions of open-mindedness, while keeping his nativist friends privately reassured. His race for a third term was especially heated. Germans had claimed for some time that they were discriminated against in municipal and state employment. One such complainant, Alexander Kayser, whose brother had been fired by Kennett, received a sour response from the Whig *Missouri Republican*, which pointed out that the Germans had come to St. Louis without an invitation; and if they did not like the way they were treated, they could go back to the "Faderland." The Benton anti-Benton Democratic split was as wide as ever, and the wounded old lion himself, Thomas Hart Benton, having lost his Senate race in 1850 because his Unionist views had divided the Democratic Party, was campaigning in righteous anger and with biting sarcasm for the district's congressional seat.

Only a spark was needed to light a fire on election day, and it was not long in coming. Early in the morning word spread through the central wards that the Germans had seized the First Ward polls and were preventing Whigs from voting. By mid-afternoon invaders from other wards were battling the Germans with fists and missiles at the Soulard Market polling place. As the afternoon wore on the crowd got larger and the action got hotter until the polls closed, when some frustrated Whigs were permitted to cast belated ballots. After dark, with the crowd still menacing them, the Germans started shooting from the houses. The nativists retaliated, first by shooting back and finally by burning down a house. The Germans had indeed intimidated the Whigs, a good old custom which they had learned from their tormentors. As early as 1838, Democratic carpenter Henry B. Miller had written that he had to go to three polling places before he was allowed to vote.

Despite their political cooperation in the 1840s, there was little love lost between the Germans and the Irish. Neither had been notably supportive of the other under fire, and while there was a religious bond between Catholic Germans and most of the Irish, and his consistent support of Catholic causes was one explanation for their loyalty to Senator Benton, their other reasons for voting Democratic were divergent. The Irish liked the anti-bank, anti-special privilege, hard-money, pro-"little man" Benton who had emerged during Jackson's presidency. Some of the Germans had initially responded to this as well, but by the late 1840s the political ground had shifted. At this point neither the Germans nor Benton were abolitionists, but they were agreed that the unchecked spread of slavery was undesirable — Benton primarily because he thought it threatened the Union, the Germans chiefly because they believed slavery was inimical to free white labor, commercial and industrial progress, and political liberty. Both would have liked to see slavery disappear, and the blacks as well, but they did not propose to destroy it where it was because that too would threaten the Union. Benton's former allies of the hard-money Fayette clique and St. Louis Democratic "Softs," like James Bowlin, Shadrach Penn of the *Missouri Reporter,* Abel R. Corbin (all former Benton men), and Trusten Polk, were now united in favor of the repeal of the Missouri Compromise, which would not only put slaves into the territories acquired from Mexico, but open the entire Louisiana Purchase territory to slavery.

Since they were in direct economic competition with blacks, most of the Irish were unresponsive to antislavery arguments. Kennett appealed to them by shedding his nativist robes and emphasizing his rather remote Irish ancestry (but not his Protestantism), prompting the

Missouri Democrat, a Benton newspaper edited by the rising star B. Gratz Brown, to accuse Kennett of "having changed his forefathers so often there is no telling how long he will remain an American." The Whig press further appealed to the Irish as well as to the Nativists by accusing Henry Boernstein, the editor of the leading German daily, the *Anzeiger des Westens,* of trying to Germanize St. Louis. Benton's successful opponent in the 1850 Senate race, Henry S. Geyer, had attracted some German support because he was of German descent, but he had been in St. Louis since 1815 and he was strongly proslavery. His victory was a hollow one for St. Louis Whigs, many of whom did not share Geyer's views, and the party was foundering on the shoals of the slavery question. In 1853 the Benton Democrat John How overwhelmed the Whig Charles P. Chouteau in the mayoralty race, proving if nothing else that there was no political magic in a proud French lineage. How was reelected in April 1854 with unified party support, but in August, Benton lost his seat in Congress in a close contest with Kennett.

This heated congressional race inspired the worst riot in the city's antebellum history. The *Missouri Republican* repeatedly indulged in a self-fulfilling prophecy that there would be violence; the *Democrat* charged a judge with deliberately delaying the issuance of naturalization papers; and the "Know-Nothings" responded that Democrats were conspiring to flood the polls with ineligible immigrant voters and asked "volunteers" to protect "the purity of the ballot box." (The Know-Nothings were old wine in new bottles—nativists who had filled the vacuum left by the disintegrating Whig Party. They avoided the slavery issue and kept their focus on economic progress and "pure Americanism"—Kennett was their local hero.) A series of fires broke out in the downtown area the week before the election, giving rise to charges of political arson. The August weather as usual was scorching hot, and partisan and cultural hatreds were boiling close to the surface (as they were in Boston, Philadelphia, New York, New Orleans, and other large cities where the immigrant tide was coming in). The *Democrat* predicted a "regular blow-up," and it came on August 7, election day. An election judge in the Irish-dominated Fifth Ward impeded the voting by minutely scrutinizing naturalization papers. The lines grew longer, the "volunteer poll watchers" swelled to mob size, fights erupted, and a flashing Irish knife found a target. The knife wielder fled the scene, and the mob raced down Second Street after him, bombarding Irish homes with missiles. When the Irish started firing down at them from windows and rooftops, the nativists shifted gears and headed for the levee, presumably for easier pickings; but a desperate line of dockhands met them, and at least two persons were

26. St. Louis, Missouri, Saturday March 22, 1856.

PREPARING FOR THE SPRING ELECTION.

Candidate—"Well, Pat, my friend, how have you been—will step in and take something to drink?"

Irishman—"Shure an' it's meself that has not had a dhrap o' the critter this many a-day an' I'll be afther votin' for yees.'

Preparing for the Spring Election. *Cartoon from* The Joker's Budget, *St. Louis, March 22, 1856. The crude humor of this cartoon brings out the ethnic stereotypes underlying the nativist movement. MHS Library.*

killed. Now faced with several thousand assailants, the Irish retreated to the boarding houses and raked the mob with gunfire. The attackers then took axes from nearby steamboats and fanned out hacking at houses and Irish saloons on Seventh Street. Others besieged Saint Louis University at Ninth and Green and the offices of the *Anzeiger Des Westens* at Third and Chestnut.

At this point, Mayor How and his tiny force of sixty-three policemen (wearing stars but not uniforms in a city of ninety-five thousand) were able to scatter some of the crowd. How had also called out six companies of volunteer militia (about five hundred men), which assembled in time to save the university and the *Anzeiger* building. These troops, some of which had served in the Mexican War, included the "St. Louis Grays," formed in 1832 and laced with socially prominent business and professional men; the equally prestigious "National Guards," who wore eye-catching uniforms of scarlet, blue, and white and shakos with gilt tassels; the "Continental Rangers," whose uniforms were replicas of those worn by Revolutionary soldiers; the German "Pioneer Corps," which sported gray and blue uniforms, leather aprons, and plumed and tasseled bearskin shakos; and the Irish "Washington Guards." Membership in these companies was as much a social as a military matter—the volunteers loved to cut a fine figure in parades. Social and political credits were earned by volunteer service, and many of the militiamen also belonged to fire companies and charitable organizations.

The militia ended hostilities temporarily, but fighting resumed the next day and continued until the morning of August 9. Rioters had not given the troops the instant respect they were accustomed to: the Grays and Continentals had suffered casualties and the Washington Guards had found themselves embroiled in hand-to-hand combat with their Irish compatriots. At this juncture Mayor How called a citizens' meeting, which was well-attended, especially by nativists. This assemblage decided to suspend the police force—a doubly motivated move. That the small regular police force had been ineffectual was obvious; that many of them were Irish was an unspoken consideration. To replace them, a volunteer special force of seven hundred men commanded by Major Meriwether Lewis Clark took over patrol duties shortly before the rioters got tired and went home. In its wake the riot had left ten dead, thirty-three wounded, and ninety-three buildings damaged. Mayor How then restored the regular police to duty, and a few weeks later, at his request, they were provided with uniforms. How did not run for reelection, and in 1855 his successor, the Know-Nothing Washington King, and the council enlarged the police force to 140. The night watch and day shifts were united under one administration; the gap in police protection between 5:00–9:00 A.M. was eliminated; the offices of chief of police and city marshal were separated and the former made appointive; and members of the force were given indefinite tenure, instead of the previous one-year appointments. In 1855, the state legislature passed a riot act, releasing police from liability for killing or wounding rioters who resisted arrest, and authorizing mayors to close saloons during elections or emergencies, and to declare curfews. A new city ordinance further required that police guards be posted at the polls.

The next two elections proceeded smoothly, despite a hot race in 1856 in which John How recaptured the mayor's office from the Know-Nothings. According to the *Republican*, which had finally disavowed nativism, the orderly voting reflected not only official reforms and precautions but the general determination to "avoid a collision at the polls." The *Democrat* agreed: "The sentiments of our community revolted at the idea of a renewal of the scenes that disgraced this city on a previous occasion. It was felt that the interests of St. Louis demanded the maintenance of Law and Order." Undoubtedly, the reforms instituted by the Know-Nothing regime had dubious origins. King used his expanded police department to enforce the Sunday saloon-closing laws that his anti-Catholic supporters had crammed down the throats of the Irish and the Germans. The new tenure provisions would protect his police appointees from removal when the opposition came back into power (King had his policemen handing out Know-Nothing ballots on street corners), and even the separation of the offices of marshal and chief was inspired by the nativists' failure to unseat the elected Bentonite marshal. Whatever his motivation, King maintained correctly that the reforms were essential to the city's welfare, as did the *Democrat*, which warned in 1856 that further violence would imperil the city's position as the western commercial emporium.

While there were no further election riots, ethnic hostility persisted. During the Civil War, with nativism politically dead, German loyalty to the Union enraged the pro-Confederates, most of them former anti-Benton Democrats and French Whigs, who, though they had been political enemies of a majority of the Germans since 1849, had not been violent nativists. But now they blamed "the Dutch" for Missouri's "desertion" of the Southern cause and for the countless humiliations and sorrows of defeat. The ex-Know-Nothings were divided on the war, but a majority of them eventually supported the Union.

Although day-to-day lawlessness was less sensational than mass rioting, it was a constant problem in St. Louis, as it was in all growing cities. Its volatile, heterogeneous population, its many transients, its swarm of incoming and outgoing steamboats with their exposed cargoes and raffish crews, its tradition (since 1804) of hotheaded violence, and its flood of impoverished immigrants kept the authorities busy. At the north end of the mile of paved levee, a line of two-story boarding houses, called "Battle Row," served a colorful melange of entertainment. A contemporary described a coffeehouse in one of these buildings as a room about sixteen feet square, with a few soiled lithographs on its dingy walls and a few shelves behind its counter lined with "vile-looking liquids," whose habitual imbibers saw "visions dire" before sinking into imbecility. Crooked gambling games, "knock down and drag out" fights, and "pigeon-drop" confidence games thrived within its walls, and its denizens made frequent visits to the calaboose at the other end of the levee, usually without restitution to their victims. West of Battle Row a nest of brothels provided frequent incidents of violence and petty thievery, but crime was not confined to these slum areas.

Competition between volunteer fire companies led frequently to stabbings and fisticuffs, and disagreements among prominent men led more often to disgraceful public beatings than to duels. One man was killed in a judge's office, a doctor murdered a judge, and a school board member and a citizen brawled during a board meeting. The most disastrous individual crime in the city's history, worse in its effects than the 1854 riots, occurred in 1858 when "Hawkeye Bill," a notorious thief, set fire to the Pacific Hotel killing sixty guests. In 1845, Ferdinand Kennett, Luther's brother, a leading industrialist and president of the Bank of Missouri, inflicted a beating on the pastor of the Centenary Methodist Church. In 1849, attorney Frank P. Blair, Jr., scion of a family powerful in national politics and Benton's "Lesser Ajax" (principal lieutenant) in St. Louis, challenged *St. Louis Union* editor Loring Pickering to a duel, whereupon Pickering ridiculed him by proposing a running fight through the streets with bowie knives. In a chance street encounter shortly thereafter, they whacked at each other with umbrellas, but apparently not to Pickering's satisfaction, because a few days later he fired three shots at Blair as the latter emerged from the courthouse, missing him from a distance of ten feet. When Pickering took to his heels, Blair got off one shot, but to his chagrin, he also missed. Pickering was arrested and charged with assault with intent to kill, but he was acquitted. The verdict seems surprising, and so does Blair's carrying a pistol in and out of the courthouse, but he had received many threats on his life, and would continue to in his controversial role as the champion of the despised immigrants.

It would be a mistake to attribute such episodes solely to the city's unique climate of violence, or to its frontier characteristics. The frontier was in its hinterland, but St. Louis was no longer the frontier—it had been less violent when it was. It was a time of violence, and the whole country was affected, except for stagnant rural eastern backwaters. Politics was whitehot, as it had been since the 1820s. Benton had been threatened with a pistol on the Senate floor by another senator in the 1830s, and in 1849 his life had been threatened before he addressed a crowd on Fayette's courthouse lawn. Boston mobs had dragged abolitionists through the streets at the ends of ropes, abetted by official complacency and encouraged by leading merchants, and even Quaker Philadelphia became notorious for its scenes of violence. In 1858 Senator James Hammond of South Carolina wrote that in the U.S. Senate itself "the only persons who do not have a revolver and a knife are those who have two revolvers." Some visitors were surprised and others disappointed when St. Louis did not live up to its notices. W. D. Bancroft wrote in 1841: "As to the inhabitants of the Western country being a set of Gamblers, Cutthroats, Murderers, and Robbers it is all humbug as far as I have seen. Indeed I cannot hardly realize that I am in the far west, the inhabitants are so different . . . from what I had heard before I left Vermont."

St. Louis's reputation for violence was based on the frontier and steamboat mystiques, the Bloody Island duels, and the nativist riots, but most of all it rested on the McIntosh affair, which received international notoriety in the writings of Elijah Lovejoy and in Theodore Weld's *Slavery As It Is*. On April 28, 1836, Francis McIntosh, a free mulatto steamboat steward, was arrested on the levee for interfering with sheriff's deputies in the conduct of their duties. As he was being escorted to the county jail at Sixth and Chestnut, he asked the officers, George Hammond and William Mull, what his punishment would be. Taking seriously Hammond's reply that he would probably be hanged, McIntosh broke free and stabbed both men, killing Hammond with a thrust to the jugular and severely wounding Mull. As a crowd gathered, several persons captured McIntosh and took him to jail. According to witnesses, when the crowd swelled to thousands, some individuals suggested a lynching party. Hanging was rejected in favor of burning, and a group of fifteen to twenty men, closely followed by the thrill-seeking crowd, rushed to the jail, expelled the sheriff, and brought out the prisoner. A "great shout" arose from the mob as the self-appointed executioners led McIntosh to Tenth and Market, chained him to a tree, and lit a slow fire around him. One anonymous eyewitness reported that when "the flames had burnt him so as to let out his bowels, some asked him if he felt any pain, and he said yes, a great deal." After eighteen minutes of burning, he died. Another witness reported that an alderman (unnamed) was "walking around and swearing he would shoot any person who would dare to loose the chain. . . ." James S. Thomas, later mayor of St. Louis, thought the crowd had wanted "excitement of some kind to get into a commotion."

In reporting the lynching, the *Republican* called it a "revolting spectacle" that would "damage the fair fame of our town," but it was understandable and could have happened anywhere, and a "veil of oblivion" should be drawn over it. There was a mighty effort to comply—in no newspaper account or other public record were the executioners ever identified. With one exception, the other local papers agreed with the *Republican*—the *Missouri Argus* emphasized the enormity of McIntosh's crime and the "heartrending cries" of Hammond's wife and children; and the *Commercial Bulletin* deplored the lynching and the effect it would have on the city's reputation. But the new German newspaper, the *Anzeiger des Westens*, fired a full broadside at the community, serving notice that it intended to uphold a different standard. Editor William Weber conceded that only a few persons had carried out the lynching and even that a majority had disapproved and left the scene before the burning, but he asked, "Why did not the well disposed citizens appear armed, the event being generally known, and continued for several hours. Where were sheltered the proud Gray civil guard, who at other times so handsomely parade through the streets with their music. It is known that you gentlemen will not fight against the Indians [a cruel blow, no doubt referring to the St. Louisans' lack of enthusiasm for the Black Hawk and Seminole Wars]; we have now witnessed that in your own town, you have been forced to fly to your bed chamber, by a handful of men."

An angry *Bulletin* correspondent, X, answered that the entire event had lasted less than an hour and a half, that the Grays had not been called out, and that Mayor John F. Darby had been ill, in no condition to dispel the mob. Even if troops had been present, said X, it would have been brother against brother, acceptable perhaps in Germany but not in St. Louis. The *Anzeiger* replied that citizens were bound to uphold the law even if blood was shed. After this exchange, and a biting critical editorial by the *Alton Telegraph*, Abel R. Corbin of the *Argus* set the lynching in its proper racial context: "The punishment was, as once said an old preacher, 'awfully emphatic,' and we trust another occasion for its administration will never present itself. It is certainly as well, however, for impudent free negroes to be cautious."

Elijah Lovejoy, editor of a Protestant religious weekly, the *St. Louis Observer,* did not believe the monstrous act was "a fair representation" of the community, but he deplored efforts to excuse it, no matter what the provocation. "We must stand by the constitution and laws or *All Is Gone*," said the fiery editor, and many agreed, now including the *Republican*. Lovejoy, however, earned the everlasting hatred of others because he kept the issue alive. On May 16, Judge Luke E. Lawless kicked off a grand jury investigation into the McIntosh affair with a long-winded, biased, and totally inappropriate charge to the jury. Conceding that McIntosh's constitutional rights had been violated, Lawless gave the jury its cue by suggesting that not the few executioners, but "congregated thousands" in a "mysterious, metaphysical, and almost electric Phrenzy" had done the regrettable deed. If this were indeed found to be true, "it would be impossible to punish, and absurd to attempt it." Lawless concluded by denouncing abolitionist religious fanaticism (Lovejoy for example), which he blamed as "the exciting cause of McIntosh's crime" and inferentially the ultimate cause of the lynching. This masterpiece of twisted logic was endorsed by the *Bulletin* and hailed by a short-lived Catholic weekly, *The Shepherd of the Valley*, as containing "much sound wisdom and discretion."

To no one's surprise, the grand jury found the lynching to have been "an act of the populace," unpreventable and unpunishable. The jurors knew, the judge knew, the community knew who the chief perpetrators were, but the crime was attributed to "thousands." Lovejoy was out of the city during the grand jury proceedings, but he came back roaring. Commenting on Lawless's assaults on "Fanatics" and the *Observer,* he said, "We court not the loss of property nor the honors of martyrdom; but better . . . that the Editor, Printer, and Publishers should be chained to the same tree as McIntosh and share his fate, than that the doctrines promulgated by Judge Lawless from the bench should become prevalent in this community." After dissecting the judge's faulty logic, endorsement of mob rule, and threats to the press, Lovejoy offered his own splenetic biases, attributing Lawless's reasoning to his Irish birth and Catholicism, seeing in his charge "the cloven feet of Jesuitism, peeping out from under the veil of almost every paragraph. . . ."

Soon after this editorial appeared, the *Observer* office was broken into and some equipment was destroyed. After another such raid, Lovejoy announced that he was moving his press to Alton, twenty miles to the north, in Illinois. Before he got away, a third and more vicious attack hurried Lovejoy along, but he left with the parting shot that his two hundred tormentors were a large enough mob to qualify for Lawless's immunity. The *Republican*, though it disagreed with Lovejoy, defended his right to print his views and denounced mob rule as a menace to constitutional liberties. When Lovejoy arrived in Alton, proslavery men threw his press into the Mississippi. After obtaining another, he published the *Alton Observer* for eleven months, until August 1837, when the mob again dumped the press into the river. So it was with the third, on the night of its arrival. On November 7, 1837, Lovejoy was killed while trying to defend his fourth press. Lovejoy had his martyrdom. To be sure, he was a flawed martyr, one who made his contribution, not only to the antislavery movement (he was not an abolitionist in the strict sense), but to the literature of nativism. As for St. Louis, it had earned an unenviable immortality. It was widely believed that some of its citizens had been in the Alton mobs; or at best, that the McIntosh atrocity had led to Lovejoy's martyrdom. St. Louis's "fair fame" was indeed tarnished. The American Anti-Slavery Society attributed the McIntosh lynching to the city's leading citizens. Theodore Weld capitalized on Lawless's logic, asserting that "the wretches who perpetrated that unspeakably diabolical murder, . . . were *her representatives* [Missouri's] and the Bench sanctifies it with the solemnity of a judicial decision." Harriet Martineau, after interviewing witnesses, reported to her English readers that "no one would have dreamed of treating any white man as this mulatto was treated." She also claimed that the authorities kept the press under surveillance to see that no antislavery opinions were printed.

Martineau was correct in treating the lynching as racially connected, but in her second charge she was in error. It was not necessary to censor the press, all that was required was to do nothing to protect it. Public opinion was a sufficient deterrent, at least until the German "Forty-Eighters" altered the St. Louis power structure. Martineau had met several persons who were appalled by the burning and by Lawless, but they did not publicly express their views. Even as late as 1860 Edwards and Hopewell's *Great West and Its Commercial Metropolis* reserved its harshest judgments for McIntosh. The near-unanimity on the slavery question in St. Louis cannot be explained in economic terms or even as a reflection of traditional lifestyles. Except for the wealthy French families and a smattering of Virginians, Kentuckians, and old Irish, most St. Louisans owned no slaves in the 1830s, never had, and never would. In 1860, there were only 497 slaveowners in the city—about 1 in 200 heads of families. The influx of New England and Middle Atlantic merchants and professional men had given the city a Yankee character, and many of the Virginians and Kentuckians who had become wealthy by 1851 came from the "mechanic" rather than the slaveholding classes in those states. St. Louis was more a western than a southern city, and it was so regarded at home and elsewhere, especially in its economic orientation. If there had ever been a "need" for slave labor in the city, the influx of immigrants erased it. Slaves were such a tiny percentage of the labor supply by the 1850s that their absence would hardly have been felt.

Slavery was an encumbrance, and despite local hostility to antislavery rhetoric, St. Louis was getting rid of it by attrition rather than by design. From 1,531 slaves (9.29 percent of the population) and 531 free blacks (3.22 percent) in 1840, the black population rose to 2,636 slaves and 1,398 free blacks in 1850, but it declined as a percentage of the total to 3.41 and 1.79 respectively. During the next decade, slavery declined absolutely to 1,542, less than 1 percent of the city's 160,733 residents, while the free black population grew slightly to surpass the slave total to 1,755 (1.09 percent). Manumissions and natural increase accounted for the latter, since free blacks could not emigrate to Missouri under an 1847 law. Male slaves declined by 56 percent in ten years, but females by only 20 percent, to 556 and 986 respectively, including children and those too old to work. Since male manumissions were less frequent than female, the greater relative decline suggests that the pull of high prices and high demand for able-bodied males in the Deep South had made the comparative advantage of alternative labor overwhelming in St. Louis. The price of a slave would buy the services of a free common laborer for several years in the city, without the necessity of furnishing shelter and clothing. The demand for slave women as domestics persisted longer, and it is possible that the bonds of affection and their reproductive capacities were also factors in their retention. Escapes by male slaves into Illinois were more frequent than female escapes, but a majority were captured and returned before they could reach Canada. Despite the presence of "slave stealers," as the St. Louis press called them, on the Illinois side, community hostility to escaping slaves (and blacks in general) was strong in that free state.

Legally and otherwise, the conditions of slavery had changed very little since 1804. The local tradition that slavery was comparatively mild in St. Louis was shared even by such moderate or strong antislavery leaders as J. B. C. Lucas, Frank P. Blair, Jr., and William Greenleaf Eliot, who spoke of the humaneness of local masters and the general disapproval of "unnecessary" cruelty. Manumissions were more frequent in the city than in rural areas, especially by those who thought slavery was damaging the economy or who favored "colonization," or both. Blair, William P. Mason, and others of this persuasion freed their slaves in the 1850s, emancipation reaching a peak of forty-nine in 1860. Even the impoverished U. S. Grant of "Hardscrabble Farm" freed his single slave in 1859. A few slaveowners illegally helped or encouraged their chattels to learn to read and write; some bondmen were permitted to "hire themselves out" so that they could buy their freedom; and slaves were guaranteed trial by jury. Yet, there were witnesses who scoffed at the vaunted benevolence of the system. William Wells Brown, a former slave, wrote that St. Louis was noted for its barbarity, and there were examples of extreme cruelty, such as hanging a woman slave by her thumbs while flogging her. Mary Armstrong, a former slave, recalled that her nine-month-old sister had been beaten to death by her mistress, and that her master would chain his slaves, beat them, and then rub salt and pepper into their wounds. Slave marriages had no legal and little customary standing; slaves were at times sold away from their families; and after 1847, they could not hold religious services unless an official was present. Gaius Paddock noted that the Biblical admonition that slaves should obey their masters "was used to a good effect, for if they did not obey, across the street stood the Court House, on one corner was the whipping post and on another corner was the slave pen . . . the place where they were sold to the highest bidder."

During the 1850s, St. Louis became a busy slave market, serving as a collecting point for slaves from outstate areas. More than two dozen dealers had agents in the city, and slave auctions at the courthouse were commonplace spectacles. At best a slave's life in St. Louis was precarious. As in other places, bondage depended on coercion or the threat of it, and even the kindest master played Jekyll and Hyde, capable of administering a beating if given provocation. Advertisements for runaways gave evidence that mutilation was resorted to. Even if the questionable premise that the institution was comparatively humane in St. Louis is accepted, the essential condition of slavery remained.

Even the free blacks were only half-free. They could not live in the city without a license, testify against a white person in court, or vote. In 1846, Circuit Judge James M. Krum (later mayor of St. Louis, mayor of Alton when Lovejoy was murdered, and a strong Unionist during the Civil War) ruled that free blacks could not plead their constitutional rights because they were not citizens *(Opinion in the Case of Charles Lyons, a Free Negro)*. Free blacks could accumulate substantial property in St. Louis, especially if they had the right lineage. According to Cyprian Clamorgan, a "colored aristocracy" of several dozen families existed in 1858, consisting chiefly of mulattoes whose forebears had been freed during the Spanish period. They had made substantial fortunes from inherited real estate, as the Creole families had, or in a few cases in the drayage business or as large-scale butchers. Some of them sent their children to private schools in Pennsylvania or abroad, partly from choice but mainly because Missouri had banned education for blacks in 1847. Ironically, these black families paid substantial taxes to support the city's public school system.

During the turbulent 1850s, demand for living and business space pushed St. Louis outward and upward. Visitors noted that the business streets were virtually blockaded with bales, barrels, boxes, and packages of merchandise. Sections of Third Street worth $1.50 a front foot twenty years earlier sold for a thousand times as much in 1859. Residential construction averaged more than one thousand units a year during the decade, and building was driving westward, especially along Chouteau Avenue. Three- and four-story business buildings had been the rule in the 1840s, many of five and six stories were erected in the 1850s, thirty-three in 1858 alone. Barnum's Hotel on Second Street, the first six-story building completed in 1854, gave the city another first class inn to rival the Planter's House, which had reigned for a dozen years as the queen of the valley, host to such noted guests as Henry Clay, Daniel Webster, Louis Kossuth, and Charles Dickens (who pronounced it excellent). Its magnificent cuisine and splendid bar, where Planter's Punch was invented, provided a setting where the city's mercantile and political elite and their allies and customers planned, traded, and played. In the 1860s, when the even larger and more elegant Lindell and Southern hotels were completed, St. Louis had what it had always lacked, enough first-class hotel space.

Planter's House Hotel. *Wood engraving, 1860. MHS-PP.*

As business grew, it edged westward. Wholesale and commission houses, concentrated on Front Street in the 1840s, moved into the vacant spaces left by the fire of 1849 on Main and Second Streets. Main retained the state and private banks and a few retailers, but a majority of the latter migrated to Fourth Street and beyond. After the St. Louis Theatre was razed in 1851, the federal customshouse and post office took its place on Third Street, which also featured a city market, boarding houses, and retail stores. The old county courthouse facing Fourth Street became a wing of the new courthouse during the latter's twenty-five-year construction period. In the early 1850s, the old east wing was razed and replaced. When completed in 1862, the project had cost $1.1 million, and its four wings faced Fourth, Fifth, Market, and Chestnut Streets (this "new" courthouse is the present "old" courthouse). Private homes, found on every downtown block in the 1840s, were rare below Fifth Street ten years later, and Fourth Street, with its "Verandah Row" ladies' shops, had become the center of the retail trade. As before, groggeries could be found on every street. St. Louis was a city of brick and stone in the 1850s, with more than two-thirds of its buildings, including residences, constructed of these materials.

Affluence, a product of commercial growth and skyrocketing real estate values, led to the building of massive, ornate private homes equipped with libraries, ballrooms, conservatories, European paintings and sculpture, imported furnishings, running water, gas lighting, and indoor toilets. Lucas Place (now Locust) between Thirteenth and Jefferson, the brainchild of James H. Lucas, was the elegant residential street. Other elite enclaves included the Compton Hill subdivision, west of Lafayette Park, and stretches of Washington Avenue and Olive Street. Several wealthy families maintained elaborate houses in the county in addition to their town houses. In painful contrast, there were poverty pockets on the northwest fringes of the downtown area, called "Wildcat Chute," "Clabber Alley," and "Castle Thunder," inhabited by what respectable people called "denizens" or "vicious characters." One entered these regions at night at risk of life and limb, but most of the crimes there were intramural.

Socially, the upper crust consisted of the French elite and a half-dozen Virginian or Kentuckian families and the Pennsylvania-German Von Phuls. Most of the wealthy French were descendants of the colonial elite, the ordinary Creoles having virtually disappeared into the masses. This elite tended to stay within a tight social circle, entertaining each other in their homes with elaborate balls and dinner parties. The French writer Auguste Laugel, who visited St. Louis in 1864, found this "friendly [to him], rich, esteemed French population" reclusive, irrelevant, clinging to slavery and their traditions. He was chagrined that they "had never given a statesman to the Republic," lacked political influence, and were ruled by people they barely knew, if they knew them at all. Laugel was a bit harsh; the French had tried politics occasionally, but except for Bernard Pratte in the 1840s, they could not win. No doubt repeated rejections and the vulgar rough and tumble of American politics stiffened their backs and encouraged their clannishness. They had lost the political game, but such names as Benoist, Bogy, Cabanne, Chouteau, Pratte, Sarpy, and Vallé still were important in the business community, and a few of them, notably Charles P. Chouteau and Louis Labeaume, were civic-minded activists. James H. Lucas, though his family had never identified closely with the Creole crowd, stood with John O'Fallon and Thomas Allen at the peak of the power structure.

There were undoubtedly those who aspired to the inner circle who could not enter, but few were bothered by what they could not see, and there were many interesting alternatives. In addition to the volunteer charitable, military, and firemen's organizations, there were other public service groups, horse racing, the annual fair, the camaraderie and singing good times of Uhrig's Cave and other beer gardens, excursions to delightful country picnic spots, and ample opportunity to participate in dramatic and musical groups. Many of the world's finest actors and singers appeared on St. Louis stages to large and appreciative audiences, and dutiful self-improvement buffs could hear

View on Lucas Place. *Wood engraving by Lossing-Barrett after a photograph by Brown, 1860. MHS-PP.*

an uplifting lecture almost every night. If all else failed, one could always watch the volunteer fire companies fight each other (until the city installed a paid department in 1856).

Professional drama had come to St. Louis in a regular basis in 1835, when N. M. Ludlow and Sol Smith, who operated theatres in New Orleans and Mobile during the winter, opened a summer theatre in St. Louis. With the assistance of Charles Keemle of the *Republican* and Meriwether L. Clark who raised seventy-eight thousand dollars in subscriptions, they incorporated the St. Louis Theatre Company in 1837 and completed a Greek-temple theatre at Third and Olive. This impressive building was 73 by 160 feet and seated fifteen hundred people in a parquet and three galleries. The floor could be removed for animal shows, the stage was 73 by 55 feet, and admission was $1.50 for boxes, $1.00 for the parquet, and $.50 for other seats. Presentations ranged from Shakespeare to American dramas such as *The Plains of Chippewa*, and from opera to individual artists such as the magician Signor Vivalla, the "wonder of the world." Usually one charity benefit was scheduled during each engagement, with seats going to the highest bidders. Ellen Tree appeared in 1839, as did Edward Forrest in *Othello* and *William Tell*. In 1845 the trained horses of the New York Circus amazed one and all, and in 1846 the Swiss Bell Ringers followed Mr. and Mrs. Charles Kean (Ellen Tree), who presented a full Shakespearean repertoire. Junius Brutus Booth was a popular favorite in St. Louis, despite an occasional erratic performance. The management reportedly locked him up during his engagements, but he occasionally outwitted them, as shown by the following: "In consequence of your having appeared on the stage last night in a state of intoxication, and disgracing the theatre and yourself by your imperfect presentation of the character of Sir Edward Mortimer, we notify you that . . . we shall hold you responsible in damages. . . . [S] Ludlow and Smith." William Clark Kennerly reported seeing Booth, in the role of *Richard III*, so inebriated that he wounded and tried to kill the actor playing the Duke of Richmond in a stage duel. Richmond fled through the stage door with Richard in hot pursuit, to the astonishment of passersby who eventually halted the carnage.

After the St. Louis theatre was razed by the federal government in 1851, its place was taken by Bates's Theater (later De Bar's) on Pine Street, the Varieties on Market, and the People's on Olive Street. In the off-season, or between professional engagements, these theatres were available to the amateurs of the American Thespian and the St. Louis Histrionic Societies, as well as local singing and instrumental groups. Among the famous artists appearing in St. Louis during the 1850s was Jenny Lind, who gave five concerts in 1851.

Bates's Theatre. *Lithograph, 1851. MHS-PP.*

Tickets for her opening performance were sold at auction for as high as $150 apiece, with balcony standing room going for $4. Not just the hall but the street, windows, and roofs of nearby buildings were jammed with thousands straining to hear the Swedish Nightingale sing "Home Sweet Home," "La Tarantella," and "The Last Rose of Summer." Even her manager, P. T. Barnum, lectured to Mayor Kennett and a group of teetotalers on the evils of drink at ten cents a ticket. Barnum also installed General Tom Thumb, the world's smallest man, in Wyman's Hall where citizens paid cash to see and talk with the two-foot nine-inch phenomenon. Other celebrated performers appearing in St. Louis in the 1850s included Lola Montez, Fanny Kemble, the Italian Opera Company, John Drew, Charlotte Cushman, and the incomparable younger Booth (Edwin) who played *Richard III* cold sober in 1857.

For the young and old alike, the highlight of the year was the October Mississippi Valley Fair, inaugurated in 1856 by the St. Louis Fair Association on fifty-five acres purchased from John O'Fallon, on Grand Avenue at Natural Bridge Plank Road, near the city's northern boundary. Exhibits in the early years included farm products and livestock, wines and whiskies, and the latest mechanical inventions.

Ten thousand persons filled the amphitheatre for the saddle horse shows and the thoroughbred racing, which attracted fast horses from all over the country to challenge the local entries of the Lucases and the Carrs. Since the Creole blades had raced their Canadian ponies past the church door at high noon on Sundays in the time of Francisco Cruzat and Father Bernard, horse racing had been a popular diversion in St. Louis, and there were several tracks near the city. The founder of Churchill Downs and the Kentucky Derby, Meriwether L. Clark, Jr., grew up not far from the Lucas track in Normandy.

Before the Germans came, public music was sadly neglected in St. Louis, except for the efforts of the cathedral choir and organist and the music teacher at Saint Louis University. A small orchestra and a brass band were organized in 1839, and the military companies featured marching bands. In 1845 the Polyhymnia Society was organized by Dr. John Woesselhoeft, primarily to encourage classical instrumental music. Among its members were the scientists George Engelmann and Friedrich Wizlizenus, Alexander Kayser, and its president, Henry Kayser. In 1846 a group of brewery workers founded the St. Louis *Saengerbund*, the *Sociales Saengerchor* was organized in 1850, and the Germania Society in 1859. These choral clubs *(gesangverein)* sang a wide range of music, from opera to *lieder* to current popular favorites, their talents earning them several national prizes in the 1850s. In 1859 the St. Louis Philharmonic Society was organized by James E. Yeatman, Henry T. Blow, James B. Eads, Dabney Carr, and others, but unfortunately it did not survive the Civil War. The energetic and public-spirited Yeatman had also helped to found the Mercantile Library Association in 1846, which a year later had collected 2,282 volumes, subscribed to 12 foreign and 12 American periodicals, and had 360 members. Its leading spirits, in addition to Yeatman, were Alfred Vinton, H. D. Bacon, Hudson E. Bridge, and George Collier. When the library's new building at Fifth and Locust was dedicated in 1854, the association had 944 members and a collection of 10,565 volumes.

Under Dr. Engelmann's leadership, St. Louis became an important center of scientific activity at mid-century. A brilliant and tireless scholar as well as a practicing physician, Engelmann took full advantage of the city's strategic location to gather cacti and other plant specimens from every corner of the West. After illness forced him to abandon arduous personal travel, he hired university-educated St. Louis German field workers who wheedled their way onto trading and military expeditions departing for the West. Engelmann's collaborator, the distinguished Asa Gray of Harvard, helped raise funds for these expeditions, and Dr. Wizlizenus, who the soldiers

Dr. George Engelmann. *Daguerreotype by Anson, New York, ca. 1855. MHS-PP.*

called "whistling Jesus," collected specimens while accompanying Colonel Stephen Watts Kearny's invading forces in New Mexico in 1846. Other mildly enthusiastic collaborators included John C. Fremont, who was mapping the West for the army, and Josiah Gregg, the chronicler of the Santa Fe Trail. Engelmann, who became Henry Shaw's principal adviser for the Missouri Botanical Gardens, first pointed out that American grapes were immune to the phylloxera that ravaged European vineyards, and he had the distinction of having three genera and several plant specimens named for him. In 1856, with Wizlizenus, Charles P. Chouteau, James B. Eads, and eleven others, Engelmann founded the St. Louis Academy of Science, which added to the world's knowledge of the botany, geology, and paleontology of the West through its publication, *Transactions*. Always the St. Louis booster, he wrote to Gray that it was "the center of North America, if not the world and of civilization! We burn one third of our steamboats, destroy one tenth of the wealth of our citizens in one night, kill one tenth by cholera . . . all only to show how much we can stand without succumbing."

6.
Rails and Mills

Pressure for the extension of St. Louis's boundaries began in 1852, with all political factions calculating their potential gains and losses. Benton Democrats, eyeing the heavy German concentration near the northern and southern limits, made expansion a political issue in 1853. After an initial referendum failed, a second passed; and in 1855 the legislature authorized an extension that more than tripled the city's area to seventeen square miles, adding more than twenty thousand to its population and 39 percent in property values. The new limits were Keokuk Street on the south, a line 660 feet beyond Grand Avenue on the west and northwest, and from the intersection of that line with Bellefontaine Road to the Mississippi on the north. Occupied and partially occupied areas annexed included south St. Louis; the town of Bremen; the village of Highland (west of Jefferson); the Union addition of L. A. Benoist, Louis Labeaume, John O'Fallon, and others, consisting of fifty-four blocks between Jefferson and Sixteenth Streets in a widening corridor to the northwest (the city's fastest-growing area); the Stoddard addition of seventy-two blocks in the same corridor; and two large sections of the city commons to the far south and west. Now measuring 2.9 miles from east to west along Market Street and 6.8 miles from north to south along the riverfront, the city was redistricted into ten wards, each extending from the river to the western boundary.

Since areal expansion did not bring a corresponding increase in revenues (property taxes in the new areas were refunded until city services reached them), the municipal debt continued to rise. From $3.2 million ($33.70 per capita) in 1854, new borrowings brought the total to $4.86 million ($38.50 per capita) in 1857, chiefly composed of harbor and sewer bonds and $1.25 million borrowed to aid railroad construction. In their efforts to avoid greater indebtedness and unable to increase the property tax because of statutory limitations, St. Louis officials had raised licenses and fees to optimum levels (the city's wharfage fees had been denounced as far away as the floor of the U.S. Senate by Stephen A. Douglas of Illinois). Also for economy's sake, and perhaps because it seemed the natural thing to do, the delivery of gas lighting had been left in private hands (the St. Louis Gas Light Company had finally started lighting lamps in 1847). The city helped the gas company by buying its stock, but its transportation subsidies were more subtle.

One- or two-horse hacks, which charged twenty-five cents per person per mile, had swarmed over the levee since territorial days, their drivers fighting each other for fares. In 1843, Erastus Wells, a twenty-year-old New Yorker, stepped off a steamboat with a few dollars in his pockets and a gleam in his eye. After sizing up the city for a few days, he approached Calvin Case, owner of a thriving river salvage business, with a proposal that they become partners. Case had salvaged the running gear from an army freight wagon—all they needed were two horses, a box frame for the wagon, and a driver, and they were in the omnibus business. Case bought the horses and the wagon box, and Wells did the driving, operating on a regular schedule between the city market and the upper ferry landing, charging one bit a passenger. Receipts averaged $1.50 a day for the first month, and small boys jeered and threw rocks, but as residents learned that Wells adhered strictly to his schedule, business picked up, and competitors entered the field. Wells dropped out of the business temporarily in 1848, ran for the city council, and was elected. In 1850 Case and Wells formed a new partnership with Lawrence Matthews and Robert McBlenis (O'Blenis) and bought out their competitors, giving St. Louis the distinction of having the first internal transportation monopoly in the nation. The partners were an ideal mix—Case and

Erastus Wells. *Steel engraving by A. H. Ritchie, 1876. MHS-PP.*

Matthews had money, Wells was the managing and political partner, and O'Blenis owned a livery stable. Perhaps more to the point, O'Blenis had a menacing reputation as the acknowledged king of Battle Row.

Case and Company opened for business with 90 omnibuses, 450 horses, 100 employees, and 4 livery stables. Their stagecoach-type vehicles, some of them double-decked, ran every four minutes during the day on four major lines: Second and Market south to the Arsenal; Third and Market north to Bremen; Broadway and Franklin west to Twenty-Seventh Street; and lower Market Street west to the Camp Spring beer garden. Subsidiary lines connected the Arsenal to Carondelet and Bremen to the river at Bissell's Point. Daily service to Alton and Belleville, Illinois, via the ferries was also provided. As evidence of their approval of the monopoly, as opposed to the brawling, racing competition that preceded it, the aldermen and delegates lowered the annual license fee for each omnibus from fifty dollars to fifteen dollars for narrow and ten dollars for wide-wheeled (six-inch) buses, which caused less street damage. Fares, which had dipped as low as five cents under competition, were restored to ten cents by Case and Company. Competitors soon reappeared, but they stuck to the outlying areas out of respect for O'Blenis and his drivers. At the peak of its prosperity in 1855, the monopoly was shattered by twin disasters: Case was killed in a train wreck, and O'Blenis went to prison for murdering a deputy sheriff. The company was divided among Case's heirs and the remaining partners, with Wells retaining the most lucrative Olive and Market Street lines.

High-toned customers had begun to complain about the elbowing democracy of the omnibuses, the discourtesy of the drivers, and the rough rides over the stony streets even before the dissolution of the monopoly; and Erastus Wells was just one of several St. Louisans who began to plan for street railways. Omnibuses were carrying fourteen thousand passengers a day by 1859, despite general dissatisfaction with them. Several horse-drawn street railways were chartered in that year, but Wells's Missouri Railway Company was first in the field. On July 4, with President Wells at the reins, a horse car loaded with company directors and city dignitaries clanked over iron rails set in the macadamized surface of Olive Street between Fourth and Tenth Streets. This halting first effort was hailed by a cheering crowd as a grand success, despite several derailments caused by stones thrown onto the rails by the horses' hooves. Wells and his directors removed the rocks, pushed the car back onto the rails, and proceeded. The derailment problem was soon solved by laying wooden ties flush with the rails on either side. Omnibuses continued to run for several years,

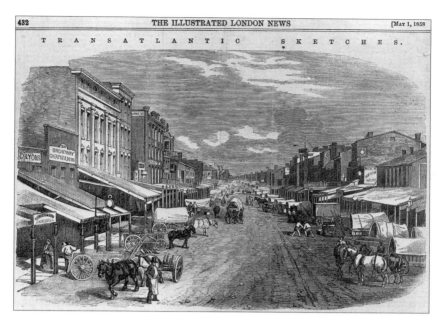

THE ILLUSTRATED LONDON NEWS

The Broadway, St. Louis. *Wood engraving from the* Illustrated London News, *May 1, 1858. MHS-PP.*

but the street railways could not be denied—they carried more passengers with far less horsepower and gave a smoother ride. Wells held the presidency of the Missouri Railway Company until 1881, in addition to his duties as alderman and then as congressman from 1868 to 1876. When the company was reorganized in 1881 under Pierre Chouteau Maffitt, it had eight and one-half miles of track on the choice Market and Olive Street lines.

High profits on high volume (plus extensive real estate investments) made Wells a rich man and attracted to the street railways a galaxy of mercantile, financial, and political stars, though none of the other lines ever matched Wells's company for profitability. Among the presidents of the St. Louis Railway Company, which owned the north-south line from Bellefontaine Road to Keokuk Avenue, were Hudson E. Bridge, founder of the Bridge-Beach Company (the Empire Stove Works); Derrick A. January, wholesale grocer and president of the Chamber of Commerce; and William Tecumseh Sherman. Three-time mayor John How, banker and land developer James H. Lucas, and Pacific Railroad Company president George R. Taylor were incorporating directors. Officers and directors of the eight other companies comprising the street-railway network during the 1860s and 1870s included B. Gratz Brown (on several street railway boards), editor, Governor of Missouri (1870–72), U.S. Senator (1863–67), and vice-presidential nominee (1872); Edward Walsh, lead, flour, and steamboat magnate; Henry Taylor Blow, founder of the Collier White Lead and the Granby Mining and Smelting Companies, a two-term congressman and minister to Brazil; James B. Eads, engineer; Julius S. Walsh, president of four of the horsecar lines; John M. Krum; Thomas M. Allen, railroad entrepreneur, state senator, and congressman; and Charles P. Chouteau. These horsecar companies cooperated, rather than competed. Their five-cent tickets (and some of their officers) were interchangeable. An experiment with a steam-powered car was abandoned in the 1870s because carriage and draft horses bolted at the first sight and sound of it, and the horsecar lines expanded with the city until steam-powered cable cars began to replace them in 1885. Total trackage in 1881 was 119.6 miles; the companies owned 2,280 horses and mules and 496 cars, employed more than a thousand workers, and carried 19.6 million passengers. Urban mass transit had become big business in St. Louis—the rocky shoals of scandal lay dead ahead.

Real and personal property in the city, assessed at $8.6 million in 1840 and $29.7 million in 1850, was valued at $102.4 million in 1860. The property tax yielded $924,427, two-thirds of total revenues. Merchants' licenses added $133,000, the waterworks $114,000, wharfage fees $68,000, and other fees, rentals, and fines $135,000. At $5.06 million ($31.46 per capita), the debt ratio had been reduced since the 1855 expansion, but Mayor Oliver D. Filley thought it was at a dangerous level because of the pressing need for further capital expenditures. Consequently, the legislature in 1860 granted the city's request to increase St. Louis's property tax limit from $1.05 to $1.50 per $100 valuation.

St. Louis became the nation's eighth largest city in 1860, having failed to pass Cincinnati by only a few hundred, New Orleans by 8,000, and Boston by 17,000. Chicago was still nearly 50,000 behind St. Louis's 160,733, but it too was moving fast. Still primarily a gathering and distributing center, St. Louis lagged in manufacturing, though not disproportionately so in comparison with other American cities. With its manufactured products valued at $27 million in 1860, St. Louis was seventh in that respect, sixth in the number of manufacturing firms, ninth in payrolls, ninth in value added by manufacturing, and tenth in manufacturing employees. Food processing was dominant, with flour and meal production valued at $4.98 million, sugar refining at $1.8 million, and meatpacking at

$1.69 million. Before the early 1830s, St. Louis had imported much of its flour from the Ohio valley, but its booming agricultural hinterland soon furnished its millers greater supplies than their Cincinnati rivals. In 1843, nine thousand barrels of flour were shipped from St. Louis to southern markets, commanding a premium of fifty cents a barrel over the Ohio product. In March 1851, a southern correspondent wrote, "Here in east Tennessee above the Muscle Shoals, and the difficult pass of the Tennessee River through the mountains we are eating St. Louis flour. If anyone had a few years ago predicted this feature of our trade, he would have been pronounced demented, but now we look forward to a more extended business, in sending flax seed and other products from this Valley to St. Louis."

St. Louis flour's reputation for quality was attributable to the lower moisture content of western wheat and the establishment of the Miller's Exchange, the first grain exchange in the nation, which instituted a rigorous system of inspection of local mills and their products. In 1850 the Miller's Exchange merged with the Chamber of Commerce, which had been established in 1837, to form the Merchants' Exchange. Here, millers, merchants, steamboat owners, and speculators exchanged information and ideas and bought and sold commodities and commodity futures. Among the leading flour millers in the 1850s were the Union Mill of James and Edward Walsh and the Star Mill on Elm Street at the levee, owned by Daniel D. Page, who boasted that every puff of smoke from his mill was worth a dollar. These puffs laid the foundation of the fortune that created the giant banking house of Page and Bacon.

Sugar refining was initiated in St. Louis by William Belcher, who built his first plant on Cedar and Front Streets in 1840. Belcher was obviously attracted to St. Louis for its market potential, since there was no substantial source of molasses nearby. Missouri and Illinois farmers grew sugar cane, but chiefly for their own consumption. Belcher shipped in his molasses from Cuba, where he had invested in sugar plantations. Nearly two-thirds of the refinery's output was consumed in St. Louis, with the rest going to the Ohio valley and the Great Lakes region as far as Buffalo. Farmers were poor customers for refined sugar; they relied upon honey and molasses ("long-sweetenin") for day-to-day purposes. After the record-breaking flood of 1844, which created a sea twelve miles wide between Second Street (south of Mill Creek) and the bluffs east of the American Bottoms, had ruined his plant, Belcher and his brother Charles built a six-story refinery at O'Fallon and Lewis Streets. In 1854 Belcher's Cuban investments were expropriated, a disaster which in combination with

Belcher Sugar Refinery, View from Across the Mississippi. *Pencil on paper by Paulus Roetter, 1854. MHS-Art.*

low sugar prices forced the partners to default on their short-term debts. Their creditors, led by D. A. January and Edward Walsh, joined with the brothers in 1855 to incorporate the Belcher Sugar Refinery, the largest such refinery in the United States and one of St. Louis's largest employers.

A special branch of food processing, the brewing and distilling industries, produced $1.76 million in 1860. Auguste Chouteau had distilled whiskey as early as the 1790s, and at least by 1809, and probably several years before, John Coons brewed and sold beer in St. Louis. In 1810 the former Spanish officer Jacques St. Vrain and his German *braumeister* Victor Habb opened a brewery on Bellefontaine Road, where they produced ale, porter, and "common beer" (these closely related top-fermented brews are differentiated by the amount of hops in the mixture—ale having the most and porter the least). In 1815 John Philipson from Philadelphia (St. Louis's first Jewish businessman) opened the St. Louis Brewery, but it was slow to begin production because of the scarcity of barley (for malt) and hops in the area. Eventually, by entering into contracts with farmers, the brewers encouraged the growing of these crops. Shortly after St. Vrain's death in 1818, Habb closed the business, leaving Philipson alone in the field for a short time. His malthouse having burned, Philipson sold the brewery in 1821 to the wealthy John Mullanphy, who controlled it until an arsonist destroyed it in 1829. James C. Lynch began to sell ale and porter at seventy-five cents per dozen bottles or $5.50 a barrel in 1826. Ellis Wainwright opened the Fulton Brewery in 1831, and in 1834 James and William Finney, successful general merchants and beer importers, established the City Brewery on Cherry Street, between Second and Third. In the following year Isaac McHose and Ezra English opened what became the most famous ale brewery in St. Louis, which prospered as the St. Louis Brewery for fifty years. The "English Cave," at what is now Benton Park, was the first subterranean beer garden in the city.

Increased production did not keep up with demand, and by 1840 thousands of barrels of beer were being imported from Cincinnati, Pittsburgh, Wheeling, and New Orleans, much of it by the Finney brothers. Total production by the City Brewery, the Fulton Brewery, and the St. Louis Brewery in 1840 was about three thousand barrels. Shortly thereafter in 1842, William J. Lemp, a German immigrant, revolutionized the city's brewing industry by introducing lager beer at his new plant on south Second Street. This light, clear, pleasant-tasting, bottom-fermented brew quickly captured the public fancy. In contrast to ales and porters, in which it rose to the top, the yeast of

William J. Lemp. *Steel engraving by Williams, New York, 1899. From Conard and Hyde,* Encyclopedia of the History of St. Louis, vol. 2, 1899. *MHS Library.*

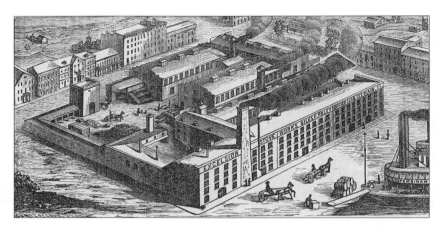

Excelsior Stove Works. *Wood engraving by William Mackwitz, 1859. From* Edwards's Programme and History of the Fair, *1859. MHS Library.*

lagers sank to the bottom of the brewing kettle. Lemp then transferred the brew to twenty thirty-barrel oak casks, where the fermentation process continued for several weeks. During this lagering or aging period, Lemp stored his casks in a large natural cave south of the city. By the 1850s *lagerbier* had captured the lion's share of the local market. Twenty-four St. Louis breweries turned out 60,000 barrels in 1854, and in 1860 forty of them produced 189,400 barrels, to slake the city's massive thirst. This phenomenon was noted by the *Republican*, which estimated that 18 million glasses of beer were drunk in St. Louis between March 1 and September 17, 1854, "when the lager beer gave out."

On June 21, 1857, the *Republican*, in a light mood, recalled that in the early 1840s, there were no beer gardens, but "when they did come in it was tempestuously; a sudden and almost unexpected wave of emigration swept over us, and we found the town inundated with breweries, beer-houses, sausage-shops, Apollo Gardens, Sunday concerts, Swiss cheese, and Holland herrings. We found it almost necessary to learn the German language before we could ride in an omnibus or buy a pair of breeches, and absolutely necessary to drink beer at a Sunday concert." The writer was grateful to the Germans for their beer, which had been "well-nigh universally adopted by the English-speaking population, and the spacious beer halls and extensive gardens nightly show that the Americans are as fond of the Gambrinian liquid as those who have introduced it. . . ."

Soap and candle-making, a companion industry to meatpacking, with a product value of $1.59 million in 1860, was just behind brewing and distilling. Heavy machinery and steam-engine manufacturing followed at a value of $1.51 million. Other industries producing more than five hundred thousand dollars annually were brickmaking, construction, men's clothing, cigar-making, boots and shoes, and stove-making. Hudson Bridge's Empire Stove Works and Giles Filley's Excelsior Stove Works were among the best-known stove companies in the West. Despite the numerous small foundries which refined pig iron and blooms (malleable wrought iron) for fashioning into machinery, the large rolling mills of Chouteau, Harrison, and Vallé, and the heavy machinery and engine-manufacturing firms such as Gaty, McCune, and Company; most of St. Louis's industries involved simple processes and low capital investment, which of course was true of the United States as a whole. The nation's flour and meal mills outproduced its textile and iron industries combined, as measured by final product value. Only in parts of the northeast did capital-intensive manufacturing predominate.

The local press, the city's chief drumbeater John Hogan, and outside observers frequently deplored St. Louis's failure to exploit more fully the vast coal and iron deposits nearby. Except for the manufacture of heavy steamboat engines and machinery, and railway rolling stock, which were prohibitively expensive to ship, local capital had too many attractive alternatives in commerce and real estate to venture into capital-intensive manufacturing (like the New England merchants who had been slow to move into textile manufacturing a few decades earlier). Capital formation for industrial investment was also hindered in St. Louis before 1857 by the constitutional prohibition against more than one bank of issue (the Bank of the State of Missouri). Note brokers, or private bankers, such as L. A. Benoist, Lucas and Simonds, and Page and Bacon, and the chartered Boatmen's Savings Bank, dealt in the notes of out-of-state banks, accepted deposits, and made loans; but they could not readily expand the monetary circulation as banks of issue could at the time by lending their own notes, or as commercial banks do now by setting up deposits against which borrowers write checks. Missouri's reputation for sound banking rested on the scarcity of "fictitious capital" in the state. The *Republican*, in a conservative mood during the depression in 1842, advanced the obvious proposition that manufacturers who generated their own capital were "much more likely to outlive the storms and embarrassments which sometimes overtake the commercial world" than those which borrowed from banks.

The state's banking policy was safe and "sound," but limited credit inhibited enterprise. As John Hogan declaimed in 1854, "If we had the banking facilities possessed by cities not containing one-fourth of our population, or doing one-tenth of our business, matters would be materially changed. . . . We also need a free banking law similar to other States, and these things being had, St. Louis with her other great advantages will become the greatest of the manufacturing cities." Even Benton was softening his anti-bank stand. The Columbia Whig leader, James S. Rollins, wrote to Abiel Leonard: "You know the bargain has been for the antis to give us banks, repeal the usury laws — satisfy St. Louis in short — and the Whigs to give them Atchison for Senator. But it seems Bullion will do as much and ask no *quid pro quo*." With all factions united except the last-ditch backcountry farmers, the legislature in 1857 amended the constitution to permit ten banks of issue. Called a free-banking amendment, the legislation was still a conservative measure, with the combined banking capital limited to $20 million, notes restricted to denominations of five dollars or more, each bank's note issue limited to twice its paid-in capital, and the state authorized to buy stock in any or all of the banks. The General Assembly promptly rechartered the Bank of the State of Missouri and created the Exchange Bank, the Bank of St. Louis, the Merchant's Bank, the City Bank, the Mechanics' Bank, and the Southern Bank, all St. Louis banks authorized to establish at least two branches outstate. Other banks were established at Lexington and St. Joseph.

The free banking law followed a period of financial stress and preceded a nationwide panic and depression. Page and Bacon, the city's (and the West's) largest private bank, overextended itself and was forced to close in 1855. With several million dollars tied up in St. Louis and San Francisco real estate and the Ohio and Mississippi Railroad, Page and Bacon could not cover the Belcher brothers' default on their short-term paper. When its New York correspondent banks declined to extend further credit, Page and Bacon thought the damage to its reputation irreparable and did not attempt to reopen. Runs on Lucas and Simonds, L. A. Benoist, and other banks followed this debacle, but depositors were reassured when John How, John O'Fallon, Edward Walsh, C. P. Chouteau, James Harrison, and several other businessmen pledged their personal fortunes, aggregating more than $8 million, to guarantee the banks' deposits.

A sterner test came late in 1857, when, after the Crimean War, Russian wheat returned to the world market, and a credit squeeze in France, which diverted British capital from American railroads and banks, embarrassed eastern banks, many of which were overextended in speculative railroad loans. New York banks first tightened and then suspended credit, with Boston, Philadelphia, and Baltimore houses closely following. By early September, nervous depositors were lined up at St. Louis banks to withdraw their savings. As the bankers pressed their business debtors for payment, several large firms, including Chouteau, Harrison, and Vallé, closed their doors. On October 5, Lucas and Simonds capitulated, to "wind up the financial horrors" of the past three weeks, according to the *Republican*. Business houses and banks had closed, adding to the confusion, "but when the house of James H. Lucas and Co. was forced to suspend yesterday by the continual run upon it, as regular as the rain which fell throughout the day, men were amazed and scarcely knew what to think." Before the "horrors" were over, several private banks had failed, and the chartered banks of issue, even the Bank of Missouri, had suspended specie payments. For several months, St. Louis was hit hard, with business faltering and thousands of workers unemployed. When the New York banks resumed in December, those in St. Louis followed suit, and by spring the mills, wharves, and warehouses were humming again.

In addition to its financing problems, St. Louis's iron industry was hampered, despite the enormous supply near at hand, by the difficulty of getting the ore to St. Louis. Iron Mountain and Pilot Knob, both virtually solid masses of ore some eighty miles to the south, were landlocked, requiring a forty-mile wagon haul to Ste. Genevieve; and the Maramec Iron Works, the city's principal supplier of high-quality blooms, seventy-five miles to the southwest, could ship directly by the Meramec River to St. Louis for only a few weeks each year during the

View of the Pilot Knob. *Steel engraving by J. M. Kershaw after R. B. Price. From the* First and Second Annual Reports of the Geological Survey of Missouri, 1855. *MHS-PP.*

spring rise. At other times the Maramec blooms and cast-iron pigs had
to be hauled over the horse-killing, stump-filled "Wire Road" to the
city, or more often, over the forty-mile "Iron Road" to Hermann on the
Missouri River for transshipment to the rolling mills and foundries of
St. Louis. Pilot Knob was owned by Louis Vital Bogy of St. Louis and
a group of Ste. Genevieve investors, while Iron Mountain belonged to
the Iron Mountain Company, organized in 1845 by James Harrison of
St. Louis, an enterprising merchant and former Santa Fe trader.
Harrison's partners were Jules Vallé of the distinguished
Ste. Genevieve lead-mining and merchant family; Pierre Chouteau, Jr.,
of St. Louis; three nearby landowners; the wealthy New York
merchant Samuel Ward, William Astor's son-in-law; and August
Belmont, the American agent for the House of Rothschild (Chouteau's
business connections with the Astors commended him to New York
capitalists). Though they were separate enterprises, the Iron Mountain
Company and its blast furnaces were obviously closely connected
with Chouteau's, Harrison's, and Vallé's rolling mills and nail factory,
located near Bremen in north St. Louis. Eventually, the mills and blast
furnaces would concentrate in Carondelet, readily accessible both to
Iron Mountain and the Illinois coal fields, but in the early 1850s the
two hundred million tons of ore at Iron Mountain, the largest mass in
the largest iron region then known in the world, waited for the coming
of the Iron Horse.

Only a few hundred miles of railroad track had been laid in the
United States on April 20, 1835, when delegates from eleven
Missouri counties met to discuss railroad construction in Missouri at
the St. Louis courthouse. Dr. Samuel Merry presided, and John
O'Fallon, Pierre Chouteau, Jr., Hamilton R. Gamble, and several
other St. Louisans attended this convention, which recommended that
two railroads be built from St. Louis, one to Fayette in the center of
the state, and the other to the iron and lead district. After the St. Louis
county court had appropriated two thousand dollars for a survey of
these lines, a second convention was called in 1836. Boston interests,
then planning a network of roads to counter New York's commercial
advantages gained from the Erie Canal, sent a representative to
St. Louis to urge Missourians to join the internal improvements
parade. After a series of enthusiastic speeches and some discussion,
the convention petitioned the Missouri legislature to charter the
previously endorsed lines and appropriate five hundred thousand
dollars toward their construction.

Dominated by the anti-bank, anti-corporation sentiments of Bentonian democracy, Missouri's lawmakers had been reluctant previously to give charter privileges to any business corporation. Now, with the exertions of James B. Bowlin in the House and lobbying pressure from Dr. Merry, William Carr Lane, John F. Darby, the lead magnate George F. Collier, Daniel Page, and Samuel Massey of the Maramec Iron Works, they changed course. At its 1836–37 session, the General Assembly chartered not only the Iron Mountain and central Missouri lines, but sixteen others as well, plus eleven turnpike companies, all intended to connect outside agricultural and mineral areas to St. Louis, either directly or via the Missouri and Mississippi Rivers. Three more railroads were chartered in 1838, but the state's slender revenues and the dampening effect of the depression precluded the appropriation of state funds for construction.

Returning prosperity had sparked a revival of the railroad fever by 1846, and for more than a decade it raged through the Missouri legislature, until eighty charters had been granted for lines running to or through every aspiring hamlet in the state. Most of these railroads were pipe dreams, but those which could attract governmental support would survive. First to be chartered in 1847 was the Hannibal and St. Joseph, projected to cross the northern part of the state. In March 1849 the Pacific Railroad was incorporated, to run from St. Louis to Missouri's western boundary. This activity coincided with, and was in part inspired by, the widespread interest in a trans-western railroad, the "passage to India," as Mississippi valley boosters thought of it, that followed the acquisition of Oregon and California. Following the California gold strike, the interest became a passion with many.

Missourians regarded the Far West as their special preserve, its interests their interests, and its development as part of their future. With Benton's unqualified support, Missouri's Lewis F. Linn devoted his senatorial career, from 1837 to 1843, to the encouragement of American settlement in Oregon, with his ultimate goal the acquisition of the entire territory by the United States. Senator Benton was considered the best-informed public man in Washington on the geography and resources of the Rocky Mountains and the Pacific Coast (very few others knew anything at all about the subject). His son-in-law, John C. Fremont, outfitted three far western expeditions at St. Louis for the Army Topographical Survey, and a fourth after his resignation from the army in 1848. With Kit Carson as his guide, Fremont mapped, observed, and collected biological and geological specimens in the Wind River Range of Wyoming, the Great Basin, the Columbia River valley, and the Oregon and California coasts. On his third expedition, Fremont engaged in subversion against Mexico, then fought against the Mexicans, served for a month as military governor there, and got into trouble for disregarding the orders of a superior officer (Colonel Stephen Watts Kearny).

When Fremont was court-martialed, found guilty of gross insubordination, and dismissed from the army, Benton pressed the president hard for a reversal. The senator had been Polk's principal adviser on the Oregon settlement and during the war; he was a power in Washington and in the Democratic Party; and few persons cared to risk the searing blast of his displeasure, or the angry tongue and pen of the fiercely loyal, talented, and beautiful Jessie Benton Fremont. The hapless president tried to compromise—he upheld the court's guilty verdict, but he restored Fremont's army commission. All to no avail— the hot-blooded Fremont promptly resigned his commission and Benton consigned Polk to political purgatory. Jessie and her Galahad returned to St. Louis, where he organized another expedition, this one financed by Benton and some of his St. Louis friends for the purpose of finding and mapping potential railroad passes through the Sierra Nevadas. When California applied for admission to the Union as a free state in 1850, Benton led a successful fight in the Senate to keep the question separate from the political hot potatoes included in Henry Clay's Omnibus Bill. Senator John C. Fremont returned in triumph to Washington later that year, representing the free state of California.

There had been public discussion of a railroad to the Pacific in the 1830s, but not until 1845 did it descend from dream-stuff to a serious public issue. Asa Whitney, a New York merchant who had just returned from China, where he had been sizing up the market for American goods (American merchants had been guaranteed access to Chinese treaty ports in 1844), suggested that a railroad be built from Lake Michigan to the mouth of the Columbia River, with the Chinese trade as its major objective. This northern route commended itself to New Yorkers for two reasons: Oregon was the only point on the Pacific accessible to Americans in 1845, and an eastern terminus on Lake Michigan would guarantee northeastern domination of the China trade, as a location at St. Louis or farther south would not. Construction costs, which Whitney estimated at $65 million, would be financed by a congressional land grant sixty miles wide for the road's entire length (2,160 miles), which he would then sell to settlers. Even Jacques Clamorgan would have paused—Whitney wanted a federal gift larger than Missouri and Illinois combined, or the six New England states plus New York and New Jersey.

Tennessee, Kentucky, and Cincinnati interests favored a southern route to the Pacific, with Memphis as its eastern terminus, while Deep South partisans supported New Orleans. When the Arkansas legislature announced for Memphis early in 1849, St. Louisans girded for battle. The city's central location and western commercial preeminence made it the logical terminus for a Pacific railroad, they reasoned, and the nation needed to be reminded of it. In February 1849 Thomas Hart Benton proposed in the Senate that a railroad be built from St. Louis to San Francisco with a branch to the Columbia River. He reminded his colleagues that he had proposed a national far western road under military protection before railroads were ever heard of, and now his Fremont had demonstrated the practicality of such routes. Instead of making "a great national work of this kind a matter of stockjobbing" with huge profits to private companies at the expense of the people, the federal government should build and own the railroad, paying for it by the sale of public lands, especially in California and Oregon. This bill astonished the editor of the Palmyra *Missouri Whig*, who asked, "What is this, ye hypocrites, but good, old . . . solid and sterling Whig doctrine? . . . the principles you have fought against and kept down by baseborn and low-flung calumniation . . . ? What has become of the doctrine that Congress had no power to make internal improvements? Is not all Missouri Locofocodom on the tiptoe of anxiety to show how devout they are in spirit to make a railroad a mile wide and 2,500 miles in length, at the cost of probably 200 millions of dollars? And is not every foot of this road to be made by Congress?"

A few weeks after Benton introduced his railroad bill, on March 12, 1849, the General Assembly chartered the Pacific Railroad Company, authorized "to construct a railroad from St. Louis to the city of Jefferson, and thence to some point on the western line of Van Buren (Cass) County, in this state, with the view that the same may be continued hereafter westwardly to the Pacific Ocean." The incorporators were twenty-one of the city's business leaders, with Thomas Allen, James H. Lucas, Daniel D. Page, and John O'Fallon the most active. Despite the cholera and fire disasters, interest in the Pacific Railroad did not wane. In June, at a mass meeting called by Major James Barry and the city council, it was decided to invite representatives from all the states to St. Louis on October 15, to consider the construction of telegraph and railroad lines from St. Louis to San Francisco Bay, convention costs to be paid by the city and county of St. Louis. Thomas Allen prepared the convention's promotional literature, which was circulated nationally. Without a convenient connection with the rest of the nation, Allen reasoned, the Pacific region might establish a separate republic which would then dominate the whale fisheries and the trade with China. A project of such magnitude required the national government to carry it out, to perpetuate the Union and extend "the noble cause of civil and

Thomas Allen. *Steel engraving by Samuel Sartain, 1883. MHS-PP.*

religious liberty, civilization and humanity." Thus was the manifest destiny of the republic enlisted in the cause of iron rails west from St. Louis. Because it was centrally located, building the national railroad and telegraph lines from St. Louis would be "useful and most acceptable to all parts of our country."

When the convention assembled in the rotunda of the courthouse on October 15, it was clear that the most distant parts of the republic were not yet fully committed to the Pacific Railroad. By the third day, 1,056 delegates had arrived; 530 from Missouri, 367 from Illinois, 75 from Iowa, 37 from Indiana, 18 from Pennsylvania, and one or more from Kentucky, Ohio, Tennessee, Michigan, New York, Virginia, Maryland, New Jersey, Wisconsin, and Louisiana. At the outset, a contest developed between Missouri and Illinois delegates, the first pressing for St. Louis as the eastern terminus, the latter endeavoring to prevent it. Knowing that it was hopeless to propose an exclusive northern route to Lake Michigan, Illinois Senator Stephen Douglas favored a compromise. Douglas was elected president of the convention, but he resigned when he sensed a St. Louis plot to keep him out of the floor debates. Former Whig Mayor John F. Darby, who carried to Benton an invitation to address the convention, recorded Benton's disdain for Douglas in his *Personal Recollections:* "Douglas can never be president, sir. His legs are too short, sir. His coat, like a cow's tail, hangs too near the ground, sir."

On the second day of the convention, to tumultuous applause, Benton rose to speak. With his usual heavy documentation, he went on for hours about the need for a central railroad to the Pacific, between the thirty-eighth and thirty-ninth parallels (where St. Louis and San Francisco can both be found). The road should be "national in its location, by being central—national in its construction, being made by the nation—national in its title, by belonging to the nation." In closing, Benton theatrically proposed a great statue of Columbus on a mountain peak above the road, "pointing with outstretched arm to the western horizon, and saying to the flying passenger, there is the East! there is India!" Benton won the oratorical honors, but the delegates, convinced by Douglas and others that designating a single eastern terminus would reduce the railroad's chances in Congress, resolved that it was the duty of the national government to provide for a central national railroad from the Mississippi valley to the Pacific, with branches to St. Louis, Memphis, and Chicago. Thomas Allen prepared the memorial to Congress, which requested that body to build a "national railroad, electric telegraph, and a line of military posts across the central parts of the continent, from the Mississippi to the Pacific Ocean . . . as a commercial link, bringing Europe and Asia into contact through the heart of our North American Continent, and becoming the greatest common carrier of the world—our own country, the half-way house upon the highway of nations. . . ."

Under its state charter, the Pacific Railroad Company was authorized to issue $10 million in capital stock. As soon as two hundred thousand dollars had been subscribed, the company could elect officers and begin to function. On January 21, 1850, at a meeting of the incorporators, James H. Lucas offered to be one of three persons to make up half of the required two hundred thousand dollars in initial subscriptions. John O'Fallon and Daniel D. Page accepted the challenge, and O'Fallon won the coin toss for the honor of becoming the leading subscriber. He took $33,400 in stock; Lucas and Page $33,300 each; Thomas Allen, Edward Walsh, Joshua Brant, and George Collier $10,000 each; James Yeatman and A. L. Mills $5,000 each; Wayman Crow $2,500; and Adolphus Meier $1,500. The books were opened to the public from February 4 to February 12. When all of the pledges were in, $350,500 had been subscribed. James Harrison, Louis Labeaume, Joseph Charless, Jr., and John Simonds subscribed $5,000 each, and John B. Sarpy and Kenneth McKenzie (king of the upper Missouri), $2,500 each. The *Republican*'s editors chipped in $2,000, and various others from $1,000 to $3,000; but most of the balance was collected in small amounts by door-to-door volunteers. In May, the city of St. Louis subscribed five hundred thousand dollars in bonds to the Pacific Railroad, underlining the nature of the enterprise as a civic project. Private subscribers had been motivated by civic duty and indirect benefits rather than direct profit, since it was assumed that no dividends would be paid for many years.

In March 1850 the stockholders elected Thomas Allen, John O'Fallon, James H. Lucas, Louis Labeaume, Edward Walsh, James Yeatman, George Collier, Daniel Page, and Mayor Luther M. Kennett directors of the company. The directors then chose Allen as president and Labeaume as secretary. Allen, who had been the leading spirit of the project from its beginning, brought promotional talent and unflagging energy to the task. Born in Pittsfield, Massachusetts, in 1813, he graduated from Union College and studied in the distinguished New York law office of Cambreling and Hatch before being admitted to the New York bar in 1835. Having contributed articles to newspapers and edited the *Family Magazine* while studying law, Allen agreed to combine his literary and legal talents to compile a digest of the court decisions of the state of New York. In 1837 Allen established *The Madisonian*, a journal of political commentary, in Washington, and shortly thereafter, he won the public printing contract for the United States. Five years later, having decided that great opportunity awaited him in the West, he opened a law office in St. Louis. Sure enough, he had guessed right. In July 1842 he married Ann C. Russell, daughter of the master land speculator of the territorial period, William C. Russell. By 1851, Allen's taxable property within the city limits was assessed at $374,600 (by no means his total wealth). Only Peter Lindell, Ann Lucas Hunt, James H. Lucas, and Daniel Page had more city property. The marriage was a boon to St. Louis — Allen invested Russell's money in productive enterprise and gave substantial sums for civic improvement, neither of which had held much appeal for his father-in-law.

As president of the Pacific Railroad, Allen traveled extensively in the state, drumming up support among the farmers in the county seat towns and in Jefferson City, and creating a constituency for himself. He sought not only subscriptions to the Pacific Railroad's stock, but also political support for state aid to railroads. Later in 1850, Allen was elected to the state senate — part of his railroad strategy. As chairman of the internal improvements committee, Allen proposed a comprehensive system of state-aided railroads, to no one's surprise. This proposal envisioned six such roads, three with terminals in St. Louis and the others connected to the first three and to the rivers.

He emphasized the superiority of rails to the shifting, snagged, and sandbarred Missouri, and the ultimate connection they would have to the East via the projected Illinoistown (East St. Louis) to Cincinnati road (the Ohio and Mississippi, in which he, John O'Fallon, Daniel Page, and other St. Louisans were interested). In February 1851 the state awarded loans of $2 million in 6 percent state bonds to the Pacific and $1.5 million to the Hannibal and St. Joseph railroads. The advantage to the companies lay in the superiority of the state's credit to their own. Initially, the railroads were required to sell these bonds at par or higher in the eastern or European capital markets—their own bonds would have been discounted heavily if they sold at all. In return for its loans, the state received first liens on the railroads, and, more important, St. Louis and the state would benefit from the rise in land values and commercial and industrial activity.

On February 9, 1850, Allen and his board also asked Congress for a donation of a right-of-way and public lands adjacent to the line, the latter to be sold to help finance construction. At the time, Congress had never given land to any railroad, but it was considering a grant to the Illinois Central, which was awarded in September. After failing at first, the Pacific and the Hannibal and St. Joseph combined their requests. The latter had strong eastern support, and the Pacific directors, having learned from their first experience, paid seventy-five hundred dollars to each of "two men who knew the proper steps to get bills through." St. Louis "won the elephant," on June 10, 1852. Each company was granted alternate sections of public land six miles deep on each side of its right-of-way, to be awarded gradually as construction progressed. The state bonds were also released in steps— fifty thousand dollars at a time after $1.5 million in stock had been sold. By December 1851, this goal had been achieved, with subscriptions from the city, county, and individuals.

After considering several routes, the Pacific selected a southwestern exit from St. Louis, from Fourteenth Street west along the Mill Creek Valley; southwest to Cheltenham (Sulphur Springs), five miles from the courthouse, and Kirkwood Station (fourteen miles); then into the Meramec valley and along the north side of the river to Franklin (now Pacific), thirty-seven miles from St. Louis. This constituted the first division, with the second projected from Franklin to Jefferson City.

Formal ground-breaking ceremonies for the pioneer trans-Mississippi railroad were held on July 4, 1851. The ritual began with a parade from Fourth and Washington to Mincke's Grove, near Chouteau's Pond at Fifteenth Street, featuring ten carriages of state, city, and railroad dignitaries; the St. Louis Grays and other militia companies; the fire companies and the benevolent societies; in all about two thousand people. At the grove the military bands played the "Grand Pacific Railroad March," composed for the occasion. More than twenty thousand people heard Thomas Allen predict that by its second year of operation the Pacific would outstrip the Missouri River in moving freight and passengers to and from St. Louis. Edward Bates, the featured speaker, predicted that the railroad would unlock an "immeasurable store of mineral treasures" and clear the way to California, Oregon, and the "Old Eastern World." Mayor Luther M. Kennett then threw the first shovelful of earth into Chouteau's Pond.

Construction contracts were let the next day, and the right-of-way to Kirkwood was purchased from private owners for $150,000. This large sum boded ill for the original estimate of $6 million for the completion of the Pacific. Labor costs also became a problem, as cholera fatalities created a shortage that drove wages from $.75 to $1.25 a day. By September nearly one thousand men were at work on the roadbed. The first shipment of rails arrived from London in April 1852 and the first locomotive, the *Pacific*, from Taunton, Massachusetts, in August. This twenty-two–ton engine cost nine thousand dollars delivered. Though its first cars were ordered from Troy, New York, the Pacific's rolling stock thereafter was manufactured by S. B. Lowe and other St. Louis carmakers. Palm and Robertson of St. Louis built their first locomotive for the Ohio and Mississippi Railroad in 1853, and by 1859 they had built seven of the Pacific's twenty-six locomotives.

On December 9, 1852, the first whistle of a moving train west of the Mississippi split the St. Louis air as the *Pacific* and two cars pulled out for Cheltenham. The road was opened to Kirkwood in May, and in July 1853 the first division was completed. Each step was an occasion for celebration, since counties along the route had subscribed to stock, and the people felt the pride of ownership and grand adventure as their first locomotive puffed down the track. High costs were a continuing problem, however, one annoyance being the speculators who dogged the surveyors, purchasing public land and preventing the company from realizing the full benefit from its federal grant (awarded only in increments after the line surveys were completed). Other costly delays were caused by fighting and rioting among the workers, on one occasion so serious that the St. Louis militia had to be called out. In December, the legislature granted another $1 million to the Pacific, and by the time the second division was completed to Jefferson City in 1855, nearly $8 million had been expended, and the rails were less than halfway across the state.

At this crucial point, the Pacific suffered its first major disaster. An eleven-car excursion train loaded with officials and prominent guests plunged into the Gasconade River near Hermann, a brand-new and well-tested 904-foot wooden bridge having collapsed as the twenty-eight–ton locomotive *Missouri* hit it at fifteen miles an hour. The locomotive, baggage car, and two passenger cars went into the river, a third car dangled from an abutment, and except for the last car, the rest of the train crunched down the steep roadbed. Thirty-one passengers were killed and seventy severely injured. Among the dead were Thomas O'Sullivan, the chief construction engineer, who had been in the cab; Calvin Case, of the omnibus company; Henry Chouteau; E. C. Yosti, a prominent merchant; and several state legislators. Mayor Washington King, John M. Wimer, L. A. Benoist, Wayman Crow, and Congressman Luther M. Kennett were among those injured. Hudson E. Bridge, who had succeeded Thomas Allen as president, was riding in the locomotive cab, but he miraculously escaped with a few scratches. As a further insult, another bridge gave way on the return trip the next day, fortunately just after those able to do so had walked across it and before the train with the injured and dead had started across.

While the Gasconade tragedy did not enhance the Pacific's reputation, it did not dampen the state's interest. In December 1855 the unflagging legislature awarded the railroad another $3 million in bonds, and the bridges were rebuilt with stronger supports. Considerable criticism of the state's generosity was developing, some of it directed at the slow progress of railroad-building and some doubting the usefulness of railroads to ordinary citizens. Columbia's *Missouri Statesman* defended public aid in 1853: "Railroads . . . pay in multiplied other forms beside the mere percent in money on their prime cost. . . . Show that the railroad will pay! Do not the opening of common roads and the building of bridges pay? Do not the erection of churches and school houses . . . pay? Not truly in percents directly paid into the pockets of those who subscribe, but indirectly in the enhancement of the value of property, the increase of facilities, religious, educational, and commercial." Governor Robert M. Stewart, one of the promoters of the Hannibal and St. Joseph, told the legislature in 1859 that "the foolish cry of oppressive taxation" had been raised, but that the completion of the trunk roads would make Missouri "the Central Empire State of the Union."

The railroad bond market, deteriorating in the mid-1850s, collapsed in 1857, virtually halting construction on the Pacific. When sales resumed in 1858, the rails began to stretch westward, and by August 1860 the line had been completed to Otterville, 176 miles west

of St. Louis. After the Civil War started, construction came to a
standstill, with the company hardpressed to repair or replace the
property destroyed or damaged by Confederate troops and irregulars.
Pro-Confederate Governor C. F. Jackson partially destroyed the Osage
and Gasconade bridges and tore up the track west of Jefferson City
before he decamped in 1861. Despite Union troops guarding the line
occasionally, General Joseph Shelby's raiders and "Bloody Bill"
Anderson's guerrillas stabbed, punched, and punished the Pacific and
its employees for the next three years. In 1864, in a last desperate
sortie into Missouri, General Sterling Price's frustrated army
demolished Pacific bridges, depots, tracks, and rolling stock worth
more than a million dollars. After Price's defeat at Westport and pell
mell retreat from the state, construction went forward, and the 283-
mile railroad reached Kansas City in 1865. Since the company had no
funds, the directors personally paid for the rolling stock added in
1865, and directors Hudson E. Bridge, Robert Campbell, and David
Rankin bought the land and paid for the building of depots and
machine shops for the Kansas City terminal.

The Pacific had spent $14.38 million in construction, rolling
stock, and capital replacements by 1867, financed by $7 million in
state bonds (sold for $6.3 million); $3.61 million in stock sales
(individuals, nearly all from St. Louis, had bought $1.38 million,
St. Louis city and county, $1.61 million, Jackson County, $275,000,

Hudson E. Bridge. *Steel engraving by A. H. Ritchie, 1883. MHS-PP.*

and other counties, $349,000); land sales, $131,860; and direct borrowing, $3.35 million ($700,000 from St. Louis County and the rest from individuals, especially after the state released its lien on the western division in 1864). Some capital expenditures had come from earnings. Since 1859 the Pacific had defaulted on its interest payments, and by 1867 it owed the state $11.33 million. Many legislators wanted the state out of the railroad business, and the Union Pacific, building westward from Council Bluffs, gave them an opening by offering $10.45 million for the Pacific, with $4 million to the state and the rest to other creditors and stockholders. Even before and during the war, the Pacific had shown a small operating profit, and its net earnings had risen to $699,000 in 1866 and $857,000 in 1867. Further large gains were probable as the rich western Missouri farmland came back into cultivation. Another favorable development was the establishment of a connection with the Union Pacific at Kansas City, though the Pacific tracks had yet to be adjusted from the wide (5' 6") gauge to the standard (4' 8.5") gauge.

In addition to the Union Pacific, the rapacious Jay Gould of the Erie and Thomas Scott of the Pennsylvania Railroads were sniffing around the Pacific, alarming the directors and stockholders in St. Louis. It would neither be fair nor reasonable, they argued, to let eastern capitalists harvest the crop that St. Louis and the state had sown. Why should the state not sell its lien to the company itself for $4 million, the amount it would receive from the Union Pacific? Unfortunately, there were problems in Jefferson City. A joint legislative committee in 1867 had recommended that the state not sell its interest for less than $8.35 million; the influential Radical newspaper, the *Missouri Democrat*, opposed selling the state's lien, especially for less than it was worth; and, most serious, the Radical majority in the legislature disliked the Pacific's directors, most of whom were Conservatives (Union Democrats) who had opposed the Radicals' punitive measures against former Confederates. Accordingly, on November 30, 1867, the directors commissioned president George R. Taylor, vice-president Daniel Garrison, and Henry Patterson to go to Jefferson City, "and there, . . . obtain such legislation as will enable this Board . . . to purchase of the state its claim upon this company" for $4 million or as near to it as possible. They could "employ such persons to assist them as they may deem useful, and in all things to do whatsoever . . . they may consider expedient or necessary to secure the success of their mission."

Pursuant to these broad-gauged instructions, the committee charted a course that could have served as a "how to" manual on railroad politics in the Gilded Age, if not on business and politics in any age. Taylor and his cohorts reported to the board after their mission that they had "first secured favorable consideration of our scheme" by the St. Louis press after "many conferences, much delay, and anxiety." Next they employed men of "such . . . standing and power with the dominant party in the legislature as would soften down or remove the 'Copperhead' character attributed to our Board." These St. Louis Radical luminaries were "willing for a 'sufficient consideration' to abandon their own business and undertake ours." When they arrived in Jefferson City in January, the committee "met hostility most violent and unaccountable" from several St. Louis legislators. "Scandalous rumors" hounded them, and they were denounced as "thieves" and "Those Railroad Kings." To combat the move for state seizure, the committee employed eminent lawyers, including Senator Charles D. Drake (the arch-Radical author of the 1865 state constitution), who testified that seizure before 1870 would be illegal. This was "somewhat costly, but we think it paid well." The "seizing fever" soon abated. Next, the committee portrayed the company as being in "crippled condition," unable to continue unless the state sold its lien. Progress was slow, but by "persevering . . . till past midnight week after week ably assisted by the numerous parties *'engaged' for the purpose* we were at length let in upon the secret of how things are sometimes done. . . . It was terribly costly for an ordinary job but as we were going for millions . . . we determined . . . not to fail." The "morality of such proceedings," the committee left "to those who have inaugurated the proceedings and divided its gains."

On March 31, 1868, the state sold its $11.33 million investment in the Pacific Railroad to the company for $5 million. This victory had cost the company $57,313.60 "already paid, and $134,865 to be paid, . . . this cost in dollars is by no means all, for it cost the committee an amount of anxious labor, pain and degradation, that they will never again willingly undergo. . . ." In closing, the committee thanked Senators George H. Rea (just made a Pacific director), Stephen Ridgeley, J. G. Woerner, and H. C. Spaunhorst, and Representatives G. C. Van Wagoner, C. H. Branscomb, C. R. Smythe, and Norman J. Colman, for their "devotion to our interests." The committee did not identify their well-paid Radical assistants. Taylor, Garrison, and Patterson had earned the gratitude of their colleagues — they had saved the company at least $3 million. Jesse and Frank James robbed a Pacific train at Otterville in the 1870s, but they took only a few thousand dollars. One disgruntled legislator had moved during the debate to retitle the bill "an act to . . . give away two million dollars to the [Pacific Railroad] company."

Widespread rumors of bribery forced the legislative leaders to appoint a joint committee to investigate and report its findings on March 24. J. G. Woerner, one of the Pacific's "devoted friends," was a leader of this committee, which heard testimony from S. W. Cox, who admitted that he had offered money to legislators for their votes, but without "the slightest assurance that the railroad company . . . would furnish a single dollar with which to buy votes." Taylor and Garrison both swore at the hearing that they knew nothing about anything improper. After the farce was played out, the joint committee reported that their one-day investigation had turned up no evidence that any legislator had taken, nor that any railroad man had offered, a bribe.

Hudson Bridge, who had been at odds with the board majority for several years, was appalled at the committee's "unblushing admission of bribery and corruption" and strenuously objected to a resolution expressing "hearty approval" of its actions. Directors James H. Lucas, James Harrison, Charles H. Peck, Oliver A. Hart, Joseph Brown, George H. Rea, Benjamin Stickney, and Timothy Edgar voted aye; Bridge and Robert Barth, nay; and the committee members abstained. Bridge then moved against further payments to the committee's "employees," and again he was supported only by Barth. His only recourse was to go outside of the board, and he promptly did so on April 16, 1868, by notifying New York bondholders of the situation and offering to join them in legal action. Bridge also asked Thomas Allen to join him in a stockholder's suit, but Allen refused, noting that stockholders would have to prove they had been personally damaged by the committee's conduct. He did point out, however, that the bribe money did not have to be paid, since an illegal contract was unenforceable. At the next board meeting, Lucas offered and the directors passed a resolution requesting Bridge to desist, as his course "reflects seriously upon each of them in their official and private relations, both here and abroad." When Bridge refused, Henry Patterson moved to censure him, saying that he wanted to injure the company "for ulterior and sinister" reasons (control of the company). The motion passed, ten ayes to one nay (Barth). Patterson's purpose was to force Bridge to resign, but he would not.

Robert Lamb, a stockholder, and the trustees for the New York bondholders, acting upon Bridge's information, then sought and obtained a temporary injunction barring payment of the $134,865 still owed to the legislators and lobbyists. In October 1868 Judge R. E. Rombauer of the United States Circuit Court made the injunction perpetual, ruling that since the Pacific's directors had not answered the allegations that they had committed bribery in incurring the debt, the charges were to "be taken as confessed by them and each of them." Taylor resigned as president in September, and Garrison was elected, confirming the dominance of the manipulators on the board. Garrison modestly declined in favor of James H. Lucas, whose immense wealth and prestige would guarantee public respectability (Garrison was a bit edgy, having been advised by William B. Napton that he would have to take the Fifth Amendment if questioned in court about his activities in Jefferson City). Although he did not believe that Lucas had or would use his position for personal gain, Hudson Bridge was not happy with the new president, knowing that Lucas would continue to support H. L. Patterson, who was not only his former employee but also the husband of his niece, the former Theodosia Hunt.

Bridge's relentless digging further revealed that Garrison and Patterson were at the head of an insider's ring that had been milking the Pacific since 1866. After a meeting with Garrison, Thomas Scott of the Pennsylvania Railroad and two of his associates had created the St. Louis and Pacific Fast Freight Express Company (the White Line). Garrison and Patterson then persuaded the Pacific's directors to approve a contract permitting the White Line to route its own cars on Pacific trains, carrying first and second class freight at third and fourth class rates. As it worked out, the White Line collected $120 a car for shipments to Kansas City and paid the railroad $56. Since it operated only on the Pacific line, the White Line performed no services for the company, obtaining no business the railroad would not have had anyway. Scott had sold Garrison, Patterson, G. H. Rea, Oliver Hart, and C. H. Peck of the Pacific's board fifty shares each of the White Line's one hundred dollars par stock and Benjamin Stickney twenty-five shares, all for fifty dollars a share. When the railroad's superintendent refused a gift of fifty shares, he was fired. The new superintendent, H. C. Moore, gladly accepted. George R. Taylor denied owning any White Line stock, but as it happened, his brother-in-law did. These shares paid dividends of 2 percent of their par value a month, or twenty-four hundred dollars a year on the directors' five thousand dollar investments. Small wonder that these insiders were willing to pay nearly two hundred thousand dollars of the railroad's money to prevent state seizure. The seven ring members controlled the board, with the unvarying support of Lucas, Harrison, Joseph Brown, and Timothy Edgar—Harrison, because of outside ties with the ring and with Lucas, according to Bridge, and Brown and Edgar out of deference to the powerful majority.

Bridge also accused Garrison of other peculations, such as submitting false vouchers and using the jerry-built Missouri River

Railroad he had laid between Kansas City and Leavenworth to enrich Taylor, Patterson, and himself at the expense of the credulous Kansans. A New Englander of Puritan background, a "real go-getter," Garrison had gained prestige as construction superintendent of the Ohio and Mississippi Railroad. He had also built the western end of the Pacific and had received a bonus of thirty thousand dollars for it (over Bridge's objections), despite having completed the job seven months after the qualifying date for the bonus.

To the majority's distress, Bridge kept worrying these issues, and eventually he exposed them in a letter to the stockholders and in a series of articles in the Missouri Democrat. There were no libel suits, but when Bridge accused Lucas of mismanaging a bond sale, Patterson, sitting next to him as if by pre-arrangement, punched and manhandled the old gadfly. Bridge had the last word, though: in 1869, when the board paid fifty thousand dollars each to Taylor, Garrison, and Patterson for their services in Jefferson City, he was impelled to buy St. Louis County's large holdings of Pacific stock, which gave him effective control of the company. First to go was the White Line; then Garrison exited; and then Bridge reorganized the board and became president. *Now* he was satisfied.

How could previously honorable men, if indeed they were, rationalize their corrupt and malodorous activities? As Bridge said, most of them could never have imagined themselves using bribery and criminal deception a few years earlier. The White Line had been imposed as a source of additional business, but Lucas and Harrison tolerated it even after it became clear that it existed only to line the pockets of the ring. True, the state had gained far more in wealth and growth from the building of the Pacific than it lost in selling its lien; the founders and original stockholders were motivated more by the larger interests of the community than by direct personal gain; and the company had performed valuable services for the nation during the recent war. But the insiders' ring had cheated the stockholders, their fellow citizens of St. Louis city and county, as the corrupt sale of the lien had cheated the state.

George R. Taylor, the Pacific's president since 1860 and a key figure in the $3 million heist, was one of a dozen men at the pinnacle of power and public respect in St. Louis. A Virginian who claimed descent from the British nobility, he had been a real estate developer since 1846 when he had married Theresa Paul, grand daughter of Auguste Chouteau. He had built Barnum's Hotel on the old Laclède block in 1854 and he had played a leading role in the building of the Merchant's Exchange. After being narrowly defeated by the Republican O. D. Filley in the mayoral race in 1859, he turned his attention to railroads.

A contemporary sketch written shortly after his death in 1880 noted that he had left his heirs a "princely fortune," but he had "also left them a prouder inheritance, that of an unsullied name, and a reputation of being one of the most active and public-spirited citizens this city ever had." This *chevalier sans peur et sans reproche* was willing to bribe and deal "because we were after millions." Lucas and Harrison, even richer and more prestigious than Taylor, gave the trio *carte blanche* and endorsed their conduct in full knowledge of its corrupt character. According to Taylor's notes taken at an informal board meeting in December 1867, Bridge had objected vigorously to bribery, but he had finally agreed to as much as one hundred thousand dollars and offered to put up ten thousand dollars himself. If true, it appears that Bridge preferred personal bribery to using company funds, but it is possible that he was leading them on, knowing that his colleagues would never match his offer.

As for the legislators, it was astonishing how Radical passion for the state's honor and distaste for "Copperhead Railroad Kings" moderated under the subtle persuasions of the Pacific's agents. Senator J. G. Woerner did not require a bribe—he was a Conservative, a partner from the beginning. Woerner was a Westphalian German, an intellectual—dramatist, poet, novelist, writer of legal treatises, and a prominent Hegelian, associated in the 1870s with William Torrey Harris and Henry Brokmeyer in the St. Louis Philosophical Society. A contemporary writer emphasized Woerner's aversion to "the tricks of politics" and his "absolutely unsullied record," yet the Senator knew that Taylor and Garrison lied to his committee—he had been helping them. Senator George H. Rea, a White Line member who joined the Pacific's board during the debates, was a well-to-do steamboat owner of New England origins, the president of the Mississippi Valley Transport Company. Another "devoted friend," Norman J. Colman, was the publisher of the nationally popular *Colman's Rural World* and a curator of the University of Missouri.

The conspirators were Protestants, Catholics, Freethinkers; Yankees, Virginians, old-line St. Louisans; Radicals and Conservatives. They shared the conviction that control of the Pacific Railroad should stay in St. Louis and the belief that appropriate ends justify even criminal means. There were no prosecutions, but after the committee had finished, who was left to do the prosecuting? The initially hostile legislature had caved in by a three-to-one margin. Mark Twain and Charles Dudley Warner, in *The Gilded Age* (1873) charged that hypocrisy and greed had conquered America in the aftermath of the Civil War. The *Credit Mobilier* and Erie Railroad scandals, and other sordid examples of railroad politics, put the Pacific's directors in plenty of company, but national moral decline, railroad politics, and venal legislators notwithstanding, several of St. Louis's most distinguished citizens connived with lesser men and a few ingenious scoundrels to defraud the state by bribery and misrepresentation. The general outlines and some of the details of this affair became generally known, but the perpetrators suffered little damage to their public reputations.

The second line in the state railroad network proposed by Thomas Allen in 1850, the Hannibal and St. Joseph, broke ground at Hannibal in November 1851. Two steamboat-loads of St. Louisans attended, headed by the Grays, Mayor Kennett, and James Lucas, the last as a featured speaker. St. Louis was expected to benefit doubly from the cross-state road, from the river connection at Hannibal and via the North Missouri Railroad, which would intersect the Hannibal and St. Joseph in Macon County, seventy miles west of Hannibal. Heavily committed to the railroads originating in St. Louis, neither the city nor the county bought Hannibal shares, most of which were snapped up by Boston, New York, and Albany interests. These eastern investors were attracted by the rich

"Missouri is Free." *Chromolithograph advertisement for the Hannibal and St. Joseph Railroad, by Matthews and Warrick, Buffalo, N.Y., 1868. MHS-PP.*

soil of the North Missouri prairie, six hundred thousand acres of it in the federal grants to the railroad (worth five to ten times as much as the land in the Pacific's grant) and by the probability that the road would be tributary to the northeast via connecting Illinois railroads. Construction began in 1853, and though it went slowly during the financial crisis, it was completed in 1859, the first to reach the Missouri River above St. Charles. This 207-mile line was financed by $3 million in state bonds, $1.3 million in stock sales, and $5 million in the railroad's own bonds sold in the East on the security of its landholdings. By 1860, the Hannibal and St. Joseph was earning enough to make its annual interest payments to the state, and it was the only state-aided railroad to keep up its payments throughout the war.

Other than the Pacific, the most important lines to St. Louis were the St. Louis and Iron Mountain, the North Missouri, and the Ohio and Mississippi. The ore at Iron Mountain had given the first impetus to railroad building in Missouri, and initially there were no plans to extend the railroad beyond the iron region. John O'Fallon, James Harrison, Jules Vallé, Hudson Bridge, James Lucas, and others organized the Iron Mountain Railroad in 1851, and in 1853, when construction began, Luther M. Kennett was elected its president. It started at Second and Lamy (the terminal was moved a few months later to Main and Plum) on the near south side and passed through the Arsenal, Carondelet, and Jefferson Barracks before heading southwest through Jefferson County to the lead district of Washington and St. François Counties, past Iron Mountain to Pilot Knob. Because of the sparse population of the mineral region, the Iron Mountain was conceived initially as an ore and freight line, but its organizers saw it potentially as a link in a continuous railroad from New Orleans to the Falls of St. Anthony (Minneapolis).

There were serious construction problems: many bridges; several tunnels, one eight hundred feet long through solid rock; and one delay because Secretary of War Jefferson Davis insisted that only horse-drawn cars could pass through the Arsenal and Jefferson Barracks (Congress overruled him in 1856). The road was completed to Pilot Knob in 1858, having cost $5.5 million (financed by $3.51 million in state bonds and $1.97 million in stock subscriptions). St. Louis had taken $500,000 in stock; St. Louis County, $1 million; Carondelet, $50,000; the Madison Iron Company at Pilot Knob, $50,000; the American Iron Mountain Company (Chouteau, Harrison, and Vallé), $75,000; and $245,000 in individual subscriptions, mostly by St. Louis businessmen. Beginning in 1859, the Iron Mountain defaulted on its interest payments, and throughout the Civil War it suffered heavily from guerrilla harassment and attacks by the

Confederate raiders M. Jeff Thompson and Joe Shelby. Price's raid and the battle at Pilot Knob in 1864 were especially destructive.

In 1866 the state foreclosed its lien on four railroads, including the Iron Mountain. State commissioners operated the road for a few weeks before accepting a bid of $550,000 for the mineral area road and $350,000 for the Cairo and Fulton in the southeast corner of the state. The successful bidders were A. J. McKay and "others," the latter believed to be St. Louis Radical politicians. Charles P. Chouteau had offered Radical Governor Thomas C. Fletcher $1.28 million for the two roads only a few days before; John C. Fremont bid $1 million and Thomas Allen six hundred thousand dollars for the Iron Mountain alone; and a Pennsylvania iron industry combination's bid of $1.9 million was rejected as having been received a few hours too late. A month later, a great hue and cry arose when McKay sold the two properties to Thomas Allen for $1.275 million. McKay, a former army quartermaster of limited means, was obviously a front man for the "others" (Joseph C. Read, John C. Vogel, Samuel Simmons, and certain unnamed Radical politicians). One of this group's agents was John Farrar, whose brother, Bernard C. Farrar, was one of the three commissioners. There were rumors of a sixty thousand dollar "slush fund," but a legislative committee headed by the "investigative specialist" J. G. Woerner found no evidence of fraud. In his report, Woerner recommended that the state drop its lawsuit against Allen, pointing out that the state had gained its major objective by the building of the road and that further delays would prevent the extension of the line to Arkansas.

The highly regarded Allen had been an unsuccessful original bidder, and he had protested the award to McKay, which tended to remove suspicions that he had conspired with the latter. Probably he had not, but there is little doubt that the ring's quick profit of $375,000 had been the result of chicanery. By August 1869 Allen and his principal associate, Henry C. Marquard of New York, had extended the Iron Mountain to Belmont, Missouri, 195 miles south of St. Louis, where it was connected by a ferry that could handle three hundred cars a day to Columbus, Kentucky, the terminus of the Mobile and Ohio Railroad. In 1874 the Iron Mountain, the Cairo and Fulton, and the Cairo, Arkansas, and Texas lines were consolidated as the St. Louis, Iron Mountain, and Southern Railway. Allen's promotional and organizational genius had brought an enormous tributary territory to St. Louis, and had given it rail connections to New Orleans, Memphis, Mobile, and Charleston, South Carolina.

The incorporators of the North Missouri Railroad were chiefly residents of St. Charles, but the financing and control of the road

quickly passed to St. Louis. John O'Fallon became its president in
1853, and construction began the next year. Originally, the North
Missouri was to run directly from St. Louis to Macon County and then
due north to the Iowa line, where it would connect with a proposed
Iowa railroad. This route had to be changed, however, under pressure
from central Missouri interests headed by Governor Sterling Price. At
considerable added cost, the road was routed west to northern Boone
County before heading north. It was completed in 1858 to Macon, 168
miles from St. Louis, but funds were not available for further
construction until after the Civil War. Construction had been financed
by \$4.35 million in state bonds and \$1.25 million in stock
subscriptions from St. Louis city and county; \$1.04 million from
St. Charles, Boone, Warren, Audrain, Randolph, Macon, and other
counties; and \$307,500 from individuals. From Second and North
Market Street the line ran north to Bellefontaine Road, then northwest
through Bridgeton to the ferry landing at St. Charles.

Proportionately, the North Missouri suffered even more heavily
from guerrilla and Confederate activity during the war than the Pacific
and the Iron Mountain. Central Missouri north of the Missouri River
was Bill Anderson's "main stomping-ground," where he harassed and
murdered the railroad's employees and destroyed its property in a
three-year reign of terror. In 1861 General Price sent out-of-uniform
troopers to the North Missouri, where they recruited sympathizers and
destroyed one hundred miles of track, four bridges, rolling stock, and
depots. In conjunction with Price's raid in 1864, Anderson destroyed
two trains and murdered twenty-six unarmed Union soldiers on leave
whom he took from a train at Centralia. Although this guerrilla band
was not a part of the Confederate army, it was operating under Price's
orders in the fall of 1864.

At the end of the war in 1865, the state exchanged its first lien on
the North Missouri for a second mortgage, to enable the railroad to
complete its main line to Iowa and to build a western branch from
Moberly to Leavenworth and Kansas City. Henry Taylor Blow, Gerard
B. Allen, and other St. Louis directors bought the state's interest (now
representing \$6.96 million) for two hundred thousand dollars and
posted a personal bond of five hundred thousand dollars, guaranteeing
completion of the main line and the west branch. Shortly thereafter,
James B. Eads and Associates (E. D. Morgan and others of New York)
invested \$4 million in North Missouri bonds. By December 1868 the
main line was completed into Iowa, 241 miles from St. Louis.
President Isaac Sturgeon and other North Missouri directors had been
instrumental in 1866 in organizing the St. Louis and Cedar Rapids
Railroad as an extension of the North Missouri, and they had

The Grand Celebration of the Ohio and Mississippi Railroad, Arrival of the Excursion Train at Midnight Opposite St. Louis, the Guests Going on Board the Steamer Provided for their Accommodation by that City for the Night Previous to the Celebration. *Wood engraving from Frank Leslie's* Illustrated Weekly Newspaper, *June 20, 1857. MHS-PP.*

subscribed six hundred thousand dollars to its stock and arranged for the Missouri road to lease and operate the Iowa line. When completed in 1869, this northern extension gave St. Louis a direct railroad link to northern Iowa, Minnesota, and Wisconsin. The west branch reached the Kansas City and Cameron Railroad, 120 miles west of Moberly, late in 1868, giving it an entry to Kansas City. In 1870–71, following a general plan suggested by James B. Eads, a North Missouri director who had obtained eastern financing for the purpose, engineer H. Shaler Smith of Baltimore, constructed a $2 million railroad and wagon suspension bridge over the Missouri River at St. Charles. With its three 300-foot central spans, 53 feet above the high-water mark, this 2,200-foot marvel was considered an advanced example of bridge construction. Unfortunately, its career was marred by tragedy: eighteen workmen were killed in a construction accident, and spans collapsed twice, in 1879 and 1881, killing six persons.

The other major St. Louis railroad commitment, the Ohio and Mississippi, received five hundred thousand dollars from the city in the early 1850s and nearly as much from local individuals. John O'Fallon was the first president of its western section (the St. Louis and Vincennes), Andrew McGunnegle was vice-president, and Charles P. Chouteau, Daniel Page, Andrew Christy, and Luther M. Kennett were directors. Page and Bacon was heavily committed in Ohio and

Colonel John O'Fallon. *Daguerreotype by Thomas M. Easterly, ca. 1850. MHS-PP.*

Mississippi bonds. This railroad, completed in 1857, stimulated the rapid growth of East St. Louis and gave St. Louis a valuable connection to Cincinnati, southern Indiana, and Illinois, and to Baltimore via the nation's oldest railroad, the Baltimore and Ohio. St. Louis interests were also active in the Southwest Branch of the Pacific, which eventually became the St. Louis and San Francisco, and the Kansas Pacific, which linked the city to Denver and the Rocky Mountain region. The Southwest Branch, headed for a time by John C. Fremont, received a state loan of $4.5 million and a huge federal land grant of one million acres in Missouri.

At the conclusion of its state-aid program in the 1860s, Missouri, primarily at the instigation of St. Louis, had committed $23.7 million to railroad construction. With accumulated interest, this involvement had risen to $33.52 million by 1867. In return, the state had 914.2 miles of railway. By surrendering its liens for a total of $6.13 million, Missouri had made possible private financing, and by 1875, the network had been extended to more than three thousand miles. In the process, a fog of corruption enshrouded the legislature, the railroad promoters, and the railroads themselves, a fog that never fully cleared. To the degree that corruption became accepted as an inevitable part of the relations between government and business, the society itself was poisoned. If "progress" is the benchmark, irrespective of means, then Missouri's policy was a success. A vast new tributary territory, shipping raw materials to St. Louis and consuming its commercial goods and industrial products, was created in the South, Southwest, and West; and railroad connections were established in all parts of the state. In the upper Mississippi valley, St. Louis lost its former dominant position to Chicago, but not for want of trying.

St. Louis and St. Louis County governments contributed $6.15 million to state railway enterprises and five hundred thousand dollars to the Ohio and Mississippi. By 1870 local individuals had invested as much or more in the state system and its external connections in Illinois, Kansas, Iowa, Arkansas, and Texas. In 1947, Wyatt W. Belcher, in an influential book, *The Economic Rivalry Between St. Louis and Chicago, 1850–1880*, attributed Chicago's rise to economic supremacy in the Middle West primarily to the progressive, wide-awake, far-seeing leadership of Chicago's businessmen, as contrasted with the conservative and complacent St. Louis business leaders. In this formulation, St. Louis was dominated by French and old southern families who clung to ancient traditions and outmoded ideas, including over-reliance on the rivers and a stubborn "meridian" (north-south) orientation in commerce and trade. The Yankee go-getters of Chicago, on the other hand, overcame St. Louis's head start and natural advantages by a sheer burst of energy. Since Chicago did indeed overhaul St. Louis in size and wealth in the 1860s and 1870s, Belcher's thesis had a certain persuasiveness.

That William B. Ogden, J. Young Scammon, James F. Joy, and other hard-driving Yankees gave Chicago powerful leadership cannot be denied, but Belcher underplayed the Windy City's natural advantages. Strategically located on the south shore of Lake Michigan, it could gather in all traffic headed East from the upper Mississippi region. In addition, when John Deere of Moline developed his steel plow in the 1840s and 1850s, making it possible for farmers to break the tough prairie sod, Chicago found itself sitting side-by-side with the deepest, richest, and most productive black loam on the continent, if not in the world. St. Louis was the chief beneficiary of this technical advance at first, but these farmers yearned for quick access to the best markets in the industrial northeast, and St. Louis could not have reversed that fact if it had built a dozen railroads to Chicago's doorstep.

Chicago was closer and more accessible than St. Louis to New York and Boston, the major sources of developmental capital in the nation, and investments in rail lines centering there would naturally pull commerce to the northeast. New York was Chicago's natural trading partner, whether it shipped through the lakes and the Erie Canal or by westward-stabbing rail lines from the East. St. Louis, on the other hand, was tied to New Orleans and Cincinnati by water, and after the mid-fifties, to Baltimore by rail. Building Chicago at St. Louis's expense made sense in the East, and location was the determining factor.

The railroads that boomed Chicago were financed and, in some cases, conceived by easterners for their own advantage, and most of the Yankee geniuses Belcher refers to came after, not before, the eastern commitment to Chicago was made—Ogden, Scammon, and a few others excepted. The first of the Chicago roads, the Galena and Chicago Union, got its first impetus from western Illinois farmers and townsmen; of the first $250,000 it raised in stock subscriptions, Chicagoans put up $20,000 (8 percent). According to A. T. Andress in *The History of Chicago*, the merchants there feared a railroad would destroy their business. The Illinois Central Railroad was organized and promoted in the 1840s by Bloomington rather than Chicago interests; its principal officers were New Yorkers, John Murray Forbes of Boston helped finance it, and its first crucial $5 million bond issue was sold to British investors by New Yorkers. Forbes and James F. Joy of Detroit were the men of imagination and capital who built the vast Burlington system, and Joy moved to Chicago eventually only to run the railroad. The Rock Island line was conceived in Davenport, Iowa, and both it and the Chicago and Northwestern were financed in the East. The Rock Island's Iowa line (the Mississippi and Missouri) held its board meetings in New York.

St. Louis did not ignore railroads because of the rivers, as has been amply demonstrated. To be sure, steamboat and ferry interests feared and opposed Mississippi bridges, but they did not dominate St. Louis. As a group, St. Louis's merchants had divested themselves of most of their steamboat interests by the 1850s, and like merchants everywhere, they favored anything that strengthened the city and enriched themselves. Neither were they burdened with a north-south fixation; they were as susceptible to the charms of the "isothermal zodiac," the magic of the middle latitudes, as Chicagoans were, and they had heard its music first. Their first railroad investments were in east-west lines (Pacific, Ohio and Mississippi). Perhaps the most pervasive and erroneous of the St. Louis myths is the generalization that Creoles and genteel Southerners dominated and paralyzed St. Louis business in the 1850s and 1860s. This common error confuses social status with power. Southerners and Creoles were not in the majority in the higher realms of business, and those Southerners

James H. Lucas. *Photograph by J. A. Scholten, 1873. MHS-PP.*

who were economically powerful tended to be Lincolns rather than Lees. Even the latter type, men such as George R. Taylor and Henry Taylor Blow, were hawkish, hard-driving, and ambitious. While some Creoles by mid-century had withdrawn from the commercial arena, their inactivity left them with little public influence. The Clarks and their Virginia connections had their proud name, but they were neither especially rich nor powerful. Those of Creole descent who were active—Charles P. Chouteau, Jules Vallé, Louis Labeaume, and Louis Vital Bogy—beat the bushes for the railroads like any Yankee.

At the apex of economic power stood Thomas Allen, John O'Fallon, and James H. Lucas. Allen was a Massachusetts native, Lucas an old-line St. Louisan, and O'Fallon's father was an Irish gentleman-adventurer who had lived in Kentucky when John was born. Their commitment to railroads and their east-west orientation need no further elaboration. Below this peak, but wealthy and powerful, was a group of New Englanders: Hudson E. Bridge and Carlos Greeley of New Hampshire; John Simonds and Sullivan Blood of Vermont; the brothers Giles and O. D. Filley of Connecticut and their cousin Chauncey of New York; George Partridge and Henry Bacon of Massachusetts; and Daniel D. Page of Maine. From New York were

Daniel R. Garrison, Henry Ames, John M. Krum, Washington King, and George Knapp of the *Missouri Republican*. Kentuckians at this level included James Harrison, Isaac Sturgeon, John S. McCune, Luther M. Kennett, and Derrick A. January. Other business leaders included Taylor and Blow of Virginia; James E. Yeatman of Tennessee; Edward Walsh, Gerard B. Allen, and Robert Campbell of Ireland; William Glasgow of Delaware; James B. Eads of Indiana; John Withnell and Henry Shaw of England; John How and George Knapp of Pennsylvania; Barton Able of Illinois; Adolphus Meier, Robert Barth, John C. Vogel, Henry Kayser, and Henry Boernstein of Germany; and David Nicholson of Scotland. These individuals, irrespective of their origins, shared an east-west commitment to the Union during the Civil War. Some of them had emotional ties with the South, and many of them were moderates (Conservatives), favoring a conciliatory stance toward the South and slavery, but they knew where their city's and their own interests lay. Although a few lawyers and politicians (notably Trusten Polk, Uriel Wright, and Thomas C. Reynolds) cast their lot with the Confederacy, and the drastic measures taken by Frank Blair and Nathaniel Lyon and their German "Wide-Awakes" in 1861 offended many businessmen, they did not let sentiment or anger override their good judgment. William Glasgow, president of the Missouri Wine Company, a slaveowner whose wife, father-in-law (William Carr Lane—a Pennsylvanian), and other in-laws were furious Confederates, adopted a stance of amused tolerance toward his family and stuck by the Union.

Belcher was wrong about the origins of St. Louis's business leadership. He underplayed Chicago's locational advantages and eastern financing, and his characterization of the St. Louisans as complacent conservatives was inaccurate and unfair. They knew that Chicago was a dangerous rival in their northern and northwestern hinterland, and they eventually lost their dominant position there because of factors they could not control. Even the Southerners and Creoles who still mattered in the business community were like Yankees in the essentials. They had to be. When their grip on northern Illinois, Iowa, Minnesota, and Wisconsin was broken during the Civil War, they turned to the South and Southwest, and they and the city prospered. They hustled for business, and they took a back seat to no one, not even in the area of railroad corruption.

7.
For the Union

In the supercharged atmosphere of the late 1850s, with the nation torn by sectional issues, politics in St. Louis grew ever more complex. Benton's henchmen, Frank P. Blair and B. Gratz Brown, were ready to shift to the Republicans in 1856. Henry Boernstein of the *Anzeiger des Westens*, who had led some Germans into an alliance with Thomas C. Reynolds in 1854, swung back into the Benton camp as politics polarized around the slavery-extension issue. To his lieutenants' dismay, Benton rejected the Republicans as a sectional party and a threat to the Union. In supporting James Buchanan over John C. Fremont, his own son-in-law, Benton hoped that "old Buck" would steer a middle course toward sectional harmony. Blair and Brown agreed not to endorse Fremont, but they would not campaign for Buchanan. It made no difference—with both the proslavery Democrats and Benton in his corner, Buchanan was certain to carry Missouri.

When his ally John How was elected mayor in April 1856, the seventy-four-year-old Benton decided to try his luck again, this time running for governor against the proslavery "Ultra" Trusten Polk. Despite Benton's forty-day swing around the state lambasting the Nullifiers and the Kansas-Nebraska Act, Polk convinced the voters that the "Old Roman" was a stalking-horse for "Black Republicanism." Though he carried St. Louis easily, Benton was overwhelmed outstate. He was politically passé, his sectional-balance arguments no longer ringing true. The voters saw what he refused to see; the logic of his course since the late 1840s led to the antislavery Republican position. Benton wanted to save the Union without war; a majority of Missourians wanted the Union and slavery without war. With a cancer growing in his vitals, Benton worked feverishly to finish his sixteen-volume *Abridgment of the Debates of Congress*. His *Thirty Years' View*, a detailed account of "the workings of government" from 1820 to 1850, completed in 1856, had been a smash hit, enriching him "as public service never had." In 1857, Benton published a scathing denunciation of the Dred Scott decision. Old Bullion's last words before he died (April 10, 1858) were "I am content." He had reason to be pleased with the reaction to his prodigious writings and political achievements, but to the end he was annoyed with Blair and Brown for their openly emancipationist views. They knew, and his enemies

Trusten Polk, Thomas Reynolds, and Claiborne Jackson knew, that there would soon be no room in the middle, but Benton never knew.

The Dred Scott case, which burst upon the nation in 1856 and 1857, was old stuff in St. Louis. Scott, a slave belonging to the widow Irene Emerson, sued for his freedom in the circuit court at St. Louis in 1846, alleging that the Emersons had held him in slavery in the free state of Illinois and at Fort Snelling in the northern part of the old Louisiana Territory (now Minnesota). Scott had been advised by Henry Taylor Blow and Taylor Blow, who had grown up with him, and their brothers-in-law Joseph Charless, Jr., Charles E. Labeaume, and Louis A. Labeaume, that he was entitled to his freedom. The lower court agreed, but Mrs. Emerson appealed; and in 1852 the Missouri Supreme Court reversed the decision, Justice Hamilton R. Gamble dissenting. The lower court's decision had been based on earlier rulings, but in the interim, slavery in the territories had become political dynamite. Judge William Scott conceded that the Supreme Court was reversing itself, but times had changed and, as Judge Lawless had in the McIntosh affair, he blamed it all on the abolitionists.

In the meantime, Irene Emerson had married Calvin Chaffee, a Massachusetts abolitionist, and had left Dred Scott in St. Louis, working for C. E. Labeaume. A brilliant local attorney, Roswell Field, then took Scott's case to the federal courts, hoping to force a ruling on the constitutionality of the Missouri Compromise. Apparently unaware that Scott still belonged to Mrs. Chaffee, Field filed the suit against her brother, John F. A. Sanford of New York, who had been handling her affairs in St. Louis. Since Field and Chaffee were both antislavery men, it has been suggested, though not proven, that the federal suit was contrived as a friendly test case. Judge Robert S. Wells, of the U.S. Circuit Court at St. Louis, directed the jury to rule against Scott; but he committed a deliberate procedural error which permitted Field to appeal to the Supreme Court on a Writ of Error. At Field's request, Montgomery Blair, now a leading Washington attorney, represented the plaintiff before the high court in December 1856. Missouri Senator Henry S. Geyer and Reverdy Johnson of Maryland, at their own request, handled the defense. Scott's fate was now to be decided at the powerhouse level.

The Court, which was dominated by Southerners, including Chief Justice Roger B. Taney, considered the arguments for several weeks while the nation waited. Although the majority could have ruled against Scott on the simple grounds that he had forfeited any claim to freedom by returning to Missouri without resisting, it chose a revolutionary course, meeting all of the issues head-on. Taney's opinion denied Scott's right to sue in the federal courts on the grounds that Negroes,

Thomas Hart Benton. *Oil on canvas by Ferdinand T. L. Boyle, 1856. MHS Art.*

slave or free, were not citizens; held that residence in Illinois could not affect his status in Missouri; and ruled that being taken to a free territory could not free a slave because the Fifth Amendment forbade Congress to deprive citizens of their property without due process of law. Therefore, the Missouri Compromise was unconstitutional and slavery was guaranteed in all the territories. This decision polarized Northern and Southern opinion and moved the nation closer to war. The Chaffees then sold Scott for a nominal sum to Taylor Blow, who promptly set him free. Dred Scott died within a year, his name destined to be better remembered than those of most presidents.

As war approached, St. Louis's course was set by the small group of younger men which had formed around Thomas Hart Benton a decade earlier: Frank P. Blair, Jr., B. Gratz Brown, John How, Barton Able, and the Filleys, Giles F., Oliver D., and Chauncey I., each of them popular with the emancipationist Germans. In 1856 Blair was elected to Congress as a Free-Soiler, How won the mayoral race, and Brown went to the legislature, where he sent shock waves through the South by proposing that slavery be abolished in Missouri. Not the moral question, said Brown, but the economic advantages of a free society were at issue. Emancipation would stimulate business, land prices, and population growth. Slavery had done nothing for Missouri except to identify it with the backward South, to which the state owed nothing. Its exports went chiefly to the North, and its imports came from there. Missouri was "the advanced leader of the Western states. Politically, she should hold the balance between North and South. . . . It would be as absurd for Missouri to ape the fanaticism of South Carolina upon the slavery issue as it would be to mimic Massachusetts upon the ultra abolitionist issues." Emancipation should be accompanied by laws favoring immigration, manufacturing, commerce, railroads, and free land. In short, Brown proposed the whole Republican program plus emancipation. His east-west emphasis and economic arguments were not new in St. Louis, and though his resolution was rejected unanimously by the legislature, it played well at home. Brown admitted that "it was framed principally to suit my own meridian." Two months later, John M. Wimer was elected mayor on the "Emancipation" ticket, a coalition of Black Republicans and Know-Nothings, according to the *Republican*, which was appalled that a party would openly declare that "agitation of the (slavery) question shall never cease until Missouri is a free state." Wimer, who tried to appease the *Republican*, was dropped in 1858 in favor of O. D. Filley, tinware manufacturer, railroad promoter, and Free-Soiler, who defeated the Democratic nominee, George R. Taylor.

For the next two years, Frank Blair's antislavery coalition and the proslavery "Ultras" struggled for control of the middle where most of the voters were, requiring them to speak more moderately than they felt. Blair had little support outstate, and his job was to create a real party, not just an opposition. Despite having promised to support Abraham Lincoln for president, Blair joined his father, his brother Montgomery, and Horace Greeley of New York in the camp of Edward Bates of St. Louis. The sixty-four-year-old Bates was a high-tariff Whig, a nationally respected party professional who had been a leader of the St. Louis bar for forty years. Although he opposed slavery extension, Bates was considered a moderate, especially compared to the leading Republican candidate, William H. Seward of New York. When it became clear that Seward could not win on an early ballot at the 1860 convention, Bates's chances looked good; but German delegates from the crucial Midwest preferred Lincoln, primarily because Bates had flirted briefly with the Know-Nothings in the 1850s. Bates correctly considered Lincoln's position to be quite like his own, but most Missourians did not agree. It was obvious that Republicans had little chance in the state in 1860.

Stephen A. Douglas of Illinois had repudiated the Southern position on slavery during his debates with Lincoln in 1858, and consequently his nomination for president by the Democrats in 1860 split the party. The bolting Southern Democrats nominated John C.

Edward Bates. *Wood engraving after a photograph by Troxell,* Edward's Great West, 1860. *MHS-PP.*

Breckenridge of Tennessee, and a group of Whigs and Conservative Democrats, calling themselves Constitutional Unionists, selected John Bell of Tennessee. Missouri's leading candidate for governor, Claiborne F. Jackson of the Howard County planter clique, was in a dilemma. He and his running mate, Thomas C. Reynolds of St. Louis, yearned for the Southern connection, but Nathaniel Paschall of the redoubtable *Missouri Republican* kept the pressure on Jackson to come out for Douglas. The Breckenridge supporters asked only that Jackson take no position on the presidential race, but when the hated Paschall threatened to sponsor a separate pro-Douglas state ticket, Jackson caved in. The disgruntled ultra-Southerners then named their own gubernatorial candidate, Hancock Jackson. The Republicans, expecting no miracles, nominated a little-known lawyer, James Gardenhire; and the Bell ticket was represented by Sample Orr.

Frank Blair, running for reelection to Congress, stole the show in St. Louis with his "Wide-Awakes," several hundred glazed-hatted, caped, singing and shouting young Germans, who escorted him everywhere, to the disgust of the Democrats. Blair was elected, as was Mayor Filley, but the moderates won the state. Claiborne Jackson, whose moderate pose fooled many voters, defeated Orr by a surprisingly small margin, with Hancock Jackson a poor third and Gardenhire last. In the presidential election, held three months later,

Frank P. Blair, Jr. *Wood engraving by J. W. Ohr after a photograph by Brown,* Edward's Great West, 1860. *MHS-PP.*

Douglas defeated Bell by only 429 votes, with Breckenridge a distant third and Lincoln last with less than 11 percent of the votes (17,028). Missourians had voted overwhelmingly for the middle ground. Lincoln carried St. Louis, with 9,483 votes to Douglas's 8,538, Bell's 4,533, and Breckenridge's 544. Ninety-eight percent of the city's voters had rejected the ultra-Southern position, but as events made the center untenable, secessionist sentiment would grow.

After South Carolina seceded in December 1860 and other slave states followed, Missourians formed into three loosely defined groups: immediate secessionists; "conditional Unionists," who opposed "coercion" of the seceding states; and "unconditional Unionists," who favored the "whole Union," by force if necessary. As the Deep South governors had done, Jackson called for a convention "to consider Missouri's relations with the Union," asserting that "the destiny of the slaveholding states . . . is one and the same." Considering this treasonous, Frank Blair reorganized his Wide-Awakes into a paramilitary Home Guard, augmented by members of the German *Turnverein,* which kept a small arsenal in Turner's Hall and emphasized physical fitness through disciplined exercise. In concert with the Filleys, Hudson Bridge, Samuel Glover, Barton Able, James O. Broadhead, John How, and others, Blair set up a "committee of safety" to cooperate with the military in enforcing federal authority. General W. S. Harney, commanding the Department of the West, urged Blair to be cautious, but the powerful congressman was in no mood for caution. Through his brother Montgomery, Lincoln's postmaster general designate, Blair kept the president-elect in touch with developments in St. Louis.

On January 1, 1861, St. Louisans received a hint of slavery's future. It had been the custom to keep the slaves of a deceased person in the county jail until the probate court ordered the sheriff to sell them at auction from the courthouse steps. On this occasion there were seven persons to be sold, and the event had been widely advertised, so the auctioneer was not surprised to find a crowd of two thousand young men on hand. When he asked for bids on the first slave, the crowd repeatedly roared "three dollars." When the bidding reached eight dollars after two hours, the exhausted auctioneer led the slaves back to jail. No one ever again tried to sell human beings at auction in St. Louis.

Meanwhile, the secessionists were busy, led by Basil Duke and Colton Greene, previously obscure political followers of Thomas C. Reynolds. Duke, who was later a daring officer in Morgan's Raiders, organized the "Minute Men," whose duties were to spy on Blair and other Unionists and harass the Home Guard. In March, the legislature removed the police from the mayor's control by establishing a Board of Police Commissioners, responsible to the governor (still a feature of St. Louis's government and still controversial). Jackson named four secessionists to the board, including Duke and John A. Brownlee, president of the Merchant's Bank and one of the few secessionist business leaders in the city. Duke recalled later that "the Police Bill was in reality a war measure, adopted to enable our people to control St. Louis. . . . I knew the meaning of the measure, . . . and tried to carry it into action."

Eighty percent of convention delegates elected in February were slaveowners, but to the governor's chagrin, they were all professed Unionists, a majority of them "unconditionals." They had defeated the secessionist ticket by 110,000 to 30,000. After a day in cramped quarters in Jefferson City, the convention moved on March 4 to the friendlier environs of the Mercantile Library in St. Louis. There is little doubt that the move affected the outcome. When not in session— in the Planter's House bar, at dinner, and in the homes of the city's business leaders—the delegates heard the persuasive rhythms of the east-west commercial song. Ex-governor Sterling Price, a central Missouri planter and a shaky Unionist, was chosen president, but former Supreme Court Justice Hamilton R. Gamble, Edward Bates's brother-in-law, dominated the convention. As chairman of the committee on federal relations, Gamble wrote a report finding no present grounds for secession, which was adopted with only one dissent. The convention also recommended that the Missouri Compromise line be extended to the Pacific and opposed coercion of the seceding states. The delegates had accurately reflected the views of most Missourians, but they had given small comfort to Claiborne Jackson or to Frank Blair, who held that the Union was indestructible and coercion unavoidable.

The *Republican* hailed the result, pointing out that secession would isolate the state in a sea of Union territory, tempt slaves to escape, and above all, ruin Missouri by separating it from its markets and sources of capital. The state's leading newspaper still opposed coercion, but this position was becoming obsolete. The zealous Home Guard stirred the embers of ethnic prejudice and helped polarize opinion. Frank Blair, who feared that the glacier-slow General Harney would lose the arsenal to the governor, kept the wires to Washington humming with his complaints. Jackson's militia commander, General Daniel M. Frost, planned to seize the arsenal at the proper time, and its commander, a North Carolinian, had assured him of his cooperation. The St. Louis Arsenal was the largest military storehouse in the slave states, and its possession was considered vital by the Confederacy. It held sixty thousand Springfield and Enfield rifles, 1.5 million cartridges, ninety thousand pounds of powder, and artillery pieces. Blair, whose agents were everywhere, was aware of the plot, and with the help of Captain Nathaniel Lyon, he was determined to block it. Lyon, a New Englander, had just arrived from Kansas, where his antislavery views had been hardened by the brutality of the proslavery Missouri "border ruffians." On March 4, Basil Duke and Colton Greene attempted to lure the soldiers away from the arsenal by raising the Confederate flag over the Minute Men's headquarters in the old Berthold mansion at Fifth and Pine. They had intended to slip into the arsenal during the uproar, but Lyon and Blair did not bite.

After the fall of Fort Sumter, Lincoln, on April 15, 1861, requested four thousand volunteers from Missouri to help suppress the rebellion. Jackson exploded in righteous anger, calling the requisition "illegal, unconstitutional, and revolutionary, in its object inhuman and diabolical, and cannot be complied with." By this time, many of St. Louis's conditional Unionists, such as George R. Taylor, had closed ranks with Blair on most of the essentials, though there were still wide areas of disagreement. Events soon to follow put this *entente cordiale* under a severe strain. The governor called the St. Louis

The Arsenal at St. Louis, Missouri. *Wood engraving by Alexander Simplot, 1861.*
MHS-PP.

Grays, the Washington Guard, and other militia companies into
training under General Frost, and nearly nine hundred of them
reported for duty, including the newly formed Southern Guard (three
hundred minute men). The last were confirmed secessionists, but the
rest were mixed and some of them did not report.

Blair's complaints having borne fruit, General Harney had been
called to Washington to explain himself. Lyon was made temporary
commander, with authority to muster the Home Guard and other
volunteers into the federal service and to declare martial law if
necessary. He promptly enrolled several thousand men, issued arms to
them, moved surplus weapons and ammunition to Illinois, and deployed
four companies in and around the arsenal. For his encampment, Frost
had selected bluffs south and west of the arsenal, within easy artillery
range, in the expectation of a shipment of guns from the Confederacy.
Greene, acting for Governor Jackson, visited President Davis at his
temporary capital in Montgomery, Alabama, on April 16. Davis agreed
to send siege guns, and wrote to Jackson: "These (guns) from the
commanding hills will be effective against the garrison and break the
enclosing walls of the place. I concur with you as to the great
importance of capturing the arsenal and securing its supplies. . . ."

Unfortunately for the secessionist plan, Lyon was a step ahead of Frost. His men were on the hills when Frost got there, and he refused to move them, even when the police commissioner quixotically ordered him to do so. There was now little point to it, but Frost played out the charade, setting up his "training camp" at Lindell Grove, a forested area near the western edge of the city, just east of Grand Avenue and south of Olive Street. Two days later, on May 8, the *J. C. Swon* arrived at the wharf with two twelve-pound howitzers, two thirty-two-pounder siege guns, and ammunition, all having been seized by the Confederates from the federal arsenal at Baton Rouge. Union agents observed the landing, and Lyon could have taken the guns on the spot, but he wanted to give Frost more rope, so he merely made certain of their destination. On May 9, Lyon toured "Camp Jackson" in a carriage, dressed in the bombazine gown and close veil of Frank Blair's mother-in-law, with two pistols concealed under his dress. He saw the camp's layout and armament, and street signs roughly lettered "Beauregard" and "Jeff Davis."

On May 10, with the Committee of Safety's approval, Lyon marched to Camp Jackson with his regulars and volunteer regiments commanded by Blair, Henry Boernstein, B. Gratz Brown, Franz Sigel, and Nicholas Schuettner, about six thousand men in all. Frost protested that his camp was lawful, which it was, and that he had no designs on the arsenal. Lyon ignored his plea and demanded unconditional surrender. Having no alternative, Frost complied. Unfortunately, Lyon was disabled by a kicking horse on his way to Frost's tent, causing a delay of nearly two hours, a delay which was the initial cause for the tragedy that followed. As news of the march on the camp had spread through the city, thousands of spectators had converged at the site, coming on horsecars and horseback, in wagons and buggies, and on foot, many carrying lunches and some carrying guns. The only group not much in evidence was the police. Several armed and mischief-minded secessionists were in the crowd, but the vast majority, such as William T. Sherman, president of J. H. Lucas's horsecar line, and Galusha Anderson, the abolitionist pastor of the Second Baptist Church, merely came to watch. If this seems an odd sort of spectator sport, it should be noted that half of Washington's elite society cluttered the scene at the First Battle of Bull Run a few months later, an error that was not repeated.

Lyon's troops marched their prisoners onto Olive Street, where they waited for further orders. As the minutes stretched into hours tensions mounted, with hecklers shouting "Damn the Dutch," "Hurrah for Jeff Davis," "Dutch Black-Guards," and other taunts, punctuated by flying rocks, brickbats, and other missiles. When the missiles became bullets and Home Guard Captain F. C. Blandowski fell wounded, some of the soldiers fired into the crowd, their tumbling minie balls doing deadly work. Sherman recalled that the first shot was fired by a drunk who had been refused passage through the line of soldiers. Other reports had the first shots coming from the hill to the west, and still others claimed that the soldiers fired first. All agreed that the regulars did not fire. When the brief volley was over, twenty-eight persons were dead, including children, and many more were wounded.

Lyon had made his point at a heavy cost, but despite his repeated denials, Frost had originally intended to seize the arsenal and the city as well, and he had received property stolen from the United States by persons in armed rebellion. Samuel Glover and John How had urged Lyon to recover the guns by a writ from a federal court, but Lyon could have had them when they hit the wharf. He wanted to assert federal supremacy and make a lasting impression in doing so. The first results were negative—several hundred persons left the city immediately, claiming to be afraid the Germans would murder them, and there was another wild shooting melee on a downtown street the next day. A good many conditional Unionists showed secessionist colors, and even those of a firmer stripe were disturbed. Revealingly, however, the Germans were the chief targets of the reaction. Witnesses hastened to absolve the "American" regulars; even Lyon and Blair were less hated than the "Dutch." Virulent nativism had found another excuse, and within a few days three Germans were murdered.

There were two interesting footnotes to the affair: the presence, as civilians, of the two future great Union generals, W. T. Sherman, who was in the line of fire at Camp Jackson, and U. S. Grant, who saw the regulars march away from the arsenal; and a colloquy that occurred as the army wagons hauled the captured militia's gear away from Camp Jackson. Galusha Anderson reported that a young secessionist woman stepped from the crowd and shouted to the soldiers, "We'll whip you yet." Two young slave women then pointed to the loaded wagons and gleefully cried out, "They've got all your tents." Anderson interpreted this episode as demonstrating that the slaves understood the real nature of the conflict from the beginning.

Most of the state guardsmen who had reported to Camp Jackson, including General Frost, eventually served in the Confederate armies. Adjutant John S. Cavender and a few other officers were Unionists. After Lyon's show of force, there was not any serious threat to St. Louis until 1864. However indignant some of the more conservative business leaders may have been, their interests lay with the Union. The legislature rushed Jackson's "military bill" through in fifteen minutes,

Battle at Wilson's Creek, Mo.—Death of General Lyon. *Steel engraving by V. Balch after F. O. C. Darley, 1865. MHS-PP.*

making all able-bodied men members of the militia, but when General Harney resumed his command on May 12 he promptly endorsed the capture of Camp Jackson and denounced the military bill. The *Republican* spoke for many when it welcomed his return. The general, a wealthy resident of St. Louis (his wife was John Mullanphy's daughter—Frost's wife was her niece) had many friends and relatives who opposed coercion, and he believed he could keep the peace.

Sterling Price, who took command of the state guard after Camp Jackson, was now privately committed to secession, though he feared he could not hold the state without outside help. If a confrontation could be avoided while he trained the militia or until the Confederacy came to his assistance, he could win the state and control the Mississippi. Accordingly, he suggested a meeting in St. Louis on May 20, at which time Harney naively agreed to restrict federal troops to St. Louis County in return for Price's guarantee to maintain order in the rest of the state. At that moment, the state guard was drilling in the western part of Missouri, the Confederate flag was flying at the governor's mansion, Unionists were being harassed in their homes and the American flag torn down in St. Joseph, and Confederate troops were reported to be massing near the southern boundary. Price assured Harney that he would resist a Confederate invasion and Harney believed him, but Frank Blair did not.

Hamilton Gamble and James E. Yeatman had visited the president to urge him to retain Harney in mid-May, but the St. Louis Committee of Safety, supported by Montgomery Blair, pressed for his removal. Lincoln sent Harney's dismissal notice to Frank Blair, to be delivered only if he found it necessary. At the same time, Captain Lyon was brevetted a brigadier general, commanding the Missouri Volunteers (the Home Guard). Predictably, Blair soon found Harney's removal necessary, and on May 30 Lyon took command of the Western Department. Jackson and Price, still playing for time, asked for another conference, which Lyon did not want but agreed to as a gesture to Conservative Unionists. At a Planter's House meeting on June 11, the state officials acted as if they were representing a sovereign nation, offering to disband the state guard if the Union Volunteers were disarmed, federal troops from other states kept out of Missouri, and Lyon's outstate recruiting activities halted. After several hours of discussion, Lyon ended the meeting with a blunt declaration:

> Rather than to concede to the state of Missouri the right to demand that my government shall not enlist troops within her limits, or bring troops into the state whenever it pleases, or move its troops into, out of, or through the state; rather than to concede for one single instant the right to dictate to my government in any matter, however unimportant, I would see you . . . and every man, woman and child in the state dead and buried.

Lyon then turned to Governor Jackson and said: *"This means war. In an hour one of my officers will call for you and conduct you out of my lines."* With this, Lyon stalked out of the room, leaving all of his hearers, even Blair, in stunned silence. When they recovered, the state officials shook hands with Blair and headed for Jefferson City as fast as the Pacific Railroad could carry them. Jackson called for fifty thousand militiamen, burned the Gasconade and Osage bridges, gathered up the state seal and some records, and left for Boonville, thought to be relatively easy to defend. Within forty-eight hours Lyon was in Jefferson City with two thousand men, having come up the Missouri by steamboat. A day later, after a brief skirmish with Jackson's green troops, he occupied Boonville, ending Price's hopes of controlling the Missouri River and forcing the governor and the state guard to retreat southward. In early July, under pressure from Gamble, who thought Lyon too rash and inexperienced for the top western command, Lincoln replaced Lyon with John C. Fremont, who Blair had suggested when he learned that Lyon was being forced out. Gamble, Lincoln, and Blair would all live to regret the change. Lyon still commanded in the field, however, until he was killed at Wilson's Creek on August 10. Lyon's loss was a severe blow to the Union. Thomas L. Snead, Jackson's aide who had been present at the Planter's House conference and was later a Confederate congressman who knew the principal officers of the Confederacy, wrote after the war that Lyon was the greatest and most powerful man he ever saw.

With its elected governor in rebellion, the state needed a government. After considering several alternatives, the Unionists recalled the state convention. In late July the delegates declared Governor Jackson guilty of treason, vacated the executive offices and the legislature, and established a provisional government. Hamilton Gamble was named governor and Willard P. Hall of St. Joseph lieutenant governor. President Lincoln promptly recognized this arrangement as the legal government of Missouri. It would not bear close scrutiny constitutionally, but it worked, and three-fourths of the state's people supported it until it was replaced by a regularly elected executive branch in 1864. On the other side, Governor Jackson proclaimed Missouri an independent state in August 1861, and what was left of the legislature passed a secession ordinance in November. The Confederacy accepted "Missouri" within a few weeks. After a year at a temporary capital in Arkansas, Jackson died of pneumonia in December 1862. When central Arkansas fell to the Union in 1863, his successor Thomas C. Reynolds moved Missouri's secession capital to Marshall, Texas, for the duration of the war.

John C. Fremont's brief term as commander of the Western Department was marked by mismanagement in the field, rigid political and social control in St. Louis, and political realignment over new issues. Egged on by his ambitious wife Jessie, the swaggering general played Caesar, vividly supported by his resplendent three-hundred-man personal bodyguard of foreign volunteers headed by Major Charles Zagonyi, a Hungarian who eventually distinguished himself in battle. Fremont was constantly at odds with Governor Gamble and anyone else who threatened his absolute authority, and he resented and at times ignored orders from Washington. While complaining of inadequate support from Washington, he was tricked by the Confederates into sending several thousand men to southeast Missouri, while Generals Price and Benjamin McCulloch with fifteen thousand men were preparing to attack Lyon, who was at Springfield with a force half as large. Soon after, Lyon was killed at Wilson's Creek in a bloody battle that ended with both armies retiring, a battle

General John C. Fremont. *Carte de visite photograph by J. A. Scholten, ca. 1861.*
MHS-PP.

that could have been won except for a blunder by General Franz Sigel,
who was known as "a bear on retreat." A month later, Fremont
dawdled while Price besieged Lexington with fifteen thousand troops
for three days, despite the presence of twenty thousand Union soldiers
within a day's march. The battle cost the Union more than three
thousand men (Mulligan's Irish Brigade), nine hundred thousand
dollars in gold, and a large quantity of guns and ammunition.

Fremont tried to block Gamble's efforts to establish a Union
militia, on the grounds that a state force would compete for recruits,
would not be under his control, and would not zealously enforce
federal authority. Gamble argued that a state militia would be less
abrasive and more effective than German or Iowan troops who
behaved as if they were in conquered territory. Lincoln backed

Gamble, welcoming the opportunity to release federal troops for battle, and the Missouri State Militia was organized. Meanwhile, St. Louis became a major training center for federal troops. On land just west of the fairgrounds at the northwestern city limits, leased from John O'Fallon for a nominal $150 a year, Fremont established Benton Barracks, which housed as many as twenty-three thousand trainees.

On August 14, determined to suppress disloyalty, Fremont declared martial law in St. Louis. The secessionist-leaning police board, Confederate recruiting activities, demonstrations against the Home Guards, and rumors of imminent Confederate attack were hampering the army command. Provost Marshal Justus McKinstry was put in charge of the city. McKinstry arrested John Brownlee, president of the police board, for consorting with the enemy, but incredibly, he then installed Basil Duke in the position. Next, the provost marshal suppressed the *War Bulletin*, the *Missourian*, and the *Morning Herald*. The Conservative *Republican* gingerly approved, noting that these journals had been publishing "the South side of the accounts of affairs, as well as . . . very improbable and wild rumors." Severe penalties were established for carrying concealed weapons, and gunsmiths and dealers were ordered not to sell or give away weapons to anyone without McKinstry's approval. Theatres, dance

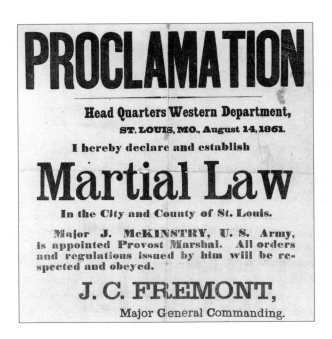

Fremont's Proclamation of Martial Law in St. Louis. *Broadside, 1861. MHS Archives.*

halls, and concert halls were closed at 10:30 P.M. during the week and all day on Sunday. If disturbances occurred during a performance, the establishment was to be closed permanently. Street assemblages were forbidden, and the sale of "spirituous liquors" was forbidden on Sundays. On August 26 McKinstry closed all saloons except those in the major hotels, which took care of the Irish bars without disturbing important citizens or the beer gardens. Two days later the *New York News*, the *Brooklyn Eagle*, and other "Seditious" papers were banned.

Citing "the helplessness of the civil authority, the total insecurity of life, and the devastation of property by bands of murderers and marauders who infest nearly every county in the State, . . . and who find an enemy wherever they find plunder . . . ," Fremont extended martial law throughout Missouri on August 30, 1861. Unauthorized persons bearing arms north of a line from Fort Leavenworth through Jefferson City to Cape Girardeau would be court-martialed, and if found guilty of hostile intent they were to be shot, as were those who destroyed railroads or telegraph lines. Anyone "engaged in treasonable correspondence," aiding the enemy, "fomenting tumults," or circulating false reports were liable to "sudden and severe punishment." His purpose, Fremont said, was to give "instantaneous effect to existing laws," not to suspend the civil tribunals where they could function peaceably.

The provost marshal forbade anyone to leave the county without a pass obtained by signing a loyalty pledge. Violation of this pledge by fighting for or aiding the enemy was punishable by death. Under the pressure of hundreds of applicants, McKinstry allowed persons to leave for the East without passes, but all Missouri and southern and western destinations required them. Young men, especially those bound for southwest Missouri, were often granted passes and then immediately arrested.

These measures were stringent, but the bombshell in Fremont's proclamation read: "The property, real and personal, of all persons in the State of Missouri who take up arms against the United States, or who . . . have taken an active part with their enemies in the field, is declared to be confiscated to the public use, and their slaves, if any they have, are thereby declared free men." The first slave so freed, and the first freed anywhere in the nation by federal authority was Hiram Reed, the property of Thomas L. Snead of St. Louis.

This bold stroke stunned the proslavery Unionists, thrilled abolitionists everywhere, and made Fremont a hero to the Germans. The *Democrat* and the German press were jubilant, and even the *Republican* was cautiously supportive, primarily because Fremont was at odds with Frank Blair. Governor Gamble, who had just announced that he would not make war on slavery, fired off a protest to Washington, and Confederate General M. Jeff Thompson proclaimed that for every person shot under Fremont's order he would "*hang, draw*, and *quarter* a minion of said Abraham Lincoln." Frank Blair had already become disgusted with Fremont's military ineptitude and resentful of his popularity with the Germans. As a further irritant, Fremont had ignored Blair's friends in awarding military contracts. Fearing that the proclamation would alienate Unionists in other border states as well as in Missouri, and believing it unenforceable and therefore ridiculous, Blair, Broadhead, Glover, and other St. Louis Unionists urged Fremont's removal. A characteristic incompetent administrator, the general had scorned his natural supporters in the city's power structure and had consulted only with his wife and a ring of imported sycophants.

Lincoln approached the situation with his usual caution. Germans and abolitionists would be enraged by a summary dismissal of Fremont, but the Union was in an even more precarious position in Kentucky than in Missouri. Fearing retaliation against Unionists in Tennessee, Arkansas, and elsewhere because of Fremont's actions, the president immediately rescinded the order to shoot armed secessionists and requested Fremont to modify his confiscation and emancipation order, noting that many border-staters would fight for the Union but not to destroy slavery. "The confiscation of property and the liberating of slaves of traitorous owners," said Lincoln, "will alarm our Southern Union friends and turn them against us." When the haughty commander refused to comply, Lincoln rescinded the emancipation order and sent Montgomery Blair and General Montgomery J. Meigs to St. Louis to evaluate the departmental administration. As soon as Lincoln's agents left St. Louis, Fremont jailed Frank Blair for insubordination. Though approved by the Germans, the *Democrat*, and the *Republican*, this act was another blunder, inviting a revival of the old saying: "When the Blairs go in for a fight, they go in for a funeral." The general had united Gamble and Blair against himself, and in Washington Edward Bates and Montgomery Blair urged his dismissal. The War Department ordered Blair's release; and Fremont, though Lincoln kept him on until November, was finished. He had finally taken the field, but he was too late. When he returned to St. Louis after relinquishing his command, Fremont was treated by the Germans as a martyred hero, but his record was stained further when at Blair's instigation massive corruption was uncovered in the accounts of Justus McKinstry, whom Fremont had promoted to departmental quartermaster. McKinstry had been selling war contracts, which helps to explain why Blair's friends had been so unlucky.

Despite his shortcomings, Fremont had really shaken the dovecotes. He had brought emancipation to the front as a war issue, and he had positioned himself among the Germans and abolitionists for a run at the presidency in 1864. In Missouri, latent differences emerged into new political groupings. Those who favored immediate emancipation, including the Germans and some other anti-Blair Republicans, were called "Charcoals." Gradual emancipationists who favored compensation to slaveowners were dubbed "Claybanks." Blair headed this faction, which included many slaveowners. Wobbly Unionists and covert secessionists who opposed emancipation in any form were known as "Snowflakes." Governor Gamble was a Claybank leaning toward the Snowflakes. In spite of themselves, the logic of events had pushed all Unionists toward emancipation. Frank Blair was consistent, but Gratz Brown had changed, and even Governor Gamble was making adjustments. Ironically, Fremont had done little in Missouri that Lincoln did not do eventually.

After Fremont left, Gratz Brown became the leader of the growing Charcoal faction, now fully committed to abolition and stern measures toward disloyalists. In late 1861 the State Convention adopted a "test oath" of loyalty to the United States and the provisional government, which was required of all officeholders, including local officials. The Charcoals were pleased, but they wanted more; secessionists within the Union lines should be treated as enemy agents and deprived of their citizenship. The *Democrat*, now controlled by William McKee, with Brown as a frequent contributor, was the major Charcoal newspaper. In 1862 Blair established his own paper, the *St. Louis Union*. Peter Foy of the *Democrat* joined him as editor, and the former *Anzeiger* editor, Henry Boernstein, attempted to promote Blair's gradual emancipation ideas among the Germans. Brown now argued that since slavery was the primary cause of the war, the rebellion could be stamped out only by its abolition. He found colonization no longer acceptable, saying, "If so many, many thousands of us have thus long borne with their presence here as slaves, surely others can endure their abiding here as free men." Brown did not object to compensation for loyal slaveowners if it did not delay emancipation.

In July 1862, the convention rejected a plan for gradual emancipation. This proposal would have prolonged slavery for thirty years, but it was not gradual enough for Snowflakes and too gradual for Charcoals. The convention also turned down Congress's offer to compensate loyal slaveowners if an emancipation plan was adopted, but it agreed to consider the proposal later. The delegates also stiffened the test oath, requiring voters to swear that they would never aid the rebels and that they had not fought against the Union since

December 17, 1861. The latter provision protected those who had believed they were defending the state early in the war, but who had left Jackson after the secession ordinance. Civil officers, jurors, attorneys, the president and faculty of the University of Missouri, public school teachers, ministers, and bank officers were also required to take this oath.

In November 1861 General Henry W. Halleck took over the Department of the West. "Old Brains," who had led his class at West Point, was an effective administrator, but he was not much better than Fremont at coming to grips with the enemy. Fortunately his subordinates, Samuel R. Curtis and U. S. Grant, were self-starters, constantly dogging the rebel armies. After Curtis had defeated Price, McCulloch, Van Dorn, and the Cherokees in a major battle at Pea Ridge, Arkansas, in March 1862 the Confederate armies stayed out of Missouri for two years, though bands of guerrillas and cavalry raiders continued their harassment.

Halleck appointed Brigadier General John M. Schofield, a former Washington University physics professor who had served as Lyon's adjutant, as commander of the Missouri State Militia. Schofield and Gamble saw eye to eye, and by April 1862 federal troops had been relieved of garrison and patrol duty by fourteen thousand militiamen. Halleck put a stop to unauthorized seizures of private property by Union soldiers, which Fremont had tolerated, but he also ordered the execution of guerrillas caught destroying bridges, railroads, and telegraph lines. Confederate regulars *in uniform* engaged in such activity would be treated as prisoners of war. Railroad officials were required to take the test oath, and many of them, such as Colonel George R. Taylor of the Pacific, were given army commissions. They also had to post bonds guaranteeing that they would not retain employees who had not taken the voter's oath.

Martial law, still in effect in St. Louis, was generally popular. Despite the inconveniences of the pass system, most citizens liked the security it provided. But Southern sympathizers, especially those of wealth and prominence, found the regime harsh indeed. Since Wilson's Creek, Unionist refugees from southwest Missouri and Arkansas had streamed into the city; and in 1862, as Grant and Sherman ground relentlessly down the Mississippi, St. Louis was inundated by Confederate prisoners, wounded soldiers, escaped slaves, and impoverished southern Unionists, who were discharged from the riverboats by the tens of thousands. The southwestern refugees, most of whom were penniless but in fairly good health, were housed, fed, and clothed in St. Louis before being transferred to Illinois or other northern states. Volunteers such as the Ladies' Union

Refugee Aid Society took care of them, but as the guerrilla persecutions increased, the incoming tide of refugees overwhelmed their resources.

Since secessionists had caused the refugees' plight, General Halleck reasoned, justice required that they be supported by secessionists. Accordingly, on December 12, 1861, he ordered that ten thousand dollars be collected from Southern sympathizers. A board of assessment, appointed to judge both financial resources and "proportion of guilt," consisted of Provost Marshal General Bernard G. Farrar, Jr., a native St. Louisan of a prominent family who knew the wealthy "secesh"; county assessor Charles Borg, who knew the value of their holdings; and General Samuel Curtis, the former city engineer, a hard-liner who also understood local society. After the list was completed, Farrar notified those chosen of the amounts due (ranging from fifty to five hundred dollars) and gave them five days to pay. If they did not, enough of their property would be sold at auction to cover their assessments plus a 25 percent penalty. Among the assessed were Erastus Wells, Alexander Kayser, Mrs. Trusten Polk (whose husband had been expelled from the U.S. Senate for disloyalty), Dr. William B. McPheeters, Juliette B. Garesche, L. A. Benoist, General Daniel Frost, Mrs. Stephen W. Kearny, Dr. L. C. Boisliniere, and about fifty others. Several of these claimed to be Unionists, but the board charged that each of them had served the enemy—financially, by verbal, written, or published words of encouragement, or by transmitting military information. This covered a lot of ground; those who had Confederate relatives or who had corresponded with rebel friends or written pro-Southern letters to the newspapers were vulnerable.

L. A. Benoist was one of several who paid immediately and some persons were excused after taking the loyalty oath, but twenty-five of those assessed refused to comply. They protested to Halleck, arguing that since "all of the officers of government, both judicial and ministerial" were functioning, they were entitled to "*a speedy* and *public* trial by an impartial jury." They had been denied due process of law "by a secret inquisitional tribunal, on what charge we know not, and condemned to pay a forced contribution levied upon us for alleged charitable purposes." The assessors had made few mistakes, if any, in identifying sympathizers, and the protestors knew very well why they had been selected, but Halleck had unquestionably violated their rights. He was outraged by guerrilla atrocities against the refugees, which had been applauded by some of those on the list. It was galling for him to hear them crow about Union defeats and predict the imminent fall of St. Louis, but he had no right to deprive them of their liberties save the right of the bayonet. None of them, except the few who were in the Confederate service, had committed an overt *act* against the United States; and if they had, there were courts to set their punishment. Some of the protectors, such as Erastus Wells, who took the test oath and was elected alderman in 1862, became fairly good Unionists, but Dr. McPheeters claimed to have been driven into the Confederate army by the action. Halleck ignored the protest, and a few weeks later, Farrar seized enough property from the recalcitrants to cover their assessments and penalties. McPheeters charged that Halleck's "Jayhawkers" took his buggy and harness, a rosewood piano, six chairs, two sofas, and a marble-topped table, aggregating $1,110 in value, as payment for his $375 assessment. Not even the Conservatives defended the protestors. The *Republican* commented that the several "fashionable and wealthy ladies" who had been penalized would have "an additional reason to indulge in their very common and delicately insinuating taunts and sneers against the 'prevailing dynasty.'"

In January 1862, Halleck ordered newspapers to submit a copy of each issue to Colonel Farrar's office for examination. Unfavorable war news and anti-administration views were thus minimized, especially after editors were required to take the test oath. Mail to and from southern points and all mail of suspected disloyalists were censored, and Blair's *Union* carried a feature called "Items from the Rebels' Mail Bag." By the summer of 1862, the army had adopted the old Spanish custom of banishment. Certain known disloyalists, wives of Confederate officers, some of whom were spies, and women who too zealously promoted Southern causes were ordered out of the state. Mrs. J. A. Coons had been permitted to give food and clothing to the Confederates held in the Gratiot Street Prison, but after several inmates had escaped in women's clothing, and Mrs. Coons had organized a public bazaar to aid needy Confederate soldiers, she and several of her associates were exiled to Illinois. Sallie McPheeters and Mrs. Daniel M. Frost were among the wives who were deposited behind the Confederate lines.

These stern measures were endorsed on July 15, 1862, at a mass meeting of Unionists of various shades which assembled at the court house. Charles D. Drake and General Frank Blair addressed the gathering, which resolved that St. Louis should contribute "the last man and the last dollar" to the war effort, and that "traitors and rebel spies" should be banished. Volunteers from each ward agreed to raise funds for recruiting and organizing the regiments for Blair's new brigade. Later, the county furnished one hundred thousand dollars to support the volunteers' families, and individuals, including L. A. Benoist, donated more than forty thousand dollars. Increased terrorist activity in the state, stimulated by officers from the Confederate command in Arkansas, inspired General Schofield, now departmental commander, to order his men to shoot armed marauders on the spot. For every Union soldier or citizen killed by guerrillas, "rebels and rebel sympathizers" would forfeit five thousand dollars, with the money to be paid to the victims' families.

Schofield appointed Giles Filley, Daniel R. Garrison, Ferdinand Meyer, John O'Fallon, James S. Thomas, Charles Borg, and Henry Moore to assess the "secessionists and southern sympathizers in St. Louis County," in the amount of five hundred thousand dollars, to support the needy families of the federal volunteers and the state militia. O'Fallon declined, but the others accepted, and by December 10, many persons had been assessed on the basis of wealth and presumed degree of guilt. Governor Gamble had borrowed $150,000 from various banks against these assessments, when to the astonishment of nearly everyone President Lincoln ordered the collections halted.

Unlike the earlier assessments and the individual seizures of the property, this huge levy had created a stench even among Unionists. In its *ex parte* proceedings the board had taken secret, unsworn, and at times malicious and false testimony, and the rationale for the selections was difficult to understand. Charles P. Chouteau, who had filled large war material orders at cost, loaned the quartermaster at St. Louis twenty thousand dollars to pay for uniforms, and supplied a Minnesota regiment for months at his own expense, was listed as a secessionist. J. H. Lucas was also selected—some of his relatives were secessionists. As a boy he had been a classmate of Jefferson Davis in a Kentucky school, and he was reported to have a Confederate flag at his home. D. A. January had been president of the Merchants' Exchange in 1861 when unconditional Unionists had withdrawn to form the Union Merchants' Exchange. Soon the older body was near collapse, and George R. Taylor had led its membership into the Union Exchange, presumably without prejudice. Chouteau, Lucas, and January had all supported Harney's efforts to maintain peace in Missouri, and, like the general, they had believed Jackson's and Price's promises. They had opposed coercion until that position became obsolete, but like most other conditional Unionists, they had not aided the Confederacy and they were guilty of little more than having anti-Republican views. But they were rich, five hundred thousand dollars was a lot of money, and the board had to cast a wide net to get it. If theirs was a Unionism of economic interest and expediency rather than an affair of the heart, and if they still disliked Lincoln and the "black Republicans," they may have deserved their neighbors' resentment; but they were neither traitors nor rebels.

For their pains, they were known as "submissionists" by the real secessionists and "dishrag Unionists" by the Charcoals.

Lincoln's attitude surprised General Curtis, who had succeeded Schofield, but though he was a determined Charcoal, he welcomed the president's action—there were too many Unionists in the net. He wired his approval to Halleck, who was now chief of staff in Washington, and on December 15 the general issued the formal reversal order. Lincoln's decision had been inspired by a letter sent to Gamble by William Greenleaf Eliot, pastor of the Unitarian Church of the Messiah, and forwarded to the president by the governor. Eliot had intended his letter as a memorial, to be signed by numerous Unionists, but he could get no signers; those asked either disagreed with his purpose or feared the consequences. Eliot's credentials were impeccable, he had been the city's only open abolitionist for many years, he had spoken and written early and often for the Union, and he was a Republican and a friend of the president.

Eliot explained that the assessments were "working evil . . . and doing great harm to the Union cause," and he pointed out that in St. Louis there were "all shades of opinion, from that kind of neutrality which is hatred in disguise, through all the grades of lukewarmness, 'sympathy,' and hesitating zeal up to the full loyalty which your memorialists . . . claim to possess." To establish the line between loyalty and disloyalty, and then to determine degrees of disloyalty, would be extremely difficult even after long investigation and hearing evidence from the accused. "It would require not only a competent tribunal, . . . possessed of full authority to examine witnesses under oath, but also a kind and degree of scrutiny inconsistent with Republican institutions." Eliot knew the assessors were upright men who had tried to be just and impartial, but their taking of "hearsay evidence, rumors, and 'general impressions,'" without requiring an oath had clouded the entire proceedings. Two classes of angry citizens had been created, the first astounded that they had been branded disloyal and the second outraged either because they had been assessed more than others or because some sympathizers had not been caught. Eliot also noted that the victims would probably recover their assessments through the courts eventually. Though he knew the Bill of Rights as well as any man, Eliot wisely based his plea primarily upon expediency. He understood the war time climate and he knew Lincoln. When the president read Eliot's appeal, it may have occurred to him that Mary Todd Lincoln could not have met the board's standards of loyalty. As for the assessed, they did not have to pay, which should have been the end of the matter, but such lists never die. Radicals in the postwar

William Greenleaf Eliot. *Carte de visite photograph by Black (Boston), ca. 1863. MHS-PP.*

period used the assessment roster to exclude individuals from voting, holding public office, or practicing certain professions.

Eliot had found a better way to help the war's victims. In preparation for the fighting he thought was sure to come, he had organized the St. Louis Provident Society to give the city's charities central direction. When more than seven hundred wounded from Wilson's Creek swamped St. Louis's three hospitals in August 1861, Eliot and James E. Yeatman organized the Western Sanitary Commission. At the suggestion of Dorothea Dix, chief of the army's nursing corps, and with Jessie Fremont's assistance, they persuaded General Fremont to give the commission official status. He authorized it, under the departmental medical director, to establish and operate hospitals, train women nurses under Dix's authority, provide male nurses, and work with army officers in improving health and sanitary conditions in military camps, with emphasis upon wholesome food and proper drainage. Never before had any army had the kind of care this privately supported adjunct proposed to provide. Fremont appointed Eliot, Dr. J. B. Johnson, and three wealthy and civic-minded businessmen, James Yeatman, Carlos Greeley, and George Partridge, to the commission.

James G. Yeatman. *Carte de visite photograph, ca. 1863. MHS-PP.*

Yeatman, the commission's president, was a banker, iron merchant, and railroad promoter who had come to St. Louis from Nashville in 1842. Though he had freed his slaves well before the war, he was not a Republican, and he had favored Harney's conciliatory approach over Blair's hard-line tactics. He was a staunch Unionist all the same, and he accomplished more during the war than a half-dozen major generals. Carlos Greeley, the treasurer, was a wholesale grocer and banker who developed extensive land, railroad, and mining interests in Missouri, Kansas, and Colorado after the war. Yeatman gave his full time and attention to the commission's work for four years, Greeley nearly so, and the others a substantial part of theirs.

By September 10, 1861, the Sanitary Commission had opened the City General Hospital in a five-story building at Fifth and Chestnut and had furnished it with five hundred beds and the necessary medical equipment. Its location near the river and the railway terminals made it an ideal receiving hospital for the wounded, including some Confederates, who were jammed into St. Louis from the southern battlefields, more than seven thousand of them after Shiloh. As the secessionist Anne Lane, daughter of William Carr Lane, wrote in May 1862, "I see by the papers that the Battle of Shiloh was a great federal victory—may they have many such. It has filled the hospitals all over the west and even yet the wounded are coming. Our streets are full of creatures who look as if they had been stolen from a graveyard." Late in 1861 the commission fitted out hospitals at Benton Barracks, at O'Fallon Street and Pratte Avenue (the Good Samaritan), and in the new Lindell Hotel on Fourth Street. By May 1864 the commission was supporting fifteen hospitals in the St. Louis area, including a huge twenty-five-hundred-bed facility at Jefferson Barracks. These institutions had already treated 61,744 soldiers, with a death rate of

A sales booth at the Mississippi Valley Sanitary Fair, St. Louis. *Stereo photograph by Robert Benecke, 1864. MHS-PP.*

under 10 percent. The commission also supplied seventeen hospitals in outstate Missouri, two in Kentucky, twenty-two in Tennessee, Mississippi, Louisiana, and Arkansas, and at least one in a half-dozen other states. Seventeen brigade and divisional hospitals, fifteen hospital steamboats, most of the Mississippi gunboat fleet, and a number of hospital railroad cars were wholly or partially supplied with medical items by the Sanitary Commission.

This massive undertaking, with all of its organizational and logistical problems, was managed by the commission and its small clerical staff. The members, Yeatman especially, made the rounds of the hospitals and battlefields, determining the areas of need and filling them as rapidly as possible. Yeatman was on hand at the siege of Vicksburg, where he furnished 250 tons of supplies to Grant's army, and the commission's shipments followed Sherman's Army of the Tennessee all the way through Georgia in 1864. Refugees from Arkansas, Tennessee, Mississippi, Alabama, Louisiana, and Texas, many of them women with little children, began to arrive in wholesale lots after the fall of Vicksburg in 1863. The Sanitary Commission opened homes for them and gave them clothing, the government paying for food and fuel. Some of the refugees were well-to-do Unionists and Confederates who had brought money with them, but the vast majority were impoverished whites. According to Galusha Anderson, they came "hatless and shoeless, sallow, lean, half-starved, . . . half-naked, shivering, penniless, dispirited." A majority were loyalists, their husbands dead or in the Union army, but others were dazed and incoherent, hardly knowing what the war was about. "Whether they were loyal or disloyal, it would have puzzled the most astute to find out."

The Western Sanitary Commission also supported the Freedmen's Relief Society; the Soldiers' Orphans Home; the Ladies' National League, consisting of twelve hundred women headed by Mrs. T. M. Post, which did voluntary work in the hospitals and other war-connected charities; the St. Louis Board of Education for Colored Schools; and the Soldiers' Homes, which were places of rest and recreation, somewhat like the modern U.S.O. By 1865, with St. Louis's black population augmented by the southern influx, the commission was aiding black schools with a total enrollment of fifteen hundred.

In 1863 Yeatman criticized the army's unsympathetic and prejudicial handling of freedmen who came within its lines and recommended that the commission support the leasing of abandoned plantations to black as well as white small farmers. He described the existing system as little better than slavery, advocated doubling the pay of freedmen who worked for large lessors, and proposed that employers be forbidden to use "the lash, paddle, and all other cruel modes of punishment." This plan was approved by Treasury Secretary Salmon P. Chase, whose department had taken over the plantation-leasing program. Chase persuaded the St. Louisan to supervise its reorganization; and in 1865 President Lincoln asked Yeatman to head the new Freedmen's Bureau, which was intended to ease the transition from slavery to freedom. Yeatman declined, reportedly because the bureau was subordinated to the War Department. A favorable response might have changed history, since the bureau accomplished very little under the incompetent and Conservative General O. O. Howard.

During its four years, the Western Sanitary Commission collected and distributed more than $4.5 million in money and goods. Except for modest appropriations by St. Louis County and the state of Missouri, the contributions came from individuals and volunteer groups from Maine to California. St. Louisans and Bostonians were the largest and steadiest contributors, with Dr. Eliot's relatives and friends promoting the cause in Massachusetts. In New York, James Roosevelt headed a fund drive; and in remote California Thomas Starr King raised fifty thousand dollars. The U.S. Sanitary Commission, which functioned in the Virginia theatre of war, also drew from these same sources, and from a series of "Sanitary fairs" held in eastern cities. With the commission's treasury almost empty and with Yeatman in the South, George Partridge and Carlos Greeley staged the Mississippi Valley Sanitary Fair for three weeks beginning on May 17, 1864. A huge temporary building, 500 feet long and 114 feet wide, with 100-foot wings extending east and west on Locust Street, was erected on Twelfth Street between Olive and St. Charles. Exhibits of the latest agricultural, scientific, and military gadgetry; patriotic speeches by generals and civic dignitaries; refreshment and recreational facilities; and mountains of donated merchandise for sale drew hundreds of thousands of visitors from the city, from rural Missouri, and from neighboring states. A local secessionist belle, upset because blacks were served at the fair's refreshment stands, commented that it was a vulgar display attended by the vulgar herd, but admission fees and sales netted $555,000 for the commission, by far the largest per capita return achieved by any of the wartime sanitary fairs.

The Civil War was a disaster for St. Louis business. When the Confederates blockaded the lower Mississippi in 1861, the city lost its southern trade and its river passage to eastern and foreign markets. Federal restrictions and discriminatory measures against its commerce, presumably because it might be tainted with disloyalty, cost the city most of its trade with the upper Mississippi valley. After martial law was declared in August 1861, shipments to Illinois, Iowa, and other loyal states required a permit from the provost marshal, and this and other regulatory delays caused a shift of Kansas, Iowa, and southern Illinois trade to Chicago. The wholesale grocers suffered heavily, but dry goods shipments held up well because of long-standing customer preferences. St. Louis merchants of New England origins, because of their superior credibility with the provost marshal, suffered less than their rivals.

Sales to the Union army partially made up for the loss of customary markets, and certain industries, iron and lead manufactories especially, were stimulated by military demand; but these were temporary gains, while much of the trade territory was lost forever. The army's commissary department spent $50 million in St. Louis for subsistence items during the war, and the chief quartermaster estimated his outlays in the city for supplies, transportation, and incidentals at $180 million. Despite the army's impact, the number of commission and forwarding merchants in the city dropped from 109 in 1859 to 52 in 1864, wholesale grocers from 80 to 69, and dry goods wholesalers from 32 to 27. As federal confidence in Missouri's stability increased, and especially after the Union armies secured the entire Mississippi valley in 1863, St. Louis's trade approached its prewar volume, but the upper Midwest market was gone. When army purchases dropped precipitately in 1865, business slowed again, and within a few months, the volume of trade at St. Louis was well below prewar levels.

As the war lengthened and the test oath began to bite, the Charcoal faction gained strength in St. Louis. The form of emancipation and the degree of tolerance of "disloyalty" became the major political issues. The Charcoals, now called Radicals, favoring immediate emancipation and no longer willing to compensate slaveowners, elected Chauncey Filley as mayor in 1863 and continued to dominate city politics through the four terms of James S. Thomas. Gratz Brown was elected to the Senate in 1863, prompting William Lloyd Garrison, the abolitionist firebrand, to ask: "Whoever dreamed that Missouri would elect him, a thorough going Abolitionist, to the Senate of the United States?" Brown had first congratulated Lincoln on his preliminary Emancipation Proclamation in 1862, but he was outraged when he learned that it applied only to areas held by Confederates. He chided the president for not calling the Southerners traitors in public as he did in private, and he was further alienated by Lincoln's plan to restore Arkansas and Louisiana to statehood as soon as 10 percent of their voters had taken a loyalty oath. "Eternal punishment for rebel traitors" was Brown's current theme, and he began to boost Fremont for the Republican nomination in 1864.

Frank Blair had been reelected to Congress over Samuel Knox in 1862, but the Radicals unseated him on a recount the following year. He devoted the next two years to his military career, distinguishing himself as a divisional commander at Vicksburg and as the major general in command of the Seventeenth Army Corps under Sherman in Tennessee, Georgia, and the Carolinas. Blair was widely recognized as one of the ablest volunteer generals in the Union army and his reckless bravery in battle as well as in personal encounters became a national legend. The *New York Sun* quoted a St. Louisan as saying: "Every man in Missouri, whatever his politics; his religion, or his beverage . . . has reason to believe that a braver man than Frank Blair never set foot on Missouri soil or any other soil. No one hereabouts whose hope of eternal life was not well assured, would ever think of drawing a knife or pistol on Frank." Blair's military duties did not keep him from flying to Lincoln's defense in print, and he flayed with impartial zeal those Democrats who supported General George B. McClellan for president in 1864 and Radicals like Brown and Daniel Drake of St. Louis, who wanted to disfranchise the rebels forever. Blair, still in his early forties, had his own presidential plans, and he gradually became a spokesman for those he had despised—the cautious Unionists who had supported Harney's policies in St. Louis. Blair held no brief for outright rebels, but they would eventually regain the franchise, and he intended to be ready.

B. Gratz Brown. *Lithograph by Joseph Keppler, 1872. MHS-PP.*

St. Louis had a major scare in 1864. Sterling Price had long advocated a strike at the city, and his superior, General Kirby Smith, agreed to an invasion as a means of blunting Sherman's drive toward Atlanta by forcing him to detach troops to protect the key river port. In preparation for the raid, Price's agents stepped up guerrilla activity all over the state, featuring the destruction of bridges and railroads and bloody terror in the towns by banditti led by such men as William Clark Quantrell and Bloody Bill Anderson. Throughout Missouri, but centering in St. Louis, a secret society called the Order of American Knights (OAK) devoted itself to two major goals: the overthrow of the Lincoln administration by securing the election of General McClellan and the capture of St. Louis and the state by General Price.

OAK was headed nationally by Clement L. Vallandigham of Ohio, and claimed more than three hundred thousand members in Ohio, Illinois, and Indiana, as well as twenty-two thousand in Missouri. Among its goals was the creation of a Northwest Confederacy, allied with but separate from the Southern Confederacy. Missouri's "Grand Commander" was Charles Lucas Hunt, James H. Lucas's nephew, who was the Belgian consul at St. Louis. Any member who revealed secrets of the Order was condemned to "a shameful death and infamy." As General Price's secret political, military, and financial agent, Hunt was to supply money and weapons to the guerrillas and lead an uprising in the state in support of Price's invasion. Unfortunately for Price, OAK was long on oaths, secret grips, mysterious incantations, and promises, but short on performance. Their boldest effort seems to have been the purchase of forty "six-shooters" from a suspended gun store for delivery to Colonel S. D. Jackman's raiders. Agents of the provost marshal had infiltrated OAK lodges, and his detectives intercepted the shipment. The irate grand commander ordered the execution of the detectives, but that order too was quickly reported to the provost marshal. The agents also heard discussions of assassinations and assaults on Union patrols at various lodge meetings, but apparently there was more bluster than courage in these discussions.

In May 1864 Provost Marshal General J. P. Sanderson arrested Hunt, "Grand Worthy Senior" Charles E. Dunn (the City Superintendent of Public Lamps), and other officers of OAK and held them in the Gratiot Street Prison awaiting trial. Appeals from Hunt's family to Commanding General W. S. Rosecrans were to no avail, but on July 22 Drs. Richard E. Bland and J. B. Johnson, the latter J. H. Lucas's son-in-law, obtained Hunt's release on medical grounds. After posting a ten-thousand-dollar bond, swearing an oath that he would "discourage, discountenance, and forever oppose secession, rebellion, and the disintegration of the Federal Union," and disclaiming "all faith and fellowship with the so-called Confederate armies," Hunt confessed to the charges against him. But he was never tried nor even banished—a tribute to his family's status and influence. Neither James H. Lucas nor any other St. Louis business or professional leader was shown to have any connection with OAK, but the affair did not improve Lucas's credibility with the Radicals. Charles Lucas Hunt, age forty-five, occupation "farmer," joined the Union militia in March 1865. Soon after, the embarrassed Belgians named a new consul at St. Louis.

Hunt's operation had its comic-opera aspects, but he had been in dead earnest. He could have sought glory as a Confederate officer, but he apparently felt that he would be more valuable at home, leading his knights along the unlit byways of subversion. Not serving in the Confederate army was quite popular with secessionist-minded scions of the St. Louis social elite. The staunch rebels Jefferson K. Clark and William Glasgow found Canada more congenial than Dixie, as did some others. Still others favored the watering places of Europe, where they could exchange views on the war with other Americans of all shades of opinion, united only by their distaste for military life in wartime.

Sterling Price entered Missouri with twelve thousand men on September 19, 1864, his objective St. Louis. This highly touted and long-awaited invasion struck terror in the countryside and blazed a path of destruction clear across the state, but militarily it was the last shriek on the road to oblivion. The frustrated Confederates blew up and tore down more than $10 million worth of railroad and other property and carried off tons of farm produce and thousands of farm animals, but nothing else went as planned. The knights, no doubt disoriented by their leader's arrest, neither rioted nor rushed to Price's banner. At Pilot Knob, General Tom Ewing with fifteen hundred men held the Confederates up for two days and punished them severely before retreating, and Price's spies informed him falsely that Rosecrans at St. Louis had him outnumbered two to one. He then switched to Jefferson City, his alternate objective, but as he neared the capital, reports that it was strongly defended caused him to bypass it too. In his headquarters at Boonville, Price received powerful moral support from admiring visitors, but not much of what he needed: recruits, guns, and money.

Rosecrans and Ewing were hot on Price's heels as he marched toward the federal installation at Leavenworth, Kansas, and in late October the Confederates met General Curtis with twenty thousand troops head-on. Curtis defeated Price at Westport, near Kansas City, and then harassed the retreating Confederates, forcing them to abandon most of their loot, until they crossed the Arkansas River on November 2, on their way to Texas. Even the guerrillas gave up for a while, and the war in Missouri was over, though the political revolution had just begun.

The slave state of Missouri had furnished well over 100,000 men to the Union army, including more than 8,000 blacks, and nearly 90,000 more had served with varying degrees of enthusiasm in the loyal militia. Because of cross-enlistments from state to state, exact figures are not obtainable, but it is clear that only New York, Pennsylvania, Illinois, Massachusetts, Ohio, and Indiana supplied more Union soldiers than Missouri. In addition, approximately thirty thousand Missourians had fought with the Confederate armies. As in other border slave states, many families had sons in both armies.

Price's defeat cleared the way for the first full-scale state election in four years. In 1863 the fifth session of the state convention, following Governor Gamble's lead, had adopted a plan to end slavery in Missouri on July 4, 1870, with those over forty years old at that time to be indentured to their masters as servants for life. Blacks under twelve in 1870 were to be indentured until they were twenty-three, and all other slaves would continue under indenture until July 4, 1876. Worn out by the stresses of his office and saddened by the incessant Radical charges that he was a pro-guerrilla "Copperhead" (only slightly more extreme than their charges against Lincoln), Governor Gamble died in January 1864. Willard P. Hall became governor, but Gamble was irreplaceable as the leader of Missouri's Conservative Unionists. In February, the legislature authorized the election of a constitutional convention to consider immediate emancipation.

Missouri was represented at the national Radical convention in May 1864, which nominated Fremont for president. The state also sent two delegations to the National Union (Republican) convention. Radicals, led by B. Gratz Brown, were pledged to U. S. Grant, and the Conservatives, acknowledging the absent Frank Blair as their leader, supported Lincoln. Surprisingly, the Union convention seated the Radicals, apparently because Lincoln wished to appease the state's dominant faction. The president feared with good reason that they might defect to Fremont and that the party split would give the victory to Democrat George B. McClellan. After the first ballot, representing the only delegation not voting for Lincoln, Brown moved to make the nomination unanimous. His price was the removal of his cousin Montgomery Blair from the cabinet. The president knuckled under, and this concession and Sherman's capture of Atlanta on September 2 prompted Fremont to withdraw from the race.

Ironically, Frank Blair had played a major role in the Atlanta campaign. In November Lincoln carried Missouri by seventy-one thousand to thirty-one thousand over McClellan, and the Radical Thomas C. Fletcher won the governorship by a similar margin. In St. Louis, Mayor Thomas was reelected, and Radicals controlled the council. A Radical split gave Conservative John Hogan one of the city's congressional seats, but Henry Taylor Blow won the other by a ten-to-one margin and the Radicals swept the state's seven other congressional races.

Radicals won three-fourths of the seats in the constitutional convention, with the test oath largely responsible. As one Conservative wrote to Lincoln, certain Confederate sympathizers, chastened by Price's rout and sniffing the future, hastened to "retrieve themselves by being more Radical than anybody else." The convention opened at the Mercantile Library Hall in St. Louis on January 6, 1865. A majority of the members were political neophytes, with only Isidor Bush, a Jewish moderate leader from St. Louis, and two others as carry-overs from the previous convention. Farmers and doctors outnumbered lawyers, who comprised only one-fifth of the sixty-six delegates. Among the extreme Radicals were former moderates from areas which had been victimized by bushwhackers. Arnold Krekel of the *St. Charles Democrat* presided, but vice-president Charles Daniel Drake of St. Louis dominated the proceedings. First a Whig, then a Know-Nothing, and finally a Democrat before the war, Drake was now an uncompromising Radical. State politics was becoming even more complex as the Radicals, having already cast moderates like Frank Blair into outer darkness, began to quarrel among themselves. The Germans disliked Drake, whom they saw as a threat to Gratz Brown. Drake and Brown disagreed over voting rights for blacks, with the former and his outside allies believing that though slavery was a curse to both races, and its abolition fitting punishment for rebels, blacks were not to be considered political and social equals. Brown's battle cry, on the other hand, was "Freedom and Franchise, one and inseparable." Having been chiefly responsible for Brown's increasingly liberal views, the German Forty-Eighters agreed.

By a vote of sixty to four, the convention on January 11 abolished slavery in Missouri and urged the state's congressmen to support the proposed Thirteenth Amendment, which would do the same nationally. Governor Fletcher immediately proclaimed that "henceforth and forever, no person within the jurisdiction of this state shall . . . know any master but God." A large, jubilant, and singing crowd, white and black, swarmed the streets near the convention hall, church bells rang, and the Stars and Stripes was raised over public buildings, businesses, and homes. Those who felt otherwise stayed out of the streets. Practically, the action merely confirmed the existing order. Most of the city's slaves had simply walked away, either to Illinois or to jobs on the levee. General Curtis, commanding in 1862–63, had shown no interest in slave-catching, and owners had eventually not even bothered to advertise for runaways.

Despite its franchise clauses, the Constitution of 1865 was in several ways a progressive document. A tax-supported free public school system was guaranteed, popular ratification of constitutional amendments was required, the often-corrupt special legislative charters were virtually eliminated, and the state was forbidden to lend its credit to private individuals and corporations. These reforms had little opposition, but the native and mostly brand-new libertarians refused to eliminate the term "white male" from the qualifications for voting and officeholding, as proposed by German delegates. Drake's major object was to disfranchise "rebels" in the broadest possible sense of the term. In this, as in denying blacks the vote, he was abetted by the rural delegates, who sat in awe as he pursued his course inflexibly, "going right forward, like a mad dog, looking neither to the left nor to the right," as one hostile reporter put it. Conservative delegate W. F. Switzler noted that Drake "hated all rebels, and hated conservatives more than rebels," and he and his followers were determined to guarantee Radical supremacy.

The Constitution's "Ironclad Oath" for voters, officeholders, corporation officers, teachers, attorneys, and ministers was much harsher than the wartime test oath. Persons in these categories had to deny eighty-six "acts or words" against the national or state government, and "desire" for Confederate success, or sympathy at any time for rebels or their cause. Even kindness to prisoners of war could be damaging. Conservatives attempted to restrict the oath to cover only the period after December 21, 1861, but the Radicals would not budge. Swearing the oath was insufficient proof of innocence; officials could reject persons on suspicion or the unsupported word of a witness (an 1866 law required all voters to register, with registrars empowered to reject oaths virtually at will). Refusal to swear for reasons of conscience created a presumption of guilt.

Not satisfied with the protections of the "Draconian Code," the convention adopted an "Ousting Ordinance" vacating the offices of all judges, circuit attorneys, sheriffs, and recorders—over eight hundred in all. Governor Fletcher reappointed Radicals, but in some counties every official was replaced. When Lafayette County officials refused to vacate, Fletcher sardonically ordered them removed by a black militia company. Because its Conservative judges might overturn Radical measures, the Supreme Court was the chief target. When the judges refused to leave the bench, they were carried away bodily by the militia.

However drastic or self-serving the Radical position may appear, it must be considered in perspective. Drake argued that "a free-State constitution" would assure the world and potential immigrants that lives and property would be protected. Lawlessness and terror had resumed their sway in the border regions, with outlaw gangs such as the James and Younger brothers emboldened by the rapid removal of the Union army. These "bushwhackers," some of them returning Confederates, others deserters, and still others plain bandits, persecuted the former slaves and any white who tried to hire them. In several instances they scalped their victims or slit their throats. Radicals asked, "Has this bloody war been fought in vain?" Drake summed it up: "We intend to erect a wall . . . as high as the eternal heavens, deep down as the very center of the earth, so that they shall neither climb over it nor dig under it, and as thick as the whole territory of Missouri so that they shall never . . . pierce through it; and never shall put upon the colored race the disqualifications which have borne them down in times past."

St. Louis was the center of the opposition. Emil Preetorius of the *Westliche Post,* a Liberal Forty-Eighter, attacked the stringency of the test oath and the "white male" provision for voting. He and other Germans detested Drake for his Know-Nothing past; they resented the constitutional provision for district instead of at-large voting for the legislature in St. Louis, since it would reduce their representation; and they thought Drake's proposal to tax church property was directed at them. Federal officeholders, who owed their appointments to Blair and Edward Bates, and Conservative lawyers and businessmen such as J. O. Broadhead, S. T. Glover, Bates, C. P. Johnson, and Isidor Bush, also assailed a code which not only violated their sense of justice and (they argued) the U.S. Constitution, but deprived them of much of their political base. In a shrewd move, Drake had insisted that ratification voters be subject to the Ironclad Oath. Bates advised all voters to swear without qualms, since this *ex post facto* requirement was unconstitutional.

Early returns from the June 6, 1865, election seemed to herald a smashing defeat for the constitution. St. Louis voted against it 10,748 to 4,822, and the eastern and central area as a whole rejected it by eleven thousand votes. But huge majorities in the northern, northwestern, and southwestern regions, all in bushwhacker country, resulting in "tomahawk" (backlash) voting, counterbalanced the eastern vote. Union soldiers in the field put the constitution across by a slim margin of 1,835 out of 85,679 votes cast. Among the disfranchised were thousands who had supported the provisional government and the Union after the first few months of the war. The effectiveness of the oath was demonstrated by the total vote, which was fifty-five thousand less than in the 1861 convention election. The *Republican* trumpeted fraud, and there was little doubt that biased application of the test oath had sealed the victory. Even so, the constitution might have failed had it not been for the reaction to Lincoln's assassination and the unfounded rumors that Jefferson Davis had been involved in the plot. Even Governor Fletcher and Senators John B. Henderson and Gratz Brown had been squeamish about the oath, finally supporting it as the alternative to Conservative domination.

The "Jacobins," as the *Republican* called them, were in the saddle, but legal challenges to their rule developed quickly. Ministers and priests, including some Unionists, refused to take the oath as a matter of conscience. Episcopal and Methodist bishops Cicero Hawks and Henry Kavanaugh spoke against it, and Archbishop Peter Kenrick advised Catholic clerics not to take it. The Missouri Baptist Association called the requirement interference with religious liberty, but the Baptist Galusha Anderson called it necessary "to hold in check the rebellious pro-slavery element . . . until the new order of things become thoroughly established."

John A. Cummings, a young priest from Louisiana, Missouri, brought matters to a head by pleading guilty to holding services without benefit of oath and then appealing his conviction to the Supreme Court. The Radical state court ruled against him, but they had a bear by the tail. Frank Blair, just back from the Grand Army's triumphal parade in Washington, described the situation: "It [the clerical oath] is inoperative. . . . In St. Louis, preachers of the gospel preach and pray and perform the marriage ceremony, and there is no Grand Jury there that will indict them for the offense." Next, Blair applied the acid test to the voters' oath by informing election judges in November 1865 that he could not swear that he had never borne arms against the state, since "in the early days of the rebellion" he had used force "against Claib Jackson and the existing government." The disconcerted judges then had to deny the ballot to a close friend of the martyred president, a distinguished major general who enjoyed the confidence of both Grant and Sherman, and who had saved the state while some of the current Radicals were denouncing him as a black Republican. Blair's attorney, Samuel Glover, then brought suit against the election officials. Both the circuit and the state supreme courts ruled against Blair, but the case embarrassed the Radicals and solidified his position as the Conservatives' leader. In 1867 the U.S. Supreme Court ruled in the Cummings case that the test oath for professional groups was both a bill of attainder and an ex post facto law in violation of Article I, Section 10 of the federal constitution. All classes subject to the oath except voters and officeholders were affected by this ruling. In 1870, after time and events had already disposed of the immediate issue, the high court upheld the Missouri ruling in the Blair case by a four-to-four vote.

In 1866, the opposition coalesced in the Conservative Union Party, led by Blair, Broadhead, Glover, O. D. Filley, T. T. Gantt, and Barton Able of St. Louis and James S. Rollins of Columbia, all former Benton Democrats or Whigs who had become Republicans by 1860. Supporting them were a group of German Radical dissenters and proslavery Unionists such as L. V. Bogy, the latter considered a Southern sympathizer by the Radicals. This broad coalition gave the Radicals a battle in St. Louis, with occasional successes aided by increasing tensions among the Radicals themselves. Ironically, a source of Radical strength in the city was the state-appointed police board, a creation of the secessionist legislature in 1861. To bolster their position, the Radical legislators in 1866 increased the number of wards in St. Louis from ten to twelve, gerrymandered them to give Radicals an edge in the city council, and created a number of new city boards, all appointed by the governor.

Though a Radical himself, Mayor J. S. Thomas had irritated party leaders by appointing a few Conservatives to office, and his appeals for the return of the police and other boards to local control went unheeded, except for the Board of Health. Not being accountable to the mayor and council, the police concentrated on Radical politics and the blackmailing of illegal gambling houses, according to the St. Louis Board of Trade. In March 1868 a legislative committee, making a show of investigating charges brought by Thomas, heard extensive testimony that top police officials were extortionists, that the police board had pressured its men to vote against Thomas in 1867 and had fired those who disobeyed, and that it had entertained official guests in "a notorious bawdyhouse." The committee exonerated the corrupt board and condemned the mayor.

The Civil War had slowed St. Louis's growth, but it had not stopped it. An increase of 43,000 in six years brought the city's population to 204,327 in 1866. Natives and second-generation

Germans and Irish were in the majority. Despite their distaste for Drake, most Germans were still Radicals, but the Irish favored the opposition. A powerful addition to the political mix arrived in 1867, when Carl Schurz came from Detroit to join Emil Preetorius as co-owner and coeditor of the *Westliche Post.* As a Union major general and the acknowledged national leader of German-American opinion, the eloquent Schurz became a potent force in the Radical Party — halfway between Blair and Drake on rebel enfranchisement but unlike either of them in favoring black political equality. More politician than editor, Schurz had his eye on the Senate. The *Post* and the *Missouri Democrat* were the leading Radical newspapers, the latter controlled by William McKee. Frank Blair, the *Democrat's* founder, charged that McKee had deserted him originally in 1861 in return for a bribe from Justus McKinstry, Fremont's crooked provost marshal. The Conservatives usually had the support of the *Anzeiger*, the *Dispatch,* the *Times,* and the *Republican*. The last, Blair's sworn enemy for fifteen years, now hailed him as a great patriot.

St. Louis's bicameral council had been reduced to a single house in 1859, but the legislature restored the two-house system in 1866. The Radicals had expected to profit from this move, but to their chagrin the Conservatives swept both houses, prompting the *Chicago Times* to crow prematurely that "the Red and Black Republicans of St. Louis have undergone the fate that should have overtaken them earlier . . . the Radicals sneaked into power and high places. While others went forward to fight, the Radicals staid home to prey." But the Registry Act went into effect before the fall election, and the Radicals swept it and several to follow. After extremists failed to unseat Mayor Thomas in the 1867 Radical convention, he was reelected over the Conservative John Finn. Thomas intended to establish a base for accelerated growth, with local control, a new waterworks, and wharf extension among his priorities. Chouteau's and Harrison's rolling mills, Filley's stove foundry, the north side warehouse district, and the North Missouri Railroad all needed improved access to the river. After much litigation with property owners, wharf extension began in 1868, and within a few years it was completed along the entire riverfront.

The waterworks constructed in the 1850s were sadly inadequate by 1865. Silt had accumulated in the reservoirs to a depth of twenty-seven feet, leaving only eleven feet for water. Tap water was muddier than ever, and in the older areas as well as in the additions, wells had to be sunk. A cholera epidemic second only to that of 1849 ravaged the city in 1866, striking hardest in the areas served by wells, which the Board of Health found to be polluted by putrid organic matter.

Typhoid fever claimed dozens of lives each year, and many buildings, including the magnificent Lindell Hotel and the *Republican* plant, were destroyed by fires which raged without sufficient water to check them. After many delays, caused in part by friction between the council and the state-appointed water commissioners, a new waterworks was completed in 1871 at Bissell's Point near the northern city limits. From a large inlet tower on the river, water was pumped to nearby settling basins holding fifty-six million gallons. From there the water was pumped to the Compton Hill Reservoir, five miles to the south at Grand and Lafayette. During slack periods water was also pumped into a large standpipe on Grand Avenue near the fairgrounds. From this point 175 feet above the foot of Market Street, gravity forced a head of water to the reservoir even in periods of high consumption, which the engines could not do. For the first time clear water flowed from the taps, a phenomenon which amazed old-timers, causing some of them to wonder what was wrong with it. The project cost nearly $5 million, financed chiefly by bond sales, but the euphoria it produced was shortlived. Industrial and population growth taxed the plant to capacity, and the water could not settle long enough to maintain its clarity. Consumption rose by 35 percent between 1872 and 1875, and effluents discharged into the river above the inlet tower compounded the problem. Not until 1904, when a filtration process was adopted at the new plant to the north at the Chain of Rocks, did St. Louis have an ample supply of pure water.

In 1871, after years of haggling and litigation with the St. Louis Gaslight Company, which had monopolized the distribution of illuminating gas since 1847, Mayor Joseph Brown agreed to divide the city into two gaslight districts, one south and the other north of Washington Avenue, the first to be served by the old company and the latter by the Laclede Gaslight Company, a new firm controlled by New York capitalists. Mayor Thomas had alleged that half of the $4.50 per thousand cubic feet rate paid by consumers under the monopoly represented profit to wealthy stockholders such as Rufus Lackland and Gerard B. Allen, and his charge seemed confirmed when both companies prospered under the reduced rate of $3.25 per thousand agreed upon in 1871. By 1879 St. Louisans, headed by Erastus Wells, had gained control of the Laclede Company.

Between 1864 and 1868, St. Louis's bonded debt ballooned from $4.8 million to $13.4 million (over $60 per capita) and city property taxes rose to $1.30 per $100, in addition to $1.55 in county and state levies. The *Republican* blamed the Radicals; and Joseph Brown, then a state legislator, complained that when the city had had no "boards," its debt was small, but now it was $14 million, "and what have we to show for it? Have we clean streets? Have we pure water? Have we fine parks? . . . There is no city in the Union where there is less cleanliness and comfort . . . and where they get less for the amount of taxes paid than in St. Louis." Brown's remarks were strictly political. The new bonded debt represented efforts to deal with the problems he complained of: $4 million for the waterworks, $2 million for land acquisition and wharf improvements, $1 million for sewer construction, and $450,000 for improvements at Tower Grove and Lafayette parks. Mayor Thomas told critics that these expenditures would "add millions to the material wealth and importance of the city," and he pointed out that county control of the city's assessments and taxes and the profligacy of the police and other state-appointed boards prevented St. Louis from making great improvements without accumulating excessive debt.

Thomas initiated an investigation of municipal departments in 1868, which led to the indictments of Comptroller Robert Deggendorf, former Comptroller Robert Wall, and ex-harbor master David Berlin. These officials had embezzled $136,000 in city funds by padding payrolls and collecting interest on the proceeds from bond sales before remitting the principal amounts to the city treasury. The mayor attributed their success to the weakness of the mayor and council under the charter. The embezzlers were Radicals, which put a period to Thomas's wavering Radicalism and gave the Conservatives political ammunition. Nathan Cole was the Radical nominee for mayor in 1869, with Thomas opposing him at the head of the "Citizen's Reform" ticket. The *Dispatch* and the *Times* supported Thomas, but the *Republican* would not forgive him his Radical past, though it endorsed the rest of the Reform slate. Cole defeated Thomas, but the Conservatives won control of the upper house, confirming the erosion of Radical strength that had appeared with the election of Erastus Wells to Congress from the First District in 1868.

Conservatives began to shed their sheeps' clothing and emerge as Democrats in 1868. Frank Blair, who had supported the Lincoln-Johnson Reconstruction plan and who had stood by Andrew Johnson during his impeachment crisis in 1867, sought the Democratic presidential nomination. But Blair was still bitter medicine for those Southerners who remembered his response to a question about his South Carolina campaign: "We left them the wells." The general had to settle for second place on the ticket behind Horatio Seymour of New York. His war record, his family, and his magnetism were assets, but his rash advocacy of using the army to overthrow Congressional Reconstruction was costly. Even so, Seymour and Blair polled 47 percent of the vote against the popular Republican candidate, U. S.

Grant. In Missouri, Grant and the state Radical ticket won easily.

Charles D. Drake replaced Gratz Brown in the U.S. Senate in 1867. Brown was ill, and he was coming around to Blair's view that the disenfranchised would eventually punish the Radicals severely. He spent his last weeks in the Senate advocating amnesty for Southerners and the franchise for blacks and women. "I stand for Universal Suffrage," he said, "and do not recognize the right of society to limit it on any grounds of race, color, or sex." Wendell Phillips called him the American de Tocqueville, but most of his senatorial colleagues thought Brown's advocacy of woman suffrage was quixotic. For the next two years, he concentrated on physical recovery, his family, and his horsecar, banking, and granite quarrying interests.

Carl Schurz stepped into Brown's shoes with the German voters. He had arrived in St. Louis as a full-fledged Radical; but he quickly sensed the shifting mood in the city, as did William Grosvenor, an editor of the *Democrat* who had been influenced by Brown. Both men gradually came around to the view that Republicans in Missouri must liberalize or perish. Consequently, Schurz advocated amnesty for ex-rebels in his campaign for the Senate in 1868. William McKee, angry because president-elect Grant had ignored his patronage recommendations, permitted Grosvenor to support Schurz editorially. The *Democrat* had suddenly discovered that "the dogma of *perpetual hate* is as un-Republican as it is anti-Christian." Senator Drake bitterly opposed Schurz, but for the first time the Radical legislature did not dance to his tune. The German bellwether was elected, and by February 1869 Liberal Republicans were calling for repeal of the test oath. Adoption of the Fifteenth Amendment in 1869 gave black males the vote; and Gratz Brown reentered the fray in 1870, demanding that voting restrictions based upon previous opinions or associations be eliminated. The Liberal position, as now advanced by Schurz, Grosvenor, and Brown, called for manhood suffrage, amnesty, tariff reduction, and civil service reform. Joseph Pulitzer, who had come to St. Louis without a penny five years earlier, gave powerful support as coeditor of the *Westliche Post.* In the summer of 1870, the Liberals bolted from the Radical convention, formed the Liberal Republican Party, and nominated Brown for governor. Blair and the Democrats, who had been "playing possum" while the Republican split developed, endorsed the Liberal ticket. Brown defeated the Radical McClurg by forty thousand votes, and the test oath repeal amendment passed by an eight-to-one margin. Drake resigned from the U.S. Senate to accept a federal judgeship, pronouncing a benediction on Brown in passing: "He has gone to the Democracy, and may the Lord have mercy on his soul."

Now cousin Gratz and cousin Frank were arm-in-arm again to the disgust of Schurz and Grosvenor, who feared that the Democrats would swallow up their new party. Blair had helped to obtain the judgeship for Drake though he believed him "no more fit for a judge than hell is for a powderhouse," because he wanted Drake's senatorial seat. The Democratic caucus nominated Blair for the Senate, and with Brown's support, he was elected. When the governor refused to follow his patronage suggestions, William McKee fired Grosvenor from the *Democrat* and made new overtures to President Grant, who now feared the Liberals enough to give McKee the appointments he wanted. By 1871 the Liberal Republican movement had spread to Illinois, Ohio, New York, and other states, attracting anti–big business elements, most of the prewar Republicans, moderates who favored amnesty, and those repelled by the corruption of the Grant regime. In 1872 a national Liberal Republican convention called by the Missourians nominated Horace Greeley for president and Gratz Brown for vice-president, and the Democrats endorsed this ticket. However, disagreement between Schurz and Brown over the latter's support of Greeley, an old-line high-tariff Whig, had disrupted the party even before the convention was over, and Grant defeated the Liberal-Democratic coalition easily. Democrat Silas Woodson was elected governor of Missouri, however, and Mayor Joseph Brown and a Democratic council controlled St. Louis. The Liberal Republican Party was dead, but the reform movement that had begun in St. Louis affected American politics for decades. Carl Schurz became Secretary of the Interior (1877–81), where he instituted improvements in the treatment of Indians. His ideas on Civil Service reform were incorporated in the Pendleton Act of 1883, the beginning of the merit system in federal employment.

Even "reform" had its darker side. There were inherent contradictions in the ideal of universal manhood suffrage. Not only were women ignored, but amnesty for ex-Confederates, short of a miraculous change in racial attitudes, meant subjugation rather than freedom for blacks, and in Missouri, blacks knew it and voted Radical. If they had doubts, the Democrats soon cleared them up. The *Republican* urged voters in 1866 to "expel those rascals, who in the bigoted spirit of Radicalism and Radical Negro equality, not only on the street cars but everywhere else, would support lazy Negroes and build fine schoolhouses for colored ABC Darians." Mayor Brown, a Union Democrat first elected in 1871, cared not a whit for black advancement, charging in his inaugural remarks that blacks "had used the (voting) privilege with all the prejudice which ignorance fostered and political partisanship encouraged." Under the Democrats, "sound judgement" would prevail.

Whether individual Radicals really believed in human equality or cynically used the black voters to punish their enemies (and there were many of both kinds in St. Louis), the defeat of Radicalism was a sad day for blacks. Their dearest friends—Brown, Schurz, and the Forty-Eighters—sounded the death-knell for their hopes by engineering the Radicals' downfall. If the Liberals could have captured the Republican Party and suppressed the seamy McKee crowd instead of making common cause with the Democrats, the story might have had a different ending, but they did not. By the early 1870s, the early promise had faded, leaving the blacks with the crumbs from the economic and political tables.

8.
The Fourth City?

Despite the stresses of Reconstruction, the St. Louis press and assorted publicists were united in their frenzy to confirm the city's title as the great city of the West. If it was not, they proposed to make it so, and if they could not, they would say it was anyway—just as their counterparts in Chicago would have done. Favored by their remoteness from the fighting, preferential freight rates on the eastern-owned railroad lines from the Hannibal and St. Joseph northward, and the iron ring thrown around St. Louis's commerce by Treasury Secretary Salmon P. Chase, Chicago's merchants during the war had seized the lion's share of the trade of the upper valley, and the Windy City's population had nearly tripled to 298,000 during the decade.

The federal census takers in St. Louis in 1870, Grant-administration appointees who owed their jobs to William McKee of the *Missouri Democrat*, carefully withheld their returns until Chicago's figures had been released. To the relief of businessmen such as Edward Walsh, the census revealed that despite the war's dislocations and the evil reputation bushwhacker activity had given Missouri, the Mound City's population had doubled to 310,000, leaving Baltimore and Boston in its dust as it became the nation's fourth largest city, behind New York, Philadelphia, and Brooklyn. The Chicago papers furiously cried fraud, as indeed it was, but the Census Bureau held its ground. The perpetrators kept their secret, and whatever their private doubts, St. Louisans basked in their triumph, though the *Republican* noted that several smaller cities had larger school enrollments. What a nasty shock it was in 1880, after a decade of apparent substantial growth including vastly extended boundaries, to discover that the city had gained only 40,000 people, for a total of 350,000, while Chicago had shot ahead to a half-million. Then there were questions raised about the previous census, led by Joseph Pulitzer of the *Post-Dispatch*, who had become the city's leading gadfly and balloon deflator. J. Thomas Scharf estimated in 1882 that the 1870 returns had been inflated by ninety-seven thousand, but the true figure was probably less, since he hoped to make the 1870–80 gain appear as large as possible. In any case, the exaggerated totals stand, without a footnote, relentlessly spawning erroneous scholarly conclusions.

L. U. Reavis. *Lithograph by Forbes and Co., ca. 1876. Preeminent St. Louis booster Logan U. Reavis promoted St. Louis in his book* St. Louis: The Future Great City of the World, *issued in at least six editions between 1870 and 1882. MHS-PP.*

Ridiculous exaggeration, or puffery, as Horace Greeley called it, was endemic in nineteenth-century cities and towns, and never more than during the Gilded Age after the Civil War. Chicago's nickname, the Windy City, referred to more than the lake breezes; and towns with no past, very little present, and no future were gaudily advertised as successors to Babylon and Rome. As has been noted, William Gilpin had touted Cairo, Illinois, as the city of destiny before he transferred the title successively to St. Louis, Independence, Kansas City, and Denver. Napoleon, Arkansas, had its moment of glory, as did Falls City, Nebraska; Chariton, Missouri; Alton, Illinois; and a host of Parises and New Athenses. Daniel Drake in Cincinnati, John S. Wright in Chicago, Jesup W. Scott in Toledo, and Robert T. Van Horn in Kansas City trumpeted the virtues of their metropolises, elaborating their locational and economic advantages and their rail and water connections.

One of the most vigorous of these town boomers was Logan U. Reavis, an Illinois newspaperman who had hustled real estate in Falls City, Nebraska, before he bought the faltering *St. Louis Daily Press* in 1866. When this paper failed after a few months, Reavis began a campaign to remove the national capital to St. Louis. The *Western*

Journal had advocated this as early as 1848, and others had taken up the theme during the 1850s, but the capital-removal scheme did not catch fire until after the Civil War. Midwestern editors asserted the region's claims to the capital as the home of the Republican Party, the contributor of more than a million men to the Union army, and the geographic and population center of the country. As Joseph Medill of the *Chicago Tribune* put it in 1869 "[the Middle West's] voice will be the voice of the nation . . . and will control, direct, and govern all interests pertaining to the Republic."

In support of St. Louis's claim, Reavis called it "the Babylon of the New World, not standing on the Euphrates, but on the banks of the great Mississippi." Washington had been located to suit the original states, he said, but now a nation which spanned the continent required a new capital. St. Louis was strategically located between New York and San Francisco, Chicago and New Orleans; the Mississippi valley would soon surpass all other sections in population, commerce, and political power; and the national interest demanded that "the ruling power of a nation be located in the midst of its material power." Medill agreed, noting that while Columbus, Ohio, was currently the center of population, that rapidly moving point would eventually rest permanently at St. Louis, which was therefore the logical site for the capital. Surprised but delighted by the Chicago editor's generosity, the *Republican* assumed that the entire Midwest would rally to the cause, and suggested that the city donate land for government buildings. Washington's federal buildings should be dismantled, moved, and rebuilt in St. Louis before additional ones could be erected in the old capital. In New Orleans, *De Bow's Review* argued that "St. Louis with its healthful climate, beautiful highlands, and metropolitan character, with its central situation in the midst of our greatest industries, and equally accessible to all parts of the country . . . should be made the Capitol of the United States."

In October 1869, at the invitation of the Merchants' Exchange, governors and delegates from twenty-one states and territories (including most of the middle-western and border states, Pennsylvania, Oregon, Alabama, Louisiana, and the territories of Colorado, New Mexico, Utah, Montana, and Alaska) met at the Mercantile Library in St. Louis to discuss capital removal. This convention urged Congress to select a central site for the capital and named Lee R. Shryock of St. Louis president and Logan Reavis secretary of the committee to publicize the cause. Reavis toured the East to promote removal, but the idea was naturally unpopular there, and, despite the efforts of Congressman Erastus Wells, the House of Representatives squashed the project by appropriating funds for new federal buildings in Washington. Reavis did not drop the subject, but everyone else did, and he eventually became an object of ridicule, not because his plan lacked merit, but because it had failed.

In his book, *St. Louis: The Future Great City of the World*, written in 1870, revised several times, and distributed widely in both English and German by the St. Louis County Court, Reavis expounded the familiar theme of the isothermal zodiac. Having followed the fortieth parallel westward from the Tigris-Euphrates valley through Europe to North America, civilization would reach its full flowering in the Mississippi valley, where "two waves of civilization, the one rolling in from the Celestial Empire, and the other from the land of Alfred and Charlemagne—will meet and commingle together in one great swelling tide of humanity, in the land of Hiawatha." More prosaically, Reavis produced commercial data from which he concluded that St. Louis, at the center of the nation's resources, was the natural hub of its commerce, and that its ultimate rivals were not the valley cities, but New York and Boston, which drew the interior's wealth to themselves through their Chicago satellite. The great valley's best outlet to Europe was the Gulf of Mexico, and St. Louis, with federal assistance, should improve the Mississippi and build railroads to the Gulf ports. The east-west railroads and the Mississippi and Missouri Rivers would facilitate manufacturing and raw-material handling at the Mound City. Reavis's emphasis on the city's strategic river location led some to conclude that St. Louisans waited complacently for an inevitable process to make them rich and powerful, but he did not say that greatness would come without effort. Unfortunately, neither did he say that the infusion of capital required to reroute the nation's commerce would have to come from Eastern sources which had a vested interest in the Chicago connection.

Reavis's influence is difficult to assess. His book circulated in Europe, especially in Germany, and it may have stimulated some of the substantial foreign immigration to St. Louis during the 1870s and 1880s. Any complacency arising from his emphasis on inevitable progress would have been negative, but it seems doubtful that many business decisions were thus affected, and commerce and public works expanded as rapidly as capital became available. Eastern investment in St. Louis enterprises did escalate after the war, the more so as the city developed its southwestern hinterland.

Compounding St. Louis's commercial problems in the upper valley, the Confederate blockade of the lower Mississippi, effective until 1863, had cut off direct access to foreign markets. After the war, the impoverished South, formerly an important outlet for the Mound City's merchants, could buy little of anything from anyone. These

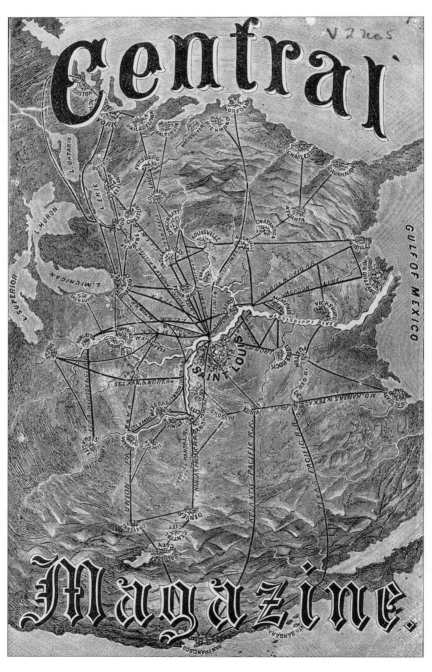

The cover of Central Magazine *for July 1874 featured the St. Louis view of the world with this map emphasizing its primacy. Wood engraving by William Mackwitz, 1874. MHS Library.*

calamities called for an organized response, and in 1866 the Union Merchants' Exchange, led by E. O. Stanard, Adolphus Meier, Henry Taylor Blow, and Isidor Bush, spun off the Board of Trade, which was charged with restoring the city's "rightful" commercial position by lobbying, information gathering, and propaganda. Federal assistance for local railroads and improvement of navigation on the Mississippi and its western tributaries were top priorities, but the board also established contacts in inland towns and sponsored experiments in industrial techniques.

In their effort to recover their prewar supremacy, merchants adopted the commercial traveler system, and by 1866 "drummers" from St. Louis competed with Chicagoans in Iowa, Illinois, Minnesota, and Kansas. They made some inroads, but, despite their better manners (according to the *Republican*), they found the well-established Chicago "rowdies" hard to handle. But as the southern economy sputtered back to life, and as the Iron Mountain and the Atlantic and Pacific Railroads opened new routes to the Southwest, old and new markets and raw-material sources stimulated business in St. Louis. By 1880, twelve hundred drummers were taking orders for the city's wares from Nebraska and Colorado to Texas and from southern Illinois to Mobile. Within a decade economic ties with the South were stronger than in antebellum days.

St. Louis had been a significant, though not major, outlet for southern cotton during the 1850s, and receipts of fifty-five thousand bales, in 1866, exceeded prewar levels. But within two years, the cotton traffic had declined sharply as downriver and Gulf ports revived economically. In an imaginative effort to reverse this decline, the Cotton Exchange offered a prize of five thousand dollars for the best grade of cotton submitted at the Mississippi Valley Fair in 1870, and within four years, three cotton compress companies were established in the city. By reducing its bulk, compressing cotton nullified the economic advantage of shipping by water, and St. Louis's rail connections to New York and Fall River gave it an edge over downriver ports. In 1874 cotton receipts exceeded one hundred thousand bales for the first time.

The St. Louis Compress Company, founded in 1873 by Colonel J. W. Paramore and W. M. Senter, was the largest of its kind in the world. Its original two-story plant, on Park Avenue at the levee, occupied fifteen acres and had a capacity of 150,000 bales. Within a few years, an even larger facility had been added near the railroad terminals in the Mill Creek Valley. Its powerful hydraulic and steam presses squeezed the five-hundred-pound bales to a thickness of nine inches, allowing fifty of them to be loaded onto a railroad car. By

1880, with receipts of 496,570 bales, St. Louis was the third largest cotton market in the nation, behind New Orleans and Savannah, and it was the largest interior market in the world. Unlike 1866, when 95 percent of its ginned cotton had arrived by steamboat, the Iron Mountain and other southwestern railroads carried 464,000 bales to the city in 1880, while steamboats and barges carried 30,200 bales. Local mills consumed only of fraction, while the bulk was compressed and shipped to the New England mills via the Ohio and Mississippi Railroad. Thomas Allen of the Iron Mountain Railroad gave the compress companies favorable rates, and their freight cars were filled in both directions. In 1879, Paramore, Senter, and other cotton men organized the Cotton Belt line, which had connections to Dallas, Laredo, and the Indian Territory. Aided by a federal land grant, this road sprouted not only cotton fields but dozens of large sawmills in its wake as it crossed Arkansas and northern Texas.

The demands of the cotton trade emphasized the need for a railroad bridge across the Mississippi. Since 1820 the Wiggins Ferry Company, which owned four miles of riverfront in Illinoistown, had virtually monopolized cross-river transportation. In 1832, Andrew and Samuel Christy, the elder Bernard Pratte, John O'Fallon, and others had bought the company from Samuel Wiggins. The Christys bought out O'Fallon in 1838, and in 1865 some twenty-five of their descendants still owned most of the company's stock, though the Wigginses retained a minority ownership and operational management. After thirty-three years as a partnership, the firm was incorporated by the Illinois legislature in 1853 with Samuel Wiggins as president. Under Wiggins and his successor, Louis V. Bogy, the company provided space for the terminals, warehouses, and yards of the Ohio and Mississippi, the Wabash, the Chicago and Alton, and other railroads, easily accessible to the Illinoistown ferry landings. In addition to eight ferry boats, it maintained three transfer boats for railroad freight in 1865.

For the railroads, the disadvantages of the ferry system were high rates, the necessity of breaking bulk to cross the river, and the long delays caused by the frozen river during severe winters. Navigation was suspended for twenty-seven days in 1865–66, for thirty-eight days the following winter, and for forty-one days in 1867–68. Coal prices in St. Louis set new records in these years. The ferry company's rates and arrogant delays constantly irritated passengers and local shippers. Illinois farmers in 1865 complained that ferry fees were costing them more than land rent: "We will take stock in the Bridge Company, if necessary, anything to free us from that nightmare Ferry, which is not only a terror, but a real vampire, sucking our very lifeblood." In 1870, in response to the threat of a railroad bridge and the example of a small ferry company upriver, the Wiggins Ferry installed inclines at Mound Street and at Chouteau Avenue, which permitted railroad cars to be run onto barges equipped with rails. By 1872 these barges could handle 450 cars a day.

A plan for a Mississippi bridge in St. Louis had been rejected as early as 1839 because of its staggering cost, but as the Ohio and Mississippi Railroad neared completion at Illinoistown in the mid-1850s, it was widely assumed that a bridge would soon follow. Josiah Dent, J. H. Lucas, John O'Fallon, John How, Andrew Christy, and Major J. R. Bissell organized a bridge company in 1855; the same year the Rock Island Railroad spanned the Mississippi with a wooden drawbridge at Rock Island, Illinois. Bissell's plan for a suspension bridge called for an investment of $1.5 million, but the Ohio and Mississippi could not afford it. Eastern capitalists, already committed to northern routes, were not interested, and the project died. During its brief life, however, the company joined steamboat captains, the Corps of Engineers, and Secretary of War Jefferson Davis in opposing the Rock Island bridge as an obstruction to navigation. They lost this battle in the courts, but the affair was more than a simple confrontation between steamboat and railroad interests. Steamboatmen feared all bridges, but the Rock Island structure would connect the East by railroad to the bonanza lands of Iowa and beyond, and it united St. Louis railroad and rivermen against their Chicago and Eastern rivals. Bissell did not oppose all Mississippi bridges, just the design of the one at hand. As if to demonstrate his foresight, the steamboat *Effie Alton* smashed into a Rock Island pier a few months later and burned to the waterline. A couple of years later, a new and less hazardous bridge replaced the original at Rock Island.

The war distracted attention from bridge building in the Mound City until February 1864, when Chauncey I. Filley, E. O. Stanard, John H. Lightner, Carlos Greeley, John M. Krum, E. W. Fox, Truman J. Homer, Senator Norman Cutter and others incorporated the St. Louis and Illinois Bridge Company, which was to build a bridge of iron and steel at St. Louis, constructed so "as not to obstruct or impede the navigation of the river." Subsequent amendments required that the bridge accommodate both railroad and common road traffic, that it be high enough to avoid obstructing steamboats at normal water stages, and that its piers be widely spaced to permit safe navigation. City Engineer Homer estimated that local citizens, railroads, and industries would save $1.8 million a year in fares and freight charges at current levels of population and commercial activity. "If we are to grow commercially," he argued, "this tax [high ferry rates] on our railroads must cease." An aldermanic committee headed by Erastus Wells then recommended that the city and county should subscribe to the bridge company's stock and urged that high steamboat chimneys be prevented from interfering with the structure. As an adjunct to the bridge, the committee urged the city to build a central railroad freight and passenger depot.

Meanwhile, the company had obtained an Illinois charter guaranteeing bridge access to all railroads terminating in East St. Louis and requiring the structure to be located within one hundred feet of the Bloody Island Causeway, directly opposite Washington Avenue. Senator B. Gratz Brown introduced the bridge authorization bill in Congress, which passed it in July 1866 without specifying a particular location or bridge company. The law permitted neither a suspension nor a drawbridge; the center of each span was to be at least 50 feet higher than the city directrix; and there had to be at least one span 500 feet long or two spans of not less than 350 feet.

By 1868 Mississippi bridges had been completed at Quincy, Illinois, and Clinton and Dubuque, Iowa, all of them serving railroads with Chicago connections. Three bridges over the Missouri were also projected or under construction — at Kansas City, Omaha, and St. Charles (the last by St. Louis businessmen, including J. B. Eads). Meanwhile, Chicago interests worked feverishly to block the St. Louis project. Southern Illinois legislators had beaten back efforts to defeat the charter in 1865, but the upstate lobby had another string to their bow. General John M. Palmer, Gustavus Koerner, T. B. Blackstone of the Chicago and Alton Railroad, Lucius Boomer, and others had decided either to stop the bridge or to control it. Boomer persuaded Chicago legislators in January 1867 to introduce bills repealing the St. Louis company's charter and incorporating the Illinois and St. Louis Bridge Company, with an exclusive right for twenty-five years, to bridge the river at East St. Louis. These maneuvers were quickly reported to St. Louis, and at an emergency meeting of the Merchants' Exchange James B. Eads, Edgar Ames, and others sounded the alarm. Ames, a meatpacker, banker, and insurance executive with a distinguished civic record, attacked the Chicago schemers and nominated General William A. Pile to head a delegation to Springfield to frustrate them. By emphasizing the common interests of southern Illinois and St. Louis, Pile helped defeat the repeal measure.

Boomer and Blackstone got their twenty-five-year monopoly, but restrictions suggested by the St. Louisans put them in a straitjacket. By requiring that the eastern end of the bridge be in St. Clair County, the legislators blocked any attempt by Chicago and Alton to isolate

St. Louis by bridging the river near Alton. If the Chicagoans' intent was merely to prevent the building of any bridge, as the *Republican* believed, they were frustrated by a provision that they must begin construction within two years and complete it in five. Like it or not, the Illinois Company was committed—they had to put up or shut up. Boomer immediately contacted his old associates of the Pacific Railroad, for whom he had built the disastrous Gasconade bridge a dozen years earlier, and through them he obtained a Missouri charter for his bridge company. Daniel R. Garrison of the Pacific's board was named president, James Harrison and Charles P. Chouteau directors, and S. S. Post and Boomer engineers of the Missouri corporation. Doubts about Boomer's intentions persisted, but despite the wily Garrison's elastic conscience and dubious record, he was still interested in the Ohio and Mississippi Railroad as well as the Pacific. It is inconceivable that James Harrison of the Pacific, a leading St. Louis industrialist and bank director, or Chouteau, who was Harrison's partner and a former director of the Ohio and Mississippi, would deliberately deny St. Louis a bridge, especially in collusion with Chicago interests. The Missouri and Illinois versions of Boomer's company quickly consolidated, and he began his surveys.

By autumn, there were three bridge companies in the field; the third, a short-lived project called the Alton and St. Charles Bridge Company, proposed to span the Mississippi at Bissell's Point, near the Chouteau, Harrison, and Vallé Rolling Mills. Its leading spirits were Isaac Sturgeon of the North Missouri Railroad, B. Gratz Brown, and G. H. Rea, giving the company a Radical Republican flavor. This bridge would complement the North Missouri's projected span at St. Charles, and Sturgeon argued that the other proposed bridges would disrupt downtown St. Louis. The Alton Bridge did not obtain an Illinois charter, and when James B. Eads and Gerard Allen, both of whom were interested in the Washington Avenue bridge, joined the North Missouri's board, the project was dropped.

There were rumors that the Wiggins Ferry had collaborated with the Chicago lobby at Springfield, and there is no doubt that its operators feared a bridge. However, the hated monopoly had little influence with downstate legislators, and its president, Louis V. Bogy, vigorously denied the charge. The *Democrat* pointed out that the ferry company would profit more from a bridge than from a continuation of its monopoly, because of the inevitable boom in the value of its vast riverfront landholdings.

Despite its uncertain legal position (Boomer cracked that Eads would end up with a bridge sticking halfway across the river), the St. Louis company proceeded. On May 1, 1867, the board was reorganized, with Charles K. Dickson, board chairman of the North Missouri and a bank official, as president. The directors were a combination of St. Louis and eastern financial and railroad luminaries, including Thomas A. Scott of the Pennsylvania Railroad, New York banker Amos Cotting, and Barton Bates, John R. Lionberger, Dr. William Taussig, Josiah Fogg, and James B. Eads. Eads was named chief engineer, responsible for planning the structure.

Since 1838, when he was eighteen years old, James Buchanan Eads had lived on and in the Mississippi River. After four years as a steamboat clerk, the self-taught engineer invented a diving bell and joined boat builders Calvin Case and William Nelson in the salvage business. For the next fifteen years, with some interruptions, Eads explored the Mississippi from St. Louis to New Orleans for sunken wrecks, personally making more than five hundred trips to the bottom, at times as much as sixty-five feet below the surface. This perilous work in the treacherous bottom currents was highly profitable, with salvage fees from shippers and insurance companies ranging from 20 to 75 percent of the value of cargoes (after five years, cargoes recovered belonged to the finder). By the 1850s Eads had a fleet of "submarines" (salvage vessels equipped with a diving bell, air hoses, and hoisting gear) operating on the Mississippi and its lower tributaries. In the process, Eads had become a walking encyclopedia of knowledge about the river bottom and the scouring action of the current.

Eads's rare talents were put to good use during the Civil War. In 1862, when the army projected a full-scale assault to break the Confederate grip on the lower Mississippi, he volunteered to build an ironclad gunboat flotilla within sixty-five days. At the Nelson-Eads shipyard in Carondelet, he built seven of these alligator-shaped monsters, making possible the capture of Island Number 10 in the Mississippi and U. S. Grant's victories at Forts Henry and Donelson on the Tennessee. At the end of the war, Eads was known nationally as a daring and resourceful engineer. He was president of an insurance company and a member of the Union Merchants' Exchange and the Board of Trade, strongly committed to civic betterment. He had not been a founder of the local bridge company, but when it was threatened by Lucius Boomer, he joined the battle.

At the Washington Avenue location, Eads had the advantage of the narrow channel at that point—fifteen hundred feet as opposed to seventeen hundred at Boomer's Cherry Street site one-half mile to the north. Washington's unusual width (the heritage of old Jeremiah Connor) made it suitable for heavy vehicular traffic and compatible

James B. Eads. *Cabinet card photograph by J. A. Scholten, ca. 1869. MHS-PP.*

with the four-lane upper level of the bridge. Its central location was convenient for vehicles and would minimally impede the maneuvers of upriver and downriver steamboats at the wharf; and most of the railroads at East St. Louis terminated at Bloody Island, directly opposite Washington. The street's high elevation provided an easy gradient to the bridge's top level at the western approach, and, most important, the layer of sand covering the bedrock upon which the piers must stand was thinner than at alternative sites.

In choosing his design, Eads sought to minimize construction problems by erecting as few channel piers as possible, thus requiring longer spans and larger piers to bear their weight. Suspension bridges, long popular because of their beauty, were dropping into rivers at an alarming rate, and Congress had ruled them out at St. Louis. Boomer and most other contemporary bridge builders favored the truss design, suitable only for spans of up to 350 feet, and requiring at least five piers at any St. Louis site. Eads had built no bridges, but he knew the river bottom better than any other man, and his two university-educated

German assistants understood the characteristics of metal under stress and the intricacies of bridge design. Henry Flad, a former St. Louis water commissioner, had been a colonel of engineers during the war, and he proved to be Eads's right-hand man. Charles Pfeifer was an expert on arch bridges. With their advice, Eads selected an upright arch design, which had twice the load-carrying capacity of the suspension or truss alternatives, enabling him to use longer spans safely. When he and his assistants had finished their computations, Eads took the precaution of having them verified by a distinguished mathematician, Chancellor William Chauvenet of Washington University.

On July 15, 1867, Eads presented his plan to his directors. There were to be three spans: the two side spans measuring 497 feet "in the clear" from the shore abutment to a channel pier, and a center span of 515 feet in the clear between the two channel piers. Actually, each span was several feet longer if measured in the usual fashion, to the center of the piers. As eventually modified, each span consisted of eight steel arch tubes, cut in twelve-foot sections eighteen inches in diameter, perfectly straight but beveled at a slight angle at each end, creating the illusion of a perfect arch, the sections coupled together by enveloping half-cylinders. Each section consisted of six steel staves crammed into a thin steel envelope. The tubes were distributed in four sets, with the arches of each set twelve feet apart vertically. Each outer arch was 16.5 feet from its interior neighbor, the interior arches were twelve feet apart, and a system of diagonal, horizontal, and vertical braces connected the tubes. The vertical separation of the two members of each set was especially important, checking the tendency of the upright arch to slip out from under its load. The two traffic levels were supported by iron beams, which were in turn supported by iron struts extending from the arch tubes. Footways bounded the upper roadway, which was thirty-three feet wide. Including the foundations, the superstructure, the approaches, the tunnel, land costs, and the double-tracked railway on the lower level, Eads estimated in 1867 that the bridge would cost $4.5 million.

Despite a condescending rejection of the Eads plan by J. H. Linville, a consultant from the Keystone Bridge Company of Pittsburgh, the directors approved the design. Now, the major obstacle was Lucius Boomer, who convened a group of engineers from all over the country at the Southern Hotel on August 21, 1867. Ostensibly, these engineers were to judge the merits of both bridge plans, but most of them were truss-bridge experts, and they ignored Eads and his design. Predictably, they endorsed the six-span truss design submitted by S. S. Post, a noted New York engineer connected with Boomer's company. Referring indirectly to Eads, they called five-hundred-foot spans "hazardous" and piers sunk to bedrock expensive and unnecessary, a scheme advanced "for his [Eads's] own personal eclat or aggrandizement. . . ." Eads knew that the "hard material" that covered the bedrock was not impervious, because he had been there. Unlike the wider channels at upstream bridges, the river at St. Louis often froze over completely, forcing descending ice floes to grind their way beneath the surface, creating currents that scoured away the hard-packed bottom sand. This was verified during construction, when chunks of coal and unpetrified bones and sticks were found deep in this layer, and the bedrock itself had been worn smooth by alluvial action.

During their deliberations, the assembled engineers heard the jarring sounds of Eads's crews tearing up the wharf at the foot of Washington Avenue. They circulated their anti-Eads report widely, hoping to impede the St. Louis Company's fund-raising efforts, but the directors stood firm, and their New York backers did not withdraw. Discouraged by their determination, his own inadequate financing, and probably under pressure from the St. Louisans on his own board, Boomer gave up the ghost. In January 1868 James Harrison of St. Louis, representing Boomer's firm, agreed with Eads to merge the two companies under the name of the Illinois and St. Louis Bridge Company. Most of the directors and officers and the chief engineer of the Dickson-Lionberger-Eads organization were retained in the merger. Illinois did not require a new charter, and in Missouri it was merely a formality.

Originally, the directors had planned to finance the project primarily by selling bonds guaranteed by the city. St. Louis voters approved this plan, but the directors, fearing interference by the city, decided not to use it. In December 1868 the board authorized $3 million in capital stock, with 40 percent of each purchase payable in cash. By selling 6 percent first mortgage bonds worth $4 million at a 10 percent discount, they would have a total of $4.8 million in ready cash. Director William McPherson, a former president of the Pacific Railroad, and Amos Cotting placed three-fifths of the stock in New York, and the remainder was sold locally in February 1869. Among the St. Louis subscribers were directors Gerard B. Allen, John A. Lionberger, Charles K. Dickson, Barton Bates, Josiah Fogg, William Taussig, McPherson, and Eads, and non-directors Hudson Bridge, S. R. Filley, James H. Britton, Carlos Greeley, and George and John Knapp of the *Republican*. In New York, the principal stockholders were the financial houses of Jameson, Smith, and Cotting; E. D. Morgan and Company; Dabney, Morgan, and Company; and Junius S. Morgan. W. R. Morrison and David Gillespie of the former Boomer Company were also directors of the reorganized firm.

Excavation for the west abutment reached bedrock, forty-seven feet below the city directrix, in February 1868. On February 25, Eads directed the emplacement of the first three-thousand-pound Grafton limestone foundation block. Work went slowly because of flooding where a coffer dam protected the site from sand but not water, and the abutment was not completed for two years. It measured 112.7 feet from top to bedrock, 94 feet by 63 feet at its base, and 64 feet by 48 feet at its top. Because the bedrock was much deeper on the east side, that abutment was 193 feet high, with a larger base but the same top dimensions as its counterpart. The limestone cores of the abutments were enclosed by layers of granite, to add strength and resistance to weathering.

During a European trip in 1868–69, Eads studied the new *plenum pneumatic* method of underwater construction, which he adopted for his channel piers. In this system, compressed air was forced into a watertight iron cylinder, or caisson, keeping the water out of the bottom air chamber and supplying the "submarines" (sand-hogs) with oxygen while they shoveled sand into suction pumps that discharged it at the surface. The outer foundation of the pier was laid inside the caisson and lowered as the caisson descended (thus the term "sinking" a pier). At the east pier, where sixty-eight feet of sand covered the bedrock, excavation began in November 1869 and was completed in four months, despite delays caused by extreme cold and ice. After setting the masonry foundation in bedrock, the submarines worked their way back up the core, filling it with concrete and leaving beneath them a solid foundation pier, 16 stories high (197 feet), with external dimensions of 82 feet by 48 feet, and 63 feet by 24 feet. Both piers were above the waterline by May 1870.

For the submarines, this pioneering venture was a killer. No one had ever worked in compressed air at such depths before, and little was known about the effects of decompression. Eads himself had been ill frequently during his career, but he had never ascribed this to his work in the diving bell. The "caisson disease," or "bends," caused by nitrogen bubbles forming in the bloodstream during decompression, could be avoided only by a gradual reduction of pressure. Since every foot of the caisson's descent required more pressure, men working at the one-hundred-foot level should have undergone more than two hours of decompression before emerging, instead of their usual five minutes. Submarines worked three two-hour watches for four dollars a day, double the prevailing wage, but hardly commensurate with the hazards involved. In March 1870, after James Riley died just after leaving the caisson, Eads shortened the watches to one hour and requested Dr. Alphonse Jaminet to study the disease. After undergoing decompression in three and one-half minutes, which temporarily paralyzed and nearly killed him, Jaminet concluded that too-rapid compression and decompression were responsible. He erred in the former and did not understand the reasons for the latter, but he set up a decompression schedule—one minute for each six pounds above normal atmospheric pressure—which reduced the effects of but did not eliminate the bends. Pressure at the east pier bedrock was nearly sixty pounds per square inch, requiring eight minutes of decompression under Jaminet's formula. Of the 600 men who worked in the air chambers, 119 suffered severely and 14 died.

Using a caisson as at the channel piers, Eads completed the east abutment within six months, and by 1871 all was ready for the superstructure. He had extended the civil engineering frontiers, and he intended the rest of the structure to meet the same standards. The Keystone Company had been awarded the construction contract, despite Linville's objections to the design. Work on the spans went slowly, primarily because American steelmakers were not ready for Eads. His exacting tolerance and quality requirements confounded an industry which was still oriented to iron rather than steel and accustomed to approximate standards with adjustments during construction instead of fabricating to exact specifications. Henry Flad had designed a testing machine which detected minute variations in measurements and tensile strength, and Eads or Flad rejected imperfect materials with monotonous regularity. When the carbon steel furnished by the Carnegie-Kloman Company consistently failed the tests, Eads turned to chrome steel, a new alloy, for the arch-tube sections. Since he did not specify chemical composition, insisting only that the steel pass his mechanical tests, the subcontractors varied the product as they saw fit. As a result, the great arches were a melange of high-grade chrome steel and a variety of carbon steels. The connecting braces were also a problem, and not until the summer of 1872 did Carnegie-Kloman furnish wrought iron that met even the compromise standards that Eads had grudgingly agreed to under pressure from a fuming Andrew Carnegie (now a shareholder in the St. Louis bridge). In other components as well, Eads often had to settle for wrought iron. In the end, the great steel bridge was more than half wrought iron.

Before the arches were closed, the company had to stave off one last attack by spoilers. Captain John McCune of the Keokuk and Northern Line Packet Company led a group of steamboatmen who registered a double-barrelled complaint. After the design had been public information for six years, the river men discovered in 1873 that an arch spanning the river would not be equidistant from the water at all points! It was not fair that there would be fifty feet of clearance only at the center of the spans, and even that was not enough for larger steamboats, they argued, unless their nine-thousand-pound smokestacks were fitted with expensive and dangerous hinged lowering devices.

Secretary of War William Belknap responded by convening a board of army engineers to recommend modifications in the bridge. Given the Corps' long-standing alliance with the boatmen and its Chief A. A. Humphreys's dislike for Eads or any civilian who understood rivers better than he did, the board's report was predictable. Major G. K. Warren, their investigator, recommended that the "monster" be razed and replaced by a drawbridge, but the board concluded that too much money had been spent to justify removal. Instead, they proposed an eight-hundred-foot canal around the bridge on the east side. Their report drew a furious blast from the *Republican*, which estimated that the "absurd [canal] project" would cost $6.5 million. Since there were only fifteen river boats high enough to be hampered by the bridge, none of them worth more than sixty-five thousand dollars, why not buy them all and end the controversy? Further, rail passenger service was making three-deckers obsolete, and the more efficient low-lying barges were capturing the freight market. By the time the canal was in service, no one would need it.

Eads refuted the engineers' report in writing, and then he and Taussig went to Washington to appeal to Secretary Belknap. Despite that slippery official's assurances to the contrary, he sent the army engineers' report to Congress with his approval. With some trepidation, because Eads had opposed Grant's reelection in 1872 and Taussig as a county commissioner in 1859 had blocked Grant's appointment as county engineer, they took their case to the president. To their relief, Grant assured them that he did not mind having lost the county appointment, since he had found a better job. Better still, he remembered Eads's gunboats and was unimpressed with the engineers' case. In Taussig's and Eads's presence, he bluntly ordered the red-faced Belknap to stop opposing the bridge, and the matter ended there.

Work had continued during the controversy, and despite problems with closing the arches because of a slight overlap, the spans were ready by December 18, 1873. The interior braces and struts and the upper roadway were completed by April 1874, and on May 24, a Sunday, twenty-five thousand persons (at five cents each) thronged the upper level, many of them enjoying the cool breezes for hours. Its construction had entertained thousands, and the bridge had become a grand social amenity. Water fountains, extra seats, and a refreshment stand encouraged and sustained the weekend crowds. In June, the structure was subjected to a series of tests. First, Joseph Gartside drove a streamered four-horse coal wagon across, then a locomotive tested the rails, and on June 14, John Robinson strolled over the upper level with an unconcerned elephant. The last reassured the multitude, but Eads had something more rigorous in mind. On July 2, fourteen locomotives pulling loaded coal tenders chugged in double file to the center of each span, paused to put a maximum strain on the arches, and then passed in single file along each span to test its side strength. When asked whether he had been relieved that the bridge survived, Eads answered that he "had felt no relief because I had felt no anxiety on the subject."

The 4,880-foot double tunnel from the west approach on Washington near Third Street to the Mill Creek Valley was completed on June 24, and on July 4, 1874, the city celebrated the bridge's formal opening. Sylvester Laflin, Barton Able, and Chauncey I. Filley were the prime movers of the colossal affair, attended by nearly everyone in the city who was not bedridden, as well as thousands from outstate Missouri, Illinois, and other states—more than two hundred thousand in all, according to press reports. The symbols of republicanism,

Eads Bridge. The Erection: The Ribs Completed and the Roadways Begun. *Photograph by Robert Benecke, 1873. MHS-PP.*

nationalism, enterprise, and inevitable progress were all in evidence. The Third Street approach featured a fifty-foot-high portrait of Eads with the caption, "St. Louis founded by Laclède, 1764: crowned Queen of the West, 1874." Beneath the portrait were symbolic figures of Missouri and Illinois clasping hands. On the Illinois side, a "great triumphal arch" loomed above the approach, with a large statue of the Goddess of Liberty beneath it. At daylight, a thirteen-gun salute honored the thirteen original states; at 9:00 A.M., one hundred guns roared, fifty on each side of the river; and at noon, thirty-seven guns saluted the states and territories.

The fourteen-mile parade required two hours to pass a given point and began with Grand Marshal Arthur H. Barret escorted by police and twenty-two uniformed boys on ponies. The procession included a U.S. cavalry company, two national guard companies, the Turners, the Knights Templar, fifteen hundred Odd Fellows and many other fraternal orders, a massive replica of the Merchants' Exchange, the Fire Department, the New Orleans Orchestra, six hundred members of the German singing societies, the U.S. customshouse officials in a full-rigged sailing ship on wheels, the Brewers' Association featuring King Gambrinus, several rowing clubs, and dozens of craft and industrial groups. To a sustained roar from the crowd, a train of thirteen Pullman cars crossed the bridge and deposited its load of dignitaries at the reviewing stand. Speeches were delivered by Mayor Joseph Brown; Governors Beveridge of Illinois, Hendricks of Indiana, and Woodson of Missouri; and Senator Thomas Ferry of Michigan. After giving full credit to Flad, Pfeifer, and his other coworkers, Eads declared that "the bridge will exist as long as it continues to be useful to the people who come after us, even if its years should number those of the pyramids."

B. Gratz Brown, the featured speaker, rang the changes on nationalism, beauty, liberty, economic growth, and inevitable progress. Though the doubters had thought it impossible, now:

> You see those spans of five hundred feet leaping agile from base to base; you see those tapering piers bedded on the immovable rock, deep down below the homeless sands, and rising to gather the threads of railways and roadways high in the upper air; and you see, caught us if by inspiration, beauty there in all its flowing proportion, and science there in its rare analysis of the strength of materials, and an endurance there for all time in its bond of iron and steel and granite to resist force and fire and flood.

William Taussig later described the bridge as "a massive and enduring bond of union between the great East and the no less great

West, the noblest monument on the continent to the commercial, industrial and artistic progress of the day . . . there is still nowhere else in the world, whether among remains of the ancients or the later works of the modern day, anything of this kind so beautiful and attractive." No longer large enough for modern trains, the Eads Bridge was closed to railroad traffic in its hundredth year (July 1974). On June 17, 1979, an official of the East-West Gateway Coordinating Council said of the old bridge, "we think it could probably withstand a nuclear attack. That bridge is very sound."

Design changes, inflated land costs, renegotiated contracts, and higher-than-expected labor costs had escalated construction expenditures to $6.5 million, 46 percent over the 1867 estimate. Bond interest and agents' commissions had swelled the total to more than $9 million by 1874, the extra funds having been raised by issuing more stock and second and third mortgage bonds, the last sold primarily in Europe. The tunnel had been spun off as the St. Louis Tunnel Railroad Company, with Taussig as president. Its cost, and five hundred thousand dollars spent by the city in widening streets to accommodate the bridge traffic, had boosted the entire project to more than $11 million.

In 1871, Taussig, Eads, Thomas Scott, Thomas Allen, and officers of the North Missouri, Ohio and Mississippi, Chicago and Alton, and other roads had formed the Union Depot Company to facilitate the transfer of passengers. Taussig supervised the erection of a brick and stone depot on Poplar Street between Eleventh and Twelfth Streets near the mouth of the bridge tunnel. The Union Depot opened in 1875, but since it could handle only fourteen trains a day, it did not eliminate existing terminals, and the ferry continued to transfer passengers.

The bridge did not annihilate the Wiggins Ferry, as many had predicted, but it wrought a marvelous change in the attitude of its operators. Shippers had been paying sixty cents a ton to move their coal fifteen hundred feet. The bridge company halved the rate. Other rates and tolls were similarly reduced, to the delight of the public. Wiggins also installed clean accommodations and pleasant service, and because of its proximity to downtown business, the ferry furnished stiff competition. The bridge had opened during the aftershock of the Panic of 1873, when farmers, already overexpanded, had been hit by reduced European demand following the end of the Franco-Prussian War. Built to serve the glorious future rather than present realities, railroads all over the West were defaulting on their bond interest. Jay Cooke's giant New York banking house collapsed under an avalanche of defaults, and lesser banks went down with it.

Unable to borrow further because of the financial stringency, the bridge company defaulted in 1875, and a federal court appointed J. P. Morgan and Solon Humphreys as receivers.

Competition between bridge and ferry, a boon to customers, was a near-disaster for both companies, but it did not last long. In 1877 Morgan and Humphreys arranged a pooling agreement with the ferry, putting passengers, shippers, and railroads (except for the Missouri Pacific and the Iron Mountain, which had their own ferry at Carondelet) at the mercy of the pool. The bridge and tunnel were to have 75 percent and the ferry 25 percent of their combined net earnings up to four hundred thousand dollars. As income rose, the bridge's share would increase to 99 percent of the net above $1 million a year. Thought necessary for survival, the pool was a typical monopolistic device of the era, often resorted to while its managers extolled the virtues of competition. This one took the edge off of the transcendent experience the bridge had been for St. Louis, and Chauncey I. Filley led a chorus of complaints against the monopoly. The price of transferring freight cars across the river rose from one to five dollars, and other rates were similarly increased. As for Eads, he was off on a new venture, again with Morgan's backing, building jetties at the mouth of the Mississippi to create a deepwater channel for ocean liners. Again, he bested the Corps of Engineers, whose alternate plan was not only more expensive, but unworkable. The channel was scouring even before the jetties were completed. Eads had made another major contribution to western commerce.

In 1878 the bridge company experienced an early form of what became famous as "Morganization." Acting for the first and second mortgage bondholders, Morgan won a federal suit for the dissolution of the firm and the sale of its assets. The only bidder at the auction was Charles Tracy, acting for A. J. Thomas of New York, who, as it happened, represented the senior bondholders. Presto! The third mortgage holders were out, the stockholders were out, and the Morgan combination had it all. As owners of the senior bonds, they got their $2 million back and a $10 million bridge as well, for a net investment of less than one-third of that amount. Solon Humphreys headed the new St. Louis Bridge Company. Gerard Allen, Julius Walsh, and several other local men served on the board, mostly for cosmetic purposes, but the Eads Bridge belonged to New York. It was a great civic asset, and it would become a greater one, but not all of its victims had suffered from the caisson disease. In 1881 the bridge and tunnel were leased to the Missouri Pacific and the Wabash Railroads, which agreed to pay all taxes, bond interest, and preferred stock dividends—nearly $750,000 annually.

Lest it be thought that Morgan had victimized the lessees, it should be noted that both railroads were controlled by Jay Gould, the most notorious speculator-shark of the century. After a dying Hudson Bridge had retired in 1874, control of the Missouri Pacific had reverted to his old enemy, D. R. Garrison, who surrendered the ailing road to Gould and Russell Sage in 1879. Gould grabbed the North Missouri for his Wabash system in that same year; leased the Missouri, Kansas, and Texas in 1880; and took over the St. Louis, Iron Mountain, and Southern in 1881. Far to the south, the once-invincible Thomas Scott coughed up the Texas and Pacific, which Gould then extended to New Orleans. His Southwestern system swept up other roads from Kansas to the Rio Grande, with the Missouri Pacific as its keystone. Within a decade, the Missouri Pacific's trackage had been extended from 421 to 5,019 miles, and its stockholders enjoyed regular dividends.

The general offices of this railroad empire were in St. Louis, but its boardrooms were in New York. Jay Gould played with railroads as other men played cards, and he had a long record of milking the assets of his acquisitions and then dropping them like dead fish—after he had quietly unloaded his stock. Not selling to Gould what he wanted was virtually impossible, and to buy a railroad from him was to buy scrap iron. Yet, on balance, he was initially an asset to St. Louis. He put the bankrupt railroads in business, he extended their lines into new territories, he took on all comers, and he seldom lost. An army of speculators followed him, and for the first time, a steady stream of New York capital flowed into St. Louis and its trade territory. The Boston and New York investors who controlled the Chicago and Iowa roads had a healthy respect for him; he took over the mighty Union Pacific on two separate occasions, and he diverted a substantial share of its traffic to St. Louis. Toward competitors, labor, and fellow speculators he was devious and ruthless, and there was not an ounce of civic virtue in him—he cared as little for St. Louis as he did for New York. His goals were money and power, but in their pursuit he filled the warehouses and made the rails hum. He differed from his fellows mostly in degree—John Murray Forbes and James F. Joy did not build the Chicago roads for love of the Windy City.

Gould did not buy the Wiggins Ferry; he did not need it. He had the pool, and since he controlled every mile of track on the west side and much of the east side trackage as well, the ferry company had to cooperate if it wanted any railroad business. He had the bridge and he had his eastern connection in the Wabash, which soon rammed its way into Chicago. An Illinois court invalidated the pool in 1881, destroying a scrap of paper. The arrangement continued in fact until 1887, when it was outlawed by the Interstate Commerce Act. Even then, the ferry company did not undercut the bridge's rates. In 1886, Gould paid $3.5 million for the St. Louis and East St. Louis transit and terminal companies and the Union Depot Company, all bridge company auxiliaries managed by William Taussig. Charges by non-Gould roads that there was discrimination in rates and facilities in favor of the Gould lines led Taussig to suggest to Gould that the auxiliaries be combined into one corporation, to be owned jointly by the major trunk lines. Gould agreed, seeing a chance for a nice profit personally, partly at the expense of his own companies.

In October 1889 the Missouri Pacific, the Wabash, the Louisville and Nashville, and the Ohio and Mississippi Railroads organized the Terminal Railroad Association of St. Louis, taking over the former auxiliaries and leasing the bridge and tunnel in perpetuity. The new corporation issued $7 million in bonds, of which $5 million was paid to Gould for the properties. Meanwhile, the Merchants' Bridge, a railroad-only all-steel structure, three miles north of the Eads Bridge at Ferry Street (Bissell's Point) had been completed in 1889. David R. Francis and some other members of the Merchants' Exchange had promoted this enterprise, and by laying track along the levee they had hoped to draw traffic away from the Eads Bridge and its smoke-choked tunnel. The formation of the association frustrated them, and in 1893 the terminal combination bought the Merchants' Bridge Terminal Railway, thereby restoring the monopoly. By this time, Gould's consolidating strategy was hurting the city. Popularly called the "bridge arbitrary" or the "kid-glove bandit," the association, by charging twenty cents per ton for moving coal across the river, had encouraged the growth of steel mills, meatpacking plants, and other industries on the Illinois side, where their noxious smoke (but not their taxes) was available to St. Louis.

Shortly after the Terminal Association was organized, Taussig had moved ahead with his dream—a grand replacement for the inadequate Union passenger depot. Despite cries of ruination from merchants near the old site, the directors chose a location six blocks to the west, at Eighteenth and Market Streets. Bids were invited from ten architectural firms, and in 1891 a plan submitted by Theodore C. Link, a German-trained local architect, was chosen for the Union Station. When completed in 1894, the building was 606 feet long and 80 feet deep, stretching from Eighteenth to Twentieth on Market, with a ten-acre train shed to the south along Eighteenth Street. Land and construction costs for the "head-house" (main building), which included the east pavilion with its tall clock tower, the central pavilion, the Terminal Hotel at the west end, and the train shed, came to $6.5 million.

The Market and Eighteenth Street facades were built of gray
Indiana limestone masonry, the west and south walls were of gray
brick above and buff brick below the roof of the train shed, and the
roof was covered with gray Spanish tile. The Romanesque style
expressed the idea that a railway station related to a modern city as a
bastioned gate did to a medieval city, a "modern elaboration of the
feudal gateway." M. Patricia Holmes has noted various architectural
influences in the building, the most pervasive being that of H. H.
Richardson's version of the Romanesque, as expressed in the massive
walls and profusion of round arches. The great visual experience of

Union Station from Eighteenth and Market Streets. *Photograph by Emil Boehl, ca. 1907. MHS-PP.*

the interior was the "Grand Hall" on the second floor of the central pavilion, an arching chamber 76 by 120 feet, with a 65-foot ceiling featuring ornamental plaster moldings and sculptures, frescoes, elaborate light fixtures, and art glass. A pictorial window over the north staircase landing illustrated a favorite local theme—the linkage of the continent from west to east by St. Louis. Three female forms seated on a wide bench represented San Francisco, St. Louis, and New York (Link's design). Following Louis Sullivan, who had pioneered the decorative use of electric lighting in Chicago, Link hung a chandelier 20 feet in diameter from the ceiling of the Grand Hall, sparkling with 350 lamps and weighing 4,500 pounds. With its brilliant ceiling and crisscrossing lights gleaming from its entrance arches, the great hall seemed charged with exciting promise.

At the opening-night reception on September 1, 1894, attended by twenty thousand invited guests, Samuel Kennard introduced a beaming Dr. Taussig as the prime mover of "this magnificent structure, the largest, grandest, and most completely equipped railroad station in the world." Brimming with pride and local patriotism, as were the guests, Kennard wished prosperity for the terminal company so that it would "never regret the expenditure which has given to the gateway to the great Southwest a station perfect, complete and

Union Station. The Grand Hall, Opening Night. *Photograph by B. A. Atwater, 1894. MHS-PP.*

commodious in all its arrangements; a building beautiful in its proportions, artistic in design and execution; a magnificent architectural conception, an ideal realization."

More railroads (twenty-two) converged at St. Louis than at any other point in the United States, though the city trailed Chicago in volume of traffic. There were nineteen miles of track in the Union Station yards, and the Westinghouse compressed-air switching system was the largest and most intricate in the country. On an average day in 1896, the station passed through 950 passenger cars, handled 2,330 pieces of baggage, and sold 1,500 tickets. Though skeptics charged that the station was far overbuilt, a steady increase in traffic required an extension of 175 feet at the west end in 1930.

The Rock Island Railroad, which had been denied admittance to the terminal association (and thus entry to St. Louis), forced the issue in 1902 by secretly bidding five hundred dollars each for the ten thousand closely held one hundred dollar par shares of the Wiggins Ferry Company through its agents in the Merchants' Trust Company of St. Louis. In collusion with the Rock Island, Festus Wade and other Wiggins stock trustees tried to encourage selling by reducing the ferry company's rates to drive down its earnings. Several stockholders took the bait, but news of the deal soon leaked out, and the Terminal Association entered the bidding through its agent, the Mississippi Valley Trust Company. The latter bought the largest individual holding (fourteen hundred shares) from a Christy heir, Mary Scanlan, for $2.14 million. After the acrimonious bidding war, punctuated by lawsuits and countersuits, had reached a stalemate, the Rock Island, five additional railroads, and the ferry company gained admission to the Terminal Association. The entire transfer and terminal business was now under one management—a rational and efficient system to railroaders, but a monster monopoly to shippers.

Since 1854, rural residents had held a majority in the county court, the administrative body of St. Louis County. After a special tax levy in 1858 had angered city taxpayers, who bore most of the burden, alderman Thomas Allen called for consolidation of the city and county governments, and Thomas T. Gantt, an associate of Frank Blair, collected four thousand signatures on a petition to the legislature asking that the court be abolished. After Governor Robert M. Stewart had vetoed abolition, David H. Armstrong, a former city comptroller, compared the court to George III and the Tsar of Russia at a mass meeting and demanded action. The legislature partially mollified urban taxpayers by increasing the city's representation on the court and setting limits on the county's taxing power, but it did not remove the major irritant, the duplication of functions and expenditures.

Another civic problem, the lack of central direction in the city administration, was tackled in 1859, when, at the request of Mayor O. D. Filley, the legislature replaced the bicameral council by a single body of two members from each of the ten wards. Filley had also asked for abolition of the long ballot, but he got less than half a loaf. Two elective offices were changed to appointive, but eight remained, making effective management still virtually impossible, with the mayoral term at one year and seven departments operating as independent satrapies.

Beginning with the police board in 1861, the legislature moved toward state-appointed departmental boards for city functions in an extension of the principle that the city was the state's agent. St. Louisans paid departments' bills without the burden of supervising their activities. This system was open to abuse, especially when the city and state governments were at odds politically, and the board's policies frequently ran counter to the popular will (legal, but hardly government by consent). As a *Republican* editor wrote in 1867, the city was "distributed among extraneous and heterogeneous bodies, acting without harmony and having no common center, agreeing with each other only in their vigorous onslaughts on the city treasury." The *Post-Dispatch* complained that the city's important functions were all entrusted to officers appointed by external authority. "The council possesses little power beyond that of cleaning streets, building sewers, paving alleys and sending to the legislature petitions and memorials which [it] . . . treats with sovereign contempt."

Since St. Louis had become a city, nearly every session of the legislature had altered, revised, enlarged, or restricted some of its functions, usually at the request of some local person or group. By 1867 the city "charter" was scattered through more than one hundred separate statutes. In 1869 a council delegation requested that tax assessment and collection be restored to the city and that some state-appointed boards be eliminated. The private Municipal Reform Association, charging past legislatures with "continual change and interference" (the council had been changed to bicameral in 1866, and changed back in 1867), urged the General Assembly to pass a general law for municipalities, as it had for private corporations, thus assuring that St. Louis would receive equal treatment. Despite the intercession of Congressman Erastus Wells, the legislature was unmoved.

In 1870, the legislature made a slight bow to St. Louis by extending the mayoral term to two years and annexing Carondelet and some adjacent land to the city, increasing its area from seventeen to twenty-one square miles. Eight of the fifteen municipal administrators were still elective, however, and no less than a dozen independent boards cluttered the scene. Even more galling was county control over real and personal property tax revenues. In a punitive mood because of rising opposition to Radicalism in the metropolis, the legislature in 1867 had transferred to the Radical county court the power to assess and collect the city's taxes. In 1869 the county collected $1.875 million from city taxpayers, while the city collected $302,000 from licenses and fees. City officers were poorly paid, and the sheriff and other county officers, including a flock of assistant collectors, enjoyed the rich fruits of the "fee system," under which they were paid according to their volume of business. Mayor James Thomas complained that the legislature had not only deprived the city of the right to tax, it had authorized "a foreign body to do it for us as though we were infants. . . ." The county board of assessors claimed that justice and economy prevailed under their regime, but even so, the situation was repugnant to St. Louisans, and charges of county corruption proliferated. At the capital, well-heeled county lobbyists beat back efforts to rewrite the charter. In the heat of the struggle, Joseph Pulitzer, then a legislator who doubled as a reporter for the *Westliche Post*, wounded a county official in a Jefferson City shootout.

By 1870, reformers had divided into three groups: one favoring further efforts to increase the city's representation in the county court, a second advocating consolidation of city and county, and a third proposing complete separation of the two. Most of the leadership believed that only extreme measures would do the job. Anthony Ittner, a legislator and former alderman, and Judge R. E. Rombauer favored consolidation, with the city limits extended to the county lines, county offices abolished, and the municipality governed by a unicameral council. Charles Smythe, another legislator, wanted "decentralization, not consolidation. We want to cut loose from the entangling alliances of the county. The city wants to go alone, to be left alone, and to let alone." Senator J. G. Woerner argued that only "total separation" would free St. Louis. He and other opponents of consolidation argued that county voters would oppose it, and that even if it did pass, the city would be burdened with the concerns of farmers and a dozen small towns whose interests it could not properly serve.

Since neither consolidation nor separation could command a majority in the St. Louis legislative delegation in 1870, the members went for charter revision again. Pulitzer proposed that the city be awarded six of the nine seats on the county court, county officers' fees reduced, and strict accountability for expenditures mandated.

This and similar bills were rejected by the General Assembly, with Liberal Republicans and Democrats generally supporting and Radicals opposing reform, the latter heavily influenced by the "courthouse ring" and its lobbyists. After the Democratic-Liberal victory later in the year, a consolidation amendment passed the House of Representatives, but the Senate demurred; and the two houses then adopted a substitute, replacing the existing county court with one slightly more palatable to St. Louis. A presiding judge would be elected at large and four associate judges by district, two each from the city and county, but neither their powers nor the fee system changed. Governor Gratz Brown signed the bill, but he knew it would not satisfy the big taxpayers and business leaders (he was one of them). In his annual message in 1872, Brown sympathized with those who were "subject to all the cost and conflict of double government, with no corresponding benefit." He decried nitpicking special legislation and county court interference with cities and advocated a home rule charter for St. Louis. He stated no preference for either consolidation or separation, but his speech helped set the stage for one or the other.

By 1873, the Democrats had gained full control of the state, and it was certain that the Constitution of 1865 had a limited future. Some advocates of reform in St. Louis feared that rewriting the organic law might jeopardize the educational system and other progressive features of the Radical document, but on the whole they welcomed the opportunity to be rid of special laws and the county court. In 1874 the *Republican* said that for St. Louis the object was "the extension of the St. Louis municipality over a large portion of the county and the reorganization of the remainder into a separate county." By the eve of the convention, the ancient distaste for the county court had been extended to the entire county apparatus, where charges that officials had overpaid contractors in return for kickbacks had been sustained by a grand jury.

Democrat Joseph Brown left the mayor's office in 1875 with a parting shot at the double government and was succeeded by Arthur Barret, who had defeated the Independent Henry Overstolz by a narrow margin. Both candidates had favored separation. When Barret died a few weeks after taking office, the *Republican* advertised for a replacement who could "handle the sweet German accent as well as command the rich Irish brogue. . . . He must be up in arithmetic, lightning on the dust, and sudden death on mud. . . . No objection on account of race, color, or previous condition of politics, the Civil Rights Bill being in full force." To fill this modest bill, the Democrats chose banker James H. Britton, a Virginian who was treasurer of the bridge company. Britton was announced as the victor, but his opponent Overstolz charged fraud and demanded a recount. Testimony revealed fraudulent voting in ten of the twelve wards, including repeating and ballot box stuffing by election judges. One witness swore that he had seen a judge chewing Overstolz ballots all day long. In all this, a harbinger of things to come, could be seen the tracks of Edward Butler, an Irish blacksmith who had bribed aldermen to get the contract for shoeing the street railway mules. In February 1876, after Britton had been in office for several months, the city council ruled that Overstolz had been elected. The new mayor, the scion of a distinguished Westphalian family, had been the first native German elected to the city council in 1849, and he had become wealthy as a banker, wholesale grocer, and insurance company president.

In the midst of this lesser scandal, Grant administration loyalists were shaken by revelations emanating from a Treasury Department investigation of whiskey frauds in St. Louis. As far back as Lincoln's day whiskey had been sold illegally in various places, but it was not until 1870 that a well-organized conspiracy had been formed at St. Louis. Initially conceived as a means of raising funds to combat the Liberal Republican threat, it was quickly diverted into a private gold mine for the conspirators. Its major figures were patronage boss William McKee, principal owner of the *Globe-Democrat*; John McDonald, supervisor of internal revenue for Missouri and the Southwest, who owed his appointment to McKee and Grant's Secretary Orville Babcock; John A. Joyce, collector of revenue at St. Louis; William Avery, chief clerk of the Internal Revenue Department of the U.S. Treasury; and Babcock. Dozens of minor Treasury functionaries, especially "gaugers," who examined the whiskey at the distillers, rectifiers who affixed the federal revenue stamps, and the distillers themselves, were necessary to the success of the scheme. The federal whiskey tax being seventy cents a gallon, the distillers paid the ring's agents thirty-five cents for each gallon of "crooked whiskey." Gaugers then attached a stamp, the serial number of which had been used before, enabling the distiller to sell the untaxed whiskey, usually at fifteen to seventeen cents below the going price. Thus the crooked distiller undersold his competitors while making an extra profit of eighteen to twenty cents a gallon. The gaugers kept one or two cents a gallon for themselves and gave the rest to McKee, McDonald, or Joyce, who then divided the loot with Avery, Babcock, and other ring members. Distillers later testified that from half to three-quarters of their output was "crooked." McKee was said to have profited as much as one thousand dollars a week from the operation for several years. Between 1873 and 1875 the Treasury was cheated of more than $4 million in revenue, more than half of it at St. Louis, and the rest at Chicago, Milwaukee, Peoria, Indianapolis, and New Orleans. Frauds at Kansas City and Colorado were part of the St. Louis operation.

To further the interests of the Grant administration, first the *Democrat*, then the *Globe*, and finally the *Globe-Democrat* were maintained as Whiskey Ring newspapers. In 1872, after the two had quarreled for years over McKee's shady connections and activities, George W. Fishback had bought McKee's and Daniel M. Houser's interests in the *Democrat*. The latter two had promptly established the *Globe*, and with the assistance of the golden stream from the whiskey frauds, they had followed an expansive (and expensive) news gathering strategy which made the *Globe* a powerful rival of the *Democrat* in the morning newspaper field. In 1873 they lured Joseph B. McCullagh, a native of Ireland who had become nationally famous as a Civil War battle correspondent, from the *Democrat* to become editor of the *Globe*. By 1874 the *Globe* had outstripped the *Democrat*, and a year later, before his conviction, McKee bought the rival paper and merged the two as the *Globe-Democrat*.

Before the merger, Fishback had fired one last volley at McKee. Treasury agents who were contemplating raids had been repeatedly frustrated by warnings sent to McDonald or Joyce by Avery or Babcock. Alerted to the size of the operation by a publication of the Merchants' Exchange, which revealed that three times as much whiskey had been distilled in St. Louis as treasury receipts showed, detectives, acting on information supplied by Fishback, conducted a lightning raid on sixteen distilleries, catching them with the goods. U.S. Attorney David P. Dyer, assisted by outside counsel led by ex-Senator John B. Henderson, immediately initiated prosecution after a grand jury returned 213 indictments. Henderson was discharged after a few weeks because of an indiscreet remark he had made about President Grant in open court, but fears that the prosecution would be hamstrung were promptly allayed when the attorney general replaced Henderson with the leader of the St. Louis bar, the prestigious Democrat James O. Broadhead.

Though juror E. W. Fox, former Radical state chairman and go-between with the legislature during the Pacific Railroad scandals, leaked every detail of the grand jury's investigation and the testimony before it to the ring, the prosecution obtained the convictions of McDonald, McKee, Joyce, Avery, and a host of lesser officials. After having said initially, "let no guilty man escape," Grant became convinced that the prosecutors were out to ruin him, and he intervened in Babcock's trial with a deposition testifying to his secretary's saintly virtues. Faced with the choice of repudiating the president or finding Babcock innocent, the trial jury backed off and chose the latter. Among the distillers indicted had been Rudolf Ulrici, Alfred Bevis, Louis Teuscher, Gordon Bingham, and J. G. Chouteau. The prosecutors had treated the distillers as victims of the rapacious officials, or at worst, as having the lesser guilt, a version the businessmen were delighted to accept. Not one of them was convicted of a crime, though they were forced to make partial restitution of the stolen funds. In fact, the "victims" had cooperated willingly with the ring, some of them even eagerly. They had not been forced at the point of a gun to defraud the Treasury, and any one of them could have blown the whistle at any time. As Joseph W. Folk and Lincoln Steffens made clear in St. Louis twenty-five years later, corrupt officials do not thrive in an atmosphere of business integrity.

Before his selection as a Whiskey Ring prosecutor, J. O. Broadhead had served as a delegate to the constitutional convention. With him in the county's twelve-man delegation were long-time advocates of home rule such as Thomas T. Gantt, H. C. Brokmeyer, Joseph Pulitzer of the *Times,* and H. C. Spaunhorst. Pulitzer immediately created a problem at the convention by demanding that urban matters be left to the St. Louis delegation, since the city was "a small state by itself," with five hundred thousand people who paid half of the state's taxes. Some outstate delegates found his condescension offensive, but the matter was smoothed over by the diplomatic Brokmeyer and Broadhead. In the end, the St. Louis delegation was designated the "Committee on St. Louis Affairs," with Broadhead as chairman. Gantt assumed the difficult task of writing a constitutional provision which would be acceptable to committee members of varying persuasions.

Gantt first took up the question of consolidation, concluding after discussion that the expense of managing a 558-square-mile area would negate most of the benefits of eliminating double government. Consolidation was kept in reserve, however, in case the convention rejected separation. After weeks of labor Gantt still lacked a consensus, partly because of his undiplomatic manner. One observer described him as "a gallant-looking man, straight and martial, and his conversation rather like that of a general officer. . . ." The county delegates resented Gantt's rigidity and his past attacks on the county court, but the timely arrival of David Armstrong, former Democratic state chairman, saved the situation. Though not a convention delegate, Armstrong became an active participant. He agreed with Gantt's plan, and though "his manners were bearish and his speech profane," he was a master persuader, respected and liked all over the state.

By proposing minor concessions to save the plan, Armstrong won over the two county delegates and then went to work on the rest of the convention. Upon the unanimous recommendation of the St. Louis committee, the convention adopted municipal home rule for St. Louis, the first time any city had been granted constitutionally guaranteed home rule status.

As approved by Missouri voters in November 1875, the constitution authorized the city and county to elect thirteen freeholders, who were to write a city charter, separate the two governments, define the new boundaries, reorganize the county government, and settle outstanding financial differences. In preparation for the Board of Freeholders' election, two tickets were put forward: a Citizens' ticket endorsed by the Merchants' Exchange and the Taxpayers' League, and including Broadhead, Armstrong, Albert Todd, August Krieckhaus, Silas Bent, Michael Phelan, Dwight Collier, George H. Shields, and five others; and a Joint ticket presented by the Democratic and Republican central committees. Broadhead, Armstrong, Phelan, and Todd were on both tickets. The political ticket included such prominent names as J. H. Lightner, Isidor Bush, and Trusten Polk (ex-governor, ex-senator, ex-Confederate), but the Merchants' slate beat it decisively.

Between April 8 and July 3, the Board of Freeholders met fifty-two times. Citizens were invited to submit suggestions; city officials gave information and advice; and the members studied the charters of New York, Philadelphia, and Chicago. They had considerable latitude, but the Gantt plan embodied in the constitution mandated a chief executive and a two-house legislature, one of which was to be elected at large. True to the assumptions of the era, Gantt had installed the check and balance system of the federal and state governments. The awkward and paralyzing bicameral legislature, the framers naively believed, "was an acutal necessity for all large cities; it made jobbery and corruption more difficult, and to a certain extent impossible." (This, despite the recent examples at both the federal and state levels.) Framers assumed that the at-large provision would assure the devotion of one house to the general interests of the city, instead of logrolling for the narrow interests of the wards. For city purposes, the tax rate was limited to 1 percent of valuation, not including debt service and the school levy; and the city was to collect the state taxes and "perform all functions in relation to the state as if it were a county. . . ."

Building on the constitutional structure, the freeholders set a four-year term for the mayor, other administrators, the thirteen members of the council (the upper house—elected at large), and the president of the council; and two-year terms for members of the House of

Delegates, one for each of the expanded city's twenty-eight wards. Administrative boards were reduced by consolidating the waterworks, streets, sewers, parks and water administrations under a Board of Public Improvements, with an elected president and five commissioners appointed by the mayor. Presumably with the best intentions, the freeholders required the mayor's administrative appointments and removals to be approved by the council. To make matters worse, these appointments had to be made in midterm, so that during his first two years, an incoming mayor would be surrounded by his predecessor's appointees. Further, the framers failed to challenge state control of the police. The city was checked-and-balanced to death, with responsible leadership virtually impossible. Reflecting the deep-seated American distrust of the executive, the freeholders gave the mayor a chance to lead with a four-year term, and then they took it away. By creating a vacuum at the top of their formal government to protect themselves from oppression, the merchants and lawyers quite unconsciously paved the way for a brutally effective informal government.

Despite the lack of precedents elsewhere, Albert Todd proposed that elements of a merit system be adopted, with subordinate employees holding their positions during good behavior and higher offices divided equally between Republicans and Democrats. Though the entire scheme was intended to hinder the growth of political machines, the spoils system was too deeply embedded to do so. David Armstrong called Todd's ideas "too pious to be satisfactory." Several of the framers were more inclined to make the city a rich man's utopia. They succeeded in requiring the mayor and councilmen to be real property owners and the members of the House of Delegates to be taxpayers. Judge Silas Bent, of the noted Indian-fighting, fur merchant family, offered an incredible "stake-in-society" plural-voting proposal, requiring voters to own at least three hundred dollars in taxable property. For each additional one thousand dollars in property, another vote would be awarded. Under this scheme, many could not have voted at all, while others would have had several thousand votes. Bent's grandfather claimed to have led the Boston Tea Party; the grandson's plan would have made George III wince. The old judge also proposed fines for qualified electors who did not vote, but these and other attempts to tinker with voting qualifications were squelched when J. O. Broadhead pointed out their unconstitutionality. The board also heard, but did not seriously consider, a request from Missouri's women's suffrage leader Virginia L. Minor that all property of women be exempted from city taxes as long as they were disfranchised.

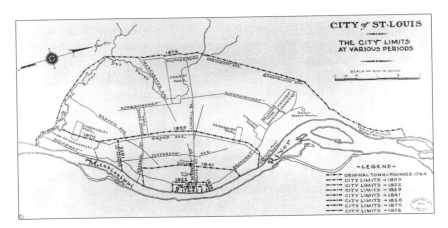

The City Limits of St. Louis at Various Periods. *Map by AS, ca. 1940. MHS Library.*

In fixing the city boundaries, there were strong differences among the freeholders. A majority wanted the limits to include the new city parks. In 1868, Henry Shaw had given the city 190 acres (later increased to 277) between Grand Avenue and Kingshighway, from Magnolia to Arsenal, which he named Tower Grove Park, after his home on the grounds of his nearby botanical gardens. A strip two hundred feet wide around the park was leased to the city, the income to be used to support the gardens. Shaw agreed to plant fifteen thousand trees and shrubs in the park (located in the old Prairie des Noyers common fields); the city appropriated $360,000 for park improvements. During Shaw's life, the Missouri Botanical Gardens were free to the public, and after his death, the magnificent collections begun by George Engelmann were to be maintained by the income from Shaw's estate and the city lease.

In 1872, after a dogged campaign by Hiram Leffingwell, who owned land near the proposed site, the legislature authorized St. Louis to buy one thousand acres or more for another public park. Various taxpayers, represented by Samuel Glover and T. T. Gantt, successfully challenged the purchase in the courts. Two years later, Andrew McKinley prepared a bill which met the judicial objections, and a heavily forested 1,375-acre tract west of Kingshighway along Olive Street Road was chosen. The southern edge of "Forest Park" had been a part of the old Gratiot League Square; the remainder was included in the J. M. Papin grant of 1796. The current owners, C. P. Chouteau and Julia Maffitt, William Forsyth, Thomas Skinker, and others, sold their land to the city for $799,995. Forest Park was dedicated in 1876 with the unveiling of the statue of Edward Bates at its southeast corner (later,

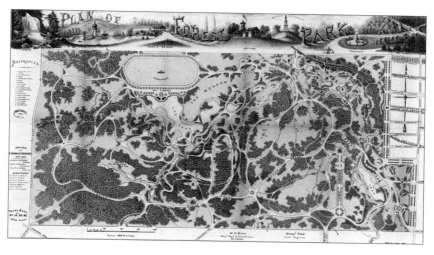

Plan of Forest Park. *Lithograph by Camille N. Dry, from the* Report of the Commissioners of Forest Park, 1875. *MHS Library.*

a statue of Frank Blair was erected at the northeast corner). Public acceptance of Forest Park was immediate, and the 1890s streetcars alone carried nearly three million visitors a year to the park, which had taken over the zoological gardens formerly located at the fairgrounds.

County and some city members of the Board of Freeholders opposed such generous boundaries. David Armstrong was against taking in "divers and sundry cornfields and melon patches and taxing them as city property," but his argument was a sham. The constitution mandated lower tax rates for the annexed areas—he spoke for large taxpayers who dreaded the cost of extending streets and services over such an expanse. Albert Todd, on the other hand, had an eye for the future, warning that "since the change would be permanent, the territory ought to be large." Finally, the board decided upon a generally symmetrical extension consistent with the outer boundaries of Forest Park on the west and O'Fallon Park on the north, with a northern extension along the river to accommodate the Chain of Rocks, where the city expected to build a new reservoir. The city's area was more than tripled, to 61.37 square miles, and it stretched along the river for 19 miles. Most of the new area was farmland—enough space, it seemed in 1876, to last forever. Yet, during the ratification campaign, a far-seeing observer warned in the *Post-Dispatch* that "there will be established in the new county and along our borders suburban villages which will grow into cities." Exactly so; inability to expand its limits after 1876 proved to be a crippling deterrent to St. Louis's development.

Supporters of the charter and separation scheme, including the powerful *Republican*, the German press, and most of the business and professional class, emphasized the lower taxes that were anticipated. The city was to assume the county debt, but its residents were already paying most of the interest on it, and the courthouse, jail, and other county buildings within the limits would become city property. Unfortunately, the city's new quasi-county status would require the maintenance of elected "county" officials, including a sheriff—a redundancy pregnant with patronage sinecures. Opponents of the scheme and charter, including the county, most of the city officeholders, and both of the party organizations, attacked them as instruments created by and for the rich. The politicians saw their jobs, especially the fat county fee-offices, slipping from their grasp.

Returns from the August balloting showed that both the scheme and charter had failed. They had passed by narrow margins in the city, but the county overwhelmingly rejected separation, and those in the area to be annexed voted four to one against the charter. Incredibly one-sided results in certain precincts and reports of voting irregularities led pro-charter attorneys D. P. Dyer and J. H. Shepley to petition the circuit court for a writ of mandamus to compel the mayor and the county court to certify that both measures had passed. Judge Louis Gottschalk delayed his decision until the allegations of fraud could be tested. Counsel then submitted an amended petition requesting that a commission be appointed to investigate the election and conduct a recount. Gottschalk complied, whereupon the opposition asked the appellate court for a writ of prohibition against a recount, which was promptly and predictably denied, T. T. Gantt being one of the three appellate judges.

Gottschalk's five-man commission found plenty of evidence of fraud. As the *Globe-Democrat* put it, election officials testified that "in the discharge of their duties they stole hundreds of ballots from the boxes and destroyed them, stuffed in fraudulent and bogus votes by the handful, swore to false returns, and by every device of perjury, corruption, and rascality did all that lay in their power to convert the election into a shameless farce." These judges and clerks had been appointed by the politicians, most of whom opposed the freeholders' plan. When asked why he had altered ballots, one judge replied: "Well, Ed Butler and Pat Kane both requested it . . . they wanted to see the scheme and charter defeated." Butler apparently believed the freeholders' claim that the charter would guarantee efficient and honest government. Ironically, he was to be its major beneficiary. No indictments were sought against the crooked officials. After throwing out fraudulent ballots and invalidating all the returns from three precincts, the commission ruled that the scheme had carried by 1,253 votes and the charter by 3,221. The mayor and the presiding judge promptly certified these results to the secretary of state. Attorney A. J. P. Garesché continued the legal battle against home rule, but finally, in April 1877, the secretary of state ordered the county court to vacate its St. Louis offices. The *Globe-Democrat* loosed an unkind parting shaft: "Lay the seven sages down, Each a bright and blessed martyr, Wearing an immortal crown, Done to death by scheme and charter."

Henry Overstolz was reelected mayor under the new charter as the choice of both political parties, an honor he may have regretted within a few months. For four days in late July, St. Louis was the scene of the first true general strike in the nation's history—an amazing, centrally directed operation which not only brought business to a standstill but controlled the streets.

Carpenters, cabinet-makers, tinners, and other craft unions had been organized in the city in the 1830s, with wages, the ten-hour day, and a mechanics' lien law their major concerns. After a union breakdown during the Panic of 1837, a short-lived Workingmans' Party had helped Democratic candidates in the early 1840s, culminating with the election of John Wimer as mayor in 1843. During the 1850s craft unionism was both stimulated and weakened by massive immigration. German intellectuals gave the unions a theoretical base, but the host of new German and Irish laborers eased the chronic shortage of workers that had kept local wages high. Labor suffered severely during the Panic of 1857, with wages reduced by one-third and unemployment reaching ten thousand during the winter. Local unions surged back in 1859 and prospered during the Civil War. By 1867, several locals were affiliated with the National Labor Union, battling against imported contract labor and pressing for the eight-hour day. Through their influence in the Radical Party the Missouri legislature passed an eight-hour law, which unfortunately could be easily circumvented; employers could require workers to contract for longer hours. In 1868, responding to local union pressure, Senator B. Gratz Brown introduced and pushed through Congress an eight-hour law for federally employed artisans and laborers. Until 1873 the crafts did well in St. Louis, despite the dissolution of the National Labor Union, commanding wages of $2.50 or $3.00 a day, more than double the going rate for unorganized common laborers.

Wages, employment, and unions were devastated by the Panic of 1873. Overcapitalized, overbuilt, squeezed by declining business and the monopoly power of giant customers such as the Standard Oil Company, and harassed politically by organized farmers outraged by high and discriminatory rates, American railroads shaved costs where they could. Rolling stock, track, and equipment were allowed to deteriorate; wages were cut twice before 1877; train crews were cut to dangerous levels; and remaining workers were forced to put in extra hours without pay. Protestors were fired and local strikes crushed by Pinkerton goon squads. In July 1877 the lid blew off. Another 10 percent wage slash by eastern roads led to massive uprisings, total stoppage of freight traffic, extensive property destruction, and pitched battles between police, militia, and strikers in Pittsburgh, Baltimore, and elsewhere. By July 22, one million men were on strike, called not by the Railway Brotherhoods but by local workers' committees and *ad hoc* unions.

Most of the St. Louis press assailed the strikers, with John Knapp of the *Republican* especially outraged by the "communistic" threat to property. The *Globe-Democrat* tempered its criticism with sympathy for the misery of the strikers. Neither the press, the businessmen, nor the authorities felt that there was any danger in St. Louis, but on the evening of July 22 railroad and bridge transit company workers elected a strike committee in East St. Louis, stopped all freight traffic, and took over the depot, yards, and streets of the town — all accomplished without property damage or personal injury. On the next day, strikers took over the St. Louis Union Depot and yards.

On July 24 the *Republican* wanted to mobilize war veterans under Generals A. J. Smith and John S. Marmaduke (the blue and the gray), to protect against *"canaille"* (dogs) who would "strike at the very vitals of society." The *Times* responded that vitals of society were on strike, "and hungry vitals they are, too." That afternoon three hundred men of the U.S. Twenty-Third Infantry arrived at the Arsenal, sent by the adjutant general to protect federal property. "Prominent citizens," with Mayor Overstolz's approval, formed a Committee of Public Safety, consisting of Judge Gantt, Smith, Marmaduke, and Generals John S. Cavender and John W. Noble. Smith and Marmaduke were to command the citizen-army, as the *Republican* had suggested. At the other end of the social spectrum, the strike in St. Louis had been taken over by the Workingmen's Party, a small socialist organization led by Albert Currlin and Peter Lofgreen. Of the party's national membership of less than five thousand, the three St. Louis sections (German, English, and Bohemian-speaking) had about one thousand. A few craft unions were involved in the strike, but the chief resources were the thousands of unemployed and ordinary workers, organized and unorganized. "Committees" from the party's Turner's Hall headquarters on Tenth Street just south of Market began to visit shops and foundries on the afternoon of the July 24 with amazing results —

workers everywhere needed only a nod to walk out. Gas works employees, coopers, and boatmen led the way; the last won immediate wage concessions.

Five thousand people had massed at the Lucas Market, at Twelfth and Olive, on July 23; a larger meeting was scheduled for the next day. Just after dark some fifteen hundred men, mostly Carondelet ironworkers, some of them carrying clubs, rolled up Olive Street four abreast, the only sounds the thump of marching feet and the fife and drum which preceded them. "Awfully suggestive," said the *Times,* which thought the crowd at the market could be measured only by the acre. Others guessed ten thousand or more. One speaker evoked the angry Parisians of the Revolution, when "hundreds of heads tumbled into the basket." A black orator asked if they would stand behind black levee workers; the crowd roared "we will." The great commercial emporium had not served the poor well. The squalor of "Castle Thunder," "Wildcat Chute," "Clabber Alley," and other degraded tenements and hovels, wage cuts, chronic hunger and unemployment, and municipal soup kitchens stood in stark contrast to the lordly mansions which loomed behind the market, the elegant ladies who descended daintily from their glittering carriages, and the rich merchants and landlords who dined on lobster and champagne at Tony Faust's Oyster House, one of the nation's finest restaurants. Even the great bridge, the pride of St. Louis, had fallen into the fat fingers of the bondholders.

The sickening political and business scandals of the Grant administration had struck especially hard at the city's sense of community. Dozens of its businessmen had connived in fraud, and a publisher whose newspaper was lambasting the strikers had gone to jail as a leading conspirator. Alienation from a nation and a city which had promised so much had been deepened by the press, especially by the *Republican*, which insulted every laboring man when it called the eastern strikers canaille. "You are just as lawabiding as those men who rob the public treasury," said a speaker, "just as decent as those lecherous bondholders who cut off coupons." Finally, H. F. Allen of the strike committee called for a general strike. The crowd roared approval, and early the next day the proclamation was distributed throughout the city.

On the afternoon of the July 25, after instructions from the strike committee to "Keep sober and orderly . . . and don't plunder," five thousand men lined up on Locust Street behind a brass band which played the *Marseillaise* as they marched off through "the miles of stone-built streets and red-brick walls. . . ." As the grim, sweating mass passed by shops, foundries, factories, flour mills, and white lead and chemical works, their employees poured out to join the marchers or the throng on the sidewalks. When recruits emerged too slowly, a thousand voices shouted, "Come out! you sons of bitches." Only at the Excelsior Stove Works, where Giles Filley had purged fifty suspected union men and put the rest to pointing rifles out of windows and manning a cannon planted at the front entrance, did no workers come out. Stunned by the size of the striking army and fearing the results of a confrontation, Mayor Overstolz kept the police in the station houses and did not ask for militia assistance.

The *Republican* shuddered at the presence of black levee roustabouts in the line of march and imaginatively reported "distressing scenes of terrified women, rudely handled by brutal negroes." But it was not what the marchers did, according to this spokesman for the "better people," but what "they barely refrained from doing" that terrified the observer. By nightfall nearly every manufacturing plant, large or small, was shut down; the downtown saloons were closed, as ordered by the mayor *and* the strike committee; and the city's food supplies were diminishing. The horsecars and waterworks were not disturbed, however. In Carondelet, where iron, steel, and zinc works were seized, businessmen met to form a safety committee, but the strikers attended, elected one of their own as chairman, and chose a committee made up of workers and a few uneasy businessmen such as Charles P. Chouteau of the Vulcan Iron Works. They agreed to protect property and even asked the mayor to designate some of their men as special police.

By Wednesday evening, the strikers ruled the city. Employers and the mayor were still mobilizing, but they shrank from the battle that was sure to follow any attempt to suppress the strike. But at a third and even larger Lucas Market meeting, speakers continued to stress long-range measures such as the election of workers to Congress and the nationalization of railroads. Now at the peak of their powers, the strike leaders were in an agony of indecision. Their articulate management had developed a controlled momentum unmatched anywhere in the nation, but they did not know what to do with it. They had shut down the city, but most employers were not disposed to make concessions. Bread *and* blood was a popular street battle cry, but the Workingmen's Party was nonviolent. Sooner or later, their antagonists or their own men would start shooting, or the movement would disintegrate. Lofgreen, Currlin, and their associates could think of nothing better than to try to maintain the status quo.

On Thursday, despite problems at its center, the strike seemed stronger than ever. An impromptu force seized the giant Belcher

Sugar Refinery; the barbers all walked out, demanding fifteen cents for haircuts; and on the levee a number of barge and packet companies agreed to wage demands. But in the evening the strike committee made the fatal error of not showing up at Lucas Market. They had nothing new to offer, and the demand for guns was growing more insistent. They had no guns, and they did not want any. At the Market, impromptu speakers called for drastic measures; they wanted to seize the Four Courts (a handsome new building on the square between Clark and Spruce, Eleventh and Twelfth, which housed the police department, the jail, and three city courts), the workhouse, the courthouse, and the U.S. Arsenal. After milling about for a while, hundreds of men walked to the new strike headquarters at Schuler's Hall, at Fifth and Biddle. To their disappointment, the committee had nothing to offer.

Meanwhile, one thousand volunteers were armed and drilling under the eyes of Generals Smith and Marmaduke at the National Armory. The strike's momentum continued on Friday, with a few remaining shops closing, but in the afternoon, constituted authority finally moved. Out of the Four Courts area came the police cavalry, followed by the mayor, Colonel David Armstrong of the police board, and General John D. Stevenson with about six hundred "citizen militia," including an artillery battery. Smith and Marmaduke opposed the foray and did not participate. They did not think it necessary, and they feared the militia would provoke armed resistance which would expose its worthlessness—there were too many officers and too few privates, and the strikers had more veteran soldiers than the militia did. There was no resistance; the strikers were unarmed; and, despite the bloodthirsty bellows of Colonel Armstrong, there was no bloodshed. Seventy-three strikers surrendered at Schuler's Hall, none of them leaders. A day or two earlier, there would have been a battle, despite the lack of weapons, but the authorities had waited until the lion was dead before entering the jungle.

The strikers were still out, but the committee made only a feeble effort to rally them. Those who had jobs were at work on Monday, with only the river workers having made any tangible gains. By the weekend the railroad strike had been broken at East St. Louis, and the trains were running. In St. Louis, workers had at least scared hell out of their "betters." Despite press hysteria, there had been no real violence. A few windows had been broken, and one militiamen had been wounded by his own bayonet when he fell off a ledge at the Four Courts. Currlin, Lofgreen, and others were brought to trial, but the prosecutors dropped the case for lack of evidence that they had advocated violence or caused property damage.

Some strikers had begged for guns, and local warehouses held plenty of Sharps, Springfields, and Winchester rifles for the western trade, but the Lassallean program of changing society through the ballotbox did not allow their use. With their central control, the Workingmen could have strewn the streets with dead bodies and made the Pennsylvania riots seem like picnics, but in the end they would have lost. With arms, the strikers could have handled the police (there were only 350) and the militia, but there were eight companies of U.S. Infantry at the Arsenal ready to march if shooting started. Knowing what they could have done, it was galling for strikers to read the crowing and chortling of the hated *Republican* after the "great citizens' raid" on Schuler's Hall. The workers had to return to their slashed wages and short rations, and the Irish cursed their German strike leaders for betraying them. The *Chicago Times* sneered that the lack of violence in St. Louis was merely further proof that it was a one-horse town. As a brief footnote to the affair, the Greenback-Labor Party polled 17 percent of the city's vote in 1878. Better times in 1879 reduced unemployment and improved wages, and if the workers never recovered their optimism of a decade earlier, neither did they return to the streets, except in officially approved rallies.

The prominence of blacks in the marching multitude underlined what many had hardly noticed: the antebellum decline in the black population had been reversed. Many of the refugees brought to the city by the Western Sanitary Commission had stayed to work on the levee and in the warehouses, and after the failure of reconstruction and the rise of the Ku Klux Klan, the refugee tide resumed. St. Louis was not very hospitable, and they got only menial jobs, but the emigrants explained themselves with the pithy saying "better to be a lamp post on Targee Street than the mayor of Dixie." Since the census of 1870 was worthless and later estimates were based on it, accurate data were not available until 1880, when the federal tally revealed that from 3,297 (2.04 percent) in 1860, blacks had increased in number to 22,256 (6.36 percent). St. Louis now had the third largest urban black concentration in the nation, behind Baltimore and Philadelphia. Since the major parties were in balance in the city, blacks had some leverage as an arm of the Republican organization.

German and Irish immigrants continued to choose the Mound City in the seventies, and it remained one of the richest ethnic mixes in the United States. Of its 350,518 residents in 1880, 54,901 were

German natives, 28,566 were Irish, and 8,762 were from Great Britain. France, Switzerland, and Bohemia had each contributed more than 2,000. Of the children sixteen and under in the public schools, 46 percent were of German, 16 percent were of Irish, and 12 percent of other European parentage. Some children of well-to-do native American families attended private schools, but a larger percentage of German and Irish pupils enrolled in parochial schools. Thus, with the second generation included, at least two-thirds of the city's population in 1880 belonged to these well-defined ethnic groups. For the public schools, this created some knotty problems.

Public education had begun in St. Louis in 1838 with the opening of two common (elementary) schools, supported in part by 5 percent of the income from the city's common lands, an arrangement made possible by Thomas F. Riddick, who had persuaded delegate Edward Hempstead to present the plan to Congress in 1813. First to open was the South School at Fourth and Spruce, with future Senator David H. Armstrong and Mary Salisbury as teachers. North School opened a few weeks later, and Benton School followed in 1841. Instruction began with the three "R's" and geography, and included "all that comes under the denomination of an English education." Classes for girls were held on the upper floor, those for boys on the ground floor. Initially, the meager common-school fund made a ten dollar annual fee necessary, but a small increment from the state under the Geyer Act of 1839, plus the return of prosperity in the mid-1840s, made it possible first to reduce and then in 1847 to abolish the fee. Citizens who equated free schools with pauperism protested, but the city moved ahead again in 1849 by levying a one-mill tax for public education. By 1854 there were 27 schools, 72 teachers, and 3,791 pupils.

The middle class was slow to accept public schools, but the addition of a high school in 1855 gave the system prestige. Built at Fifteenth and Olive for fifty thousand dollars, it was the most lavish public schoolhouse west of New York. Superintendent John Tice defended it as "an expression of the refinement, public spirit, and taste of the community." The rich and their imitators responded as expected, and within a year the schools were turning away hundreds of applicants. Ancient and modern languages, history, and natural sciences were offered, a curriculum as ambitious as that of many colleges, and the level of instruction was probably higher than at most small colleges, where three or four ministers taught everything. By 1860, nearly 12,000 pupils were enrolled, including 301 in high school, but the Civil War rudely interrupted the system's progress. Governor Jackson and the secessionist legislature promptly grabbed the state school fund for the use of the militia, and the slackening of

High School. N.E. cor. 15th & Olive Sts.

The Public High School (later, Central High School), Northeast Corner, Olive and Fifteenth Streets. *Photograph by Emil Boehl, 1870. MHS-PP.*

business reduced the city's rental income. The school board was forced to assess fees again: six dollars for the district schools and twenty-eight dollars for the high school and normal school (founded in 1857). Enrollment fell drastically to 5,520 in 1861–62. The overall drop was 53 percent, but it was 67 percent among the children of laborers. In 1863 the state school fund was restored, and in 1864–65 fees were eliminated. Enrollment rose to 14,000, and wartime salary cuts were restored to an average of $657 annually per teacher (under $600 for women, over $750 for men).

In 1865 the school levy was raised to two mills, in 1867 to three, and in 1868 to four (.4 percent of the assessed valuation of property). Thereafter, at least three-fourths of public school revenues were derived from the property tax. By 1870, there were 24,347 pupils in public and 4,362 in parochial schools, including "colored" public schools, the latter an innovation of the Radical Republicans. John Mason Peck had taught local black children religion and the three "R's" in the 1820s, and his associate, John Berry Meachum, had managed a day school for blacks for several years before the sheriff broke in, arrested a white teacher, and closed the doors. In 1845 the Sisters of St. Joseph of Carondelet began to teach the basics, French, and needlework to black girls, but after two years a mob destroyed their convent. In 1847 antiabolitionist fury and the national debate over slavery extension led the Missouri legislature to outlaw schools "for the instruction of free negroes and Mulattoes . . . in this State."

Meachum had then opened his "Freedom School" on a steamboat anchored in the middle of the Mississippi. During the late 1840s and 1850s dozens of black pupils rafted back and forth daily to these water-borne classes taught by teachers imported from the East. Elizabeth Keckley, an ex-slave, taught "sewing classes," which were covers for lessons in reading and writing. Lookouts warned of approaching strange or unfriendly whites, whereupon books would disappear and needles would fly. The five black churches had schools in their basements, and in 1860 Hiram H. Revels, who was to become the nation's first black U.S. senator (from Mississippi during Reconstruction), opened his school near the levee, which was said to have 150 pupils. Blanche K. Bruce, the second black senator-to-be, took over this school in 1861.

While there were no legal changes favoring black education before 1865, William Greenleaf Eliot and James Yeatman led a group of Unionists who were pressing for change. In May 1863, the American Missionary Society set up a school, primarily for fugitive slaves, in the Missouri Hotel. Soon the influx of "most earnest young scholars" required larger quarters at the Ebenezer Church on Washington Avenue. After two days a mob of "unknown perpetrators" (according to the police) burned the church. Another site was found, and soon daily attendance at the "American Freedom School" was over one hundred. Samuel Sawyer, the superintendent of "Contrabands," was amazed by their rapid progress, which Lydia Hess, a teacher, attributed to superior motivation. Yet only 10 percent of the city's black children were in school in late 1863. Refugees had nearly tripled the black population, aggravating the school situation in unanticipated ways. Native blacks were reluctant to mix their children with the newcomers, many of whom were adults and most of whom they considered their inferiors.

Blacks and well-disposed whites joined in 1864 to form a Board of Education for Colored Schools, to provide free education for all black children. Without public funds, this was a difficult goal, but the Western Sanitary Commission helped by contributing one hundred dollars a month to the board and establishing nine schools of its own, chiefly for refugees. W. G. Eliot chipped in with high school classes for blacks in the basement of his church at Eighth and Locust. By 1865, the various black schools served fifteen hundred pupils.

The Radical Constitution of 1865 required school boards to support black education, and the St. Louis board hastened to comply by appropriating five hundred dollars (.2 percent of its budget) to the Colored Board, and in 1866 three black district schools were created. A year later, there were 437 pupils in these schools, and a similar number in tuition schools partially supported by the Freedmen's Bureau and various benevolent societies. Even these modest efforts met implacable white hostility. The Democratic press marched out an army of complaints about wasted tax money, and tumble-down quarters for the black schools were not found for several months after classes were supposed to begin. By 1875 there were twelve such schools, but there had been few qualitative improvements. They were relocated frequently, district boundaries were irrational, and many pupils had to walk long distances to classes, often passing several white schools enroute. Teachers were paid barely half as much as those in white schools. R. B. Foster, founder of Lincoln Institute in Jefferson City, wryly pointed out that teachers of black children were in less danger of becoming rich than other teachers, "How many school-houses in the state have dusky faces for occupants?" he asked. "Houses that would be suitable for white children? Are there any forty-thousand dollar school-houses in St. Louis for the 5,000 colored children?" In 1880, the value of land, building, and furnishings for sixty-eight white schools serving 52,270 pupils was $2.67 million, or $39,330 per school, while eight properties serving 3,100 black pupils averaged $14,600 in value. Another 500 blacks attended classes in rented buildings.

Black parents' complaints usually went unheeded, especially after the decline of Radicalism. In one instance, they built a school at their own expense and donated it to the board. They pleaded for kindergartens, trained teachers, and a high school. In 1875 a few high school classes were offered, but they were discontinued after a month. Parents then demanded that they be resumed or the students admitted to white high schools. In response, the board cited the constitutional ban on mixing the races in schools, but its attorney R. E. Rombauer reminded the members that the state constitution also required a black high school. Reluctantly, they complied by establishing Sumner High, on Eleventh Street between Poplar and Spruce. For several years, this educational landmark was only another monument to inequality. White high school teachers were the best paid in the system, but Sumner's were "third assistants," the lowest rank. Three times as much per pupil was spent on the white school in 1880. Despite these and other inequities, black parents valued education. Before the Missouri compulsory school attendance law of 1905 black children enrolled in St. Louis schools in larger numbers than whites of similar economic status.

During the 1850s and 1860s, public education was profoundly affected by the "St. Louis Movement," a philosophical society which drew international attention through its publications. Its originator and most profound thinker was Henry C. Brokmeyer, a young German who had studied at Brown University before coming to Warren County, Missouri, to live in the woods after the fashion of Thoreau. In 1858, needing a larger audience for the ideas of Immanuel Kant and

Henry C. Brokmeyer. *Carte de visite photograph by J. C. Downing, 1875. MHS-PP.*

William Torrey Harris. *Steel engraving by J. C. Buttre, after a photograph by J. A. Scholten, ca. 1878. MHS-PP.*

Georg Hegel, which had become his ruling passion, Brokmeyer moved to St. Louis, where he worked as a stove-molder. In some chance fashion he met young William Torrey Harris, who taught shorthand classes in the downtown district. Harris had attended Yale, and he had some knowledge of German idealism, but for the next several years he and a small circle of friends were to Brokmeyer as pupils to master. In 1860 Brokmeyer completed his English translation of Hegel's *Larger Logic*, and in 1866 he and his now well-seasoned disciples founded the St. Louis Philosophical Society, one of its aims being the publication of Brokmeyer's work. Brokmeyer was chosen president, and Harris, now a high school teacher, was named secretary. Teachers, lawyers, ministers, aspiring students, and even politicians were drawn to the group. Brokmeyer himself served as the unlikeliest lieutenant governor Missouri ever had, from 1877 to 1881. The society quickly established classes in Hegel, Kant, Plato, and Aristotle, and in 1867 Harris launched the *Journal of Speculative Philosophy,* an ambitious departure from the plan to print the Hegel translation. This quarterly featured articles by movement writers and by philosophers of widely divergent views, such as Josiah Royce, C.

S. Peirce, William James, and John Dewey. Always prominent, however, were translations by Brokmeyer and others of the works of Hegel, Fichte, Schelling, Kant, Schopenhauer, Goethe, Descartes, and the Greeks.

Just behind Brokmeyer and Harris in influence, the movement's most prolific writer was Denton J. Snider, author of *The System of Shakespeare's Dramas, Delphic Plays, The American State,* and some fifty other works on philosophy, history, and the fine arts. Others of prominence were F. Louis Soldan, principal of the Normal School and later superintendent of schools, who published articles on Darwinism, Dante, and pedagogy; Susan Blow, who founded America's first public school kindergarten; J. G. Woerner, state senator and probate judge, who wrote legal treatises and drama; James S. Garland, an attorney who collaborated with Harris on *Hegel's Logic*; J. K. Hosmer, a German literature professor at Washington University who published widely; H. H. Morgan, high school principal who contributed to the *Journal* and other periodicals; Anna C. Brackett and Sue V. Beeson, high school teachers and educational writers; George Howison, author of *The Limits of Evolution* and later founder of the University of California's philosophy department; W. M. Bryant, author of *Hegel's Esthetics*; and Thomas Davidson, the movement's most distinguished scholar, who eventually founded the organization in London that became the Fabian Society. Davidson, who wrote *Aristotle and Ancient Educational Ideals* and *The History of Education,* was an idealist, but he opposed Harris's prescriptive rigidity for the classroom. His ideas influenced the thought of William James and John Dewey.

Dozens of young men and women came to the city because of the Philosophical Society. They joined its clubs, discussion groups, and classes, worked in the city's offices, and taught in the public schools. Wives and daughters of business and professional men thronged to classes in idealist philosophy, and their husbands and fathers gave the movement moral and financial support—James Yeatman, G. E. Leighton, Henry T. Blow, Thomas Allen, and Albert Todd among them. The movement spread its influence afar—affiliates were organized in Milwaukee, Chicago, and Massachusetts, where Harris and Davidson joined with Bronson Alcott and Ralph Waldo Emerson to found the Concord School of Philosophy. The *Journal* was read as widely in Europe as in America. There were plenty of critics, one of the strongest at home, where the *Republican,* distrusting all forms of social mechanics, referred to the society as a "clique."

The St. Louis philosophers were the heralds of an industrial-urban society. An earlier generation of intellectuals had tried to withdraw from a materialistic world in ideal, self-abnegating communities. By their example, they hoped to create a humane society, but as Margaret Fuller observed after the failure of Brook Farm, the human ego, "mountainous me," had defeated them. The lines of descent were clear. Harris, Garland, Hosmer, and others were New Englanders, shaped by transcendentalism as Brokmeyer had been as a student at Brown. Transcendentalism was itself grounded in Kantian idealism, and Brokmeyer's studies of Kant and Hegel in his Warren County Walden had convinced him that humanitarian goals could be attained by the application of Hegelian logic to an industrial, democratic society. That Hegel himself had not believed this did not bother Brokmeyer. Significantly, the first outside speakers to address the society were Alcott, Emerson, and Julia Ward Howe, all veterans of perfectionist communities.

As editor of the *Journal* and superintendent of the St. Louis schools (1868–80), Harris became the movement's central figure. As he saw it, American society was torn by disintegrating forces. The materialism from which reformers had recoiled in the 1840s was now compounded by corruption and unrest, the theories of Darwin and Huxley threatened religion, and the old moral values were melting away in the hurly-burly of industrialization and urbanization. Far from being dismayed by all this, Harris believed that the opposites could be reconciled to create a better society. As superintendent of schools he would lead the community in this effort. With the necessary resources and loyal, well-trained teachers, a generation of children could be immersed in the values that would make them valuable citizens. Self-realization, Harris's goal for every child, required the individual to understand his responsibilities to others and to the whole. Such a person would be free in the truest sense; that is, he would suppress his selfish instincts to become a cooperative and productive member of society. This was all part of God's plan; Harris was not a bible Christian, but he detested atheism and agnosticism.

Unlike Alcott and other perfectionists, Harris did not believe that humans were basically good, but rather that by the use of their reason, they could devise a system in which all would choose to be good. Hegel's view that the ideal could be achieved only in an authoritarian state was denied, but his dialectic was essential to the creation of a good society. The agrarian order and its moral values (thesis), was threatened by an amoral and complex scientific-industrial intruder (antithesis). These opposites should be seen as complementary—the best of the old could be retained in an efficient, free, republican, and bountiful political-industrial order (synthesis). Karl Marx, applying Hegel's dialectic, proposed a different synthesis. Harris and his colleagues did not deliberately glorify the state at the expense of the individual, but in their construct, the dimensions of freedom and democracy were squeezed a bit.

Having experienced unbridled freedom in their families, children came to the school as little savages. Thus, it was necessary that they be tamed quickly, that the process of learning to be good citizens start on their first day. They must learn their lessons perfectly and be prepared to recite them without hesitation. Punishment for those who upset the order was automatic. If enforced without exception, submission would become a habit; if comprehension was slow to come, disciplined study would bring it eventually. Since neither children nor their parents knew enough to select a course of study, there were no electives in grammar school, save German, and none for boys in high school. In the primary and grammar schools, Students were thoroughly grounded in the basic skills and some exposed to the universal truths contained in the writings of Shakespeare, Homer, Goethe, Plato, Aristotle, and other greats. Harris, who was a dynamo of energy and an organizational genius, expected corresponding grades in every school to be studying or reciting exactly the same lessons at any given moment, and so it was. Noise was not permitted, and when the pupils recited, they stood in line, their toes pointing exactly to the front, their bodies erect, their eyes on the teacher. If any little foot was out of line, its owner was called to account. This rigid discipline was harsh, but it was logical and purposive, and its aim was to produce eager, cooperative, and productive citizens.

In high school, where the more talented and usually more affluent pupils prepared for the leading roles in society, Greek and Latin language and literature, ancient and modern history, English history and literature, geography, mathematics, and the natural sciences were offered. Until 1887 German was taught in the high and grammar schools, mandated not by Harris, though he approved, but by the German constituency. It was finally dropped in the grammar schools for political reasons, thinly disguised as economic. Since the schools existed to prepare children for intelligent citizenship, no hint of vocational preparation was to intrude. Nor was religion, at any level.

The St. Louis schools under William Torrey Harris were widely admired and emulated. No educator in the United States stood higher than he in public and professional esteem. Though they existed, those who flinched from his rigid discipline were in the minority. The most remarkable feature of the schools was not the discipline or the quality of instruction but the systematic and purposeful administration. The superintendent so overawed the school board that his will prevailed without question. He had enlisted a superior corps of teachers, most of them trained in his own Normal School, and he marched them all toward his well-defined objectives like a good general. Every teacher knew where to go and how to get there, and free-wheeling was not encouraged. They did not often refuse the bit, because they believed in Harris, his views, and his methods.

The most innovative development of the Harris era was the result of his reaction to the difficult adjustments children had to make during their first year. After studying the living conditions of preschool children in the city, Harris concluded that many of them, especially those in the levee and factory districts, were lost to education between the ages of three and five. In 1871, he became interested in the kindergarten movement which had spread through western Europe, deriving from the ideas of the Swiss educator Friedrich Froebel, who believed that a child's intellect and personality could be developed through directed play. Immigrants had established German play-schools in St. Louis, Cincinnati, and Milwaukee, and private kindergartens thrived in New York and Boston. Fortunately, Harris had the proper instrument at hand. Susan Blow, the expensively educated, world-traveling twenty-eight-year-old daughter of Henry Taylor Blow, was back in town with a burning social conscience, working as an unpaid substitute teacher. As she wrote forty years later, upon first hearing Harris lecture on Hegel: "The open secret was revealed and I knew that I stood upon the delectable mountains and discerned from afar the shining pinnacles of the Eternal City. . . . I was a novice admitted to a school fellowship." She was indeed a true believer; Denton Snider wrote irreverently that she used "ponderous Hegelian nomenclature" in explaining babies' games.

In 1872, with Harris's encouragement, Susan Blow went east to study with Maria Kraus-Bolte, an educational leader from Holland who had opened a private kindergarten in New York. After a year she returned to St. Louis, where she and Harris designed a kindergarten program to bridge the gap between the family and the primary school. Children would be taught punctuality, silence, obedience, and self-control, virtues which would enable them "to combine with [their] fellow man in civilized society and the state." Unlike street play, kindergarten "games" would develop specific skills. The manipulation of blocks of various shapes, drawing, weaving, clay modeling—all would equip the child with tools that would be useful in school, or later in his work or leisure time. The pilot kindergarten, conducted by Blow with three unpaid assistants and sixty-eight pupils, was set up in the foundry district at the Des Peres School in Carondelet. In 1874 Blow established a training school for kindergarten teachers, and

Susan Blow. *Photograph of a pastel on paper by C. F. Maury, 1906. MHS-PP.*

despite objections to the program as unlawful, too expensive, and too German, it was generally popular. In 1878 the board declared the kindergartens a regular part of the public school program. By 1880, they were in all sections of the city, serving the rich as well as the poor, with 166 paid and 60 unpaid teachers and 7,828 pupils, and in 1881 they were extended to the black schools.

Success bred imitation, and St. Louis–trained educators supervised the opening of kindergartens in Baltimore, Boston, Chicago, and a dozen other cities. By 1900, nearly two hundred thousand children were enrolled in public kindergartens. Meanwhile, the St. Louis movement was dispersing. Irritated by pressures for economy and "practicality," capped by board member Calvin Woodward's campaign for manual training, but primarily because he wanted to devote more time to philosophy, Harris resigned in 1880 to lecture in and direct the Concord School of Philosophy. He took the *Journal* with him and published it until 1893. As U.S. Commissioner of Education from 1889 to 1906, he increased the stature and usefulness of the bureau, collecting and publishing national and international educational data on a scale never attempted before. He was honored by dozens of international awards and medals, and his was a powerful voice in the National Education Association. Apparently, his style never changed; one of his associates in Washington wrote that whenever Harris spoke for a motion, it passed; when he opposed one, it was "as dead as a dodo."

Howison went to California; Snider to Chicago, where he conducted "literary schools"; and Davidson to Concord, to England, and finally to New York. The movement philosophy dominated the St. Louis schools until the 1890s, when Woodward's manual training program was installed. By then the school board had become one of St. Louis's several centers of corruption, and the rancid atmosphere at City Hall seemed to suggest that education for leadership had failed. On the other hand, most of the businessmen and politicians of Ed Butler's "boodle ring" were either private-school products or had never attended school at all. None of this bothered Henry Brokmeyer; he had long since decided that America was not ready for philosophy, and four years at the statehouse had not improved his outlook. After his term expired, he practiced law for a time, and then went to the Indian Territory to live with the Osages and the Cherokees.

9.
Meet Me in St. Louis

In his celebrated study, *The American Commonwealth*, published in 1888, Lord James Bryce pointed to the governance of its cities as "the one conspicuous failure" of the United States. He blamed this deplorable condition on crooked and incompetent officials and the influence of state and national politics in municipal affairs. If St. Louis was not the prize example of Bryce's analysis, it was a worthy contender. By the 1890s the highly touted home rule charter had not only failed to guarantee honest and efficient government, it had encouraged corruption and mismanagement.

Paradoxically, the Lion of the Valley had in some respects surpassed its early promise. Despite newspaper envy of the Chicago phenomenon, St. Louis had grown substantially in population and wealth during the last quarter of the nineteenth century. Still a leading agricultural entrepôt and commercial hub, it was second only to Chicago as a railroad center, and it was a humming industrial metropolis. From 350,518 in 1880, the city's population grew by 29 percent to 451,770 in 1890, and by an additional 27 percent to 575,238 in 1900, to rank fourth in the nation behind New York, Chicago, and Philadelphia. By 1890 St. Louis was also fourth in the gross value of its manufactured products and fifth in the amount of capital invested in manufacturing. Industrial establishments increased in number from 2,984 to 6,148 in the 1880s, and the number of "hands" employed in them from 41,825 to 82,911. Manufacturing capital had risen from $50.8 million to $141 million during the decade and industrial production from $114.3 million to $229.1 million.

The pattern of St. Louis's industry changed rapidly during the 1890s, and its industrial growth came virtually to a halt. A shift from raw-material forwarding to manufacturing in the smaller cities of its trade was partly responsible, as well as the diversion of some industries to other regions as capitalists utilized the fully developed national railway network to locate near the best markets, raw materials, and cheap labor supplies. East St. Louis, for example, assisted by the high freight transfer rates of the Terminal Railroad Association and the availability of relatively cheap land, grew from less than $2 million annually in product value in 1890 to $32.7 million in 1900. Kansas City, Kansas; South Omaha, Nebraska; and

St. Joseph, Missouri, all in the St. Louis–Chicago hinterland, and all
beneficiaries of the shift in cattle-finishing from Texas to the rich
grasslands of the northern Great Plains, became major slaughtering
and meat-packing centers—the last two emerging from insignificance
in the 1890s. Having been heavily dependent upon Texas cattle,
St. Louis lost more to the newcomers than Chicago, which, like
Indianapolis, concentrated upon the slaughter of corn-fed hogs from
the upper Midwest. From fifth in meat-packing in 1890, behind
Chicago, Kansas City, New York, and Philadelphia, St. Louis slipped
to sixth, following Chicago, the three western centers, and
Indianapolis. The introduction of refrigerated railroad cars had made
long-distance shipping of livestock unnecessary, and slaughtering
declined even more drastically in the East.

Among other factors hampering industrial development was the
crushing economic depression of 1893–97. This crisis exacerbated the
long-standing malaise of the cotton and wheat growers of the South
and West, both of key importance to St. Louis. Heavily indebted
farmers had for years overplanted and overproduced for a saturated
world market. Vast new wheat regions in Canada, the Ukraine, and
elsewhere pressed down world grain prices, while protective tariffs
and federal hard-money policy savaged the wheat and cotton farmers
as consumers and debtors.

Between 1890 and 1900 the gross value of St. Louis's
manufactures grew by only 2 percent, to $233.6 million. Most other
older cities were also hard hit; several, including Boston and
Cincinnati, suffered substantial overall declines. Brooklyn having
been absorbed by New York City, St. Louis "rose" in industrial
production, from fifth to fourth; but in capital invested in
manufacturing, despite a 15 percent increase to $162.2 million, it
slipped to fifth, behind the resurgent steel capital, Pittsburgh. The most
marked decline was in flour and grist mill products. St. Louis had
surrendered the national leadership in milling to Minneapolis a decade
earlier, and in the 1890s, the economic depression eliminated the
premium the local flour had previously enjoyed. Production fell from
$12.5 million to $4 million, nearly half of the city's mills closed their
doors, and its rank in the industry slipped from second to fifth. Men's
clothing, construction, fruit and vegetable canning, agricultural
machinery, and lumber production also declined, as apparently did the
city's largest industry—brewing. According to the census reports,
St. Louis's beer production dropped from $16.2 million in 1890 to
$11.7 million in 1900, and its rank in the industry from second, behind
New York, to fifth, below Chicago, Milwaukee, and Philadelphia as
well. The introduction of pasteurized bottled beer and national

Anheuser-Busch Brewery, Boiler House with Refrigerator Cars. *The use of the refrigerator car enabled St. Louis breweries to open new markets outside the region. Photograph by Emil Boehl, 1892. MHS-PP.*

advertising by Anheuser-Busch, closely followed by Milwaukee brewers, had created a national market and a drastic reduction in the number of breweries. Yet, the industry was still predominantly local in orientation, as attested to by the presence of the nation's three largest cities among the major producers, although their beers were qualitatively inferior to the St. Louis and Milwaukee products.

Because of increasing capital requirements and the economies of scale in production, only nineteen of the forty breweries in operation in 1860 in St. Louis survived in 1900. Large-scale enterprises, including Anheuser-Busch, with its fifty-square-block plant, the largest in the world, and the pioneering Lemp Company, produced nearly one million barrels and five hundred thousand barrels respectively in 1900. Since the two combined reported more than $10 million in sales in 1900, and the city's nineteen breweries $20 million in 1901, it seems conclusive that the low census figure for 1900 was in error.

Both major companies, Anheuser-Busch especially, had extensive foreign sales, chiefly in Mexico and South America. The remarkable success of Anheuser-Busch was attributable to the organizing genius and imagination of Adolphus Busch, a German immigrant who had become a full partner and president of the firm four years after marrying Lilly Anheuser in 1861. One of the world's first super-salesmen, Busch had responded quickly to advances in science and

Adolphus Busch. *Busch, a salesman and promoter, divided his time between America and his native Germany. Photograph by Adler, Carlsbad, ca. 1908. MHS-PP.*

technology. After pioneering in the use of refrigerated railroad cars to capture a large share of the southern market shortly after the Civil War, he introduced pasteurized bottled beer in 1873, and in 1876 he began marketing Budweiser, a bottled beer of unusual clarity, which quickly became one of the world's leading beers. Budweiser's appeal was enhanced by its attractive label, which resembled that of a fine vintage wine, and Busch dedicated himself to making it the best-known brewery product in the world. Picturing himself as a merchant prince, he looked and lived like one, at Number One Busch Place on the brewery grounds, at Tony Faust's Oyster House, at the Waldorf in New York, on his private railroad car, the Adolphus, and at his palatial homes at Pasadena, New York City, and Langenswalbach on the Rhine. He was a familiar figure in Berlin, where he consorted with the Prussian aristocracy and consulted with Otto von Bismarck about the spread of German cultural influence and the common interests of the Fatherland and those of German descent throughout the world. Wherever he went, he advertised by giving away pocket-knives and other trinkets stamped with his picture and the brewery's name, but most of all by a device perhaps never surpassed in effectiveness—the distribution of hundreds of thousands of prints of Cassily Adams's *Custer's Last Fight*, with "Anheuser-Busch Brewing Association" spread across the bottom of the painting. Busch reportedly paid Adams thirty-five thousand dollars for the work and the right to distribute prints of it. The painting's claim to artistic merit was modest, but as an eye-catching back-bar display in a hundred thousand saloons, it was a Rembrandt.

By the turn of the century, St. Louis had responded to relative or absolute declines in some of its older industries by a shift in emphasis toward those industries characteristic of maturing cities with large populations and high local demand, approximate equality in numbers of men and women, and relative cultural maturity. It ranked fifth or six nationally in dress manufacturing, furniture-making, book publishing and job printing, boots and shoes, lumber products, and newspaper and periodical publishing. With the exception of Grand Rapids, Michigan (third in furniture), those ahead of St. Louis in these categories were older eastern cities.

Ironically, though the city was still, as it had been for three decades, the national leader in chewing and pipe tobacco manufacturing, the local industry's survival was threatened by the formation of the giant tobacco trust. Tobacco had been manufactured locally since territorial days, and by 1867 the city led the world in the production of fine-cut and plug tobacco. Formerly a leading tobacco-growing state, Missouri found its crop reduced to one-third of its prewar size as the abolition of slavery led farmers to turn to the less labor-intensive grain crops. This had not deterred St. Louis manufacturers, who found new sources of leaf in Kentucky, Tennessee, and southern Ohio, where the soil was less suitable for grain. The everlasting federal excise tax on tobacco, originally a Civil War revenue measure, accelerated the decline of the less efficient smaller factories, and as the industry boomed, the larger firms grew even faster. In 1873, John E. Liggett, whose family had been in the industry in St. Louis for fifty years, formed a partnership with George H. Myers. Soon after its incorporation in 1878, the Liggett and Myers Tobacco Company was the largest manufacturer of plug tobacco in the world. Only the Lorillard Company of New York and the Drummond Company of St. Louis rivaled it in size. The Brown and Catlin companies, both local firms, were also major plug and pipe tobacco manufacturers. By 1890 St. Louis was producing more than twice as much chewing tobacco as its nearest rival. Each of these firms manufactured snuff as well, and A. S. Stickney was a major maker and distributor of fine Cuban-leaf cigars. Dozens of retail stores in the city rolled their own cigars from domestic and Cuban tobacco for the local trade.

In 1893, James B. Duke, whose American Tobacco Company dominated cigarette production—a tiny fraction of the tobacco industry—began to move into the plug tobacco field. At a heavy cost, made possible only by the high profit margins in cigarette manufacturing, Duke's firm bought out most of the plug manufacturers, including the Drummond, Brown, and Catlin establishments in St. Louis. Liggett and Myers, still the plug industry giant, held out until a Wall Street syndicate gained control of the

Continental Tobacco Company, a plug-tobacco spinoff from
American. Faced with the threat of a ruinous price war against an
opponent with overwhelming financial resources, Liggett and Myers
succumbed. Most of the tobacco industry was consolidated as the
American Tobacco Company in 1904. Seven years later, the Supreme
Court held that the tobacco trust was in violation of the Sherman Anti-
Trust Act. In the reorganization that followed, Liggett and Myers was
designated as one of the four "competing" successor companies, but
its operations had been moved to North Carolina and its ownership
remained in New York, though its plant in the Mill Creek Valley still
led the world in plug tobacco.

After the Whiskey Ring scandals, several St. Louis distillers had
shifted their plants to Kentucky, others had dropped out of the
business, and still others had become chiefly wholesalers of whiskeys
and wines. Rebstock and Company exported its "Old Stonewall," a
sour-mash Kentucky-distilled bourbon, to the South and Southwest
and to foreign customers. Charles Schiele distributed his "Autocrat"
and "Geisha Malt" ryes in Illinois, Missouri, and the broader region;
and Stracke and Caesar were the regional distributors for "Old Crow,"
the nation's leading bourbon. In addition to sour-mash Kentucky
whiskey, the Bardenheier Company marketed Missouri, Ohio,
California, French, and German wines and Holland bitters over a wide
territory. The city's largest and best-known winery, the American
Wine Company, headed by Douglas Cook, bottled Cook's Imperial
Champagne, advertised it as the premier domestic champagne, and
sold it from coast to coast. Its large plant at Cass and Garrison
Avenues had a capacity of ten thousand bottles a day and storage
capacity for one million bottles in 1900.

As noted, St. Louis businesses, with the indispensable assistance
of the Missouri Pacific system, pushed aggressively into a rapidly
expanding hinterland from Mississippi to the New Mexico Territory
and from Colorado to the Rio Grande during the last three decades of
the nineteenth century. Jobbers and retailers all along the tracks, in the
small towns and in Little Rock, Wichita, Pueblo, Denver, Dallas,
Houston, Fort Worth, Laredo, and San Antonio relied heavily upon
St. Louis wholesalers for their supplies. The city's largest hardware
wholesaler, the Norvell-Shapleigh Company, formerly A. F. Shapleigh
and Company, conducted a million-dollar annual business in cutlery,
guns, mining machinery, chains, anvils, nails, and other items from its
warehouses occupying the entire block between Washington and
Lucas Avenues, Third and Fourth Streets in 1903 (the present
"Laclède's Landing" area) and from other warehouses along the
Terminal Railway tracks.

Estimated locally at $70 or $80 million annually, grocery distribution was the largest branch of the wholesale trade. Of the principal grocery staples, these firms in 1901 handled 150 million pounds of sugar, 37 million pounds of coffee, 20 million pounds of rice, and 14 million pounds of sugar and molasses. St. Louis's water connections to the primary producing areas and to New Orleans gave it a competitive advantage in these staples, and its trade territory for them encompassed much of the upper Mississippi valley and the Northwest, as well as the Southwest. Conversely, New Orleans competed strongly in these items along the St. Louis hinterland's southern periphery. In addition to bulky staples, the city's full-line wholesalers distributed flour, soap, tobacco, spices, woodenware, and other household items throughout the area. From its large building on Seventh Street at Clark Avenue, which housed can and box factories and storage facilities, the C. F. Blanke Tea and Coffee Company had forty drummers traversing a territory extending from British Columbia to Mexico City and from the upper Midwest to California. It was the largest coffee distributor west of the Mississippi; its principal brands were the Faust Blend and Exposition Coffees and Kafeko, a malted-grain coffee substitute "recommended for children and nervous people." Its expensive Faust brand was also sold in the East and in Europe after 1900.

Other large wholesalers included William Schotten and Company, a full-line distributor specializing in its own mustards and catsups; the Sternweger-Stoffregen Coffee Company, whose branch was established in New York in 1885 and became the nation's fifth largest coffee distributor; the Western Tea and Spice Company, whose drummers traveled from Canada to Texas; Haas, Lieber, and Coste, a full-line distributor; and Adam Roth and Company, which concentrated on the local and western trade. The Moll Company, the city's largest grocery retailer, located on Third Street between Market and Chestnut, distributed its full line in Arkansas, Texas, Illinois, Tennessee, and Florida. Moll's occupied warehouse space at Cupples Station, as did most local wholesalers. Samuel Cupples, the country's leading woodenware distributor, and Robert S. Brookings had established this giant freight depot in 1891, consisting of a group of seven-story buildings covering thirty acres and providing 1.5 million square feet of floor space, located between Seventh and Eleventh, Spruce and Poplar Streets. The Terminal Railroad's Eads Bridge tunnel ran through Cupples Station, connecting it with all the railroad lines. Hydraulic pressure elevators transferred goods from the warehouse floors to track level. Most of the city's heavy wholesale trade, amounting to more than $200 million annually at the turn of the century, was handled there, eliminating the need to cart it through the streets. Incoming freight was

Cupples Block from the South. *The Cupples Station development by Samuel Cupples and Robert S. Brookings gave St. Louis light industry a boost by creating a rapid, cheap means of transshipment of goods from rail to warehouse and back again. Photograph by Emil Boehl, ca. 1895. MHS-PP.*

billed directly to the Station, and outgoing items were shipped from there, giving the wholesalers a time and cost advantage. In 1900 Cupples and Brookings donated Cupples Station, nominally valued at $3 million but worth considerably more, to Washington University.

Second only to the grocery trade in sales volume, dry-goods wholesaling averaged between $50 and $60 million annually. The pioneer dry-goods wholesalers in St. Louis had been Wayman Crow and Samuel C. Davis, each of whom had opened for business in 1835. One of the most active early philanthropists in the city, Crow operated a private academy for boys, strongly supported the public school movement, helped found Washington University and served as its first vice president, and donated to the city its first art museum. With various partners, he stayed in the wholesale business until the 1880s. S. C. Davis eventually outstripped Crow, and by 1878 his firm was selling dry goods, boots, and shoes in the Nevada and New Mexico territories, in Louisiana and Texas to the south, and in the Midwest from Nebraska to Indiana. After his death, his grandsons, preferring other careers, sold out to Hargadine and McKittrick in 1895. One of them, Dwight F. Davis, became Secretary of War in 1925 and governor general of the Philippines in 1929. He also established tennis's Davis Cup competition.

In 1900 the city's major dry-goods wholesalers were Hargadine and McKittrick; Ely and Walker at Eighth and Washington; Rice-Stix at 1000 Washington Avenue (former army sutlers who had moved from Memphis in 1879 to escape the yellow fever and to take advantage of St. Louis's western railroad connections); and Carleton's, which claimed one-third of the wholesale dry-goods business, primarily serving the Southwest. Each of these companies maintained full-time buyers in New York, London, Paris, and Brussels. Rapid change in dry-goods marketing techniques put a premium on adjustment, and those who survived did so by integrating, either forward into retailing or backward into manufacturing or both. Giant retail firms, called department stores, had developed such heavy volume by the 1890s that they could wring concessions from manufacturers by dealing directly with them, and their pricing policies and quality merchandise drove smaller urban retailers to the wall. The wholesalers' best customers, small-town retailers scattered through the trade territory, were under pressure from Sears-Roebuck, Montgomery Ward, and other mail-order houses, which were able to undersell them because of their volume purchases and low overhead. A new threat appeared in 1902, though not so perceived at first, when J. C. Penney opened the first of what was to become a national chain of department stores at Kemmerer, Wyoming, closely followed by W. T. Grant in the East. Now the wholesalers had to fight to save their customers in the medium-sized cities.

In 1900 Hargadine and McKittrick bought the William Barr Company, St. Louis's first and largest department store, which occupied the entire block bounded by Sixth, Seventh, Olive, and Locust Streets. This firm, which had bought much of its stock directly from manufacturers, had also conducted a large mail-order business. Its principal rivals, the Grand Leader (Stix, Baer, and Fuller) and the Famous Company, also offered local customers a large stock of dry goods and clothing at all ranges of price and quality. Famous had been acquired in 1892 by the May Company of Cleveland, the nation's largest retailer in 1900 with its stores in St. Louis, Denver, and Cleveland. Ely and Walker, which had been a major supplier of Sears-Roebuck, stopped selling to them in 1900, in an effort to protect its retail customers, but in 1902 it picked up the Penney account, and by 1910 it was doing a $5 million annual business with Penney's, amounting to one-third of the wholesalers' annual sales. Shortly after breaking off with Sears, Ely and Walker began to manufacture overalls and work shirts, in order to bring these items to retailers at the lowest possible cost while widening its own margins. Rice-Stix, an even larger firm capitalized at $4 million in 1903, had begun to manufacture shirts, overalls, and pants in the 1890s, and in 1906 it began to make skirts, petticoats, and muslin underwear. In 1907 this house employed 175 traveling salesmen in 13 midwestern, southern, and western states.

Flushed with success in 1908, Hargadine and McKittrick undertook construction of the city's tallest building, the twenty-story "Railway Exchange." Barr's was to occupy the first eight floors; the rest was to be leased to the railroads for their executive suites. Construction costs ran much higher than expected, the railroads did not cooperate, and in 1911 the staggering wholesaler had to sell Barr's to the May Company. The Cleveland firm promptly merged its two St. Louis stores as Famous-Barr, then as now the city's largest department store. By 1920, Carleton's had merged with Ferguson-McKinney, another large firm, and the wholesale dry-goods business was concentrated in four companies: Ely and Walker, Rice-Stix, Carleton-Ferguson, and Butler Brothers, a branch of a Chicago firm.

Railway Exchange Building. *Opened in 1914, the Railway Exchange Building dominated the city skyline until overshadowed by the skyscrapers of the late 1920s. The lower floors still house Famous-Barr's downtown store. Photograph, ca. 1915. MHS-PP.*

Ely and Walker then dropped J. C. Penney to protect its customers and began to convert (manufacture) cloth percales and wash goods. Having overtaken Rice-Stix as the leading local jobber, Ely and Walker now did business in more than thirty states; and in 1923 it acquired a shirt factory in Kennett, Missouri, the first of several small-town operations, which included retail stores as well as factories. Rice-Stix did the same, and under the pressure of their competition, Carleton-Ferguson succumbed in the mid-1920s.

Wholesalers had become a standby resource for the larger retailers, useful only when unexpected shortages arose. Those surviving in 1930 had succeeded by absorbing competitors and integrating in both directions. They still considered themselves primarily as wholesalers who had assured themselves of stable markets and supplies through integration. People were singing the death song for wholesaling in 1930, as they had for decades, but St. Louis's dollar volume was higher than it had ever been. As a veteran executive put it in 1930: "To know how long the wholesaler has been going out of business and still staying in it, you will have to ask someone older than I am, but I well recollect hearing the matter discussed . . . as far back as 1888. When I asked an old merchant, who was then over 80, if it was likely to happen very soon, [he] said 'Don't worry, Johnny, I heard the same thing when I was a boy.'"

While the wholesalers had been moving into manufacturing and retailing, manufacturers and retailers were assuming the wholesaling function. Formerly a branch of dry-goods wholesaling, ready-made clothing had become a major item of manufacture in St. Louis in the 1880s. In 1901, at its eight-story building at Eighth and Lucas, N. and J. Friedman's employed five hundred persons in the making of cloaks, suits, skirts, and fur garments, which it distributed to retailers and wholesalers in the West and Midwest. Hughes and Company, the Singer Brothers, Bry and Brothers, and F. B. Hauck, specializing in women's and children's clothing; S. Grobinsky, in the new and daring field of women's underwear; and the St. Louis Corset Company all had drummers beating the bushes throughout the trade territory, selling the products of Eastern and European manufacturers as well as their own. In addition, another dozen or so St. Louis clothing manufacturers distributed only their own makes. Schwab's sold its men's and boys' lines in the Midwest and West, and the Marx and Haas Jeans Company's two thousand workers at its Thirteenth and Washington plant produced more than a million of its Rabbit Brand jeans and corduroys in 1901 for a nationwide market. Other large makers of men's clothing included Baer, Oliver and Singer; A. Haas and Sons; the Loth Jeans Company; and Smith and Schroder.

Watches, clocks, jewelry, and silverware were also major wholesale items. The principal distributors were Bauman and Company, the largest; Sol Loewenstein; and Mermod-Jaccard, the most elegant and expensive. In china, glass, and queensware the leader was E. F. W. Meier, which outfitted clubs, restaurants, bars, and hotels and distributed domestic ware and fine imports such as Haviland, Sevres, and Dresden china and Bohemian cut glass throughout the Mississippi valley and the West.

Although the wholesale trade approximately equalled manufacturing in sales volume at St. Louis in 1900, distribution no longer dominated the local economy. Of the 245,348 workers over ten years of age in the city, 37.8 percent were in manufacturing, 31.8 percent were in the retail and wholesale trade and transportation, 24.5 percent were in domestic and personal service, 5 percent were in the professions, and 0.9 percent were in agriculture. Primarily because of the growth of the clothing industry, women's share of the manufacturing labor force had doubled to 19 percent in twenty years. They comprised 23.3 percent of the gainfully employed; 40 percent of those employed in domestic and personal services; 28 percent of the professionals; and 11.1 percent of the commercial workers. In the large eastern industrial cities, manufacturing typically employed nearly one-half of the labor force, and in the newer western cities, the mining centers excepted, trade was predominant. Similarly, the mature cities, excepting those where heavy industry predominated, had a higher proportion of employed women than St. Louis, and the western cities had a smaller one. Since only a fraction of these dissimilarities were accounted for by the percentage of women in the general population, they apparently reflected the rise of light industry in the older cities, with the consequent opportunity to exploit a cheap labor supply. Thus, in the early twentieth century, St. Louis was temporarily in balance between trade and manufacturing.

In 1900, St. Louis was still a place of rich ethnic diversity, though it no longer led the nation in the proportion of its foreign-born, as it had on the eve of the Civil War. Of its 575,238 people, 111,356 (19.7 percent) were foreign-born, and another 239,170 (41.6 percent) had foreign-born parents. Only 189,249 (32.3 percent) were native whites with native parents, and 35,463 (6.4 percent) were native blacks. Among the second-generation ethnics, Germans predominated, with Irish as distant second. Among the foreign-born, 58,781 (52.8 percent) were German; 19,421 (17.5 percent) were Irish; 5,800 (5.2 percent) were English; 4,875 (4.3 percent) were Russian—primarily Jewish; 2,857 (2.6 percent) were Poles; 2,752 (2.5 percent) were Swiss; and

2,590 (2.3 percent) were Bohemians. Other foreign-born groups of more than one thousand included Austrians, Italians, French, Scots, and Swedes. St. Louis was now seventh among the twenty-five largest American cities in number of foreign-born, seventeenth in percentage of foreign-born, fourth in German-born, and fifth in Irish-born.

Most of this large ethnic population, including the second generation, was still crammed into the north and south sections near the river and along the periphery of the expanding business district. In the absence of planning, the growth of commerce, industry, and population after mid-century had created a ramshackle crazy-quilt place not unusual among American cities, but despite the handsome brick and stone public and business buildings and the islands of beautiful homes of the well-to-do, the houses of the poor were meaner, uglier, and more miserable than most, according to local writers and visitors. Charles Dickens in 1842 had noted the "tumble-down galleries" and "crazy old tenements" of old Frenchtown south of Market Street, adjacent to the business district. Again and again, single-family residences gave way to multifamily tenements and boardinghouses in the path of advancing commerce. The newest immigrants and a majority of blacks tended to live in these fringe areas or in seamy little pockets scattered through the older sections of the city. William Morris, an English visitor to St. Louis in the 1870s, found "black stinking slums" in the downtown area, where the "women and children . . . are as squalid and dirty as you would find people of the same class in the back slums of an English city." The famous Irish "Kerry Patch," a place of stark poverty and raucous violence, "floated" on the near north side, giving way to the west just ahead of the wreckers' hammers.

Living conditions for most St. Louisans in 1900 were fairly typical of the large American industrial city; that is, they were a good deal worse than those in the smaller and medium-sized cities. As a measure of the relative instability of home life, only 22.8 percent of the families owned their residences. Among the nation's five largest cities, St. Louis trailed Chicago in its proportion of homeowners but was ahead of New York, Boston, and Philadelphia. Among the first twenty-five cities, the Mound City was seventeenth. In Detroit, half as large as St. Louis, 40 percent were homeowners; and in the small (34,159 people) city of Springfield, Illinois, the ratio was 49 percent. Only 38 percent of the occupant-owned houses in St. Louis were mortgaged, considerably under the urban average, attributable perhaps to the sturdy self-reliance of the local burghers, but more likely a reflection of the unavailability of loans. In most cities where homeownership was more prevalent, the proportion of mortgages was considerably higher. In Cleveland and

Rochester, for example, where 38 percent owned their homes, more than half were mortgaged. With an average of seven persons per dwelling, St. Louis was higher than Philadelphia in residential density, but behind Boston, New York, and Chicago, and eighth from the top among the twenty-five largest cities. In Indianapolis, about one-third as large as St. Louis, density averaged 4.7, and in Denver, still smaller, the figure was 4.9. In eastern coastal cities, Baltimore excepted, density per dwelling was considerably higher.

Another hazard of life in the river city was the everlasting smoke from Illinois soft coal that poured from factories, trains, and the houses of poor and rich alike. Despite sporadic efforts to control it, nothing was accomplished until 1893, when a smoke abatement ordinance had some effect until the state supreme court declared it unconstitutional in 1897. It was widely believed that the smoke was responsible for consumption (tuberculosis), pneumonia, and other death-dealing diseases. One of the more graphic descriptions of the quality of this phenomenon was delivered by the Frenchman Charles Croonenberghs in 1885: "The air is so rich along the Mississippi, the pasty dust from American coal smoke falls so thick in the streets, that one is satisfied by an afternoon walk in St. Louis as if one had eaten a heavy dinner. . . . Everyone coughs . . . what an atmosphere charged with chimney emanations, in this capital, the name of which seems to betoken only charm and poetry."

Despite its housing and smoke problems and its hot and humid summer weather, St. Louis was not an unhealthful place by the standards of the time or in comparison with other cities. Its annual death rate from disease was 628 per 100,000 population, lowest among the five largest cities, and tenth lowest among the twenty-five largest. New Orleans was the deadliest city, with an annual rate of 1,040, with Washington, Pittsburgh, and Boston close behind. Minneapolis, St. Paul, and Rochester were the healthiest, with rates of under 400. With respect to the three major killers—consumption, pneumonia, and "diarrheal diseases"—St. Louis was tenth, thirteenth, and seventh lowest respectively. It was third highest among the larger cities in deaths by malaria, behind New Orleans and Washington; but that disease was not a leading cause of death in 1900, except in smaller southern cities such as Shreveport, Savannah, and Memphis—all of which had rates at least ten times that of St. Louis. In Missouri, St. Louis was slightly more healthful than Kansas City, but less so than St. Joseph.

Since the 1840s the wealthy had responded to the intrusions of commerce, disease, and the poor by fleeing to the outskirts of the city. By the 1840s many of the well-to-do had moved to fashionable

"Walsh's Row" on Fifth Street, or to the hills rimming Chouteau's Pond. As business invaded their sanctuary in the late 1840s, Walshes, Von Phuls, Vallés, and the like migrated south and west to Chouteau Avenue, just south of the pond. This wealthy enclave was dominated by the "veritable palace" built by J. B. Brant and occupied by General Fremont and his glittering retinue in 1861. The Vallé home, later sold to Carl Schurz; the marble-front villa of Benjamin Stickney of the Planter's House; the "Cracker Castle," at Fourteenth and Chouteau, built by James Pearce, who had made a fortune selling hardtack to the army during the Civil War; the "elegant residence" of Charles K. Dickson of the Eads Bridge Company; and the mansions of E. O. Stanard, Charles Stifel, William Glasgow, and James Barry were also on Chouteau Avenue. Just off Chouteau on Eighth Street was the "beautiful, white stone, Italian villa style" residence of George Knapp of the *Republican*. Forty years later, lamented a former resident, the area was covered by railroad yards, mills, and factories.

In the 1860s, Washington Avenue was a fashionable residential area. Bankers who lived there, by various financing maneuvers, tried but failed to divert the tide of commercial development after the Eads Bridge was under construction, and the fine homes disappeared. More carefully planned and longer lasting, Lucas Place was for decades the showplace of the city. This exclusive enclave was laid out in the 1850s by the financial titan James H. Lucas to insulate the homes of the wealthy from business and immigrants. Lucas Place was located west of the business district, from Fourteenth to Eighteenth Street, four blocks north of Market. Traffic from the east was blocked by Lucas's Missouri Park, extending from Thirteenth to Fourteenth, between the Place and Locust Street. This island of elegance, at its peak in the 1860s and 1870s, was especially popular with Yankee manufacturers and merchants, though it attracted several Southern and old Irish families as well. The Filleys, Carlos Greeley, Thomas T. Gantt, the Colliers, Thomas Allen, Edgar and Henry Ames, the Lacklands, and the Lionbergers lived there, as well as the Lucases and their relatives the Turners, Bernard Farrar, General William Harney (John Mullanphy's son-in-law), Dr. William Maffitt and his wife Julia Chouteau Maffitt, and Trusten Polk. One of these fine houses, outwardly rather unpretentious, the home of the noted fur trader Robert Campbell, has been preserved as an example of nineteenth-century genteel living. The First Presbyterian Church and Mary Institute, a girls' school connected with Washington University, were the only nonresidential buildings.

A mighty share of the city's wealth and power was concentrated in Lucas Place and in Carr Square, a half-dozen blocks to the north.

Washington Avenue West from Tenth Street. *St. Louis's thriving garment industry established itself on Washington Avenue in the western central business district. Photograph by George Stark, 1903. MHS-PP.*

William C. Carr, a Virginian who had come to St. Louis in the early territorial days, had created a select residential district protected by deed restrictions against all sorts of "nuisances." The Carrs, Bents, General D. M. Frost, and Colonel George Hayward were prominent residents of Carr Square. These exclusive "places" began to decline in the late 1880s. Some older residents, such as Rufus Lackland, clung stubbornly to their homes after 1890, but "high-toned" boarding houses, quickly followed by shabby ones, had begun to intrude. In 1898 the city cut Missouri Park in two, making Lucas Place a mere extension of Locust Street. Lackland, who lived until 1910, saw the Presbyterian Church become the Gayety Theater. Years later Isaac Lionberger fondly remembered the palmy days of the 1870s: "We who have lived a little while, recall the quiet charm of Lucas Place: the pleasant park upon the east, the rows of stately trees and stately houses, the aristocratic tide which streamed from its doors, the smart carriages, and the constant hospitality of its gracious inhabitants."

In 1850, a contemporary who also hoped to combine personal profit and the creation of a stable upper-class environment, attorney Charles Gibson, acquired land adjacent to Lafayette Park, west of

Eighteenth Street and south of Chouteau Avenue. After Gibson had persuaded the aldermen to forbid "nuisances"—dram shops, iron foundries, hemp, soap, candle, and vitriol factories, livery stables—in the park area, rows of expensive town houses were built, most of them in the late 1850s and 1860s. These narrow, deep, two- and three-story brick houses faced with stone lined the 120-foot-wide Lafayette, Missouri, Park, and Mississippi Avenues that surrounded the park and formed Lafayette Square. Off these streets, private places, closed to through traffic, such as Benton, Waverly, and Kennett were developed during the 1860s and 1870s. William Torrey Harris, railroad executive Stephen Barlow, and Mayor James Thomas were early residents, and dozens of the well-to-do joined them, but the extension of the city limits in 1877 and new housing to the south and west made Lafayette and nearby Jefferson Avenue into major thoroughfares. Crowds in the park added to the noise and confusion, and the former Thomas home was converted into a private school in 1877. Barlow moved away, and several others quit the area during the next few years; but Lafayette Square held its ground until 1896, when the century's most devastating tornado struck the corner of Lafayette and Missouri, flattening many homes and destroying the park facilities and leaving the statue of Senator Benton standing in solitary grandeur. The great storm killed at least 140 persons and severely injured over 1,000 more, most of them in the homes of the poor lying between the Square and the river. It missed the downtown business district, but it struck the Eads Bridge—without damaging the piers or main structure. The three-hundred-foot eastern approach was destroyed, however, and trains were blown off sidings on the east side. Contemporary estimates of property damage ranged upward from $10 million, with more than eight thousand buildings demolished. There were no more complaints that the bridge was overbuilt.

Most of the Lafayette Square houses were rebuilt, and some of them replaced by huge Romanesque mansions, but most of the first families moved to the West End. The introduction of cable street railways in 1886, followed in the 1890s by electric streetcars, had destroyed the advantages of the Square's close-in location. It was too large and not exclusive enough to give it quite the tone of Lucas Place, and those who succeeded the original families could not restore its status. In 1918 the area was zoned for business.

Many affluent families maintained country homes as cool summer retreats, and others preferred their country estates or isolated city residences to close living with the often richer and frequently Yankee Protestant parvenus of Lucas Place. Lucas's prices, $120 a front foot and up for raw land, undoubtedly deterred some whose social standing exceeded their resources. Others chose to live in splendid isolation, like Charles P. Chouteau at 6800 South Broadway, near his Vulcan Iron Works, and Mary Scanlan, the Wiggins Ferry heiress and the city's leading Victorian hostess, who entertained Mrs. Grover Cleveland, France's "man on horseback," the reactionary General Georges Boulanger and his retinue, and other luminaries at her palatial residence on Grand Avenue.

After Erastus Wells completed his West End Narrow Gauge Railway, from near Grand and Olive to Normandy in 1876 and to Florissant, a total of sixteen miles, two years later, the country squires had easy access to the city. This tiny steam engine and cars rocked and swayed to Wells's home, "Wellston," before passing the estates of D. R. Francis, the Kennetts, and Jefferson Clark's "Minoma." Along Natural Bridge Road it served passengers from the mansions of George R. Taylor, John O'Fallon, William Glasgow, and those of the silver titans, Charles Clark and Charles McLure, before arriving at Normandy, the bailiwick of Anne Lucas Hunt's heirs— Hunts and Turners and their Lucas cousins. Up the Florissant valley were the large estates of Charles Chambers, Daniel Frost, General W. S. Harney and Richard Graham (Hazelwood), all of whom had had the good sense to marry Mullanphys. Thomas January, the founder of Ferguson, also owned much of the valley and lived there. Fashionable social clubs, such as the Florissant Valley and the Kinloch Country Clubs, the Glen Echo Country Club (social and golf), and the Normandie Golf Club were located near the Narrow

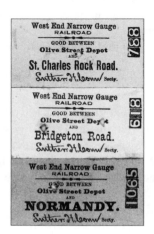

West End Narrow Gauge Railway Tickets from the 1870s, Showing the Various Stops. *These tickets were collected by Rolla Wells, son of Erastus Wells and general manager of the road during the late 1870s. Rolla Wells Scrapbook, MHS Archives.*

Gauge. Glen Echo was the first and Normandie the second golf course west of the Mississippi.

Distance protected the country estates from the intrusions of the vulgar, but in the city, rigorous deed restrictions had become necessary. Vandeventer Place, laid out in 1870, had become the city's grand address by the late 1880s. It was a three-quarter-mile private street, extending from Grand to Vandeventer Avenue a few blocks north of Olive, set down in the middle of what was already a prime residential area known as the Stoddard addition. Unlike nearby streets, which had little protection against unwelcome developments, Vandeventer Place's deeds mandated single-family residences, with control of the entire tract in the hands of trustees who hired watchmen, enforced maintenance standards, and levied assessments. Residents of the declining streets, such as the Lionbergers and the Carrs, fled to the new retreat; and newer moguls, such as Henry Clay Pierce of the Waters-Pierce Oil Company; plug tobacco millionaire Daniel Catlin; ammonia manufacturer Edward Mallinckrodt; tinware maker Thomas K. Niedringhaus, the founder of Granite City, Illinois; and the New York native Charles Clark, the principal figure among a group of St. Louisans who had developed the Granite Mountain silver mines in Montana, built ornate mansions there. Yesterday's *nouveaux riches*, such as the stovemaking Bridges and Filleys, had become today's solid old families, and a new generation of hustling outsiders was at the gates. An embittered Harry Turner hated to see "the bourgeoisie of yesterday become the pseudonymous aristocracy of today." For those like Turner who were keeping score, beaver-skinning, real estate speculation, and banking, in that order, were genteel sources of fortunes; the grocery trade and iron-smelting were all right if one's grandfather had started them; but lager-brewing would never do. In the last instance, even the "pseudonymous aristocracy" agreed.

When the streetcars were electrified in the 1890s and Grand Avenue changed from a residential to a commercial street, Vandeventer Place was subjected to noise, smoke, and the rapid deterioration of the neighboring residential streets. It was still elegant in 1910, but the exodus had begun. Isaac Lionberger mourned that "progress has been accompanied by horrid waste." Each generation had been forced to move three times, leaving abandoned houses built for small wealthy families, not suitable for working people. "Pleasant neighborhoods" lasted for only a short while before they were "besmirched by smoke and dust and dirt." The "roar of street cars" assailed them, and "no forethought, no restrictions can prevail. Those who have the means move continually, leaving behind what they cannot endure."

Another effort to create an island of luxurious homes which would survive was laid out near the Eads home, "Compton Hill," in 1889. Compton Heights, just east of Grand and two blocks south of Lafayette, featured as its principal streets "Hawthorne" and "Longfellow." In addition to this literary advantage, its houses, unlike those of Vandeventer Place, faced and therefore enhanced the surrounding streets, and the neighborhood was not in the direct line of the central commercial corridor. Despite the heavy damage inflicted by the great tornado, its owners persisted; their successors have remained vigilant, and Compton Heights survives with integrity. Lager brewers were not only welcome there, they and their wealthy compatriots were in the majority. In 1901, the owners' association included Henry Griesedieck, W. F. Woerner, E. A. Busch, Hugo Muench, H. M. Von Starkloff, and William Heinrichshofen.

Though less spectacular than Vandeventer Place in the sheer massiveness of its structures, the most ambitious effort of the wealthy to wall off the outside world was the cluster of "places" built at the turn of the century just north of Lindell Boulevard and Forest Park, primarily between Kingshighway and Union Avenue. The first of these, Portland Place, was laid out in 1888 by Julius Pitzman, a former city engineer who had planned Vandeventer Place and Compton Heights. Westmoreland Place followed Portland, and in the general area, though perhaps a shade less elegant, were Hortense and Lenox Places, just east of Kingshighway; Westminster Place, in three sections, one east of Kingshighway, one parallel with Portland and Westmoreland, and one farther west; and Kingsbury and Cabanne Places, also to the west.

Among these mansions, whose carriage houses were more splendid than ordinary homes, were those of the younger Hudson Bridge, banker and railroad magnate W. K. Bixby, Dwight F. Davis, John J. O'Fallon, Dr. William Glasgow, John D. Filley, Howard Benoist, carpet manufacturer and director of the Mechanics' Bank S. M. Kennard, Pierre Chouteau Maffitt, A. B. Lambert, Walter McKittrick, George Brown, Breckinridge Jones, and Edward Faust, whose magnificent Number One Portland Place was a wedding gift from his father-in-law, Adolphus Busch. Near the West End places were other choice residential streets such as Maryland; West Pine, the western reaches of Washington and McPherson; Berlin, straddling the city limits north of Washington University; and Lindell Boulevard, from Sarah Street to its western terminus. In 1907, Governor Francis and publisher C. W. Knapp lived on Maryland; R. S. Brookings and Mayor Rolla Wells on Lindell; Samuel Cupples on West Pine; and Charles Nagel, the city's most politically potent attorney, on Washington.

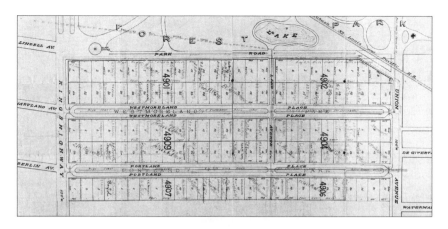

Plat Map of Westmoreland and Portland Places, Showing Names of Original Lot Owners. *Ink and wash on linen by Julius Pitzman, 1890. MHS Library.*

For at least three decades after 1900, the city's economic power, wealth, and social elite were concentrated within a half-dozen blocks of Lindell and Kingshighway. Of the 324 members of the St. Louis Country Club, the most exclusive of the larger social organizations, over 90 percent lived in this limited area and on Vandeventer Place in 1907. Ancient lineage (three generations of relative affluence) or current wealth and power, even if recently acquired, were qualifications for membership—with certain exceptions. An eastern education and professional stature helped too, if one could afford a good address. Carrs, Glasgows, Maffitts, Turners, O'Fallons, Walshes, and Lucases hobnobbed at the Clayton and Hanley Roads location with Pierces, Mallinckrodts, Niedringhauses and Huttigs. Busches, Lemps, and Griesediecks were not admitted, however, no matter how many German princes they knew. Neither were Stixes, Baers, nor other Jewish merchants. On the other hand, C. P. Chouteau's son Pierre and the powerful attorney, General John W. Noble, Secretary of the Interior from 1889 to 1893, were not members either, presumably because they chose not to be.

The downtown bankers, lawyers, merchants, and manufacturers of this elite, known locally as the "Big Cinch," were powerful and resourceful enough to protect their silk-stocking preserve from the consequences of municipal growth. Having learned from past failures, they controlled their environment by building luxurious hotels and apartments along Kingshighway, by purchasing the nearby Rock Island Railroad yards and erecting apartments there, and by extracting a promise from the Wabash Railroad not to lay out yards

W. K. Bixby. *A prominent capitalist and philanthropist, Bixby controlled the American Car and Foundry Company. He negotiated an agreement preventing the further encroachment of railroad operations on the Central West End. Photograph by Evans, 1903. MHS-PP.*

or sidings along its tracks in the area. Federal Judge Elmer Adams, who lived on Westmoreland Place, had at one time appointed W. K. Bixby, board chairman of the American Car and Foundry Company and a director of several banks and railroads, as receiver of the Wabash Railroad. Bixby lived on Portland Place.

These West End homes were widely admired. Ex-Governor David B. Hill of New York expressed surprise at the city's "beautiful streets, great Union Station, parks, residences, hotels, and business buildings. Everything is on a grand scale." Count Apponyi of Hungary, visiting during the World's Fair in 1904, extravagantly credited the city with more beautiful residences than all of continental Europe. In 1903 the *National Magazine* ranked St. Louis first anywhere in this respect, saying that it outshone any combination of three cities in the world. Many homes were "veritable palaces in every particular of richness, appointment, and setting—even in size." Each was "surrounded by stretching green lawns, fresh and sparkling . . . diversified and enriched by luxuriant shrubs, flowers, and trees." The long stretches of these streets created "an atmosphere, a setting for a mansion . . . that cannot possibly attach to an isolated house and grounds—St. Louis had planned for its homes—planned with a result in effect that is marvelous that is inconceivable by those who live away from the city."

The West End elite seemed to be the indisputable masters of St. Louis. They believed they were entitled to rule even when denying the fact, their detractors believed they conspired to rule, and most observers agreed. It seemed appropriate—the tradition was as old as the city itself. Chouteaus, Gratiots, Cerrés, Papins, Sarpys, DeMuns, and Prattes were the downtown leaders of Creole St. Louis; they had learned, grudgingly at first, to share with Hempsteads, Eastons, Carrs, Lucases, O'Fallons, Mullanphys, Clarks, and Walshes, who in their turn made room for Lanes, Darbys, Pages, Allens, Kennetts, Hows, Blows, Taylors, Bridges, Filleys, Yeatmans, Blairs, and Harrisons. At this point the Germans made their mark too, in war, politics, business, and journalism, if not in society. Yankee merchants and lawyers and their German cohorts kept Missouri in the Union, and they kept coming when peace came.

The downtown elite of the early 1900s was a modern revision of an old writ. Correlation between social and economic status was high but not absolute, and the divergence between the religious and ethnic backgrounds of the Big Cinch and those of the larger community forced accommodation with other power centers. Among sixty-five powerful downtown businessmen and capitalists in 1902, forty-five were Protestants, five were Catholics, and fifteen expressed no religious preference. Episcopalians, Presbyterians, and Methodists were most numerous. Twenty-four of this sampling were Democrats, twenty-four were Republicans, and seventeen were independents or gave no preference. This apparently even division was deceptive, however; the Democrats were nearly all of the conservative "goldbug" variety, out of step with the rank and file. Rolla Wells, Democratic mayor from 1901 to 1903, had openly opposed William Jennings Bryan and the national ticket in 1896. The group's academic background covered the spectrum: thirty-two had earned college degrees, including advanced degrees; two had attended but not completed college, and thirty-one had elementary or high school (including academy) educations, supplemented in several instances by "commercial" courses. Washington University had attracted nine, Yale eight, Princeton three, Harvard and Saint Louis University two each, and midwestern, eastern, and foreign universities the rest. Twenty-two of the sixty-five were born in St. Louis, three in outstate Missouri, eighteen in eastern and midwestern states, seven in border states, six in Germany, six in southern states, two in Canada, and one in Bohemia. Forty members of this informal group were millionaires, and most of the remainder were soon-to-be.

The large German Republican vote and the economic power of the brewers and other German businessmen precluded the extension of the prevailing social ostracism to most business and civic matters. On the Democratic side, Boss Edward Butler and his Irish legions had to be placated. With a majority of the working people in its fold, the Catholic hierarchy had to be taken into account. When these factors were ignored, things had a tendency to go wrong. When Mayor David R. Francis, a self-made wealthy grain broker who came to be the symbolic Big Cinch leader, ran successfully for governor in 1888, he lost St. Louis by a sizeable margin, largely because he had courted the outstate Protestant and anti-saloon vote by vigorously enforcing the state's Sunday saloon-closing law. As a result he came perilously close to being the first Democrat to lose a gubernatorial race in eighteen years. Again in 1897, German dissatisfaction with elite rule came into play. They had blamed West End "aristocrats" in 1887 when F. L. Judson, a corporation attorney, led a successful fight to remove the German language requirement from the public school curriculum. To many Germans this seemed a violation of a long-standing community compact. In 1895, hoping to obtain a consensus for clean government across religious, ethnic, and class lines, Judson had been the principal founder of the Civic Federation, a conservative reform group which espoused honesty and economy in government and election-law reforms. As the first president of the federation, Joseph Charless Cabanne, with a name that promised more than it delivered, expected to convince the leading businessmen to join. To doubters, good government under such auspices meant that the wealthy would get their franchise monopolies free rather than having to bribe councilmen for them.

The tornado of 1896 gave the federation its opportunity to broaden its appeal. Republican Cyrus Walbridge, wholesale druggist and president of the older of the city's two telephone companies, the Bell Telephone Company of Missouri, had been elected mayor in 1893 with heavy German support, not only from the solidly Republican and middle-class Lutherans, but from the Democratic-leaning German Catholics who were sick of the corruption in Ed Butler's Democratic machine. The brunt of the great tornado fell on the hundreds of German homes and shops that lay between Lafayette Square and the river. When the victims appealed to the city for disaster relief and loans, the mayor responded with homilies about courage and self-reliance. Walbridge, who lived on Westminster Place, had enthusiastically supported improvements to Kingshighway and other West End streets. Walter

Vrooman, the federation's secretary, appealed to the south siders to organize, pointing out that if the city would stop "giving franchises worth millions to men who deserve no favors, we could save in 10 years the value of all the property destroyed by the tornados."

Union workers headed by David Kreyling, president of the Central Trades and Labor Union, and middle-class Germans led by Emil Preetorius of the *Westliche Post,* formed community groups which affiliated with the federation. They found their mayoral candidate in the person of Lee Meriwether, the state labor commissioner, who published a report in 1896 which showed that while real property in St. Louis was assessed at an average of 40 percent of value, street railways were assessed at only 11 to 25 percent. Meriwether belonged to the Jefferson Club, a group of reformist Democrats who were trying to loosen Edward Butler's grip on the ward and precinct organizations. Though officially a Democrat, Butler supported Republicans when it suited him. His control of the House of Delegates was seldom challenged. As he put it, "I don't have to induce 'em—I own 'em." Some of the Jeffersonians were "reformers" not as much because the boss was corrupt as because he was unreliable. The club apparently had its origins with a small group of independent Democrats called "Solar Walkers," led by James L. Blair, General Frank Blair's son. By 1898 its principal figure was a young attorney, Harry B. "Handsome Harry" Hawes, who had been appointed president of the Board of Police Commissioners in that year.

Harry Hawes. *Hawes was the leader of the Jefferson Democratic Club, a reform group which compromised with Boss Butler to elect Rolla Wells mayor in 1900. Photograph by Evans, 1903. MHS-PP.*

In the 1897 mayoral primary, the gold Democrats in the Civic Federation, led by D. R. Francis, Rolla Wells, and C. C. Maffitt, persuaded the federation's executive committee to endorse Edward Harrison of the iron and steel family, the quintessential West Ender, for the Democratic nomination. Harrison, a clean government conservative, had no intention of altering the municipal tax structure. Offended because Harrison would not offer him his customary patronage guarantees, Butler at first supported ex-mayor Edward Noonan. In the primary, Meriwether ran a strong second to Harrison, with the support of the federation groups on the north and south sides, which stayed with him despite their executive committee's desertion. Sensing that the voters were tired of Noonan, Butler quietly switched to Meriwether, while making a patronage deal with the Republicans in return for splitting the Democrats. With high hopes and Butler's encouragement—the boss did not ask him for a thing—Meriwether tried again on a Reform ticket in the general election. The Republican nominee, Henry Ziegenhein, played on the frustrations of the German voters. He said he would make the utilities pay for their privileges and would initiate a public works program on the south side using local labor. Meriwether had promised these things first, but Ziegenhein promised them in German and broken English. Capturing most of Meriwether's original supporters, "Onkle Henry" defeated Harrison easily, leaving the reformer a bad third, with only the hard-core Butler vote. That the boss was not very serious was obvious when his "Indians" did not bother to repeat their votes or intimidate anyone at the polls.

Ziegenhein's victory appeared to be a repudiation of the elite, but the business leaders had little to fear. Despite his spending promises, he was an "economy" mayor. The city debt decreased by $2.7 million during his term, and per capita expenditures were among the lowest of the large cities. St. Louis bonds, bearing an interest rate of 3.65 percent, had been sold to Kuhn, Loeb of New York in 1895 at better than par. Since the charter had gone into effect in 1877, the net bonded debt had fallen from $23.1 million to $18.5 million in 1900, a per capita reduction from $74.30 to $32.19. The tax rate for general revenue and debt retirement was only 40 cents on the $100 valuation, and under the charter, outlays could not exceed revenues in any year. Solvency was a cause for congratulations, and it was gratifying to be considered a model city by New York bankers, but the happiest of all were the wealthy taxpayers, especially the favored utilities. Charles Turner's Suburban Railroad Company, with a market value of $3 million, paid less than two thousand dollars a year for its privileges. At the same time, the streets were still muddy and unpaved in poorer sections, and the sewers were clogged and did not extend to all the settled areas.

The mayor had won his share of support from downtown interests, and his alliance with Butler guaranteed business as usual. He was applauded for completing the new city hall, but he was to be remembered chiefly as the "one candlepower" mayor, because of a story concocted by Carlos Hurd and Harry James of the *Post-Dispatch*. Fascinated by the Ziegenhein brand of English, the reporters wrote that he had responded to demands for better street lighting with "We got a moon yet, aindt it."

There was trouble around the corner, but neither Butler nor the moguls dreamed of it. A young attorney named Joseph W. Folk, who had come upriver from Tennessee in 1893, had made his presence felt in 1896 by leading a successful fight to keep the Jefferson Club in line for Bryan and the national ticket. In 1898 he became president of the club, but he stepped aside the next year for Harry Hawes. The coincidence of Hawes's two presidencies, the other being the Police Board, had a marvelous effect on the size and power of the Jefferson Club. Soon it had effective organizations in every precinct, and even the Francis-Maffitt sound money clique and the Bryan loyalists declared an armistice. Thomas C. Hennings, the campaign chairman for 1900, Isaac Lionberger, F. N. Judson, D. R. Francis, and other downtown lawyers and businessmen were active in the organization. With Boss Butler at his worst and hand-in-hand with the Republicans, the stage was set for an all-out attack on bossism, but Harry Hawes, preferring victory to reform, made an arrangement with Butler. The Jefferson Club was to select the top of the ticket, leaving the House of Delegates to Butler. Hawes then assigned the choice of the mayoral candidate to James L. Blair and the silk-stocking Solar Walkers, who picked Rolla Wells, millionaire son of the founder of the street railways, who was president of the American Steel Foundry Company and a director of two downtown banks.

William Marion Reedy, who had emerged from Kerry Patch to become the publisher of an internationally respected literary magazine, *The Mirror*, and who admired the cultured, silky-smooth Hawes, described the new political order: "His strength in the Jefferson Club is the crowd of young men of education . . . and distinctive gentlemanliness, as opposed to the crap-game, bar-tending, touting, sporting characters. . . . He has them to put up a respectable front . . . and at the same time Hawes takes especial pains to ingratiate himself with the elements that come up from the groggeries." Hawes would need all his art to prevail; the former dead-even political

William Marion Reedy. *Reedy, editor and publisher of* The Mirror, *called for political reform in St. Louis in the period preceding the World's Fair. Photograph by J. C. Strauss, 1904. MHS-PP.*

balance had shifted toward the Republicans as the city had swung to manufacturing and protectionism, and as the national democracy had become identified with agrarian radicalism. With Bryan heading the ticket again in 1900, local Democrats would be hard-pressed. In their favor, however, was the malodorous character of the heavily Republican municipal assembly, which had raised the art of "Boodle" to new heights. Boodle was the local term for the practice of bribing city officials or legislators to win utilities franchises, licenses, low tax assessments, garbage contracts, or other special privileges. The Republicans, who had certainly earned their share, got nearly all of the blame for corruption in 1900–1901, while the master boodler, Butler, was working for the Democratic ticket.

The West End–downtown elite, both Republicans and Democrats, were in an ambivalent position. In the first place, their common interests were more compelling than their political differences; and in the second, they themselves were involved in boodle. Honest government had a fine sound to it, and a physical cleanup would be good for business and essential to the community image if there was to be a World's Fair. It was expensive to bribe a franchise from the assembly, but it would be much costlier to pay a fair price to the city and be assessed for taxes at reasonable rates. Most of these gentlemen had never had direct dealings with the legislative thieves, but the interlocking relationships between the banks and the real estate and utilities firms made it virtually impossible to be an officer, director, or stockholder in the major financial houses without having benefited from boodle. For example, one of the larger firms, the Commonwealth Trust Company, headed by Charles Turner of the old elite, was primarily an umbrella for the dubious activities of Turner's real estate and traction interests. Its directors included A. D. Brown of the Hamilton-Brown Shoe Company; August A. Samuel, president of Wagner Electric and a director of the city's biggest bank, the National Bank of Commerce, as well as two real estate and two insurance firms; Samuel Kennard, a carpet manufacturer and a director of the Mechanics' Bank; Henry Nicolaus, president of the Brewer's Association and a director of the Kinloch Telephone Company and the Mechanics' Bank; Otto Stifel, brewer and coal company president; and L. B. Tebbetts, a carriage manufacturer and a director of the National Bank of Commerce.

There were many other examples of the cosy relationship between the banks and utilities. Charles Huttig, president of the Third National Bank, was a director of the Mercantile Trust, the St. Louis and Suburban Railroad, and the Laclede Gaslight Company. Adolphus Busch was on the board of the St. Louis Union Trust, the Third National Bank, the Kinloch Telephone Company, and the North American (utilities holding) Company. Grain broker and former Governor D. R. Francis held vice presidencies in the Mississippi Valley Trust and the Terminal Railway Association and was vice president of the Union Electric Company and three traction companies before their consolidation in 1899. Julius Walsh of the Mississippi Valley Trust and several transit boards was one of the old territorial elite, the son of Edward and Isabella (DeMun) Walsh. Dry-goods wholesaler Murray Carleton, a director of the Boatmen's Bank and the Mississippi Valley Trust, was a chief organizer with John Scullin of the St. Louis Transit Company consolidation.

The towering figure of this group was James Campbell, a major stockholder of the Mercantile Trust. Dubbed by the press "the Morgan of the West," Campbell was a Scots-Irish immigrant lad who had first seen St. Louis as a messenger on General Fremont's staff. After the war he was a surveyor for Fremont's Atlantic and Pacific Railroad, at which time he seized the opportunity to speculate in Missouri lands. With one hundred thousand dollars in profits thus acquired, he bought heavily

James Campbell. *One of the most powerful men in St. Louis finance at the turn of the century, Campbell was behind utilities consolidation and a key figure in the "Big Cinch." Photograph by J. Edward Roesch, 1903. MHS-PP.*

discounted local railroad bonds. When they were redeemed at par, he invested the proceeds in St. Louis street railways. By 1900 he was a multimillionaire with a palatial home on Westmoreland Place. Having little education and less social finesse, Campbell was contemptuous of society, but he enjoyed making money with its representatives. He was the principal owner of the Welsbach Company, which "won" the ten-year contract for most of the street lighting in 1899; he was involved in the traction company consolidation; and he managed the acquisition of the resulting United Railways by the North American Company, a utilities holding combine that operated in several midwestern cities. Campbell became president and then chairman of this firm, which also controlled the Laclede Gas and Union Electric companies.

These and a few dozen other bankers, lawyers, and investors comprised the Big Cinch. Scot McConachie, who has made a careful analysis of this elite, attributes the origins of the popular view that a clique of self-anointed leaders ruled the city in its own interest and to the detriment of the public to Joseph Pulitzer of the *Post-Dispatch*. McConachie points out that after Pulitzer had been betrayed by Ed Butler during his congressional campaign against Thomas Allen in 1880, he had charged his loss to a bribe given Butler by Allen's rich friends and business associates. The editor had pursued an unrelenting campaign against the city's rulers thereafter. Actually, Pulitzer had gone after the power brokers from the *Post-Dispatch*'s founding in 1878. After reporting that J. B. C. Lucas II, one of the city's wealthiest men, had declared only $2,735 in property to the assessor, Pulitzer wrote: "Millions and millions of property in this city escape all taxation. When people like Charles P. Chouteau, the Lucases, or Gerard B. Allen swear that they do not have a cent in cash or in the bank, don't own one cent's worth of bonds or stocks or notes or other securities, they commit . . . a falsehood both ridiculous and monstrous. . . ." This kind of news sold papers, earned the publisher and his staff the undying hatred of his targets, and sometimes got unexpected results.

In 1882 managing editor John A. Cockerill charged that J. O. Broadhead, the dean of the St. Louis bar and the first president of the American Bar Association, had committed a serious and perhaps criminal breach of ethics ten years earlier. Broadhead's partner, Alonso Slayback, burst into the newspaper office the day after the charge was printed, armed and threatening Cockerill's life. The editor, a hotspur himself, promptly shot and killed Slayback. There were cries for Cockerill's blood, but he had his defenders, including Joseph McCullagh of the *Globe-Democrat.* Eventually, Cockerill was forced to leave town, but the *Post-Dispatch* continued to harass the "ruling class" without mercy. For two decades before *McClure's,* the *Atlantic,* and other magazines undertook the exposés that Theodore Roosevelt dubbed "muckraking," this St. Louis newspaper was exposing big boodlers and little grafters in St. Louis. The *Republic,* formerly the *Republican,* still controlled by the Knapps, was the organ of the Francis Democrats and the status quo. Joseph McCullagh of the *Globe-Democrat* was committed to the national Republican Party, but

Joseph McCullagh. *McCullagh was editor of the* St. Louis Globe-Democrat *and a leader in St. Louis journalism. Cabinet card photograph by J. A. Scholten, ca. 1890. MHS-PP.*

his cutting blade was as sharp as Pulitzer's or Cockerill's, and he fired away at everybody who displeased him. He was offended more often by the *Republic* and the Francis-Maffitt crowd than by the middle-lower-class stance of the *Post-Dispatch.*

Around 1900, fiery articles attacking the Big Cinch began to appear, a reflection of the atmosphere of a Progressive reform. In a small magazine, the *Iconoclast,* a pseudonymous writer attacked James Campbell, D. R. Francis, Ed Butler, C. C. Maffitt, Edwards Whitaker, Thomas West, Julius Walsh, John Scullin, and a few others as the "local nobility," which controlled "everything worth owning," especially the banks, transit companies, and the gas, telephone, and electric franchises. They bought aldermen "like cattle" and the city was "at their mercy." Yet they were all "religious and moral men, their crookedness purely commercial and political." McConachie attributes this article to W. M. Reedy, and it may be so, but it is at least questionable, in view of the inclusion of Reedy's benefactor, Campbell. McConachie also believes that Reedy invented the term "Big Cinch." In any case, within a few years, he had become an indefatigable critic of those who by economic interest or bias opposed "anything that might threaten their supremacy of clutch upon the resources and opportunities of this city." Reedy did not oppose profits; his point was that the "snaps" of the Big Cinch were based upon fraud and injustice. Applying Henry George's analysis, he stressed that the wealth of the franchise holders and their coterie of bankers, lawyers, and investors was based not upon earned income but upon monopoly of what the community's growth had created.

A transit workers' strike in 1900 led indirectly to the sensational exposures of the boodle ring that came two years later. In response to the consolidation of the transit lines in 1899 that weakened their bargaining position, union members stepped up their organizing efforts, asking for recognition of Local 131 of the Street Railway Employees of America and demanding a ten-hour day and reinstatement of men previously fired for union activity. On March 10, President Edwards Whitaker of the St. Louis Transit Company (Boatmen's Bank and Bell Telephone vice president) and his board, in order to stave off embarrassment while they were floating a bond issue, agreed to reinstatement and the ten-hour day, and a strike was averted. Turner's St. Louis and Suburban would not negotiate, however, and half of its employees walked out. On May 8, their bosses having reneged on their promises, 3,325 St. Louis Transit workers struck, Whitaker brought in strike breakers from Cleveland, and siege warfare began, to the rhythms of escalating violence. Strikers, their wives, children, and sympathizers threw dead frogs and

St. Louisans crowd onto a wagon at Fifteenth and Franklin Streets during the streetcar strike of 1900. Improvised transport such as this was patronized by supporters of the transit workers. Photograph, 1900. MHS-PP.

water-soaked bread at the scab motormen and rocks at the cars at first. Then they graduated to cutting trolley wires, blocking the tracks with rubbish and stones, and building bonfires on and dynamiting the rails. These actions were deplored west of Grand Avenue, but the north and south sides favored the strikers. Union members rallied behind them, restaurants near the car barns refused to serve the scabs, and seven hundred grocers and other retailers published a flier attacking the transit trust.

Seizing upon the temporary stoppage of cars carrying mail, Federal Judge Elmer Adams enjoined fifty strike leaders from further such action and authorized the formation of a *posse comitatus*, to be drawn from the "better elements." Service was mandatory if called on, and despite an epidemic of disqualifying disabilities, twenty-five hundred citizens were enrolled as guardians of the traction company. This took some heat off of Harry Hawes, who hated to use the police too prominently in view of the impending election, especially in an unpopular cause. The sheriff's posse was stationed in squads throughout the city, its principal function being to interfere with the horse-drawn buses the strikers were running in competition with the streetcars.

The venerable Emil Preetorius, respected publisher of the *Westliche Post* for thirty-five years, led a south side protest denouncing the scabs as "alien enemies, imported to shoot down

Four Members of the Sheriff's Posse during the Streetcar Strike. *Second from left is restaurateur and Busch son-in-law Edward A. Faust. Photograph, 1900. MHS-PP.*

citizens" (they had fired into crowds from the cars), and the transit trust as promoting government "of monopoly, by monopoly, and for monopoly." On June 10, a battle between the posse and the strikers left three dead and fourteen wounded. Samuel Gompers, president of the American Federation of Labor (AFL), tried but failed to obtain a settlement and then called a general boycott of the transit company. By the end of June, with their strike funds and donations from sympathizers depleted and their families hungry, the workers were desperate for a compromise. On June 2, Joseph W. Folk and the Reverend Willard Boyd, the city's leading Social Gospel minister, representing the workers, made a tentative settlement with the company reaffirming the March 10 agreement. President Whitaker refused to fire the strikebreakers, but he agreed to fill all vacancies from a list prepared by the union. Folk was praised by labor and the press, but the slippery Whitaker kept on hiring nonunion workers, and after a week, the weary strikers resumed the battle. In September, their misery forced them to surrender. It was small comfort to them, but for the city, it had not all been in vain. The six-month confrontation had highlighted the poor municipal services, corporate arrogance,

Rolla Wells. *Wells was elected mayor of St. Louis on a reform platform in 1901 and led the city through the World's Fair. Photograph by Evans, 1903. MHS-PP.*

Joseph Folk. *Popularly known as "Holy Joe," Folk went after the "Boodlers" and parlayed his crusading zeal into a term as governor. Photograph by J. C. Strauss, 1902. MHS-PP.*

legislative corruption, and the need for fair taxation of utilities, with public ownership as an alternative. Despite the settlement's short life, it had made Folk a popular figure. As evidence of the effectiveness of the moral issue, when Rolla Wells became mayor in 1901 he divested himself of his large block of stock in the North American Company, which owned the gas and electric companies and the United Railways, the last of which controlled the St. Louis Transit Company. Wells' sacrifice turned out well—North American stock never again reached the price he sold it for.

By selecting Wells over Lee Meriwether as their nominee for mayor, Harry Hawes and the Jefferson Club demonstrated that they were interested only in weeding out the little crooks at City Hall. Serious reform would have undermined their own foundations. Because of Folk's popularity with the unions, Hawes chose him as the Democratic candidate for circuit attorney. Butler had picked another for the post, but when Hawes brought his "little man" around, as Butler put it: "I looked him over, and there didn't seem to be anything the matter of him, and I says all right, and he was nominated. An' look what he done—spent four years trying to put me in the penitentiary. . . ."

In the campaign, the Democrats came out boldly for a world's fair, better streets and services, and improvement of the Mississippi channel. They were against payroll padding. If Folk had anything more in mind, he did not say so. In November he defeated Republican Eugene McQuillin by 2,000 votes out of 121,000 cast, with substantial help from Butler's repeaters. Whatever he owed the boss, Folk quickly made it clear that he would be slow pay by refusing to appoint as his assistants two lawyers to whom Butler had already promised the positions. The Democrats swept the city offices in April and gained a three-vote plurality in the House of Delegates over the Republicans, with Lee Meriwether's Public Ownership Party picking up six seats. Smarting from his own defeat in the presidential race in November, William Jennings Bryan had intervened in the St. Louis mayoralty campaign; he denounced Rolla Wells as a goldbug traitor to the party and urged his supporters to vote for Lee Meriwether. Many of them did, but many middle-class Republicans, embarrassed by Ziegenhein, delighted at the prospect of the American Steel Foundry's president as mayor and pleased to take one last swipe at Bryan, deserted their ticket for Wells. At the other end of the scale, several thousand Republican union members voted for Meriwether. The Republicans and Democrats both feared the Public Ownership Party more than each other, and both committed large-scale fraud at the polls. Hawes's policemen were accused by many witnesses of helping Butler's Indians vote again and again. Wells won, with 43,012 votes, to

Republican G. W. Parker's 34,846 and Meriwether's 30,568. The city
was safe in the hands of the Big Cinch. W. M. Reedy, still a political
schizophrenic, hailed the outcome as the last rites for Ziegenheinism
and free silver in one stroke.

Mayor Wells took as his inaugural theme the "New St. Louis," a
better, cleaner, friendlier, and more beautiful city, bound together by a
sense of shared purpose, with the coming World's Fair as the capstone.
He began by inviting the Municipal Assembly and the leading social
and business club presidents to a New St. Louis banquet at the
St. Louis Club. The invitation flustered the members of the House,
who were once reported to have bolted out of the chamber to a man
when a young boy rushed in shouting "Mister, your saloon's on fire."
They were unaccustomed to dining with the elite, and most of them
had never worn evening dress. One reporter wrote that after a long
discussion the members voted to wear full dress. "All except the Hon.
Snake Kinney, who declares he never wore a dress suit in his life and
don't intend to now." The Honorable Snake, who represented a central
river ward, finally decided to brave the gibes of his constituents; he
attended, in resplendent full dress, to hear the mayor advocate charter
revision to increase the city's borrowing power and remove the many
impediments to responsible and orderly government.

As the new mayor put it, public buildings, hospitals, the jail, and
the "poor and ill-kept streets" must be brought to a condition that
would be a source of pride rather than embarrassment. Not additional
taxes, but prudent borrowing, reassessments, and economical
administration would do the job. Overstaffed departments, swarming
with patronage employees, must be reduced to efficient working
levels. Wells implied that he expected lower charges from franchise
holders and winners of city contracts, and that he would not be above
using the threat of municipal ownership to bring them into line. Like
most members of the elite, especially those with inherited fortunes,
Wells saw himself not as a member of a privileged "nobility," but as a
responsible "leading citizen" rendering unselfish service. He would
not attack the roots of the city's problems in the Meriwether style; he
believed that "business government" was a solution rather than a
problem. When circuit attorney Folk exposed as crooks some of the
"better people," Wells supported him, but he did not change his
fundamental assumptions. The sensational aspects of the
investigations, especially when the national press took them up,
distressed him as damaging to the city's image and tending to social
disorder. That his own large fortune and those of his friends were
based in part upon unfair exploitation of the community, he would not
believe, except where individual illegal acts could be proven.

Ed Butler. *"Boss" Butler, an Irish immigrant and blacksmith by trade, used his native political acumen and business sense to attempt to dominate the Democratic Party in St. Louis. Steel engraving by Central Biographical Publishing Company, 1894. MHS-PP.*

Folk investigated the election frauds and caught a number of small fries, a majority of them Democrats, to the distress of the Jefferson Club, but it was Wells who first tried to bring down Ed Butler. The boss owned the St. Louis Sanitary Company, which had held the contract for hauling and reducing St. Louis's garbage for many years. Under the existing contract, which was to expire in September 1901, Butler was paid sixty-five thousand dollars a year for garbage reduction. Wells told the assembly in April that he would insist on competitive bids before signing a new contract. The upper house (council) was no longer dominated by the combine, but the delegates were, and by a series of delaying maneuvers, authorization was withheld until six days before the old contract expired. Butler gleefully bid $130,000 a year, and, lacking an alternative, the Board of Public Improvement had to award him the contract for three years. After biding his time for two years, the mayor quietly bought a small island in the Mississippi, twenty-two miles south of the city, using his own money. Then he bought Butler's hauling firm for the city at an inflated price. Butler suspected nothing, assuming that the garbage would still have to be hauled to his reduction plant, but to his consternation, Wells informed him that the city would handle St. Louis's garbage. Butler reduced his price to eighty thousand dollars, but to no avail. The garbage was hauled to barges and then taken to Chesley Island, which Wells had stocked with hungry hogs. In 1908, during Wells's second term, a new contract was awarded to a firm financed by "several prominent St. Louis businessmen" headed by Lawrence Pierce, a director of several railroads and utilities and a former partner of Charles H. Turner in the real estate business. Wells exulted that he had ended boss rule in city hall and had proven that "a community can have business government if it is ready to make the effort and sacrifice to procure and preserve it."

On January 21, 1902, the *St. Louis Star* carried a back-page report of a dispute between assemblymen and a traction company over an unpaid bribe. The circuit attorney promptly ordered the members of the assembly and the officers of the Suburban Railway Company to appear before the grand jury then in session. Nearly one hundred persons were questioned, but no one knew a thing, and the assemblymen treated the proceedings as a joke. Despite their bravado, Folk sensed that they were badly frightened and decided to attack at the most vulnerable point—those who had the most to lose. He called to his office C. H. Turner, the Suburban's president, and Philip Stock, lobbyist for the St. Louis Brewing Association. Pulling a monstrous bluff, Folk asserted that he had evidence that would send them to prison. They swallowed the bait, and upon his promise of immunity, they talked.

In 1900, Turner had proposed to extend the Suburban's tracks for several miles to Union Station; his purpose in invading the St. Louis Transit Company's territory was chiefly to force it to buy his company for twice its current value of $3 million. To put the deal across, he first approached Ed Butler, who asked for $145,000 to escort the franchise extension through the assembly. Thinking Butler's price too high, Turner hired Stock to bribe the boodlers individually. Through Councilman Charles Kratz, the combine set its price at seventy-five thousand dollars for the delegates and sixty thousand dollars for the council. Turner borrowed the money from the German Savings Bank on a note signed by millionaire brewers Ellis Wainwright and Henry Nicolaus, and then put the two sums in safety deposit boxes awaiting the completion of the deal. Unfortunately, Councilman Emil Meysenburg, a broker who did not belong to the combine, had smelled a rat, and he refused to discharge the bill from his committee. Not sure what the wealthy Meysenburg wanted, Turner sent Stock to see him. It turned out that he wanted nine thousand dollars. After Turner and Nicolaus obliged, the bill slid right out of committee and passed easily, Meysenburg righteously voting nay. Four days later, on petition from affected property owners, who may have been acting on behalf of the St. Louis Transit Company or Butler, the circuit court enjoined the House of Delegates from approving the franchise extension.

Arguing that they had done their part, the boodlers demanded payment, but Turner refused.

When Folk heard this story, he asked A. A. B. Woerheide and Julius Walsh of the Lincoln and Mississippi Valley Trusts to hand over the safety deposit boxes. When they refused, he threatened to seek indictments against them and their officers and directors. Their scruples thus allayed, they delivered. A few days later the grand jury indicted Wainwright, Nicolaus, Meysenburg, Kratz, and Delegate John K. Murrell for bribery and two other delegates for lying to the grand jury. Each of the defendants was apprehended, except Wainwright, who extended a European vacation to nine years. Nicolaus's claim that he had not known what Turner planned to do with the money did not persuade the grand jury, but Adolphus Busch stated to the *Post-Dispatch* that his fellow brewer had "the entire sympathy of the best element in St. Louis." Reedy believed Nicolaus "a gentleman," but he yearned for Butler's scalp and scorned Turner as representative of a dozen "socially distinguished and politically corrupt" citizens. Turner counted among his ancestors J. B. C. Lucas and a clutch of Creole founding families. He had succumbed to what his kinsman Harry Turner called the "heavy, sodden determination to make money," and his propensity to talk about it constantly marked the ascendancy of the vulgar parvenus who had seized St. Louis's economic and social bastions.

As he must have expected, Folk encountered opposition, surreptitious at first, ranging from the "go slow" advice of Jefferson Club types (who wanted him to catch only little crooks, preferably Republicans) to threats of political retaliation and murder. Few tears were shed for Turner, even among the elite, perhaps because he had turned states' evidence, or perhaps because his attempted coup had been aimed at the transit trust, where most of the real power lay. Folk lost no time in going after Turner's rivals.

In 1898 Robert M. Snyder, a Kansas City banker-speculator, seeing a target of opportunity in St. Louis's decentralized transit lines, had organized the Central Traction Company and sought a citywide franchise. If granted, such a charter could ruin the existing independent lines. First, Snyder contacted Ed Butler and the boodle combine, but they stonewalled him, because the street railways had guarded against such raids by paying seven council members $5,000 each and an eighth, Frederick Uthoff, $25,000 to keep the seven from straying. In turn, Butler was to hold Uthoff on course, but when Snyder offered that larcenous gentleman $50,000, he changed sides and honorably returned the $25,000. Having thus breached the defenses, Snyder picked off majorities in each House with bribes totaling about $250,000. The bill passed and Snyder promptly sold his trackless, carless franchise to the local transit men and some outside backers for $1.25 million. Net gain to Snyder for a few weeks of interesting work totaled more than $1 million. Uthoff, with terrible timing, had returned his $50,000 and demanded $100,000. While Snyder was mulling it over the bill passed, and he waved Uthoff away with a $5,000 consultation fee.

The *Post-Dispatch* had revealed most of these machinations while they were occurring, but despite the widespread knowledge of the case, Folk was able to obtain only one indictment. Except for Snyder, everyone involved—councilmen, delegates, traction officials, bankers, and lawyers—was protected by Missouri's three-year statute of limitations. Having spent most of his time in New York since 1898, Snyder was treated as a fugitive from justice, and therefore was not covered by the statute. In fact, he had visited his children frequently in Kansas City, and no effort had been made to apprehend him.

The grand jury also found that while Henry Ziegenhein was city collector he had made illegal loans from city funds and pocketed the interest (not indictable under the statute of limitations), and that local gas companies had bribed assemblymen in 1898–99 to mandate ten-year street lighting contracts, for the purpose of preventing a New York lighting firm from entering St. Louis. It was reported to Folk that forty-seven thousand of the seventy-five thousand dollars paid had been handed to Ed Butler by the powerful James Campbell, whose Welsbach Company had been granted the ten-year contract in 1899. No indictment was possible; Butler would not talk, and Speaker of the House Charles Kelly, to whom Butler had passed the money, toured Europe until the statute of limitations took effect. This did not give immunity to the fugitive Kelly, but it did to Butler and Campbell.

On March 28, 1902, a circuit court jury found Emil Meysenburg guilty of bribery in the Suburban franchise case and recommended a five-year sentence. Councilman Kratz and Delegate John K. Murrell were to be tried next, but they fled the country. When the *Post-Dispatch* learned that Murrell was homesick, reporter Frank McNeil went to Mexico and brought him back, having given assurances that Folk would exchange leniency for testimony. John Murrell, Edward Murrell, and George Robertson then testified for the state, and fifteen members of the House were indicted for bribery on two counts in the Suburban and lighting cases. By the fall of 1902, Folk's relentless probing had attracted widespread national attention, capped by the appearance in *McClure's Magazine* in October of the first of the famous muckraking exposés of urban corruption, "Tweed Days in St. Louis," by Claude Wetmore and Lincoln Steffens. Actually written by

Wetmore and edited by Steffens, the article was of the same tenor as a dozen published by Wetmore when he was city editor of the *Post-Dispatch* in the 1890s.

With the spotlight on St. Louis, it remained to be seen whether any big fish would follow the minnows into the net. Folk pressed ahead, with some *pro forma* support from Mayor Wells, but for the downtown elite and the Democratic professionals, the circuit attorney was a public nuisance. Wells and Hawes had both supported the boodler Kelly for the House speakership, and Wells had some kind of tie with every big businessman who came before the grand jury, Snyder excepted. Hawes was thoroughly alienated by early 1903, and Wells left Folk off the invitation list at gatherings of prominent Democrats. As usual, when the prosecutor's boot came too close to the wrong toes, he was charged with publicity-seeking and with placing himself ahead of the party and the city. The mayor was a man of impeccable reputation, yet his whole world was threatened by the crusading circuit attorney. Undoubtedly, Wells would not bribe an alderman, and probably he would not knowingly permit others to do so in his behalf; yet, his large fortune rested upon the transit empire built by his father Erastus Wells, who had almost from the beginning enjoyed a special relationship with the city assembly, over and above his many terms of service as an alderman.

In the Snyder trial in October 1902, Uthoff testified that the Kansas Citian had bribed him, a fact confirmed by George Kobusch, a wealthy streetcar manufacturer, who admitted to having personally acted as a go-between for a ten thousand dollar bribe. Snyder did not deny his guilt, resting his case on the fact that he had not been a fugitive, and was therefore immune from prosecution under the statute of limitations. This was a strong argument, and it might have prevailed except for an incredible and revealing blunder by Snyder's attorney, H. F. Priest, one of the "big four" corporation lawyers, who numbered among his clients the Wabash and the Missouri Pacific Railroads. In his closing argument Priest said that bribery was "after all, not such a serious crime. It is a conventional offense, a mere perversion of justice." Folk, in his summation, hit this one right out of the park. Bribery was "treason, and the givers and takers of bribes are traitors of peace." The jury found Snyder guilty and he was sentenced to five years in prison. Witnesses in this trial also mentioned questionable activities by other business leaders, especially John Scullin, the steel, finance, and traction magnate. Allusions of this kind were upsetting to W. M. Reedy, who had an excellent appetite for derogatory information about bluebloods such as C. H. Turner, for whom he had a caste-born aversion, but he was defensive about rugged, "self-made" types such as Scullin and James Campbell. The latter had financed the beginnings of *The Mirror.*

Ed Butler was next to be tried, at Columbia, Missouri, on a change of venue. His distinguished trial lawyers, C. P. Johnson, Chester H. Krum, and Thomas J. Rowe, were supported by three leaders of the central Missouri bar. They tried everything: Butler wore a prosperous farmer's costume, including a broad-brimmed hat; his wife and small grandson were at his side at all times; and the attorneys repeatedly alluded to their client's advanced years (late sixties). The trial was based on Butler's indictment for attempted bribery of Dr. H. H. Chapman, a member of the Board of Health, in connection with the 1901 garbage contract. Chapman's testimony was supported by his wife and family and a colleague, and Butler was given a three-year prison term. During the trial Butler was indicted a second time for bribing Charles Kelly in the lighting contract deal. None of this bothered Butler politically—he was active as usual in the sweeping Democratic triumph in the November elections, where he worked arm-in-arm with Hawes and occupied center stage at Democratic rallies with Mayor Wells.

By this time, the circuit attorney was low on funds, and the House of Delegates turned down the mayor's request for a supplementary appropriation. Part of the amount needed was supplied by Wells from his contingency fund, and the rest was donated by the public in response to appeals by the *Post-Dispatch.* By December 31, 1902, Folk had won thirteen convictions and lost only one case, that of Henry Nicolaus, in which the trial judge had directed a not-guilty verdict when C. H. Turner, reversing himself, testified that Nicolaus had not known the purpose of the notes he had signed in the Suburban Railway extension affair.

Folk won ten more bribery and perjury convictions in 1903 and 1904, losing only the Butler lighting case. A third indictment against Butler, for causing Kelly to become a fugitive from justice, was quashed by the Missouri Supreme Court under the statute of limitations. In all, Folk had obtained indictments against twenty-four persons for bribery or perjury or both, but only eight of them went to prison. Butler's attempted bribery conviction was reversed by the high court on technical grounds, and Snyder's on procedural errors. Meysenburg and a dozen others were freed because of errors by the trial judge or the prosecutor. Folk's biographer, Louis Geiger, suggests that the court took an extremely narrow view in most of these reversals, and the Butler case especially drew a storm of criticism from all over the country. President Theodore Roosevelt, who frequently wrote encouragingly to Folk, consoled him with a letter critical of the Butler decision. The court had ruled that the Board of

Health was not constitutionally empowered to issue garbage contracts, despite the fact that it had been doing so for twelve years. Butler had tried to bribe the wrong people, that is, those who customarily performed the function, rather than the Board of Public Improvements, which had the power but did not know it.

This judicial stance was chiefly the work of Justice James Gantt of St. Louis, son of the principal author of the 1876 charter, who was a clamoring critic of Folk away from the court as well as on it. Gantt had his eye on the 1904 Democratic gubernatorial nomination, for which Folk was being boomed all over the state. Steffens wrote after this reversal that "the machinery of government had broken down under the strain of boodle pull"; and it did seem curious to thoughtful observers that errors were found in the cases of the wealthy Butler, Snyder, and Meysenburg and all of the "higher class" councilmen but not in the trials of the eight lowly delegates. Several major criminals were given immunity in return for their testimony by Folk himself, but in view of the high court's performance, it seems possible that Turner, Stock, and Murrell would never have seen the inside of a prison even if they had been tried.

The boodle cases were only the most spectacular aspects of Folk's incumbency. He and his associates, W. Scott Hancock, Andrew Maroney, and C. Orrick Bishop, closed the policy shops and other gambling operations, ferreted out police graft (to Hawes's displeasure), drove out phony "investment" firms, and furnished evidence to the state attorney general, which led to the breaking up of the baking powder trust and to the arrests of the lieutenant governor and several legislators for bribery. A United States senator from Kansas was jailed, and former Missouri Governor William Joel Stone, thereafter known as "Gumshoe Bill," was badly embarrassed in these investigations.

Folk's enemies and some of his friends called him "Holy Joe," but he was a national as well as a local sensation. The "Missouri Idea," a term describing what Folk called "aggressive honesty," joined the Wisconsin, Iowa, and Oregon Ideas as a symbol for Progressivism. He was not only the most popular Democrat in the state, but also mentioned prominently in the national press for the presidency, which cooled Theodore Roosevelt's enthusiasm for him. When Folk was to speak in Philadelphia, he could not enter the hall until he had addressed the huge crowd outside, and when he returned to his hotel at midnight, two thousand people gathered in the streets and on the sidewalk demanded and got another speech. In St. Louis, the Jefferson Club and most of the downtown business elite were solidly against him; the notable exception being the shoe manufacturers and merchants of Washington Avenue's wholesale row, who provided most of the funds for his gubernatorial campaign. John C. Roberts, of the Roberts, Johnson, and Rand (International) Shoe Company, was his largest contributor, and Nelson McLeod, a lumberman, was his early campaign chairman. Murray Carleton, the dry-goods wholesaler, was the only prominent country club insider to support him. Roberts and McLeod were Tennesseans, and, like Folk, they were relative newcomers to St. Louis, well-to-do but not yet among the super-rich. It is probable that as shippers the wholesalers and shoe manufacturers identified with Folk as the enemy of the Terminal Railway monopoly and its financial partners. For obvious reasons, the brewers were allied with the Big Cinch in opposition. W. M. Reedy did not yet like Folk much, despite their mutual distaste for Butler and Turner. He thought the circuit attorney was a glory-grabber who was hurting the city. The *Post-Dispatch* was his only consistent newspaper supporter; the *Republic,* the *Star,* and the *Times* wavered back and forth depending upon Folk's target, and after the first few weeks the *Globe-Democrat* was usually in opposition, although it disliked Hawes, Butler, Francis, Wells, and all other Democrats as much as it did Folk. Though a Republican paper, the *Kansas City Star* was very supportive, and the Democratic rural press sang his praises. The latter had long resented D. R. Francis and the St. Louis monopolists, especially after the goldbugs had deserted Bryan in 1896.

The Democratic bosses worked up an anti-Folk strategy for the 1904 gubernatorial campaign, in which Harry Hawes would challenge him in eastern Missouri for convention delegates and Mayor James A. Reed of Kansas City would do the same in the west. If the nominating convention deadlocked, as they hoped, Justice Gantt could slip in as the compromise nominee. But they were fighting the whirlwind—the rural democracy had reveled in Folk's onslaughts against the city crooks, and he was nominated on the first ballot with 77 percent of the vote. Machine Democrats prevailed for the other state offices, however, and the factions put a cosmetic patch over their differences for the general election. No one was fooled by Folk's tepid endorsements of his running mates, and in November he carried the state by more than thirty thousand, while the Republicans won the presidential and U.S. senatorial elections, a majority of the congressional and legislative seats, and all of the other statewide offices. Roosevelt was the first Republican presidential winner in Missouri since Grant, and William Warner of Kansas City was the first Republican senator since Carl Schurz (over thirty years in both cases). Folk had a bigger majority than the Republicans, and the nearly sixty-thousand-vote split-ticket swing vividly demonstrated the reform mood of the electorate.

As governor, Folk fulfilled his promise, worked well with the Republican legislature, and in partnership with Attorney General Herbert S. Hadley of Kansas City put Missouri in the vanguard of the antitrust movement. Among those caught for massive antitrust violations was Henry Clay Pierce of St. Louis, whose Waters-Pierce Oil Company turned out to be a front for Rockefeller's Standard Oil Company. Ultimately, the resourceful Hadley forced the dissolution of the huge Standard Oil Trust. Folk backed him vigorously, even though the attorney general's quick thrust to national fame dimmed some of the governor's lustre.

Folk's investigations provided an ambiguous backdrop for the St. Louis World's Fair. Since 1855 the city had promoted itself in the region through its annual Agricultural and Mechanical Fair. After the Civil War, the role of the agricultural exhibits gradually diminished as the industrial increased, and more emphasis was placed on the carnival midway, musical presentations, and horse racing and betting, the last being the principal drawing card by the 1880s. In 1883, attention was partially diverted from the fairgrounds by the formation of an exposition association, which built a million-dollar exposition and music hall at Thirteenth and Olive. In its first season, the downtown exposition drew five hundred thousand people during the fair and Veiled Prophet week in October. Industrial exhibits were transferred to the hall, and many of them remained on permanent display there. John Philip Sousa's great concert band made annual appearances in the hall during the late 1880s and 1890s. These fall festivities served as a unifying instrument for businessmen and as tourist attractions, and the exposition hall physically supported the city's claim to national and world prominence.

The Veiled Prophet celebration began in 1878, when Alonso and Charles Slayback, former residents of New Orleans, bought all of the floats and costumes used at the Mardi Gras and convinced St. Louis businessmen that an annual event modelled on the Mardi Gras would enhance the fall festivities by its colorful display. The Mystic Order of the Veiled Prophet of the Enchanted Realm was created, and membership in the order was reserved for those who contributed to community accord and civic progress, as defined by the business leaders. According to the official myth, the prophet had chosen St. Louis because of its high-quality citizens and its strategic location, which made it the best place on earth to live and conduct a business. Charles Slayback described the order as "a social organization with a

Exposition and Music Hall. *Opened in 1883, the Exposition and Music Hall provided a permanent attraction for exhibitions and concerts. The 1888 Republican convention was held in it. The site is now occupied by the St. Louis Public Library. Photograph by Emil Boehl, 1883. MHS-PP.*

broader vision of citizenship—a pure altruistic order," and its colorful parades provided an exciting spectacle for the people and tourists, but it was chiefly a booster's scheme and a bonding instrument among business and social leaders. Though officially secret, membership attested to one's importance, and being selected as the Veiled Prophet of Khorassan was the highest accolade (another putative secret). Beginning officially in 1894, the most breathtaking event for the social elite was the unveiling of the Queen of Love and Beauty at the Veiled Prophet Ball. Wealthy men scrambled and politicked to have their daughters elected as queen or at least as maids of honor, primarily as a tribute to their own status and influence. Dark rumors circulated about bribes offered during these secret campaigns, but if so, they probably had little effect. Keen observers noted from the beginning that the selection system tended to produce queens with the kind of beauty that radiated from within rather than the more obvious physical kind—a tradition that has stood the test of time.

In 1890 David R. Francis led an ambitious effort to capture the Columbian Exposition—the celebration of the four hundredth anniversary of the discovery of America. St. Louisans raised more

David R. Francis. *Francis, a commission merchant and civic promoter in the 1880s, moved into politics, serving as mayor of St. Louis and governor of Missouri. His greatest prominence, however, was his service as president of the Louisiana Purchase Exposition Company between 1901 and 1904, when he became St. Louis's ambassador to the world. Photograph, 1903. MHS-PP.*

than $4 million in subscriptions in anticipation of the award, but the hated rival, Chicago, captured the prize. When the Windy City threw the biggest bash America had ever seen in 1893 (a year late), Francis burned to get even and reminded Congress that within a decade there would be another occasion for a national celebration.

Little more was said until 1896, when Pierre Chouteau, at a meeting of the Missouri Historical Society, proposed that a memorial to Thomas Jefferson be erected in Forest Park, where documents relating to the Louisiana Purchase could be housed. Later, he suggested recreating the old Creole village, on the riverfront if possible, where a centennial observance of the purchase could be held. Nothing so small suited the Businessmen's League, and it was pointed out that Congress would support a celebration only if the site were vast and the scope international. The *Post-Dispatch* saw in the project a chance to "eclipse the Columbian Exposition of 1893." In January 1899, delegates from the states and territories of the Louisiana Purchase met in St. Louis and chose the host city over New Orleans as the Exposition site. A logical choice, according to Francis, since St. Louis was by far the largest and wealthiest city in the purchase. More important, its citizens were prepared to raise $5 million by private subscription and $5 million in their corporate capacity. The visiting delegates pledged their states to apply pressure on Congress to appropriate a matching $5 million. The $15 million total was symbolic—it equaled the amount paid to Napoleon for the Louisiana Territory.

In March 1899, more than $4 million was pledged in one night in a mass meeting in Exposition Hall, and by December 1900 the subscription was completed. Subscribers bought stock, at ten dollars a share, in the Louisiana Purchase Exposition Company. Before the city could make its contribution, the state constitutional limit on borrowing had to be amended and the city charter revised, both of which were approved by the voters in 1900. In 1901, the city floated a $5 million issue of World's Fair sinking-fund bonds, which required a special ten-cent tax levy, beginning in 1903. Subscribers to the stock elected a 118-man board of directors, which was virtually an elite honor roll with a scattering of journalists, professors, architects, art experts, and out-of-town members. Small business, the clergy, ethnic and black leaders, and the unions were not represented. Half of the directors were also directors of large downtown banks and trust companies, thirty-three were known millionaires and a half-dozen more probably were, and forty belonged to the St. Louis Country Club. Only a few were of German origins, including the world-class millionaire Adolphus Busch and highly assimilated types such as Frederick Niedringhaus. Obviously, such an enormous undertaking required the vigorous support of these men and the resources at their command, but the nature of the directorate demonstrated their assumption that major civic enterprises did not require broad representation at the decision level.

In Congress there was stiff opposition at first. There were objections to the lack of union representation on the board, and New England congressmen did not see much to celebrate. This was logical enough, since their great-grandfathers had not wanted the Louisiana Territory in the first place. But James Tawney of Minnesota, chairman of the House Exposition Committee, argued that "nowhere in the history of the World" had there been "a more marvelous development" in a single century than in the former Louisiana Territory, which would be shown to the world at the proposed exposition. Crippling riders were attached to the bill in the Senate, the final one removed only after the veteran Missouri free-silver senator George Graham Vest called in some old markers from "Pitchfork Ben" Tillman of

South Carolina. On March 4, 1901, the federal appropriation passed, to be applied only after St. Louis had spent its $10 million.

Having been offered sites at Carondelet, O'Fallon Park, and the western half of Forest Park, the directors chose the last, after hearing arguments for it from James Campbell, D. R. Francis, Murray Carleton, L. D. Dozier, and C. W. Knapp of the *Republic.* Streetcar lines and the Wabash Railroad already served Forest Park, and by building short spurs the Missouri Pacific, Iron Mountain, Cotton Belt, and the Frisco could reach it. Seventy-five percent of the sewer construction required was immediately necessary without the Fair, and the beauty of the site and its surroundings would counterbalance the city's corrupt and smoky reputation. Not mentioned, but most important, a majority of the city's most powerful men wanted it there. Some families living in the private places objected because of the inevitable noise and bustle, and John Scullin argued vigorously for the Carondelet site, where he was a big landowner, but Francis and his colleagues prevailed. When owners of the one-hundred-acre Catlin tract near the park objected, the Lincoln Trust Company bought the property, leased sixty acres of it to the Exposition Company, and reaped a harvest in rising land values. When the Exposition Realty Company bought a tract north of the park and west of DeBaliviere on de Giverville on both sides of the Wabash tracks for five hundred thousand dollars, land in the park area immediately doubled in value. The biggest haul went to the Parkview Realty Company, headed by A. A. B. Woerheide, president of the Lincoln Trust and a director of the Exposition Company. Capitalized at $10 million, the Parkview group bought seven large tracts totalling more than one thousand acres adjoining the park to the south, southwest, and northwest.

To accommodate the expected hundreds of thousands of visitors, more than a dozen permanent hotels were built. A group associated with ex-mayor Cyrus Walbridge, an Exposition director, erected a $750,000 posh, nine-story, fireproof hotel at Kingshighway and West Pine overlooking the park. They called it the Buckingham Club (later Kingsway) and sold limited memberships to wealthy families. Some of the members took up permanent residence there, and others loaned their suites to out-of-town friends for the Fair. Downtown interests built the Jefferson Hotel at Twelfth and Locust Streets, a twelve-story structural steel building with four hundred rooms and baths. To supplement the more than one hundred old and new hotels in the city, the Exposition Company allotted free space for twenty-one temporary structures. Some of these were inexpensive wooden buildings, one was a collection of board-floored, electric-lighted tents, and others were permanent buildings which could be converted to other uses. Within the fairgrounds, the Statlers, in their first-ever hotel enterprise, built the Inside Inn, a giant structure which accommodated over four thousand guests and one thousand employees throughout the Fair. Necessarily built of combustible materials, it required a constant firewatch, which was so successful that a dozen or so fires that were started during the Fair never burned so much as the contents of a room. Each of the temporary hotels was required to sign a contract holding its room charges to the pre-Fair city levels.

It was obvious by 1901 that the western half of Forest Park, from DeBaliviere to Skinker Road, would not be large enough for the Fair as planned. Consequently the directors added to its 657 acres by leasing the 109-acre campus and buildings of Washington University to the west, which were nearly completed but not yet occupied, and ten other parcels north and west of the park, giving the Exposition grounds 1,272 acres in all, half again as large as the Philadelphia Centennial and Chicago Columbian Expositions combined. The grounds then measured 1.75 by 1.05 miles.

The St. Louis Transit Company, still in disarray because of the recent strike, added 450 new cars, equipped with air brakes, for the Fair; the Terminal Railroad built a belt line from the northern city limits, which skirted the western edge of the grounds to expedite the movement of equipment and materials during the construction period; and four major railroads built freight terminals, which would be converted to passenger use during the Fair, to the south of the grounds for the same purpose. Inside the grounds, the Intramural Railway, a third-rail electric streetcar line, traversed the hills and valleys from near the main entrance at DeBaliviere to the west and back by a southern route before returning to the main entrance. There were fifty-six of these cars, which made the 6.6 mile outer loop in thirty-five minutes. Two inner loops added another 6.5 miles of track. Except on very heavy days, they departed singly, at three-minute intervals.

In keeping with the "New St. Louis" and "City Beautiful" themes that accompanied preparations for the Fair, Mayor Wells tackled the city's major service problems. He startled his friends on the United Railways board and delighted nearly everyone else by denouncing the shoddy service and maintenance on the car lines, and then he proposed that the twenty-five dollars per car annual tax be replaced by a 1 percent levy on each fare. Perhaps with tongue in cheek, Wells asserted that the change would improve relations between the transit company and the city, but his prospective "partners" squealed in anguish at what would amount to a quadrupling of their taxes. When the bill passed the assembly, the United Railways fought it all the way to the U.S. Supreme Court, which ruled for the city. The mayor also argued that since rapid transit could never be achieved on the street surface, subways should be built, one along the central corridor from Third Street to Jefferson or Grand Avenue, and a north-south line from Chouteau to Cass Avenue (about twenty blocks). Wells conceded that subways cut through solid rock would be expensive, but well within the city's capacity, especially if the Eads Bridge tunnel could be purchased and used as a nucleus for the system. Unfortunately, the free-bridge controversy that erupted during Wells's second term relegated this idea to obscurity. Another Wells proposal, the creation of the office of transit-line inspector, was killed by boodle in the House of Delegates, and his plan for a city public utilities regulatory commission lingered in the House until the last weeks of his second term in 1909. As soon as the commission was ready to function, the Missouri legislature co-opted it by establishing the Missouri Public Service Commission.

In 1901 Wells attacked the water purification problem. The settling basins at Chain of Rocks and Bissell's Point precipitated the heavy material that had given St. Louis water the consistency of gruel, but the fine particles remained in suspension, leaving a coffee-colored liquid that the uninitiated found repellent. The frequent typhoid epidemics, it was assumed, were traceable to Chicago's practice of dumping raw sewage into the Illinois River, depositing bacilli that clung to the particulates. The water commissioner favored a filtration plant, others favored new works on the Missouri River, and a private group offered to dam the Meramec River and sell the sparkling Meramec Spring water to the city. Wells proposed to the Municipal Assembly that a board of engineers be appointed, and they agreed on behalf of their constituents, though as he put it, they personally "used water sparingly for libation." Two of the engineers recommended the Meramec plan, which would have furnished clear water without a need for pumps, but the project would have cost the city $30 million, or if left to private interests, it would have meant dealing with another giant utility. It could not have been done in time for the World's Fair, and no one could guarantee that the flow would be sufficient as the city grew or that the spring would last forever. The Missouri River plan, which would also have eliminated pumping, was obviously the ultimate solution, and as the water was purer and less complex than that of the Mississippi, it would have been less difficult to treat. However, it too would require an outlay beyond the city's current capabilities, and it could not be completed in time for the Fair.

The perpetual problem of St. Louis's muddy water was solved in 1902 by adding calcium carbonate as a precipitant. Here, the chemical is added to water at the city's Chain of Rocks water plant. Photograph, ca. 1902. MHS-PP.

Exposition President D. R. Francis was putting daily pressure on Wells, since one of the major highlights of the Fair was to be the water display, consisting of three giant cascades of leaping, sparkling water, two great fountains, a grand basin, and radiating lagoons. Dark brown waterfalls haunted the dreams of the directors. Wells kept assuring them that he would furnish twenty million gallons of clear water a day, though he did not yet know how. Most people favored the water commissioner's plan to construct huge sand filters at the Chain of Rocks. Many businesses and private homes had small filtering systems that performed well, but again the mayor objected to a large expenditure, which the city's own experience indicated might not work for long on a large scale.

Privately, Wells had long favored treating the water with a coagulating agent, such as alum, but as the object of a current popular prejudice, alum was politically impracticable. Early in 1903 he learned that ferrous sulphate (iron) and milk of lime were being used successfully in the Lorain, Ohio, and Quincy, Illinois, water systems. After an engineering study had shown that the plan was feasible at Chain of Rocks, machinery to produce the mixture was installed. On March 21, 1904, only weeks before the Exposition opened, every tap in the city was discharging an unfamiliar clear and pure liquid. A filtering plant which the anxious directors had installed at the fairgrounds was never used. After the Fair, water commissioner Ben C. Adkins made further improvements which raised the plant's efficiency, and water consumption per person dropped, which ironically was attributed to its improved quality. New turbine pumps replaced the old reciprocal ones, which doubled pumping capacity. The total additional cost had been $155,000, including the pumps, and the building of a larger plant, originally thought necessary by 1910, was deferred for another twenty years, when the Missouri River installation was constructed. Wells claimed he had saved the city $30 million.

Also important to the New St. Louis–World's Fair plan were street improvement, smoke abatement, and a general citizens' cleanup. The *Post-Dispatch* pointed out that these were "absolutely essential to the success of the World's Fair. All are regarded as a public necessity regardless of the Fair." Before they could be achieved, charter revisions and constitutional amendments were necessary. First, the drain on the general fund produced by the expensive and partially redundant county offices was to be remedied by a special tax levy of thirty-five cents on the one hundred dollar valuation. Second, an effective increase in the constitutional debt limit of 5 percent of the assessed valuation of all private property was to be achieved by excluding from the computation the $6.1 million county debt assumed in 1876 and the $5.8 million waterworks debt. Any future borrowing for the water system was to be accomplished by issuing revenue instead of general obligation bonds. Assisted by public enthusiasm for the Fair, voters of the state and city approved these measures overwhelmingly in 1902.

Since there was no bridge crossing the Mill Creek Valley west of Grand Avenue and only two dangerous grade crossings over the maze of railroad tracks in the West End, the city built a temporary wooden bridge over the Kingshighway crossing to give the southern half of the city better access to the Fair as well as to make Shaw's Botanical Gardens accessible to the Fair visitors. This stopgap measure was prefatory to a master plan for the completion and paving of Kingshighway Boulevard, the old royal road separating the village's common fields from the King's domain. Ultimately, Kingshighway was to form a semicircular parkway around the city, connecting Carondelet, Forest, and O'Fallon Parks and the outlying cemeteries and tying semi-isolated sections of the city together. The Civic Improvement League, which was organized in 1901 by Mrs. Louis Marion McCall, gave much time and service to the boulevard and other New St. Louis projects. Claiming 1,576 members in 1902, the league was represented throughout the middle- and upper-class sections of the city. Its rolls included architects, engineers, and members of men's and women's social clubs, but its officers reflected its close ties with the Businessmen's League. George Leighton, an iron foundry president, headed the league, and downtown bankers dominated its board. William Marion Reedy, though he was no fan of the Businessmen's League on its record, trumpeted the virtues of the Civic League's City Beautiful program, no doubt because most of it was his idea in the first place.

The league urged popular support of health and safety standards and personal involvement in government and law enforcement—each citizen was asked to pledge himself to appear as a witness against criminals of whom he had knowledge. With the World's Fair in mind, prizes were offered for the most improved front yard in a neighborhood and citizens were pledged to "advise" immigrants on home maintenance and political involvement. McCall published an article in the *Chautauquan* in 1903, crediting the beautification campaign with inspiring a "MORAL AWAKENING which is all a part of the New St. Louis. . . ." The league's "Ladies' Sanitary Committee" entered unpainted homes and asked owners to cooperate, vacant lots were cleaned up and turned into playgrounds for slum children, and men and women volunteers rolled up their sleeves to help refurbish unsightly tenements. In 1903 the Civic League enlisted the children by distributing a pamphlet in the schools called *Keep Our City Clean*, which explained the sanitation ordinances and put uncooperative parents at risk of the moral disapproval of their offspring.

Delays in bond authorization and property owners' suits against condemnation held up the boulevard project at first, and indifference and opposition to what many considered to be a scheme of, by, and for the rich, helped to delay its completion until the 1930s. But from 1901 to 1904, a strenuous street improvement program moved ahead. Much of the downtown district was already paved with stone, but adjacent streets and especially those leading to Forest Park were macadam or gravel, some of them in very poor condition. Property owners, who shared in the costs, were often reluctant or opposed to improving their fronting streets. Lindell, which was to be the main western artery for the Fair traffic, was a gravel road. Mayor Wells, whose home was on Lindell, told a group of "vociferous" objectors at a Board of Public Improvements hearing that the boulevard "had to be reconstructed, and that any property owner who could not afford to pay the slight cost of such necessary improvement, was living there, in my judgement, under false pretences and should move to another street." This challenge irked his neighbors, but it ended the debate. In the four years before the Fair, in 227 projects, more than 70 miles of streets were rebuilt and 30 miles of new streets or extensions were constructed. As a result the amount of solid matter in the air showed a marked decrease by the opening of the World's Fair.

In March 1901, Wells signed an ordinance declaring the emission of dense smoke to be a public nuisance, and in August the Chief Smoke Inspector's office was established and empowered to issue warnings, which if not heeded were subject to a fine of twenty-five dollars. In 1902 the Smoke Abatement Department's authority was extended to steamboats and barges at the levee. Many larger firms installed smoke-consuming devices, then just being developed, and the inspectors reported a 70 percent decline in dense smoke by the end of the year. This level reportedly held throughout the Fair. Not only was St. Louis's air a bit thinner, it was lighter in color. But not for long—more industry and people were coming, including the automobile.

Assisting President D. R. Francis in managing the Exposition were William H. Thompson, treasurer; Walter B. Stevens, secretary; James L. Blair, general counsel (replaced in 1903 by Franklin Ferris); and eight vice presidents. The Executive Committee, which worked closely with the principal officers, included Francis, Thompson, C. W. Knapp, Murray Carleton, L. D. Dozier, James Campbell, Rolla Wells, John Scullin, Breckinridge Jones, C. H. Spencer, Nathan Frank, A. L. Shapleigh, W. F. Boyle, C. G. Warner, and Howard Elliott. In planning for the grandest World's Fair ever seen, St. Louis drew upon the recent experiences of the Columbian and Paris Expositions. Frederick J. V. Skiff, director of the Colorado exhibit at Chicago in 1893 and the American exhibits at Paris in 1900, was chosen director of Exhibits. Most of the sixteen department heads who worked with him had also been involved in one or both of the other fairs. Isaac Taylor of St. Louis was chief architect and Director of Works, Norris B. Gregg of the Mound City Paint Company directed concessions and admissions, and Walter B. Stevens was Director of Exploitation (publicity). Halsey C. Ives, director of the St. Louis School of Fine Arts, who had headed the art department at the Columbian Exposition, was chief of the Department of Art.

Fortunately, the officers had available for their headquarters the just-completed buildings of Washington University, which delayed its move from Seventeenth and Eighteenth Streets. As the Fair's grand centerpiece, they conceived and erected the "Ivory City," twelve gigantic exhibition "palaces," the smallest of which, the Forestry Building, covered 4.1 acres. The largest, the Palace of Agriculture, was 1,600 feet long and 500 feet wide—18.4 acres. D. R. Francis illustrated their magnitude:

> Suppose a freight train to consist of forty cars eighteen of these cars were required to haul the lumber . . . to St. Louis for the construction of a single exhibit building. The structured iron for that building called for two trains of twenty cars each. . . . Three trains of one hundred cars of plaster and two trains of fifty cars of sand entered into the construction of the palace; eighteen carloads of roofing material, ten cars loaded with glass and four carloads of nails were the smaller items. . . .

To erect the average palace, 670 carpenters, plasterers, staff workers (plaster moulders and shapers), and laborers worked for seven months before 100 painters applied 3,000 gallons of paint. Wages had improved since Eads Bridge construction, but not by much. Plaster moulders were paid up to a dollar an hour; plasterers, 75 to 87.5 cents; plumbers and bricklayers, 70 cents; painters and two-horse teams with wagon and driver, 50 cents; carpenters, 55 cents; and common laborers, 20 to 25 cents. At the same time, at least one hundred millionaires lived within twenty blocks of the work site!

Of the twelve buildings, only the Palace of Fine Arts, made of stone and steel, was intended to be permanent. Though it was one of the smaller palaces, it cost nearly $1 million, naturally more expensive than its plaster-covered neighbors, and it occupied center stage atop "Art Hill," with the Palaces of Liberal Arts, Manufactures, Mines and Metallurgy, Electricity, Machinery, Education, Transportation, and Varied Industries fanned out below. Agriculture, Horticulture, and Forestry were located to the west of Skinker Road. The palaces were all about sixty-five feet high, but as Francis described them, the facades, entrances, and towers were of "charming variety." Education had "a great Corinthian Colonnaide," and "across the Grand Basin the towers of Electricity were . . . pedestals for daring sculpture above the sky-line." Manufactures featured a triumphal arch, Spanish steeples graced Varied Industries, Gothic towers decorated Machinery, and quadrigas (four horse chariots) loomed above the arched entrances to the Liberal Arts. Transportation had a "union-station" look, with a domed roof and pylons; Mines and Metallurgy sported obelisks, globes, and overhanging roofs; and Agriculture was deliberately plain, a third-of-a-mile of unadorned facade interspersed with piers.

Ivory was the predominant hue, but the steeples, towers, and domes ran the spectrum from light gray to deep orange. Francis rhapsodized: "Between sunset and the slow coming out of hundreds of thousands of incandescent lights there was a half hour of deepening twilight in which the World's Fair scenes assumed new beauties."

Ivory changed to "sombre gray" and "the human currents on the plazas and pathways grew sluggish and quiet. . . . The bustle of the World's Fair day was gone. The singing of the gondoliers on the lagoons and the music of the bands in the early evening sounded sweeter."

Even to the sophisticate, the sheer beauty of the Louisiana Purchase Exposition was overwhelming. Henry Adams, whose enthusiasm for the Middle West and for St. Louis in particular was quite limited, wrote in *The Education of Henry Adams:*

> The world had never witnessed so marvellous a phantasm; by night Arabia's crimson sands had never returned a glow half so astonishing, as one wandered among long lines of white palaces, exquisitely lighted by thousands on thousands of electric candles, soft, rich, shadowy, palpable in their sensuous depths. . . . One enjoyed it with iniquitous rapture. . . .

In April 1902, the palace construction had been nearing completion, but there was some doubt whether the federal and some of the state exhibit structures could be ready by the centennial date,

Festival Hall, the Grand Basin, and the Palaces of Electricity and Machinery from the German Pavilion, Louisiana Purchase Exposition. *Photograph by F. J. Koster, 1904. MHS-PP.*

April 30, 1903. Several foreign nations, believing that the Exposition business was wearing thin and doubting whether they could make the deadline, had already sent regrets. Consequently, in June 1902 Congress approved a one-year delay in the beginning of the Exposition, though the dedication ceremonies were to be held as scheduled. The new date seemed apropos in St. Louis, since it approximated the centennial of the upper Louisiana transfer at St. Louis. President Theodore Roosevelt, whose special affinity for the West dated from his Dakota ranching days, stressed the Exposition's national importance to the foreign service, and the embassies and consulates hustled to promote it. D. R. Francis's visit to the European capitals in February 1903 was virtually a triumphal tour. He met with the principal governmental and business leaders in London, Paris, Berlin, Madrid, and Brussels, made two speeches to assemblies of notables in Paris, and had audiences with Kings Edward VII of England and Leopold of Belgium, Kaiser Wilhelm II of Germany, and President Loubet of France. Edward VII loaned him Queen Victoria's Diamond Jubilee presents for exhibition at the Fair. Francis was especially impressed with the German Emperor's wide-ranging knowledge, vigor, and admiration for Theodore Roosevelt and all things American. Other Exposition representatives visited Rome, Vienna, the Scandinavian capitals, St. Petersburg, Latin America, and East Asia.

Equally important was the worldwide newspaper publicity given the Exposition, chiefly through the efforts of Walter Williams, commissioner to the foreign press, who covered twenty-five thousand miles in nine months, visiting one thousand newspaper offices in twenty-five countries in Europe, Asia, Latin America, and North Africa. Williams, later the founder of the University of Missouri School of Journalism, also organized the World Press Parliament's first meeting at St. Louis during the Exposition, which was attended by five thousand journalists. He observed that in Europe during his tour, the best-known Americans were "President Roosevelt, Pierpont Morgan, David R. Francis, and the Missouri mule."

The ceremonial dedication of the Exposition's buildings and grounds took place as scheduled on April 30, May 1 and 2, 1903. Twelve thousand regulars and state troops marched to the Exposition grounds through streets lined with three to four hundred thousand cheering people. The dedication speaker, President Theodore Roosevelt, spoke knowledgeably of the history of national expansion and favorably of courage, tenacity, virility, and honesty. Ex-President Grover Cleveland eulogized Thomas Jefferson and the Americans, "a people favored of God."

A year later, on April 30, 1904, D. R. Francis shouted, "Enter herein ye sons of men!" and William Howard Taft, representing the president in St. Louis, made a speech before Roosevelt pressed a telegraph key in the White House which set the Exposition's machinery in motion. To those gathered in the East Room, the president said the Exposition would show "the progress in the industry, the science and the art, not only of the American nation, but of all the other nations," during the century since the Louisiana Purchase. He was also pleased that the third Olympic Games of the modern era were being held in conjunction with the Exposition. The 1904 Games, at the Washington University stadium (Francis Field) within the Exposition grounds, were the last to adhere to the original Olympic ideal. Instead of national "teams" marching under flags into chauvinistic combat, the athletes entered as individuals, or in the case of team events, as clubs.

Forty-three foreign nations erected exhibit buildings. All of the principal European countries were included, each displaying examples of their most advanced technology as well as their traditional arts and crafts. Britain's dominions: Australia, Canada, India, New Zealand, and South Africa; Mexico, Argentina, Brazil, and most of Latin America (still smarting over Roosevelt's Panama grab, Colombia declined); and Egypt, China, Persia, and Japan showed the world their best.

The Plateau of States occupied the southeastern part of the grounds. Forty-five states and territories built exhibit "pavilions," the most elaborate and largest of which was Missouri's. Only Delaware and South Carolina were totally unrepresented, though several other states did not have pavilions. Each had a "day" devoted to it with delegations from home, welcoming speeches, responses from their governors, special events, music, receptions, and a ball, but there was a wide variety in their efforts to put their best foot forward. Alabama featured an antebellum mansion and a fifty-six-foot-high, sixty-ton statue of Vulcan; Pennsylvania brought the Liberty Bell; Oregon reproduced Lewis and Clark's old Fort Clatsop; Tennessee's pavilion was a detailed copy of Andrew Jackson's "Hermitage"; fifteen hundred of California's "Sons and Daughters of the Golden West" gave away seven thousand bottles of wine in the courtyard of their old Jesuit mission; and Louisiana reenacted the Louisiana Purchase at its Cabildo, to the music of Paris's *Garde Republicaine* band, with their descendants playing the roles of the original participants.

One of the more popular state days was that of Colorado, which gave away one hundred thousand Rocky Ford cantaloupes and lapel ribbons with tiny silver potatoes attached. The Virginia pavilion was

The Missouri State Building at the Louisiana Purchase Exposition. *The building burned in late November 1904, shortly before the close of the Fair. Photograph by the Official Photographic Company, 1904. MHS-PP.*

a faithful replica of Jefferson's Monticello, and three thousand Virginians arrived by train for their day. At its Theodore Roosevelt ranch cabin, North Dakota served thousands of visitors ice cream shaped as cabbages, strawberries, corn, apples, and other vegetables. Fifteen thousand Kansans paraded on their day, and their governor "cackled" (it was reported) that his state produced enough eggs and dairy products each year to pay for the Louisiana Purchase. Missouri Day featured tens of thousands of free sandwiches and a speech by Governor A. M. Dockery praising the millions of Missourians who were not boodlers. Philippines Day, the million-dollar brainchild of the islands' former governor W. H. Taft, focused attention on the forty-seven-acre Philippines Reservation at the southwest corner of the grounds. The walls of Manila and villages of the headhunting and diminutive Negritos, the slightly less "primitive" Igorots, the "semi-civilized" Moros and Bagobos, and the "civilized" (Christian) Visayans, more than eleven hundred Filipinos in all, with their exhibits of products and native animals, illustrated the glories of empire. The exhibit was an ambiguous demonstration of the power of American arms and the mission to the "little brown brothers" as shown by the model school taught by Christian women, attended dutifully by all the children except the Negritos. The most prominent features were the crack Philippine Constabulary and the marching band, which paraded the Exposition grounds daily. There must have been some lingering Bryanite anti-imperialism about, since President Francis was moved to stress in his almost daily speeches the beneficial effects of civilization on the Filipinos, which should be noted without reference to politics.

Greatest among the foreign days was the German, attended by 184,000 people, a figure which was exceeded only by St. Louis Day, Labor Day, and Francis Day (closing day, December 1). Prince Hohenlohe and Mrs. Adolphus Busch headed the dedication receiving line at the pavilion, a massive reproduction of the Charlottenburg Castle. Carl Schurz, Emil Preetorius, and the German ambassador all stressed the unbreakable bonds between America and the German Empire. French Day at the Grand Trianon pavilion was held on July 14, to commemorate the fall of the Bastille, and the French emphasized their roles in the American Revolution and the Louisiana Territory. The Japanese pavilion was a collection of pagodas and teahouses in a garden of winding walks, rustic bridges, rare dwarf trees, flower beds, a mountain stream, a waterfall, and a lake, all "suggestive of a fairyland." Japanese exhibits, some eighty thousand in all, included silks, ceramics, jewelry, carvings, embroideries, electrical machinery, and railway tracks with miniature trains. The India pavilion was an artistic gem, including reproductions of the great mosque and the Taj Mahal at Agra. Italian Day on October 12 celebrated the discovery of America, and the pavilion was decorated with scenes depicting the grandeur of ancient Rome. Other "days" and pavilions were equally striking, interesting, and instructive.

Each nation also presented the exhibits of firms and individuals, which were shown in the palaces to stimulate interest in their exports. Ireland housed its industrial exhibits separately, in "Blarney Castle" and the Irish village. Its ancient arts and crafts were displayed, but Ireland's chief aim was to replace its potato farmer image with that of a busy industrial society. China's pavilion, a copy of Prince Pu Lun's palace at Peking, was graced for a time by Pu Lun himself, the nephew of the reigning and last Manchu Emperor, Kuang Hsu. China's three-acre space in the Palace of Liberal Arts exhibited fine textiles, bronzes, jade, silverware, porcelains, silks, furs, ancient cannon, junks and other boats, carvings, screens, and paintings. Thirty-four nations exhibited in the Palace of Manufactures, forty-five showed their wares along the four miles of aisles in Agriculture, and similar numbers exhibited in the other palaces. German, French, and American manufacturers supplied the steam engines, generators, and boilers which operated the Exposition's power plant.

View along the Pike, Louisiana Purchase Exposition. *The Pike, an avenue of amusements and attractions, sometimes looms larger in memories of the Fair than the educational and industrial exhibits held most important by the organizers. Photograph by the Official Photographic Company, 1904. MHS-PP.*

For most people, young and old, the major attraction was the "Ten Million Dollar Pike," an enchanting street of private concessions stretching for nearly a mile along the northern edge of the grounds. Even at ten to fifty cents per thrill, a small fortune could be spent in the hundreds of concessions that lined the street. Near Jim Key, the educated horse, who could spell and do sums with blocks, was Battle Abbey, a large, turreted and towered building containing huge cycloramas of the battles of Gettysburg, Manassas, Custer's "Massacre," Yorktown, New Orleans, Buena Vista, and Manila. The "Boer War," a reenactment with hundreds of real Englishmen and real Boers, featured much shooting and shouting, climaxed by a daring dive off a high cliff by a horse and rider (into a water tank). The naval battle of Santiago de Cuba depicted the American victory over the decrepit Spanish fleet, all acted out with miniature ships and real sailors. One reporter wrote that it was a lot more exciting than the original. The "Galveston Flood" was an uncomfortably realistic portrayal of the tidal wave that had killed five thousand people in 1900. Through mechanical contrivances, roaring waters and shrieking winds convinced even the skeptical that they were in real danger.

Other "notable amusements" on the Pike included the Hagenbeck Wild Animal Show; mysterious Asia; the Creation of the Earth (Bible version); the Wild West Indian Congress, with representatives of fifty-one tribes; the Rough Riders; Paris on the Pike; Old St. Louis; Cairo, with twenty-six buildings, a bazaar, camels, monkeys, and snakes; the Cliff Dwellers; the Esquimaux Village; Twenty Minutes to the North Pole, a 250-foot ship on tracks, grinding through ice fields by the light of the Aurora Borealis; the Holy City, an eleven-acre Jerusalem; Hunting in the Ozarks; and the Hereafter, where sinners could see their futures in the "shades of Hades, depicted with startling realism by the most advanced mechanical and electrical ingenuity."

The most popular concession was the Tyrolean Alps, a scenic restaurant which was a miracle of the molder's art, where "Snow-capped masses of the Ortler with the wild and jagged Jugspitze threw

The Beer Garden at the Tyrolean Alps. *The largest grossing attraction on the Pike was the Tyrolean Alps, partly owned by native St. Louisan Edward A. Faust. Photograph by Jesse Tarbox Beals, 1904. MHS-PP.*

their cooling shadows over a verdant scene of Alpine life." There were "massive castles with gray towers and embattled walls," a Tyrolese village council hall, and "groups of peasants singing as they worked." Beneath the mountains a tram car took passengers through a "massive cyclorama" of painted Alpine scenery. This concession grossed more than $1 million, second only to the Inside Inn.

The Exposition was a smashing success. Scientific and technological advances gave it a wide edge over the Columbian Exposition as a spectacle, and in a stunning reversal of form, balmy, resort-like weather held throughout. It was comfortably warm in May, stayed in the 70s and low 80s through the summer, and autumn was a repeat of May. St. Louis's reputation for miserable summer weather was shattered, much to the delight of the local press. Including those given passes, primarily workmen and the military, 19.7 million people attended in seven months, with the grounds closed on Sundays. On September 15, St. Louis Day, 404,450 people came through the turnstiles. Francis claimed that Chicago's larger attendance (more than 20 million) was due solely to its having more than twice as many people in 1893 as St. Louis had in 1904. More than half of St. Louis's customers had come from elsewhere, while 70 percent of Chicago's crowds were local people. The Pacific Coast had sent three times as many to St. Louis, and the number of foreign guests was also much larger. True to an ancient local tradition, Mayor Wells announced that the Louisiana Purchase Exposition had also drawn more than 20 million, a figure he arrived at by counting the thousands of concession and pavilion people who left and returned to the grounds each Sunday.

Another Exposition bonus was the swarm of conventioneers. Local fraternal, business, and professional groups had worked diligently to bring the national meetings to the city in 1904. The biggest plums, each with five-figure attendance, were the National Democratic and the National Education Association's conventions, but there were 153 others, including the World Congress of Arts and Science, the World Press Parliament, the National Federation of Women's Clubs, the Ancient Order of Hibernians, the Catholic Total Abstinence Union, and the National Nut Grower's Association.

To the surprise and delight of its planners, the St. Louis World's Fair finished in the black. Receipts from all sources, including the national and municipal subventions, came to $32.16 million. Construction expenditures, not including the federal, state, foreign, and concession buildings, amounted to $17 million; the power plant cost more than $2 million; repayment of short-term loans over $5 million; and rental fees to Washington University, $750,000. Other rental charges and expenses for sewers, water, a security force, park

Jefferson Memorial Building. *Built with the profits from the exposition as a memorial to Jefferson and the Louisiana Purchase, the Jefferson Memorial provided a modern home for the Missouri Historical Society and the records of the Exposition Company. Photograph by Emil Boehl, 1913. MHS-PP.*

St. Louis Art Museum. *The central portion of the exposition's Palace of Art was designed as a permanent structure for the city's Art Museum. Photograph, ca. 1906. MHS-PP.*

restoration, and a host of smaller items left a balance of more than six hundred thousand dollars.

In 1909, at Francis's request, Congress and the city relinquished all claims upon this surplus with the understanding that it would be used to erect a monument to Thomas Jefferson. In 1911 Francis laid the cornerstone for the magnificent Jefferson Memorial, a granite and Bedford limestone building featuring a statue of Jefferson flanked by its two wings. The Missouri Historical Society, founded in 1866 by the business and professional elite, which had already collected many valuable documents relating to the Louisiana Territory and Purchase, was to be housed in the Memorial. Isaac Taylor, the Exposition's Director of Works, drew the plans for the building, which was completed at a cost of $484,000 and turned over to the city in 1913. The society, a private corporation which had abandoned its dilapidated quarters at Sixteenth and Locust two years earlier, moved in promptly, and its excellent research library, manuscript collections, and museum have become one of the community's major assets.

Other permanent bequests of the Exposition Company were the Art Museum (the Palace of Fine Arts less its temporary wings), which was operated jointly by the company and Washington University until 1909, when it was accepted by the city; the gigantic bronze equestrian statue of Saint Louis the Crusader on Art Hill, a reproduction of the plaster version that had stood near the main gate during the Fair; four buildings at Washington University, built before the Fair by the Exposition Company with the $750,000 due the university for the use of its campus; the World's Fair Pavilion, erected after the Fair on the site of the Missouri Pavilion as a public shelter house; and the giant birdcage, which now graces the St. Louis Zoo. Forest Park itself was vastly changed. Under the direction of George Kessler of Kansas City, the Exposition's landscape architect who had designed the fine parkway and boulevard system in Kansas City, the swampy wilderness near the west end of the park, where one party of dignitaries had been lost for hours in 1901, had been cleared and drained. Thousands of trees were replanted but with a regularity that left long vistas of grassland where the palaces had been. A permanent system of paved roads, underground water pipes, drinking fountains, sewers, and a chain of five lakes also remained in place. Not many regretted these changes.

In the longer perspective, the heritage of the Exposition was mixed. Officially, its chief thrust had been education, as expressed by Helen Keller in a speech at the Fair in October 1904: "The Louisiana Purchase Exposition is a great manifestation of all the forces of enlightenment and all of man's thousand torches burning together. The value of everything here . . . is educational . . . what its distinguished founder intended it to be—a world's university." In this respect the Fair's influence is difficult to measure, though it may be significant that Governor Folk signed the state's first compulsory school attendance law, for children between eight and fourteen, in April 1905. Rolla Wells wrote in 1933 that the Fair had been "in its incomparable splendor and magnitude, one of the greatest expositions ever held. It left an indelible impression of rare beauty and human triumph. The . . . entrancing picture lingered with everyone as lasting treasures. . . ." In 1906 the mayor attributed to the Fair's momentum an additional $12 million in investments in St. Louis industry and a $50 million increase in bank deposits. It had created "a solidarity of movement" in the community, Wells believed. W. M. Reedy agreed that the Fair had triggered a civic revival, though he was to have second thoughts within a few years when the clutch of the Big Cinch seemed stronger than ever. The *Post-Dispatch* was so delighted that it presented both Joseph W. Folk and D. R. Francis, who hardly spoke to each other, with silver loving cups, noting that "on weekdays we read about the horrors Folk had uncovered and on Sunday we watched the progress of the Fair."

On the other hand, the tremendous one-shot effort destroyed the city's annual fall festivities except for the Veiled Prophet's visit. The Agricultural and Mechanical Fair and the Exposition were gone, never to return; as if having done the almost impossible, the city would not try anything less. This cost the city a valuable link with its hinterland. From still another viewpoint, St. Louis novelist Winston Churchill wrote in 1918 that while the Fair had shown that St. Louis could handle great projects, "if the city had spent all that money that it spent on the fair on city planning commission recommendations . . . the results would have shown substantial benefits more enduring."

Perhaps so, but whether the Fair was responsible or not, its decade was one of substantial if not spectacular growth. St. Louis was still the nation's fourth city in 1910, its population having increased by 19.4 percent to 687,029. Capital invested in manufacturing had grown by 15 percent to $269.3 million, and value of manufactured products by 79 percent to $430.2 million. Those more than ten years of age in gainful employment had increased by 30.7 percent to 320,714. Male employment had risen by 23.7 percent to 190,842; and female by 42.4 percent to 77,628. One British visitor during the Fair reported that the city's most striking quality was the large number of brisk, bright, and competent young women at work in downtown businesses.

Whether the New St. Louis was real remained to be seen, but in the haunting realms of nostalgia the Louisiana Purchase Exposition would never die. "Meet Me in St. Louis," a popular song at the Fair which caught on nationally, was made immortal by Judy Garland in a movie of the same name in 1944. As Stephen Raiche has put it, "for seven months in 1904, St. Louis had become the most cosmopolitan city on earth." In 1960, C. R. Leighton, a descendant of one of the leaders of the New St. Louis movement, published "The Year St. Louis Enchanted the World" in *Harper's*. In 1979 the Missouri Historical Society, the guardian of two of the city's nostalgic treasures, the World's Fair and the Lindbergh legend, led the celebration of the Fair's seventy-fifth anniversary. Nonagenarians wistfully recalled the golden days of 1904 as St. Louis's and their own time of glory. The shrouded mists of the past seem scarcely worth the parting to those more concerned with brilliant halfbacks and four million dollar shortstops, but the underlying thrust remains the same—"Beat Chicago!" It has been done by stealing Lou Brock from them, for example, but never so well as in 1904, when the nation sang:

Meet Me in St. Louis, Louis [pronounced Looie]
Meet Me at the Fair
Don't Tell Me the Lights Are Shining
Anywhere but There . . .

10.
The Decline of the Inner City

In the glowing aftermath of the World's Fair, visions of glamorous growth danced before the eyes of St. Louis boosters. In December 1904 the "One Million Population" club gave symbolic emphasis to the Businessmen's League's primary goal: to stimulate growth and attract new industry through "scientific" honest government, reduced business taxes, and public improvements, chiefly the creation of a parkway and boulevard system. Mayo Fesler, the secretary of the Civic League, admitted that businessmen operated through organizations such as his because of the "distinctive prejudice existing . . . toward the interference of business in public affairs." The Civic League hoped that with its broader membership and somewhat more diverse goals, it could accomplish its purposes without being accused of ulterior motives. The league advocated "the City Beautiful" program, which provided for parkways, public playgrounds and baths, a riverside drive, clearing the dilapidated levee district (the old village) to make way for a civic center and new commercial development, and revision of the city charter.

John H. Gundlach, a north St. Louis Republican businessman and politician who was a member of the league's city plan committee, argued that successful cities must have a "democratic business leadership" working not only for commercial growth but also for better living conditions for everyone. He pointed to Kansas City, which had built a fine park and boulevard system that had in turn spurred the building of inexpensive new homes. Gundlach did not propose public slum clearance as a general rule, assuming that public improvements would encourage private investment in new housing. He thought some of the City Beautiful advocates were naive in assuming that West End boulevards, exclusive Places, and industrial growth would "compel the world's homage," when a visitor could not reach them without "twisting and turning through sections that suggest an abandoned village," with "tenement conditions which are a reproach to our intelligence, to our sense of humanity."

Luther Ely Smith, a successful Republican lawyer, believed with Gundlach that by a persistent application of energy, responsible leaders could produce a better city and a more just society. His persistent advocacy of a riverfront center led eventually to the creation

John H. Gundlach. *Gundlach, a realtor, was one of the driving forces of the Civic League, which proposed reforms based on Progressive ideas and City Beautiful notions of planning. One of his projects was the Pageant and Masque of St. Louis, from which came the Muny Opera. Photograph by J. C. Strauss, 1922. MHS-PP.*

of the Jefferson National Expansion Memorial, but initially he emphasized immediate people-oriented projects such as playgrounds. In the latter he was associated with Charlotte Rumbold, secretary of the Public Recreation Committee, a city agency appointed by the mayor from the ranks of socially concerned groups. In 1910 Rumbold was appointed with Jane Addams and others as officers of the Playground Association of America. As a thoroughgoing social-justice activist, Rumbold believed that the city was failing its people, especially the poor, and that all social problems could be solved by rational, democratic means.

Labor unions, socialists, and the Wednesday Club, an elite women's group, were active in the playground movement; the last believed that providing the poor with "breathing spaces" would reduce crime. By 1901 the club had established summer playgrounds that its members supervised, and in 1903 the Civic League opened six playgrounds in a twenty-four-block slum area between Sixth and Tenth Streets, where directed activities and free play took place. By the end of Mayor Wells's second term, in 1909, the city had by purchase or donation acquired an additional sixteen parks and playgrounds with a total area of 152 acres, costing $1.43 million. Except for the 129-acre Fairgrounds Park at Grand and Natural Bridge, they ranged in size from one-tenth of an acre to five acres. The wealthy Philip Scanlan, a Christy descendant who was director of parks after 1906, turned them over to the people. Mayor Wells admiringly credited Scanlan with having "no caste prejudice" and with being "equally esteemed in the downtown tenement localities and the fashionable clubs." He installed baseball diamonds and tennis courts in Fairgrounds and Forest Parks and removed the "Keep off the grass" signs in all of the parks. In a self-congratulatory mood, Wells wrote that never had the wealthy "mingled with" and "shown such conscientious interest" in the poor and their recreational needs, and never had the latter so much appreciated the generosity of the rich.

If the well-meaning, paternalistic Wells believed that the recreational programs had substantially changed the public attitude toward elite leadership, he was doomed to disappointment. These palliatives may indeed have earned the gratitude of the recent immigrants and blacks who lived in the downtown fringes, but the articulate middle- and laboring-class ethnics of the north and south sides, where unionism flourished and socialism and the single-tax movement had taken root, remained adamantly opposed to the Big Cinch. The issues about which this opposition coalesced were the municipal free bridge, which it favored, and charter revision, which it opposed.

Irrespective of party or economic status, St. Louisans had long resented the "bridge arbitrary," through which the Terminal Railroad Association levied tribute upon railroad freight, passengers, and wagon traffic. Strictly speaking, the arbitrary was a levy on shippers and consumers as their share of the operational and capital costs of the bridge, but in St. Louis the charge was larger than necessary for these purposes. The Terminal Railroad Association belonged to the railroads, and it was an additional source of profit to them. Averaging four cents a hundred pounds on freight, depending upon bulk and distance, the arbitrary could represent as much as a third of the cost of transportation, even from several hundred miles to the east. Not only did it raise the price of goods, it diverted some through traffic away from the city. Local shippers had long argued that the railroads should absorb the arbitrary in their overall rate structure, but the Interstate Commerce Commission had approved the existing system. Thus local shippers had to swallow the extra charge in order to compete in eastern markets, and St. Louis firms had to charge higher prices for eastern goods. Because it affected everyone, the extra cost of Illinois soft coal had been an especially sore point for decades. As previously noted, the arbitrary had been largely responsible for the development of heavy industry on the east side. Granite City, Illinois, for example, owed its existence chiefly to the arbitrary. The Niedringhauses had founded the city and located their American Stamping Company plant there, and

Edward Goltra's and Rolla Wells's American Steel Foundry Company mills were in Granite City.

Given the general dislike of the arbitrary, the issue became how to get rid of it. David R. Francis and others had built the Merchants' Bridge to break the monopoly, but they could not force the railroads to use it; and during the Panic of 1893, they sold it to the Terminal Railroad to save their financial skins. Lee Meriwether's Public Ownership Party advocated a municipal free bridge in 1901, and in 1905 the *Post-Dispatch* joined the cause. In April voters rejected a $9 million bond issue for a city hospital, an insane asylum, extension of public sewers, and Kingshighway Boulevard. Wells blamed this defeat on "the free-bridge cyclone," voters chanted "no bridge, no bonds," and the *Globe-Democrat*, speaking for many small businessmen and workers, blasted the "30 or 40 persons" who thought they were the true St. Louisans whose "predatory schemes" were hatched under the pretext of serving the public. Currently, said the *Globe*, this cabal was upset over the failure of a bond issue providing "millions for one small section of the city. . . ."

Soon after the bond issue's defeat, Mayor Wells appointed a Municipal Bridge and Terminal Commission made up of engineers, big shippers such as Hugh McKittrick, bankers, and himself to negotiate with the railroads. In response to a suggestion that the commission should sample public opinion, Wells snorted that he would not listen to the views of "every crank in the city." After several meetings, which antagonized the press because they were secret, the parties reached an agreement. St. Louis would be a freight-rate basing point, and the arbitrary differential over East St. Louis was cut in half. Toll rates on coal were cut by one-third, a savings of $160,000 a year, and other freight reductions amounted to $800,000 a year. Some St. Louis shippers did not want the total abolition of the arbitrary, because it would eliminate their advantage over eastern competitors for the western trade. The commission then suggested that the city make land available for a massive freight terminal and depot on the levee south of the Eads Bridge and other smaller terminals to be scattered through the greater St. Louis terminal district. The railroads were receptive to this plan, which the engineers claimed would give St. Louis "the greatest terminal system in the world."

The railroads were not only committed to huge expenditures on land and buildings, but they also proposed to construct a four-track cantilever railroad bridge, probably at Poplar Street. The Businessmen's League (Chamber of Commerce after 1916) and the Merchants' Exchange endorsed this plan, but the municipal assembly, in response to the overwhelming free-bridge sentiment, refused to enact the necessary ordinances. Middle-class voters saw the plan as the ultimate Big Cinch scheme, designed to line the pockets of big railroad stock and bondholders such as Francis, John Scullin, and Wells himself, and bankers like Festus Wade, Edwards Whittaker, and Julius Walsh. Wells undoubtedly believed that he was working in the public interest as well as private interests, and in retrospect it seems that he was. But he and his colleagues never understood the symbolic importance of the free bridge to the neighborhoods, who felt that they had been systematically robbed by downtown interests and were determined to put a stop to it. Neither side could have had an inkling of the vast changes to come in transportation, but in the meantime the railroad expansion scheme would have accelerated economic growth and employment. Only a few such as Luther Ely Smith objected to the terminal as an obstacle to the restoration of esthetic values to the riverfront.

When the bond-issue proposal was resubmitted, this time for $11.2 million, the assembly set aside $3.5 million for bridge construction. The bonds were approved by the necessary two-thirds of the voters in June 1906. W. M. Reedy of *The Mirror*, by this time a confirmed single-taxer, opposed the planners, making both economic and esthetic objections to the arbitrary "settlement" and the terminal plan. He had become a friend of the blueblood rebel Harry Turner, a strange alliance of boosterism and Creole nostalgia. Several of those who romanticized the "leisurely" southern and Creole past (one part fact and nine parts imagination) made common cause with the Germans and working-class free-bridge advocates. Local novelist Kate Chopin, once the "littlest rebel," of Creole (Charleville) and Old Irish descent and who the *Republic* in 1910 called the "most brilliant, distinguished, and interesting woman who ever graced St. Louis," thought the common laborer superior to the cold-hearted, money-grubbing monsters who devised the terminal scheme, the "short, round, blond, and bald" types who dominated the city.

Wells and the Businessmen's League continued to fight the free bridge even after the bond issue passed, but the tide was running against them. In 1910 Roger Baldwin, a professor of sociology at Washington University, who later founded the American Civil Liberties Union, replaced Mayo Fesler as Civic League secretary. Baldwin, John Gundlach, Luther Ely Smith, and other dissident north and south side businessmen and lawyers were joined by the southern-oriented former "Solar Walker" attorney Frederick Judson in bringing the Civic League around to the popular side of the bridge controversy. Big businessmen dropped out as Baldwin, Gundlach, social-gospel ministers such as Willard Boyd, and other social-justice advocates changed the league's emphasis from honest, efficient government, public improvements, and growth to "Democratizing the city instead of just a city beautiful." As Roger Baldwin put it in 1915, the city's "entire progress" had been shaped by the free-bridge issue, "for it has been the chief local issue in the country-wide struggle between monopoly and the people. . . . The issue of the 'Big Cinch versus the people' came to the front. . . ." And again in 1967, in a letter to Jack Muraskin: "Following the end of overt graft . . . it was influence and pressure rather than corruption that kept the business interest dominant."

In 1912 Baldwin led in organizing the Civic Federation, which united business, professional, labor, and religious groups in the reform movement. He felt that success would come only if a wide variety of interests were convinced that reform would benefit them directly as well as improve the city. Real estate man John Gundlach, Civic League president in 1914, told his colleagues that overall planning would provide terminal facilities, low taxation, jobs, and advantages to real estate firms. Rolla Wells had charged that the desire of real estate operators to gouge the city for land for the bridge approaches was the prime mover in the free-bridge crusade.

By a margin of seven to one, voters approved another $2.75 million in bridge bonds in 1914, and in 1923 the project still required another $1.5 million. The highway section of the bridge opened in 1917, and in the following year railroads could use it but seldom did, primarily because additional approaches were needed both in the Chouteau Avenue area and on the east side. To complete the approaches, the city called on the Terminal Association to supply $3.25 million, in return for which it could use the bridge without charge until it had recovered this amount. Thereafter, tolls were to be collected by the city. The net effect was as if the bridge arbitrary had been continued, but under municipal auspices. The reformers had won, but the "free bridge" was not free except on the vehicle level; the big freight terminals were still across the river; the maintenance bill was nearly $1 million annually; and, including interest, the project had cost nearly $17 million by 1933. After the Terminal Railroad and the city had disagreed over the details of their arrangement, a fourth bond issue was floated in 1935. Rolla Wells, in retirement in 1933 after many years with the Federal Reserve System, was still bitter about the "bridge folly." In 1940 the through lines began to use the Municipal Bridge regularly.

In 1908 the Civic League began a campaign for a new city charter, which would institutionalize Wells's "business government," chiefly through a strong mayor and a unicameral legislature. Six Democrats and six Republicans, selected by their party organizations from the business and legal elite, were elected to the Board of Freeholders, which would write the charter. They selected as their chairman Frederick W. Lehmann, attorney for the United Railways transit monopoly and the Terminal Railroad. After eighteen months of deliberation the board released its handiwork, subject to the vote of the people on January 31, 1911. A broad coalition of labor, socialists, Germans, moderate reformers, and small businessmen immediately mounted a root-and-branch attack on the proposed charter. The People's League, headed by Dr. William P. Hill, plastered the city with broadsides denouncing the "Plutocratic-Oligarchic" plot to make the people "serfs of the Big Cinch." The opponents feared the vast expansion of the mayor's appointive powers and thought the elimination of the House of Delegates in favor of a "plutocratic" fifteen-member council elected at-large would deny ordinary people access to their government. They liked neither the abolition of the elective auditor's office nor the creation of an appointive civil service commission. Above all, the reformers in the opposition were angered by the absence of workable initiative, referendum, and recall provisions. It would have been hard to devise a document less appealing to voters, as the 65,324 to 24,817 margin of defeat demonstrated. It failed by three to one in the Democratic Irish wards, and by as high as eleven to one in the more numerous German Republican areas. Only in the silk-stocking twenty-sixth and twenty-eighth and transitional twenty-fourth did the proposal carry. The voters had rejected the endorsements of both major party organizations and Republican mayor F. H. Kriesmann, but neither party had tried to impose discipline in the wards.

City Beautiful–scientific government planners had some rethinking to do. Somehow a sense of mission and unity had to be created. In October 1909, in emulation of Boston, which the *Post-Dispatch* claimed had responded to St. Louis's inroads into its shoe business by marking "another batch of historic spots, and sending picture postcards of them to its customers," the Million Population Club, the Civic League, the Missouri Historical Society, and various business organizations had sponsored a week-long celebration of St. Louis's incorporation as a town. It was a "royal purple week," said the *Globe-Democrat*, with hundreds of mayors and tens of thousands of other visitors joining St. Louisans to view a series of pageants portraying the major events of the city's history, from the arrivals of Laclède and Piernas to the World's Fair. A fur-trade episode afforded the opportunity to remind the spectators that St. Louis was still the largest primary fur market. Among the extra attractions, some viewed by crowds estimated at three hundred thousand, were the U.S. navy torpedo-boat flotilla, an industrial parade, an aeroplane flight by Glenn Curtiss, a dirigible race, and a balloon race for distance, the last nearly ending in tragedy when north Missouri farmers, mistaking the low-flying racers for advertising balloons carrying ten-dollar bills, blasted away at them with shotguns.

Promotional articles carried the centennial message to five thousand newspapers on five continents, and the local press believed that the affair had instilled a sense of civic pride. The *Globe-Democrat* commented that the people were united by the drama of the early settlers and that the marking of twenty-one historic sites, such as Fort San Carlos and the Laclède-Chouteau home, had produced "a marvelous effect." But like the Veiled Prophet ceremonies, which were a part of the celebration, the booster effort was to most people primarily an interesting spectacle, the plaything of the rich.

After the 1911 charter fiasco, the now more democratically oriented Civic League took over the unity effort, determined to involve as many elements of the community as possible. Led by Charlotte Rumbold, Luther Ely Smith, John Gundlach, and Roger Baldwin and supported by the Missouri Historical Society and the Businessmen's League, the reformers involved seven thousand people in an ambitious historical drama, the sesquicentennial Pageant and Masque of May 28–June 1, 1914. As Donald Oster has written, the Pageant was intended to present a clear picture of the reasons for the city's existence and growth, to "explain the city to itself," as Percy MacKaye, the drama's writer-director, put it. The French and older American families were pleased with the inevitable emphasis upon their ancestors, and for a small fee families could furnish a family history and be enrolled in the native-born registry, with the chance that one's ancestors would be included in the Pageant. Businessmen saw the Pageant and Masque as an opportunity to advertise the city and its products and as a part of the battle to retain St. Louis's rank as the fourth city against the onslaughts of Boston and Cleveland, which had crowded closer in the 1910 census.

As a part of the fund-raising effort, Charles A. Stix wrote, "as a business proposition alone the Pageant appeals to everyone who thoroughly understands its immense possibilities." Oster suggests that the urban progressives of the newer upper class were motivated in their community efforts by their wish to replace the decentralized, horse-trading, middle- and lower-class political system by a centralized, efficient, professional government that was quick to respond to civic needs, especially as defined by themselves. Thus, the Pageant's organizers thought it wise to delay the 1914 charter election

The Pageant and Masque of St. Louis. *This view is from the back of the stage set toward the crowd on Art Hill. Photograph by E. Warwick Harmon, 1914. MHS-PP.*

until after the sesquicentennial celebration's work was done. There was more to it, of course; Rumbold and Baldwin, and to a lesser degree Gundlach and Smith, really wanted a more democratic city, and not just in the political sense. Rumbold's slogan, "If We Play Together, We Will Work Together," was a basic tenet of the Pageant and Masque.

Percy MacKaye, an experienced eastern playwright who had been recruited for the sesquicentennial drama by Rumbold, believed in the socially conscious theater. Industrialization having destroyed much of the satisfaction in work, the only hope for self-fulfillment lay in participatory arts and recreation. Intrigued by St. Louis's "Mound City" nickname, he visited the then little-appreciated Cahokia Mounds, which so impressed him that he put the mound-builders at the center of a gigantic Masque presented in a great natural amphitheater below Art Hill in Forest Park. The stage was 880 feet wide in front by 200 feet deep. The Pageant, written by Thomas Wood Stevens, featured the mound builders, the Osages, the black-gowned Marquette, LaSalle claiming the valley for France, Chouteau and Taillon building Laclède's village, Laclède admonishing the Missouris, St. Ange confirming Laclède's grants of land, Piernas taking over for Spain, the 1780 Indian attack with the usual erroneous portrayal of de Leyba, Stoddard accepting upper Louisiana from DeLassus, Gratiot urging loyalty to the United States, Lewis and Clark, Lafayette's visit, Thomas Hart Benton, the Mexican War, Sanitary Commission nurses caring for the Civil War wounded, and finally an exultant crowd greeting the news of peace.

MacKaye's Masque was a visual and aural spectacular presenting the forces of nature, geography, history, and the human spirit. Individuals represented Cahokia, Mississippi, Saint Louis, the Pioneer, Gold the villain with his minions War and Poverty, and the great cities: Washington representing the nation, New York the eastern sea, Chicago the lakes, New Orleans the rivers, Denver the mountains, and Honolulu the islands. In the foreground was the great river with real, rushing water, beyond which lay a vast plaza dominated by a large flattened mound topped by a ruined shrine. Behind the screen at the rear was a five hundred-voice chorus and a one hundred-piece orchestra, and hundreds of dancers and actors swarmed over the stage.

Cahokia began the Masque with a reflection on past glory and a premonition of death. Then the mighty Mississippi entered, carrying a white child. Cahokia chanted, "Ah, he is stripling, bold and wildly fair; My dream is a strong child and shall restore me!" The wild forces of nature threatened the child, but he was saved by a host of Frenchmen and Spaniards, led by the Knight, the Trapper, and the Priest, all come to do the child homage. To the kneeling child, the Priest said, "Now in the name of Christ . . . Rise and receive thy name: Rise–Saint Louis." Thousands of voices roared "Saint Louis," as a "colossal cross" burned with a white fire. Cahokia departed, saying, "For I am old, old-forgotten. But not my dream. My dream is a strong child, and shall survive me." Then came a host, led by the Pioneer, shouting, "Here are fields waiting to sow; here are forests to fell, floods to span, mines to shaft, blood to spill, wives to wed. . . . Lead us, Saint Louis." Saint Louis responded, "Who shall defy us?"

Then an earthquake felled the Pioneers. A "tall athletic form" emerged, shouting, "We the earth spirits defy you." Saint Louis asked, "What are you?" "Gold, I am Gold. I am the . . . Master and maker of men." Then Saint Louis chose the Pioneer to wrestle with Gold. After Gold had won the first fall, Saint Louis handed his champion a star, saying, "None can down Gold who fights for himself. Fight for our star!" Gold was vanquished, but he shouted that he would return to forge new chains. Next came the immigrants, singing "Give welcome to the World Adventurers, Who come to blend their blood and toil with yours. . . ." Again Saint Louis cried, "Who shall defy us now?"

Amid flame and thunder, a rider in blood-red mail rode in at the head of a demon horde, boasting "War—War defies!" The World Adventurer and the Pioneers routed the horde, but Gold returned with Poverty and gained the crest of the mound. Saint Louis then called upon the League of Cities, each played by its representative to the Pageant and Masque. The league came forward with its battalions of industry, science, the professions, and the arts, the last including the playgrounds, the dance, and the civic theatre. At St. Louis's request, the child Love ascended the mound, and Gold knelt before him as his servant. With Love in the temple and the elements subdued, Saint Louis and the League of Cities closed the Masque with a triumphant chorus: "Out of the formless void, Beauty and order are born; One for all, all in one, We wheel in the joy of our dance. Brother with brother sharing our light, Build we new worlds with ancient fire!"

MacKaye had invoked all the symbols: the golden age of the garden (Cahokia), the triumph of good over evil, the doctrine of progress, and the heavenly city of the eighteenth-century philosophers. With love and unity, the League of Cities would march to the just and beautiful society, led by St. Louis. The Pageant and Masque's organizers and city boosters were ecstatic; more than 455,000 people had seen the production in five nights, and 7,700 had appeared in it in various capacities. Such phrases as "greatest city in the nation," "inherent capacity for united action," and "new spirit of cooperation" floated about. John Gundlach believed that the production had brought "a sustained public spirit for a more humane city"; and Roger Baldwin credited the "great democratic civic pageant and masque" with having assured victory in the charter election a few weeks later.

St. Louis had made another major effort to enhance its image and improve the quality of life, but tangible results were elusive. There was no sustained participatory arts program. Profits from the Pageant were used to construct another amphitheater, much smaller than George Kessler's one-hundred-thousand-seat giant, at another location in Forest Park, but the civic theatre had a short life. After producing *As You Like It* in 1916, with one thousand local and a few professional actors, the new Municipal Theatre's major effort was to establish the Municipal Opera in 1919. This outdoor summer amenity became an ornament to the city, but its professional road-show emphasis was a far cry from the Rumbold-MacKaye concept, another spectacle, not even a homegrown one.

On the other hand, the recreation and playgrounds program, spurred by the same impulse as the Pageant and Masque, thrived mightily under the leadership of Rumbold and Dwight F. Davis, the former national doubles tennis champion who had succeeded Philip

Dwight F. Davis. *Davis's term as parks commissioner (1911–15) saw an expanded emphasis on recreational programs and park uses. Following service in World War I, he became secretary of war under President Coolidge. Photograph by Pirie McDonald, 1917. MHS-PP.*

Scanlan as parks commissioner. New playgrounds, parks, pools, and baths were opened and equipped, and by the end of Davis's tenure in 1914, attendance averaged several million a year, including nearly one hundred thousand at the tennis courts. In Forest Park, the middle class could even play golf, the rich man's game. The Triple-A nine-hole course, a private club which had been located first near the west end of the park, had moved to seventy acres in the southeastern section to make room for the World's Fair. It operated under a permit from the city and subsequently became semi-public. The long vistas provided by George Kessler's replanting program after the Fair had made the northwestern section ideal for golf, and Davis, who was as committed to the strenuous life as Theodore Roosevelt, constructed an eighteen-hole public course where the great exposition palaces had stood. Much later the commitment of so much of the park's area to golf created considerable controversy, but Davis thought any healthy recreational use of the parks that did not require the erection of buildings was compatible with their purposes.

Thus, Davis was not enthused about building a municipal zoo in Forest Park. A zoological gardens had been established at the Fairgrounds by Julius Walsh in the 1870s, and when the collection was sold in 1891, a few animals were purchased by local citizens and housed in Forest Park. In 1910, at the instigation of shirt manufacturer Cortlandt Harris and taxidermist Frank Schwarz, the St. Louis

Zoological Society was organized with Professor James F. Abbott of
Washington University as president. Broker George Dieckman became
interested in 1911 and began a whirlwind collection campaign with his
own money, apparently believing that a glut of animals would force
the city to build a zoo. Davis reported in 1912 that with the recent
addition of a camel and a llama, the small space in the park was
overcrowded. He believed that a zoo should be built, but preferably
not in a city park. If it were to be in a park, the collection should be
limited to deer and other range animals not requiring buildings.

Several sites were suggested for a zoo, but most people preferred the
central location at Forest Park, in the area of the birdcage sold to the city
for six thousand dollars by the Smithsonian Institution after the World's
Fair. During his successful mayoral campaign in 1913, Republican
Henry Kiel endorsed a Forest Park zoo, and the press backed the plan. In
November 1913, the Municipal Assembly set aside seventy-seven acres
in the park and established a zoo board of control. Still opposed to
invading the park with more buildings, Davis urged Kiel to veto the bill,
arguing that it would create conflicting jurisdictions within the park. As
the *Post-Dispatch* reported it, the mayor told Davis, "the people of
St. Louis want a zoo awfully bad. . . . They don't know whether you
cut the grass or not—and they don't give a damn. What the people want
is a lot of elephants, lions, tigers, and monkeys. . . ."

Animals kept pouring in, though there was little money for
maintenance and shelter, and by 1914 there were bison; elk; a camel; a
llama; zebras; twenty-two deer; a kangaroo; twelve monkeys; polar,
grizzly, black, and cinnamon bears; mountain lions; a dozen small
American animals; and two dozen varieties of birds. Conditions were
miserable, the animals were dying, and in 1915 Health Commissioner
Max Starkloff called the zoo "a menace to the public and the animals'
health." George Dieckman and others haunted the state legislature
until, at the end of the 1915 session, it passed St. Louis Senator
Michael Kinney's bill authorizing the city to levy a one-fifth mill tax
to support the zoo, subject to the approval of the voters. The bill
provided for a board of control, and the zoo was to be "forever free to
the usage of the inhabitants."

There was considerable opposition to the zoo tax, but George
Dieckman had persuaded Superintendent Ben Blewett to allow
schoolchildren to contribute their pennies for the purchase of an
elephant. They raised $2,385 and, with another $3,000 added by the
board, purchased a female elephant. To meet a commitment to name
the young animal for school board president James Harper without
violating the facts, she was dubbed "Miss Jim." She was installed at
the zoo in April 1916, and in October, with the assistance of battalions

Bear Cage, St. Louis Zoological Garden. *These barred cages housed the Zoo's bears from 1906 until 1921, when the first of the current Bear Pits were opened. Photograph by O. C. Conkling, 1918. MHS-PP.*

of little partisans, the zoo tax passed by nearly a two-to-one margin. The widely admired and copied bear pits were completed in 1919, after Director George Vierheller had conferred with the Hagenbecks in Germany, and under his leadership for the next four decades, the zoo earned a reputation as one of the finest in the world. Its superb spaciousness and design, the remarkable blending of its structure into the natural setting—all have earned the plaudits of experts. In no way is it an ugly intrusion into the park, perhaps a tribute to Dwight Davis's early objections.

Charter revision finally succeeded in 1914, but only after a major concession had been made by the freeholders. Initiative, referendum, and recall were installed to appease the Baldwin-Gundlach Civic League reformers, but even with this provision and the endorsements of the major parties, the charter met strong opposition. The Pageant and Masque undoubtedly helped, and the reform support was crucial, but many voters still regarded revision as a self-serving Big Cinch scheme. Initiative, referendum, recall, and the merit system seemed newfangled and threatening to ward politicians and their constituents.

In the predominantly black river wards, the charter was rejected, despite the probability that Republicans would dominate the unicameral council. To the west, where the Negro Civic League and the

Nineteenth Ward Republican Club were influential, blacks gave the charter solid majorities. Even though it was supported by the German-American Alliance and Edward Preetorius of the *Westliche Post*, the charter lost in ten of the twelve predominantly German wards, in some by margins of three to one. The well-to-do highly assimilated Germans of the thirteenth and fourteenth (southwestern) wards gave the charter a margin of 2,100, but the total German-areas vote was 15,641 for and 21,760 against. This negative vote reflected in part the frustrations of the Socialists, who could never hope to win an aldermanic seat in an at-large electoral system, but even more telling was the opposition of brewer Henry Kolkschneider's Taxpayers' League, which distributed handbills predicting higher taxes to pay for the City Beautiful schemes of the charter's elite proponents. W. M. Reedy, still smarting over the lopsided rejection of the Single Tax by Missouri's voters in 1912 and thoroughly alienated from the business leadership despite his active support of the Pageant and Masque, combined conviction with profit by writing Kolkschneider's material for pay.

Despite the probability that the at-large provision would guarantee a Republican monopoly of the council, especially with the influx of blacks to the city, the Irish Democrats favored the charter by a small majority. But it was the heavy vote in the western silk-stocking wards that squeezed the charter through by a citywide tally of 46,839 to 44,158. Not until twenty-five years later, in 1941, was the charter amended to provide for representation by wards (twenty-eight in all), plus an aldermanic president elected at-large.

Ironically, the first use of the "reform" provisions of the new charter was to initiate a reactionary racial policy. Attitudes toward blacks in St. Louis had not been especially hostile since Reconstruction. As described by one observer, the white point of view was "one of patient endurance toward an inferior but necessary creature." Race conflict had been minimal because the ratio of blacks to the population had remained at a stable 6 percent for four decades. With minor exceptions, blacks had stayed in place in the central river wards and downtown fringes, and those who ventured beyond Eighteenth Street moved into declining "boarding house" areas just being vacated by ethnic minorities. The Deep South migrants occupied vacant houses and shacks that no one else wanted in the downtown wards, and in the black community itself there was a gulf between old St. Louisans and the scorned and often illiterate "Mississippi" types. There were fairly well-defined social distinctions among St. Louis blacks, with the upper strata including the professional, business, and skilled laboring classes. Occupation, income, and education were especially important, with light color and antebellum St. Louis origins (especially free black origins) considered assets. Newcomers had to be well-educated and willing to conform to the existing social structure to be accepted.

Legally, the pattern of segregation was inconsistent. Schools were segregated, but libraries were not. Blacks were excluded from white hotels, restaurants, and barber shops (except as barbers), but they rode crowded department store elevators and attended the legitimate theatre—if they cared to squint at the stage from the peanut gallery. They could sit where they pleased on the streetcars, but most whites would rather stand than sit by them. The arrival of Poles and southern Europeans since the late 1880s had not moderated white attitudes. Not only did the immigrants adopt the prevailing prejudices, they tended to feel them more intensely as they competed with blacks for jobs. Despite the importance of the black vote to the Republican Party, German attitudes toward blacks had deteriorated to some extent with the decline of Radical idealism in the 1870s.

After one of the most violent decades in American history, Baltimore passed a residential segregation law in 1910, and many other southern and border-state cities had followed suit by 1915. In St. Louis, neighborhood associations in white communities, which were close to black areas, organized the United Welfare Association (UWA) in 1911, found a powerful, well-heeled ally in the Real Estate Exchange, and began a persistent campaign for a segregation ordinance. After repeated rejections by the Municipal Assembly, the UWA circulated an initiative petition in 1915 to enact "an ordinance to prevent ill feeling, conflict and collision between the white and colored races" by requiring "the use of separate blocks for residence" and mandating segregation in churches and dance halls. The UWA was not prejudiced, it claimed, it only sought the greatest good for the greatest number by protecting property values. Presumably to demonstrate this absence of prejudice, it collected signatures in front of theaters that were showing D. W. Griffith's *Birth of a Nation*, a grossly distorted film version of Reconstruction that portrayed black men as beasts who lusted after white women. By early December 1915, the UWA had obtained the signatures of the 10 percent of the registered voters required for the petition, and the election was set for the following February 29.

Roger Baldwin coordinated the activities of the several committees that were formed to oppose the Baltimore Law. Of these the most active was the National Association for the Advancement of

LOOK At These Homes NOW!

An entire block ruined by negro invasion. Every house marked "X" now occupied by negroes. ACTUAL PHOTOGRAPH OF 4300 WEST BELLE PLACE.

SAVE YOUR HOME! VOTE FOR SEGREGATION!

 73

Literature such as this flier mailed by the United Welfare Association in 1916 promoted St. Louis's residential segregation ordinance, passed later that year but thrown out by the courts in 1917. MHS Archives.

Colored People (NAACP), led in St. Louis by Charles Pitman, Homer G. Phillips, George L. Vaughn, and Thomas A. Curtis. Kathryn Johnson of the national office organized public meetings and house-to-house canvasses. Literature was distributed attacking segregation as moral slavery, dangerous and un-American. Daniel R. Fitzpatrick's "The Great Divide," a *Post-Dispatch* cartoon portraying blacks and whites glaring over an alley at each other, was disseminated widely in a brochure. In its major effort, the NAACP filed a lawsuit charging that legislation by initiative petition was unconstitutional. Charles Pitman appeared as the plaintiff, represented in court by Phillips and Vaughn, but the court ruled against them.

As the election neared, segregationists presented their case as a matter of racial pride and patriotism. Polish-American organizations formally endorsed this position on January 28. One segregationist warrior asked, "How can we afford to let the Negro whip the white man in this election?" Blacks were rumored to be driving to the registration center in limousines by the thousands, some of them supposedly from Memphis. Against this drive, twenty-three of the twenty-eight aldermen and Mayor Kiel publicly aired their views opposing the ordinance; the *Post-Dispatch*, the *Globe-Democrat*, and the *Argus* (a leading Black newspaper) attacked it vigorously and

D. R. Francis's *Republic* mildly; Congressman L. P. Dyer, of Radical Republican antecedents, spoke and wrote against it; the powerful Democratic state senator, Michael Kinney, had his troops circulating anti-ordinance handbills; and the Socialist Party and many Jewish leaders opposed it, the latter calling it a first step toward segregating all minorities. Kathryn Johnson's effort to enlist the Catholic hierarchy struck a snag when Father John McGuire, pastor of the St. Elizabeth's Negro parish, made it clear that he favored segregation. Reportedly, a number of priests felt otherwise, but it was only after Johnson had appealed to the papal delegate at Washington that Archbishop John Glennon came out publicly against the ordinance, too late to make a difference. The various Protestant ministers kept a low profile as well.

Despite the impressive public opposition, the segregationists were confident of victory, especially after a poll of the City Club membership showed a majority for the ordinance. One leader exulted that if the silk-stocking class, who were sheltered behind restrictive deed covenants excluding blacks, favored the ordinance, "you can count on the common people, living in homes they buy on the installment plan to be in favor of the measure." He was right. The first segregation law ever enacted anywhere by initiative petition passed by a vote of 52,220 to 17,877. The Republican leadership could not deliver the result it had promised its black constituency. Only the wards with large black populations, two of them in Mike Kinney's district, rejected the ordinance. Those areas on the rim of black settlement voted eight to one for segregation, and the elite western wards went four to one. In those German wards where Socialism was strongest, the eighth, ninth, and tenth, the margins were held to less than two to one.

Under the new law, no person of any race could move to a block where 75 percent of the residents were of another race. In a quick move to block its enforcement, the NAACP's Charles Pitman conferred with Colonel Wells Blodgett, a Union veteran who was an attorney for the Wabash Railroad. In a meeting which might have recalled one of General Frank Blair's staff sessions, Blodgett; Judge Leo Rassieur, who had headed both the Missouri and national organizations of the Grand Army of the Republic; Judge Selden P. Spencer; and the city's leading lawyer, Charles Nagel, who had been secretary of commerce and labor under Taft, agreed to seek a restraining order to prevent enforcement of the ordinance, for a fee of one dollar. Federal Judge D. P. Dyer, the Union veteran who had prosecuted the Whiskey Ring, issued a temporary injunction in April 1916. After the Supreme Court had declared a similar Louisville ordinance unconstitutional, Dyer made the injunction permanent in March 1918. The colonel had done in the segregationists, but the NAACP's victory was of little practical use. The rapid spread of private but legally enforcible restrictive covenants against selling houses to blacks effectively hemmed them in.

Ironically, the influx of southern blacks accelerated rapidly after the adoption of the segregation ordinance. War having virtually halted European immigration, northern industry drew black laborers to its industrial centers. To the southern newcomers, survival rather than the residential addresses of better-educated, upward-bound, cultural strangers was the immediate issue. Thousands of them had been recruited by railroad agents and East St. Louis officials, offering false promises of high wages and adequate shelter. The east side city was a sinkhole of municipal corruption; some of its officials owned brothels in the notorious "Valley" district, and special tax breaks were given to its biggest corporations, such as the Aluminum Ore Company and the Terminal Railroad's bridge, terminal, and ferry properties. The big meatpackers operated tax-free in National City, an enclave set aside

St. Louis Republic, Front Page, July 3, 1917. *Use of African American workers as strikebreakers led to horrifying scenes in East St. Louis as whites rioted, burned, and murdered blacks in the streets. St. Louis received refugees who fled across the Eads Bridge. MHS Library.*

for them for the purpose. They expected and received full East St. Louis services, however. The Chicago, St. Louis, and eastern capitalists who owned the industrial base of the east side paid its labor seventeen to twenty cents an hour, barely half of the prevailing area wages.

Workers at the Aluminum Ore Company had been on strike for many weeks by mid-summer 1917, but the plant had continued to operate with imported black laborers. The immediate cause of the disturbances, which culminated on July 2 in the bloodiest race riot of a violent era, was never established, but corrupt government and management greed superimposed upon the underlying racism of American whites were at the roots. Official post-riot reports listed thirty-nine blacks and eight whites killed, hundreds wounded, and three hundred houses burned. Other estimates put the dead as high as one hundred, but given the frequent disposal of black bodies by burning or consignment to the river and their lack of local identity, an accurate count was impossible. Not only did police and National Guardsmen not stop the massacre, they participated in it. Carlos Hurd, a veteran *Post-Dispatch* reporter, was an eyewitness to the June 30–July 2 events:

> For an hour and a half last evening I saw the massacre of helpless Negroes at Broadway and Fourth Streets in downtown East St. Louis where a black skin was a death warrant. . . .

> I saw man after man, with his hands raised pleading for his life, surrounded by groups of men . . . who knew nothing about him except that he was black—and saw them administer the historic sentence of intolerance, death by stoning. . . .

> I saw Negro women begging for mercy . . . set upon by white women . . . who laughed and answered the coarse sallies of the men as they beat the Negresses' faces and breasts with stones and sticks. . . .

> It was not my idea of a mob. . . . The East St. Louis affair, as I saw it, was a man hunt . . . there was a horribly cool deliberateness and spirit of fun about it. . . . It was no crowd of hot-headed youths. Younger men were in the greater number, but there were the middle-aged, no less active in destroying every discoverable black man. . . .

> "Get a nigger" was the slogan, and it was varied by the recurrent cry, "Get another!"

St. Louis gained a reputation for righteousness during the riot. Reporters Paul Anderson of the *Post-Dispatch* and Russel Froehlich of the *Globe-Democrat* risked their lives to get the story to an outraged readership. Froehlich was jailed but not intimidated by the East St. Louis police, and Anderson's Grand Jury testimony led to the conviction of certain corrupt officials. During the slaughter, St. Louis policemen were stationed on Eads Bridge, protecting the hundreds of fleeing black men, women, and children from their pursuers. Housing and food was provided by the city, the Red Cross, and other relief agencies; and most of the refugees never recrossed the river. St. Louis had indeed acted decently on this occasion, though some of its citizens had a substantial economic stake in the vicious world of the east side.

Not surprisingly, the census of 1920 showed that for the first time in a half-century, the black population had accelerated more rapidly than the whole. From 43,960 in 1910 (6.4 percent) it had increased by 60 percent to 69,854 (9 percent) in 1920. What the boosters dreaded had come to pass; the growth of Cleveland and the booming motor city, Detroit, had dropped St. Louis to sixth in population, though the Mound City had made a respectable gain of 11.1 percent to 772,897. The county, chiefly in its close-in suburbs of Wellston, University City, and Kirkwood, had grown by 22 percent, from 82,417 to 100,737. The neighboring counties of St. Charles and Jefferson, still reflecting a declining rural rather than a metropolitan character, had actually lost population.

Despite slight increases in the number arriving from southern Europe during the 1910–1915 period, the foreign-born component of St. Louis's population had decreased from 18.3 percent to 13.4 percent during the decade. There were 30,089 native Germans; 13,067 Russians (primarily Jewish); 9,244 Irish; 9,067 Italians; 6,637 Hungarians; 5,587 Austrians; 5,524 Poles; and a scattering of Czechs, Swiss, Greeks, English, and Canadians. There were some changes in residential patterns; German Jews, largely of the highly assimilated third generation, were widely distributed through the west-end wards twenty-five through twenty-eight, many of them in the most exclusive areas. Many of the Ukrainians, Poles, Lithuanians, and Rumanians, usually lumped together as "Russian" or "eastern" Jews, remained in the "ghettoes" (not the real thing, since they were not legally mandated) of the downtown fourth and fifth wards and the nineteenth just east of Grand Avenue. They shared space with the blacks in all three wards and with the Sicilians and Neapolitans downtown—as well as a few remaining Irish.

Deep cultural, economic, and religious differences divided temple and synagogue. The Germans, about twenty-five thousand in number, were firmly established in the business, professional, and political life of the city, many of them in leadership roles. They dominated the department store business and much of the clothing manufacturing, for example, and there were many prominent doctors, lawyers, and local and state politicians among them. They did not know Hebrew or Yiddish, having abandoned the Orthodox ritual for the vernacular "Reform" Judaism, which had discarded much of the ancient ritual and observances. German Jews were alarmed by the segregating tendencies of the Russians, which they felt drew hostility toward all Jews, and they did not identify with their poverty, except now and again as an object of philanthropy. The Russians, for their part, did not regard the Germans as proper Jews. Trained to regard the synagogue as the center of their existence and revering Talmudic learning and ritual, they disliked the "gentile" orientation of the Germans and resented their assumptions of social superiority. Yet, even in 1920, they too were on the move. Some were moving west, first to the nineteenth ward, then along Page and Easton Avenues toward Wellston, bringing their synagogues and Kosher markets with them. In the 1920s, the vanguard of this westward movement spilled into University City and Wellston.

In addition to "Little Italy," an enclave of southern Italians centering on Columbus Square at Tenth and Carr Streets, a cluster of Milanese, other Lombards, and Piedmontese lived in the twenty-fourth ward's "Italian Hill" section, just west of Kingshighway in the old Gratiot League Square. The southerners of Little Italy had first arrived in the 1890s, most of them to work for the Genoese fruit dealers, merchants, and manufacturers who had come to St. Louis before the Civil War. At the heart of the Hill or "Fairmount" district was the St. Ambrose Catholic Church, at Wilson and Marconi Avenues. Not only was there a cultural gap between what some perceived as the volatile and demonstrative southerners and the Lombards, the nature of their neighborhoods was quite different. Little Italy was near the heart of downtown, subject to the disintegrating pressures of crowding neighbors and rapid changes in the commercial and industrial environment, with its people living in former commercial buildings or homes abandoned by other ethnic groups, while the Hill was five miles to the southwest—farmland before the northern Italians built their own sturdy homes there, for decades lacking city services and not requiring them.

The Fairmount district and neighboring Cheltenham, or Sulphur Springs, which had boasted the first Pacific Railroad Station west of St. Louis and had been the site of Etienne Cabet's French Icarian colony in the 1850s, had first been an area of large farms and estates, including those of D. A. January and the noted fur trader William Sublette. English Quakers had mined fire clay there in the 1840s, and during the Civil War the St. Louis Smelting and Refining Company had brought German and Irish labor to its precious metals refining plant on Manchester. Booming demand for terra cotta and firebrick in the 1890s brought northern Italians from the Illinois coal fields to work in the clay mines, and they gradually displaced most of the German and black miners and farmers in the Fairmount area. Makeshift residences sprouted on the Hill, gradually replaced by brick homes as the miners acquired the means. By 1920 the area bounded by Macklind, Kingshighway, Pattison, and Southwest Boulevard was well built up. The community was self-contained, with groceries, restaurants, saloons, barbers, bakeries, salami and spaghetti manufacturing, a bank, and other businesses. Snug behind their Kingshighway and railroad barriers, many of them found it unnecessary to go outside the area for any reason.

In the early years the atmosphere between Lombards and Sicilians crackled with tension, with the northerners tending to look down upon the southerners, as they had in Italy. Socializing and intermarriage were discouraged, but as the southerners filled the downtown interstices and as more blacks crowded into Little Italy, older residents moved out, some of them to newer sections of the Hill. Separate social clubs still existed there in 1920, but the St. Ambrose Church was a unifying factor, and gradually the old hostilities eased, helped along by intermarriage and the passing of the first generation. But even in 1980, Hill residents of pure northern descent tried not to keep it a secret.

During Prohibition, which was an insult to Italians, illegal wine and other beverages were produced in basements all over the Hill. Most of it was for home consumption, but there was some bootlegging and connections with downtown groups identified with national criminal activity. Because it was an easily identifiable ethnic unit, the Fairmount community became a target for the intolerance of the anti-foreign, anti-Catholic, anti-Jewish, and anti-black mentality that produced the Ku Klux Klan and a host of other self-anointed guardians of "true Americanism." Some younger families left the Hill to try to escape this undeserved odium, but most remained, and the embattled community withdrew even further in the face of external disapproval. But World War II widened perspectives; Italian servicemen and war workers, and non-Italians as well, adopted new attitudes toward cultural differences. This softening process had a centrifugal effect on the Hill. The exodus was on in earnest as some veterans and women who had worked in war industries married non-Italians and even non-Catholics, and as others, impatient with the old language and the old ways and anxious to minimize the qualities that set them apart, headed for the new subdivisions. The area took on a seedy look and a more standard American appearance, and vacant houses were rented to transient non-Italians who cared not a whit for the physical appearance of the neighborhood or whether it survived. The remarkable athletic program that had produced Yogi Berra, Joe Garagiola, and several international soccer stars was in the doldrums.

In the 1960s the people of the Hill decided to save it. The catalysts were a proposed drive-in movie, a lead company's plan to dump its wastes in the abandoned mines, and the routing of the new highway, Interstate 44, through its northern section. In 1965 the newly formed Improvement Association blocked the theater and waste disposal plans, but efforts to relocate the highway failed. Finally, in 1971 Father Salvatore Polizzi, Paul M. Berra, and others visited the Transportation Department in Washington and presented officials with fifty thousand dollars they had collected locally to help pay for a vehicular overpass connecting the 150 families north of the highway with their friends and businesses in the main section of the Hill. The government could not accept the money, but the delegation had made its point. The Hill got its overpass, and a walkway as well.

The rallying against external threats helped to bond the community. In 1969 Father Polizzi and a group of businessmen founded a civic organization called Hill 2000 "to plan effectively and creatively for the future welfare of the area as regards to the continued quality of community life. This will encompass the social, economic, commercial, religious, physical, cultural, and moral welfare of the area and its residents." "Pride builds" was the theme, and soon a rash of new porches, roofs, and sidewalks appeared. This regeneration was applauded by the news media, and soon by all of St. Louis.

A new dimension had been added locally to the concept of ethnic awareness. At a time when multimillion-dollar housing schemes and renewal projects were failing, one small community was bucking the tide and winning. Now the Hill became a showcase; one of the highlights of any year in St. Louis was "Hill Day," when tens of thousands of people gathered in a carnival mood to sample the Italian cuisine, drink wine and beer; watch fireworks, grape-stomping, and residents in old-country costumes; visit handicraft displays; dance; and have a smashing good time. The proceeds were used for community projects and to aid individuals in home improvements. In 1979 the Hill 2000 committee announced that the festival of that year would be the last. Apparently, they had achieved their objectives. Their example had sparked neighborhood preservation and restoration projects all over the city. Father Polizzi, the founding and guiding genius of the organization, also played a significant role in the development of the Carondelet, Soulard, and other neighborhood revival projects that followed the Italian Hill's lead in the 1970s.

On April 7, 1923, St. Louis's bonded debt stood at $19.7 million ($25.50 per capita), by far the lowest of any major American city. Boston, Cleveland, and Baltimore, all approximately St. Louis's size, had debts of $48.3 million, $76.3 million, and $96.7 million respectively; and New York City's per capita debt was $220. The Mound City's appearance reflected its parsimony, as testimony before the City Plan Commission in 1918 demonstrated. Among the commission's recommendations, which included proposals for improving transit, transportation, recreation, housing, civic arts, public buildings, and the River des Peres, was a zoning plan submitted after consultation with New York City officials and engineers. Among the major American cities, only New York had adopted citywide, industrial-residential zoning; St. Louis was to be the second.

The Plan Commission, headed by Ernest J. Russell and including J. A. Ockerson; Charles E. Goltermann; E. R. Kinsey of the Board of Public Service; Louis P. Aloe, president of the Board of Aldermen; Parks and Recreation Commissioner Nelson Cunliff; and Public Safety Director J. N. McKelvey heard Isaac Lionberger state bluntly: "The town is a very ugly town, and the downtown part of it is not only excessively ugly but excessively dirty. . . ." His family had moved five times:

> We were groping toward the sunlight. . . . Westmoreland Place, where I now reside, was twelve years ago a charming, clean, and quiet retreat; it is today as unclean atmospherically, and almost as noisy, as was my boyhood's residence on Chestnut Street [downtown] in the year 1860. . . . The motive to be clean is a human motive, in all respects praiseworthy. The financial consequences of what I have mentioned can be seen between 17th and 14th streets on Olive. There seems to be no use for this property. It cannot be rented for enough to pay taxes; the neighborhood is deserted, business will not thrive there.

Dr. M. A. Bliss argued that zoning laws were essential, because nervous and mental disorders were created by congestion and the juxtaposition of businesses and residences. "How, by planning, may we save . . . our nervous systems (from) the incessant blows of countless little hammers that never cease day or night." With the growth of industry, "more and more people attempt to occupy the limited area of cities; as the squeeze increases we find ourselves struggling up into the air to get breath and light; the result is the skyscraper. Then we produce deep valleys, ever shadowed by the tall structures. . . ." Realtor John Gundlach argued for "rational expansion of the city to take the place of the . . . senseless waste in building up the new by abandoning of old sections . . . the section east of Fourth Street has to a large extent been abandoned. . . . Even today there is no . . . greater opportunity for civic enterprises with its splendid economic returns than in this almost forgotten and shunned front terrace of St. Louis." The Reverend Doctor W. C. Bitting emphasized what could not be measured: "A city is more than an assemblage of buildings with streets between them. It has a soul, and an atmosphere, and a social significance to which all material things should be made to minister."

With the enthusiastic support of the *Globe-Democrat*, the *Star,* and the *Post-Dispatch*, the zoning ordinance won aldermanic approval easily, and Mayor Kiel signed it on July 16, 1918. It established five use, five height, and four area categories. To protect the wealthy and the professional classes, top residence classification was assigned to relatively small sections of primarily high-value homes in the West End and the north and south sides, permitting one-family use, doctors' and dentists' offices, and a garage holding as many as four automobiles. The second and much larger residence district allowed multifamily dwellings, boarding houses, hotels, churches, clubs, and hospitals. In the commercial category were retailers and wholesalers, studios, and fire and police stations. The industrial district, primarily the high-density area adjacent to the Mill Creek Valley as far west as Grand Avenue, included factories which did not emit undue quantities of smoke, gas, odors, or noise. Everything was permitted in the unrestricted district, in the Mill Creek Valley, along the west belt of the Terminal Railroad, and along the river.

First and most second residence districts were limited to 45 feet in height, commercial generally to 60 feet, and most industrial areas to 80 feet. Unrestricted and industrial buildings surrounding the downtown highest-value business district could be 120 feet high, and in the central district itself, bounded by Washington and Market, Fourth and Twelfth, the limit was 150 feet, or about twelve stories. There were twenty existing buildings thirteen to twenty-one stories high, which were of course unaffected, since the ordinance was not retroactive in any of its parts. Area restrictions, to preserve open space, ranged from permitting full-lot occupancy for 120–150 foot buildings to 60 percent in first residence districts.

Zoning was a painless reform—it cost very little and tended to confirm, rather than disturb, existing land-use patterns, but in 1923 the

Mayor Henry Kiel Signing an Official Document. *During Kiel's term from 1913 to 1925, zoning legislation was enacted, and a major campaign of public improvements was approved and begun. Photograph by W. C. Persons, ca. 1918. MHS-PP.*

city plan burst into full bloom. For decades small and middle-class property owners, especially in the heavily German wards, not trusting the big-business leadership and feeling that increased taxes would fall most heavily upon themselves, had maintained a conservative stance that amounted to civic neglect. Now, at last the businessmen, the reformers, and the people got together to pass the largest bond issue that had ever been adopted by an American city. Voters approved twenty of twenty-one proposals totaling $87.4 million by margins averaging four to one.

All of these projects were intended to improve the quality of life in one way or another, and several embodied the City Beautiful dreams of the "New St. Louis" and Civic League reformers, though nothing was done about the riverfront. With a two-thirds majority required for passage, only the $1 million National Guard Armory failed, and that by a narrow margin, a defeat attributable primarily to labor opposition in four south side German wards. Mayor Kiel, aldermanic president Louis P. Aloe, the Chamber of Commerce, both political parties, and the newspapers applied political and economic pressure and hammering publicity to the campaign. The Chamber of Commerce revived a slogan first conceived by its predecessors in 1913, "the Spirit of

St. Louis," presenting the issues as a crusade for the good, the true, the beautiful, and the proud. More pragmatically, Mayor Kiel and Alderman Aloe promised attorney Homer G. Phillips and other black leaders a separate hospital for blacks in the heart of the black district in return for their support of the entire project. Not surprisingly, the primarily black wards supported the bond issue by a 4.5 to 1 average margin, as did the German by just under 3 to 1, the Irish by 3.5 to 1, and both the Jewish and silk-stocking wards by over 5 to 1.

The most popular and expensive project, $12 million for waterworks extension, provided for construction of a new plant on the Missouri River, a less expensive source than the Mississippi because the water was cleaner and could be moved primarily by gravity flow. Also urgently needed was the River des Peres $11 million bond issue, because of that stream's polluted condition and propensity for destructive flooding. In 1919, for example, during the second week of the municipal opera's maiden season, the stage had been damaged and the cast of *The Bohemian Girl* and the audience routed by the surging waters in Forest

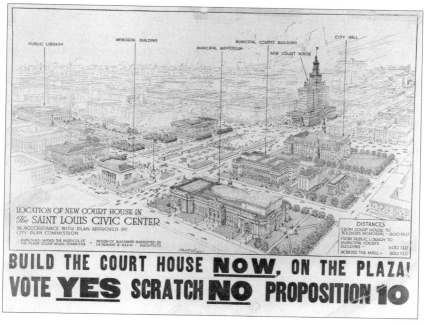

Build the Courthouse Now, On the Plaza! *The bond issue of 1923 funded a massive program of public improvements, including new civic buildings, promoted in this advertisement, a new water plant, the River des Peres Sewer project, and a host of others totalling $87.4 million dollars. Advertisement, rendering by Fred Graf, 1923. MHS-PP.*

Park. The solution adopted was to get rid of the noxious open sewer by digging a deep channel and forcing it underground.

Other projects included two bond issues totaling $14.45 million for street paving, new construction, and the widening of the two major arteries radiating from downtown, Natural Bridge to the northwest and Gravois to the southwest; $8 million to install electric streetlights throughout the city; $8 million for sewer extension and repair; $3.8 million for new parks, playgrounds, and improvements; $4.5 for hospitals; $6 million for a Soldier's Memorial and plaza; $5 million for a municipal auditorium (Kiel Auditorium); and $2.6 million for widening Market Street and constructing a plaza across from the Union Station (for years an area of ugly blight). When finally completed in 1940, the Aloe Plaza, featuring a beautiful and lively fountain group of bronze nudes, which its sculptor Carl Milles called "The Wedding of the Rivers," created a colossal row. The aggressive maleness of the Mississippi figure which approached the shy bride Missouri was too much for the prudes, who wanted to put proper clothes on the wedding couple and the naiads who attended them. All they received for their pains was a new title, "The Meeting of the Rivers." Still other bonds provided for an aquarium in Forest Park; new approaches for the Municipal Bridge; a new courthouse; elimination of railroad grade crossings, especially in the Mill Creek Valley; new fire stations; and public market improvements.

As enacted by the Board of Aldermen, $12 million in revenue bonds were issued for the waterworks, and $73.9 million in 4.5 percent serial bonds were floated over a ten-year period, to be serviced by general property taxes. One of the bridge approaches was cancelled, and the four hundred thousand dollars for the aquarium was never issued because of high maintenance estimates. The impact of this ambitious program on tax levels was surprisingly light. Despite substantial additional issues for cost overruns, further improvements, and for unemployment relief in the 1930s, the property tax only rose from $2.55 per $100 valuation in 1923 to $2.77 in 1936. Net debt during the period advanced from $19 million to $82 million ($98.25 per capita).

The late 1920s were great years for St. Louis and its boosters. The city had adopted baseball as a source of civic pride as early as 1875, when J. B. C. Lucas assembled a professional team from all over the country to break a string of defeats by Chicago, Boston, Cincinnati, and Philadelphia professionals who had humiliated the homegrown clubs. On May 6, 1875, ten thousand proud St. Louisans watched their

Brown Stockings shellack the mighty Chicago White Stockings by a score of ten to nothing. "We have met the enemy, and they are ours," trumpeted the *Democrat*, and the *Republican* exulted: "Time was when Chicago had an excellent baseball club, the best in the West, but that was before St. Louis decided to make an appearance on the diamond field and there, as everywhere else, attest her supremacy. . . ." A week later the Browns repeated their triumph, prompting "Jack Frost" to write in the *Democrat:* "A village, once, of low degree, a city's rival tried to be. The city now in triumph stands. The village— leveled to the sands." The *Chicago Tribune* grumbled that St. Louisans seemed to believe that "the fate of the cities had been decided by eighteen hired men."

Since the beginning of baseball's modern era in 1901, St. Louis had been a two-team major-league city, with its American League Browns and National League Cardinals. Neither had won a pennant through 1925, though the powerful 1922 Browns, featuring the incomparable George Sisler, had barely been nosed out by the Yankees. Each club had its local partisans, with the Browns having an edge because they usually had better teams. Based in the westernmost city in the majors, both had a strong following in its vast southwestern and southern trade territory, and at weekend games out-of-towners often greatly outnumbered the local fans. Not only were the clubs symbols of local pride, they represented the West and South against the arrogant Northeast.

In 1926 the twenty-five-year famine broke. Led by the game's best-ever right-handed hitter, manager Rogers Hornsby, and a pair of right-handed pitching aces, Jesse Haines and Grover Cleveland Alexander, the latter winding down an illustrious career as the peer of Walter Johnson and Christy Mathewson, the Cardinals swept to the pennant and, wonder of wonders, to a World Series victory over the mighty Yankees. The New York club, conceded even in 1980 to have been the greatest team ever assembled, had a fine pitching staff led by Waite Hoyt and Herb Pennock, and the fearsome "Murderer's Row" hitting lineup of Babe Ruth, Bob Meusel, Lou Gehrig, and Tony Lazzeri. The seventh game, in New York, was a classic of World Series history, embodying all the elements of the David and Goliath legend. Jesse Haines, pitching in his third game, developed a blister on his middle finger in the seventh inning. With two outs, the bases full, and Lazzeri at the plate, Hornsby called upon "Old Pete" Alexander, who was snoozing in the bullpen after having beaten the Yankees the day before, followed by his customary night on the town. As Hornsby told it to J. Roy Stockton, he walked from his second-base position to meet his thirty-nine-year-old pitcher "to find out if he could see."

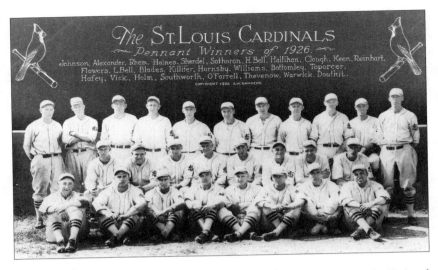

St. Louis Cardinals, Pennant Winners, 1926. *The Cardinals not only won the National League Pennant in 1926, as touted in this commemorative photograph, but went on to win their first World Series in a tense seven-game match with the New York Yankees. Photograph by A. W. Sanders, 1926. MHS-PP.*

Encouraged because Alexander recognized him, Hornsby described the game situation, and "after I saw that he could see and walk and didn't have anything in his hip pocket, I told him to go in and pitch."

The veteran pitcher, who had won 327 regular-season games in his sixteen-year career and would later win another forty-six, had told Hornsby he would give Lazzeri a lot of trouble, and after five tosses to catcher Bob O'Farrell to be certain he was facing in the right direction, he struck out the Yankee slugger while sixty thousand frustrated New York fans watched in disbelief. As if this were not enough, he set the Yankees down in order in the eighth; and in the ninth, when Babe Ruth tried to steal second with two outs, O'Farrell threw him out to end the game. In St. Louis and half the nation Alexander and Hornsby were epic heroes, with their deeds compared favorably in the press with Thermopylae, Horatio's stand at the Bridge, and Wellington's victory at Waterloo. The spirit of St. Louis had triumphed; the insufferable eastern metropolis had been brought to its knees; and every obscure soul who had ever suffered indignities or petty tyranny was vindicated. The Chamber of Commerce claimed that the World Series victory "was the one thing needed to cement St. Louis's leadership among great cities." Probably the least impressed was Alexander himself; not realizing the cosmic significance of his artistry, he tied another one on.

Hot on the heels of this booster's bonanza came an even bigger one. Since the nineteenth century, St. Louis had been a center of interest in aviation. In 1859 Captain John Wise had set a 1,150-mile world balloon distance record that lasted for a half-century, and glider and balloon pilots had competed for $135,000 in prizes at the World's Fair. In 1907 Thomas W. Benoist became the first St. Louisan to fly an airplane at the Aero Club Field in Kinloch Park, which had been established by pharmaceuticals manufacturer Albert Bond Lambert and Andrew Drew. In 1911 Benoist began to manufacture airplanes at his small factory on Delmar Avenue in University City and opened a flying school at Kinloch which attracted students from a wide area, including the Japanese Navy. In Benoist's biplane, which would fly for three hours at sixty miles an hour, John Berry in 1912 made the first successful parachute jump from an airplane. In 1914 Benoist and Albert Jannus designed a flying boat to compete for the fifty thousand

Thomas Benoist at Kinloch Field Air Meet. *Benoist, one of St. Louis's aviation pioneers, developed a sea plane and established the nation's first scheduled air service in Florida. He was killed in a street car accident in Tampa. Photograph by David Boyd, 1910. MHS-PP.*

dollar prize offered by British newspaper baron Lord Northcliffe for the first successful transatlantic flight, but the World War interfered. Shortly after losing a contract to manufacture planes for the British military to Glenn Curtiss in 1917, Benoist was killed in a freak streetcar accident. The St. Louis Car Company, the world's leading streetcar manufacturer, had agreed to build Benoist's planes at its Baden factory. Jannus, who was training Russian pilots in Crimea, went down without a trace in the Black Sea in the same year. St. Louis's pioneer professional pilots were gone, and the city's interest in aviation waned for a few years, but it had revived again by 1924, when the International Air Races were held at Lambert Field.

J. W. Alcock and A. W. Brown won Northcliffe's prize in 1919 with a nineteen-hundred-mile flight from Newfoundland to Ireland, but French-born Raymond Orteig of New York promptly offered twenty five thousand dollars for the first successful flight between France and the United States. In 1926, Charles A. "Slim" Lindbergh, a twenty-five-year-old Minnesotan who was chief pilot for the Robertson Aircraft Company, a St. Louis firm which held the air mail contract between St. Louis and Chicago, decided to compete for the Orteig Prize.

After Lindbergh had failed to obtain financial backing in New York, he turned to St. Louis and his friend A. B. Lambert, the pioneer pilot for whom the city's airport was named. Lambert added one thousand dollars to Lindbergh's two thousand dollars, and between them they raised another twelve thousand dollars from J. D. W. Lambert; Earl Thompson; William and Frank Robertson; Harry H. Knight, a broker who was president of the St. Louis Flying Club; Harold M. Bixby, president of the Chamber of Commerce; and E. Lansing Ray, publisher of the *Globe-Democrat*. O. K. Bovard of the *Post-Dispatch* would have no part in a one-man, single-engine quixotic enterprise. Neither would most airplane manufacturers.

Lindbergh had been a daredevil "gypsy pilot" or barnstormer, who had barely escaped by parachute from four crashes and had flown under the Eads and Municipal Bridges in an air show, but his youth, his lack of experience with long-distance flights, and his plan to fly alone in a single-engine plane scared the big firms off. Finally, a shoestring operation in San Diego, the Ryan Aircraft Company, agreed to build Lindbergh's plane for $10,580, which included a 220-horsepower Wright Whirlwind engine. When completed, fully loaded with Lindbergh and 450 gallons of gasoline, it weighed 5,250 pounds. Just under ten feet high and twenty-eight feet long, it had an oversized wing span of forty-six feet.

Meanwhile, several of the world's greatest pilots had entered the competition, all with copilots and larger and more expensive planes. In

New York, Commander Richard E. Byrd, who had flown over the North Pole; Clarence Chamberlin, whose Wright Bellanca held the world's endurance record of fifty-one hours; and Major Noel Davis, war ace and test pilot, were about ready to go. In Paris wartime flying heroes Charles Nungesser and Francois Coli took off for New York on May 8, were sighted over Ireland a few hours later, and were never seen again. On May 10, Lindbergh left San Diego in his *Spirit of St. Louis*, which he had named to honor his backers, his adopted city, and the French people. In 14 hours and 25 minutes he flew the 1,550 miles to Lambert Field, having broken the nonstop record for a one-man flight and the speed record from the West Coast. After a day's rest he went on to New York, breaking the coast-to-coast flying time record by 5.5 hours.

In the meantime, Noel Davis had crashed to his death in a test flight, leaving only Byrd, Chamberlain, and "Lucky Lindy," as the crowd had dubbed him. The experts thought Lindbergh's lone flight a reckless gamble and gave him very little chance of surviving. On May 20, 1927, with favorable weather but dangerously overloaded with fuel, the *Spirit of St. Louis* labored into the air at Roosevelt Field, Long Island, barely missing a tractor just beyond the runway. For the next thirty-three-and-one-half hours and 3,610 miles Lindbergh had the world's attention. Before sunset on May 21, he was sighted over the southern tip of Ireland, squarely on course after more than twenty hours of navigating by dead reckoning—an astounding feat. At 10:24 P.M. Lindbergh set his plane down at Le Bourget Field to the roaring welcome of one hundred thousand Parisians.

The *Spirit of St. Louis* and its pilot were the marvels of the western world. Never was there such a hero, and there was no other news—the first 16 pages of the May 22 edition of the *New York Times* was devoted to the flight, and in St. Louis every true heart thrilled in vicarious triumph. The *Globe-Democrat*, justly proud of its own role, the *Star-Times*, and the instantaneously converted *Post-Dispatch* competed for superlatives to describe the hero and St. Louis's part in making him. It would have been better had he lived in the city longer, but it could not be denied that without St. Louis there would have been no flight. Boosters could not have imagined a better script. With his boyish good looks, clean-cut and modest demeanor, and refusal to drink anything even as strong as coffee, the Lone Eagle seemed the antithesis of Pete Alexander, but the two had something in common—they were experts, and they were good for St. Louis.

In a cynical era with the old gods and the old values seemingly discarded, Lindbergh was hailed as a redeemer, the reincarnation of Saint Louis. For the pilot himself, there was vast disillusionment.

He had been in physical danger from his admirers from the moment he landed at Le Bourget; young women had tried to tear off his clothes in New York; and during the grand homecoming at St. Louis, sloppy adoration reached a climax when at an alfresco banquet a society matron collected his discarded corncobs and stuffed them in her purse. The redemption theme ran through the four thousand poems that were entered from a dozen countries in the Spirit of St. Louis poetry contest. The man was exalted in all of them, the saint and the city in many. A sample from Nathalia Crane's first-prize poem entitled "The Wings of Lead" illustrates the mood:

> *The gods released a vision on a world forespent and*
> * dull;*
> *They sent it as a challenge by the sea hawk and the*
> * gull. . . .*
>
> *And then one night there landed on a Mineola swale*
> *A plane that looked like pewter, with a carrier of*
> * mail. . . .*
>
> *"The Spirit of St. Louis" was inscribed upon the lea;*
> *It came from out a province that had never seen the*
> * sea. . . .*
>
> *He listed in as "Lindbergh"—just one pace beyond*
> * the ranks;*
> *He had a moon-stained paddle and some star gas in*
> * his tanks. . . .*
>
> *He made the course the gods had sent, the quarter*
> * quadrant glide;*
> *He flew the full Atlantic and the tag ends of the*
> * tide. . . .*
>
> *We hear the clinking tambourine of Miriam anew,*
> *We believe in every miracle since Lindbergh flew the*
> * blue. . . .*

Baseball's contribution to St. Louis's image of excellence in 1926 was not a one-shot affair. The Cardinals were consistently strong contenders thereafter, dominating the league with pennants in 1928, 1930, 1931, and 1934 and winning the World Series in 1931 and 1934. The "Gashouse Gang" of the 1930s, featuring the irrepressible Dizzy

Lindbergh and *Spirit of St Louis. Photograph, 1927. MHS-PP.*

The 1934 World Champion St. Louis Cardinals relax in their spring training dugout in Florida. Photograph, 1935. MHS-PP.

Dean, Pepper Martin (the "Wild Horse of the Osage"), Rip Collins, Joe Medwick, and manager Frank Frisch, was the most colorful aggregation of major-league players ever assembled as well as one of the best. With the positive visible symbols of baseball, Lindbergh, the Municipal Opera, the zoo, the free bridge, civic improvements, the bond issue, and an economic base that had never seemed stronger, boosters were in a confident mood on the eve of the Great Depression.

The city's population growth was slowing down, having increased during the 1920s by only 6.3 percent to 821,960, dropping from sixth to seventh in the nation. But the industrial district, which included St. Clair and Madison Counties in Illinois, was growing faster than the national average, having increased by 19.5 percent to 1.34 million. For the first time in nearly a century, blacks outnumbered the foreign-born, the two groups comprising 11.5 and 9.8 percent of the total respectively.

The city's largest ethnic group, the Germans, had never formed a homogeneous, closed community. Despite their numerical dominance in both north and south side areas, they had lived in neighborhoods interspersed with other immigrants and native Americans, and they had moved with the flow to the western sections. Early German immigrants had clung to the mother tongue, and several German-language newspapers had persisted throughout the nineteenth century, as had numerous German and German-English private schools. But the public schools, without strong opposition from the Germans, had followed a system of instruction (one German class a day, with all other classes taught in English) that encouraged the rapid assimilation of the second generation into the English-speaking population.

In 1887, despite the pleas of the German-language press, German voters had not united to defeat a "Citizens' Party" school board, which pledged to eliminate German from the elementary public school curriculum. The *Anzeiger*'s charges that the Citizens' Party was a nativist front went unheeded, and most Germans did not bother to vote. Of those who did, many supported the elimination slate, persuaded by the fear of higher taxes or by the fact that their own children were in private schools. The new school board quickly carried out its pledge, leaving German instruction to the high schools, private schools, and homes. Sporadic efforts to repair the loss by after-school and Saturday classes met a meager response. In 1915 the *Westliche Post* complained that many persons of German descent seemed ashamed of their mother tongue.

German churches—Evangelical, Lutheran, and Catholic—were bastions of the German language until the twentieth century, but the twenty German Catholic and twenty-two German Lutheran schools in existence on the eve of World War I used English textbooks, and instruction was only occasionally in German. German-language services, intended to hold young people in the faith, were having the opposite effect, and in 1909, some Lutheran churches began to hold evening services in English twice a month. In Catholic churches, where only the sermon and announcements had been involved, German was dropped from the services altogether in 1915 at the request of Cardinal John Glennon, who was responding to anti-German pressures.

Aspects of German culture had been preserved in St. Louis since the 1840s through a wide variety of *vereine*, or societies, which were unifying agencies only in the sense that they were purveyors of *gemütlichkeit*, a spirit of friendliness, conviviality, and appreciation of things German, including frequent celebrations and lager beer. The vereine included benevolent societies, which paid sickness and death benefits to their dues-paying members; provincial societies, which represented the various parts of Germany from which St. Louisans had emigrated; various craft unions, which had insurance features; the *Turnverein*, or gymnastic societies, with their women's auxiliaries, which emphasized body building, fellowship, and occasional political activity (Turners had rallied to Blair, Lyon, and the Union in 1861); and singing societies. By 1900 there were hundreds of vereine in the city, but according to Sister Audrey Olson, historian of the St. Louis German community's growth, these societies tended to fragment rather than unify the ethnic group. Only the Turners had an effective citywide organization in 1911 with some five thousand members. The proliferation of vereine operating in virtual isolation reflected the wide dispersion of the Germans and the jealousies and animosities of the north and south siders. This rivalry resulted from local geographic separation rather than old-country origins, since Prussians, Oldenburgers, Bavarians, and Saxons were numerous in both sections.

The eruption of war in Europe in 1914 created a dilemma for ethnic Germans. The fatherland was at war with their ancient French enemy and with England, the latter identified with Puritanism and the hated temperance movement. On the other hand the American government, though it professed neutrality, tilted toward the Allies; and public opinion, led by the inflammatory tales of German atrocities against women and children in Belgium that were relentlessly cranked out by the British propaganda machine, was decidedly pro-Ally. In August 1914, after a series of anti-German editorials had appeared in the *Post-Dispatch*, the *Star*, and the *Republic*, several thousand Germans assembled at the central Turner Hall to urge fair play for Germany and to demonstrate their unity in the cause. The climax of the evening, according to the *Westliche Post*, came when the crowd rose as one to sing *Die Wacht am Rhein*. The *Post* thought "the old disharmony" among St. Louis Germans had been destroyed.

Shortly thereafter, representatives of many of the German societies proposed to raise one hundred thousand dollars for the widows and orphans of German soldiers. Direct contributions were meager, but in October 1915, a gigantic bazaar featuring numerous exhibits, theatrical performances, band music, dancing, and Turner exhibitions put the drive over its funding goal. Smaller sums for German relief were collected from time to time in St. Louis until the United States entered the war.

More important to St. Louis Germans was their effort to hold the United States to strict neutrality. Since the British navy could block any shipment of arms to Germany, they argued that only an embargo on the sale of war material to belligerents would guarantee real neutrality. Their common hatred for the British brought old antagonists together in St. Louis in December 1914, as the Germans and Irish joined to establish the Neutrality League. On January 10, 1915, a league-sponsored demonstration against arms shipments attracted twelve thousand people. Speakers attacked Britain as the "bully of the world"; the crowd roared in song as the band played *Deutschland Uber Alles*; and hawkers sold German, Irish, and American flags. Despite this impressive show of strength, the demonstration apparently had a sobering effect. Subsequent gatherings were less partisan, and attendance dwindled to a few hundred.

After attorney Kurt von Rippert publicly attacked President Wilson as a pro-British jackass and crook, deep divisions appeared among Germans. Despite the opposition of the German-language press and the Turners on the grounds that a military buildup would lead to war against Germany, August A. Busch and several prominent bankers and lawyers led a large contingent of Germans who marched in Wilson's "preparedness-day" parade on June 3, 1916. In the fall presidential election, despite the urgings of the Republican *Westliche Post* and the Democratic *Amerika* to repudiate Wilson, the president took 41.2 percent of the vote in the eleven heavily German wards, a slight gain over his 1912 total. While a shift in the non-German vote may have been partly responsible for this, there was obviously no united German-American opposition to Wilson's course.

Unfortunately, while their press had not united the Germans, it had convinced many non-Germans that the ethnic group placed the interests of the fatherland first. Latent nativism became frenzied and foolish persecution when the United States entered the war. German men and women who had only their first naturalization papers were required by the government to register as enemy aliens, and the German newspapers were ordered to submit their war reports and editorials to the postmaster to be censored. In St. Louis the city government stopped publishing its proceedings in the German papers; the teaching of German in the high schools was prohibited; the Symphony Orchestra dropped the works of German composers from its concerts; and books written in German were removed from the public library shelves. Because it "reeked of Hunism, Kaiserism, and Hohenzollernism," Berlin Avenue was renamed Pershing, and Van Verson Avenue became Enright.

On the citizens' level, self-appointed "Hun-Watchers" listened for pro-German remarks on streetcars, in the streets and parks, and at work, seeking ammunition for prosecution under the Espionage Act or for vigilante action. William Stiefer, a streetcar motorman, was forced by his coworkers to stand on a table and give three cheers for Wilson and three for America, curse the Kaiser, and kiss the American flag. He was alleged to have predicted a German victory and to have carried a newspaper that reported the capture of some American troops. On April 13, 1918, the *Post-Dispatch* reported that Dr. Charles Weinsberg, Missouri president of the German-American Alliance, had predicted the defeat of the Allies. He was promptly arrested and charged with violating the Espionage Act. Weinsberg was eventually freed by a federal judge, but several less prominent citizens were jailed for similar remarks.

St. Louis Germans were stunned by this hostility. Their record of loyal service in the Civil War, their role in the growth of the city, their sons in the armed forces, and their large contributions to the Red Cross and the Liberty bond drives seemed to count for nothing. August A. Busch had bought more Liberty bonds than anyone in the entire Eighth Federal Reserve District, yet he was constantly under fire. His mother had remained in Germany after Adolphus Busch died there in 1913 and had returned to St. Louis only after the United States entered the war. This was held against him, as were the portraits of noted Germans which were hanging at the Anheuser-Busch brewery.

The *Westliche Post* attributed anti-Germanism to the unfortunate tendency to associate everything German with the Kaiser and to the opportunism of nativists whose forebears had hated and scorned Germans since the Civil War era. The *Post* charged that the principal purveyor of hate, David R. Francis's *Republic*, had been pro-Confederate in 1861 and that anti-German sentiment reflected in part the resentment of descendants of Confederates. As its editors must have known, the *Post* was rewriting history. The former *Republican* had never advocated secession. It had opposed the Radical Republican program, with which the Germans were identified during and after the Civil War, as had Frank P. Blair and many other St. Louis Unionists. Old hatreds were undoubtedly involved in World War I anti-Germanism, but the implication that St. Louis had been a Confederate city was demagoguery. The origins of nativism in the city were not so simple.

The efforts of the German-language press to unify its constituency on the war issue had failed even before the United States entered the war. Once the nation was directly involved, Germans endured the hate campaign against them and supported the war effort at least as enthusiastically as other Americans.

World War I and its illegitimate offspring, the Prohibition Amendment, ruined the beer industry. Most of the brewers went out of business, and even the mighty Anheuser-Busch was reduced to peddling malt syrup; a yeasty drink called Bevo; ginger ale; and near beer (real beer with its alcohol content reduced to .5 percent). August A. Busch, who had attempted to appease the super-patriots during the war by purchasing $1 million in Liberty bonds and by turning over his Busch-Sulzer Diesel Company to the government for the production of submarine engines, found that his efforts availed him little when he carried his battle for repeal of the amendment to Washington, where he met a blank wall in the person of President Calvin Coolidge. When Franklin Roosevelt and the Democratic Congress initiated the repeal of Prohibition in 1933, the Busches became instant Democrats.

Other industries filled the vacuum left by the temporary loss of the brewing giants. Despite the relative decline of wholesaling nationally, the city's jobbing trade set new records in the 1920s, and light manufacturing, especially the making of shoes and women's clothing, was booming. Electrical manufacturing, represented locally by the Century, Moloney, Knapp-Monarch, Emerson, and Wagner firms, had grown rapidly since the 1890s, and Ford and General Motors had found that St. Louis's railroad connections and large trade territory made it an ideal location for their assembly plants. Nine firms had been established in the city to manufacture auto parts. With the shift to cigarettes and the absorption of local firms by the eastern tobacco trust, St. Louis was no longer the center of the tobacco industry, but the Liggett and Myers plant in the Mill Creek Valley was still the world's largest plug tobacco producer. By moving into the remote regions of Alaska and northern Canada shortly after 1900, St. Louis had recaptured its position as the nation's leading fur market.

Business publicists in the 1920s dubbed St. Louis the capital of the forty-ninth state. The *Globe-Democrat* proclaimed itself the newspaper of the forty-ninth state on its masthead until 1959, when it was forced to choose between moving to Alaska or dropping the title. St. Louis dominated a primary trade territory which at the end of World War I covered an area roughly 150 to 200 miles to the east, south, and west, and to Hannibal on the Mississippi to the north.

Based upon railroad package car deliveries (wholesale and light manufacturing items), which of course did not include truck short hauls, the city's major distributing area covered fourteen states, with Missouri accounting for 22.7 percent of the total, Illinois 13.4 percent, Texas 10.4 percent, and Arkansas, Oklahoma, Tennessee, Louisiana, Indiana, Ohio, Iowa, Alabama, and Kentucky, ranging from 5.7 to 2 percent. The secondary interregional area, which received 10 percent of St. Louis's shipments, included California, Pennsylvania, New York, Georgia, Nebraska, Florida, and Minnesota.

With $1.542 billion in products in 1929, the St. Louis industrial district ranked seventh in the nation in manufacturing, after New York–Newark, Chicago, Philadelphia-Camden, Pittsburgh, Detroit, and Boston, and just ahead of Cleveland and Los Angeles. In order of local importance, the major industries were food products, including meatpacking and bakery items; chemicals and drugs; iron and steel products, not including machinery; clothing, especially women's; boots and shoes, chiefly by the Brown, International, and Hamilton-Brown companies, which produced 5 percent of the nation's output in St. Louis and a lesser amount in small-town factories scattered through Missouri and southern Illinois, where labor costs and taxes were lower; aluminum, zinc, and other non-ferrous metals; electrical machinery and supplies; and printing and publishing. The St. Louis district's industrial base was highly diversified; the next twenty-nine industries employed as many workers as did the eight largest.

The district was composed of nine clearly identifiable subdistricts, most of them occupying the low-lying valleys that marked railroad approaches to downtown. The North Broadway district had lumber mills, woodworking, Mallinckrodt Chemical, Mississippi Glass, St. Louis Car (streetcars), grain elevators, stockyards, meatpacking, boiler works, machine shops, and the yards, shops, and terminals of the Wabash, C. B. and Q., and the Missouri, Kansas and Texas railroads. South Broadway had Monsanto Chemical, Anheuser-Busch, American Car and Foundry (railroad cars), Busch-Sulzer Diesel, smelters, boiler works, and the yards and shops of the Iron Mountain Railroad. Mill Creek had the Missouri Pacific, Frisco, and

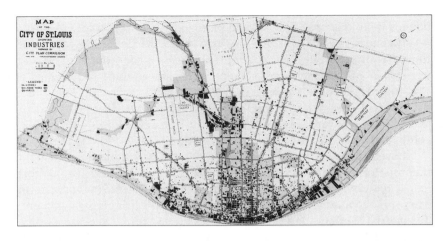

Map of the City of St. Louis Showing Industries, from *The Zone Plan,* published by
the City Plan Commission. *The shaded areas denote the industrial areas proposed
under the zoning plan of 1918. Black areas represent existing industries. Map by
Harland Bartholomew, City Engineer, 1918. MHS Library.*

Terminal Railroad yards and shops, two large meatpacking plants,
Liggett and Myers, glue works, foundries, and warehouses. River des
Peres had firebrick, tile, terra cotta, Scullin Steel, National Lead
Company, and a brass foundry. Oak Hill (southwest) had clay products
and light manufactures. Northwest (the Harlem River drainage basin)
had brick plants, Chevrolet and Fisher Body, United Drug, Pullman
Car shops, and the Bridge-Beach stove company. Carondelet had steel
smelters, foundries, railroad yards and shops, shipbuilding, and grain
elevators. Downtown had most of the city's light manufacturing,
including pharmaceuticals, shoes, hats, and clothing, electrical
machinery manufacturing, the major wholesale and retail firms, and
the banks and insurance companies. East side had the largest steel
smelters, the Aluminum Corporation, American Zinc, chemical plants,
Swift and Company and other meatpackers, Kettle River Creosote,
Beaver Asphalt, cottonseed cake, the Union Electric steam plant, and
the terminals and yards of eighteen railroads.

   Light manufacturing favored the west side for the same reason
that heavy industry had migrated to the east side—the bridge arbitrary.
The great market for its products was in the city itself and to the west
and southwest; it did not consume huge quantities of coal as the steel
mills did; and its finished products, if they had been shipped across the
bridge from the east side, would have cost more in tolls than had been
saved in fuel. As far as the Illinois market within the one-hundred-
mile zone was concerned, the arbitrary could be avoided by using

trucks over the free bridge. The market for steel, zinc, and aluminum, on the other hand, was primarily in the East; and these firms saved the bridge tolls, and their lesser distance to the coal fields saved time and money, as did avoidance of the delays involved in the Terminal Railroad's transfer system. Clay and stone products were the exceptions to the rule that heavy industry sought the east side. Their raw material was in St. Louis; their markets were on the west side; and the arbitrary charge for clay and stone was higher than for coal.

As measured by product value in 1929, the city accounted for 66.3 percent of the district's manufactures, St. Louis County for 2.9 percent, and the Illinois side for 30.8 percent. The Illinois share had actually declined since 1919, at least partly because the Union Electric Company had built a 240,000 kilowatt steam generating plant on the river shore at Cahokia between 1923 and 1927. By locating there, the company had acquired forty acres of land cheaply, and it saved $350,000 a year in bridge tolls. With its transmission cables under the river, it was only two miles from the center of its power load. As Union Electric's president L. H. Egan put it in 1924: "The fact is, that Cahokia established, no coal can ever again pass the Mississippi to the fires of industry in St. Louis without a great monetary loss. Thousands of tons of coal whose destiny was smudging the city with a black pall must stop . . . at Cahokia, for conversion into cleaner, more dependable, more flexible power." Electrification of some west side plants began almost immediately. In 1939 the Illinois share of the district's manufacturing output had declined further, to 29.8 percent, though the greater relative decline in demand for steel as opposed to consumers' goods during the depression was apparently the chief factor.

One of the comfortable and recurring myths of the local tradition presents the Great Depression as less severe in St. Louis than elsewhere because of the highly diversified local economy. In support of this thesis, worst-case comparisons are made with "one-industry" cities such as Pittsburgh and Detroit. To be sure, St. Louis had its Hoovervilles and Happy Valleys on the levee, where the evicted, penniless, and hopeless huddled in cardboard and wooden cartons or galvanized metal shacks, scrounging a little food from garbage heaps to supplement the fare of the municipal soup kitchens, but things were even worse in other cities, or so the story goes. Unfortunately, the evidence does not support this view.

At the peak in 1929, the St. Louis district's manufactures produced 2.26 percent of the U.S. total. By 1933, when national manufacturing output had dropped by 55 percent, St. Louis's output had fallen by 57 percent to 2.18 percent of the national total. In 1935, when a slight recovery was evident, St. Louis's share had fallen

Hooverville. *Photograph by Isaac Sievers, 1934. Sievers Studio Collection, MHS-PP.*

further to 1.97 percent, and in 1939, when national industrial production was back to 84 percent of its 1929 level, local industry was still languishing at 70 percent of its 1929 level or 1.91 percent of the national total. The supposedly less-resilient Detroit and Pittsburgh were at 78 and 75 percent of their 1929 performances. Kansas City stood at 65 percent of its 1929 level, having dropped from 1.1 to 0.8 percent of the U.S. total, and highly diversified Chicago was at 77 percent, down from 8.2 to a 7.15 percent share. Part of the drop in output as measured by product value was accounted for by deflation, but the reduced shares of these midwestern and such eastern urban centers as New York, Boston, and Philadelphia was attributable to the dispersion of light industry to smaller cities and towns and to the southern and western states. Los Angeles's share of U.S. manufacturing rose from 1.9 to 2.1 percent during the depression, for example. In the shoe industry, the accelerating trend toward locating plants in Missouri towns such as Kirksville and Eldorado Springs had a direct effect upon St. Louis. Its share of U.S. shoe manufacturing fell by 30 percent, though the companies with headquarters in the city increased their market shares.

But for the return of the brewing industry and the growth of women's clothing and electrical manufacturing, the St. Louis economy would have done even worse during the depression. Like Kansas City, its dependence upon a far-flung hinterland that included the devastated agricultural regions of Arkansas, Oklahoma, southern Missouri, and southern Kansas, from which flat-broke farmers were fleeing by the tens of thousands, made St. Louis especially vulnerable.

St. Louis held its share of the nation's wholesale business during the 1930s, at 2.1 percent of the total, but its value declined from $1.4 billion in 1929 to $900 million in 1935 before a partial recovery to $1.2 billion in 1939. New York, Boston, Kansas City, and Chicago lost ground relatively, but Detroit and Los Angeles passed St. Louis as wholesale distributors. As the measure of the impact of a metropolis upon its hinterland, wholesale volume is misleading, since wholesale demand depends to a greater extent than manufacturing upon the size of the local population. Per capita volume, on the other hand, is a fairly reliable indicator of the extent of a city's trade territory. St. Louis was eighth in the nation in wholesale volume in 1939, but on a per capita basis it was fourth below only San Francisco, Boston, and New York. Far more dependent than St. Louis upon primarily agricultural products, Kansas City's wholesale trade had dropped from 2 to 1.4 percent of the U.S. total by 1939. That St. Louis's share of this market had not declined, as its manufacturing share had, was apparently due to the increasing use of trucks by its merchants to reach northern Missouri and central Illinois towns which were linked to Chicago, but not to St. Louis, by rail.

Unemployment figures for the 1930s not only illustrated the excessive severity of the depression in St. Louis, they demonstrated the negative impact of hard times on an ancient problem—race. In 1930, with national unemployment having risen from 3.2 to 8.7 percent in one year, the city's 35,089 unemployed represented 9.8 percent of the workforce: 8.4 percent of the white workers and 13.2 percent of the black. A year later, with the national figure at 15.9 percent, 92,666 St. Louisans—24 percent of the work force—were unemployed, with the ratio for whites at 21.5 percent and for blacks at 42.8 percent. By the spring of 1933, when the Bureau of Labor Statistics reported that national unemployment peaked at 24.9 percent, St. Louis's was estimated at over 30 percent; and 80 percent of black workers were either unemployed or underemployed.

Blacks were being fired in wholesale lots, in some cases to be replaced by white workers. In November 1933, the entire force of eighteen black women in the filling and labeling department of the Conferro Paint and Varnish Company was laid off without stated reasons. As required by the National Recovery Act (NRA) code, their wages had been raised from nine to fourteen dollars a week shortly before they were discharged. An Urban League representative who visited the plant a week later saw that these experienced workers had been replaced by white women. In response to a league inquiry, company officials stated that they would not pay such high wages to blacks.

In some cases, whites received the required pay increases, but blacks did not. If black employees would not swear to compliance officials that they had been awarded the raise, they were discharged. An office building porter was fired because the tenants urged that his position be given to a white man, and another was replaced because he would not split his pay with management. In the meatpacking industry, the labor force was reduced chiefly by discharging blacks, one plant having cut its number of black employees by 70 percent by 1934. Of 591 laborers laid off by the rolling mills in 1931, 401 were black, and when the New Deal codes took effect the situation worsened. Thus, the federal legislation, which had been intended to raise the purchasing power of all workers, had the effect of intensifying racial discrimination. Despite the latent prejudice against them, blacks had been hired in the first place because they were cheaper. When the codes mandated non-discriminatory wage floors, white solidarity reasserted itself. Once the most ethnically diverse of major American cities, St. Louis had become one of the least so, and one black observer believed that the city's failure to attract large numbers of Slavic and southern European immigrants after 1910 had intensified the distinctions between blacks and whites in employment.

Since a majority of black workers were in personal and domestic service, many of them lost their jobs because of forced retrenchment by their employers. Some apparently stayed in domestic service for board and room only, since the Urban League announced in 1933 that it would no longer recommend names for such positions. For these and the unskilled workers in industry and commerce, employers were the problem. For skilled black craftsmen, the major difficulty lay with union policies. Blacks were totally excluded from the boilermakers and the machinists unions; the railway engineers, conductors, firemen, clerks, and expressmen; and all of the building trades except for the hodcarriers, even though the building trades were open in the other large industrial cities. In some St. Louis locals, such as the Musicians', black members were allowed to form a subsidiary totally dominated by the white organization. Some trades, such as the longshoremen and the hodcarriers, in which radical leadership was strong, did not discriminate. The Sleeping Car Porters and Dining Car Stewards were black monopolies, but very weak in dealing with their employers, apparently because they feared the railroads would hire white labor. Tips were supposed to augment their wages, which were as low as eight cents an hour.

Whatever their qualifications, blacks were not wanted in the building trades. When the national headquarters of one union raised questions about local policy in 1933, John J. Church of the Building

Trades Council responded that there were few Negroes in St. Louis who were qualified to work in construction. If there were such "qualified mechanics . . . the affiliated local union would not hesitate having them in their organization." Yet among fifty-one black bricklayers who were denied work on closed-shop jobs, forty-seven had been union members elsewhere and carried journeymen's cards. In one notable instance, thirty-five electricians, thirty-one carpenters, forty-four painters, and twenty plasterers, all blacks who either had union cards or were qualified to join, were denied work in the construction of the municipal hospital for Negroes (City Number Two). Even in black-owned private construction projects, such as the Poro Beauty College and the Peoples' Finance Company, blacks were employed only as common laborers. The Board of Education, despite its public stance favoring the Urban League's equal-employment objectives, could not or would not hire black craftsmen to build its segregated black schools. Still, the president of the St. Louis Building Trades Council asserted to the U.S. Department of Labor in March 1934 that there was no discrimination in his construction unions.

Between 1930 and 1932, before the federal government took any responsibility for direct relief, both public and private charities were strained to their limits. The city allocated $1.48 million from operating revenue for relief purposes, and another $2 million was distributed by the Salvation Army, the St. Vincent DePaul Society, and the Provident Association. These expenditures and an extraordinary number of tax defaults had created a municipal deficit, and further large expenditures for relief were thought impossible. Banker Tom K. Smith of the Citizens' Relief Committee and Mayor Victor Miller initiated a "Command Campaign" in February 1932 which raised $1.1 million from individual and corporate donors, but the regiments of unemployed had become armies. In November, voters passed a $4.6 million relief bond issue. Various economies and a 10 percent wage cut for municipal employees in 1933 enabled Bernard F. Dickmann, the first Democratic mayor since 1909, and the Board of Aldermen to reduce the budget by 11 percent to $38.4 million. Rolla Wells, in retirement, must have experienced a certain wry satisfaction when the new regime augmented relief funds by levying tolls on motor vehicles crossing the free bridge.

The federal emergency relief program got under way in May 1933, but local aid was still needed, even after WPA work relief began in 1934. In February 1935, a second relief bond issue of $3.6 million was approved. Between 1932 and 1936 approximately $68 million was expended for relief in St. Louis: some $50 million by the federal government, $6 million by the state, and about $12 million by the city

African American WPA workers constructing the River des Peres enclosure extension through University City. Photograph by W. C. Persons, 1940. MHS-PP.

and voluntary agencies. In addition, thousands who would otherwise have been jobless were at work for the Public Works Administration (PWA) and on civic government projects: the $87 million bond issue improvements, airport construction, and a $16.1 million supplemental civic improvements program adopted in 1934. By 1936 the relief rolls were down from well over one hundred thousand to thirty-five thousand, most of whom were considered unemployable. After the WPA had started a premature retrenchment in 1937 the downtown bankers W. C. Connett and J. Lionberger Davis, who dominated the Relief Committee, and Mayor Dickmann agreed that the hardcore unemployed and unemployables were the permanent responsibility of the city.

Despite the pervasive discrimination against black workers, the direct relief programs, both city and federal, were handled equitably, and though there were instances of administrative bias in the WPA, they were usually corrected on appeal. Among the casualties of these unprecedented welfare efforts was the black voters' ancient allegiance to the Republican Party. The Democrats dispensed lifesaving largesse in the city, in the state, and in Washington; and they reaped a harvest.

Senator Mike Kinney delivered one-hundred-to-one majorities in his primarily black downtown district for the 1934 bond issue—it passed in the city by four to one, and by 1936 black Republicans were in short supply. With some exceptions, the newer ethnics had already tended to be Democratic, and the New Deal turned tendency into commitment. While the basic Republicanism of the German middle class remained, it was shaken temporarily by Prohibition's repeal, and German trade-unionists liked the pro-labor stance of the Roosevelt administration.

The census of 1940 was a shocker for St. Louis. For the first time in 120 years the population had declined, though by less than 1 percent to 816,048. Immigration was only a trickle after the restrictive federal legislation of the 1920s, and the rush to green suburbia, which had more than doubled the county's population during the prosperity decade, continued, though at a reduced pace during the depression. The county had 274,230 people in 1940, a 12 percent increase. Among the major suburbs, University City had become the state's sixth largest city in 1930, after nearly tripling in size in ten years. Another increase of 28 percent brought its population to 33,023 in 1940. Webster Groves had grown by 11.6 percent to 18,394, and Clayton, the county seat, by 22 percent to 16,035. Maplewood, larger than University City in 1920, had neared its peak in 1930 and grew by only 1.7 percent during the thirties. Its neighbor, Richmond Heights, was still in its peak growth period during the depression, showing an increase of 40 percent to 12,802. Kirkwood, the child of the Pacific Railroad and the oldest of the larger county towns, gained by 32 percent to 12,132 in 1940. Latecomers to the suburban scene, such as Berkeley, Brentwood, and Overland, were still under 5,000. Ferguson, still more properly a thriving country town than a suburb, had grown by 50 percent to 5,724. The old colonial village of Florissant was still slumbering in the far north county, larger by only a few hundred than it had been at the time of the Louisiana Purchase.

Even more striking than the suburban migration had been the westward movement within the city itself. The grim sequence of settlement, growth, maturity, blight, and rot, which had been in process for a century as Isaac Lionberger had pointed out in 1918, was described by the City Plan Commission in 1942 as "a wave-like action from east to west." Before the 1930s, the vast open areas in the western section of the city had contained the movement, but now the breakers were beyond the city limits. Eighty percent of new construction in the metropolitan area between 1935 and 1940 had occurred outside the city, and the planners foresaw the prospect of catastrophic decline. Other cities, no more wisely managed but with much larger areas and the ability to expand by annexation (a device not available to St. Louis), masked their deteriorating cores more effectively. Boundary expansion had many advantages, but it did not solve the problem of blight.

In 1900 the area bounded by the river, Angelica Avenue, Jefferson, and South Broadway, comprising 14.3 percent of the city's land area, had 281,159 residents, 48.8 percent of the total population. It had declined steadily thereafter to 169,815—20.8 percent of the city's total. The area between Jefferson and Grand and including Carondelet, with 14.3 percent of the land area, had 135,988 residents in 1900. After peaking at 179,210, it had dropped to 166,276 in 1940. The area between Grand and Calvary-Kingshighway-Gravois had 32.7 percent of the city's area and a population of 116,272 in 1900. It had doubled in population by 1920, but it grew more slowly during the next decades to 269,515 (33 percent of the total). On the western edge, the area from Kingshighway to the city limits, with 38.7 of the land area but only 41,869 people in 1900 (7.3 percent), had grown steadily to 210,442, or 25.8 percent of the population in 1940, but it too was levelling off.

With 30.2 persons per acre, the area east of Jefferson was still the most densely populated, because most of its impoverished residents were crowded into slum tenements—former large homes or business buildings fifty to sixty years old or more. In the downtown district and along the central corridor beyond Jefferson more than 90 percent of the homes were substandard, and the north and south side districts were little better. More than 80 percent of these homes were heated with coal stoves, as were a majority of those between Jefferson and Grand. On the south side near the river 20 percent of the units had no running water, and the ratio was above 10 percent in the entire city east of Grand Avenue. Seventy percent of the dwellings east of Jefferson were without baths, and over 60 percent had no inside toilets. Every section near the river had outside toilets, and there were substantial numbers of them almost to the city's western limits, especially in the Des Peres valley and along Natural Bridge Road.

Using these measures of substandard housing, St. Louis was the worst among the nation's twelve largest metropolitan areas. The plan commission argued that there was no sound reason why this should be so. With its excellent external transportation facilities, strong and diversified industry, and thriving wholesale and retail trade, the city had a sound economic base. The planners denied the charge that the city was rotting at the core. With $100 million expended on public improvements since 1923, they claimed that the problem was not in the public sector. Private housing had expanded in a haphazard and irresponsible fashion, leaving desolation in its wake. When the speculative developers had exhausted the cheap land in the city's far reaches, they had jumped to the country, creating parasitical suburbs which fed on the city and its services. To reverse this trend, obsolete (slum) areas had to be reconstructed and the vast blighted district of twenty-five- to forty-year-old homes between the slums and the newer subdivisions rehabilitated. In the obsolete area large blocks of land, one hundred acres or more, would need to be acquired by the Housing Authority, since piecemeal reconstruction was useless. Land prices had to be reduced to reasonable levels and private capital encouraged by tax abatement to undertake new construction.

The zoning plan of 1918 had allowed too great an area for industry and had permitted historic nuisances and nonconforming uses to persist, and more to the point, it had been declared unconstitutional in 1924. A new and more stringent plan was needed. In any case, the 1942 plan commission argued that deed restrictions such as those used in the private places and in the city's newest and finest subdivision, St. Louis Hills, would help check undesirable development. In tacit recognition that more than cheap land was drawing people to the suburbs, the commission urged continued vigilance against smoke, establishment of a community center in each of eighty-two residential neighborhoods, and additional parks and playgrounds, especially in the older sections of the city. Chairman Gregory Nooney, Lon V. Hocker, and other members recognized that one of their most serious problems was the political separation of the city and county. Efficient delivery of services and rational distribution of industry was virtually impossible in a city flanked by half a hundred self-centered municipalities. Reunification was desirable but apparently impossible, as had been demonstrated in 1926, when a state constitutional amendment had authorized a Board of Freeholders to submit a scheme whereby the city would have absorbed the entire county. City electors had approved consolidation by seven to one, but county voters had rejected it by three to one. In 1930 an amendment authorizing a consolidation of certain services was defeated statewide, with county voters again in opposition.

Air pollution had always plagued St. Louis. It was known in 1822 as the dirtiest place in the Mississippi valley, and in January 1823, the *Missouri Republican* wrote that smoke had been "in some instances so dense as to render it necessary to use candles at midday." Mayor William Carr Lane proposed measures to check pollution without success, and as the city grew, the smoke grew with it. Anti-smoke ordinances in the 1890s helped a little, but growth soon wiped out the gains. In 1906 the public library spent ten thousand dollars to repair smoke damage to its collection, and "sulphuric gases from smoke" were killing trees in Forest Park. By the 1920s growers would not sell evergreens to be planted in the city, and the botanical gardens was considering a move to the county. John Gundlach, chairman of the Chamber of Commerce's Committee on Smoke Abatement in 1923, pressured the newspapers, gave public lectures, and harassed the Terminal Railroad, trying to convince residents to use proper stoking and other techniques to cut down smoke emissions. An ordinance in 1924 created a smoke regulation commission empowered to inspect and license new furnaces. Smoke emission other than during a daily start-up period of twenty minutes was outlawed, but there was no provision for prosecution.

Exasperated by half-measures, Edward Flad, son of James B. Eads's associate Henry Flad, stated bluntly in 1925 that only smokeless fuel would do the job. He urged the construction of a municipal distillation plant, which would convert bituminous coal into coke and gas to be sold at prices competitive with coal, with the extra cost to be borne by the taxpayers. This and other suggestions involving alternatives to Illinois coal were rejected out of consideration for taxpayers, the poor, the "best citizens" (industrialists), and the soft-coal industry.

Engineers did not agree as to the major source of the smoke pall. One of them, Erle Ormsby, president of the Donk Brothers Coal Company, predictably found that it was the homes of the poor. In a humanitarian vein, he argued that only Illinois bituminous would enable the poor to save on fuel costs, "in order that they may have as much as possible left for the enjoyment of life and the education of their children." Professor Franz Berger of Washington University agreed that at least 50 percent of the smoke came from dwellings and that industries and residents could be taught to create less of it. Outraged by this reasoning, David Larkin argued that since householders burned only 10 percent of the coal, they probably produced only 10 percent of the smoke.

In 1926 the Citizens' Smoke Abatement League chose Erle Ormsby as president, a move not unlike hiring a bear to watch over the honey. The league, which raised funds from coal dealers, furnace manufacturers, and railroad executives, was sincerely against smoke, but it was even more against efforts to replace soft coal as the city's fuel. Meanwhile, the press, which knew the problem but not the answers, carried such headlines as "St. Louis, 3 times as smoky as Pittsburgh," and "Smoke Kills Evergreen Trees in Shaw's Gardens." On December 23, 1926, the *Post-Dispatch* cracked, "Presumably the sun rose, but whether it did nobody knows." After estimating the cost of smoke to St. Louisans at $15 million a year, the league established a school for training householders and janitors in firing and banking their furnaces and stoves and sponsored an engineering survey, which revealed that St. Louis's annual soot deposit came to 870 tons per square mile, compared to 450 for Chicago and 250 for Pittsburgh. To the chagrin of some members of the league, the report also claimed that dwellings contributed only 5 percent of the smoke nuisance. Ormsby and the other coal merchants soon resigned from the league, and department store magnate Sidney Baer took over as president. The educational campaign had some effect initially, but the "Black Christmas" of 1927 underlined the failure to get at the root of the problem. Flad's plan for a synthetic fuel plant was brought up again, but Mayor Victor Miller ruled it out as prohibitively expensive.

For another dozen years St. Louis had to endure the killing smoke. As the long ordeal continued, the public outcry mounted, spurred by the *Globe-Democrat*, the *Star-Times*, and the *Post-Dispatch*, the last eventually winning the 1941 Pulitzer Prize in Journalism for its efforts. In 1934 Mayor Bernard Dickmann appointed Raymond Tucker, a Washington University engineering professor, as assistant for smoke. After dismissing the voluntary approach as a waste of time, Tucker recommended that coal should be washed to reduce the ash and sulphur content of the smoke. The Board of Aldermen mandated coal-washing in 1937 and created the office of Smoke Commissioner with adequate enforcement powers. Sulphurous smoke was reduced somewhat, but the volume was still so high that the improvement escaped the senses. Angry coal merchants, charging Dickmann and Tucker with corrupt dealings with stoker manufacturers, betraying the poor, and various other crimes, attacked the ordinance in the federal courts, but Judge George H. Moore found it to be a constitutional use of the police power.

Despite his strenuous enforcement efforts, Tucker knew that washed Illinois coal was not the answer. After three suffocating weeks in late 1939, featuring the midnight-at-noon "Black Tuesday" on November 28, a quick response was imperative. Tucker recommended standards that would outlaw Illinois coal except when mechanical stokers were used, forcing householders to burn expensive Arkansas coal. Anticipating an enraged reaction from coal interests and citizens, Mayor Dickmann appointed a Smoke Elimination Committee with banker James L. Ford, Jr., as chairman. As expected, Ford's group endorsed the Tucker plan and launched a publicity campaign to counter the assaults of the coal interests. Dickmann shook the patronage stick at the aldermen, and in April 1940, after the mayor squelched an attempt to exempt one of the worst offenders, the Terminal Railway Association, the board enacted Tucker's recommendations.

With the cooperation of the Frisco Railroad, which reduced its coal-hauling rates from Arkansas by one-third, residents could buy clean-burning fuel without a great financial sacrifice. The Manufacturers' and the Terminal Railways changed to diesel-powered switch engines, and Tucker's inspectors stopped coal smuggling at the bridges and cracked down on emission offenders, large and small. The results were spectacular; in the winter of 1940–41 there were only 19 hours of thick and 178 hours of moderate smoke, as compared to 177 and 599 hours respectively during the previous winter. Most of the heavy smoke now came from the east side, on the infrequent days when the wind blew from that quarter. For the first time in a century, St. Louis's buildings, after cleaning, looked as they did when built. Fortunately, the real long-range solution was provided at the same time by the completion of the Mississippi Valley Fuel Company's pipeline from the South. Now, the Laclede Gas Company could furnish cheap clean fuel to all comers, whenever they could afford to install gas furnaces.

St. Louis had taken an important step toward rehabilitation of its environment, with a powerful assist from the pipeline. But much remained to be done—city services were inadequate; many of those who had benefited most from its past successes continued to run from its problems, leaving the ruined areas to the poor; and solutions to the problem of blight were hampered by physical and political barriers. There were elements of strength: able individuals willing to attack the city's problems, pride in the city's past and identification with its successful symbols, the location in the great valley and the city's large hinterland, and the range and diversity of its business and cultural components. St. Louis had been a "major-league" city—it still was. It would remain so if the dynamics of change in the region, in the nation, and in the world permitted, and if its citizens had the tenacity and the imagination to remedy past omissions and adjust to changed conditions.

Black Tuesday. *The Civil Courts Building is barely visible through the smoke at noon-time on October 24, 1939. Photograph, 1939. MHS-PP.*

11.
The New Spirit of St. Louis

In December 1933, Mayor Bernard Dickmann called together a group of businessmen to set in motion plans for Luther Ely Smith's cherished riverfront rehabilitation and memorial project. At that meeting the Jefferson National Expansion Memorial Association was formed, which immediately began a campaign to make the project a national effort. By joint resolution in 1934, Congress created a Federal Memorial Commission to plan the construction of a permanent memorial "at or near the site of old St. Louis," to honor "the men who made possible the territorial expansion of the United States . . . Thomas Jefferson and his aides Livingston and Monroe, who negotiated the Louisiana Purchase, and the hardy hunters, trappers, frontiersmen, and pioneers . . . who contributed to the territorial expansion and development of the United States of America." Members of the Federal Commission appointed by Congress, President Franklin D. Roosevelt, and St. Louis's Jefferson Memorial Association included Professor Charles E. Merriam of the University of Chicago; William Allen White of the *Emporia Gazette*; Luther Ely Smith; Congressman Lloyd Thurston of Iowa; Senator Alben W. Barkley of Kentucky; banker William T. Kemper of Kansas City; J. Lionberger Davis of St. Louis; General Jefferson Randolph Kean, a direct descendant of Thomas Jefferson; and Senator Frederick Van Nuys of Indiana.

At its first meeting in the Adolphus Room of the Jefferson Hotel on December 19, 1934, the commission elected Senator Barkley as chairman. After each member had pledged his devotion to Jeffersonian ideals and the commission's purpose, Professor Merriam set the tone by urging that it "make no little plans." The memorial should be comparable to the greatest in the world, "to the great column at Trafalgar Square in London," the Arc de Triomphe at Paris, and to the "great towering monument" to George Washington at the capital. Louis Labeaume, chairman of the St. Louis chapter of the American Institute of Architects, proposed a tentative plan for the Memorial involving the demolition of the buildings in the area of the original village, from the Eads Bridge south for a half-mile and one-third of a mile deep, from Third Street to the levee. A memorial group to be in direct line with the Old Court House would feature a large central building of stone, 140 feet high to its dome and 60 to 75 feet high at

Luther Ely Smith. *Smith, a prominent attorney, was deeply involved in civic affairs and was the foremost advocate of clearance of the riverfront and a memorial park with a symbolic monument. Photograph by Strauss Studio, 1936. MHS-PP.*

its cornices, flanked by two smaller buildings, each of the three to extend 750 feet from Third Street toward the river. The area at the foot of the buildings, along the levee, would be reserved for gardens. Murals illustrating westward expansion, sculptures, and the main exhibits were to be housed in the central building, with the flanking buildings devoted to individual museum and display rooms for each of the states of the Northwest and the Southwest. Obelisks commemorating the Oregon and Santa Fe Trails would stand outside the buildings. Labeaume estimated the cost of the project, exclusive of site acquisition, to be at least $20 million. It was presumed that these costs would be shared by St. Louis and the federal government. Chairman Barkley closed the meeting with the hope that the mission would be completed within five years.

In 1935, the city passed a $7.5 million bond issue, which, with $9 million in WPA funds committed by President Roosevelt, made possible the acquisition and clearance of the forty-block area. The site of the Creole village was eventually to be buried under thousands of tons of landfill. Most of its original character had been destroyed in the nineteenth century anyway—the limestone bluffs having been leveled to build up the wharf, and many of the brick replacements of the old houses of posts having been destroyed by fire in 1849. Their successors by the 1930s were mostly warehouses and seedy tenements. Beyond the Eads Bridge, the northern edge of the village was saved, its cobblestone streets lined with mid-nineteenth-century brick structures, retaining the street lines approximately as laid out by Laclède, making it possible for the curious to reconstruct in their minds the layout of old St. Louis. The Old Cathedral, completed in 1834, was preserved on Laclède's church lot between Second and Third on Walnut, but sadly and indefensibly, the much older stone warehouse of Manuel Lisa's fur company was destroyed.

The project withstood several tests in the 1930s. Taxpayers in 1936 challenged the bond issue as having been adopted in a fraudulent election. They had a strong case, but the judge, impressed by the importance of the project or perhaps by its powerful sponsors, refused to kill the memorial. In 1939 Congressman John Cochran, under heavy pressure from Smith and Dickmann, staved off a Congressional move to repudiate the federal commitment. War put the riverfront plan on the shelf for five years, and the postwar Congress, in a budget-balancing mood, showed no interest. Meanwhile, the cleared area was used as a forty-five hundred-car parking lot, and housing developers, sports stadium promoters, and a host of others clamored for the land. To complicate matters further, the Terminal Railroad refused to remove the elevated tracks which loomed over the levee, connecting the Eads Bridge with the Union Station.

Aerial View of the Riverfront Area before Clearance. *Photograph, 1932. McCrea Collection, MHS-PP.*

Undaunted by the lack of action in Washington, Luther Ely Smith and James L. Ford raised $225,000 in 1945 to conduct an architectural competition for the memorial design. Having pumped his energies into the cause for more than thirty years, Smith was determined to persevere. A distinguished panel of architects, including the director of the Philadelphia Museum, the dean of architecture at M.I.T., Louis Labeaume, and Charles Nagel of the St. Louis Art Museum selected Eero Saarinen's catenary arch design for the memorial in 1948.

Saarinen described the genesis of his concept to the *Post-Dispatch:*

> I can remember thinking how, in Washington, the memorials to our three greatest men, Washington, Lincoln and Jefferson, each has a distinct geometric shape. The Washington Monument a vertical line, the Lincoln Memorial a cube; and the Jefferson Memorial a globe. There is something simple and satisfying in that, and I wondered whether St. Louis should not have a shape along similar lines. . . . We thought of a huge concrete arch. . . . Then . . . we began to wonder whether one leg should be placed on each shore of the river. No, there seemed to be enough bridges. . . . We tried it obtuse, close to a semicircle, and it looked too much like a rainbow. We tried it vertical and pointed and it looked too ecclesiastical. Anyway, we chose an archform which was neither flat and round nor too pointed.
>
> More and more it began to dawn on us that the arch was really a gateway and, gradually we named it the *Gateway* to the West.

Aerial View of the Riverfront Area after Clearance. *Photograph by Ted McCrea, 1948. MHS-PP.*

After 1949, when the railroads finally surrendered their elevated tracks, it remained only for Congress to deliver on its three-to-one matching commitment for construction. In 1954 Missouri Senator Thomas Hennings, supported by Senator Stuart Symington and Representatives Frank Karsten and Leonor Sullivan, persuaded Congress to appropriate $5 million. Subsequently, with Sullivan and Congressman Thomas L. Curtis applying pressure, $12.25 million (1958), $6 million (1965), and $9.5 million (1976) were added to complete the Gateway Arch and the Museum of Westward Expansion. To supplement the city's original $7.5 million, the Terminal Railway put up $500,000, the Bi-State Development Agency $800,000, and the private Jefferson Memorial Expansion Association $200,000. In March 1967, the city's voters approved another Arch and Museum bond issue of $2 million.

The Arch was topped out on October 28, 1965, its construction having taken seven years. Towering 632 feet from base to apex, it was a shimmering steel wonder for all the world to see, and a good part of it has. Skeptics and wiseacres who had called it the "big hairpin" and a "giant croquet wicket" during construction began to see and feel what millions of visitors would experience. Not only was the Arch a successful symbol of westward expansion and the latest "New St. Louis," it had a presence and a mystique all its own. The observer notes that visitors seem impelled to enhance the visual experience by touching or caressing the structure itself. In 1967 the National Park service, which managed the twenty-two-acre park, made an inspired addition to the original plan by installing trains in the north leg which carried passengers to the observation platform at the top. So enthusiastic was the response that the south leg was similarly equipped in 1968, but the lines only grew longer. During its first ten years, 16.25 million people visited the memorial. In 1976 the Museum of Westward Expansion, with forty-two thousand square feet of floor space, the largest museum in the National Park System, opened in the underground section of the Arch.

Part of the landscaping plan was yet to be completed, but the theme and purpose of the memorial has been magnificently realized. As a result, St. Louis became one of the world's major tourist centers. It was claimed in 1975 that only Lenin's Tomb and the two Disney theme parks recorded more visitors than the Gateway Arch (a claim supported only by a rough turnstile count). At the same time it was estimated that the project stimulated $503 million in downtown construction. The Arch certainly was partially responsible for the downtown renaissance, but some of the rebuilding would have gone forward in any case. Famous-Barr and the First National Bank were committed to renewal

Busch Stadium and the Gateway Arch. *Photograph by Ted McCrea, 1967. MHS-PP.*

before Arch construction began. Nonetheless, the Arch was the symbol of progress in St. Louis, as was evident from the eagerness of business to be associated with it. The 1980 St. Louis telephone directory listed seventeen "Arch" business firms, from the Arch Bootery to the Archview Cafeteria, an "Archable" real estate firm, a plain Archco, an Archland Dome, and forty-nine "Archway" companies, including a funeral home, a massage parlor, and a brokerage house. There was also a "Big Arch" leasing firm and 131 "Gateway" enterprises, including a bartending school, a Bible fellowship, a loan company, a bank, an Oriental herb company, and a corkball club.

In 1958, when there had been no new construction downtown for many years and Eero Saarinen was complaining about the rundown character of the Arch's setting, Charles Farris of the Federal Land Clearance Authority proposed the building of a downtown stadium. Unlike most major-league cities, St. Louis elected to do the job with private capital. James Hickok, president of the First National Bank, headed a fund-raising drive which collected $20 million for the project, including $5 million from the Cardinals' owners, Anheuser-Busch, and $2.5 million from the May Company (Famous-Barr). Architect Edward Durell Stone repeated the Gateway Arch design ninety-six times in Busch Memorial Stadium's exterior. In 1965 the Cardinals moved to their new home, leaving old Sportsman's Park at

Grand and Dodier, the scene of the spectacular feats of the "Gashouse Gang" of the 1930s; the Browns' only pennant-winning team (1944), which lost the World Series to the Cardinals; and the brilliance of Stan Musial and Enos Slaughter in the 1940s and 1950s. After their long drought, the Cardinals had won ten pennants and seven World Series between 1926 and 1964, by far the best record of any National League team. Especially satisfying were the World Series triumphs, as many as all of the other teams in their league combined had won during the period, and including three out of five over the Yankees.

The new stadium's playing surface was well below ground level and consisted of artificial turf, a combination which produced a marvelous effect on warm July and August days. In 1966, during the Major-League All-Star Game, Casey Stengel, the irrepressible Yankee manager, summed it up by commenting that St. Louis's fine new stadium held the heat well. With a seating capacity of nearly fifty thousand, some 50 percent greater than that of the old park, the handsome home of the baseball and football Cardinals became a major asset to downtown St. Louis, especially to the weekend hotel, restaurant, and entertainment business. As a high-volume visitor attraction, in combination with the Arch, the Zoo, and the new (opened in 1971) Six Flags over Mid-America Amusement Park, the stadium helped to make the tourist industry one of the city's most important assets.

Six Flags (so-called with a little poetic license) presumably derived its name from the Spanish, French, British (on the east side), United States, Confederate, and Missouri flags. Located just off Interstate 44 in southwest St. Louis County, thirty-five miles from the Arch, the 250-acre park attracted 1.7 million visitors in 1979. At the juncture of Interstate Routes 44, 55, and 70, St. Louis's location was ideal for tourism. Although attractive primarily to local citizens, another tourist asset was the excursion steamboat *Admiral*, which cruised the Mississippi along the city's front several times daily during the warm months. In April 1980 its future was uncertain because of the insolvency of its owners, but a "Save the *Admiral*" fund-raising drive was under way.

Of equal or greater concern than the city's riverfront face in the post–World War II period was the quality of life for its residents. A 1937 study had revealed that obsolete housing areas, chiefly within fifteen blocks of downtown, with one-fifth of the city's area and one-third of its population, accounted for three-fourths of the illegitimate children, half of the infant deaths, and two-thirds of the tuberculosis and delinquency in the city. Beaumont, Mill Creek, Soulard, and the downtown fringe were the worst areas. In 1939 the city embarked upon its first federally assisted, low-rent housing projects. Carr Square Village, in a once-elegant neighborhood on the near north side, and Clinton-Peabody Terrace, just west of Fourteenth Street near City Hospital Number One, were completed in 1942.

In 1947, the City Plan Commission reported that despite the two low-rent developments and the civic improvements completed under the bond issues of the previous two decades, St. Louis was not a "livable" city. There were still 33,000 homes with shared toilet facilities, and 88,000 families living in pre-1900 buildings. Obsolete and blighted districts covered half of St. Louis's residential area, and they were expanding rapidly. The commission recommended that if private interests continued to ignore the problem, the city should buy the obsolete properties and undertake reconstruction and rehabilitation itself. Assuming that construction costs would decline after the postwar boom (a vain hope), the planners estimated that the new and rehabilitated housing would cost no more than current street, sewer, and airport improvements and additions. Costs could be recovered by the higher taxes collected from the upgraded areas and from federal subsidies. Citizen identification with community purposes would follow if the projects were treated as neighborhoods, provided with parks, playgrounds, recreation areas, and shopping centers. Minimum standards should be established, said the commission, requiring indoor toilets, adequate air, lighting, screens, elimination of overcrowding, and eradication of rats, roaches, and other vermin.

Anticipating an early end to the war and an immediate depression, Republican Mayor Aloys Kaufmann and a Citizens' Committee on Postwar Improvements and Employment proposed a $43.5 million bond issue in 1944 "to help provide jobs for discharged servicemen and war workers through necessary expansion of municipal facilities and services." Chairman Walter W. Head, Powell B. McHaney, J. Wesley McAfee, and the Citizens' Committee presented eleven proposals headed by airport expansion; completion of the River des Peres drainage project; street improvements; water system repair; and Parks and Recreation expansion, the last to include new athletic fields and new swimming pools at Fairgrounds Park, Vashon Center, and Market Street at Compton. A new central police station, fire engine houses, hospital improvements, new elephant quarters at the Zoo, a new Grand Avenue viaduct over Mill Creek valley, and Art Museum repairs were also included. Joseph Darst, former City Welfare director and a Democratic mayoral candidate, attacked the bond issue as hopelessly inadequate, not "the type and kind of progressive master plan that the citizens were entitled to." He noted that most of the funds would be spent for work relief that might not be necessary, and that the plan did not attack the core problems of blight and decay. But labor endorsed the bond issue, and Comptroller Louis Nolte assured the public that no tax increase would be required. Jobs and patriotism at no cost were irresistible, and the propositions passed by margins averaging 4 to 1, ranging downward from 4.5 to 1 for hospitals to 3 to 1 for art. As Darst had predicted, there was no depression and little need for make-work projects, and labor and construction costs soared instead of dropped. The funds were inadequate, even for their modest objectives.

Mayor Kaufmann had succeeded William Dee Becker, who had been killed in a glider crash at the airport. The fallout from an attempt to steal the governorship in 1940 was still plaguing the Democrats, and Kaufmann won a full term in 1945, as of 1980 the last Republican mayoral victory in St. Louis.

The voters had turned sour on civic improvements in 1948, defeating bond issues of $15 million for sewers and $16 million for slum clearance and redevelopment, the latter failing to win even a simple majority. The sewer bonds went down again in 1949, and a $17.2 million school construction issue passed in 1951 after first being rejected. On other fronts, Darst was successful. With federal matching funds, the Land Clearance and Redevelopment Authority in 1953 bought and cleared a slum area between Chestnut and Olive Street near the Civic Center. This "Plaza Square" project was then sold to private developers, who built six attractive thirteen-story apartment buildings for middle-class tenants. In 1953, a $1.5 million bond issue realized a forty-year-old City Beautiful dream, the completion of a continuous green-belt mall from Aloe Plaza to the Soldier's Memorial at Thirteenth Street. But low-rent housing was Darst's major objective. Federal legislation provided the funding, and public housing was declared tax-exempt by a court decision in 1949, breaking the slum clearance logjam. Five major low-rent housing projects were soon under way, all primarily high-rise buildings, chiefly because of federal insistence on minimizing land costs. The structures were of steel and concrete faced with brick.

Cochran Gardens, just north of the central business district, completed in 1953, included 704 dwelling units in two six-story, two seven-story, and four twelve-story buildings. South of Chouteau Avenue, the Darst-Webbe complex was built on 28.5 acres between Park and Lafayette, Twelfth and Fourteenth Streets. Eight high-rise buildings were to provide 1,238 units for low-income white tenants. Of the 515 old homes that had been razed for the project, 362 had lacked inside toilets and 131 had no running water. The complex opened in 1956 and 1957 with no racial bars, discrimination in public housing having been outlawed by the United States Supreme Court.

The Pruitt and Igoe Apartments, on the northwest fringe of the downtown district, consisted of thirty-three eleven-story buildings each 170 feet long. Their combined capacity was nearly three thousand families. The first units opened in 1954 and 1955, theoretically unsegregated but primarily black in fact. The 657-unit Vaughn Apartments, consisting of four nine-story buildings just east of Pruitt-Igoe between Eighteenth and Twentieth Streets, opened in 1957. St. Louis now had 6,138 postwar public dwelling units costing $80.4 million, in addition to the two prewar projects, which had provided 1,315 apartments for only $7 million.

Each of the new complexes opened auspiciously to the plaudits of the press, self-congratulations by local leaders and federal housing officials, and enthusiastic comments by tenants contrasting their spacious and sparkling new quarters with their previous slum homes. Pruitt-Igoe, as one of the largest projects in the nation, attracted wide and favorable comment from architects and planners as a model for other cities. But alas, there was trouble from the beginning. The first residents at Darst were harassed by gangs of stone-throwing boys, and it was soon obvious that there was too little recreational space,

The Pruitt-Igoe Housing Project Shortly after Completion. *Photograph by Ted McCrea, 1955. MHS-PP.*

especially for the thousands of children who were stacked in the high-rises. There were neither nearby shopping facilities nor health services, public transportation was inadequate, and nearby job opportunities were limited. Crime and vandalism plagued all of the complexes, but at Pruitt-Igoe, they were of catastrophic proportions. In 1965 another $5 million was invested in its renovation, but families who could get out did so. By 1971 only seventeen of the thirty-three buildings had any occupants at all—six hundred families were scattered through them. The halls stank of urine and feces, plumbing was ripped out and the pipes sold, and even the toilet bowls had been torn from their moorings. In 1972, with Washington's permission, the Housing Authority dynamited two buildings to make room for playgrounds, but to no avail. Total demolition began in 1975, and the empty and sterile seventy acres became a stark reminder of good intentions gone wrong.

Assessments of the reasons for the Pruitt-Igoe fiasco have been of two principal types, one blaming it on the character of the residents, and the other emphasizing the physical-environmental factors. The first points out that in all of the projects, the Housing Authority's plan called for a careful screening of applicants for family solidarity, respect for property and education, and for other middle-class attitudes. This screening was carried out at first in Pruitt-Igoe as well as the others, but later, when a tornado ripped through the city's most degraded slum, a rat-infested one-hundred-block agglomeration of shacks and falling-down mansions in the Mill Creek valley, the policy changed. During and after World War II, the Mill Creek area had soaked up thousands of rural blacks from Mississippi, southeast Missouri, and eastern Arkansas, many of them sharecroppers displaced by agricultural mechanization. Without roots in the city, neither understanding nor sharing the values of the older black community, they were on the nether rim of existence. Many of the families were barely surviving on Missouri's meager welfare payments. When the tornado struck, hundreds lost their slum homes, and under heavy pressure from Mayor Tucker and the community leadership, the Housing Authority admitted them willy-nilly to Pruitt-Igoe. Of more than eight thousand residents after this influx, only twelve hundred were adult males. For those who believed that clean and attractive surroundings would make proud and orderly citizens, the results were shattering. In this view, the humanitarian decision to admit the poorest of the poor doomed Pruitt-Igoe.

The above analysis was rejected entirely by St. Louis's KMOX–TV in 1971, in an editorial endorsed by Congressman William Clay, who inserted it into the Congressional Record. Not the residents but the concept itself was at fault, "doomed from the day it left the drawing boards," because it crowded thousands of families into too small an area, surrounded by blight and bereft of the services and facilities necessary for a decent life.

Professor Eugene Meehan of the University of Missouri–St. Louis, the most thorough student of the question, has called public housing in the 1950s "programmed disaster." While he conceded that "the culture of poverty" and the large number of juveniles from single-parent families exacerbated the problem, Meehan concluded that despite its location in devastated surroundings Pruitt-Igoe might have succeeded had it been better designed and constructed. Other than location and a generally unhelpful attitude in city government, the chief culprits were the federal government and the construction industry. To hold construction costs down, the government insisted on "mean, shoddy, and cheap" economies that eventually irritated or enraged the residents and escalated maintenance costs. Some units were reduced in size by as much as 20 percent below comparable units in Cochran Gardens. Doorknobs and locks that broke on first use; window frames that could not stand the wind; thin plywood kitchen cabinets; plain wood kitchen counter tops; tiny sinks, stoves, and refrigerators; small bathrooms; dangerously non-insulated water pipes, and the omission of most playground space and landscaping all added to the problem. Worse perhaps were the skip-stop elevators, with exits only on the first, fourth, seventh, and tenth floors, which, as Mayor A. J. Cervantes (1965–73) pointed out, made a majority of the residents vulnerable to the assaults of criminals lurking in the stairwells. The elimination of a central corridor that produced cross-ventilation in the other housing developments made the heat virtually unbearable at Pruitt-Igoe.

Largely responsible for these devastating economies were the rapacious and sloppy construction industry and its unions. Because of the economic and political power of the Steamfitters, virtually the only item that was not pared down was an elaborate and expensive steam-heating system. Despite the corner-cutting, construction costs at Pruitt-Igoe were 60 percent above the national average and 40 percent over the New York City average. According to Professor Meehan, luxury homes in the suburbs could have been built for less per square foot. Site owners, contractors, and the unions grabbed the federal bonanza and ran, leaving the Housing Authority to deal with the problems created by their greed. This "legal larceny," said Meehan, was glossed over with the fiction "high construction cost area."

The other high-rise complexes of similar vintage were still in operation in 1980, Darst with 78 percent occupancy, Webbe with 82 percent, and Vaughn with 74 percent. They were only marginally better built than Pruitt-Igoe, and they too had suffered crime and vandalism, especially during the 1969 rent strike, but they survived. Perhaps, as Meehan has suggested, they would have been considered disasters if Pruitt-Igoe had not been so much worse, but others have argued that screening for occupancy made the difference. Since most of the violence and vandalism at Pruitt-Igoe, though not the fouling of the corridors, was attributed to intruders, the crystal ball remained clouded. Cochran Gardens, with its superior construction, was relatively successful, and the thirty-eight-year-old Clinton-Peabody and Carr Square apartments were fully occupied in 1980. If the latter is accounted for by their one and two-story design, then what about the rigorously screened Blumeyer complex, which opened in 1967 west of Compton Avenue between Delmar and Easton? Its forty-two two-story townhouses, two fifteen-story and two fourteen-story buildings were fully occupied in 1980.

Low-rent public housing was Joseph Darst's major goal, a part of the general framework of revitalizing the city. His successor would be the chief catalyst for the rest. Raymond Tucker had left his classroom again, first to work for Darst and then to run for mayor himself. As chairman of the Board of Freeholders in 1949, he had helped draft a new city charter, which would have eliminated the "county" offices and transferred their few real functions to regular departments. Hundreds of patronage jobs would have come under the merit system, to the distress of hacks of both parties. Because the city could levy only those taxes authorized by its charter, the freeholders listed a variety of them, including an earnings tax. The state legislature authorized a temporary levy of .5 percent during the Kaufmann administration, but the risk that later lawmakers might not extend the privilege made permanent authorization desirable. The need would grow as urban renewal created ever-larger tax-free or tax-abated areas. The politicians convinced many voters that all of the taxes mentioned in the charter would be levied immediately, which insured its defeat. Despite Tucker's role in this losing cause, the voters respected him for his work as smoke commissioner and liked him for his straightforward honesty and unpopularity with the political bureaucracy. He was elected mayor in 1953 by a margin of fifty thousand, a record for the city.

The General Assembly had killed the earnings tax just before the new mayor took office, leaving him with a $7 million budgetary gap. With Aloys Kaufmann's help, Tucker persuaded the legislature to make the tax authorization permanent, and the St. Louis voters enacted the levy. Now, the city was guaranteed some return on the services it provided to those executives, professionals, and workers who had moved to the suburbs. In 1959 the earnings tax was increased to 1 percent.

During the last year of his term, Mayor Darst approached a group of businessmen in an effort to get St. Louis moving. No new office building had been erected downtown in two decades, traffic in the central business district was a nerve-shattering mess, and half of the city was blighted. To lead the attack on these problems, Darst appointed eight men from the city's business elite to "Civic Progress, Incorporated." In 1953 Mayor Tucker expanded the group by ten, and eventually there were twenty-five members. As close to a "Big Cinch" as St. Louis could muster at mid-century, the Darst appointees included David R. Calhoun of the St. Louis Union Trust Company; J. W. McAfee of Union Electric; Powell McHaney of the General American Life Insurance Company; Ethan A. H. Shepley, chancellor of Washington University; Sidney R. Baer of Stix, Baer, and Fuller; Arthur Blumeyer of the Bank of St. Louis; James Douglas, a prominent lawyer; and ex-mayor Kaufmann. Tucker added August A. Busch, Jr.; Edwin Clark, a dynamic newcomer who headed Southwestern Bell; Donald Danforth of Ralston-Purina; Morton D. May of the May Company; Edgar M. Queeny of Monsanto Chemical; Sidney Maestre of Mercantile Trust; William McDonnell of McDonnell Aircraft; Tom K. Smith of Boatmen's Bank; Edgar Rand; and Clarence Turley. McHaney was the first president, succeeded in 1955 by Clark.

According to Howard F. Baer, a prominent businessman and civic leader, several members of Civic Progress were powerful enough to commit their companies without the risk of being reversed by their boards, notably Busch, Calhoun, Clark, McAfee, Queeny, Maestre, Smith, and Danforth. Baer referred admiringly to some of them as "swashbucklers," though none of them had the flair, the overwhelming personal community recognition, or the political and economic power of the leaders of a less complex era, such individuals as David R. Francis, James Campbell, Robert Brookings, Rolla Wells, and "Prince" Adolphus Busch. But they did still cluster in the exclusive insiders' clubs created by the turn-of-the-century elite, the small, exclusively male and predominantly Anglo-Saxon domains such as the Bogey and Log Cabin Clubs. The St. Louis Country Club had been joined by Bellerive and Old Warson as their playgrounds, and it was an article of faith that informal decisions made in these elite enclaves and in the St. Louis Club had a powerful effect in St. Louis. Unlike their predecessors, however, the insiders of the 1950s, led by their more liberal members such as David R. Calhoun, admitted a few Jews (usually under 10 percent) to their councils. Formerly, the Jewish elite

David R. Calhoun. *Calhoun, president of the St. Louis Union Trust Company (since absorbed as Centerre Bank into Boatmen's Bank and now NationsBank), was an original member of Civic Progress and led the campaign for the 1955 bond issue which financed land clearances and improvements. Photograph by Edwyn Studios, ca. 1955. MHS-PP.*

had been confined to their own bastions such as the Columbian Club (a downtown business fraternity) and the Westwood Country Club.

Civic Progress hired the powerful Fleishman-Hillard firm, headed by the highly regarded Jewish leader Alfred Fleishman, to handle the publicity, and assisted by the churches, the League of Women Voters, the unions, and the press, it launched a massive civic improvement bond issue campaign in 1954. According to Sidney Maestre, chairman of the Bond Issue Screening Committee, the bond issue was essential because St. Louis had been "tolerant too long of inadequacy, too complacent in the face of growing slums and congested traffic, of rundown playgrounds for children and dilapidated quarters for aged and chronic patients." David R. Calhoun presided over a campaign blitz that saturated every level and corner of the community, backed by an all-out effort by the press. The *Globe-Democrat* awarded a weekly prize for the best letter embodying the spirit of the bond issue. One of the fifty dollar winners said, "Let those who pass through St. Louis the Gateway to the West, see the 'Arch of Triumph' that we voters will erect. . . ." For several years the *Post-Dispatch* had challenged the city with a series of editorials and articles headed "Progress or Decay," which the civic leaders acknowledged as a major catalyst for the campaign.

On May 26, 1955, the voters approved twenty-three propositions amounting to $110.6 million by stunning margins averaging nearly six to one. Among the major items were three expressways: the Daniel Boone (U.S. 40), $7 million for one-half of the land costs for eight miles of divided highway from the west boundary to Tenth and Clark Avenues downtown; the Mark Twain (alternate U.S. 40—later I-70), $6 million for eight miles from the northwestern limits to Third and Locust; and the Ozark (U.S. 66—now I-44), $5 million for 7.9 miles from the southwestern limits to Eleventh and Geyer. The federal and state governments were committed to $75 million for one-half of the right-of-way and all of the construction costs. Other important propositions were $11.6 million for streets; $11.4 million for bridges and viaducts; $10 million for slum clearance; $11 million for parks and playgrounds; $7.5 million for hospitals; $6 million for street lighting; $5.2 million for juvenile and other correctional centers; $7.5 million for flood control, to be matched by a $112.5 million federal appropriation for eleven miles of waterfront improvement; and $22.3 million for neighborhood rehabilitation, street resurfacing, voting machines, fire stations, public building improvements, rubbish disposal facilities, a Forest Park planetarium, a lion house and a children's zoo, library branches, air conditioning for the Art Museum, municipal docks, and miscellaneous items. The least popular propositions (planetarium and Art Museum) had margins of better than three to one. Despite their knowledge that many black residents would be displaced by slum clearance, the primarily black wards passed that proposition by a vote of 15,243 to 878. In addition to the civic improvements, a $16.4 million school bond issue was approved by five to one.

Local leaders and newspapers and the national press hailed this magnificent achievement. The "new Spirit of St. Louis" was in full flower. "They voted for progress—and against decay," exulted the *Post-Dispatch*. "They voted for the new and clean—and against the outmoded and dirty. They voted for a moving, growing, advancing future—and against a blighting, killing past." The *Minneapolis Tribune* congratulated St. Louis: "It is an aroused citizenry which has a bold and imaginative vision of the future . . . ready and willing to pay the cost. . . ." The *Kansas City Star* wrote, "In the history of every great city, certain events stand out as decisive turning points. . . . The smashing St. Louis bond victory was one of those civic peaks." In Baltimore, the *Evening Sun* hoped that its city would profit from St. Louis's example. Prodded by scores of business and civic groups, city agencies, and newspapers, the awakened citizenry had done "something drastic about the downtown strangulation and the flight to the suburbs." The *Louisville Times* hailed the bond issue as "an example of civic spirit to make cities throughout the U.S. sit up and take notice." In an article entitled "St. Louis Wakes Itself Up," *Harper's* applauded the "energetic midwesterners who have yanked the community out of its long slide into decay."

In 1951, the Land Clearance for Redevelopment Authority of St. Louis had been established "to undertake the acquisition, relocation, demolition, and site improvements of the urban renewal areas . . . which needed Federal assistance." The Redevelopment Authority was to be governed by a five-person board appointed by the mayor. Except for a three-year hiatus in the late 1960s, C. L. Farris was its director from its founding to 1980.

With $7 million of the 1955 bond issue proceeds and $21 million in federal funds, the authority began clearing the 454-acre Mill Creek valley site between Lindell-Olive and Scott Avenues, Twentieth Street and Grand Avenue in February 1959. Slum homes and ancient buildings were razed to make way for industrial (132 acres), commercial (26 acres), and residential construction (83.5 acres), the Ozark Expressway and streets, and for a 22-acre extension of Saint Louis University onto the old Camp Jackson site. In what an NAACP official called a "Negro Removal" project, the poorest blacks in the city, 1,772 families and 610 individuals, were displaced. Some moved into public housing, but the majority crowded into sections between Delmar and Natural Bridge on both sides of Grand Avenue, and south along Chouteau. The Ville (once Elleardsville), a relatively prosperous black community of single-family homes west of Grand, was near the center of the major area, and the flood of newcomers accelerated a migration that was already underway to University City, Wellston, and Pine Lawn.

Mill Creek redevelopment went slowly at first, causing it to be dubbed "Hiroshima Flats," but in 1962 the first dwelling units were completed, and construction came on with a rush. Private developers, supported by Teamsters' and Teachers' Pension Fund money, built Laclède Town, a "stylish and colorful" 655-unit townhouse development for middle-income whites and blacks; Grand Forest, 122 units; Grand Towers Apartments, 264 units; Heritage House, 251 units; and the Council Plaza high-rise apartments for the elderly, 600 units. The federal government built an additional 454 subsidized units to demonstrate the feasibility of prefabricated housing in the early 1970s, a program known as Operation Breakthrough. These attractive developments were a source of civic pride and an example of smooth-working social and economic integration, but by the late 1970s the area had taken on some of the character of a neighborhood in transition. By 1974 private investment in the Mill Creek commercial, industrial, and residential redevelopments had reached $106 million, in addition to the

Mayor Raymond Tucker and Sidney Maestre of Mercantile Trust Company overlook Mill Creek Valley shortly before clearance began. Photograph, 1956. MHS-PP.

$25 million in federal expenditures for the Breakthrough-sponsored apartments. The Redevelopment Authority estimated that the city's return in taxes after the twenty-five-year abatement period would exceed its 1957 collections in the area by four to one.

In 1959, the 221-acre Kosciusko redevelopment got under way, between Second and Seventh Streets on the near south side. A one hundred-year-old shopping district, old residences, and industries were cleared to make room for thirty-four commercial buildings, twenty-six industrial buildings, and extensive parking and loading facilities. Some twenty-two hundred people were forced to relocate to other blighted areas.

Most significant of all for St. Louis's rejuvenated image was the Civic Center Redevelopment Project between Third and Eleventh Streets, Poplar and Market, plus Market to Pine between Broadway and Seventh. The Civic Center Redevelopment Corporation, a downtown businessmen's group, contracted with the Land Clearance Authority and the city to carry out the project, with no federal involvement. As previously noted, the business leaders raised $20 million in gifts, and in June 1961 the Redevelopment Corporation borrowed $30 million

Mayor Alphonso Cervantes, James Hickok of the Civic Center Redevelopment Corporation, and Roy L. Tartar of Carondelet Savings and Loan display plans for the Spanish International Pavilion, which Cervantes obtained from the 1964 New York World's Fair. Photograph by Lou Phillips, St. Louis Post-Dispatch. *MHS-PP.* © St. Louis Post-Dispatch, *1966.*

from the Equitable Life Assurance Society, the largest loan in the city's history. In 1962 the city floated a $6 million bond issue for streets, lighting, and the two-block landscaped Gateway Mall. Before demolition, tax revenues in the area had amounted to $147,000 annually. The new construction was granted tax abatement for twenty-five years, but in 1970 the Redevelopment Corporation began paying the city $225,000 annually in lieu of taxes.

Busch Stadium was the Civic Center's centerpiece, and the Gateway Arch was its inspiring influence. As its southern hinge, the massive Poplar Street Bridge, named with a total absence of historical sense, funneled traffic from the expressways to and from Illinois. In addition to the stadium's cost of more than $50 million, a group of distinguished new business buildings were erected at a cost of $65 million by 1976. They included Stouffer's Riverfront Tower at 200 South Fourth, an eye-catching twenty-seven story hotel topped by a revolving restaurant, plus a second tower completed in 1975; the handsome national headquarters of Pet, Inc. at 400 South Fourth; the Equitable Life Assurance Society's shimmering twenty-two-story building at Tenth and Broadway, with mirrored walls reflecting its neighbors and the passing scene; and the national headquarters of the

General American Life Insurance Company on the Gateway Mall at 700 Market Street.

Major A. J. Cervantes brought the Spanish Pavilion to St. Louis from New York, where it had been the most beautiful building at the 1965 World's Fair. Of Spanish descent himself, the mayor thought it appropriate to acknowledge St. Louis's Spanish heritage in this fashion, but once it was in place, on Broadway north of the stadium, no one knew what to do with it. Don Breckenridge eventually came to the rescue by erecting a twenty-two-story hotel above it, which he then sold to a rival chain. Cervantes's folly, as it had been called, was in 1980 the Marriott Pavilion Hotel, both an ornament and an asset to the city.

West End redevelopment began in 1965 in a 693-acre area from Union Avenue to the city limits between Delmar and Page. The Redevelopment Authority spent $35.8 million and private investors $19.4 million by 1974 for 610 multifamily and 21 single-family residences, commercial structures, a nursing home, and an addition to St. Luke's Hospital. At Grand and Delmar, a group of black businessmen constructed the Grandel Square shopping center for about $1 million in federal and private funds. On the near south side, between Gratiot and I-55, Seventh and Twelfth Streets, the Ralston-Purina Company whose "Checkerboard Square" world headquarters were at the north edge of the area, initiated the LaSalle Park renewal project. The company assumed the $2 million share of the renewal funds and assumed the role of developer for the commercial, industrial, and residential project. Ralston-Purina Chairman R. Hal Dean vigorously and effectively denied charges that the company and the Redevelopment Authority were acting arbitrarily in condemnation proceedings, which aired in the *Post-Dispatch* in 1980. The DeSoto-Carr project, potentially comparable in importance to the Civic Center redevelopment, covered 370 acres of the old Prairie St. Louis common fields between Delmar and Cass, I-70 and Jefferson, excluding the public housing complexes. Multiple dwellings and business structures were planned, and the program received funding despite HUD's objections to some details of the developer's plans. Considerable industrial construction was completed in the western section of the project, but the catalyst for development came in 1972, when the voters approved a $25 million bond issue for a convention center.

Mayor Cervantes, who lost his race for a third term to John Poelker in 1973, had pushed hard for the bond issue, especially after its initial failure, and the Civic Center was named for him. Ground was broken in 1974 and the huge structure was completed in 1977. Construction costs ran higher than expected, but an additional $9 million was

Entrance to the Cervantes Convention Center. *Financed by a $25 million bond issue in 1972, the convention center was one of Mayor Cervantes' pet projects. After he was defeated for reelection in 1973, the center was named for him. Photograph by Ted McCrea, 1978. MHS-PP.*

furnished by the Redevelopment Authority and a group of businessmen headed by August A. Busch, Jr. The two-story building had 240,000 square feet of exhibit space, three eight-thousand-seat auditoriums, and forty-three meeting rooms each seating up to fifteen hundred. Attendance at conventions and public events reached 461,450 in the fiscal year 1978–79 and 531,540 in 1979–80. The American Foundrymen's Society's twenty-thousand-person convention in April 1980 required all of the exhibit space and filled all of the available and suitable hotel and motel rooms in the city and most of the county.

According to Marie Portell, the convention and schedule manager at the center, many additional downtown hotel rooms were essential if St. Louis was to continue to attract large conventions. The 20-story, 614-room Sheraton–St. Louis Hotel just east of the center on Seventh Street, which opened in 1977, and the 2-story, 350-room Radisson–St. Louis, under construction at Ninth and Convention Plaza, were the first of several to be located nearby. The Westin

International world-class luxury chain considered building in downtown St. Louis, and the May Company proposed a $100 million shopping mall between the Famous-Barr and Stix, Baer, and Fuller department stores, in an area bounded by Sixth and Seventh, Locust and Washington, which was to include a triangle-shaped luxury hotel towering above the seven-story mall. The future of the latter project was uncertain in July 1980, but something of the kind seemed essential if St. Louis was to capitalize fully on the fast-growing convention and tourist business.

Much of the downtown construction from the 1950s through the 1970s was made possible by Missouri 353, the Urban Developments Corporation Law, which the legislature passed in 1943 and amended in 1945. This measure was originally intended to encourage private developers to build new housing in blighted areas by allowing major cities to grant tax abatement on such property for a period of twenty-five years, but St. Louis adopted an expanded interpretation of the statute. Under the modified procedure, the city was first to declare an area blighted, then a private redevelopment corporation would submit a plan for the renewal of all or part of the blighted area. If the city approved the plan, the corporation could acquire the needed properties by "borrowing" the city's power of eminent domain. Once the property was its own, the redevelopment corporation received tax abatement for twenty-five years.

The Missouri Supreme Court endorsed a broad definition of "blighted," which made it possible to include vacant land and sound buildings within such an area. Under a 1974 ruling, there were virtually no limits on what could be declared blighted. Though federally funded projects were not actually covered by Missouri 353, the tax abatement provisions of the statute were applied to the Plaza Square development in 1951 and subsequently to four other federal urban renewal areas. The Civic Center Redevelopment Corporation's stadium-area project in 1960 was the first non-housing development carried out under the statute. Since the area was truly blighted, and the city's need for the stadium, and the parking garages, hotels, and office buildings that were included was so obvious, the project caused little controversy. It was the entering wedge, however, for other developments that were controversial.

From 1967 through 1969, five city blocks, including the site for the new Boatmen's Bank, were declared blighted, but the most radical move was yet to come. In 1967 Mayor Cervantes had advocated blighting the entire downtown area between Third and Twelfth, Delmar and Highway 40 (public property and new buildings excepted). The plan commission recommended this action in 1970, and the city adopted their report in 1971. J. Arthur Baer, president of "Downtown St. Louis, Incorporated," which represented the leading downtown firms, was reported to have said, "What a wonderful gesture—to hand me a completely blighted downtown St. Louis!"

By 1975, tax-abated projects completed or under construction included the Mercantile Bank's office tower; the 500 Broadway building; Boatmen's; Stouffer's two riverfront towers; the Amax Company's $10 million expansion; the Spanish Pavilion and tower; the stadium and garages; the First National Bank, the Pet, Equitable, and General American Life buildings; the Mansion House and Gateway Tower; and the five federal projects. The value of these properties was in excess of $300 million.

For the first ten years after the private redevelopers acquired the blighted properties, they were to pay to the city in lieu of taxes the amount the properties had paid before acquisition. During the next fifteen years, they were to increase their payments to one-half of the taxes based upon current valuation, including improvements. Thereafter, they were to assume their full share of taxes. Deemed essential to the survival of a viable central business district by its advocates, the freewheeling use of Missouri 353 was bitterly opposed by Alderman Bruce Sommer and others as a windfall for big business at the expense of homeowners, small businesses, and the public schools.

Defenders of the policy argued that even during the abatement period the city would gain revenue through larger earnings-tax collections. More important, the renewal of the downtown area would not have occurred without the program. The Clayton and Westport industrial and business centers, where land was cheaper, were attractive alternatives for the insurance companies and other investors as compared to the seedy, rundown, and crime-ridden downtown area, and these county areas continued to be more attractive even after the 353 program was well under way. A report sponsored by the St. Louis Community Development Agency in 1978 revealed that a majority of those who had invested in renewal under Missouri 353 would otherwise have considered Clayton or West County locations. Fifteen percent would have moved away from the St. Louis area, and 15 percent would not have built at all. Amax officials, for example, claimed that their company would have transferred its entire operation to another city.

The report also pointed out that 37 percent of all property in St. Louis was tax-exempt, 89 percent of such property belonging to churches, schools, hospitals, and governments. Property abated under Missouri 353 represented a mere 3 percent of the value of St. Louis real estate and abated revenues only 2 percent of the city's tax receipts

Westport, a combined office, entertainment, and industrial center, exemplified the development of St. Louis County in the mid-1970s. Photograph by Ted McCrea, 1976. MHS-PP.

in 1977. One-half of one percent of the city's land area was abated, yet the central business district furnished 51 percent of its tax revenues. The case for abatement was well-founded. Without the injection of capital made possible by this program, the city's core would have rotted with disastrous consequences for the entire area. Historically hampered by its difficulties in attracting outside capital, St. Louis had made imaginative use of the law to reverse its decline.

Population growth had resumed in St. Louis in the 1940s, chiefly because of the influx of rural blacks and whites attracted by war industries and cheap slum rents. The city proper grew by 5 percent to 856,796 in 1950, but its share fell from 57 to 51 percent of the residents of the metropolitan area. The county gained 48 percent to 406,349; St. Charles County grew slightly; and Madison and St. Clair Counties grew by 22 percent to 388,000. Blacks increased in number by 41 percent in the city to 18 percent of the total. Most striking was the direction of suburban expansion. Older western and southwestern suburbs were still thriving; and University City, now heavily Jewish in population, had become the state's fifth largest city with forty

James S. McDonnell. *McDonnell founded his aircraft company at Lambert Field in
1939. By 1980 McDonnell Douglas was the St. Louis area's largest manufacturing
employer and one of the largest defense contractors in the world. Photograph by
McDonnell Douglas Corp., 1979. Courtesy of McDonnell Douglas Archives.*

thousand people. But middle- and working-class whites were
choosing the less expensive areas to the northwest, building neat
brick bungalows on the former baronial estates of the nineteenth-
century elite. Jennings, not even a decimal point in 1940, boasted
15,282 people in 1950; Ferguson shot up by 50 percent to 11,573;
and a few city families even invaded Florissant, shades of Mullanphy,
O'Fallon, Frost, Graham, Clark, and Harney!

Ironically, the civic improvement explosion of the 1950s, so
essential to the city's survival, accelerated the rush to the suburbs. Block
after block of middle-class homes melted in the path of the
expressways. Having automobiles and little choice in the matter, those
ousted headed north and west to a new ring of suburbs, and the retail
shopping centers followed them. With improved streets, high-speed
highways, and larger and larger trucks, land costs became more
important in industrial site selection and proximity to the labor supply
and railroad freight terminals relatively less so. Light industry began to
disperse to formerly remote corners of the metropolitan area. Thus, in
microcosm, the story of the great hinterland was repeated. New
industrial-commercial centers in the county rivalled the central business

district, as Kansas City, Wichita, Oklahoma City, Tulsa, Houston, and Dallas rivalled the entire metropolis in the larger trade territory.

Suburban growth reawakened interest in governmental consolidation. The city and the urbanized portion of the county united to form the Metropolitan Sewer District in 1954, but an area-wide transit authority was rejected at the polls in 1955. Alderman A. J. Cervantes then led a drive to form a city-county Board of Freeholders to work out some form of consolidation. Mayor Tucker, who favored total consolidation or reentry into the county and motivated in part by a desire to cut the energetic Cervantes down to size, helped Washington and Saint Louis University political scientists obtain grants of $50,000 from the McDonnell Charitable Trust and $250,000 from the Ford Foundation to set up the Metropolitan St. Louis Survey. Convinced by extensive interviews in city and county that nothing stronger would succeed, the researchers recommended a plan that would not require charter amendments or other state action. An area-wide government would control arterial highways and streets, mass transit, zoning for industry and economic development, the sewer district, civil defense, and all property assessment in the city and county. No existing governmental unit would be eliminated. The freeholders consisted of nine city and nine county appointees and one outside member appointed by the governor. Charles Vatterot, a contractor and realtor from the county, was chosen chairman. By a margin of ten to nine, after long debate, the freeholders selected the district plan recommended by the survey instead of a full city-county merger.

In the campaign for adoption, Cervantes took a leading role, joined by Edwin Clark of Southwestern Bell, the chairman of Civic Progress; the heads of the city and county chambers of commerce; the mayor of University City; Civic Progress as a group; the Metropolitan Church Federation; professional groups; the *Globe-Democrat* and the *Post-Dispatch*; the League of Women Voters; and the Building Trades Union. Efficient administration of services, orderly growth, better crime control, and a better business climate were most often cited in support of the district plan. In opposition was the Central Labor Council, the county Democratic and Republican organizations, most county officeholders, and the suburban newspapers, which took their usual dog-in-the-manger attitude toward the evil city. But Mayor Tucker delivered the killing blow. He objected to the plan as inadequate: it did not eliminate the host of governmental units in the county, and it continued city-county separation. His stance deflated the enthusiasm of his friends in Civic Progress, most of whom faded out of sight after their initial cash contributions to the campaign. The anti-tax arguments against the district plan were effective, and city voters said "no" by two to one and the county by three to one. Large-scale consolidation seemed doomed thereafter, but the campaign has been credited with setting the stage for the establishment of the Bi-State Transit Authority and the reorganization of the St. Louis County government.

The extent of out-migration from the city was painfully apparent in the Census of 1960. St. Louis lost 12.5 percent of its people, dropping to 750,026. The Standard Metropolitan Statistical Area (SMSA), which included the city and the counties of St. Louis, St. Charles, Franklin, and Jefferson in Missouri and Madison and St. Clair in Illinois, increased by 20 percent to 2.015 million; but it had dropped to tenth place among the nation's metropolitan areas. St. Louis County almost caught up with the city, gaining by 73 percent to 703,532. Natural increase accounted for one-third of its growth, with most of the rest coming from the city. The outlying counties were beginning to receive the migrants as well, as shown by St. Charles and Jefferson Counties, which had nearly doubled in population to 52,970 and 66,377, respectively. In a continuation of the northwestern trend, Florissant had become the new middle-income mecca, showing a 1,000 percent increase during the decade to 38,166. Berkeley had tripled to 18,676; Bridgeton had grown from 202 to 7,820; St. Ann from 4,577 to 12,155; and Ferguson and Overland had each doubled to nearly 23,000. Near the river, north of the city, the new suburb of Bellefontaine Neighbors had erupted into being with 13,650 people, and there were nearly two dozen growing villages in the Normandy area. In the older western suburbs, University City peaked at 51,249 and Webster Groves and Kirkwood at about 29,000 each. South of Clayton, Brentwood had grown to 12,250, and in the southwest, Crestwood had jumped from 1,645 to more than 11,000.

Clayton, which had become a second central business district rivaling the downtown area, had actually lost population in the 1950s as it made room for business buildings, dropping by 5 percent to 15,245. Many of its elite families had moved to Ladue, just to the west, which had previously succeeded it as the site of the exclusive St. Louis Country Club. With 9,466 people, Ladue had also drawn the last of the diehards from the West End private places. Portland and Westmoreland were still beautiful though declassé, but most of the private streets had succumbed to blight. Mid-twentieth-century swank was not quite the same; neither Ladue nor adjoining Frontenac captured the panache and breathtaking elegance of the turn-of-the-century rich men's rows.

In the city, the rural poor had filled up part of the space left by the out-migration. The black population had increased by 60,000 to

By the mid-1970s Clayton, Missouri, the county seat of St. Louis County, had developed a complex of offices and services which became a second central business district for the St. Louis region. Photograph by Ted McCrea, 1977. MHS-PP.

214,539 (28.8 percent of the total). These demographic changes were reflected dramatically in retail sales. With $1.17 billion in sales in 1958, central city merchants accounted for 48 percent of the SMSA total. After dropping to 37 percent in 1963, the city's share, though sales were $1.2 billion, fell to 32.7 percent of SMSA's retail volume in 1970, trailing St. Louis County for the first time by $273 million.

Not only was the central city declining within the SMSA, the latter was slipping nationally. The 1970 census revealed that St. Louis had dropped in population from tenth to eighteenth among American cities, and the metropolitan area from tenth to eleventh, because of the separation of the Nassau-Suffolk County (Long Island) complex from New York City as a statistical area. With only 622,236 people, comparable to its size during the 1904 World's Fair, St. Louis had declined by another 17 percent. The SMSA had gained 10 percent in population to 2.4 million. Most other older central cities had lost population as well, though not quite as dramatically as St. Louis. Among the more conspicuous were Cleveland, with a 14.2 percent loss; Pittsburgh, 14 percent; Detroit, 9.3 percent; and

Boston, 8 percent. The last had only 16.6 percent of its SMSA's population. Kansas City, following an aggressive annexation policy, had managed a 7 percent gain to 507,000, but its SMSA had grown only at the St. Louis rate to 1.27 million, just over half of the older area's size.

As in other central cities, there was reason to believe that not all of St. Louis's poor had been counted, but even with a 10 percent negative error in the blighted areas, the loss had been substantial. The 1976 Census Bureau estimates offered no relief; St. Louis was credited with 519,345 people, another 17 percent drop to twenty-fourth in the nation, and the SMSA had declined to twelfth nationally. The sunbelt was chipping away at all of the older metropolises. The Pittsburgh, New York, Newark, and Cleveland SMSA's had declined substantially between 1970 and 1976, and Philadelphia, Cincinnati, Buffalo, and Detroit declined fractionally. Dallas–Fort Worth, Houston, Atlanta, Miami, Phoenix, and Anaheim–Santa Ana were the big gainers, along with the Denver-Boulder complex.

Within the SMSA in 1970, the central city was down to 26.4 percent of the population; St. Louis County, with 951,671 people, was up to 40 percent; the "Metro East" (Illinois) counties were down slightly to 22.5 percent; and the rapidly growing St. Charles, Jefferson, and Franklin Counties comprised 11 percent of the total. With 65,912 residents, Florissant had become the largest county municipality, followed by University City, which was now participating in the central city's decline (down 10 percent to 46,309); Kirkwood, 31,769; Ferguson, 28,759; and Webster Groves, 27,455. Elsewhere in the SMSA, East St. Louis had 69,996 residents; Belleville, 41,699; Granite City 40,440; Alton 39,700; and St. Charles, 31,834.

Municipal redundancy had reached the ridiculous in St. Louis County, as tiny enclaves scrambled to establish an identity separated from dangerous neighbors. There were ninety-three of them in 1970. Many were smaller than Laclède's St. Louis had been two centuries earlier. Champ had 19 residents; Twin Oaks, 41; Country Life Acres, 60; Norwood Court, 122; Clarkson Valley, 167; MacKenzie, 224; and Glen Echo Park, 268. Velda Village had its Velda Village Hills; Pasadena Hills its Pasadena Park; Vinita Terrace its Vinita Park; and Bridgeton its Bridgeton Terrace, the latter known chiefly in 1980 for the erratic and unprofessional conduct of its police. The caliber of services in the ninety-three jurisdictions was not exceptionally high, as a rule.

The depressing census data underlined St. Louis's major problems in 1980. Almost all of the negatives related in one way or another to the understandable and well-intentioned decision in 1876, which erected an insurmountable barrier against central-city growth after the first quarter of the twentieth century. Separation from the county guaranteed that St. Louis would eventually lose its position as one of the nation's half-dozen largest cities. The universal suburban phenomenon made the metropolitan area (SMSA) a more meaningful economic unit than the central city, but St. Louis's meager sixty-one-square-mile area, by far the smallest of any important American city, created extraordinary difficulties for overall planning and disciplined growth. Among the first to develop a planned approach, St. Louis suffered when the suburban exodus put many of its most productive citizens out of reach before the plan was fairly started. Worse yet, the political leaders of the county and its myriad of municipalities adopted a "damn the city" stance, with unsubtle overtones of racism, which if it prevailed would either create a new central city in the county or bring down the entire structure. In the various city-county and regional joint enterprises, parochial jealousies have at times made cooperation difficult. For example, St. Louis County Supervisor Eugene McNary and Mayor James Conway were reported as barely speaking to each other after McNary advanced a plan in 1979 which would have created a competitive sports complex in the far county.

After many past disappointments, advocates of a unified approach to metropolitan problems found at least a partial solution in 1965, when federal legislation made possible the creation of the East-West Gateway Coordinating Council. The first such regional planning group in the nation, East-West was in essence a council of governments, including the city of St. Louis and the counties of St. Louis, St. Charles, Franklin, and Jefferson in Missouri and Madison, St. Clair, and Monroe in Illinois. Its executive board consisted of the chief administrative officers of each of the counties, the mayor and aldermanic president of St. Louis, the mayor of East St. Louis, the chairman of the Bi-State Development Agency, other Missouri and Illinois state and regional representatives, and a full-time executive director.

Funded by various federal agencies with matching amounts from St. Louis and the seven counties of the region, East-West Gateway assumed a variety of planning responsibilities, eventually including land use and highway improvements, water and sewage facilities, port development, rapid transit, solid waste disposal, parks, housing, transportation planning including railroad relocation and airports, and many other regional concerns. Armed with federal A-95 review powers after 1969, East-West became a potent power center with authority to pass upon all applications for federal aid from municipal and county governments within the region. It described itself as a clearinghouse for such applications, a source of assistance rather than an impediment, but it insisted that local planning not be in conflict with state or regional comprehensive plans. A-95 had a marvelous effect on the attitudes of local governments toward regional interests.

Because East-West Gateway had the planning function but lacked the bonding or implementation authority granted to the Bi-State Development Agency by the states of Missouri and Illinois, close cooperation between the two regional bodies was essential and was usually achieved. Similarly, the council worked closely with the Regional Commerce and Growth Association (RCGA), a businessmen's development and booster organization formed in 1973 by a merger of the Chamber of Commerce, the Regional Development Association, and the St. Louis Research Council.

Probably the most controversial position taken by the Gateway Council was its advocacy of a regional airport to be located in Illinois. As an early indication of things to come, the council recommended in 1967 that a metropolitan airport system be established to be operated by Bi-State, with the city of St. Louis to be paid $12,183,000 for surrendering Lambert Airport to the regional agency. In July 1970, during St. Louis Mayor A. J. Cervantes's term as chairman of the Gateway Council, the directors voted twelve to two in order to draw up a plan for a $350 million airport to be located on the east side. St. Louis County Supervisor Lawrence Roos voted against the proposal and attempted to gain support from fellow Missourians on the council by asking why several Missouri sites, such as Foristell in St. Charles County, Eureka in St. Louis County, and Cedar Hill in Jefferson County, each of which had been proposed, were rejected.

By this time, a massive public debate was under way. Mayor Cervantes; Governor Richard Ogilvey of Illinois, who pledged that his state would finance construction of the regional airport; and the *Post-Dispatch*, supported by downtown St. Louis and Illinois interests, argued that if St. Louis were to be competitive in transportation by the turn of the century, another commercial airport of not less than ten thousand acres (Lambert had two thousand acres) was essential. In 1967 the Federal Aviation Administration (FAA) had pointed out the need for two major airports in the region. According to the FAA, Lambert was already becoming overcrowded both in the air and on the ground, and there was little room for expansion. Even if all conceivable measures were adopted to expand its capacity, Lambert would not be adequate beyond 1985.

Another powerful argument for the Columbia-Waterloo site, which was endorsed by the Gateway Council in 1971, was that it would attract capital to and create jobs in the region's most depressed area, the broken-down, poverty-stricken, crime-ridden slum that was East St. Louis, Venice, Madison, and Brooklyn, Illinois. This economic and social wasteland was a liability to Illinois, to St. Louis, and to the entire metropolitan complex. The location in Monroe County was close in, only nine miles from the Eads Bridge, as was Lambert. Feasible Missouri sites, such as Wentzville and Cedar Hill, were more than thirty miles from the metropolitan core.

More concerned with the state and county's immediate interests than with the region, a host of public officials and businessmen raised the specter of lost jobs, profits, and tax revenues. County Supervisor Lawrence Roos, who had been the Gateway Council's president during its first two years; Wallace Persons, the chief executive of Emerson Electric, which was located in Jennings, less than five miles from Lambert; Senator Stuart Symington, formerly Emerson's president; the state of Missouri; most of Missouri's congressional delegation; and the *Globe-Democrat* led the opposition to the Illinois location. Some of them spoke vaguely at first in favor of a second airport on the Missouri side, but they finally came together in what the *Post-Dispatch* called a "Lambert Forever" stance. They argued that the FAA had overestimated the need for expansion, that Lambert's capacity for growth was greater than their opponents' claimed, and that St. Louis's investment in Lambert should not be wasted.

County motel and business interests and Lambert's passenger customers, the last chiefly businessmen who lived in the county, joined the chorus of opposition to Columbia-Waterloo. Howard F. Baer, an acerbic critic of what he called the "Missouri xenophobes," stressed the irony of the county's sudden protective and proprietary attitude toward Lambert. The city had purchased the northwest county site from Major A. B. Lambert in 1928 at his cost, and it had supported the airport for decades when it was a losing proposition. Having made no contribution to the airport except to subject it to a series of petty harassments, the county now perceived it as a major asset which must be protected from regional planners. Baer hinted that the long-standing jealousy of countians toward the city was a factor in their attitudes.

Though Illinois would finance the construction of the new regional airport, Columbia-Waterloo would eventually be merged with Lambert, bringing the latter under regional authority. This was a sticking point. In perceiving that regionalism offered a solution to many of St. Louis's problems, Mayor Cervantes had wakened an old ghost. Some Lambert-only partisans demonstrated the ancient fear of the city and its consolidation schemes, seeing the airport plan as a threat to the county communities' independence. Others, including some city opponents of Columbia-Waterloo and Governor Warren Hearnes, apparently did not want to make any concessions to Illinois. If Bi-State were to be the operating agency, its bonding power raised the specter of Missourians paying taxes for the benefit of Illinois. After two centuries, the Mississippi was still a mighty psychological barrier.

In 1976 the federal Department of Transportation ruled in favor of the Illinois site. Immediately, lawsuits were filed against the plan, but they were unnecessary. In 1977, President Carter's Secretary of Transportation, Brock Adams, under heavy pressure from Senator Thomas Eagleton and other Missouri politicians, reversed the decision. Events to follow seemed to have vindicated, at least temporarily, the Lambert-only partisans. Lambert was expanded in capacity, larger planes required fewer flights, the increasing cost of energy put a premium on efficiency, and advances in computer technology made it possible to safely reduce the time and space between flights. In addition, the verdict on some of the huge airports built by other cities was still not in by 1980. Yet the big questions were still in order. Would Lambert meet the region's needs forever? If not, should Columbia-Waterloo have been acquired when it was offered? Could anti-city and anti-regional attitudes prevail indefinitely without bringing down the entire metropolis?

In another area of joint concern, cooperation was finally achieved. George Vierheller's successor at the St. Louis Zoo, the controversial genius Marlin Perkins, whose world-renowned outside activities created some friction with his board, worked diligently to improve revenues. When he took over in 1960, the inflated costs of animal procurement, care, and feeding had delayed essential maintenance and repairs. If this had continued, the zoo would have been reduced to second-class status. The flight to the suburbs had removed many of the zoo's patrons from its taxing authority, and both law and tradition ruled out admissions charges. Perkins and the zoological board's president Howard F. Baer led a drive to extend the zoo's tax base, and finally in 1971, just after Perkins had resigned, the St. Louis Zoo-Museum District, coterminous with the city's and the county's boundaries, was overwhelmingly approved at the polls. The proceeds of a four-mill tax furnished about 50 percent of the zoo's budget; the rest came from concessions and donations.

Among its peers, which included the Bronx and the San Diego Zoos, only the St. Louis Zoo was free. Since the 1920s it had been a shared amenity and a source of pride for the people and a major attraction for the hinterland. Of an estimated two million visitors in 1979, some two-thirds came from outside the tax district, a ratio that had prevailed for decades. Again in 1980, however, rising costs had created a crisis. With the chances of extending the district's boundaries slim, the zoological board was faced with the uncomfortable choices of asking for a tax increase, charging admission, or worst of all, allowing the zoo to sink to second-class status.

In still another critical area, its problems also reflecting in part the barriers between city and county, the St. Louis public school system had degenerated from one of the best in the nation in the days of Harris, Blow, and Soldan to one of the worst. As in other major cities, segregation and "white flight" were complicating factors. The city's black population had risen by another 20 percent in the 1960s to 254,191 (41 percent of the total) with the probability that a substantial number of blacks had not been counted. Middle-income black migration to University City, Wellston, Pine Lawn, and other near western and northwestern suburbs had been well under way before 1960; and thereafter, low-income families had followed with a rush.

Yet in the city, except for isolated pockets, the area north of Delmar was solidly black; the central corridor and the near south side were mixed; and the south and southwest were predominantly white, reemphasizing the historic two-cities-within-a-city pattern. By building almost all of its public housing on the north side, the city's planners had encouraged this trend. Thus, the *Brown vs. Board of Education of Topeka* school desegregation decision in 1954 had little practical effect in St. Louis because of housing segregation. If segregated education is inferior education, as the Warren Court ruled, the resulting decline in quality was inevitable. Despite assumptions that school integration caused white flight, the exodus in St. Louis was well under way before the *Brown* decision and was only marginally affected by it.

Under a federal court ruling that St. Louis was not in compliance with *Brown vs. Board of Education of Topeka*, Superintendent Arthur Wentz and the Board of Education, assisted by citizens' panels and advised by nearly everyone, were patiently trying in 1980 to integrate a school population that was 76 percent black in a situation where most of the pupils of the two races were widely separated geographically, and where there was strong opposition to being bussed out of their neighborhoods by some persons of both races. Although Catholic schools after 1974 would not accept pupils who were fleeing from integration, 73 percent of their pupils were white. Thus, not including Lutheran elementary pupils and those attending schools outside of the district, 43 percent of the white school population was beyond the reach of public school integration efforts. To some it appeared that only a wide-ranging metropolitan approach would make real headway. Judge James Meredith's suggestion that county schools could help by agreeing to a voluntary exchange of pupils met a cool reception, several close-in districts pointing out that they were already well-integrated, and most of the others saying in effect that it was not their problem. Again at the roots of the problem, side-by-side with racial prejudice, cultural and economic deprivation, and historic housing policy, lay the unfortunate legacy of 1876.

Another problem of the 1970s was the loss of manufacturing jobs, the most powerful generators of secondary employment. From a peak of 294,100 in the SMSA in 1967, manufacturing employment fell to 253,000 in 1974 and 244,100 in March 1980. This decline reflected a national trend, but there was a further shock in 1980 when General Motors announced that it was abandoning its Corvette plant on Natural Bridge; that news was partially alleviated by the company's decision to build a new x-car assembly plant near Wentzville, on the northwestern rim of the SMSA. But Corvette was moving to Kentucky, and St. Louis would lose some jobs and all of its tax revenues from General Motors. Having Ford and Chrysler plants as well, the district had been for years second in the nation in automobile assembly (a tribute to its central location), but the cyclical nature of the industry had kept it fluctuating from the second to the fourth or fifth largest within the SMSA. With the General Motors move, Chrysler's weakness, and the energy crunch, automobile manufacturing did not seem an element of great strength in 1980.

Still, there was cause for optimism. The district's largest manufacturing employer, McDonnell-Douglas Aerospace, with thirty-one thousand employees, had a big new Canadian military contract and confidently expected to win a major share of the rising United States defense budget. Next in manufacturing employment, less cyclically vulnerable than motor vehicle production, was the non-electrical machinery industry, followed by fabricated metal products.

Thirty companies, each with sales of more than $100 million annually, had headquarters in St. Louis in the late 1970s. Twelve of these averaged more than $1 billion in sales, and nineteen were among the Fortune 500. Twenty-four of the top twenty-five largest American firms had offices, plants, or other operations in the area, as did 296 others among the top 500. Some of the largest, such as General Dynamics, which employed only 450 of its 83,000 workers at its world headquarters, brought more prestige than revenue to the city. Some local firms of long standing had fewer workers in St. Louis than elsewhere. Anheuser-Busch, the giant of the brewing industry, which had supported a payroll of five thousand people in 1950, had grown to twelve thousand employees nationally in 1980, but its local employment had declined slightly. It had been advantageous to reduce transportation costs by distributing bottling plants throughout its national market (St. Louis loyalists claim that beer from the parent brewery tastes better). Monsanto Chemical, the city's largest firm in sales volume in 1979, had 62,250 employees worldwide, including

44,100 in the United States, 9,000 of them in the three St. Louis SMSA plants. Manufacturing in the area was highly diversified, however, with fifteen industries each employing more than 10,000 workers, and with more than 3,300 manufacturing plants.

Offsetting the loss of 50,000 manufacturing jobs since 1967, the trade, service, transportation, and financial sectors gained 106,000. Services, with 204,000 workers in 1979, had added 48,000, led by hospital and health services, which had grown to 35,000 employees; the convention and tourist business; hotels and restaurants; and amusements. Wholesale and retail trade employment had grown during the decade by 26,000; governments had added 13,800 jobs; and insurance and real estate firms 7,000.

According to the RCGA, service jobs in the SMSA would increase by 82,500 between 1980 and 1995, and the manufacture of transportation equipment, chemical products, fabricated metals, and machinery would grow in output and employment. Declines were expected in food processing and steel. Employment in trade, at about two hundred thousand in 1979, would rise slightly. The convention business, which brought in $31 million in 1973, $80 million in 1976, and $100 million in 1979, was projected to increase further, depending upon additional downtown hotel space. Mayor John Poelker, who had defeated A. J. Cervantes's bid for a third term in 1973, agreed with his predecessor in emphasizing conventions and tourism as the wave of the future. Although its impact is difficult to measure precisely, tourism at least equaled conventions as an economic asset in 1979, with nearly seventy thousand persons employed during the peak season. Future growth depended in part upon the extent to which high gasoline prices would encourage those living within a day's journey to choose St. Louis over distant vacation spots.

While charges that St. Louis had depended too heavily in the past upon its natural advantages may have been partly justified, local boosters and planners in the 1970s still counted its location a major asset, with good reason. The nation's center of population in 1970 was within the SMSA, near Mascoutah in St. Clair County, and it seemed probable that the 1980 census would place it even closer to the central city. Half of the population of the United States lived within a five-hundred-mile radius of St. Louis, and its central location and the availability of comparatively inexpensive office space in new buildings downtown (assisted by Missouri 353) were of prime importance in attracting corporate headquarters and branch offices. General American Life, for example, found that locating in St. Louis made major branch offices unnecessary. When Washington University Chancellor William Danforth asked James S. McDonnell why he had selected the city as the site for his new aircraft company in 1939, the founder replied that "he saw a war coming on so he decided the best place to build war planes would be smack in the middle." And so it had been with the automobile companies. As Mayor Poelker put it, St. Louis had not stolen the assembly plants from Detroit, the plants had simply sought out the best access to markets.

Transportation was also largely a function of location. Despite antiquated yards (sixty-three of them) and the agonizingly slow transfer time for freight cars (thirty-four hours), the nineteen railroads serving St. Louis made it one of the world's leading rail centers, still second only to Chicago in the United States. Consolidation and relocation of yards and terminals, according to one estimate in 1975, would save local shippers $6 million a year, attract new business, and free thirteen hundred acres of prime riverfront land in East St. Louis for redevelopment.

Called the "Gateway to the World" by its publicists, the St. Louis riverport, the largest in the United States, covered seventy miles from St. Charles on the Missouri in the north to the Kaskaskia River in the south. Some twenty-four million tons of commodities, primarily coal, petroleum, chemicals, and grain were handled at the port's eighty-six docks in 1979. Volume had increased substantially and was expected to gain further because shippers of low-sulphur Wyoming coal had discovered that as the nearest major port with lock-free and ice-free water downstream, St. Louis was the best route to the Gulf of Mexico. From the Powder River basin via the Burlington Northern, along the ancient paths of Lisa, Sublette, and Campbell, the coal came to the new terminal at Hall Street, where it was transferred to barges. With an annual capacity of eleven million tons, this single terminal could handle more freight than the entire port of Memphis. There were seven port districts in the St. Louis complex, employing twenty-one thousand workers and affecting forty-three thousand manufacturing jobs. The Bi-State Development Agency was charged with encouraging port development by helping port districts carry out plans and improve facilities and by providing coordinating and technical assistance. As previously indicated, the East-West Gateway Coordinating Council was responsible for overall port planning.

Of crucial importance to the port and to the construction industry was the fate of the Army Corps of Engineers' plan to rebuild and expand Lock and Dam 26 at Alton at a cost of $500 million, which had been blocked, at least temporarily, by a federal suit brought by the Santa Fe Railroad and environmentalists. Barges from the upper Mississippi, under existing conditions, suffered delays averaging more than twenty hours in waiting their turn to pass through the locks.

According to Wayne Weidemann of the Metropolitan Port Authority, St. Louis in 1980 enjoyed significant locational advantages as a transportation break-point, just as it had in the steamboat era, abetted in the modern era by the concentration of railroads and interstate highways in the metropolis. Plans for future port expansion included the building of synthetic fuel plants and industrial parks, all of which would rely heavily upon barge transportation.

Once "the jewel in St. Louis's crown," the trucking business, though still of major importance, had slipped from second in volume to seventh nationally between the 1950s and the late 1970s, reflecting the decline in light manufacturing in the city, especially in the garment industry. Though less so than regional planners had anticipated, airline volume had expanded as trucking declined. Approximately 4.4 million passengers emplaned at Lambert International in 1979, ranking it the eleventh busiest airport in the nation. The Airport Authority aspired to the top ten in 1980. Incoming freight express and mail amounted to 76,398 tons in 1979, and outgoing cargo to 78,761 tons. St. Louis–domiciled TWA led the way with 40 percent of the traffic, and locally headquartered Ozark Airlines was second. Nine other airlines operated from Lambert, including a newcomer, British Caledonian Airways, which featured nonstop flights to London. Terminal expansion and improvements begun in the mid-1970s were to cost $30 million when completed. A multimillion-dollar land acquisition and runway extension program was under way, proceeding at high cost because of the nature of the terrain and existing construction on its periphery.

In professional sports after mid-century, St. Louis lost its perennially second-division baseball Browns to Baltimore, but it gained major-league status in other sports. In two attempts, first with a well-run and successful team and later with a disappointing club, professional basketball failed to win the hearts of St. Louisans. Football was another story. The dream of sports editor Robert L. Burnes of the *Globe-Democrat* and many other boosters and publicists was realized in 1960, when the Chicago Cardinals moved to St. Louis.

Initially, the "Big Red," as the team came to be called informally to distinguish it from the baseball Cardinals, had only modest success. Forced to play in old Busch Stadium (formerly Sportsman's Park) as paying guests of the baseball club, the team was denied use of the field for practice and had to delay its home opener each year until the baseball season was over. The stadium was small (thirty-four thousand seats), and substantial parts of the playing field were obscured from the view of many spectators.

Partly because of this, the team did not draw well despite a slightly better-than-average record of forty-two victories, thirty-eight defeats, and two ties during its six seasons in the old stadium. In 1963 the Cardinals led their division with only three games to play, but they dropped two of their last three games to finish second to the New York Giants. Despite an even better record in 1964 (10–3–1) they were second again, this time to the Cleveland Browns. The baseball Cardinals had won the pennant and World Series in the latter year, and football had not yet reached parity as a symbol of city pride.

After the 1963 season, faced with the prospect of continued second-rate status in the new stadium, the football Cardinals considered a move to Atlanta, which offered them a new stadium on favorable terms. But through the good offices of Morton D. "Buster" May, a powerful member of the downtown business community, the owners (William and "Stormy" Bidwill) were persuaded to stay, and their team was put on an equal footing with baseball in the new Busch Stadium. In their new quarters after 1965, the team quickly captured the seemingly undivided attention of many St. Louisans each season, and the seats were usually sold out for home games.

With the exception of an excellent season in 1974, when the

The St. Louis Cardinals and the Chicago Bears match up in a preseason exhibition game. Photograph by James Carrington, 1970. MHS-PP.

"Cardiac Cardinals" under Coach Don Coryell won the National Conference's eastern division title with a 10–4 record (and lost their first playoff game to Minnesota), the Cardinals of the 1970s were an up-and-down team with more downs than ups. Great individual performances by one of the game's better quarterbacks, Jim Hart, and by such all-league stars as Larry Wilson, Roger Wehrli, Jim Bakken, Dan Dierdorf, Bob Young, Tom Banks, Jackie Smith, Terry Metcalf, and Mel Gray did not produce a consistent team effort. Perhaps because the baseball Cardinals were an established local institution with many past glories to recall, or because of the game's slower pace and usually non-violent nature, or because many of them went to see a game as much as a victory, baseball followers seemed to accept losing seasons in the 1970s with a degree of patient understanding. Seldom, and then usually for off-the-field reasons, did they boo their own players. The merciless, mercurial, and fickle football crowds, on the other hand, made life miserable on and off the field for players, coaches, the general manager, and even the president of the Big Red. It was said that football ticketholders were generally more prosperous, better-dressed, and of a higher social rank than baseball fans. Perhaps that was the explanation. In any case, they came to the games.

St. Louis was represented in professional hockey by the Blues. Winners at first, they attracted the largest crowds in the game for several years, and even after a string of indifferent seasons, the skaters still had a large nucleus of committed fans in 1979. In soccer, although the city was the national hotbed at the amateur level, professional teams did not draw well until the Steamers went indoors with a mini-version of the sport in 1979.

With the wealth of talent available from the Catholic and public school leagues, Saint Louis University reigned as the kingpin of college soccer for decades. Its rivals had to stock up with St. Louis players to compete at all. In the 1970s another area school, Southern Illinois University at Edwardsville, achieved the front rank winning the NCAA Division I title in 1979. The University of Missouri–St. Louis became a Division II power, and both the Florissant Valley and Meramec campuses of the St. Louis Community College were national leaders among the junior colleges. Quincy and several other colleges near and far drew heavily upon the St. Louis playgrounds and schools for their better players.

In basketball Saint Louis University was a strong source of local pride for many years after World War II, but interest diminished substantially in the 1970s as university officials cut back in emphasis upon the sport—a step made necessary by the difficulty in attracting the better local players in the face of seductive recruiting pressures exerted by the Big Eight, Big Ten, and Kentucky schools and glamorous independent universities led by Notre Dame. Washington University had dropped basketball and was content to compete in football against like-minded schools on the amateur level.

While St. Louis was not the intellectual capital of America, as it may have had some claim to be a century earlier, and while its high crime rate, one of the worst in the nation, and consistently high black unemployment spoke poorly for the overall quality of life, the city was rather well-served culturally in the 1970s. Chartered in 1832 as a Jesuit institution, Saint Louis University offered a range of undergraduate and graduate programs and professional training. Its Pius XII Memorial Library featured the only complete collection of Vatican Library Documents on microfilm to be found outside of Rome. About half of the university's 6,811 undergraduates and 3,685 graduate and professional students in 1979–80 were from the metropolitan area—the rest represented fifty states and sixty foreign countries.

Founded in 1853 as Eliot Seminary by the abolitionist Unitarian minister William Greenleaf Eliot, Wayman Crow, Hudson Bridge, John How, and others, chiefly merchants of Yankee origins, Washington University acquired its permanent name in 1857. At the turn of the century, wholesale merchants Samuel Cupples and Robert S. Brookings made large contributions to the university, and the latter arranged for its spacious new campus on the World's Fair site, west of Skinker Boulevard. Brookings hoped the campus would be the educational mecca of St. Louis's great southwestern trade territory, but the student body remained chiefly a local one until E. A. H. Shepley and Arthur Holly Compton made it a national university in the 1950s. In 1979–80 there were 4,438 undergraduates and 3,338 graduate and professional students. The professional schools included the medical school, which operated one of the world's leading medical research facilities at its medical center complex on Kingshighway. Nearly 80 percent of the full-time undergraduates were from outside the metropolitan area, but evening programs attracted 2,761 chiefly local students.

Both Washington and Saint Louis Universities benefited substantially from the Danforth Foundation and other local philanthropists. James S. McDonnell, founder of the McDonnell-Douglas Corporation, gave millions in the 1970s, chiefly to the Washington University Medical School. According to the RCGA in 1975, the out-of-town students at the two private universities contributed more than $21 million annually to the local economy.

In 1963 the University of Missouri established a campus on Natural Bridge Road in Normandy as part of its coordinate-campus system, which consisted of campuses in Columbia, Kansas City, Rolla, and St. Louis. Led by district superintendent Ward A. Barnes, the Normandy Board of Education had encouraged this development by transferring land for which it had paid nearly seven hundred thousand dollars to the university for a nominal sum. In its early years the University of Missouri–St. Louis (UMSL) had recognition problems in the St. Louis community, but students, many of whom were the first in their families to attend college, found their way to the campus in substantial numbers. Of the 9,409 undergraduates and 1,644 graduate students enrolled in 1979–80, nearly all were from the metropolitan area, and 72 percent were employed part- or full-time. By the late 1970s, substantial formal and informal cooperation had been established among the three local universities, and more was expected.

The Florissant Valley, Forest Park, and Meramec campuses of the St. Louis Community College, established in the early 1960s, enrolled twenty-six thousand students in 1979–80 in a wide variety of one- and two-year career and college transfer programs. Harris-Stowe State College, a 1955 merger of William Torrey Harris's pioneering normal school with the post–Civil War Stowe Teacher's College for blacks, became a state college in 1978, after more than a century under the St. Louis Board of Education. In 1979–80 Harris-Stowe had eleven hundred students working toward B.S. in Education degrees, most of them preparing to teach in the city's public schools. Southern Illinois University at Edwardsville, Webster College in Webster Groves, Lindenwood College in St. Charles, Maryville and Fontbonne Colleges in St. Louis County, Belleville Area Junior College, Jefferson Junior College in Jefferson County, East Central Missouri Junior College in Franklin County, and Lewis and Clark College in Madison County were among the thirty-six other post-secondary institutions that enriched the cultural and educational opportunities of the metropolitan area in 1980.

Among the high-cultural amenities, the Art Museum in Forest Park, by its nature, its location, and free admission, reached the largest numbers. Attendance averaged more than five hundred thousand annually in the 1970s (including weather-driven drop-ins) and reached a peak of seven hundred thousand in 1978, because of a special exhibit of French Impressionist paintings. The museum traced its origins to the philanthropy of the wholesale merchant and part-time educator Wayman Crow, who donated a building for the city's first art museum at Nineteenth Street on Lucas Place near Washington University in 1881. The museum and school of art there, attached to the university, was directed for many years by Halsey C. Ives, the guiding spirit behind the building of the magnificent Palace of Fine Arts at the World's Fair in 1904. In 1909, the Art Hill building and collection were dedicated to the city with William K. Bixby, president of the American Car and Foundry Company, and David R. Francis as its first president and vice president. In 1971 the Art Museum became a part of the new Zoo-Museum District, supported by a four-mill tax. It was considered to be among the better art museums in the United States, notable especially for the fact that its building was itself a superb work of art. The nineteenth-century French Impressionist collection on the main floor attracted the most attention, along with the American section, including some of the major paintings of the nineteenth-century Missourian George Caleb Bingham. Perhaps most highly prized, with a more specialized appeal, was the museum's fine collection of primitive art.

Also of respectable rank in its field, the more-than-a-century-old St. Louis Symphony Orchestra performed in the fall, winter, and spring seasons in its plush Victorian Powell Hall, a converted movie palace on Grand Avenue. Pop concerts were performed in the summer at Queeny Park in west county. Like the Art Museum, the orchestra has suffered from a lack of funding, and in the 1970s it was not one of the top half-dozen in America. Apparently, the wealthy St. Louisans who were its patrons were satisfied with its status, because they did not provide the large gifts and bequests which have helped to sustain

The St. Louis Symphony in Its Opening Concert at Powell Symphony Hall. *The renovation of the St. Louis Theater into a permanent home for the St. Louis Symphony led the way for the redevelopment of the Midtown area as an arts center. Photograph by Ralph D'Oench, 1968. MHS-PP.*

the great Cleveland Orchestra, one of the nation's golden cultural assets, representing a city comparable to St. Louis in size and wealth.

In the realm of dramatic art, the Loretto-Hilton Repertory Theater at Webster College, the fastest-growing professional theatre in the United States, had gained national stature by the mid-1970s. The American Theatre, downtown at Ninth and St. Charles, brought Broadway touring companies to St. Louisans and convention visitors, and the universities and colleges offered a variety of musical, dance, dramatic, and artistic presentations. The highly touted Municipal Opera's programs featured touring companies starring popular-media performers. By this technique and by frequent repetition of proven box-office winners, usually the sirupy kind, the management continued to please a large audience. If it will play in Peoria, it will play at the Muny, seemed to be the standard. As a result, the Municipal Opera's impact upon St. Louis, while large indeed, was hardly different in kind from that of professional sports or large movie theaters.

In the spring of 1980, Chase Econometrics of New York predicted that like other cities of the industrial Northeast and Midwest, St. Louis would experience slow growth in the 1980s, with employment increasing by only .5 percent a year, better than New York, Jersey City, Cleveland, and Buffalo; slightly worse than Chicago; and far behind such Sunbelt cities as Tucson and Houston, which were expected to grow by more than 4 percent annually. In response, Stephen J. Taylor, research chief of the RCGA, predicted that employment in St. Louis would expand by more than 1 percent annually, a pace slightly better than that of the 1970s. Economist Murray Weidenbaum of Washington University cited as reasons for optimism St. Louis's diversified economy; its increasing attractiveness to tourists; its relatively low cost of living—$729 a year under the national urban average and $3,500 less than Boston's for a family of four; the volume of water flowing past the city, ninety-three times greater at low water than current demand; and the increasing importance of the city's central location as energy and transportation costs climb.

Two hundred and sixteen years after Pierre Laclède picked a choice location for his fur-trading outpost, the quality of St. Louis's future seemed only marginally favorable. There was nothing unusual about that in urban America, but the city carried the additional burden of a restrictive, suffocating, and apparently everlasting charter. Until the voters finally approved a change in August 1980, salaries of city officials (except for policemen and firemen) were limited to twenty-five thousand dollars annually, condemning the mayor, comptroller, and other top officials to vows of eternal poverty. Any further significant changes, however, especially those in the direction of metropolitan government, requiring the approval of county voters, seemed unlikely.

After all, the civic patriots had done their best and the scoundrels their worst, those who spoke for St. Louis still defined salvation in terms of location. For some this was a counsel of despair, an echo of past failures, but St. Louisans had never assumed they could carry the day without effort. After all, the locational advantages could not be denied. In 1980 the players had changed since Manuel Lisa ventured into the domain of the Arikaras, and again since Thomas Hart Benton and Thomas Allen dreamed of and drafted plans for the great Pacific Railroad, and yet again since Rolla Wells and David R. Francis's "New St. Louis" played host to the world during the glorious exposition summer, but the game was the same.

12.
Urban Renaissance

The 1970s were embarrassing times for those concerned with St. Louis's image. For the majority, life had continued much as before, and the metropolis had much to offer. There was a self-conscious, romantic sense of a grander past that might return; there were outstanding cultural amenities; major-league baseball and football were still in place; rehabilitation and restoration were under way in the neighborhoods; housing costs were lower than in comparable areas; the convention and tourist business was thriving; the central location still held promise for the future; and for those so inclined who could afford it, residence in outer suburbs or protected inner enclaves offered a comfortable way to enjoy the city's advantages without suffering its inconveniences. But as their tradition decreed, St. Louisans were sensitive to the view from outside. The steady barrage of negative publicity flowing from the city's national leadership in population decline was a heavy load to bear. Whether the flight from the city was caused by racism, poor schools, fear of crime, a longing for green space, or a combination of these and other factors, it was a bleeding wound and a prescription for pessimism.

A Brookings Institution study in the late 1970s characterized St. Louis as the nation's most distressed large city and East St. Louis as the most distressed small city. Such comparisons ignored the metropolitan area, a more meaningful measure of urban growth or decline. But the 1980 federal census revealed more alarming statistics. The city had lost 27.2 percent of its population in a decade, down to its 1890 level at 453,084. Nationally, the city of St. Louis had dropped in rank from fourth largest in 1910, sixth in 1920, and eighteenth in 1970 to twenty-sixth in 1980. Less drastically but yet disturbingly, the metropolitan area had also declined during the 1970s, from tenth to twelfth among SMSA's, with a 2.3 percent loss in population, to 2,356,460. The New York, Boston, Cleveland, Pittsburgh, and Newark areas had bigger losses, but only Cleveland approached St. Louis's decline within the city limits.

Mayors John Poelker (1973–77) and James Conway (1977–81) were able, experienced, and well intentioned, but they had the misfortune to be in office during this crisis in civic confidence. They were also hampered by the archaic presences of the elected "county" patronage offices inherited from the 1876 charter and the state-appointed police board, which dated from the short-lived pro-Confederate control of the state in 1861. Peculations and derelictions in the elective offices were beyond the reach of the mayor and aldermen, and the police board could dispense salary increases at will without reference to the city's budgetary difficulties. More immediately troublesome, there was an army of municipal employees, created to serve the population of more than eight hundred thousand that had existed between 1920 and the 1950s. According to the conventional wisdom and the word from the precincts, any serious attempt at reduction in force would be political suicide.

As he approached the 1981 city election, Mayor Conway believed that he had a strong case for reelection. He had campaigned as a reform candidate in 1977, and he had tried to live up to that label. Conway had pressed the city's cause at home and abroad, featuring several trips to Europe to establish or strengthen "sister-city" and other cultural, industrial, and market relationships. But his efforts to improve services and attract corporate investment and relocation to St. Louis had been diminished by his feuds with County Executive Eugene McNary and Comptroller Raymond Percich. There were substantive reasons for disagreeing with both of these officials, but their differences had degenerated into rancorous and unproductive personal animosity.

Conway and downtown interests perceived McNary's aggressive promotion of county locations for organized sports, business, and entertainment as a threat to the city's traditional role as the heart of the metropolitan community. The county executive denied any such intent, but he was not believed east of Skinker Boulevard, and the lack of accord between the top elected officials was unproductive and unedifying. Those who blamed the problem on Conway's stubbornness would find future developments instructive.

The mayor's problems with Comptroller Percich were more threatening politically. Percich, an irascible fiscal conservative, opposed any initiative that threatened the budget. He personified the venerable south side tradition which regarded grand schemes for civic improvement as plots against middle-class taxpayers. As a member of the Board of Estimate and Apportionment, along with the mayor and the aldermanic president, the comptroller shared control of the budget process. Since Thomas Zych, the president of the Board of Aldermen, was a Percich protégé who usually sided with his mentor, the mayor's public housing and downtown development efforts were frustrated. Publicly, Zych attributed his opposition to the mayor's dictatorial manner, but the alderman was busily building his own power base.

Alderman Vincent C. Schoemehl, Jr., Conway's opponent in the 1981 Democratic primary, seemed a long shot at the outset. Schoemehl, a thirty-four-year-old graduate of the University of Missouri–St. Louis, had begun his campaign more than a year before the election, concentrating his efforts on neighborhood face-to-face meetings. But Conway had the backing of most of the Democratic leaders, including some black leaders in the north side wards; the quiet support of most of downtown business, and both the *Globe-Democrat* and the *Post-Dispatch*. The latter characterized the incumbent as a tough leader who had consolidated wasteful programs, improved health services, and worked hard for neighborhood housing and new construction downtown.

Some observers perceived Schoemehl as a novice, overmatched against an incumbent with a creditable record and organizational support. But the challenger had been an active alderman with a maverick reputation and headlong style reminiscent of Alphonso Cervantes in his aldermanic days. His engaging presence and open manner contrasted favorably with Conway's reserved demeanor, misconstrued by some as unfriendliness. When Comptroller Percich died a few months before the election, Schoemehl appointed Mrs. Percich as honorary chairperson of his campaign, and his south side voters' guide included her endorsement. On the north side, his campaign kit featured a supporting letter from the powerful black congressman William L. Clay. The congressman had been a hero of the local civil rights struggle, which did not commend him to social conservatives. Consequently, he did not make a public pronouncement for Schoemehl.

By allying himself with Conway's opponent, Clay was representing his black constituents' resentment of the closing of Homer G. Phillips City Hospital Number Two. But black state legislators Fred E. Williams, Elbert E. Walton, Jr., and Charles "Quincy" Troupe charged that Clay had struck a deal with Circuit Clerk Joseph P. Roddy, a Schoemehl ally, because he wanted to extend his congressional district to the near south side, to which many blacks had recently moved. Clay dismissed the charge as an "ego trip" by the three legislators.

Citing the redundancy of two city hospitals and the necessity for economy, Conway had transferred Homer G. Phillips's in-patient services to the older but larger and better-equipped City Hospital Number One on the near south side. The major newspapers and the medical community approved, but Phillips had been promised to black leaders in 1923 in return for their support for a huge bond issue, and the black community regarded the hospital as its own. Schoemehl

Democratic Congressman William L. Clay in His Washington Office. *Photograph courtesy of the office of Congressman William Clay.*

agreed that the city no longer needed two public hospitals; he promised to close City Number One and reopen Phillips. More than the hospital issue was at stake from Clay's point of view. An alliance with an incoming mayor could increase black participation in city government substantially.

Conway was reported to feel that votes lost on the hospital issue would be countered by approval of the cost reductions effected by the consolidation of health services. If so, he miscalculated; consolidation was popular south of Chouteau Avenue, but few people there cared deeply about the hospital's location—they did not use it. They did care about police protection, and Schoemehl seized that issue by capitalizing on a newspaper report that Conway favored reducing the nineteen-hundred-man police force by five hundred officers. Conway denied any such intention, but the issue hurt him, especially after a Schoemehl television spot featuring a disappearing police cruiser aired repeatedly. What Conway really wanted, according to an aide, was some degree of city control over the police department.

Lacking ward organization support, Schoemehl created his own organization of hundreds of volunteers who blanketed the city door-to-door. Even Conway's supporters were impressed; they heard Schoemehl's footsteps, especially after Aldermanic President Thomas

Mayor Vincent Schoemehl. *Photograph by Martin Schweig III, 1982. Courtesy of Schweig Studios. MHS-PP.*

Zych abandoned his neutral stance to endorse the challenger. With two days to go before the election, Conway realized that he did not have a lock on the nomination, though he believed he still had an edge. Some of his backers had no doubts at all; Alderman James Signaigo of the Second Ward predicted a Conway margin there of four to one.

Schoemehl won a smashing victory on March 3, by a vote of seventy thousand to thirty-two thousand. Stunned by the size of his majority, the winner attributed it to "the elderly, the blacks, and organized labor." Conway graciously called it a slaughter. He had lost twenty-seven of the twenty-eight wards, winning only his own, the Eighth, by a small margin. Signaigo's Second Ward went to Schoemehl by nearly three to one, and black legislator J. B. "Jet" Banks, who had endorsed Conway, saw his Nineteenth Ward "fiefdom" go for the winner by six to one.

For three decades, the Democratic nomination for mayor had been tantamount to election, but in 1981 the Republicans put up a strong young candidate, Jerry Wamser, who hoped to capitalize upon the bitterness engendered by the Democratic primary. Schoemehl expected to win, and he gave the city a preview of his operating style by seeking advice and help on city problems from a variety of sources: neighborhood organizations, labor unions, small-business executives, corporate leaders, bankers, and political leaders north and south. Not only was this evidence of careful planning, it was a campaign technique. He talked about "creative financing" to improve the city's health system, not just to reopen Phillips because he had promised it. For this approach, though he had no detailed plan as yet, Schoemehl obtained the approval of the Saint Louis University School of Medicine, which operated City Hospital, and the two most powerful bankers in the city, Donald Lasater of Mercantile Bank and Clarence Barksdale of Centerre Bank. In endorsing Schoemehl over Wamser, the *Post-Dispatch* hailed the former for seeking positive solutions rather than lamenting the city's shortcomings.

With a basic Republican constituency of less than one-third of the voters, Jerry Wamser had to make substantial inroads among conservative Democrats. He stressed the high cost of reopening Phillips, the need to reduce expenditures, the untouchability of the police and fire departments, and the prospect of Clay influence in a Schoemehl administration. He was well financed and he made a strong showing on the south side, carrying five of its twelve wards. But Schoemehl swept the north side wards by margins ranging up to twenty to one, and he prevailed in the racially mixed Central West End by more than two to one. Overall, Schoemehl received seventy-three thousand votes, Wamser thirty-seven thousand. Despite his easy victory, Schoemehl faced possible trouble ahead, especially if a rift developed with Zych, who had expressed an interest in running for mayor in 1985. In that event, City Treasurer and Democratic Party Chairman Paul M. Berra, who had won the race for comptroller, would hold the balance of power on the Board of Estimate and Apportionment.

The health services issue was not settled by the election. An amendment to the city charter for the reopening of Phillips Hospital, which required 60 percent of the vote for adoption, received only 56 percent. The new mayor was in a tight squeeze. At the current level of expenditures, the city's deficit was estimated at $54 million for the year ahead, which a transfer of indigent services to Phillips would exacerbate. Furthermore, a double-digit inflation and recession was under way, which was reducing revenues and ballooning energy and other costs of government while new administrations in Washington and Jefferson City were slashing aid to cities. According to medical authorities at Saint Louis and Washington Universities, reopening Phillips would cost millions of dollars, and some of the services available at City Hospital Number One could not be duplicated at Phillips because of limited space. With local medical opinion and cost considerations weighing against the transfer, Schoemehl ordered an independent study of its feasibility. Black aldermen hoped that the study would support their case, but it did not. With the support of the aldermanic majority, the mayor then decided not to reopen Phillips. Some in the black community felt they had been betrayed, and the brand-new Clay-Schoemehl political accord was at some risk.

In other respects, the new city hall regime began auspiciously. Schoemehl's ebullient confidence and pro-development stance impressed Civic Progress and the downtown business community. He brought in experts from outside the local party organization to deal with community relations and economic development and initiated programs to improve the environment and external appearances of St. Louis. Most encouraging of all, Mayor Schoemehl and County Executive McNary frequently appeared in public together—smiling, shaking hands, speaking of a shared vision of a greater St. Louis. Shortly after taking office, the administration asked residents what they disliked about St. Louis. Respondents to the survey placed crime in the streets high on the list, but even more frequently they complained that the city was dirty. After seeking and getting help from business, labor, church, and neighborhood groups, the mayor launched "Operation Brightside," a massive cleanup campaign involving as many as seventy-five thousand volunteers. Grants from Civic Progress and Anheuser-Busch funded eight hundred summer jobs for disadvantaged youths, who worked primarily on arterial streets. Within two years, the mayor reported nearly fifty million tons of trash had been removed from the streets. Private contractors and the operating engineers union helped to clean up, grade, and seed thousands of vacant lots, and in 1985 volunteers planted one million flowers in municipal parks and along the streets. By 1988 some 5.5 million daffodils graced the highway margins and another five million flowers had been planted in the parks and streetsides. Under the plan, all of the city's twelve thousand vacant lots would be graded, seeded, and put under regular maintenance by 1991. The public, visitors and residents alike, responded enthusiastically. What had been an occasion for apology had become a source of pride.

Under "Operation Safestreet," which got under way in 1984, the city installed dead bolt locks, peepholes, window bars, and other security devices in homes at $150 per unit (free for older residents). Police officers trained residents to identify potential criminal activity, and block captains coordinated the efforts of their neighbors and the police. Traffic patterns were redesigned in some areas by blocking streets to discourage cruising and loitering by strangers to the neighborhood. This last program, which was a familiar device in the suburbs, drew fire from some south side residents because of the disruption of their customary routes. In the target areas, murder, rape,

"Operation Safestreet." *Concrete planters blocking through traffic from residential streets were one visible feature of "Operation Safestreet," a Schoemehl administration initiative. Photograph by David Schultz, 1998. MHS-PP.*

assault, burglary, and larceny were down by an average of 30 percent in 1984, marking the fourth straight year that the rate had declined. Even after a slight rise in 1985, the St. Louis crime rate was below the average for comparable cities. In the broader metropolitan area, crime had declined for twelve consecutive years in 1984; the St. Louis SMSA was fifth in violent crimes and eighth in crimes against property among ten areas of comparable size. From 1985 to 1988, the city's rate was fairly stable, but in the first quarter of 1989, led by a 32 percent rise in auto thefts, it increased by 9.1 percent.

In other initiatives, the city helped developers and owners renovate dilapidated housing, boosted expenditures for street construction and repair, boarded up or demolished dangerous vacant buildings, and set up a central response service for city departments. The demolition program created a confrontation between safety and historic preservation. Criminals using vacant buildings posed a threat of violence, and some rickety interiors were hazardous to children. But some of these buildings were structurally sound and in historic districts, potential candidates for rehabilitation. The city's Heritage and Urban Design Commission had to approve such demolitions, but after changes in the federal tax laws in 1985 virtually eliminated restoration incentives, more buildings came down. Preservationists protested that some significant buildings in the Central West End were destroyed chiefly to make room for new construction. The commission's decisions, after it had heard from various interested parties, were based upon its assessments of the public interest.

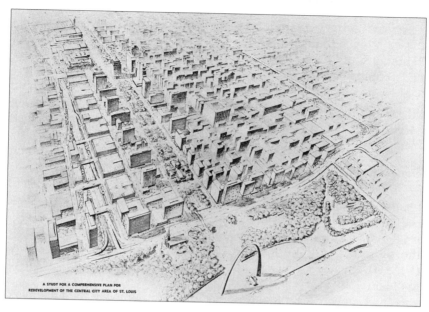

Study for a Comprehensive Plan for Redevelopment of the Central City Area of
St. Louis. *This plan was the first visualization of a Gateway Mall stretching from the
Old Courthouse to the Civil Courts, eliminating the Buder, Title Guaranty, and
Western Union Buildings. Rendering by Russell, Mullgardt, Schwarz and Van Hoefen,
1954. MHS-PP.*

By far the most important of the rehabilitation controversies,
the Gateway Mall project, reflected a complex mix of interests and
personalities. The idea of a green-belt mall with parks and fountains
and a few low-rise public buildings stretching from the Union
Station to the Old Courthouse originated with the City Beautiful
planners in the heyday of urban progressivism before the First
World War. A green belt had been completed from Twentieth to
Thirteenth Street in 1953, and Eero Saarinen later urged that it be
extended to Fourth Street to enhance the environment of his
Gateway Arch. For years the funereal quiet of the downtown streets
after working hours had embarrassed civic patriots. Various
schemes for the mall were discussed in the late 1960s, and during
the Poelker administration (1973–77) the linear mall became a
planning priority. Poelker's successor, Mayor James Conway,
working closely with downtown interests, had the Land Clearance
for Redevelopment Authority prepare a federal grant application for
the project in 1980.

The 1980 proposal, like early concepts of the mall, stressed open space and greenery, with a bit more commercial activity. After razing the existing buildings between Chestnut and Market Streets, from Tenth to Sixth Street, the plan would replace them with an 875-space underground parking facility, cascades and fountains, green space, and a glass-covered commercial mall filled with specialty shops and restaurants. Presumably, large crowds from outlying areas would want to enjoy this amenity in the fashion of the central piazzas, plazas, and places of Europe. Some critics thought the covered mall would feel like home to suburbanites, not unlike Chesterfield Mall, a bland concrete semi-continent twenty miles to the west.

St. Louis's request was denied by the HUD in December 1980, primarily because local matching funds were not in hand. After reducing its asking from $20 million to $16.8 million, the city resubmitted its proposal, but in April 1981, HUD rejected it again for the same reason. Without an Urban Development Action Grant (UDAG), greater incentives for investors would be needed—a threat to the original open-space concept.

The Gateway Mall Redevelopment Corporation and the Landmark Redevelopment Corporation were the chief competitors for the redevelopment contract for the four-block area. Former Mayor John Poelker was the titular head of Gateway, but Robert Hyland, general manager of KMOX Radio and regional vice president of CBS, Richard Ford, president of the Centerre Bank, and H. Edwin Trusheim, president of the General American Insurance Company, were the most active members of its board. Downtown powerhouses Zane E. Barnes, chairman of Southwestern Bell, and Clarence Barksdale, chairman of the Centerre Bancorporation, were also members. These linear-mall enthusiasts not only wanted to revitalize and beautify downtown, they wanted to improve their neighborhood. Except for Hyland, whose CBS building was down Chouteau's Hill from the courthouse, the redevelopment area was in their front yards. Centerre's 31.5-story building, the largest in the state, was nearly completed at 800 Market Street; General American's headquarters were at 700 Market; and Southwestern Bell's new forty-story One Bell Center was under construction in the block bounded by Tenth and Eleventh, Chestnut and Pine Streets. From their viewpoint, the existing tall buildings in the redevelopment area were mediocre examples of an outmoded architectural style.

Donn Lipton, president of the Landmark Corporation, did not agree. He owned or had options to buy several buildings in the blocks in question, and he thought three of them were distinguished representatives of turn-of-the-century architecture. His plan, which would save these buildings, had the support of his associate, S. Lee Kling, chairman of the Landmark Banks, the St. Louis Landmarks Association and other preservationists, Mayor Schoemehl, and the construction unions. Lipton proposed to rehabilitate the "Real Estate Row" skyscrapers just south of the Wainwright Building. The latter, located at 111 North Seventh Street, was an 1892 Louis Sullivan masterpiece. It had been rescued by the state in the 1970s and converted into a state office building. In 1980 the Missouri Department of Natural Resources certified the Wainwright–Real Estate Row cluster for inclusion in the National Register of Historic Places, noting at the time that the linear-mall plan threatened the historic fabric of downtown St. Louis. These structures had been St. Louis's first skyscrapers, the most distinguished "wall" of tall buildings in the nation, according to their partisans. Vincent Scully, Yale University's eminent architectural historian, called their exteriors "the major architectural achievement of St. Louis in present, no less than in historical terms."

The Title Guaranty (Lincoln Trust) Building at 706 Chestnut Street, designed by William Eames and Thomas C. Young and built in 1899, had a two-story base and a ten-story shaft. With its intricate terra-cotta facade and elaborate interior, it had been called one of the most extravagant buildings in the West. The Buder (Missouri Pacific) Building at One North Seventh Street, designed by W. Albert Swasey and built in 1903, was 12.5 stories high and also featured a lavish display of terra-cotta. The International (Liggett) Building, west of Title Guaranty at Eighth and Chestnut Streets, was a 16.5-story Eames and Young design, built in 1906. In 1981 these buildings provided inexpensive office space for a variety of firms and professionals. Even those who appreciated their distinction conceded that after eight decades they had a rather down-at-heels appearance.

Lipton planned to renovate these buildings and build others on the western blocks of the area, including a six-hundred-room hotel and a bank. He played the underdog David confronting a big-business Goliath, but with labor and the mayor behind him, he was in the running. Labor liked his plan because it would produce more construction jobs than its competitor. In early July, a *Post-Dispatch* poll showed thirteen of the twenty-eight aldermen for Lipton, seven for Gateway, and the rest undecided, the last including those who were awaiting commitments to minority participation in construction.

By April 1982 Gateway's linear mall had become a half-mall. Citing economic considerations for the shift, Gateway now proposed to replace the old buildings on the Chestnut Street (north) side with six- or seven-story office buildings and underground parking. Green space, outdoor cafes, and an amphitheater would occupy the Market Street side of the blocks. At this point, Seventh Ward Democratic committeeman Sorkis Webbe, Jr., a downtown hotel owner with strong labor connections, came forward with a compromise plan. The younger Webbe was ambitious and articulate, and he considered downtown his turf. He suggested removing everything from the southern half of the blocks to maintain the linear mall, but he would save the Title Guaranty and International Buildings and erect new ones west of Eighth Street that could be as tall as the International's 16.5 stories. Mayor Schoemehl was uncomfortable with Webbe's proposal because Buder would be destroyed. Still determined to take down all of the old buildings, the Gateway Mall board ignored Webbe's offering at first.

With both Gateway and Landmark mounting strenuous public relations campaigns and pressuring aldermen, Mayor Schoemehl and the Community Development Agency (CDA) drew up a plan that kept all three of the historic buildings but created a block and a half of open space west of Buder on the Market Street side. When Lipton agreed to the CDA solution, the Gateway board promptly signed on with Webbe. Ironically, the Webbes had traditionally regarded the Civic Progress businessmen as enemies, a sentiment that had been heartily reciprocated. A *St. Louis Business Journal* article cited an anonymous observer who attributed Webbe's shift to the management side to a desire to restore his family's credibility after his father had been indicted in Nevada for gambling irregularities. The Gateway leaders may have had reservations about their new ally, but as one businessman told the *Journal*, Webbe had saved them.

Mayor Schoemehl wanted the matter settled without a bitter fight in the Board of Aldermen, but the linear-mall people would not compromise on the Buder Building, and neither side would concede management control to the other. Hyland, Ford, and others rejected the CDA plan at a meeting with the mayor on July 2, but after a low-profile meeting at Pipefitter's Hall with construction union leaders John Lawler (Pipefitters), Richard Mantia (Construction Trades Council), Ollie Langhorst (Carpenters), and Jack Martorelli (Operating Engineers), the Gateway leaders were ready to deal.

On July 8, representatives of Gateway, Landmark, labor, and Mayor Schoemehl agreed to create the Pride of St. Louis Redevelopment Corporation, which would attempt to reconcile the competing plans. The *Post-Dispatch* reported that there had been hot words between Mayor Schoemehl and Robert Hyland during the discussions, apparently because the mayor resented Gateway's alliance with Webbe, who was perceived at the time to be a threat to

Schoemehl's downtown political base. Both Schoemehl and Hyland later dismissed their argument as inconsequential.

The labor leaders involved in the founding of this new organization had been among the founders of Pride, a joint labor-management effort that had kept the peace for ten years, rehabilitated the construction industry's formerly negative image in the St. Louis area, and contributed to the recent construction boom. Richard Mantia, executive secretary of the Construction Trades Council and co-chairman of Pride, was especially effective as a peacemaker.

Mayor Schoemehl pointed out that the Pride of St. Louis Corporation's only purpose was to develop an acceptable compromise, but on the same day, July 9, the *Globe-Democrat* hailed its formation as a victory for the linear mall, citing an anonymous inside source. Lipton promptly withdrew, charging the *Globe* with trying to discredit the Landmark plan. The mayor deplored the *Globe* article, regretted Lipton's departure, and reiterated his confidence in the Pride of St. Louis organization. Richard Mantia and H. Edwin Trusheim were chosen as co-chairmen of the thirteen-man board, a majority of whom were Gateway Mall members. Labor's five members said they would protect Landmark's interests, but they were no longer its advocates, having been promised that the half-mall plan would produce more jobs than Landmark's renovations would.

Lipton offered to sacrifice the Buder Building in late July in return for certain concessions, but by the end of August, Pride had decided to eliminate all three of the historic buildings. The Title Guaranty and International Buildings would be replaced by a new ten-story building. Eleven- and nine-story structures would be built between Eighth and Tenth Streets, with a clause permitting a 25 percent variance in height. In the weeks that followed, the Pride board, citing "economic realities," took a more flexible view of permissible building heights, aesthetics, and the view of the Arch. On October 8, the Board of Aldermen approved a plan that did not mention building heights, limiting each building to 350,000 square feet plus the 25 percent variance. When reporters pointed out that twenty-story buildings would now be possible, some aldermen admitted that they had not known this, but that they trusted Pride to do the right thing. But Alderman Dan McGuire of the Twenty-Eighth Ward was outraged. "Pride," he said, "is saying that we should trust them, and I think that is a hell of a way to run a railroad."

Mayor Schoemehl, with whom McGuire had usually agreed, was more trusting. He believed that Pride officials would "exercise their flexibility in the best interest of the public." Aldermanic President Thomas Zych was quoted in the *Post-Dispatch* as saying, "We're not going to get . . . a completely open parkway. . . . Aesthetics are one thing. When you're talking about a $100 million project, you can't go on aesthetics." Carolyn Toft, executive director of the St. Louis Landmarks Association, said the elected officials had abdicated their responsibilities, and called their expressions of faith in Pride "hogwash."

The *Globe-Democrat* was delighted with the outcome, but the *Post-Dispatch*, which had also supported the mall plan and Pride, found the latest developments involving buildings in the twenty-story range "disquieting . . . instead of a sweeping vista west of the arch, set off by a low range of buildings to the north, the view from the mall would be like that from the mouth of a canyon." But the *Post* took comfort from the fact that Pride directors Robert Hyland and Edwin Trusheim were committed to a "visually inspiring, credit to the community" kind of mall development. Hyland and Trusheim had issued comforting statements to that effect.

Within three years, Real Estate Row was down, Buder the last to go. Gateway One, a shiny fifteen-story structure of steel-and-glass towers over underground parking, built by the Turco Development Company and the Paragon Corporation, a prestigious national developer, soon stood in the place of the Title Guaranty and International Buildings. In 1989, new construction had not begun on the two western blocks of the redevelopment area. A grassy plot occupied Buder's former space. To the east, between Sixth and Seventh Streets, the Morton D. May Amphitheater and plaza, dedicated in 1987, took up the entire block. It featured a sunken courtyard, with the amphitheater on the west and a cascade fountain on the east, the latter flanked by steps rising to connect with the Kiener plaza block. The amphitheater and plaza was intended to be a gathering place, featuring game-day pep rallies, lunch-hour concerts, and the like. In good weather, it attracted visitors even without special events, with children especially drawn to the fountain, and others responding to the spectacular view of the Old Courthouse framed by the Gateway Arch.

Did the city do well by adopting the half-mall plan? Was it the wisest use of these "most important blocks downtown," as Richard Claybour, designer of Lipton's Landmark plan, had called them? The amphitheater, in 1989 the most attractive feature of the eastern part of the mall, had not been excluded by the Landmark alternative. The historic buildings were gone, and so was the block-wide mall. Did Gateway One and its anticipated counterparts (Gateway Two and Three) speak to St. Louis's expansive past, as the Gateway Arch and the Union Station did, or would they have served better in Miami, or Tulsa, or Westport? Many visitors and residents did not ask these

Kiener Plaza and Gateway One. *Photograph by David Schultz, 1998. MHS-PP.*

questions; they preferred the eastern blocks of the mall to its center, the much-maligned composition of seven steel slabs between Tenth and Eleventh Streets called "Twain," designed by Richard Serra. Preservationists will never forgive the half-mall's planners, but by the mid-1980s the mall controversy had faded in the glow of more successful developments.

The mall controversy aside, 1982 was a triumphant year for St. Louis. In addition to city hall initiatives, and despite the failure of a developmental sales tax proposition, major private efforts brought favorable national attention to the city. A group of energetic businessmen, headed by Robert Hermann, chairman of the Hermann Group, and including William Maritz of the Maritz Companies; Donald Lasater, chairman of the Mercantile Bank; Clarence Barksdale, the Centerre chairman; Charles Wallace; and Robert Stolz, had organized and carried out a huge civic celebration on the riverfront in 1981. In planning the event, which was to become an annual affair, Hermann had combined aspects of the city's tradition with the national Independence Day celebration.

The Veiled Prophet parade, ball, and coronation had been staged by the city's social elite in the autumn since 1878, in conjunction with the Mississippi Valley Agricultural and Mechanical Fair, which had originated in 1856. The annual fair had perished in the afterglow of the Louisiana Purchase Exposition, but the Veiled Prophet celebration had persisted. Its sponsors agreed in 1981 to conduct its parade, though not its ball and coronation, in conjunction with the Fourth of July riverfront extravaganza, which was to be called the VP Fair. In response to the flood of negative publicity the city had suffered because of Pruitt-Igoe and population decline, Hermann and his associates were determined to throw the biggest Fourth of July bash in the nation and to let the nation know it. Enormous crowds would be necessary, which in return required emphasis on big-name entertainers, fireworks, and other spectaculars. Except for the Veiled Prophet parade, a crowd pleaser in spite of its elitist tradition (or perhaps because of it) the VP Fair as it developed had little to do with the city's past and its traditions.

Its inaugural year had met all expectations. Crowds were in the millions, according to the organizers, and 1982 was to be even better. The main stage, located in the shadow of the Gateway Arch in the National Park Service's Jefferson National Expansion Memorial grounds, featured St. Louis's own Chuck Berry, Dionne Warwick, the Beach Boys, Bob Hope, Elton John, and Roy Clark, with the Mamas and the Papas performing on the Laclède's Landing stage. The three-day affair on July 3, 4, and 5 drew more than three million people, said the fair authorities, with the police guessing a smaller figure. Since there were no turnstiles and no strict boundaries, the count could not be precise, but all who attended knew they were in an enormous crowd. Two innocent bystanders were shot and killed in what had begun as an exchange of racial insults, and considerable damage was done to the National Park grounds, but the latter could be fixed, and was, with the fair authorities paying all expenses. Each year thereafter, there was some tension between the Park Service and the fair's management because of the environmental stress created by the huge crowds, especially when the grounds were muddy. But to many in the metropolitan area, especially children and younger adults, the fair was great fun, the highlight of the year—except perhaps in pennant-winning seasons. As its organizers had hoped, the event attracted considerable media attention, with the ABC television network giving it almost full coverage in 1988.

St. Louis city and county supported the fair in various ways, including direct financial subsidies through 1988, but the larger part of its revenues came from concession fees and corporate and private support. In 1989 County Executive Gene McNary, still smarting because downtown business and city hall had opposed his efforts to build a domed stadium in the Missouri River flood plain, decided that

An Afternoon at the VP Fair. *Photograph by Glenn S. Hensley, 1984. MHS-PP.*

the county's budget could not accommodate a further subsidy. The county had contributed $150,000 in 1987 and $50,000 in 1988. In a split vote, the Board of Estimate and Apportionment increased the city's contribution from $300,000 to $400,000 in 1989, representing 10 percent of the fair's total budget. Mayor Schoemehl and Aldermanic President Thomas Villa favored the subsidy, but Comptroller Virvus Jones opposed it, citing financial reasons. As an alderman from 1981 to 1985, Jones had charged that the fair provided insufficient black participation, but he conceded that the situation had improved in recent years. The fair's accumulated debt was $690,000 in 1989, considerably less than it had contributed to riverfront improvements such as lighting for the Eads Bridge and building a balcony and promenade overlooking the wharf in front of the Gateway Arch. After eight years the VP Fair's impact on the nation may have been less than expected, but it had been a smash hit at home, likely to be part of the St. Louis scene as long as its board retained the enthusiasm and the National Park Service its tolerance.

In another phase of the civic-improvement drive, Mayor Schoemehl and County Executive McNary proposed a five-eighth of a cent sales tax increase in 1982. Of the $40 million generated by this tax in its first year, $24 million would go to economic development and tourism and $16 million to cultural institutions. As a sweetener for property owners, the nine-cents-per-one-hundred-dollar-valuation zoo-museum tax would be rescinded by the proposition. A labor-community leaders' coalition, calling itself People for Jobs and Growth, managed the tax campaign. Despite a lavish promotional effort, loaded with hyperbole and featuring television scripts read by professional actors, county voters turned down the tax at the August primary by a 54 to 46 percent margin. The city approved the proposition by 52 to 48 percent, but the county rejection killed it. Given the expensive promotion and its laudable purposes, the tax probably should have passed, but the scripts were inane and the imported actors lacked credibility. The opposition, volunteers virtually without funds but with the advantage of the FCC's equal time provision, stressed the regressive nature of the tax and played upon village suspicions of downtown and Clayton business interests. The *Post-Dispatch* took comfort from the narrow defeat during a recession and in the face of nationwide anti-tax sentiment.

Black voters and candidates shocked the political pundits at the same primary by dominating citywide races as never before. Factionalism and voter apathy had long characterized north side politics, but the results of congressional redistricting, after the 1980 census reduced the Missouri delegation from ten to nine, energized the community. The Missouri legislature, not notably friendly to Congressman William Clay, had extended his district into the white enclaves of north and northwest county. State Senator Alan G. Mueller, a good campaigner with a creditable record, challenged Clay for the First District Democratic nomination. When early polls showed that Mueller was a serious contender, Clay and his cohorts went to work. Black leaders, some of whom had opposed him in the past, united behind Clay. With strong support from organized labor, which appreciated his pro-labor record, Clay swept to a smashing victory, by 72,896 votes to 45,692. He had won 80 percent of the total in the city part of the district and 40 percent in the county, much of the latter attributable to his effective targeting of interest groups such as seniors and environmentalists.

Experts had predicted the usual 30 to 35 percent primary turnout in the city's predominantly black wards; instead, about 45 percent of those registered had voted. Not only had the returns demonstrated that Clay could win substantial white support, but they also revealed the length of his coattails. City Treasurer Larry Williams, a friend and ally of Clay's, said that blacks were defending against a perceived conspiracy to steal their congressional district. The heavy turnout also won the City License Collector's office for Billie A. Boykins, the first black woman ever to be nominated by a major party for a citywide office. For more than a dozen years, that office had been notoriously corrupt, with one incumbent serving a seven-year sentence for bribery and another saved from an indictment by the death of the chief witness against him. Boykins promised to "clean up" the staff problems, conduct regular audits, and "maximize the revenue-gathering potential" of the collector's office.

In an even more surprising upset, attorney Freeman Bosley, Jr., son of the veteran alderman Freeman Bosley, defeated Joseph P. Roddy for the Democratic nomination for Circuit Clerk. Roddy, the incumbent, was chairman of the Democratic Central Committee and a close associate of Mayor Schoemehl. He had been endorsed by most of the ward organizations, including the north side wards. Bosley squeezed through with the aid of the heavy black vote, his name recognition through his father, and the "candidacy" of one Clara Roddy, who drew a vote total larger than Bosley's plurality, presumably because of voter confusion. As usual, the Democrats won easily in the November general election. For the first time in its history, St. Louis had three black citywide officeholders: Bosley, Boykins, and City Treasurer Larry Williams. As elected "county" officers, Bosley and Boykins were outside the mayor's direct control, not a part of his administration.

The construction boom, the VP Fair, and rising black political power were all striking examples of a changing St. Louis, but to many people, the resurgence of Cardinal baseball in the 1980s was even more exciting. After winning three National League pennants and two World Series in the 1960s, the team had lapsed into mediocrity for more than a decade, failing even to capture an eastern division title after divisional play began in 1969. But in 1982, after a few key player trades and the arrival of manager Whitey Herzog (in 1980), the Cardinals won their division, swept the Atlanta Braves in the playoffs, and won a nail-biting World Series from the Milwaukee Brewers, four games to three. Manager Herzog, first baseman Keith Hernandez, and outfielders George Hendrick and Willie McGee were consensus local heroes. A few visiting reporters, apparently unhappy with a midwestern World Series, outraged local residents by referring to the event as a "beer bust" and criticizing St. Louis's inadequate public transportation, taxicab "ripoffs," and limited downtown night life. That there was truth in some of these barbs was no help. Nonetheless, the dominant mood was upbeat. The *New York Times* quoted Mayor Schoemehl as saying, "I couldn't be happier. . . . I've got a billion dollars in rehabilitation going on, we just received a $10 million federal grant for redevelopment, and the Cardinals are in the World Series." Other interviewees told the *Times*: "It ties it all together . . . the city is in the midst of a boom, just like the Cardinals"; and "the Cardinals were lousy for years, and now things have turned around, just like they have for the city." Some St. Louisans took the reporters' questions as an opportunity to stress institutional strengths: the Botanical Gardens, the zoo, the symphony, the Art Museum, the "healthy university community," and "outstanding rail transportation and more river traffic than any other American city."

A *Chicago Tribune* reporter concluded that St. Louis's often-cited conservatism was assumed modesty, considering the city's many cultural assets, its seventeen Fortune 500 corporate headquarters, and its "friendly and charming atmosphere." The *Kansas City Star* called William Maritz, the founding genius of the Laclède's Landing redevelopment and chairman of the VP Fair, a living denial that St. Louis was conservative, a "veritable one-man symposium on momentum." Maritz had informed the *Star* that "in the downtown core area . . . more than $500 million in construction is going on—we have the new Centerre Tower, . . . several major office buildings being built, the new Serra Sculpture, the Radisson and Sheraton Hotels completed, a major new addition to the Marriott, and the VP Fair." The earlier sources of local pride—the museums, the symphony, the universities, the great research hospitals, the Arch and its symbolism, a sense of tradition held quietly but firmly by the older families and others who had caught its spirit, which was strengthened now by a revitalized downtown, the fair, and the Cardinals' championship season— reasserted themselves with the public, and the embarrassments of the recent past began to recede. Civic spirit in St. Louis had always had its ebbs and flows; in the early 1980s it was on the rise, and in 1985 it reached a peak.

Confidence in the city's political leadership was an important part of the public's sense of well-being. Mayor Schoemehl, whose relationships with County Executive McNary and Congressman Clay were still in good working order, had won the confidence of Civic Progress and the corporate leadership generally. The most important labor leaders, including Richard Mantia of the Construction Union Council and Robert Kelly, the Central Trades and Labor Council chief, trusted the mayor and were in his confidence. Schoemehl's occasional truculence when pressed hard in public may not have endeared him to everyone, but it had a kind of Trumanesque quality to it, not a disadvantage in St. Louis. He had become the champion, and to a good many people the symbol, of the urban revival. He had the good fortune to be in office when good things were happening, but a substantial part of the civic resurgence was attributable to him, and he did not mind saying so.

As his reelection drive began in 1984, the mayor's position seemed impregnable, but with his own upset victory in 1981 in mind, he took no chances. "Citizens for Schoemehl," his campaign organization, raised $1.44 million for him, by far the largest sum ever amassed in St. Louis for a mayoral candidate. The A. G. Edwards brokerage house gave five thousand dollars, and a host of major corporations, including Anheuser-Busch, Monsanto Chemical, the Mercantile Bancorporation, Alberici Construction, and McDonnell Douglas, donated five-figure sums, as did a large number of individuals. Through media advertisements, pamphlets, and "coffees" in private homes, Schoemehl made his case. He reminded the voters of his initiatives already under way, such as Operations Brightside and Safestreet, and stressed the fact that sixteen UDAG grants had been awarded to St. Louis by HUD since 1980, totalling $56 million and providing 7,895 permanent and 3,343 construction jobs. St. Louis led the nation in taking advantage of this federal program. Looking ahead, the mayor promised that his administration would spend $30 million in the next five years on repaving 167 miles of streets, building two thousand blocks of new sidewalks, and planting thirteen thousand trees—all without a tax increase.

Fiscal stability was perhaps Schoemehl's most effective weapon. Facing a $54 million deficit in 1981, he had cut the oversized civic payroll by one thousand jobs immediately and fifty-five hundred in all by 1984, nearly 40 percent of the total. Annual savings had been $17 million because of the force reductions and, according to the mayor, the installation of a computerized revenue and expenditure system, obtained with the help of a grant from Civic Progress. A new budget office, headed by a graduate of the Wharton School of Finance, managed this operation. Even after these reductions and efficiencies, a deficit of nearly $20 million had remained because of lost revenues, police and fire department raises, and higher energy costs. If city services were to be maintained, the budget problem had to be attacked from the revenue end. On June 5, 1984, despite warnings to the mayor that no tax increase had a chance in the existing tight economy, the voters approved a combined business and sales tax. In that year the city's budget was in balance for the first time since 1980, and the budget office estimated that with a 4 percent annual growth in the revenue base, deficits would be avoided for the next five years.

Four candidates challenged Schoemehl for the Democratic mayoral nomination in 1985. His leading opponent, Freeman Bosley, Sr., had begun his campaign shortly after his son's surprise victory in 1982. Bosley charged Schoemehl with breaking faith by not reopening Phillips Hospital and attacked him for laying off too many city employees. Schoemehl refused to debate him, instead pointing out that he had tried in November 1982 to reopen Phillips, but that the voters had rejected a $64 million bond issue for the purpose. Actually, more than 53 percent of those voting had favored the proposition, but this was far short of the margin required.

The result was a landslide: Schoemehl polled three-fourths of the votes, with 62,751 to Bosley's 18,600. Schoemehl carried four of the twelve north side wards; his total there was only fifteen hundred less than Bosley's. The mayor may have overstated the case, according to a *Post-Dispatch* editorialist, when he called the election outcome the end of racial politics in St. Louis. But he had shown that "a skillful incumbent could make accomplishment count for more than race in all parts of the city."

Comptroller Paul M. Berra was renominated over Alphonso Jackson by nearly three to one, and on the near south side, Seventh Ward voters read the last rites over the Webbe-Leisure machine by selecting political newcomer Phyllis Young over a last-minute replacement for Sorkis Webbe, Jr. Webbe had resigned as alderman and from the race because the law was hot on his heels. In another reversal of the past, voters buried the city's venerable Sunday closing law by a three-to-one margin.

In the April general election, Schoemehl and Berra both won landslide victories. Schoemehl's opponent, Curtis Crawford, won only 29 percent of the vote in the predominantly black wards and 15 percent of the total, carrying not a single ward. He was bitter in defeat, complaining that despite the Republicans' talk of helping him in order to attract black voters, neither the state nor the national party had given a cent to his campaign.

As previously noted, 1985 was a shining year for St. Louis. After a long wait for the "May Mall" and for something to be done about the Union Station, which had closed as a railroad terminal in 1978, both projects burst into flower. Before the end of the year, the public hospital dilemma appeared to have been solved, and the Cardinals had won another pennant. The downtown revival had actually begun in the 1970s, chiefly through initiatives by Mercantile Bank Chairman Donald Lasater and William E. Maritz of the Maritz Companies. To keep Mercantile's key operations downtown and thus to slow—and if possible reverse—the business slide to the county, Lasater made a decision that he called "30 percent emotional." He undertook a six-block redevelopment project, which was to include a shopping mall, an office building, and a hotel. The thirty-six-story Mercantile Tower was completed in 1975. The shopping mall, which became the St. Louis Centre, took shape in 1980 when the May Company brought in Melvin Simon and Associates of Indianapolis as the managing partner for the project.

The Mercantile Tower Shortly after Completion. *Photograph by Mac Mizuki, 1975.*
MHS-PP.

Maritz created his Laclède's Landing Redevelopment Corporation
in the mid-1970s, and with the assistance of tax abatement and a 25
percent tax credit for historic rehabilitation, he brought to life the
long-neglected area just north of the Eads Bridge's western approach.
The nineteenth-century brick warehouses were converted into offices,
restaurants, night clubs, and shops. With its cobblestone streets and
alleys, brick structures hung with decorative ironwork, a smattering of
eighteenth-century street names, and the river rolling below, the
Landing captured a whiff of the distant past, all with a suggestion of
adventure and good times. Downtown workers and tourists crowded
its restaurants at lunchtime, and in the late afternoon and evening the
tempo increased as tourists, conventioneers, and younger adults from
the entire area converged on it. As a visiting writer put it, "music
blares from open doors; young women in heels walk carefully across

cobblestone streets. The Landing swings until 3 A.M. Your cab driver can tell you where to go for the best blues (or) shrimp and oysters." Ironically, a part of the past preserved in the Landing is the name of St. Louis's most dedicated enemy in the 1860s, Lucius Boomer, etched boldly across the front of a popular restaurant. In 1985, an out-of-town writer compared the Landing's ambiance to San Francisco's Ghirardelli Square "with a few riverboats thrown in."

Herman Simon, president of Simon Associates, became interested in the St. Louis Centre when he determined that the regional economy was strong despite the city's negative image. The risk that shoppers accustomed to outlying shopping centers would not come downtown was mitigated by an $18 million Urban Development Action Grant and city property tax abatement that accompanied the project. After approval by the Land Clearance for Redevelopment Authority (LCRA), which also agreed to finance and build a six-level, $14.5 million parking garage, Simon began clearance and construction in August 1982. LCRA's garage was financed by revenue bonds purchased by Boatmen's Bank and $6 million of LCRA equity. A twenty-one-story office building, One City Centre, was constructed above the mall's fourth level.

The mall proper, bounded by Broadway, Locust, and Seventh Streets, and Washington Avenue, was anchored on the north and south by the flagship stores of Dillard's and the May Company's Famous-Barr. These older buildings were renovated and integrated with the mall. Famous-Barr operated on ten levels, connected by bridges to the mall; Dillard's reduced its space to its first four floors; the rest of its eleven-story building was to be converted to a suite size hotel, scheduled for opening in 1991. When completed, the complex had 1.5 million square feet of retail space, 350,000 square feet of it in the mall—the largest enclosed urban mall in the country. Including the parking garage, the office tower, the mall, and the projected hotel, the complex was to cost $176.5 million.

Expanses of glass, including two glass atria and a vaulted skylight, gave shoppers a view of the streets and allowed pedestrians outside to see the retail activity—an invitation to enter. Clear glass walkways connected at several levels with the department stores, the parking garages, and several nearby office buildings. There were twelve escalators and a central glass-enclosed elevator, the latter overlooking a reflecting pool and fountain.

On opening day, August 8, 1985, thirty thousand people crowded the escalators, sampled the wares of the seventy-seven shops and restaurants, heard Mayor Schoemehl hail the civic resurgence and Bob Hope adjust his venerable repertoire to the occasion. A few months

St. Louis Centre under Construction. *Photograph by Ted McCrea, 1984. MHS-PP.*

later, Edwin Faltermayer of *Fortune* magazine described St. Louis Centre as "an eye-popping four-story arcade," with an urban rather than a suburban atmosphere. Other visiting writers called it "a Crystal Palace," "steamboat surrealism," and "a four-level fantasy, crowned by a block-long glass skylight." Paul Goldberger, in the *New York Times*, thought that the Centre was not architecturally remarkable, as the Union Station was, but "it was striking that it was there at all, in a retail district that seemed a few years ago to be grinding to a halt." Its great features were "the vaulted rooms and the considerable degree of glass fronting on the street, tying the activity within the mall to the outside, and avoiding the street-deadening effect of so many interior malls."

The main question, of course, was whether the crowds would come after the novelty wore off. They did. Soon, the Centre was a major hub of downtown activity. Finding a place to sit down and have lunch in its 750-seat, fourth-level, fast-food arena was an accomplishment. There were some withdrawals and shifting of tenants, as in any mall, but on the whole, business met or exceeded expectations. In May 1989 there were 132 retail tenants, more than 90 percent of capacity, and more than thirty-five hundred retail employees. The future looked bright, with a convention center expansion and light-rail system coming right to the doors of the Centre and new high-quality hotels nearby accommodating more visitors each year. In the more distant future, the mall's prosperity may be linked to the city's success in providing housing for and attracting more downtown residents. In that effort, the St. Louis Centre itself will be a major asset.

From the day it opened in 1894 until the Gateway Arch was completed in 1965, the St. Louis Union Station was the city's signature landmark (having succeeded the Eads Bridge, which had succeeded the Big Mound). It was both an aesthetic and commercial triumph. Frank Lloyd Wright called it and the Wainwright Building St. Louis's finest structures. It was the nation's largest train station, the window through which as many as one hundred thousand people a day saw St. Louis, and the gate through which St. Louisans went into the world. Passenger traffic peaked during World War II, but during the 1950s it began a disastrous decline. In 1961 the last commuter train left the station, and in 1970 Fred Harvey's Restaurant and the Terminal Hotel closed. In 1973 a Florida developer outlined a $100 million plan to convert the station into residential housing and a hotel, but nothing came of it. By that time the interior walls were badly cracked and there were holes in the roof. The building's admirers everywhere deplored its impending demise. The *Baltimore Sun*, as quoted in the *Post-Dispatch*, wrote: "Air pollution threatens the Parthenon, and a paucity of railroad trains threatens the Union Station in St. Louis, the Western Hemisphere's only comparable structure."

Various proposals for redevelopment of the station were offered in the 1970s. One would have transformed the site into a soccer stadium; another, requiring government funding, would have made it a transportation museum. In 1976, the U.S. Department of the Interior designated the Union Station a national historic landmark, and two years later Amtrak abandoned it. Local bankers shunned it, and their attitude discouraged out-of-town interest. But in January 1979 a quirk of fate intervened. Delayed in St. Louis because a heavy storm had shut down Lambert Field, James Levi, president of Oppenheimer Properties of New York, stopped at the station while touring downtown in a taxicab. He was excited by its medieval-castle exterior, and he saw possibilities in the Grand Hall and the train shed, in spite of the fetid odors and decaying interior of the two-block-long building. "But it was a truly grand piece of property," he told an interviewer, "and in my view St. Louis was a real sleeping giant."

Oppenheimer bought the property for $5 million, less than the station had cost to build nearly ninety years earlier, but the hard part was ahead. No St. Louis bank would touch the redevelopment, but when the Rouse Corporation of Baltimore agreed to manage the project, outside capitalists showed interest. Rouse had made an international reputation with several successful redevelopments, the most spectacular being the "festival marketplaces" of Faneuil Hall in Boston and Harborplace in Baltimore. But Oppenheimer wanted a hotel and shopping center at Union Station, discouraging investors accustomed to one or the other. Steve Miller, Oppenheimer's senior vice president, thought the St. Louis bankers were provincial. "The attitudes I faced in this community from the day I walked in here was that the world was flat and it ends at Twelfth Street." But despite the negatives and the economic recession, the great building eventually sold the project.

The Bank of Montreal invested first, sharing a first mortgage of $65 million with the Bank of America. A London investment house took a $25 million second mortgage, and in 1983 Oppenheimer organized the St. Louis Station Associates with itself as general partner and some three hundred limited partners, who invested $34,875,000. The financing was rounded out with $10 million in federal funds, a UDAG obtained through the St. Louis Land Clearance for Redevelopment Authority. A 25 percent federal historic rehabilitation tax credit made the limited partnerships a bonanza, and they were quickly oversubscribed.

Shops on the Midway at St. Louis Union Station. *Photograph by Glenn S. Hensley, 1986. MHS-PP.*

Rouse intended to create a festival atmosphere at Union Station to attract people not primarily to shop but to enjoy themselves. If they had a good time, they would reward themselves by shopping. Impulse items, providing instant gratification, would be readily available. According to a Rouse official, the station would not resemble a mall, either urban or suburban. A luxury hotel, sock shops, gourmet dining rooms, hot-dog stands, high-tech fixtures, and cocktails in paper cups would coexist in "a city within a city." Only New Orleans' French Quarter, San Francisco's Farmers' Market, and Manhattan's Greenwich Village, all of which had distinct personalities and generated their own energy, could match the Union Station, according to a Rouse spokesman. Except that at St. Louis, Rouse was spinning a web of fantasy, fed only by an extraordinary building and memories of a distant and romantic past.

Architects Hellmuth, Obata, and Kassabaum faced the challenge of creating unity out of a mix of shops, restaurants, entertainment facilities, and a hotel. A tower next to the Headhouse would be incongruous and separated from the retail area, so Rouse and the architects chose to renovate the Terminal Hotel and erect a connecting wing under the train shed. The result was the 550-room Omni International Hotel, with 70 rooms and suites in the restored area and 480 smaller and less elegant rooms in the new section.

"Join the celebration" was the rallying cry at the Union Station's opening on August 19, 1985. And celebrate St. Louisans did: six thousand of them at thirty-five dollars a head at the Arts and Education Council's benefit-preview the night before, and tens of thousands at the main event. The crush continued for days, and even the skeptics knew that they had witnessed a *tour de force*, and that St. Louis was riding high. Paul Goldberger of *Fortune* called the station a "truly sumptuous piece of elegance," highlighted by its Grand Hall, "a huge, barrel-vaulted room in green and gold heavily influenced by the architecture of Louis Sullivan." The room, now serving as the lobby of the hotel, had been "lovingly and respectfully restored. . . . Not since the Palm Court of the Plaza was the favored meeting spot in New York had there been so architecturally pleasing a centerpiece for the city's social activity as this room. The most expensive complex ever to qualify for the federal restoration tax credit was worth the expense—a truly grand hotel and a veritable town square for a city that had been desperately in need of both." Though it was similar in some ways to Baltimore's Harborplace and other food and retail marketplaces that had been built in other cities, it rose above their "clichéd quality" because it was "inside one of the most exuberant pieces of 19th Century American architecture ever created."

After four years the Union Station was a success by any standard. Retail units had increased from the opening day's 70-plus to 120, and most of them were prospering. Surprisingly, the larger, somewhat more conventional retailers were the most successful, and there were plans to increase their number. Apparently, shopping had become an important incentive for coming to the station, though the setting and variety of experiences available there still made the difference. In the spring of 1989, the Hyatt Regency chain took over the operation of the hotel. The Station Associates, according to Donna Laidlaw, their chief representative at the site, had made the change because of Hyatt's superior resources and name recognition.

In 1985 the St. Louis Centre and the Union Station were perceived by some observers as rivals, perhaps deadly rivals, but in 1989 there was little evidence that one had hurt the other, and more reason to believe that they were complementary symbols of a vibrant city. But they were not the only new civic assets. On Grand Avenue in Midtown, Mary and Leon Strauss put the "Fabulous Fox" back in business in 1982. With the usual tax incentives, they restored the four-level forty-five-hundred-seat movie palace to its 1920s-style lush extravagance. One observer, an admirer of its "red-marble columns rising to an opulent vault," said that one's eyes were "practically blinded by the jewel-studded light fixtures." A grand staircase and velvet throne chairs, done in the "Siamese Byzantine" style, added to the effect. In this glamorous setting, crowds filled the house to see and hear media stars and to admire the theater. As the novelty diminished, so did attendance, but it averaged more than two thousand a performance year after year. A half-dozen Municipal Opera presentations each winter and a weekly classical musical series in the summer became regular offerings in the mid-1980s.

Metropolitan Square, a vital symbol of a different kind, was completed in 1988 and had its grand opening in January 1989. Gregory Nooney, chairman emeritus of the Nooney Company, a major commercial development and management firm, called it the most significant evidence of St. Louis's renewal in the decade. The 42-story, 597-foot-high skyscraper, which filled the block bounded by Broadway, Olive, Sixth, and Pine Streets, represented a vote of confidence in the city's future by the giant Metropolitan Life Insurance Company. With more than one million square feet in rental space, it was the largest building in the state, having eclipsed One Bell Center, which had just acquired the title from One Centerre Plaza. Hellmuth, Obata, and Kassabaum, St. Louis's leading architectural firm and one of the nation's largest, had designed at Metropolitan Square a massive pile which filled its square-block site at its lower

Metropolitan Square Building. *The forty-two-story post-modern bulk of the Metropolitan Square Building now dominates the downtown skyline. Photograph by David Schultz, 1998. MHS-PP.*

level and half of that area above the eighth floor. The exterior at the base of the building was granite of varying textures and hues and the tower 60 percent golden granite and 40 percent bronzed glass. The pitched copper roof culminated in a series of glass-enclosed pinnacles. Some critics charged that the building lacked refinement or distinction, but to the less sophisticated, it was an energetic and impressive giant on the St. Louis skyline.

For more than a decade, one of the hindrances to the growth of St. Louis as a convention city had been its shortage of first-class hotel space. The Marriott, the Clarion, the Sheraton, and other downtown hotels built in the 1960s and 1970s were of good quality, but there was still a shortage of rooms and meeting space for the larger conventions. The Omni (now Hyatt Regency) at the Union Station, especially the elegant suites in its renovated section, improved the situation, but the biggest breakthrough came in March 1986, when the Adam's Mark Hotel opened on Chestnut Street between Fourth Street and Memorial Drive. It was large by St. Louis standards, with 910 rooms and 94 suites, 75,800 feet of meeting space, including two large ballrooms — one nearly a half-acre (20,000 square feet) in size and the other slightly smaller. Built at a cost of $110 million, it was eighteen stories high on three sides (Fourth, Chestnut, and Pine Streets) and six stories high at Memorial Drive. During construction there were complaints that it was too close to the Gateway Arch and that its boxy shape added nothing of beauty to the city. Other critics thought the twin, oversized horse statues in the lobby, presumably an Adam's Mark signature, were in bad taste. Certainly its big bustling lobby and escalators could not match the classic elegance of the Grand Hall lobby at the Union Station, but the Adam's Mark's prime location, interior arrangements, luxury features, and size made it a major asset to St. Louis's convention and tourist business. As one convention visitor put it: "When you go in the Fourth Street doors of the Adam's Mark, you know you are in town."

George H. Walker, chairman of Downtown St. Louis, Inc., noted at the Adam's Mark opening that the hotel would add seven hundred permanent jobs to the downtown work force. This and the emergence of the St. Louis Centre, the Union Station, and the new headquarters buildings of Southwestern Bell and Edison Brothers stores had increased downtown jobs from 102,000 to 110,000 in a little more than a year. The twenty-three new and renovated buildings scheduled for completion in 1986 represented an investment of $390 million.

During the ceremony some twenty members of the Association for Community Organization for Reform Now (ACORN) picketed outside the hotel, charging that the management would make no commitment to hire poor residents. The hotel responded that it was working with a city agency to arrange for employment for minorities and the poor. This question had arisen repeatedly during the past two decades, especially since the city had blighted the whole downtown area, except for existing new buildings in 1971, making new construction and renovation eligible for tax abatement. Was it fair to the residents of St. Louis to pick up the tax bill for wealthy developers? This question was raised by ACORN and other groups seeking quid pro quo in jobs for the poor. Were small property owners and businessmen and poor families uprooted by rehabilitation projects paying the price for upscale condominiums and downtown hotels and office towers? Interest-free or low-interest loans and tax abatement for redevelopers drew the fire of some social activists who charged that "welfare for the rich" was part of "a policy to drive the poor out of St. Louis."

Alderman Bosley, during his mayoral campaign in 1985, claimed that redevelopment was overrated. "What we get out of it is a beautiful skyline, . . . what we need is jobs, a piece of the action." Deborah Patterson, director of the Community Development Agency, retorted that all developers who had been subsidized by the city had promised to interview any job applicant who had passed a city-run training course. But as ACORN pointed out, interviews were not jobs, and not every applicant had passed a training course. The winners were the developers, the investors, the architects, the bankers, the political leaders, and the construction unions—the middle and upper classes, as usual, according to ACORN.

As noted above, nearly eight thousand new jobs were created downtown by the building boom in 1985 and early 1986, and a good many of them went to minorities and the poor, especially at Union Station, St. Louis Centre, and the hotels. Most of them were relatively low-paying service jobs, some of them seasonal, and they were not the equivalent of the jobs lost or transferred to Wentzville by the closing of the Chevrolet plant on Natural Bridge. But they were a lot better than nothing, and they represented nationwide trends in an economy in transition. Unemployment on the north side was still in double digits, and among black youths it exceeded 25 percent. In November 1985 the unemployment rate in the SMSA was 7.4 percent, lower than in Chicago or Cleveland but a half point higher than the national average. Despite the erosion of manufacturing jobs, St. Louis was still an industrial city; its unemployment rate tended to fluctuate more than the national average. In April 1988, with national unemployment at 5.4 percent, St. Louis's was 6 percent. One year later, with the economy approaching full employment, the national rate was 5.3 percent; St. Louis's, 5.2 percent. Yet the double-digit numbers for black youths persisted. Perhaps better educational and training opportunities—and some changes in attitudes and priorities on all sides—would ameliorate the problem. But the dismal state of public education in St. Louis did not offer much encouragement.

As Mayor Schoemehl put it in 1985, it was "cruel" to pretend to those "who are cruelly disadvantaged in a competitive society" that the construction boom would break the grip of poverty when it would not. But it was worse to imply that they would be better off without the revival. All that the city could do "was to try to leverage the opportunities . . . into further opportunities and try to skew some of those benefits toward some of the most needy."

In addition to the impoverished who wanted jobs, there were the desperately poor and homeless, some of whom were not looking for work and who were not included in the unemployment statistics. To rationalize the effort to help the homeless, in December 1985, upon the recommendation of a homelessness task force he had appointed, the mayor created the Homeless Services Network, a coalition of more than seventy social service agencies, charitable institutions, and other interested parties. The Department of Human Services coordinated the effort, using city funds and federal and state grants to purchase services from the social agencies.

The task force had recommended that the city not add temporary shelter beds, concentrating instead upon assisting existing charitable agencies and finding permanent housing. But as a part of the settlement of a lawsuit brought against it by the Legal Aid Society, the city agreed not only to find permanent homes for one hundred families a year, but to add two hundred shelter beds. The Homeless Services Network's Reception Center, a twenty-four-hour walk-in, call-in facility operated by the Salvation Army, kept a daily count of available beds and collected data on homeless individuals. In 1989 there were thirty-eight shelters being coordinated by the Reception Center. The Christ Church Cathedral Mission (Episcopalian), the Catholic Charities, the United Methodist Metro Ministry, and other agencies provided day and night shelters, meals, transportation, laundry facilities, child care, training programs, counseling and placement, and classes in home management. Through the Homeless Services Network, the city maintained Hope House, a fifty-unit apartment building where homeless families lived rent-free for up to three months while preparing to move into permanent housing. Agencies also provided other transitional apartments where meals, counseling, and socialization were available. In these activities, the network relied heavily upon unpaid volunteers.

In its first two years, Homeless Services made available its promised 200 new emergency beds, helped nearly 1,000 persons find permanent housing, and subsidized 250 families to enable them to keep their homes. Harvard and Tufts Universities, the Ford Foundation, the U.S. Conference of Mayors, and the National League of Cities cited the St. Louis program for its comprehensive and innovative approach. The city increased its budget for homeless services from $310,000 in 1986 to $785,000 in 1989, but there seemed to be no end to the problem. Only about half of those seeking permanent homes had been accommodated, and those not helped, if not on the streets, were back with relatives in overcrowded apartments or other miserable quarters. Some attorneys who worked with the poor traced the homeless problem to the series of redevelopment projects which had begun with the Mill Creek urban renewal development in 1958. Mill Creek alone had forced twenty-six hundred families to move, and a 1979 study had reported that redevelopment had displaced more than five thousand people in St. Louis.

On the other hand, many of those displaced had been living in miserable falling-down slums without indoor toilets or hot water. Leon Strauss, one of the city's major redevelopers, pointed out that projects such as his DeBaliviere Place had been devoted partly to low-income housing. He might have added that many of its ruined buildings had been vacant and the area a dangerous center of violent crime. Strauss attributed the shortage of affordable housing to the federal government's abandonment of support for redevelopment. Ironically, at the same time, the Federal Department of Housing and Urban Development had co-insured Gatesworth Manor in University City, where apartment rents ranged from $1,700 to $2,550 a month. Despite its efforts, which according to some of the homeless made St. Louis one of the best places in the nation in which to be homeless, some critics charged the administration with doing too little. One attacked Operation Brightside in the press, calling it a waste of energy that should have been expended to help the poor. Operation Brightside was largely a voluntary effort, privately funded, and how it could have been turned to another cause was not explained. Other critics, notably the Reverend Larry Rice of the New Life Evangelical Center, kept up a drumfire of attacks on city hall in the media and staged street demonstrations to stress the "inadequacy" of the city's efforts. Rice worked outside the Homeless Services Network, and perhaps because of this, he kept his cause, and himself, in the public eye as much as possible.

In the public health area, Mayor Schoemehl made every effort to keep his campaign promises. In midsummer 1982 he proposed to renovate and reopen Phillips Hospital with the proceeds of a $64 million bond issue, along with an amendment to operate the hospital. The Board of Aldermen approved, ordering both propositions to be placed on the November 2 ballot. Black voters gave them better than two-to-one majorities, but they failed citywide. The bond issue received 53 percent of the vote, with 66.6 percent required, and the charter amendment 59 percent, with 60 percent required.

After this setback, the mayor explored a wide range of alternatives to the existing health-care structure. He appointed a task force headed by Robert F. Hyland and Laclède Gas Company chairman Lee Liberman to study the question, and he pursued other possibilities on his own. In April 1983 the task force recommended the construction of a $40 million municipal hospital, to be funded by a bond issue and a federal grant, and with teaching and research facilities to be operated by the Saint Louis University Medical School. This plan was dead on arrival. Congressman William Clay charged that the medical school was racist and promised to oppose federal funding for any project involving it in city health services. City Hospital had lost its accreditation a few months earlier, requiring a good deal of effort and expenditure to regain it, at least temporarily, while still other solutions were sought. In December 1983 accreditation was restored, but the Saint Louis University Medical School announced that it would no longer operate the facility after July 1, 1985.

Meanwhile, media reports of inadequate nursing care, shortages of drugs and supplies, managerial laxness, and a shocking absentee rate of 30 to 35 percent among its employees thoroughly discredited City Hospital. In 1984 the city hired National Medical Enterprises, a private firm, to manage St. Louis's primary and acute care operations and health clinics. In April 1985 the firm agreed to provide staff physicians for City Hospital after the medical school departed. This arrangement required a broad interpretation of the city's powers under its charter, but in a somewhat different context, the principle was later upheld by the courts. But this apparent commitment to City Hospital was not the end of the matter. The mayor surprised nearly everyone on June 22 when he announced that the city and county jointly had agreed to purchase Charter Hospital at 5535 Delmar Boulevard for $15 million. The Charter Corporation had just bought the 275-bed facility from St. Luke's Hospital, and was not anxious to sell it, but the mayor made Charter an offer it could not refuse, involving the city's power of eminent domain.

On June 24, in what some doctors called a tour de force, Schoemehl closed City Hospital and moved the entire operation to Charter within two weeks. There had not been time for a smooth transition, since the hospital could have lost its charter during a longer delay, and stringent relicensing guidelines could have forced the city to undertake extensive remodeling. Initially, serious problems plagued the new location: communications breakdowns, nurse and doctor shortages, inadequate emergency room space, and many lesser deficiencies in what some harassed and exasperated doctors called "St. Schoemehl's." But Dr. Edward Vastola of Washington University, who became chief neurosurgeon at the city-county facility, thought that instead of complaining, the doctors should "light candles in the chapel" for the move from the rundown City Hospital to a modern, air-conditioned building.

County Hospital closed on November 1, its patients having been transferred to the Regional Medical Center, as it was called. Some of the county employees had petitioned the County Council to reject the move, but to no avail. County Executive McNary and the council were tired of the high per-patient cost at their hospital, and they wanted out of the acute-care business. McNary and Schoemehl contracted with the Regional Health Care Corporation (RHCC), a private nonprofit organization formed for the purpose, to run the hospital. The partners had shared the cost of purchasing Charter Hospital equally, but renovation and operating costs were to be assigned on a patient-usage basis, considerably larger for the city than for the county. In December 1985 Schoemehl and McNary appointed a fifteen-member board which took control of the RHCC, and within a month the board named Robert Johnson of Washington University as the Medical Center's chief executive officer. The medical staff was drawn primarily from the Washington University Medical School.

The Regional plan was endorsed by the Urban League, the League of Women Voters, the Metropolitan Medical Society, Confluence St. Louis (a volunteer organization devoted to civic improvement), various business groups and some mayors of county municipalities, and the *Post-Dispatch* and *Globe-Democrat*. The Missouri Health Services Review Committee had quickly approved the transfer. On the other hand, several health-care groups, including the Missouri Nurses' Association, expressed concern about public accountability and access for the indigent. Former employees were naturally outraged. The support staff at Regional, though it was drawn chiefly from Charter, City, and County Hospitals, required less than one-third of the more than twenty-five hundred employees of the three institutions. Many of those displaced were from the black community. Black leaders, mostly associates of Congressman Clay, joined with the health-care groups in petition drives to force a referendum on the issue. The county drive failed for lack of signatures, and the courts struck down the city referendum. The Public Employees' Union brought suit against the Regional plan as well, but neither the trial nor the appeals court found merit in its position.

Professor George Wendel of Saint Louis University, a public policy specialist, doubted the legality and viability of the Regional plan when it first became public, and as late as March 1987 he found serious shortcomings in the hospital's financial management and questioned its lack of accountability and long-term financial viability. Wendel did see advantages in its cleaner, more modern building, better facilities, and location nearer than City Hospital to its indigent clientele. "Hands-on" patient care at Regional was at least equivalent to that of its predecessors, but in certain areas, services were less accessible. In a professional paper coauthored with Mary Collins Wendel, he objected, however, to the way public acute care in St. Louis had been privatized. The decisions had been made, not by the popular will, but by an elite: Civic Progress, the mayor and county executive, and certain members of the medical community. It appeared that all involved, including the media "watchdogs" and the city and county legislatures, had avoided raising embarrassing questions.

Certainly Regional Medical Center was the product of a "let's get it done" administrative philosophy. City and county hospitals were liabilities and cooperation seemed to promise better care at less cost. For a majority of the electorate, as the failed county petition drive demonstrated, the location of indigent health care was not a burning issue. Both McNary and Schoemehl won overwhelming majorities in subsequent reelection races without evidence that voters were angry that they had been bypassed in the hospital decision. The two officials had been high-handed and undemocratic, or bold and imaginative, depending on one's point of view. They had happily distanced themselves from health-care management, but unhappily, that achievement was the last of their partnership.

McNary and Schoemehl's productive relationship had been remarkable from the beginning. Rivalry approaching hostility between county and city was typical at least as far back as the Cervantes administration, or the 1870s, or the 1850s, depending upon one's sense of history. The mayor and county executive, though of opposite political parties, apparently agreed in 1981 that cooperation was good for the community and for themselves. They appeared frequently together for the next few years, speaking favorably of St. Louis's potential. But in 1986, underlying tensions broke to the surface. As former Mayor Conway could have told his successor, the county executive would not be satisfied without concessions that no mayor could afford. From the Clayton perspective the metropolis was bipolar, with authority, rewards, and amenities equally shared. City hall thought differently. The city, downtown especially, was the heart of the region; its vigorous health essential to the success, even to the survival of the entire area. Unless those who had fled to the suburbs fulfilled their obligations to the city, they would suffer with it. Unfortunately, there was still another view, one which cared little for city hall or Clayton.

Among other things, McNary wanted a big sports complex for the county and an equal share in the operation of Lambert International Airport, owned by the city but located in the county. St. Louis County contributed the larger share of the funding of the Bi-State Development Agency, despite the fact that the Bi-State buses served the city primarily, and McNary wanted quid pro quo. From time to time, when Bi-State proposed initiatives he did not like, such as a light-rail system, or when he wanted a larger role for the county government in an area-wide activity, McNary temporarily withheld or threatened to withhold county funds.

County government was in an anomalous position. Its domain had grown rapidly but irrationally, and efforts to impose order on it had failed repeatedly. Voters did not want consolidation with the city, and McNary's plans to reduce the ninety-plus cities, towns, and villages to a sensible number confronted a persistent petty localism. Tiny villages just big enough to have municipal employees fiercely defended their turfs, digging frantically into semi-old records in search of an identity—human nature perhaps, but a trait that had bedeviled General Washington in the dark days of the Revolution and doomed the Southern Confederacy. At the other extreme, sprawling artificial "communities" with no past and little present purpose beyond grabbing shopping-mall tax-cows and extorting fines from motorists ate away at the county's tax base. McNary's efforts to keep up by levying new taxes were repeatedly rejected by the voters, who would reelect him but would not follow him.

Finally, McNary saw what he thought was an opportunity to make his mark. William Bidwill, owner of the football Cardinals, was unhappy with Busch Stadium because the fifty-four-thousand-seat facility (for football) could not produce enough revenue to enable him to accumulate the kind of estate he thought was fair to his family. So he said on one occasion; on others, he stressed the high cost of winning. Consequently, if the city did not build him a seventy-thousand-seat stadium in St. Louis, he would consider moving his franchise to another city, such as Jacksonville, Baltimore, or Phoenix. Bidwill did not explain why St. Louisans would fill a seventy-thousand-seat stadium to watch his unfailingly mediocre teams, when they had rarely in recent years filled Busch Stadium. The community's disenchantment with the "Big Red" was well founded. The team led the league in incompetent first-round draft choices, it never made the playoffs, and Bidwill's public personality, charisma in reverse, was matched only by that of his quarterback, Neil Lomax, who had never concealed his dislike for St. Louis.

Whether Bidwill was sincere in his desire to stay in St. Louis, as he claimed, was never quite clear. He may have believed that he would get his new stadium, but if not, his delaying tactics were maximizing offers from aspiring cities, and his "patience" would stand him in good stead with the other National Football League owners when he sought their permission to move. When the city administration and Civic Progress did not respond promptly to his threats, McNary leaped into the breach with an offer of a privately funded domed stadium in the county. With county funds, he bought land in the Missouri River flood plain for a stadium site. Bidwill professed interest in the proposal, but the city and downtown interests attacked its feasibility. Even if the financing was forthcoming, football receipts would fall far short of the amount needed to service the stadium debt. Rock concerts, other sports events, and a variety of attractions would have to be offered at "McDome" to keep it afloat, even if pumps and paddles were not required. This, the detractors argued, would mean that the locus of entertainment, except for baseball, would be shifted to the remote suburbs, with disastrous results for downtown restaurants, night spots, and hotels. Environmentalists too were alarmed, arguing that the additional levee engineering needed to guarantee a dry stadium, as well as the constant pressure of the stadium activity itself, would upset the balance of life on the flood plain. They brought suit to stop construction, with funds furnished to them by Civic Progress, according to McNary. Apparently the downtown boosters had become sensitive to the natural environment in timely fashion.

Probably McNary's opponents need not have bothered. There was no groundswell of support for a county stadium among county residents, and raising the $150 to $200 million required without any public financing was a "quixotic dream," according to a *Post-Dispatch* editorial. McNary and Bidwill blamed the mayor and Civic Progress for killing the county stadium, but as the editorialist said, "it collapsed of its own weight." In December 1987 Charles "Chuck" Knight of Emerson Electric Company, representing Civic Progress, Mayor Schoemehl, Missouri Governor John Ashcroft, and a somewhat ambivalent County Executive McNary offered Bidwill, if he would stay in St. Louis, $5 million a year in cash, rent-free use of Busch Stadium, a share in concession revenues, and a new $5 million practice center. If construction of a seventy-thousand-seat domed stadium downtown was not committed immediately, Civic Progress would make another $20 million available until the stadium was under way. Governor Ashcroft thought this was "a spectacular offer," but as Knight put it later, "Bidwill never really negotiated." On January 15, 1988, Bidwill announced that he was moving his team to Phoenix.

Thomas J. Guilfoil, Bidwill's attorney, told the *Post-Dispatch* that "finances were not the controlling factors." He attributed the move to Phoenix's rapid growth and warm climate and the Cardinal players' affinity for the West Coast. Then he got to the heart of the matter. Arizona State University's compact seventy-two-thousand-seat stadium would provide a great home-field advantage because the fans could make more noise to disturb the other team's play-calling, and that stadium had a lot of high-priced luxury boxes plus twenty-seven-thousand other premium-priced seats.

Finally, the city-stadium group laid their quite reasonable proposal before the NFL owners on the unlikely chance they would block the team's move. As expected, the owners backed their fellow club member, and the Cardinals were gone. A *Post-Dispatch* editorial predicted that Schoemehl would undeservedly bear the brunt of the blame, and he did, at least initially. Bidwill and McNary blamed him, and so did local sportswriters and broadcasters, including some of the *Post*'s own columnists. For those in the public who cared one way or the other, Bidwill's image and actions took a lot of heat away from the mayor. One revealing comment was that of veteran Eighth Ward Alderman Martin Aboussie, who was reported as saying "Bidwill's leaving doesn't bother me, if you were telling me that we were losing the baseball team, I'd jump off the bridge." Neil Lomax, who resented baseball's hold on the city, hailed the move, complaining that Fredbird, the baseball team's mascot, had more endorsements than he did.

Before Bidwill's announcement, a bill committing the state to aiding construction of a St. Louis stadium had passed the Missouri House of Representatives. With the Cardinals gone, it was almost certain that St. Louis would not obtain another NFL franchise without first building a stadium and that the stadium would not be built without state involvement. Since Governor Ashcroft would not agree to state funding for a stadium until a franchise was assured, the stadium project hung fire through 1988. Jerry B. Clinton, who headed the Anheuser-Busch distributorship in St. Louis County, and Francis W. Murray, a minority partner in the New England Patriots, had formed the NFL Partnership, committed to obtaining an NFL franchise for St. Louis by 1993. With the backing of St. Louis business and political interests, strongly supported by Kansas City and Springfield legislators, they led the effort which drove a stadium bill through the Missouri General Assembly in May 1989. St. Louis was to get a stadium and convention center expansion, Kansas City a convention center expansion and repairs at its Truman Sports Complex, and Springfield a minor-league baseball park.

The stadium bill introduced a "new net fiscal benefit" concept to justify state, county, and municipal expenditures for the projects. In principle, this "new" rationale resembled that which used to justify millions of dollars in state and local aid to railroads in Missouri in the 1850s, the important difference being that the railroads were privately owned and the stadium and convention centers public property. (The Missouri Constitution of 1865 and its successors had forbidden lending to private enterprise.) Net fiscal benefit meant that the participating governments would collect more in tax revenue engendered by the improvements than they would spend in paying for them. Construction costs would be paid by $225 million in revenue bonds issued by the St. Louis Regional Convention and Sports Complex Authority (created by the bill), which would have eleven commissioners, five appointed by the governor and three each by the mayor of St. Louis and the county executive. The Sports Complex Authority would have title to the stadium, but NFL Enterprises (Clinton and Murray), backed by Sanwa Bank of Tokyo, would operate it.

In a study released by Clinton and Murray, Professor James D. Little of Washington University estimated that debt service and maintenance costs for the stadium would be $24 million a year over a thirty-year period. The state would pay $12 million and the city and county $6 million each. In the first year, the state would receive $8.4 million more than its contribution in added tax revenue, the city $7 million more, and the county $3.1 million more. In each subsequent year, the net gain to each of the governments would rise. If any of the jurisdictions in any year collected less stadium-induced revenue than its contribution, it would pay only the amount collected. The shortfall would be met by the NFL Partnership, which had a $28 million letter of credit from the Sanwa Bank.

After keeping the bill's supporters squirming for weeks, during which time he expressed doubts about its financing provisions, Governor Ashcroft signed it on the last day possible, July 19, 1989. He believed it would boost the St. Louis and Missouri economies, and he had been persuaded in part because the federal authority to issue $175 million in tax-exempt stadium revenue bonds, which would save the project $93 million, would expire in eighteen months. Backers of the bill were ecstatic. Senator John Scott of St. Louis, who had sponsored the bill in the Upper House, called the project "the biggest economic development package to hit this state this century." When completed, the complex would be one of the largest convention and exhibition centers in the country, suitable for national political conventions, the Super Bowl, and NCAA Final Four basketball. Clinton and Murray claimed that there was no doubt that St. Louis would have an NFL expansion franchise by the time the stadium was completed in 1993. With the stadium, the largest television market in the country without NFL football, and the world's largest television sports advertiser in its pocket, St. Louis could not miss. Mayor Schoemehl was confident that the city would gain far more than its contribution to the stadium. The development, on the east side of the Cervantes Convention Center, would add two hundred thousand square feet of space for conventions and would be used two hundred times a year in addition to football. Schoemehl was sure that the complex would spin off more construction. The ink had hardly dried on the bill before inquiries from groups interested in building one-thousand-room hotels downtown had started coming in.

Executive McNary was less comfortable. He still blamed the mayor for McDome's demise, and he had kept up a tattoo of criticism throughout the legislative discussions of the bill, calling it "half-baked" on one occasion. Now that the governor had signed the bill, he would go along, but for his cooperation, the county should be given the majority voice in the Bi-State Development Agency and an equal share in the management of Lambert Airport. McNary was dubious about the revenue projections, and he pointed out, correctly, that the plan was seriously flawed as it applied to the county. The county government would have to pay the entire $6 million a year assigned as their share, but the county municipalities that would receive 75 percent of the new revenue would pay nothing. As the governor had said, the stadium bill was only the first step; construction could not begin until the three governments involved had signed contracts guaranteeing their annual payments. Imbalances had to be ironed out before this occurred.

McNary's objections were directed to aspects of the plan; the Reverend Larry Rice hated it in principle and in detail, as he apparently did all downtown development. He had delivered to the governor a ten-thousand-signature petition opposing it, and he charged that Ashcroft had surrendered to special interests by signing it. Governments would not help the homeless, said Rice, "but they have money to subsidize the rich." Net fiscal benefit apparently did not impress Rice; he charged instead that the stadium financing plan would dry up the market for first-time owners' housing bonds. Several outstate editors criticized the state's commitment; Jack Stapleton of Kennett, head of the Missouri News and Editorial Service, called Ashcroft's approval of the stadium bill "good politics but bad policy." Special interests, he argued, had been placed above the collective interest in education, mental health, and the eradication of poverty.

It had been obvious throughout 1988 that Mayor Schoemehl would seek a third term. The city had made noteworthy progress during his administrations, and he had been responsible for a good deal of it. Even those who used the term "wheeler-dealer" to describe him, a term attributable largely to his unpredictability and personal style, had to admit that he got things done. On November 28, he formally announced his candidacy.

Since the four-year mayoral term had been introduced more than a century earlier, only two mayors had served three terms: Republican Henry Kiel (1913–1925) and Democrat Raymond Tucker (1953–1965). Schoemehl's record made him an odds-on favorite to repeat, but he had intra-party problems that needed fixing. His alliance with Congressman Clay had weathered several storms, but it had not withstood their disagreement over health-care issues in 1985. Recorder of Deeds Sharon Q. Carpenter, chairwoman of the

Democratic Central Committee, was in Clay's corner. As the holder of one of the city's "county" patronage offices, Carpenter, who had a good record in office and in the party, understood the key role played by these offices in the Democratic organization. It was no secret that Schoemehl, like many of his predecessors, found these anachronistic offices impediments to responsible and effective administration. Many St. Louisans, including the *Post-Dispatch*'s editorial cartoonist, did not understand that incompetence and corruption in the patronage offices were not within the mayor's purview. But to their partisans, they were bastions of democracy, protecting the people against power-hungry mayors.

In 1986, fresh from his landslide victory over Freeman Bosley in his second mayoral race, Schoemehl had overreached himself by backing several candidates in the August primary against the Clay-Carpenter slate, including state representative William L. Clay, Jr. This effort failed, and the rift between the city's political powerhouses widened to a gulf. In 1988 Carpenter even considered running against Schoemehl, but after testing the waters, she decided against it. Schoemehl had made a conciliatory gesture. After having backed Congressman Richard Gephardt of St. Louis for the Democratic presidential nomination, he relinquished his seat at the Democratic National Convention to a Jesse Jackson supporter when Gephardt dropped out of the race. Clay was backing Jackson, who had finished second to Gephardt in the Missouri presidential primary. This overture by Schoemehl was merely a prologue. On November 24, after a meeting at city hall, Clay, Carpenter, Comptroller Paul Berra, City Assessor Virvus Jones, and the mayor revealed the details of a startling political deal that, for the time being at least, marked the end of the Clay-Schoemehl split.

Comptroller Berra and Assessor Jones were to resign their offices on December 15, whereupon the mayor would appoint Jones comptroller and name Berra assessor. Berra, for whom the change was a demotion, would serve at the mayor's pleasure, and Jones would have the advantage of incumbency in the upcoming Democratic primary — and Clay, Carpenter, Berra, and Schoemehl would support him. In turn they would all back Schoemehl in his primary race against Michael Roberts, a black ex-alderman who had run strong but losing races for aldermanic president three times. Jones had not been a Clay protégé, but the congressman wanted an African American on the Board of Estimate and Apportionment. He was happy that north St. Louis would be represented in city government "at the highest echelon." With reference to his relations to the mayor, Clay cited the maxim that in politics "there are no permanent enemies, just permanent interests." In his turn, Schoemehl said that blacks "could not perpetually be denied a voice where the highest decisions are made."

Michael Roberts, comptroller candidate Stephen J. Conway, several aldermen, and even the cross-state *Kansas City Times* called the political coup a cynical "job swap" to ensure the mayor's reelection, but the rationale was not that simple. Schoemehl did not need the deal to defeat Roberts, who was no favorite of Clay's anyway. With good relations with Clay and Carpenter he could attain his third-term goals more readily. He wanted to reduce racial tensions in city politics, and another landslide win would enhance his standing among Democrats statewide. Clay told an interviewer that he too welcomed a working alliance with the mayor, though he had not changed his mind on health-care matters.

In the March 6, 1989, primary Schoemehl won 62 percent of the vote, decisive but smaller than his margin over Bosley four years earlier, but much larger than the third-term victories of Kiel and Tucker. Eleven inches of snow the day before had reduced the vote totals considerably, especially on the south side. Roberts, a more credible candidate than Bosley had been, defeated Schoemehl by two to one in the north side wards and claimed a moral victory for it, but his margins there were much less than they had been in his aldermanic president races. The mayor took the so-called racially mixed central wards handily and won on the south side by ten to one.

The big surprise was Jones's large plurality in the comptroller's race. Stephen Conway, whose father was former Mayor James Conway, had been expected to give Jones a hard battle, especially after it was revealed during the campaign that Jones had not graduated from Antioch College as he claimed—nor even attended it. But Jones's management of the assessor's office had won high praise for efficient professional management by the state auditor, his allies had stood their ground, and Conway's south side base was eroded by the late entry into the race of Peter R. Percich, son of Mayor Conway's old sparring partner, former Comptroller Raymond Percich, now deceased. Percich was considered to be a friend of Schoemehl's, which worried Conway a lot, but Jones not at all. Jones won 48 percent of the total vote to Conway's 32 percent and Percich's 20 percent. The victor carried the north side, with 90 percent of the total, and the central wards, with 52 percent. Conway won all the south side wards, most of them by small margins over Percich.

Roberts considered his strong race on the north side to have been a repudiation of the ward organizations, but Jones, with organization support, had done much better there. As for the mayor, it was conceded by most politicians and the press that he had positioned himself well for a successful third term and a future statewide race. He swept to an easy victory over token Republican opposition in the April general election. Jones was unopposed for comptroller. Sharon Carpenter thought Schoemehl was at his strongest point ever, having solidified his base in the city and gained name recognition across the state.

In his inaugural address on April 18, without referring to County Executive McNary, who was expected soon to be appointed to a position in the Bush administration, Schoemehl stressed city-county cooperation. "We cannot continue a war of attrition with St. Louis County," he said. "I can tell you the county will not find a separate destiny from the city." He mentioned the need to reconcile black and white, rich and poor, and to improve the quality of public education, the last not only imperative for children now, but also essential if the city was to reverse its population decline. Before the inaugural, in a talk to the Board of Aldermen, the mayor stressed the need to improve neighborhood housing and refurbish city hall's reputation.

The latter referred to revelations made by Republican State Auditor Margaret Kelly, who had conducted an audit of city offices during the previous winter. Kelly praised then-Assessor Virvus Jones and Collector of Revenue Ronald Leggett for their professionalism, but she found financial irregularities in City Treasurer Fred Williams's office and gross mismanagement by License Collector Billie Boykins. According to Kelly, Boykins had failed to collect millions of dollars in license fees and had used city funds for speculative investments that had lost money. Boykins, who was absent from her office most of the time, claimed at first that Kelly had partisan motives, but after Circuit Attorney George Peach had brought action in the Missouri Supreme Court to oust her and the mayor had publicly denounced her, she charged her critics with racism. On June 23, on a motion by Aldermanic President Thomas Villa, the Board of Aldermen voted sixteen to thirteen to reduce Boykins's staff from fifty-three to two employees and to turn over most of the license collector's functions to the comptroller. Within an hour, on the mayor's orders, the locks had been changed on the license collector's office and two of the three corridor entrances to it had been barricaded. On June 26, Comptroller Jones took over most of the space in Boykins's office suite. Boykins was left with her personal office, her chief assistant, her secretary, and the responsibility for a couple of minor license-collecting categories. Collector of Revenue Leggett called it "a municipal coup."

All of the black aldermen had opposed stripping Boykins of her duties. Comptroller Jones, under heavy pressure, belatedly agreed with them, but once the ordinance had passed, he carried out its mandate with alacrity. Senator John Bass and other black leaders assailed Schoemehl and Villa and publicly vowed to stay the course with her, but Congressman Clay did not join them. It was not certain that the mayor and aldermen had the authority to act as they did, but neither was it certain that they did not. The state legislature had created the license collector's office in 1901, and Boykins argued that it could not be eliminated or reduced without the legislature's consent. But the city's legal staff held that constitutional revisions in 1945 had outmoded the statute. Boykins's attempts to nullify the action by injunction failed twice at the circuit court level. On July 25, a "special master," appointed by the state supreme court to hold hearings on the ouster suit initiated by Circuit Attorney Peach, reported to the court that Boykins should be ousted for failing to collect at least $3 million in revenues and other "willfully neglectful acts." Final action by the state supreme court was expected in the fall.

Boykins's case did not present the ideal cause upon which to take a do-or-die stand, but the measures taken against her suggested to black leaders the possibility of an assault upon the entire patronage system. As Senator Banks put it, "the mayor and city council can eliminate every office in City Hall." Although it had not been established by the "separation" charter, the license collector's position was a "county" office, a part of the suffocating divided government St. Louis had fastened upon itself in 1876.

In the summer of 1989, despite the evidence that serious problems remained, notably in the area of public education, housing for the poor, and drug-related crime (a national study ranked the city the seventh most dangerous in the nation), St. Louisans could be proud of much of their recent past. Downtown had become a source of gratification rather than shame, though the "renaissance" was not an unqualified success. The Washington Avenue and Old Post Office renovations had not attracted many tenants, Laclède's Landing had not fully met expectations, and the *Admiral* had foundered again. But the new office and headquarters buildings, the clean streets, the St. Louis Centre, and the Union Station testified that St. Louis was a vital going concern.

The city's cultural institutions were thriving as well. The Missouri Botanical Gardens, so long a jewel in St. Louis's crown, had built upon its magnificent base to become a world leader in botanical and environmental research. Director Peter Raven directed a staff of Ph.D. scholars, scattered over the globe from Brazil to Madagascar, investigating especially the impact of the depletion of the rain forest on the rest of life on the planet. This research program was a major source of information for governments and individuals concerned with environmental quality and long-range survival. At home, the Garden's

Ridgeway Center, the Missouri Botanical Gardens. *In the 1980s the Missouri Botanical Gardens built a new entrance, the Ridgeway Center, to complement the Climatron. Photograph by Glenn S. Hensley, 1986. MHS-PP.*

membership was at an all-time high, and the community looked forward to the completion of a new and more stable and secure version of its chief attraction, the tropical-plants Climatron.

The St. Louis Symphony Orchestra delivered a sparkling series of successes in the 1980s. It expanded its itinerary, and Director Leonard Slatkin and the orchestra impressed audiences and critics in Europe, in New York City, and elsewhere. By mid-decade the symphony made everybody's list of distinguished American orchestras. Its standing in that exclusive category ranged as high as second and seldom below fourth or fifth, depending upon the individual critic. Since world-class status was expensive, the Symphony Association decided in 1989 to seek inclusion in the Zoo-Museum Tax District. In appealing to city and county voters, the symphony's strongest assets were its high quality, the prestige it brought to the community, and its role in attracting national firms and their executive personnel to St. Louis. In making its case, the symphony had to combat the perception that it was an elitist institution with limited appeal to most of the district's people—unlike the museums, the zoo, and the Gardens.

The St. Louis Art Museum was a major asset to the community. It was free, and it attracted sizeable crowds year-round. Its Pre-Columbian Art Collection was excellent, and it featured a representative display of good-quality European and American art. Its friends claimed that it ranked among the better American museums, but some local critics thought it did not always live up to its publicity. To the ordinary viewer, the collections seemed magnificent, as did the building itself and the museum's educational programs. To many St. Louisans, with its grand location on Art Hill and the statue of St. Louis guarding its approaches, the Art Museum was the key symbol of the city itself, the Gateway Arch notwithstanding.

As would be expected, the zoo, now directed by Charles Hoessle, was the most popular St. Louis cultural institution. Everyone in the metropolitan area and most people within a two-hundred-mile range of it had enjoyed its exhibits and shows. Perhaps it could no longer claim to be the nation's best, as it once had, but it was among them. It had maintained its standing under the handicap of limited space. In Forest Park, any institutional expansion, however worthy its purpose, was an intrusion, sure to be opposed by those who wanted to preserve what was left of the park's natural environment. But without expanding its area, the zoo took a giant step in 1989, with the opening of its dramatic presentation of life as it has developed on earth, called the Living World.

The Missouri Historical Society, at the Jefferson Memorial in Forest Park, sought to be included in the Zoo-Museum District in 1987. For more than a century, it had been a rich resource for research scholars interested in the history of St. Louis, the Mississippi valley, and the West, and its museum displays and paintings had drawn the attention of visitors to the park. Among scholars, archivists, and museum professionals, it had considerable national visibility. Its support had come chiefly from the descendants of its founders, St. Louis's nineteenth-century mercantile and professional elite. In the mid-1980s its director and trustees mounted a successful capital-improvements fund-raising drive, with good support from area businesses. Simultaneously, its education department, led by Katharine T. Corbett, developed an excellent local history curriculum, took it to the classroom teachers and their pupils, and brought the classrooms to the Society's archives and artifacts. The Society was being transformed, but its small professional staff was grossly underpaid, its vast holdings could not be properly catalogued and exhibited, and the operation was running on empty.

Just as the Board of Trustees of the Society was preparing to ask the voters for public funding, the *Post-Dispatch* reported, in considerable detail, that the U.S. Attorney was investigating allegations that Director Raymond Pisney had improperly disposed of some of the museum's artifacts. In the fall of 1987, without citing specific reasons for doing so, the board first suspended and then dismissed Pisney. The *Post-Dispatch* had stressed the organization's lack of internal controls and its board's lack of vigilance. Under the circumstances, it was risky to go to the voters, but considering the alternative, which was to close down all or most of the time, the trustees decided they must put the proposition on the November ballot.

With the newspaper and much of the intellectual and cultural community alienated, the prospects seemed dim, especially since an unpopular Metropolitan Sewer District tax was on the ballot, which was certain to energize anti-tax voters. On the other hand, the history museum proposition had been endorsed by Congressman Clay in a letter to his constituents, the suburban newspapers supported it, and the Society's staff members were working the neighborhoods. It was also helpful that the other museums were in the tax district. To some voters the recent mismanagement revelations were not sufficient reason to pass the death sentence on a long-time major cultural asset.

The history museum proposition passed, narrowly in the county and somewhat more comfortably in the city, with the north side providing the margin. There was little doubt that relatively unpublicized factors, such as the education department's outreach programs, had played a crucial role. Unnoticed by the press and some of its own constituency, and without denigrating its past, the institution had grown new roots in the community. The change had not been from the top, and the director's abrupt departure had no negative effect upon it. Led by Acting Director Karen M. Goering, with the strong support of a new financial officer and an energized if somewhat chastened Board of Trustees, operational procedures, security, and accountability were brought up to professional standards. In 1988 the trustees approved and their president, Earl K. Dille, persuaded the history museum subdistrict to purchase the former United Hebrew Temple on Skinker Boulevard, three par fours and an out-of-bounds to the west of the Jefferson Memorial. After both buildings were renovated, the temple would house the library and archives; the Jefferson Memorial, the museum exhibits and education department.

Later that year, Robert Archibald, director of the Montana Historical Society, was appointed executive director of the Missouri Historical Society.

For the local universities, the 1980s were neither the best nor the worst of times. Washington University, one of the better-endowed universities in the nation, continued to demonstrate its excellence in medicine and business administration—the latter gained a magnificent new building. A new library was in the works in 1989, a development eagerly awaited by the Arts and Science faculty and students. The administration had never been able to commit the funds necessary to develop and maintain library holdings commensurate with the institution's status as a major university, and the situation had deteriorated in the 1980s. Some of the liberal arts departments had lost ground by attrition during the decade as well, partly because administrators made several mystifying negative tenure decisions. Then in the spring of 1989, the administration pronounced the last rites over the Sociology Department. With a distinguished faculty, highly ranked nationally, sociology had been a major strength at the university two decades earlier. The department had wounded itself grievously by intramural bickering over the years, and only a shadow remained, but the announcement of its demise stressed budgetary considerations. Some faculty members and students protested that a university without sociology was a contradiction in terms, and the usually supportive *Post-Dispatch* questioned the decision. In a letter to the editor, Chancellor William Danforth reassured all concerned by pointing out that he had been and would continue to be committed to the liberal arts and sciences.

Rising costs were a problem everywhere in higher education, and Saint Louis University was no exception. In areas where student demand had declined, especially in graduate fields, the university reduced or discontinued programs. One of the reductions, actually initiated in the 1970s, was in its basketball program. But the declining competitiveness of its teams and the loss of national status in the sports distressed some alumni, local fans, and sportswriters. St. Louis did not have professional basketball, and as the only Division One university in the area, the Billikens in their heyday had been everybody's team. After 1985 the Billikens began to improve, and in 1989 they reached the NIT finals in New York. They would have preferred the more prestigious NCAA playoffs, but with the exception of *Post-Dispatch* sports editor Kevin Horrigan, St. Louisans applauded anyway.

At the University of Missouri–St. Louis, within a few months of her arrival as chancellor in 1986, Marguerite Ross Barnett, a dynamic young administrator from the City University of New York, had made a dramatic impact on the community. Earlier chancellors had concentrated on internal matters and the campus's role within the University of Missouri. Arnold Grobman, her immediate predecessor, had established ties with the business community through support groups such as the Chancellor's Council, but these efforts had not borne fruit financially or in effective local pressure on Jefferson City and Columbia decision makers. Barnett built upon this foundation to persuade a half-dozen major corporations to make six-figure grants to UMSL and to commit them to the university's future. Soon, she was invited to become an ex-officio member of Civic Progress, putting the university on a par with Washington and Saint Louis Universities in that powerful organization for the first time. Similarly, state legislators from the city's north side, who had not been on good terms with Grobman, responded quickly and favorably to Barnett and her ideas. These developments were noted in the state capital and by the university's central administration, and substantial funds were allocated to UMSL's Partnerships For Progress, a community-oriented package that included a "bridge program" which committed faculty and staff members and resources to the improvement of the quality of the public schools in St. Louis.

Despite these developments, UMSL had deep-seated problems. Missouri was one of the worst states in per capita support for higher education, and the University of Missouri, though it had excelled in some disciplines from time to time, had never been in the front rank among state universities. Recent governors and legislatures had exacerbated the situation by steadily reducing higher education's share of the state budget. Faculty salaries were not competitive, and each year good scholars left all four University of Missouri campuses for greener pastures.

UMSL had an intramural handicap as well. When its program proposals threatened the older campuses, their chancellors rushed to defend their turfs, and they usually prevailed with presidents and curators. Dormitories at St. Louis were forbidden because they might divert students from Columbia. In 1988–89 a limited program for part-time students in engineering, proposed to be carried out in cooperation with Washington University, caused tremors in Rolla. Preferring no program at all in St. Louis, University of Missouri–Rolla (UMR) offered a weak substitute managed at Rolla and relying heavily on television lectures by Rolla professors. It appeared that another UMSL initiative had been shot down, but this time President C. Peter Magrath and the curators authorized UMSL and UMR jointly to develop a program at St. Louis with a live faculty and a director reporting to both chancellors.

Union Electric Chairman William L. Cornelius and other Civic Progress members had been fully informed about the original proposal, as had the St. Louis legislative delegation, and their interest had made a difference. This event may have marked a shift in the wind, but generally neither the state's Coordinating Board for Higher Education nor the central administration in Columbia had been willing to expand UMSL's offerings to a level commensurate with its responsibilities as an urban university. Local students who for economic or other reasons could neither leave the city nor attend the private universities had a choice between programs they did not want or no university education at all. In 1989 UMSL's share of the University of Missouri's student population was 20 to 23 percent; its share of the operating budget, under 12 percent.

In the early summer of 1989, another development controversy erupted. The Civic Center Redevelopment Corporation, now a wholly owned subsidiary of Anheuser-Busch, announced plans to buy an interest in the St. Louis Blues hockey team and to build a $70 million hockey arena in the existing parking area south of Busch Stadium. To replace that space, the brewery proposed to buy the ten remaining warehouses of the Cupples Station complex between Eighth and Eleventh Streets south of Clark Avenue, raze them, and build a huge surface parking lot. Washington University, which owned the complex, had been systematically refusing to renew long-term leases, according to preservationists, in order to make a case for destruction of the historic buildings, and it was anxious to sell. Apparently to both parties' surprise, Mayor Schoemehl refused the brewery's request to "short-cut" the approval process, whereupon Anheuser-Busch, in a corporate snit, withdrew its plan to buy the team and build the arena, claiming that it could not proceed without the Cupples property.

Various interested parties brewed up a storm because the mayor had defied the sports establishment and the brewery. Michael Shanahan, the principal Blues owner whose visions of sugarplums were fading; a clutch of sports enthusiasts accustomed to swallowing anything poured by the brewery; Senator John Danforth, whose favorite university had lost the sale; Aldermanic President Tom Villa, who was displaying a sudden penchant for distancing himself from the mayor; and the chronically cranky sports editor Kevin Horrigan all charged that Cupples Station was nothing more than a collection of dusty old warehouses, not comparable to ice hockey as a civic asset. Villa, an instant expert, dismissed Cupples Station as having neither architectural nor historical significance. On the other hand, Carolyn Toft of the St. Louis Landmarks Association called the complex "an unparalleled grouping of national significance," which *Inland*

Architect magazine said had "brought warehouse design to a point where little improvement is possible." *Scientific Design* had called it technically outstanding, on "a scale of elaborateness with a perfection of detail unequaled by any similar institution in the world."

Mayor Schoemehl stressed that there were other places in St. Louis where a hockey arena could be built, but he was concerned with a lot more than hockey. Seven years after he had finally endorsed the Pride of St. Louis Gateway Mall plan, he was no longer sure that he had been right to consent to the destruction of the Real Estate Row skyscrapers. He had consulted with experts around the country, and he knew that "vibrant downtowns are created by distinctive buildings, not by surface parking lots . . . downtown could not compete with suburban markets if it looks and acts just like them."

Architects at their national convention at the Adam's Mark Hotel earlier in the spring had been impressed that St. Louis had saved so much of its large stock of historic buildings, but they were appalled at the redundancy of surface parking lots. Not only were they aesthetically offensive, they and the large brood of high-rise parking garages bore witness to an inefficient transportation system and invited people not to stay in the city, but to drive away from it in a polluting machine. Those who wanted "a vibrant downtown" had at first hailed the hockey arena *because* it would have eliminated some surface parking. The MetroLink Light Rail System, based upon the Eads Bridge tunnel, which would connect the east side to Lambert International Airport via St. Louis Centre, the Union Station, the University of Missouri–St. Louis, and other points, would have a station between Cupples Station and Busch Stadium, near the mouth of the tunnel. Less available parking would increase ridership on MetroLink, encourage its expansion, improve air quality, and spur the redevelopment of Cupples Station for productive uses.

MetroLink. *A MetroLink train exits the Eads Bridge on the Illinois side. Photograph by David Schultz, 1997. MHS-PP.*

As examples of Eames and Young's architectural designs, the Cupples Station warehouses attracted preservationists' support, all the more because of the recent loss of the Title Guaranty and International Buildings. Some with a sense of history also thought of the complex as a monument to a time when St. Louis led the nation in its ability to transfer goods rapidly and efficiently. The fact that Cupples Station was the brainchild of Robert S. Brookings, Washington University's principal benefactor at a crucial time in its history, added to the irony of the situation. Perhaps Brookings, like Chancellor Danforth, would have preferred parking lots to historic buildings, if he thought the university's welfare was involved.

According to the Federal Reserve Bank of St. Louis, which in June 1989 was celebrating its seventy-fifth year as a vital part of the city, St. Louis in 1987 had ranked thirty-sixth among one hundred metropolitan areas in per capita income ($16,487 a year) and twenty-fifth in per capita discretionary income ($9,348 a year), the difference in the two rankings attributable to cost-of-living factors. The area's manufacturing payroll had fallen at an annual rate of 1.4 percent in ten years, but its total nonagricultural payroll had risen during the same period by 1.4 percent annually. Since the recession of the early 1980s, manufacturing employment had actually risen, by 1.1 percent in 1988, for example. But predictions of another national economic downturn for the early 1990s were afoot, not good news for St. Louis because so many of its jobs were in durable goods manufacturing, automobiles especially, highly vulnerable to cyclical economic fluctuations. In addition, the area's largest employer, McDonnell Douglas, which had experienced substantial growth in the 1980s, was vulnerable to expected military budget cuts in the next few years.

This analysis did not attempt to take into account the impact of the convention-center complex, which would add jobs during construction and after its completion. Other construction would follow, presumably, in addition to the rapidly expanding convention and tourist business. These service-related jobs, although less potent economically than manufacturing jobs, would help to insulate the St. Louis economy from the effects of short, sharp cyclical downturns. There was also the prospect of new jobs in printing and publishing. St. Louis had become a one-newspaper town with the demise of the *Globe-Democrat* in 1986, but in July 1989 another daily, the *St. Louis Sun*, was just below the horizon. Whether the new journal would be a credible replacement for the *Globe-Democrat* was conjectural, but its publisher, who said in a television interview that the *Sun* would emphasize the positive, had made a spectacular start by hiring away Kevin Horrigan from the *Post-Dispatch*.

Among other signs of the future, the population trend seemed favorable. The area was still growing, especially St. Charles County, and the city's downhill plunge had flattened out. It appeared that St. Louis would hold the line above four hundred thousand in 1990, representing a 10 percent drop during the decade. This was rather cool comfort, considering that it resembled somewhat the decline in bank failures in 1932, which Will Rogers attributed to the fact that the country was running out of banks. Yet the loss was considerably less than the direr predictions of 1980. On the whole, St. Louisans could claim to have turned things around in the 1980s, and they looked ahead to the next decade with more confidence than they had ten years earlier.

Abbreviations

MHS-PP   Missouri Historical Society Photograph and Print
       Collection

MHS-Art   Missouri Historical Society Art Collection

MHS Library Missouri Historical Society Library

MHS Archives Missouri Historical Society Archives

Notes on Sources

The most ambitious general history of St. Louis is J. Thomas Scharf's massive two-volume *History of St. Louis City and County*, Philadelphia, 1883. This account has serious flaws, such as extraneous discussions of European dynastic history, some wild guesses about early St. Louis which later research has contradicted, unfailingly adulatory assessments of the author's prominent contemporaries (and subscribers) and repetitions and contradictions which suggest it was written by a committee. But within its vast reaches are a good many nuggets of useful data, and for the half-century preceding its publication, it is full and generally accurate.

Walter B. Stevens's *St. Louis, the Fourth City*, is less satisfactory. Published in 1909 by a veteran journalist who had for decades been a close friend or associate of the city's movers and shakers, it has some of the strengths and more of the weaknesses that might be expected of such an author. There is much interesting anecdotal material, and good use has been made of nineteenth-century newspapers, but the *Fourth City*'s organization, if any, is incomprehensible, it includes little valuable economic or social data, and Stevens was too loyal to expose any of the chinks in the city's armor. His friends among the elite escape scot free, with criticism reserved for the "knockers" who had caught some of them with their hands in the till.

McCune Gill's three-volume *St. Louis Story*, published in 1952, is primarily biographical, befitting its status as a *Library of American Lives* publication. Though there are snippets of general history scattered helter-skelter through the first volume, there is no running account as is implied in the title. John Devoy's *A History of St. Louis and Vicinity*, St. Louis, 1898, has some interesting photographs but little else of value. Elihu Shepard's *The Early History of St. Louis*, St. Louis, 1870, is short, anecdotal, and disappointing. Richard Edwards's *Great West and Her Commercial Metropolis*, St. Louis, 1860, includes a brief history of the city, numerous pictures and sketches, and short biographies of prominent men. It is a worthy example of mid-nineteenth-century boosterism, and as such it still has its uses. Especially valuable is William Hyde and Howard L. Conard's *Encyclopedia of the History of St. Louis*, Louisville, 1899, an enormous four-volume compilation of lives, institutions, and events, with emphasis upon the last half of the nineteenth century. Some of the entries must be approached with caution, since they were written by the principals themselves, or other interested parties.

Of the more recent general works, Ernest Kirschten's *Catfish and Crystal*, New York, 1960, is a lucidly written and affectionate informal history of St. Louis, enriched by the author's first-hand knowledge of the city, its people, and its leaders. Unlike his fellow journalist Walter Stevens, Kirschten hit hard at governmental, corporate, and individual chicanery, and he displayed an insider's knowledge of certain twentieth-century events. But the work is episodic and highly selective, and it does not present a systematic historical account. Unfortunately, this widely read book repeats certain ancient myths about Creole St. Louis, despite their previous demolition by the historian John McDermott. Kirschten's treatment of the Civil War era reflects some bias, but for post-bellum and twentieth-century St. Louis it is often instructive and always entertaining.

Father William B. Faherty's beautiful pictorial history, *St. Louis Portrait*, 1978, includes a necessarily brief but historically sound series of vignettes of the city's past. His *Dream By The River: Two Centuries of St. Louis Catholicism, 1766–1967*, St. Louis, 1973, is a thorough and competent account of the early church, the rise to diocesan status, and the administrations of the succession of prelates from Bishop Louis DuBourg to Cardinal John Carberry. Not yet published but by far the most sophisticated treatment of a major segment of the history of St. Louis is Glen Holt's "The Shaping of St. Louis, 1763–1860," University of Chicago Ph.D. dissertation, 1975. This study presents in detail the city's economic and social development in a clear and convincing style, supported by an impressive array of economic and demographic data. With Selwyn Troen, Holt has also written *St. Louis*; New York, 1977. As a volume in the *Documentary History of American Cities* series, this work presents important documents accompanied by insightful commentary. For the city's booster image-making, an excellent study is Donald B. Oster's "Community Image in the History of St. Louis and Kansas City," Ph.D. dissertation, University of Missouri, 1969.

Several histories of Missouri cover St. Louis topics in some detail. Two are outstanding in quality, style, and depth of research. David D. March's *History of Missouri*, 4 volumes, Chicago, 1967, is a much-neglected *tour de force*, written by a scholar whose knowledge of the state's past is unmatched. The University of Missouri Press's multi-volume history, under the editorship of William E. Parrish, displays the expert talents of William E. Foley, Perry McCandless, and Parrish himself, respectively the authors of the first three volumes. Still useful though neither well-written nor well-organized is Floyd C. Shoemaker's encyclopedic 5-volume *Missouri and Missourians*, Chicago, 1943. Duane Meyer's *The Heritage of Missouri: A History*, St. Louis, 1963, is comprehensive, reliable, and worthwhile. A shorter, highly readable new volume is William E. Parrish, Charles T. Jones, Jr., and Lawrence Christenson, *Missouri: The Heart of the Nation*, St. Louis, 1980.

Essential to the student of St. Louis history are the publications of the Missouri Historical Society: *Glimpses of the Past*, 10 volumes, 1933–1943; and the *Bulletin of the Missouri Historical Society,* now *Gateway Heritage*, 1944–present (referred to hereafter as BMHS); the first a treasury of documents, letters, reminiscences, and manuscripts from the Society's voluminous files, and the latter containing hundreds of articles on the history of St. Louis and the Mississippi valley. The Society's library features a magnificent array of manuscript materials, books, and documents, especially valuable on the nineteenth century, with several significant collections rooted in the territorial period. The newspaper files, some available on microfilm and others in the original, beginning with the *Louisiana Gazette* in 1808, are invaluable, as is the excellent photograph collection.

The State Historical Society of Missouri's journal, *The Missouri Historical Review*, 1906–present, (MHR hereafter) is rich in articles on St. Louis topics, and the Society's collection of Missouri and St. Louis newspapers is unsurpassed. The archival and manuscript holdings of the University of Missouri's Western Historical Manuscripts Collection, both at the Columbia and St. Louis campuses, are also extensive and relevant to St. Louis. Perhaps the least appreciated (and most valuable for the twentieth century) is the Municipal Reference Library at City Hall, which has a comprehensive body of documents, clippings, and other materials, especially important for city government and federal, state, and regional agency materials. The venerable and accommodating Mercantile Library has many holdings of value to the historian of St. Louis, as do the City and County Libraries. Olin Library at Washington University and the Pius XII Library at Saint Louis University are especially useful for their collections of theses and dissertations.

CHAPTERS 1 AND 2—BORDERLAND CAPITAL AND COLONY IN TRANSITION

Dominating the literature of the French and Spanish period are the works of Louis Houck and John F. McDermott. Houck's pioneering *The Spanish Regime in Missouri*, 2 vols., Chicago, 1909, opened the door to Creole Upper Louisiana. It features translations of relevant documents in the Spanish archives, with detailed explanatory footnotes reflecting the author's indefatigable research. His two-volume *History of Missouri*, Chicago, 1908, is rich in detail, though there are gaps and some errors in the text. Both works are indispensable to the historian. McDermott has tirelessly retrieved lost knowledge about the period and corrected the errors of earlier writers. His erudite and felicitous style enhances his *The Early Histories of St. Louis*, St. Louis, 1952; *Private Libraries in Creole St. Louis*, Baltimore, 1938; and his edited volumes: *Frenchmen and French Ways in the Mississippi Valley*, Urbana, 1969; *The French in the Mississippi Valley*, Urbana, 1965; and *The Spanish in the Mississippi Valley, 1762–1804*, Urbana, 1974. The last includes his definitive long article, "The Myth of the Imbecile Governor, Captain Fernando de Leyba and the Defense of St. Louis in 1780," which was reproduced in shortened form in BMHS, April, 1980.

Lawrence Kinniard's *Spain the Mississippi Valley, 1765–1794*, 2 vols., Washington, 1945, 1949; and A. P. Nasatir, *Before Lewis and Clark: Documents Illustrating the History of Missouri, 1785–1804*,

St. Louis, 1952, round out Houck's work with documents from the Spanish and British files. In *Colonial St. Louis: Building a Creole Capital*, St. Louis, 1949, Charles E. Peterson expertly delineates the geographical plan, the architecture, and the occupations of the village. Frederick E. Billon's *Annals of St. Louis in its Early Days under the French and Spanish Dominations*, St. Louis, 1886, contains much valuable data not available elsewhere.

Relevant for aspects of Creole St. Louis are John F. Bannon, *The Spanish Borderlands Frontier, 1513–1803*, New York, 1970; Abraham P. Nasatir, *Borderland in Retreat*, Albuquerque, 1976; and *Spanish War Vessels on the Mississippi, 1792–1796*, New Haven, 1968; and with Noel Loomis, *Pedro Vial and the Roads to Santa Fe*, Norman, 1967; James B. Musick, *St. Louis as a Fortified Town*, St. Louis, 1941; Paul E. Beckwith, *Creoles of St. Louis*, St. Louis, 1893; Elinor M. Coyle, *Old St. Louis Homes, 1764–1865*, St. Louis, 1979; Arthur E. Whitaker, *The Mississippi Question, 1795–1803*, Washington, 1934; Amos Stoddard, *Sketches, Historical and Descriptive, of Louisiana*, Philadelphia, 1812; Carl H. Chapman's long article, "The Indomitable Osage in Spanish Illinois, 1763–1804," in McDermott, *The Spanish in the Mississippi Valley;* and Richard E. Oglesby, *Manuel Lisa and the Opening of the Missouri Fur Trade*, Norman, 1963.

Washington University A.M. Theses for the period include Rachel F. Vogel, "Social Life in St. Louis (1764–1804)," 1921; and Willis W. Marshall, "Geography of the Early Port of St. Louis," 1932. Also useful is Warren Lynn Barnhart, "The Letterbooks of Charles Gratiot, Fur Trader: The Nomadic Years, 1769–1797," Ph.D. dissertation, Saint Louis University, 1972.

Pertinent BMHS articles are William E. Foley, "St. Louis, the First Hundred Years," July, 1978; John C. Ewers, "The Indian Trade of the Upper Missouri Before Lewis and Clark," July, 1954; Charles Van Ravenswaay, "The Creole Arts and Crafts of Upper Louisiana," April, 1956; John F. McDermott, "Pierre de Laclede and the Chouteaus," July, 1965, and "St. Louis as Military Headquarters," January, 1967; Arlene Black, "Captain James Mackay, Early St. Louis Settler," January, 1955; and Russell M. Magnaghi, "The Role of Indian Slavery in Colonial St. Louis," July, 1975. Articles in MHR include John F. Bannon, "Missouri, a Borderland," January, 1969; Lemont K. Richardson, "Private Land Claims in Missouri," Part I, January, 1976; Jack D. L. Holmes, "A 1795 Inspection of Spanish Missouri," October, 1960; and Don Rickey, Jr., "The British-Indian Attack on St. Louis, May 26, 1780," October, 1960.

For the early fur trade, the Chouteau Collections of the Missouri Historical Society are invaluable.

CHAPTER 3—THE FRONTIER TOWN

For the American territorial period, Frederick L. Billon, *Annals of St. Louis in its Territorial Days, from 1804 to 1821*, St. Louis, 1888, has the flavor of personal reminiscence supported by thorough research. See also William E. Foley, *A History of Missouri, 1673 to 1820*, Columbia, 1971; Thomas M. Marshall, ed., *The Life and Papers of Frederick Bates*, 2 vols., New York, 1926; John Bradbury, *Travels in the Interior of North America in the Years 1809, 1810 and 1811*, London, 1819; Henry M. Brackenridge, *Views of Louisiana Together With a Voyage Up the Missouri River in 1811*, Pittsburgh, 1814; Timothy Flint, *Recollections of the Last Ten Years Passed in Occasional Residence and Journeying in the Valley of the Mississippi*, Boston, 1826; John Mason Peck, *Forty Years of Pioneer Life: Memoirs of John Mason Peck*, Philadelphia, 1846; and Richard C. Wade, *The Urban Frontier, The Rise of Western Cities, 1790–1830*, Cambridge, 1959.

Halvor G. Melom's Ph.D. dissertation, "The Economic Development of St. Louis, 1803–1846," University of Missouri, 1947, includes a good discussion of early banking and economic development, as does Holt's "Shaping of St. Louis." Important also are the following Washington University dissertations and theses: Robert L. Kirkpatrick, "History of St. Louis, 1804–1816," A.M., 1947; Floyd O. Becherer, "History of St. Louis, 1817–1826," A.M., 1950; John L. Loos, "A Biography of William Clark, 1770–1813," Ph.D., 1953; Robert R. Russell, "The Public Career of William Clark, 1813–1838," A.M., 1945; Georgeann Tracy, "Frederick Bates and his Administration of the Louisiana Territory," A.M., 1936; Edward F. Rowse, "Auguste and Pierre Chouteau," Ph.D., 1936; Ruth M. Engler, "The Development of the Missouri Valley, 1813–1820", A.M., 1933; and Dorothy G. Brown, "Early St. Louis Newspapers, 1808–1850," A.M., 1931. Relevant theses at Saint Louis University include Humbert H. Gavin, "The Decline of Creole Life in Missouri to 1820," A.M., 1954; Mary D. Kramer, "The First American Administration of the Louisiana Purchase, 1803–1825," A.M., 1944; John D. Finney, "The Public Life of Judge John B. C. Lucas in St. Louis, 1805–1821," A.M., 1962; and Marshall Smelser, "Folkways in Creole St. Louis: The Transition from Creole to American Customs," A.M., 1938.

BMHS articles for the period include Clarence E. Carter, "The Burr-Wilkinson Intrigue in St. Louis," July, 1954; De Witt Ellenwood, Jr., "Protestantism Enters St. Louis: The Presbyterians," April, 1956; William E. Foley, "Justus Post: Portrait of a Frontier Land Speculator," October, 1979; "James Wilkinson: Territorial Governor," October, 1968; and with Charles D. Rice, "Compounding the Risks: International Politics, Wartime Dislocations, and Auguste Chouteau's Fur-Trading Operations, 1792–1815," April, 1978; John F. McDermott, "William Clark's Struggle with Place Names in Upper Louisiana," April, 1978; Kenneth W. Keller, "Alexander McNair and John B. C. Lucas: The Background of Early Missouri Politics," July, 1977; Mrs. Dana O. Jensen, ed., "'I At Home,' the diary of Stephen Hempstead, Sr.," 9 parts, intermittently from October, 1956 through July, 1966; William B. Faherty, "St. Louis College: First Community

School," January, 1968; and Maximilian Reichard, "Black and White on the Urban Frontier: The St. Louis Community in 1800–1830," October, 1976.

Applicable MHR articles are William E. Foley and Charles D. Rice, "Pierre Chouteau, Entrepreneur as Indian Agent," July, 1978; R. L. Kirkpatrick, "Professional, Religious and Social Aspects of St. Louis Life, 1804–1816,' July, 1950; Jerome O. Steffen, "William Clark: A New Perspective of Missouri Territorial Politics, 1813–1820," January, 1973; Eleanora A. Baer, "Books, Newspapers, and Libraries in Pioneer St. Louis, 1808–1842," July, 1962; Harry S. Gleick, "Banking in Early Missouri," July and October, 1967; William E. Foley, "The American Territorial System: Missouri's Experience," July, 1971; William T. Hagan, "The Sauk and Fox Treaty of 1804," October, 1946; and Lemont K. Richardson, "Private Land Claims in Missouri," January and April, 1956.

The Chouteau Collections and the Darby Papers at the Missouri Historical Society are useful for this period, as is John B. C. Lucas, ed., *The Letters of Hon. J. B. C. Lucas from 1815 to 1836*, St. Louis, 1905.

CHAPTER 4—THE GATEWAY CITY

William N. Chambers's *Old Bullion Benton*, Boston, 1956, is a fascinating portrait of St. Louis's great man, rich in details of the frontier city, its politics and its westward thrust. John F. Darby's *Personal Recollections*, St. Louis, 1880, presents the views of one of the era's major figures. Hiram M. Chittenden's *The American Fur Trade of the Far West*, 2 vols., New York, 1935, is the definitive work on the subject; and Bernard De Voto's *Across the Wide Missouri*, Boston, 1947, is a brilliant account of St. Louis's Rocky Mountain Fur Company. For the local fur magnate of the 1825–1835 period, see John E. Sunder, *Bill Sublette: Mountain Man*, Norman, 1959. The greatest of the trapper-explorers is given his due in Dale L. Morgan, *Jedediah Smith and the Opening of the West*, Indianapolis, 1953; and for an interesting personal account, Charles Larpenteur, *Forty Years A Fur Trader on the Upper Missouri*, Elliot Coues, ed., New York, 1898. For the Santa Fe trade, Josiah Gregg, *Commerce of the Prairies*, Max L. Moorhead, ed., Norman, 1954, is excellent; as is James J. Webb, *Adventures in the Santa Fe Trade, 1844–1847*, Ralph P. Beiber, ed., Glendale, California, 1931. For the retail and wholesale trade, see Lewis Atherton, *The Pioneer Merchant in Mid-America*, Columbia, 1939; and for commerce and banking, Melom's "Economic Development of St. Louis." James N. Primm, "Economic Policy in the Development of a Western State: Missouri, 1820–1860," treats the role of state and local governments. John Ray Cable, *The Bank of the State of Missouri*, New York, 1923, is the classic work on banking. For political matters, see Floyd C. Shoemaker, *Missouri's Struggle for Statehood*, Jefferson City, 1916; John V. Mering, *The Whig Party in*

Missouri, Columbia, 1967, and Marvin R. Cain, *Lincoln's Attorney-General: Edward Bates of Missouri*, Columbia, 1965. The William Gilpin Papers at the Missouri Historical Society are revealing for the Hard-Soft political struggles.

Washington University theses and dissertations for the period include Alma E. Burneson, "Steamboating on the Missouri River, 1819–1837," A.M., 1945; Virginia DeLiniere, "The Santa Fe Trail," A.M., 1923; Isabel F. Dolch, "Calendar of the Pierre Chouteau Maffitt Papers Concerning the Fur Trade," A.M., 1922; Walter O. Forster, "Settlement of the Saxon Lutherans in Missouri, 1839–1847," Ph.D., 1947; Ralph E. Glauert, "The Life and Activities of William Henry Ashley, 1822–1826," A.M., 1950; Paul W. Brewer, "The Rise of the Second Party System in Missouri, 1815–1845," Ph.D., 1974; Dorothy Longan, "History of the Santa Fe Trail, 1829–1844," A.M., 1964; Thomas E. Parks, "The History of St. Louis, 1827–1836," A.M., 1948; Lewis W. Spitz, "The Germans in Missouri," A.M., 1930; and Herbert T. Mayer, "History of St. Louis, 1837–1847," A.M., 1937. Saint Louis University theses include Mary H. McNally, "Manuel Lisa, a Pioneer St. Louisan," A.M., 1945; Chris Kuhn, "The Influence of Steamboats in the Development of the Upper Mississippi Valley (1810–1840)," A.M., 1960; Walter J. Ksycki, "The Missouri Fur Company, 1807–1832," A.M., 1942; and Richard E. Mueller, "The History of Jefferson Barracks, 1826–1900," A.M., 1967.

BMHS articles for the period include Dale L. Morgan, ed., "The Diary of William H. Ashley," October, 1944, January and April, 1945; Charles H. Rehkopf, "The Beginnings of the Episcopal Church in Missouri, 1819–1844," April, 1955; George R. Brooks, ed., "The Private Journal of Robert Campbell," October, 1963 and January, 1964; *The Missouri Saturday News*, March 10, 1938, "Senor Don Manuel Lisa," October, 1966; William G. B. Carson, "Night Life in St. Louis a Century Ago," April and October, 1945; Charles E. Peterson, "Manuel Lisa's Warehouse," January, 1948; Mrs. Max W. Myer, "Dr. William Beaumont Comes to St. Louis," July, 1952; and *The Missouri Saturday News*, April 14, 1938, "Biographical Notice of Genl. William H. Ashley," July, 1968.

From the MHR: Stephen Sayles, "Thomas Hart Benton and the Santa Fe Trail," October, 1974; Perry McCandless, "The Political Philosophy and Personality of Thomas Hart Benton," January, 1956, and "The Rise of Thomas Hart Benton in Missouri Politics," October, 1955; Donald J. Abramoske, "The Public Lands in Early Missouri Politics," July, 1959; James E. Moss, "William Henry Ashley, A Jackson Man with Feet of Clay," October, 1966; Cynthia DeHaven Pitcock, "Doctors in Controversy: An Ethical Dispute between Joseph Nash McDowell and William Beaumont," April, 1966, and "The Darnes-Davis Case, 1840," October, 1964; Richard E. Mueller, "Jefferson Barracks, the Early Years," October, 1972; William E. Foley, "The Political Philosophy of David Barton," April, 1964; Peter J. Rahill, "St. Louis under Bishop

Rosati," July, 1972; David D. March, "The Admission of Missouri," July, 1971; William E. Lass, "Tourists' Impressions of St. Louis, 1766–1859," Part II, October, 1958; Maximilian Reichard, "Urban Politics in Jacksonian St. Louis," April, 1976; and Alice H. Finckh, "Gottfried Duden Views Missouri," July, 1949.

CHAPTER 5—GROWING PAINS

Holt's "The Shaping of St. Louis" thoroughly depicts and analyzes economic and population growth patterns and attendant problems for the antebellum decades. Louis C. Hunter's *Steamboats on the Western Rivers*, Cambridge, 1949, is definitive, and the intricacy and romance of river piloting and keen observations about aspects of St. Louis life feature Mark Twain's *Life on the Mississippi*. For slavery and related topics, see Harrison A. Trexler, *Slavery in Missouri, 1804–1865*, Baltimore, 1914; and Merton L. Dillon, *Elijah P. Lovejoy, Abolitionist Editor*, Urbana, 1961. For the Germans in St. Louis, the best study is George Kellner, "The German Element in the Urban Frontier: St. Louis, 1830–1860," Ph.D. dissertation, University of Missouri, Columbia, 1973.

Relevant Saint Louis University theses and dissertations include John P. Dietzler, "Sewage and Drainage in St. Louis, 1764–1954," A.M., 1954; Arlen P. Dykstra, "A History of St. Louis Firefighting, 1850–1880," Ph.D., 1970; George J. McHugh, "Political Nativism in St. Louis, 1840–1857," A.M., 1939; James F. Robinson, "St. Louis in the Gold Rush Era, 1848–1858," A.M., 1940; Mary Martina Stygar, "St. Louis Immigrants from 1820 to 1860," A.M., 1937; and Kenneth A. Williams, "The Mullanphy Emigrant Relief Fund," A.M., 1952. Washington University theses are Wesley F. Diem, "Steamboating on the Upper Mississippi River, 1823–1845," A.M., 1932; and Oscar Mervene Ross, "The History of St. Louis, 1848–1853," A.M., 1949.

BMHS articles are Emil Oberholzer, "The Legal Aspects of Slavery in Missouri," January, April, and July, 1850; No author, "St. Louis in 1849," April, 1950; No author, "Big Thursday: Gala Days of the Old St. Louis Agricultural and Mechanical Fair," October, 1955; Walter P. Hendrickson, "The Western Academy of Natural Sciences of St. Louis," January, 1960; Ruth Ferris, "Steamboat Art, Decoration, and Elegance," January, 1962; Lloyd A. Hunter, "Slavery in St. Louis, 1804–1860," July, 1974; Judy Day and M. James Kedro, "Free Blacks in St. Louis: Antebellum Conditions, Emancipation, and the Postwar Era," January, 1974; Charles Van Ravenswaay, "Years of Turmoil, Years of Growth, St. Louis in the 1850s," July, 1967; N. Webster Moore, "John Berry Meachum (1789–1854): St. Louis Pioneer, Black Abolitionist, Educator and Preacher," January, 1972; John G. Gill, "Lovejoy's Pledge of Silence," January, 1958; and George A. Joyaux, "August Laugel Visits St. Louis," October, 1957.

MHR articles include Mary K. Dains, "Midwestern River Steamboats: A Pictorial History," July, 1972, and "Steamboats of the

1850s–1860s: A Pictorial History," January, 1973; Patrick E. McLear, "The St. Louis Cholera Epidemic of 1849," January, 1969; A. B. Lampe, "St. Louis Volunteer Fire Department, 1820–1850," April, 1968; Douglas D. Hale, Jr., "Friedrich Adolph Wizlizenus," April, 1968; John C. Schneider, "Riot and Reaction in St. Louis, 1854–1856," January, 1974; Arlen R. Dykstra, "Rowdyism and Rivalism in the St. Louis Fire Department, 1850–1857," October, 1974; Brad Luckingham, "The Mercantile Library Association," January, 1963; Laura Langehennig, "The Steamboat, Playground of St. Louis in the Fifties," January, 1946; and Helen Davault Williams, "Social Life in St. Louis, 1840–1860," October, 1936.

CHAPTER 6—RAILS AND MILLS

The principal work on railroads is still John W. Million, *State Aid to Railways in Missouri*, Chicago, 1896. Cable's *Bank of the State of Missouri* explains the shift in state banking policy in 1857, and Scharf's *History of St. Louis City and County* includes details on banking, railroad, and industrial development. Primm's, *Economic Policy in Missouri* is relevant both for banking and railroads. In addition to his mistaken version of the Chicago–St. Louis theme, Wyatt Belcher, in *Economic Rivalry Between St. Louis and Chicago*, New York, 1943, presents a wealth of detail about St. Louis's economy. For contemporary booster views, see John Hogan, *Thoughts About the City of St. Louis, Her Commerce and Manufactures, Railroads & Co.*, St. Louis, 1854; and Richard Edwards, *Edwards's Great West and Her Commercial Metropolis*, St. Louis, 1860. The George R. Taylor Papers at the Missouri Historical Society are revealing for the Pacific Railroad scandals.

Three University of Missouri–Columbia theses are relevant: Ethel Osborne, "Missouri's Interest in the Transcontinental Railroad Movement, 1849–1855," A.M., 1928; Dorothy E. Powell, "History of the Hannibal and St. Joseph Railroad," A.M., 1942; and Lucinda de Leftevich Templin, "The Development of Railroads in Missouri to 1860," A.M., 1915. Washington University theses include Dorothy Jennings, "Railroad Development in Missouri Before the Civil War," A.M., 1930; Margaret L. Fitzsimmons, "Railroad Development in Missouri, 1860–1870," A.M., 1931; Cyril Clemens, "The History of St. Louis, 1834–1860," A.M., 1949; Lura M. Gard, "East St. Louis and the Railroads to 1875," A.M., 1947; James Lindhurst, "History of the Brewing Industry in St. Louis, 1804–1860," A.M., 1939; and Helen Davault Williams, "Factors in the Growth of St. Louis from 1840 to 1860," A.M., 1934. See also Mary Louise Adams, "A History of the North Missouri Railroad Company," A.M., Saint Louis University, 1951.

BMHS articles: J. Christopher Schnell and Patrick E. McLear, "Why the Cities Grew . . . 1850–1880," April, 1972; and Lyle and Mary Dorsett, "Rhetoric vs. Realism: 150 Years of Missouri Boosterism," January, 1972. MHR articles: J. Christopher Schnell,

"Chicago Versus St. Louis: A Reassessment of the Great Rivalry," April, 1977; Jim A. Hart, "The *Missouri Democrat, 1852–1860*," January, 1961; G. C. Broadhead, "Early Railroads in Missouri," April, 1912; R. S. Cotterill, "National Railroad Convention in St. Louis, 1849," July, 1918; Paul W. Gates, "Railroads of Missouri, 1850–1870," January, 1932; and Edward J. White, "A Century of Transportation in Missouri," October, 1920.

CHAPTER 7 — FOR THE UNION

War and reconstruction themes abound in the literature. A good running account of the period is William E. Parrish, *A History of Missouri, 1860–1875*, Columbia, 1973; and see his *Missouri Under Radical Rule*, Columbia, 1965. Participant narratives with a Union tilt are Galusha Anderson, *A Border City During the Civil War*, Boston, 1908; and Robert J. Rombauer, *The Union Cause in St. Louis in 1861*, St. Louis, 1909. Guerrilla warfare and martial law from the Southern viewpoint are ably presented in Richard S. Brownlee, *Grey Ghosts of the Confederacy: Guerrilla Warfare in the West, 1861–1865*, Baton Rouge, 1958. Norma Peterson's *Freedom and Franchise: The Political Career of B. Gratz Brown*, is an insightful treatment of St. Louis's Unionist editor and leading emancipationist, with considerable attention also to the city's first and most powerful Unionist, Frank P. Blair. There is much of interest in William E. Smith's *The Francis Preston Blair Family in Politics*, New York, 1930. For the Dred Scott case, see Walter Ehrlich, *They Have No Rights: Dred Scott's Struggle for Freedom*, Chicago, 1979, an excellent study of the St. Louis and Missouri background of the case, including its progress through the Missouri Courts. Charles Daniel Drake is thoroughly and competently covered in David March, "The Life and Times of Charles Daniel Drake," University of Missouri Ph.D. dissertation, 1949. Radical Rule and the genesis of Liberal Republicanism are handled best in Thomas S. Barclay's classic, *The Liberal Republican Movement in Missouri*, Columbia, 1927.

Saint Louis University theses and dissertations include Virgil C. Blum, "The German Element in St. Louis, 1859–1861," Ph.D., 1945; Francis H. Burke, "The Missouri State Convention of 1861," A.M., 1968; James Covington, "The Camp Jackson Affair, 1861," A.M., 1943; Leo S. Donati, "Secret Societies in Missouri During the Civil War," A.M., 1950; and Philip R. Salga, "St. Louis Newspapers in the Election of 1860," A.M., 1958. Washington University theses are Ruth C. Cowen, "Civil War and Politics in Missouri, 1863," A.M., 1954; Marian F. Hixson, "Freemont's Hundred Days," A.M., 1926; Harold E. Iverson, "The History of the St. Louis Arsenal, 1826–1861," A.M., 1963; Harry C. Koelling, "The Civil War in Missouri in 1861," A.M., 1937; Louis H. Ledoux, "The Civil War in Missouri in 1862," A.M., 1949; Janie C. Mason, "The Civil War in Missouri, 1864–1865," A.M., 1937; Benjamin Merkel, "The Antislavery Movement in

Missouri, 1819–1865," Ph.D., 1939; and Areola Reinhardt, "The Gunboats of James B. Eads during the Civil War," A.M., 1936.

BMHS articles: Milan James Kedro, "The Civil War's Effect on the Urban Church: The St. Louis Presbytery under Martial Law," April, 1971; William G. B. Carson, "Anne Ewing Lane," October, 1964; Marvin R. Cain, "Lincoln's Attorney-General Views the Secession Crisis: The Edward Bates Letters," October, 1964; and Harvey Saalberg, "Dr. Emil Preetorius, Editor-in-Chief of the *Westliche Post*, 1864–1905," January, 1968; MHR articles: Arthur R. Kirkpatrick, "The Admission of Missouri to the Confederacy," July, 1961, and "Missouri in the Early Months of the Civil War," April, 1961; Marvin Cain, "Edward Bates and Hamilton R. Gamble: A Wartime Partnership," January, 1962; Harold C. Bradley, "In Defense of John Cummings," October, 1962; William F. Zornow, "The Missouri Radicals and the Election of 1864," July, 1951; Ray W. Irwin, ed., "The Journal of Captain Albert Tracy, 1861," October, 1956, January, 1957, and July, 1957; Jasper W. Cross, "The Mississippi Valley Sanitary Fair," April, 1952; William E. Parrish, "General Nathaniel Lyon: A Portrait," October, 1954; and Joe M. Richardson, "The American Missionary Association and Black Education in Civil War Missouri," July, 1975.

CHAPTER 8—THE FOURTH CITY?

Booster literature for the Gilded Age in St. Louis is dominated by Logan U. Reavis's *Saint Louis: The Future Great City of the World*, St. Louis, 1870, 1871, 1873, 1875, and 1881; *The Railway and River Systems of the City of St. Louis*, St. Louis, 1879; and *A Change of National Empire; or, Arguments in Favor of the Removal of the National Capital from Washington City to the Mississippi Valley*, St. Louis, 1869. Outstanding among the several studies of the Eads Bridge is Quinta Scott and Howard S. Miller, *The Eads Bridge*, Columbia, 1979, a brilliant photographic essay with an equally valuable history and analysis of the bridge's construction. See also Calvin M. Woodward, *A History of the St. Louis Bridge*, St. Louis, 1881; Gerald R. Polinsky, "The Construction of the Illinois and St. Louis Bridge at St. Louis, 1867–1874," Washington University thesis, A.M., 1954; Estell McHenry, comp., *Addresses and Papers of James B. Eads, Together with a Biographical Sketch of James B. Eads*, St. Louis, 1884; James B. Eads, *Report of the Engineer-in-Chief of the Illinois and St. Louis Bridge Company*, St. Louis, 1868, and *Chief Engineers Report*, St. Louis, 1870; and Alphonse Jaminet, *Physical Effects of Compressed Air, And of the Causes of Pathological Symptoms Produced on Man, by Increased Atmospheric Pressure Employed for the Sinking of Piers*, St. Louis, 1871. For the Whiskey Ring scandals, see W. B. Hesseltine, *U. S. Grant, Politician*, New York, 1935; and L. E. Guese, "St. Louis and the Great Whiskey Ring," MHR, July, 1942. The railroad and general strike of 1877 is colorfully presented in David

Burbank, *Reign of the Rabble: The St. Louis General Strike of 1877*, New York, 1966. For the separation of St. Louis and St. Louis County see Thomas S. Barclay's *The St. Louis Home Rule Charter of 1876*, Columbia, 1962, and *The Movement for Municipal Home Rule in St. Louis*, Columbia, 1943. See also the St. Louis Board of Freeholders, *Scheme for the Government of the County and City of St. Louis, and Charter for the City of St. Louis*, St. Louis, 1876. The St. Louis school of philosophy and its impact on public education are covered in Charles M. Perry, *The St. Louis Movement in Philosophy*, Norman, 1930; Denton J. Snider, *The Early St. Louis Movement in Philosophy, Literature, Art and Education*, St. Louis, 1921; and Selwyn K. Troen, *The Public and the Schools: Shaping the St. Louis System, 1838–1920*, Columbia, 1975.

Washington University theses: Corine Hachtman, "The History of the Wiggins Ferry Company," A.M., 1931; Florence F. McDermott, "The Southwestern Railway Strike of 1886," A.M., 1942; Odon F. Moehle, "History of St. Louis, 1878–1882," A.M., 1954; Catherine V. Soraghan, "The History of St. Louis, 1865–1876," A.M., 1936; Loretta Mae Walter, "Woman Suffrage in Missouri, 1866–1880," A.M., 1963; Howard L. Hibbs, "The Governmental History of Saint Louis before 1876," A.M., 1931; and David Horton, "The Problem of the Unification of St. Louis and St. Louis County," A.M., 1936. Saint Louis University theses and dissertations: Joseph P. Blough, "Southwestern Railroad Strike of 1886," A.M., 1949; Mary Kaaren Conati, "The St. Louis Movement: Reconstruction of the Individual and the Nation through Speculative Philosophy," Ph.D., 1970; Lyle J. Fisher, "The Whiskey Ring in St. Louis," A.M., 1952; Frederick A. Hodes, "The Urbanization of St. Louis," Ph.D., 1973; Henry J. Schmandt, "A History of Municipal Home Rule in St. Louis," A.M., 1948; and Agnes Mary Wallace, "The Wiggins Ferry, 1795–1902," A.M., 1945.

BMHS articles: Toni Flannery, "The Cupples Warehouse Block," January, 1972; N. Webster Moore, "James Milton Turner, Diplomat, Educator, and Defender of Rights, 1840–1915," April, 1971; M. Patricia Holmes, "The St. Louis Union Station," July, 1971; William N. Cassella, Jr., "City-County Separation: 'The Great Divorce' of 1876," January, 1959; John P. Dietzler, "The Mill Creek Sewer Explosion, July 26, 1892," January, 1959; No author, "St. Louis Business and Industry, 1877," January, 1960; David Burbank, "The First International in St. Louis," January, 1962; Julius S. Rammelkamp, "St. Louis in the Early Eighties," July, 1963; Charles M. Dye, "Calvin Woodward, Manual Training and the St. Louis Public Schools," January, 1975, and "Calvin Woodward and Manual Training, The Man, The Idea, and the School," January, 1976; John A. Kouwenhoeven, "Eads Bridge: The Celebration," April, 1974; J. Christopher Schnell and Katherine B. Clinton, "The New West: Themes in Nineteenth Century Urban Promotion, 1815–1880," January, 1974; and Glen E. Holt, "St. Louis

Observed from Two Different Worlds: An Exploration of the City Through French and English Travelers' Accounts, 1874–1889," January, 1973. MHR articles are Richard Ives, "Compulsory Education and the St. Louis Public School System, 1905–1907," April, 1977; Benedict K. Zobrist, "Steamboat Men Versus Railroad Men: The First Bridging of the Mississippi River," January, 1965; Patrick E. McLear, "Logan U. Reavis: Nineteenth Century Urban Promoter," July, 1972; Selwyn K. Troen, "Operation Headstart: The Beginnings of the St. Louis Public School Kindergarten Movement," January, 1972; Craig Miner, "The Colonization of the St. Louis and San Francisco Railway Company, 1880–1882," April, 1969; Kevin C. Kearns, "The Acquisition of St. Louis's Forest Park," January, 1968; Arthur E. Lee, "The Decline of Radicalism and its Effect on Public Education in Missouri," October, 1979; and A. F. Holland and Gary R. Kraemer, eds., Richard B. Foster, "Some Aspects of Black Education in Reconstruction Missouri," January, 1976.

CHAPTER 9—MEET ME IN ST. LOUIS

The United States *Census of Population* and *Census of Manufacturing* for 1880, 1890, and 1900 include full details on St. Louis's development, including some analysis of growth patterns. Individual firms are listed and described in Ernest D. Kargau, *Mercantile, Industrial, and Professional St. Louis*, St. Louis, 1902. See also the *St. Louis Star, The History of St. Louis and its Resources*, St. Louis, 1893; Roland Krebs, *Making Friends is Our Business: 100 Years of Anheuser-Busch*, St. Louis, 1953; Eugene T. Wells, "St. Louis and Cities West, 1820–1880," University of Kansas Ph.D. dissertation, 1951; Sylvester Waterhouse, *The Westward Movement of Capital, and the Facilities which St. Louis and Missouri Offer for its Investment*, St. Louis, 1890; St. Louis Merchant's Exchange, *Annual Statement of the Trade and Commerce of St. Louis*, for 1865 to 1900; Mahlon F. Yeakle, *The City of St. Louis Today: Its Progress and Prospects*, St. Louis, 1889; and *Gould's Commercial Register, 1873–1880.* For a balanced yet devastating account of the boodle ring and its prosecution, see Louis Geiger, *Joseph W. Folk of Missouri*, Columbia, 1953. Lincoln Steffens' and Claude Wetmore's "Tweed Days in St. Louis," *McClure's Magazine*, October, 1902, was reprinted in Steffens's *Shame of the Cities*, New York, 1904. For a conservative view of these events and of the preparation for the World's Fair as well, see Rolla Wells, *Episodes of My Life*, St. Louis, 1933. A sophisticated analysis of the business elite, its manipulations and its residential enclaves is presented in Scot McConachie, "The Big Cinch: A Business Elite in the Life of a City, St. Louis, 1895–1915," Ph.D. dissertation, Washington University, 1976. Contemporary accounts of the business leaders include John W. Leonard, *The Book of St. Louisans: A Biographical Dictionary of the Leading Living Men of St. Louis*, St. Louis, 1906, 1912; and James Cox, *Notable*

St. Louisans, St. Louis, 1900. The fullest account of the World's Fair is the official version: David R. Francis, *The Universal Exposition of 1904*, 2 vols., St. Louis, 1913. See also the Exposition Board's *The Universal Exposition of 1904; Exhibits, Architecture, Ceremonies, Amusements*, St. Louis, 1904; Mark Bennett, *History of the Louisiana Purchase Exposition*, St. Louis, 1905; and Dorothy D. Birk, *The World Came to St. Louis*, St. Louis, 1979.

Washington University theses and dissertations are Ann C. Harrison, "Edward Butler, the Beginnings of a Boss," A.M., 1969; Mabel Mulkey, "History of the St. Louis School of Fine Arts, 1879–1909," A.M., 1944; Delphine R. Meyer, "Joseph W. Folk, Governor of Missouri," A.M., 1932; Wilber C. Bothwell, "History of Banking in Missouri from 1875 to the Establishment of the Federal Reserve System," degree unknown, no date; and Frederick L. Deming, "The Boatmen's National Bank, 1847–1941," Ph.D., 1942. Saint Louis University theses include James Lee Murphy, "The Consolidation of Street Railways in the City of St. Louis, Missouri," A.M., 1964; and Clara Rose Mutschnick, "St. Louis Prepares for a World's Fair, 1898–1904," A.M., 1945.

BMHS articles include Doris Henly Beuttenmueller, "The Granite City Steel Company," January, 1954 (a condensed version of her Saint Louis University Ph.D. dissertation, 1952); Katherine Lindsay Franciscus, "Social Customs of Old St. Louis," January, 1954; author unknown, "The First Veiled Prophet Carnival, October 8, 1878," October, 1952; author unknown, "Big Thursday: Gala Days of the Old St. Louis Agricultural and Mechanical Fair," October, 1955; Robert James Terry, "Memories of a Long Life in St. Louis," October, 1954; April, 1955; January, 1956; and January, 1959; author unknown, "St. Louis Celebrates: the World's Fair of 1904," October, 1954; Edward J. Coffman, "A Boy's-Eye View of the World's Fair," October, 1954; Per E. Seyersted, "Kate Chopin, An Important St. Louis Writer Reconsidered," January, 1963; Frederic L. Niemeyer, "The Cabanne Place That Was," January, 1969; Robert C. Williams, "The Russians Are Coming: Art and Politics at the Louisiana Purchase Exposition," April, 1975; James G. Horgan, "Aeronautics at the World's Fair of 1904," April, 1968; Henry S. Iglauer, "The Demolition of the Louisiana Purchase Exposition of 1904," July, 1966; Eugene F. Provenzo, Jr., "Education and the Louisiana Purchase Exposition," January, 1976; Charles Van Ravenswaay, "Lafayette Park," July, 1958; Stephen J. Raiche, "Lafayette Square: A Bit of Old St. Louis," January, 1973; Jane Ann Liebenguth, "Music at the Louisiana Purchase Exposition," October, 1979; Scot McConachie, "Public Problems and Private Places," January, 1978; Steven L. Piott, "Modernization and the Anti-Monopoly Issue: The St. Louis Transit Strike of 1900," October, 1978; Julius S. Rammelkamp, "St. Louis: Boosters and Boodlers," July, 1978; and Jack S. Muraskin, "St. Louis Municipal Reform in the 1890s: A Study in Failure," October, 1968.

MHR articles: Irene E. Cortinovis, "China at the St. Louis World's Fair," October, 1977; John T. Flanagan, "Reedy of the Mirror," January, 1949; Steven L. Piott, "Missouri and Monopoly: The 1890s," October, 1979; Myra Himelhoch, "St. Louis Opposition to David R. Francis in the Gubernatorial Election of 1888," April, 1974; Stephen J. Raiche, "The World's Fair and the New St. Louis, 1896–1904," October, 1972; A. L. Thurman, Jr., "Joseph Wingate Folk: The Politician as Speaker and Public Servant," January, 1965; C. Joseph Pusateri, "Public Quarrels and Private Plans," October, 1967; Ted C. Hinckley, "When the Boer War Came to St. Louis," April, 1967; Lee Meriwether, "Labor and Industry in Missouri During the Last Century," October, 1920; George S. Johns, "Joseph Pulitzer," January, April, July, and October, 1931; January and April, 1932; and Walter B. Stevens, "The New Journalism in Missouri," April, July, and October, 1923; January, April, July, and October, 1924; January, April, July 1925.

CHAPTER 10—THE DECLINE OF THE INNER CITY

For a conservative, narrowly defined version of municipal reform see Rolla Wells, *Episodes of My Life*, St. Louis, 1933. More comprehensive in viewpoint are Jack Muraskin, "Municipal Reform in Two Missouri Cities," BMHS, January, 1969; Julian S. Rammelkamp, "St. Louis: Boosters and Boodlers," BMHS, July, 1978; Norman L. Crockett, "The 1912 Single Tax Campaign in Missouri," MHR, October, 1961; and Curtis H. Porter, "Charter Reform in St. Louis, 1900–1914," A.M., Washington University, 1966; Scot McConachie, "The Big Cinch"; Louis Geiger, Joseph W. Folk, and Donald B. Oster, "Nights of Fantasy: The St. Louis Pageant and Masque of 1914," BMHS, April, 1975. See also St. Louis Board of Freeholders, *Charter for the City of St. Louis*, St. Louis, 1910; *Proposed Charter for the City of St. Louis*, St. Louis, 1914; St. Louis Civic League, *An Abstract of the Provisions of the Old and New Charters of St. Louis*, St. Louis, 1971; St. Louis City Plan Commission, *Central Traffic Parkway, Recommended by the City Plan Commission*, St. Louis, 1912; *Problems of St. Louis*, St. Louis, 1917; and *The River Front: Possible Municipal Ownership of a Railway from the Chain of Rocks to the River Des Peres*, St. Louis, 1913. Percy MacKaye, *St. Louis: A Civic Masque*, Garden City, N.Y., 1914; and William E. Rolfe and Lucius H. Cannon, *The Municipal Bridge of St. Louis*, St. Louis, 1922.

Twentieth-century immigration and ethnicity are ably covered in Merle Fainsod, "The Influence of Racial and National Groups in St. Louis Politics, 1908–1928," A.M. thesis, Washington University, 1927; and Audrey Olson, "St. Louis Germans, 1850–1920: The Nature of the Immigrant Community," Ph.D. dissertation, University of Kansas, 1970. In addition to the census reports, there are several excellent business and economic studies, including Lewis F. Thomas, *The Geography of the St. Louis Trade Territory*, St. Louis, 1924, and

The Localization of Business Activities in Metropolitan St. Louis,
St. Louis, 1927; and Harry L. Purdy, *An Historical Analysis of the
Economic Growth of St. Louis*, St. Louis, 1946. For the booster
bonanza in sports and aviation, see Kenneth F. Davis, *The Hero:
Charles A. Lindbergh and the American Dream*, New York, 1959; and
J. Roy Stockton, *The Gashouse Gang and a Couple of Other Guys*,
New York, 1947. For urban rehabilitation in the 1920s and 1930s, see
St. Louis City Plan Commission, *The Kingshighway*, 1917; *The Zone
Plan*, 1919; *A Plan for the Central River Front*, 1928; and *Plans for
the Northern and Southern River Front*, 1929. See also Stanley R.
Suchat, "Sinking Fund and Bonded Debt of the City of St. Louis,"
A.M. thesis, Washington University, 1937. The last also portrays the
city's unemployment relief program during the depression, as does
William J. Harrison, "The New Deal in Black St. Louis, 1935–1940,"
Ph.D. dissertation, Saint Louis University, 1976.

Washington University theses: Maxine F. Fendleman,
"Saint Louis Shoe Manufacturing," A.M., 1947; Esther L.
Aschemeyer, "The Urban Geography of the Clay Products Industries
of Metropolitan St. Louis," A.M., 1943; Henry F. Stratmeyer, "The
Fiscal Program of St. Louis," A.M., 1947; Herbert J. Vogt, "Boot and
Shoe Industry of St. Louis," A.M., 1929; Elmer S. Wood, "Fairmount
Heights, an Italian Immigrant Colony in St. Louis," A.M., 1936; and
Joan Loraine Seeger, "The Rhetoric of the Muckraking Movement in
St. Louis," A.M., 1955. Saint Louis University theses and
dissertations: Lawrence H. Boxerman, "St. Louis Urban League:
History and Activities," Ph.D., 1968; Daniel M. Hogan, "The Catholic
Church and the Negroes of St. Louis," A.M., 1955; James J. Horgan,
"City of Flight: The History of Aviation in St. Louis," Ph.D., 1955;
Susan Croce Kelly, "Zoos in St. Louis," A.M., 1973; and Ronal Jan
Plauchan, "A History of Anheuser-Busch, 1853–1933," Ph.D., 1969.

BMHS articles: Richard H. Lytle, "The Busch-Sulzer Brothers
Diesel Engine Company, 1911–1939," January, 1969; Elizabeth W.
Owens, "The Year was 1908: A Personal Reminiscence," October,
1976; George R. Brooks, "The First Century of the Missouri Historical
Society," April, 1966; Eugene F. Provenzo, Jr., "Thomas W.
Benoist–Early Pioneer St. Louis Aviator (1874–1917)," January, 1975;
Susan Croce Kelly, "The Beginnings of the St. Louis Zoo," July, 1974;
Charles E. Burgess, "Henry James's Big Impression: St. Louis, 1905,"
October, 1970; Burton A. Boxerman, "Louis Patrick Aloe," October,
1974; Margaret Lo Piccolo Sullivan, "St. Louis Ethnic Neighborhoods,
1850–1930," January, 1977; Timothy O'Leary and Sandra Schoenberg,
"Ethnicity and Social Class Convergence in an Italian Community, The
Hill in St. Louis," January, 1977; Jay Corzine and Irene Dobrowski,
"The Czechs in Soulard and South St. Louis," January, 1977; and
Sandra Schoenberg and Charles Bailey, "The Symbolic Meaning of an
Elite Black Community: The Ville in St. Louis," January, 1977. MHR
articles: Irene Cortinovis, "The Golden Age of German Song," July,

1974; and Robert Dale Grinder, "The War Against St. Louis's Smoke, 1891–1924," January, 1975.

CHAPTER 11 — THE NEW SPIRIT OF ST. LOUIS

Howard F. Baer's *St. Louis to Me*, St. Louis, 1978, is an interesting insider's view of the city's institutions, issues, leadership, and problems since the 1940s, with personal reflections on the status and role of the Jewish elite. Alphonso J. Cervantes's *Mr. Mayor*, Los Angeles, 1974, illuminates major aspects of the city's growth and survival efforts, discusses in detail racial and housing problems, and mounts a spirited defense of Cervantes's role and activities. Eugene Meehan, *The Quality of Federal Policymaking: Programmed Failure in Public Housing*, Columbia, 1979, is a hard-hitting scholarly study of the Pruitt-Igoe housing fiasco, including a thorough analysis of the causes of the failure and pungent criticisms of local and federal officials, the construction industry, and the building trade unions. In the area of popular culture, see Robert Burnes, *Big Red*, St. Louis, 1975, a good account of the Cardinal football team from its Chicago beginnings to the Coryell era. Mary Kimbrough, *The Muny: St. Louis' Invisible Curtain*, St. Louis, 1978, tells the story of the city's popular amenity. Henry J. Schmandt, Paul J. Steinbicher, and George Wendel, *Metropolitan Reform in St. Louis, A Case Study*, New York, 1960, describes and analyzes the last failed effort at city-county consolidation.

For urban redevelopment and planning and various civic problems see the many reports and studies of the City Plan Commission and the St. Louis Housing Authority; St. Louis Civic Progress, Inc., *An American City: Four Years Progress*, St. Louis, 1953; Sue Dubman, *Poverty in St. Louis*, 1953; Irwin Sobel, Werner G. Hirsch, and Harry C. Harris, *The Negro in the St. Louis Economy*, St. Louis, 1954; and the Social Planning Council of St. Louis and St. Louis County, *Selected Social and Economic Characteristics of the Population*, St. Louis, 1953. For economic conditions and regional planning, see the *Reports of the East-West Gateway Coordinating Committee*, 1967–present, and the publications of the Regional Commerce and Growth Association, including *Spotlight on the St. Louis Economy*, 1979. The *Globe-Democrat* and *Post-Dispatch* usually carry summaries of the reports of the regional planning groups and other civic organizations. Elinor M. Coyle, *St. Louis' Portrait of a River City*, 3rd Edition, St. Louis, 1977, is a dramatic visual portrayal of the old and new, accompanied by a brief informed commentary.

Washington University theses and dissertations are Joseph S. Kimerling, "Value Systems and Group Differentiations Within the St. Louis Jewish Community," A.M., 1955; Virginia A. Henry, "The Sequent Occupance of Mill Creek Valley," A.M., 1947; Donald C. Mundinger, "An Appraisal of the Fiscal Autonomy of St. Louis, A Home Rule City: The St. Louis Earnings Tax, A Case Study," Ph.D., 1956; William P. Battiste, "History of the St. Louis Brown Stockings,"

A.M., 1962; Peter C. Scrivener, "The Politics of Urban Renewal Project," A.M., 1967; and Charles Bailey, "The Ville, A Study of a Symbolic Community in St. Louis," Ph.D., 1978. Saint Louis University theses and dissertations: Oscar Hugh Allison, "Raymond R. Tucker: The Smoke Elimination Years, 1934–1950," Ph.D., 1978; Robert L. Gronemeyer, "The History of Professional Football in the City of St. Louis," A.M., 1963; Anthony B. Lampe, "The Background of Professional Baseball in St. Louis," A.M., 1950; William Marsh, "The St. Louis Municipal Opera," A.M., 1954; and Richard E. Mueller, "The St. Louis Symphony Orchestra, 1931 to 1958," Ph.D., 1976.

BMHS articles: Gregg Lee Carter, "Baseball in St. Louis, 1867–1875: An Historical Case Study in Civic Pride," July, 1975; Glen E. Holt, "The Future of St. Louis: Another Look Ahead," July, 1978.

Chapter 12 — Urban Renaissance

Civic, cultural, economic, political, and social developments generally are covered in the *St. Louis Post-Dispatch*, 1981–1989, and in the *St. Louis Globe-Democrat*, 1981–1985. Relevant topics are also treated in the *Riverfront Times*, the *St. Louis Business Journal*, *St. Louis Magazine*, the *St. Louis Sentinel*, and other weekly or periodical publications. Civic development, redevelopment, and historic preservation issues are dealt with by Carolyn Hewes Toft, ed., the "Landmarks Newsletter," published bimonthly for the St. Louis Landmarks Association membership.

St. Louis Currents: The Community and Its Resources, St. Louis, 1986, published by Leadership St. Louis, Carolyn W. Losos, director, is an excellent review of the state of the city in the early 1980s. E. Terrence Jones, Ann Carter Stith, Patricia Rice, Peter Grandstaff and John Hinrichs, Susan Glassman, John E. Farley, George Dorian Wendel, Donald Phares, Charles Korr, Gary K. and Chris L. Wright, Sheila Aery, Bryan Jackson with Elaine Morley, A. Michael Klein and John J. Stretch, and Phil Sutin contributed articles.

Articles and books on special topics: Michael Bosc, "Beating Blight in St. Louis," *U.S. News and World Report*, August 4, 1986; Edmund Faltermayer, "How St. Louis Turned Less Into More," *Fortune*, December 23, 1985; J. Terrence Farris, "Threat to St. Louis' Revitalization," *Post-Dispatch*, August 25, 1985; Gregory B. Freeman, "Cleanup Theme in Collector Race," *Post-Dispatch*, July 22, 1982; John Garrity, "Flying High: The Spirit of Downtown St. Louis," *Travel Holiday Magazine*, March, 1985; Mary Henderson Gars, "The Morton D. May Amphitheatre," *Inland Architect*, January/February, 1988, and "St. Louis Light Rail; Using What's There," *Inland Architect*, January/February, 1989; Paul Goldberger, "A Crowded Downtown Marks St. Louis Revival," *New York Times*, December 26, 1985; Thomas B. Mandelbaum, "The Relative Performance of the District's Major Metropolitan Areas," in *Pieces of Eight, An Economic*

Perspective on the 8th District, St. Louis Federal Reserve Bank, June, 1989; George McCue, "The 3-Year-Old Quarrels of Serra's 'Twain;' With People Who Look at it the Wrong Way," *Post-Dispatch*, August 25, 1985; Howard Mansfield, "Housing the Homeless," *Inland Architect*, January/February, 1989; E. F. Porter, Jr., "Metropolitan Square: Treasure or Common Place," *Post-Dispatch*, November 13, 1988, and "Schoemehl Confident in Downtown Plan," *Post-Dispatch*, August 6, 1989; Mark Schlinkmann, "Clay Accuses Schoemehl," *Post-Dispatch*, January 19, 1986; E. R. Shipp, "St. Louis Image Shines With a Cardinal Red Glow," *New York Times*, October 12, 1985; Roger Signor, "Growing Pains for Regional Hospital," *Post-Dispatch*, August 25, 1985; Carolyn Hewes Toft, *St. Louis: Landmarks and Historic Districts*, St. Louis, 1988; Tom Uhlenbrock, "Enigma: Image was Always a Problem for Bidwill in St. Louis," *Post-Dispatch*, January 16, 1988; George Dorian Wendel, "Is the Hospital Merger Legal," *Post-Dispatch*, July 2, 1985; George Dorian Wendel and Mary Collins Wendel, "The Public Hospital Crisis in St. Louis City and County; The Privatizing Reconfiguration of 1985," paper presented to the American Public Health Association Public Hospitals Caucus, September 30, 1986, revised March 1, 1987.

Other sources: *The Arts at Metropolitan Square*, pamphlet, 1989; *Focus on the Issues*, Citizens for Schoemehl campaign pamphlet, 1984; letter, Mayor Vincent Schoemehl to author, August 17, 1988; *The Homeless Services Network, A National Model*, pamphlet, 1988; *St. Louis Centre: At the Heart of Downtown*, St. Louis Centre pamphlet, January, 1989.

Index

A. F. Shapleigh Company, 332

A. G. Edwards Company, 517

A. S. Stickney Cigar Company, 331

Abbott, James F., 408

ABC television network, 512

Able, Barton, 226, 229, 232, 289

Abolition, Antislavery. *See* Slavery, abolition of

Aboussie, Martin, 536

Abridgment of the Debates of Congress (Benton), 227

Acadians, 31

Adam Roth and Company, 333

Adams, Brock, 484

Adams, Cassily, 330

Adams, Elmer, 348, 359

Adams, Henry, 384

Adams, John Quincy, 110

Adam's Mark Hotel, 526–27, 549

Adams-Onis Treaty, 69, 110

Addams, Jane, 397

Adkins, Ben C., 380

Admiral (riverboat), 458, 542

Aero Club, 427

African Americans. *See* Blacks; Slavery

Air pollution, 132, 340, 345, 380, 382, 448–50

Alabama, 254, 274, 386 437

Alaska, 274, 437

Alberici Construction Company, 517

Alcock, J. W., 428

Alcott, Bronson, 322

Alexander, Grover Cleveland "Pete," 425–26, 429

Allen, Gerard B., 220, 225, 267, 281, 285, 292, 357

Allen, H. F., 311

Allen, Thomas, 183, 192, 203–9, 213, 217–19, 278, 291, 297, 321, 341, 349, 356

Aloe, Louis P., 420, 422–23

Aloe Plaza, 424, 460

Alton and St. Charles Bridge Company, 281

Alton, Ill., 177, 180, 190, 272, 281, 480, 488

Alton Observer, 177

Alton Telegraph, 176

Aluminum Corporation, 438

Aluminum Ore Company, 415

Amax, Inc., 474

American Anti-Slavery Society, 178

American Bar Association, 357

American Baseball League, 425

American Bottoms, 46, 119, 132, 160, 193

American Car and Foundry Company, 348, 437

American Civil Liberties Union, 400

American Commonwealth, The (Bryce), 327

American Federation of Labor, 360

American Foundrymen's Society, 472

American Freedom School, 317

American Fur Company, 85, 128–29, 135

American Institute of Architects, 452

American Iron Mountain Company, 218

Americanization of St. Louis, 83–86

American Missionary Society, 317

American Party, 164–65, 167

American Red Cross, 416, 435

American Revolution, 37–47, 52

Americans in Spanish Louisiana, 52–55, 64, 72

575

American Stamping Company, 398

American State, The (Snider), 321

American Steel Foundry Company, 353, 362, 399

American Theatre, 495

American Tobacco Company, 331

American Wine Company, 332

Amerika, 434

Ames, Edgar, 280, 341

Ames, Henry, 226, 341

Amtrak, 522

Ancient Order of Hibernians, 391

Anderson, Galusha, 237, 264

Anderson, Paul, 416

Anderson, William "Bloody Bill," 210, 220, 258

Andress, A. T., 224

Angelrodt, E. K., 144

Anheuser, Lilly. *See* Busch, Lilly Anheuser

Anheuser-Busch Brewing Association, 328–30, 435, 437, 457, 486, 503, 517, 536, 548

Anti-abolitionism, 173–80, 317

Anti-Catholicism, 173, 176–77, 418

Antioch College, 540

Anzeiger des Westens, 170–72, 176, 227, 245, 266, 432

Appalachian Mountains, 43, 53, 68, 139

Arch. *See* Gateway Arch

Archibald, Robert, 546

Architecture: of Cupples Station, 548–50; distinctive, St. Louis, 294–96, 507, 524–26, 548–49; of Gateway Arch, 455–57; of "Real Estate Row," 507, 510, 549. *See also* specific landmarks

Argus, 412

Arikara Indians, 57–59, 124–26

Aristotle and Ancient Educational Ideals (Davidson), 321

Arkansas Post, 25, 35

Armstrong, David H., 297, 303–5, 313, 315

Armstrong, Mary, 180

Army Corps of Engineers. *See* U.S. Army

Army of the Tenness*see*. *See* U.S. Army

Arsenal, 144–45, 190, 218–19, 234–36, 310, 313–14

Art Hill, 383, 393, 404, 493, 544

Art Museum, 383, 467, 493–94, 516, 543–44

Arts and Education Council, 524

Ashcroft, John, 535–38

Ashe, Thomas, 85

Ashley, William H., 125–27, 136, 143

Ashley and Henry Fur Company, 125–26

Association for Community Organization for Reform Now (ACORN), 527

Astor, John Jacob, 85, 110, 128

Astoria (Irving), 85

Atchison, David R., 208

Atlanta, Ga., 258, 261, 480, 490

Atlanta Braves, 515

Atlantic and Pacific Railroad, 277, 355

Atwater, Caleb, 133

Aubry, Charles P., 18–19

Aull, James, 140

Aull, Robert, 140

Austin, Moses, 54, 79, 106

Automobile: manufacturing of, 486, 550

Avery, William, 301–2

Babcock, Orville, 301–2

Bacon, Henry D., 186, 225

Baer, Howard F., 465, 483–84

Baer, J. Arthur, 474

Baer, Sidney, 449, 465

Baer family, 347

Baking Powder Trust, 370

Bakken, James, 491

Baldwin, Roger, 400, 403, 406, 411; and Baldwin-Gundlach Civic League, 409

Baltimore, Md., 310, 325, 420; as competitor of St. Louis, 272, 314, 340; investors from, 198, 221; and segregation law, 411–12

Baltimore and Ohio Railroad, 222

Baltimore Evening Sun, 467, 522

Bancroft, W. D., 175

Bank of America, 523

Bank of Illinois, 139

Bank of Missouri, 106–8

Bank of Montreal, 523

Bank of St. Louis, 465–66; and free banking law, 198; territorial bank, 105–6

Bank of the State of Missouri, 137–40, 174, 197–99

Bank of the United States, 105; St. Louis branch, 136; Second, 107, 137

Banks, 355, 473–74, 550; failure of, 106–8, 139; formation of, 105, 197–98; and fraud, 356, 358, 365–66; and free banking law, 198; and hard money versus soft, 138–40, 169, 201; and private note brokers, 138, 197; and "rag" notes, 136–37, 139; and redevelopment, 523

Bank War, 136–37

Banks, J. B. "Jet," 501, 542

Banks, Tom, 491

Baptiste (slave), 24

Baptists, 91, 94–95, 116, 146, 264

Bardenheier Wine Company, 332

Barkley, Alben W., 452

Barksdale, Clarence, 502, 506, 511

Barlow, Stephen, 343

Barnes, Ward A., 493

Barnes, Zane E., 506

Barnett, Marguerite Ross, 546–47

Barnum, P. T., 185

Barnum's Hotel, 181, 215

Baron, Pierre, 32

Barrett, Arthur H., 290, 300

Barry, James G., 156, 165–66, 203, 341

Barth, Robert, 213, 226

Barton, David, 112, 115–18

Barton, Joshua, 114

Baseball: and beginning of professional team, 424–26. *See also* St. Louis Browns; St. Louis Cardinals

Bates, Barton, 282, 285

Bates, Edward, 89, 208, 306; political career of, 116, 230–31, 244, 263

Bates, Frederick, 78–79, 82, 84, 89, 91, 93, 100–101, 106, 127

Bates's Theatre, 184

"Battle Row," 167, 173, 190

Battles (Civil War): Bull Run, 236; Lexington, 241; Pea Ridge, 246; Pilot Knob, 219; Shiloh, 253; Vicksburgh, 254, 257; Westport, 259; Wilson's Creek 240, 246, 251

Bauman and Company, 338

Beach Boys, 512

Béarn, France: and Laclède, 11, 52

Beaumont, William P., 140, 150

Beautification plan, 503, 513–14, 517

Beaver Asphalt Company, 438

Becker, William Dee, 460

Becknell, William, 130

Beckwourth, Jim, 126

Beer: and early breweries, 108, 194–96, 328. *See also* specific breweries

Beeson, Sue V., 321

Belcher, Charles, 193

Belcher, William, 193–94

Belcher, Wyatt W., 223, 226

Belcher Sugar Refinery, 193–94, 198, 312–13

Belknap, William, 288

Bellefontaine Neighbors, 478

Bellerive Country Club, 465

Belleville, Ill., 190, 480, 549

Belleville Area Junior College, 493

Bell Telephone Company of Missouri, 350, 358

Belmont, August, 200

Belmont, Mo., 219

Benoist, François, 61

Benoist, Howard, 346

Benoist, Louis A., 167, 188, 209; and private bank, 138–39, 197–98; and secession, view of, 247–48

Benoist family, 183

Bent, Charles, 130

Bent, Silas, 304, 305

Bent, William, 130

Benton, Thomas Hart, 156, 343, 404; as attorney, 82, 93, 106; and bank failure, 107, 139; and duel with Lucas, 113–14, 117–18; as newspaper editor, 110–18; political career of, 125, 131, 136–37, 148, 150, 165, 167–70, 174–75, 201–3, 227–28; statue, 343

Benton Barracks, 242

Benton Park, 195

Benton Place, 343

Benton School, 315

Bent's Fort, 130

Berard, Antoine, 32

Berger, Franz, 448

Berkeley, Mo., 445, 478

Berlin Ave. (now Pershing), 346, 435

Berra, Paul M., 419, 502, 518, 539

Berra, Yogi, 419

Berry, Chuck, 512

Berry, John, 427

Berthold, Bartholomew, 83

Berthold and Ewing Company, 167

Berthold mansion, 234

Bevis, Alfred, 303

Biddle, Nicholas, 136

Biddle, Thomas, 136

Biddle-Pettis duel, 136

Bidwill, "Stormy," 490

Bidwill, William, 490, 534–36

"Big Cinch," 347–50, 354–58, 363–64, 368–70, 376–77, 383, 396–402

"Big Eight," 492

"Big Four," 294

Bighorn River, 125

Big Mound. *See Grange de Terre, La*

"Big Ten," 492

Billikens (Saint Louis University), 546

Bingham, George Caleb, 494

Bingham, Gordon, 303

Bingham, Henry Vest, 110

Birdcage (Forest Park), 393

Birth of a Nation (Griffith), 411

Bishop, C. Orrick, 370

Bismarck, Otto von, 330

Bissell, Daniel, 106

Bissell, J. R., 279

Bissell's Point, 190, 267, 281, 294, 378

Bissette, Charles, 30

Bissette, William, 30

Bissonet, François, 15

Bissonette, Louis, 31

Bi-State Development Agency, 481–84; and county control, 533, 538; and Gateway Arch, 456; and port, 488–89

Bitting, Rev. Dr. W. C., 421

Bixby, Harold M., 428

Bixby, William K., 348, 494

Blackbird (Omaha chief), 59

Blackfeet Indians, 125–26, 128

Black Hawk War, 176

Blacks: free, rights of, 180, 229, 270–71, 410–15, 485; and jobs, 311, 415, 442–43, 507, 527–28; population of, 148, 179, 314, 416, 432, 462, 475, 479, 485, 514; violence against, 175–77, 415–16; and the vote, 270–71, 409–10, 423, 444–45, 467, 501, 514–15, 518, 530, 539–42. *See also* Slavery

Blackstone, T. B., 280

Blair, Francis P., 230

Blair, Francis P. Jr., 174, 226, 307, 436; and abolition, view on, 179, 227; and loyalty oath, 264–65; political career of, 229–39, 244–45, 248, 257, 260–61, 265–66, 268–69

Blair, James L., 351, 353, 382

Blair, Montgomery, 190, 228, 230, 239, 244, 252, 261

Blair family, 349

Blanchette, Louis, 62

Bland, Richard E., 258

Blandowski, F. C., 237

Blewett, Ben, 408

Bliss, M. A., 420–21

Blodgett, Wells, 413

Blood, Sullivan, 225

Bloody Island, 114, 136, 141, 149–51, 156, 175, 280, 283

Blount Conspiracy, 64

Blow, Henry Taylor, 186, 192, 220, 225–26, 228, 261, 277, 321, 324

Blow, Susan, 324–25, 485

Blow, Taylor, 228

Blow family, 349

Blumeyer, Arthur, 465

Blumeyer housing project, 464

Board of Aldermen, 498, 507–10, 530, 539–42

Board of Education, 443, 485, 493

Board of Education for Colored Schools, 318

Board of Estimate and Apportionment, 498, 502, 513, 539

Board of Freeholders, 304–8, 401, 464, 477

Board of Health, 265; and cholera epidemics, 155, 266; and corruption, 369

Board of Land Commissioners, 79–80, 84

Board of Public Improvements, 305, 364, 370, 381

Board of Trade, 57, 265, 282

Board of Water Commissioners, 267

Boatmen's Bank, 355, 358, 465, 474, 520

Boatmen's Savings Bank, 197

Boernstein, Henry (Heinrich), 170, 226–27, 236, 245

Bogey Club, 465

Bogy, Louis Vital, 200, 225, 265, 278, 281

Bond Issues: for hospital, 499–50, 517–18, 530; for Pacific Railroad, 206; public improvements (in years following), 1827–1828, 150; 1839, 152; 1849–1853, 153–54; 1854, 158–59, 188; 1858, 188–89; 1864–1868, 267–68; 1905, 399–400; 1906, 400; 1914, 401; 1923, 422–23; 1935, 453–54; 1944, 459–60; 1948 and 1953, 460; 1954, 467; 1955, 466–68; 1962, 469–70; 1967, 456; 1972, 471; for stadium, 536–37

Bonhomme bottoms, 63, 97

Bonneville, Benjamin, 128

"Boodle" (bribery), 326, 354, 363–71, 387

Boomer, Lucius, 280–82, 284–85, 520

Boone, Daniel, 80

Boone County, Mo., 220

Boonslick area, 137, 139; immigration to, 104, 112, 115

Boosterism, 8, 110, 142–43, 272–73, 372–73, 377, 393–94, 396, 402–406, 422–32, 452–58, 465–70

Booth, Edwin, 185

Booth, Junius Brutus, 184

Bootlegging, 418

Border Ruffians, 234

Borg, Charles, 247, 249

Bosley, Freeman Jr., 515

Bosley, Freeman Sr., 515, 517–18, 527, 539, 540

Boston, Mass.: as competitor of St. Louis, 272, 275, 328, 339–40, 402, 420, 424, 437, 441, 480, 497; investors from, 198, 200, 217, 224, 293

Boston Mirror, 86

Boston Tea Party, 305

Bouis, Pascal Vincent, 73

Boulanger, Georges, 344

Boundary extensions: of St. Louis (in years following), 1811, 96; 1823, 120; 1841, 145–46; 1855, 188; 1870, 298–99; 1876, 307

Bourgmont, Étienne de, 2, 6, 11

Bovard, O. K., 428

Bowlin, James, 137, 169, 201

Boyd, Rev. Willard, 360, 400

Boykins, Billie A., 514–15

Boyle, W. F., 383

Brackenridge, Henry M., 83, 89, 124

Brackett, Anna, 89, 124

Bradbury, John, 83

Brady, Thomas, 83, 93, 104, 164

Branscomb, C. H., 212

Brant, Joshua B., 205, 341

Breckenridge, Don, 471

Breckenridge, John C., 230–32

Bremer, Frederika, 160

Brentwood, Mo., 445, 478

Bridge, Hudson E., 186, 191, 197, 209–10, 213–16, 218, 225, 232, 285, 293

Bridge, Hudson E. Jr., 346

Bridge and ferry pool, 292–94

"Bridge arbitrary," 294, 398–400

Bridge-Beach Company (Empire Stove Works), 191, 197, 438

Bridge family, 345, 349

Bridger, Jim, 126–28

Bridgeton, Mo., 63, 220, 478

Britton, James H., 285

Broadhead, James O., 232, 244, 263, 265, 303, 305, 357

Broadway Avenue: in 1858, 191

Brock, Lou, 395

Brokmeyer, Henry C., 216, 319–21, 326

Bronx Zoo, 484

Brook Farm, 322

Brookings, Robert S., 333, 346, 465, 492, 550

Brookings Institution, 497

Brooklyn, Ill., 482

Brooklyn Eagle, 243

Brown, A. W., 428

Brown, Alanson D., 355

Brown, B. Gratz, 170, 192, 227, 229, 237, 245, 256–57, 260–61, 264, 269–70, 280–81, 309

Brown, George, 346

Brown, Joseph, 213–14, 267, 270, 290, 300

Brown, William Wells, 179–80

Brown Shoe Company, 437

Brown Tobacco Company, 331

Brown University, 319

Brown v. Board of Education of Topeka, 485

Browne, Joseph, 78–79, 81

Brownlee, John A., 233, 242

Bruce, Blanche K., 317

Bruehl, J. B., 144

Bruff, James, 79

Bryan, William Jennings, 349, 353–54, 362

Bry and Brothers Company, 337

Bryant, W. M., 321

Bryce, James, 327

Buchanan, James, 227

Buckingham Club, 376

Buder (Missouri Pacific) Building, 507–8, 510

Buffalo, N.Y.: as competitor of St. Louis, 480, 495

Bull Run, Battle of. *See* Battles (Civil War)

Burlington Northern Railroad, 488

Burlington Railroad, 224

Burnes, Robert L., 489

Burr, Aaron, 78; and conspiracy, 80–81

Busch, Adolphus, 329–30, 347, 366, 375, 435, 465

Busch, August A., 434–36

Busch, August A. Jr., 465, 472

Busch, E. A., 346

Busch, Lilly Anheuser, 329, 388, 435

Busch Memorial Stadium, 457–58, 470, 489–90, 534, 535, 548, 549

Busch-Sulzer Diesel Company, 436–37

Bush, George: administration of, 541

Bush, Isidor, 261, 263, 277, 304

Bushwhackers, 263–64, 272

Business district, 181–82, 475, 478, 506

Businessmen's League, 374, 381, 396, 399, 400

Butler, Edward, 301, 326, 350–53, 354, 356, 362–70

Butler Brothers Company, 336

Butler's "Indians," 353, 362

Byrd, Richard E., 429

C. F. Blanke Tea and Coffee Company, 333

Cabanné, Jean P., 52, 96

Cabanné, Joseph Charless, 350

Cabanné family, 52, 93, 183

Cabanné, Rasin and Company, 167

Cabanné Place, 346

Cabet, Étienne, 417

Cache Valley, 126

Caddo Indians, 25

Cadillac, Antoine de la Mothe, 4

Cahokia, Ill., 1, 3, 9–11, 16–17, 22, 25, 31, 38, 42–43, 47, 50, 62, 77, 439

Cahokia Ferry, 145

Cahokia Mounds, 404

Cairo, Arkansas, and Texas Railroad, 219

Cairo, Ill., 138, 149, 161

Cairo and Fulton Railroad, 219

Caisson disease, 286–87, 292

Calhoun, David L., 465–66

California, 68, 127, 131, 201–3, 208, 255, 333, 386, 437; gold rush, 165, 201

Calvé, Joseph, 41–43

Cambreling and Hatch, 206

Camden, Peter G., 165

Camp, Ann, 55

Campbell, James, 356–58, 367, 376, 465

Campbell, John, 108

Campbell, Robert, 130, 139, 167, 210, 226, 341

Camp Jackson, 236–38, 468

Camp Springs, 190

Cape Girardeau, Mo., 72, 101, 243

Capital, U.S.: removal campaign, 273–74

Carleton, Murray, 355, 371, 376, 382

Carleton Wholesale Dry Goods Company (Carleton-Ferguson), 335–36

Carnegie, Andrew, 287

Carnegie-Kloman Company, 287

Carondelet, Baron de, 55–56, 64, 67, 110

Carondelet Commons, 112

Carondelet Park, 380

Carondelet (town), 16–17, 61–62, 67, 70, 132, 149, 190, 200, 218, 282, 292, 298, 311–12, 376, 420, 446

Carpenter, Sharon Q., 538–40

Carpenters Union, 508

Carr, Dabney, 186

Carr, William C., 79, 83, 93–96, 342

Carr family, 186, 345, 347–49

Carr Square, 342

Carr Square Village, 459, 464

Carrow, Henry, 156

Carson, Kit, 201

Cartabona, Francisco de, 41–42, 44

Carter, James Earl "Jimmy," 484

Case, Calvin, 189–90, 209, 282

Case and Company, 190–91

"Castle Thunder," 182, 311

Catholic Charities, 529

Catholicism, 166, 216, 349, 413, 435; after 1804, 89, 91, 93; and the Creoles, 31–33, 54; under DuBourg, 93–94; and early churches, 93–94; and Jesuits, 3, 33, 94, 492

Catholic Total Abstinence Union, 391

Catlin, Daniel, 345

Catlin Tobacco Company, 331

Catlin tract, 376

Cavender, John S., 237, 310

CBS radio, 506

Censuses: and fraud of 1870, 272, 314; of St. Louis (in years following), 1773, 25; 1791, 62–63; 1800, 63; 1818 and 1820, 104; 1830, 132–33; 1835, 133; 1840, 135, 142–43; 1845, 143; 1850, 165–66; 1860, 192; 1866, 265–66; 1880, 272; 1890 and 1900, 327; 1910, 394; 1920, 416; 1930, 432; 1940, 445; 1950, 475–76; 1960, 478; 1970, 478–80; 1976, 480–81; 1980, 497, 514

Centenary Methodist Church, 174

Centennial Exposition, 374

Centerre Bank, 502, 506

Central business district: expansion, 181–82; decline, 475–79; revitalizing efforts, 504–506; St. Louis Centre, 518–21

Centralia Massacre, 220

Central Traction Company, 366

Central Trades and Labor Council, 477, 516

Century Electric Company, 436

Cerré, Catherine, 50

Cerré, Gabriel, 47–50, 53, 58

Cerré, Julia. *See* Soulard, Julia

Cerré, Marie Anne (Panet), 49

Cerré, Pascal, 49

Cerré, Thérèse, 49

Cerré family, 49, 50, 63, 72, 89

Cervantes, Alphonso J., 464, 470–71, 477, 487, 499, 533

Cervantes Convention Center, 472, 522, 537, 550

Chaffee, Calvin, 228–29

Chain of Rocks, 267, 307, 378–79

Chamberlain, Clarence, 429

Chamber of Commerce, 191, 193, 399, 422, 426, 448, 482. *See also* Businessmen's League (before 1916)

Chambers, Adam B., 139–40, 165

Chambers, Charles, 344

Champlain, Samuel de, 2

Chancelier, Louis, 40

Chancellor's Council (UMSL), 547

Chapman, H. H., 369

"Charcoals," 245, 250, 256

Charettes, 17

Charles III (king of Spain), 20, 33, 44

Charles IV (king of Spain), 61, 68

Charless, Edward, 122

Charless, Joseph, 86–89, 97, 100–103, 106, 111–13, 116–17

Charless, Joseph Jr., 164, 205, 228

Charter Hospital. *See* Hospitals

Charters: of St. Louis (in years following), 1809, 96; 1823, 120; 1839, 146–47; 1855–1876, 297–300; 1876, 303–9, 327, 495, 498; 1902–1911, 380, 398–99, 401–3; 1914, 403, 409–10; 1941, 410; 1949, 464

Chase, Salmon P., 272

Chase Econometrics, 495

Chautauquan, 381

Chauvenet, William, 284

Cheltenham area, 207–8, 417

Cherokee Indians, 246, 326

Chesley Island, 364–65

Chevrolet Plant, 438, 486, 528

Cheyenne Indians, 59, 125

Chicago: rivalry with St. Louis, 256, 272–75, 277, 280–81, 284–85, 314, 373–74, 391, 395, 424–25

Chicago and Alton Railroad, 224

Chicago and Northwestern Railroad, 224

Chicago Times, 266, 314

Chicago White Stockings, 425

Chickasaw Bluffs, 64

Chickasaw Indians, 64

Chihuahua, Mexico: and the silver trade, 131

China: trade with, 110–11, 202–5

Chippewa Indians, 40

Choctaw Indians, 64

Choiseul, Étienne de, 17–18

Cholera: epidemics of, 146, 154–57, 167, 203, 266

Chopin, Kate, 400

Chouteau, Auguste, 8–10, 13, 15, 35–36, 45, 49–51, 53, 56–57, 61, 72–74, 77, 81–82, 85, 89, 93, 98–99, 102–5, 107, 110–11, 120, 135–36, 215, 404

Chouteau, Auguste P., 73, 130, 194

Chouteau, Charles P., 170, 183, 187, 192, 198, 219, 221, 225, 249, 281, 306, 312, 344, 357

Chouteau, Francis, 124

Chouteau, Gabriel, 124, 146

Chouteau, Harrison and Vallé, 197, 199–200, 218, 266, 281

Chouteau, Henry, 167, 209

Chouteau, J. G., 303

Chouteau, Marie Louis, 13

Chouteau, Marie Thérèse, 10, 12–13, 23, 35, 51–52

Chouteau, Pelagie, 13

Chouteau, Pierre, 9, 50, 52, 56–57, 61, 67, 74–76, 80–81, 90, 93, 98, 102, 110–11, 124, 157

Chouteau, Pierre, Jr., 52, 110, 116, 128, 136–38, 167, 200

Chouteau, René Auguste, 13

Chouteau, Veuve, 24

Chouteau, Victoire, 13, 50–52

Chouteau family, 50–52, 56–57, 67, 72, 123–24, 133, 183, 349

Chouteau-Lucas addition, 104, 109, 120

Chouteau's Hill, 82, 506

Chouteau's Pond, 35, 66, 145–47, 151, 157, 207–8, 340–41

Christ Church Cathedral Mission, 529

Christy, Andrew, 221, 278–79

Christy, E. T., 144
Christy, Samuel, 278
Christy, William, 96, 104, 144–45, 164
Chrysler Motor Company, 486
Church, John J., 442
Churchill, Winston (novelist), 394
Church of the Messiah, 250
Cimarron Desert, 131
Cincinnati, Ohio, 88, 134–35, 137, 141, 154–55, 161, 165, 192–93, 195, 202, 207, 222, 224, 273, 324, 328, 424
Cincinnati Commercial Agency, 137
Cincinnati (steamboat), 134
Citizens' Committee on Postwar Improvements, 459
"Citizens for Schoemehl," 517
Citizens' Party, 432
Citizens' Smoke Abatement League, 448–49
"City Beautiful," 377, 381, 396, 402, 410, 505
City Club, 413
City-county separation-consolidation issue. *See also* St. Louis County
City Hospital. *See* Hospitals
City Hotel, 136
City Plan Commission, 420, 445, 447, 459
Civic Center Redevelopment Corporation, 469, 470, 473, 548
Civic Federation, 350, 352, 401
Civic improvement, 503, 513, 517
Civic Improvement League, 381, 396, 400–1, 403, 409
Civic Progress, Inc., 465–66, 477, 503, 508, 516–17, 532, 534–35, 547–48
Civic Theatre, 406
Civil War, 227–66, 282; and conservatives, 211, 216, 226, 239, 248, 260–66, 268; guerrilla activity in, 210, 218–20, 246–51, 258–60; assessments, 247–51. *See also* Battles (Civil War); Confederate Army; Confederacy
"Clabber Alley," 182, 311
Claiborne, William C. C., 69
Clamorgan, Cyprian, 180
Clamorgan, Jacques, 58–61, 73, 77, 110, 202
Clamorgan family, 148
Clarion Hotel, 526
Clark, Charles, 344–45, 476
Clark, Edwin, 465, 477
Clark, George Rogers, 39–41, 44–46, 48, 50, 55–56, 64
Clark, Jefferson K., 248, 259
Clark, Meriwether L. Jr., 186
Clark, Meriwether Lewis, 172, 184
Clark, Roy, 512
Clark, William, 81, 83, 93, 102–3, 111–12, 117, 124, 136, 405
Clay, Henry, 115, 118, 165, 181, 212
Clay, William L., 462, 499–500, 502–3, 514, 516, 530, 532, 538–41, 545
Clay, William L. Jr., 539
"Claybanks," 245
Claybour, Richard, 510
Clay mines, clay products, 417–18, 438–39
Clayton, Mo., 446, 478, 480, 514, 533
Clemens, James, 136
Clemens, Samuel L. *See* Twain, Mark
Cleveland, Grover, 386
Cleveland, Mrs. Grover, 344
Cleveland, Ohio: as competitor of St. Louis, 339–40, 416, 420, 437, 479–80, 495, 497; and retail stores, 335–36; and strikebreakers, 358

Cleveland Browns, 490

Cleveland Orchestra: as competitor of St. Louis's, 495

Climatron, 543

Clinton, Jerry B., 535, 537

Clinton-Peabody Terrace, 459, 464

Clothing: production of, 331, 335–37, 436, 440

Clyman, James, 126

Coal: mining of, 132, 145, 200, 398–99, 447–50

Cochran, John, 454

Cochran Gardens, 460, 463–64

Cockerill, John A., 357–58

Coignard, Louis, 67–68

Coldwater Creek, 38, 62

Cole, Nathan, 268

Coli, François, 429

Colleges. *See* specific colleges

Collier, Dwight, 304

Collier, George F., 186, 201, 205–6

Collier family, 341

Collier White Lead Company, 192

Collins, James "Rip," 432

Collot, Victor, 66–67

Colman, Norman J., 212, 216

Colman's Rural World, 216

Colorado, 252; and capital removal campaign, 272; and trade with, 277, 332; and whiskey ring, 302

Columbia, Mo., 369

Columbia Club, 466

Columbian Exposition (Chicago World's Fair), 374–75, 377, 382, 391

Columbia River, 59, 201–2

Columbus Square, 417

Comanche (Padouca) Indians, 5, 57, 130

Commercial Bulletin, 176–77

Committee of Public Safety, 310

Committee of Safety, 232–33, 236, 239

Commons, common fields, 15–17, 63–64, 471

Common School fund, 315

Commonwealth Trust Company, 355

Company of Explorers of the Upper Missouri, 57–61

Company of the West (Royal Company of the Indies), 4–5

Compromise of 1850, 202

Compton, Arthur Holly, 492

Compton Heights, 346

Compton Hill, 346

Compton Hill Reservoir, 261

Compton Hill Subdivision, 182

Compulsory school attendance law, 319, 394

Concord School of Philosophy, 325, 326

Concordia Seminary, 144

Condé, Andre, 19, 30, 90

Condé, Marie, 58

Confederate Army, 210, 218–20, 237–38, 240–41, 246–49, 253, 258–60; and blockade of the Mississippi, 255, 275, 282

Confederacy, 234, 238–40, 258, 534

Conference of Mayors, 529

Conferro Paint Company, 441

Confluence St. Louis, 532

Congregational Church, 95

Connecticut Missionary Society, 95

Connett, W. C., 444

Connor, Jeremiah, 93, 97, 106, 109, 120, 164

Conservatives, Civil War, 211, 216, 226, 239, 248, 260, 262–65, 268

Conservative Union Party, 265–66, 268

Constitutional conventions: of 1820, 116–17; of 1865, 260–66; of 1875, 303–4

Constitutional Union Party, 231

Constitutions (Mo.): of 1820, 117; of 1865, 260–66, 300, 318, 536

Construction industry, 132, 181, 463, 515–16, 527–28, 550; and unions, 508, 516, 528

Construction Trades Council, 508, 516

Continental Rangers, 172

Continental Tobacco Company, 332

Conventions and tourism, 391, 471–73, 487, 495, 519–20, 526–27, 536–37, 550

Conway, James, 481, 497–501, 505, 533, 540

Conway, Stephen, 540

Cook, Douglas, 332

Cooke, Jay, 291

Cook's Imperial Champagne, 332

Coolidge, Calvin, 436

Coons, John, 55, 143, 194

Coons, Mrs. J. A., 248

Coordinating Board for Higher Education (CBHE), 548

"Copperheads," 260

Corbett, Katharine T., 544

Corbin, Abel R., 140, 169, 176

Cornelius, William L., 548

Coronado, Francisco, 2

Corruption, 211–20, 222–23, 226, 268, 270, 326, 350–72. *See also* "Boodle"

Coryell, Don, 491

Cotting, Amos, 282, 285

Cotton Belt Railroad, 278, 376

Cotton Exchange, 277

Council Plaza, 468

County Court, 132, 298–300, 309

County Hospital (Regional Medical Center). *See* Hospitals

"County" offices (of St. Louis). *See* Patronage system

Coureurs de bois, 3, 5

Courts: at county level, 132, 299–301, 309; in the territory, 73, 76–79, 85

Coutumes de Paris (customs of Paris), 33

Cox, S. W., 213

"Cracker Castle," 341

Crane, Nathalia, 430

Crawford, Curtis, 518

Credit Mobilier, 216

Creek Indians, 64

Creoles: culture of, 38, 51–55, 61–62, 66, 70–72, 77, 81–83, 85–86, 89–93, 98–99, 133, 143, 147–48, 167–68, 178, 180, 224–25, 400; elite of, 46–55, 58–59, 61, 63–66, 70–72, 79–81, 85–86, 89, 97, 100, 111–12, 114–15, 182–84, 225; homes, 15–16, 82–83, 85, 132

Crestwood, Mo., 478

Crime, 83–86, 111–14, 140–41, 174–77, 182, 461–62, 483, 497, 500, 502–4, 512, 529, 542

Crimean War, 198

Croonenburghs, Charles, 340

Crow, Wayman, 205, 209, 334

Crozat, Antoine, 4

Cruzat, Don Francisco, 27–28, 32–34, 37, 44–45, 51, 66, 93, 154, 186

Cuba: and the Louisiana Territory, 19, 22, 53, 193

Cul de Sac, 17

Cummings, Fr. John A., 264

Cunliff, Nelson, 420

Cupples, Samuel, 333, 346, 492

Cupples Station Complex, 333–34, 548–50

Currlin, Albert, 310, 312–13

Curtis, Samuel R., 150, 158, 246–47, 250, 259, 262

Curtis, Thomas A., 412

Curtiss, Glenn, 403, 428

Cushman, Charlotte, 185

Custer's Last Fight (painting), 330

Customs House, 182

Cutter, Norman, 279

D'Abbadie, Jean Jacques, 8, 11
Daggett, John F., 164
Danforth, Donald, 465
Danforth, John, 548
Danforth, William, 487, 546, 550
Danforth Foundation, 492
Darby, John F., 15, 152, 154, 176,
   201, 204, 349
Darnes, William P., 139–40
Darst, Joseph, 459–60, 464–65
Darst-Webbe Apartments, 460
Darwin, Charles: and Darwinism,
   321–22
Davidson, Thomas, 321, 326
Davis, Andrew Jackson, 140
Davis, Dwight F., 334, 346, 406–7,
   409
Davis, J. Lionberger, 444, 452
Davis, Jefferson, 218, 235, 264, 279
Davis, Noel, 429
Davis, Samuel C., 333–34
Davis Cup, 334
Dean, J. H. "Dizzy," 432
Dean, R. Hal, 471
DeAndreis, Fr. Felix, 93–94
Deaver and Cromwell Company,
   141
Deaver's Clothing Store, 134
DeBaliviere Place, 529
De Bar's Theater, 184
De Belestre, Picote, 41, 44
Deere, John, 223
De Fossat, Guy, 19
Deggendorf, Robert, 268
De Lassus, Charles de Hault, 51,
   61, 69, 79–80, 106, 129–30, 405
De Launay, David, 73, 100
Delaware Indians, 66
De Leyba, Don Fernando, 37–38,
   40–44, 69, 405

De Leyba, Teresa, 37
Delor de Tregét, Clement, 61–62
Democrats, 137, 146, 154, 164–65,
   167–70, 202, 230–32, 258, 261,
   268–70, 299–300, 349–55, 358,
   362–65, 367–72, 391, 402, 410,
   436, 443–45, 477, 538; anti-
   Benton faction, 169–70, 173,
   198, 227–28; and city
   organization, 499–501, 508,
   515, 517, 538–39, 541; national
   conventions of, 391, 539; pro-
   Benton faction, 151, 169–70,
   173, 188, 200–201, 227,
   229–30, 265
De Mun, Jules, 52, 129
De Mun family, 52, 349
Dent, Josiah, 279
Department of Transportation, 484
Descartes, René, 321
Des Moines (Mua) River, 38, 41,
   52, 55, 67, 70, 110
Desnoyers, Veronique, 24
De Soto, Hernando, 2
De Soto-Carr Redevelopment, 471
Detailly, Denau, 29
Deutschland Uber Alles, 434
De Villiers, Neyon, 8, 10
Devol, Charles, 163
De Volsay, Pierre, 24, 30
Dewey, John, 321
D'Iberville, Pierre Le Moyne,
   Sieur, 4
Dickens, Charles, 162, 181, 339
Dickman, Bernard F., 443, 449,
   452, 454
Dickson, Charles K., 282, 285, 341
Didier, Fr. Marie Joseph, 92
Didier, Pierre, 98
Dieckmann, George, 408
Dierdorf, Dan, 491
Die Wacht Am Rhein, 434
Dillard Department Stores, 520
Dille, Earl K., 545

Discrimination: against blacks, 410–16, 441–45, 485–86, 499, 540; against Catholics, 164–66; against Germans, 164–66, 168, 432, 434–36; against Irish, 164–67; against Italians, 418; against Jews, 20, 347, 465; against Protestants, 20

Dispatch. See St. Louis Dispatch

Dix, Dorothea, 251

Dockery, A. M., 387

Dodier, Mme., 23

Donaldson, James L., 79, 84

Donk Brothers Coal Company, 448

Dougherty, John, 128

Douglas, James, 465

Douglas, Stephen A., 150, 188, 204–5, 232

Downtown St. Louis, Inc., 474, 527

Dozier, L. D., 376, 382

Drake, Charles Daniel, 212, 248, 257, 261–63, 266, 269

Drake, Daniel, 273

Dred Scott case, 227–29

Drew, Andrew, 427

Drew, John, 185

Drummond Tobacco Company, 331

DuBourg, Louis William (bishop), 90, 92–94

Dubreuil, Clarissa, 81

Dubreuil, Louis, 58

Dubreuil family, 52, 72, 89

Ducharme, Jean Marie, 26, 42

Duchesne, Mother Rose Philippine, 93–94

Duden, Gottfried, 143

Duels, 85, 88, 113–14, 136, 174–75

Duke, Basil, 233–34, 242

Duke, James B., 331

Dunand, Fr. Marie Joseph, 91

Duncan's Island, 149

Dunn, Charles E., 258

Duralde, Martin Miloney, 25, 30

Durocher, Laurent, 58

Du Tisne, Charles C., 5

Dyer, David P., 302, 308

Dyer, L. P., 413

E. D. Morgan and Company, 220

E. F. W. Meier Company, 338

Eads, James B., 186–87, 192, 221, 226; and bridge, 280–92, 448; and railroads, 220; and ironclads, 282, 288; and diving bell, 282, 286

Eads Bridge, 279–291, 311, 343, 398–99, 416, 428, 452–54, 483, 513, 519, 522

Eagle Powder Works, 145

Eagleton, Thomas, 484

Eames, William: of Eames and Young, architects, 507, 550

East Central Missouri Junior College, 493

Easton, Rufus, 73–74, 79, 84, 89, 101, 112, 349

East St. Louis, Ill.: as distressed area, 414–16, 497; growth of, 222, 327–28, 481–83; and railroads, 283, 310, 313, 399, 401, 438–39, 488; race riot of 1917, 415–16. *See also* Illinoistown

East St. Louis Terminal Company, 294

East-West commercial orientation, 224, 230, 233

East-West Gateway Coordinating Council, 488; and A-95 review power, 481–82

Ebenezer Church, 317

Economy: budget deficits, 502–3, 517; condition of (in years following), 1818–1819, 104–8, 109; 1820s, 132; 1830s, 133–35, 141–43; 1840s, 158–60; 1850s, 180–82; 1860s, 275–79; 1870s, 293, 309–14; 1880s–1890s,

327–39; 1900, 358–62, 383; 1910, 394; 1920s–1930s, 436–45; 1940s, 459–60; 1970s, 486–89, 495–96; 1980s, 497, 520, 527–30, 550–51; and wage levels (in years following), 1851, 208; 1873, 309; 1904, 383

Economic Rivalry between St. Louis and Chicago, 1850–1880, The (Belcher), 223

Edgar, Timothy, 213–14

Edison Brothers Stores, 527

Education: for blacks, 270, 315–19, 385, 443, 493, 528; in Catholic schools, 91, 94, 433, 485; in Lutheran Schools, 144, 433, 485; in public schools, 121, 180, 262, 315–17, 323, 350, 393–94, 485, 497, 528, 541–42, 546–48; in the territory, 89–91, 93

Education of Henry Adams, The, 384

Edward VII (king of England), 385

Edwards, Marcellus, 157

Edwards, Ninian, 103

Effie Alton (steamboat), 279

Egan, L. H., 439

Eldorado Springs, Mo., 440

Elections: and "Butler's Indians," 352; in seventh ward, 508, 518; in nineteenth ward, 410, 501; in St. Louis (in years following), 1856, 173; 1860, 230–32; 1864, 260–61; 1900, 361–63; 1904, 370–72; 1981, 498–503; 1985, 516–18, 533, 539; 1989, 538–41; and ward boundaries, 147

Eliot, William Greenleaf, 179, 250–51, 317–18, 492

Elliott, Howard, 382

Elliott, R. S., 156

Ely and Walker Company, 335

Emerson, Irene, 228

Emerson Electric Company, 436, 484, 535

Empire Stove Works. *See* Bridge-Beach Company

Engelmann, George, 186–87, 306

English, Ezra, 195

English Cave, the, 195

Episcopal Church, 95–96, 264, 350

Equitable Life Assurance Society, 470, 474

Erie Canal, 224

Erie Railroad, 212, 216

Erin Benevolent Society, 164

Espionage Act, 435

Essex, James, 145

Ewing, Thomas, 259–60

Exacte Description de la Louisiane (DeBourgmont), 2

Excelsior Stove Works, 197, 266, 312

Exchange Bank, 198

Exhibition Palaces (World's Fair), 382–84, 388

Exposition Realty Company, 376

F. B. Hauck Company, 337

Fabian Society, 321

Fairgrounds Park, 397–98, 459

Fairmount district. *See* "Hill, the"

Falls of St. Anthony, 218

Faltermayer, Edwin, 521

Famous-Barr, Famous Company. *See* May Company

Faneuil Hall (Boston), 523

Farmer's Market (San Francisco), 524

Farrar, Bernard Jr., 219, 247, 248, 341

Farrar, Dr. Bernard G., 111, 156

Farrar, John, 219

Farris, Charles K., 457, 468

Faust, Edward, 346

Fayette planter's clique, 139, 170, 231

Featherstonhaugh, George, 142

Federalist Party: and the Louisiana Purchase, 169; and the Missouri constitution, 116

Femme Osage Settlement, 80

Ferguson, Mo., 344, 445, 476, 478, 480

Ferguson-McKinney Company, 336

Ferry, Thomas, 290

Fesler, Mayo, 396, 400

Field, Roswell, 228

Fifteenth Amendment, 269

Filley, Chauncey I., 225, 229, 256, 279, 289, 292

Filley, Giles, 197, 225, 229, 249, 266, 312

Filley, John D., 346

Filley, Oliver D., 192, 197, 225, 229, 265, 298

Filley, S. R., 285

Filley family, 229, 232, 341, 345, 349

Fine, Philip, 55

Fink, Mike, 126

Finn, John, 266

Finney, James, 195

Finney, William, 195

Firebrick: production of, 418, 438

Fires: and city fire department, 502; and Great Fire of 1849, 167–68; protection from, 98, 290, 467; and volunteer companies, 166–68, 174, 183–84, 208

First National Bank, 456, 474

First Presbyterian Church, 342

Fishback, George W., 302

Fitzpatrick, Daniel R., 412

Fitzpatrick, Thomas, 126–28

Flad, Edward, 448–49

Flad, Henry, 284, 287, 290, 448

Flaget, Bishop Benedict, 91

Fleishman, Alfred, 466

Fleishman-Hillard, Inc., 466

Fletcher, Thomas C., 219, 261–64

Flint, Rev. Timothy, 95, 133

Flood of 1844, 193

Florida Territory: Spain's rule of, 38, 44, 52, 55, 64, 68

Florissant, Mo., 62, 94, 344, 445, 476, 478, 480

Florissant Valley Country Club, 344

Flour: milling of, 192–93, 328

Flynn, Fr. Thomas, 91

Fogg, Josiah, 282, 285

Folk, Joseph W.: and campaign against "boodlers," 303, 361, 363–64, 366–71; political career of, 353, 360, 362, 372–94

Follenius, Paul, 143

Fontbonne College, 493

Forbes, John Murray, 224, 293

Ford, James L. Jr., 449, 455

Ford, Richard, 506, 508

Ford Foundation, 477, 529

Ford Motor Company, 436, 486

Forest Park, 51, 306–8, 346, 376–77, 381–82, 393, 404–9, 424, 448, 493–94, 544

Foristell, Mo., 482

Forrest, Edward, 184

Forsyth, William, 306

Fort Armstrong, 133

Fort Bellefontaine, 38, 96–97, 102, 105, 133

Fort Carondelet, 56–57

Fort Cavagnolle, 6

Fort Crawford, 133–34

Fort de Chartres, 5, 8–9, 11, 31

Fort Don Carlos, 19, 26, 38–41

Fort Donelson, 282

Fort Henry, 282

Fort Laramie, 128

Fort Leavenworth, 133–35, 151, 259

Fort Lisa, 125

Fort Mandan, 125

Fort Manuel, 125

Fort Orleans, 5–6, 11

Fort Osage, 115

Fort Pitt, 37

Fortress Monroe, 52

Fort St. Louis, 13

Fort San Carlos, 45, 66, 69, 97, 403

Fort Snelling, 133–34, 228

Fort Sumter, 234

Fortune: on St. Louis architecture, 521, 524; and the 500, companies in, 486, 516

Fort Vancouver, 127

"Forty-Eighters," 164, 178, 261, 263, 271

Foster, R. B., 318

Four Courts Building, 313

Fox, Abraham, 151

Fox, E. W., 279, 302

Fox Indians. *See* Sauk and Fox Indians

Fox River, 2

Fox Theatre, 525

Foy, Peter, 245

Fraeb, Henry, 127

France: empire of, 1–8, 17–18, 26, 38, 63–64, 68–69, 200, 385, 404

Francis, David R., 294, 344, 352–53, 355, 371, 373–76, 378–80, 382, 385–86, 394, 399, 413, 435–36, 465

Franco-Prussian War, 291

Frank, Nathan, 382

Franklin County, 478, 480–81, 493

"Fredbird," 536

Fred Harvey's Restaurant, 522

Free Bridge movement, 399–401

Freedman's Bureau, 255

Freedmen's Relief Society, 254

"Freedom School," 317

Freeman, Daniel, 97

Free-Soil advocates, 229–30

Freethinkers, 216

Fremont, Jessie Benton, 202, 240, 244, 251

Fremont, John C.: military career of, 202, 239–45, 251, 266; political career of, 227, 256, 260; and railroads, 219, 222; and western expeditions, 187, 201–2

French and Indian War, 6

French Quarter (New Orleans), 524

French Revolution, 311; views of, in Louisiana, 66–67

Frisch, Frank, 432

Froebel, Friedrich, 324

Froehlich, Russell, 416

Frontenac, Mo., 478

Frost, Daniel M., 234–38, 247, 342, 344

Frost, Mrs. Daniel M., 248

Fuller, Margaret, 332

Fulton Brewery, 194

Fur factories, 74, 115, 125

Fur trade, 5, 9, 17–21, 25–28, 30–31, 38–40, 48–49, 51–52, 53–55, 62, 70, 73, 76, 111, 115, 123–25, 131, 135, 402, 436; and rendezvous system, 126–30

Gabriel and Francis Chouteau Fur Company, 124

Galena and Chicago Union Railroad, 224

Galena-Dubuque lead district, 160

Gallatin, Albert, 76

Gálvez, Don Bernardo, 28, 34–35, 37–38, 44, 51, 55

Gamble, Hamilton R., 200, 233, 239–45, 249–50, 260

Gantt, James, 370–71

Gantt, Thomas T., 265, 297, 303–4, 306, 308

Gantt and Blackwell Fur Company, 128

Garagiola, Joe, 419

Gardenhire, James, 231

Garesche, Juliette, 247

Garland, James S., 321–22

Garland, Judy, 395

Garnier, Joseph, 100

Garrison, Daniel R., 211–12, 214–16, 226, 249, 281, 293

Garrison, William L., 256

Gartside, Joseph, 288–89

"Gashouse Gang." *See* St. Louis Cardinals (baseball)

Gatesworth Manor, 530

Gateway Arch, 455–56, 505, 509–10, 512–13, 516, 521, 527, 544

Gateway Mall project, 504–12, 548

Gateway Mall Redevelopment Inc., 505–8, 510

Gateway One, 510–11

Gateway Tower, 474

Gateway Two and Three, 510

Gaty, McCune and Company, 197

Gayety Theatre, 342

Gayoso de Lemos, Manuel, 51, 66

Gehrig, Lou, 425

Geiger, Louis, 369

General American Life Insurance Company, 465, 471, 474, 487, 506

General Dynamics Corporation, 486

General Motors Corporation, 436, 486; Chevrolet plant, 438, 528; Corvette plant, 486

General Strike of 1877, 309–14

Genèt, Edmond, 55, 64

George, Henry, 358

George III (king of England), 88

Georgetown College, 92

Gephardt, Richard, 539

German-American Alliance, 410, 435

Germania Society, 186

Germans: and anti-British sentiment, 434; churches and schools of, 432–33; and choral clubs, 186; and the German language, use in schools, 323; and German- language newspapers, 175, 266, 432–34; and the vote, 188, 226–27, 229–30, 237, 269, 349–50, 352, 402, 410, 413, 434–35, 445. *See also* "Forty-Eighters"; Immigrants

German Savings Bank, 365

Gervais, Jean Baptiste, 127–28

Gesangverein (choral clubs), 186

Geyer, Henry S., 140, 143, 170, 228

Geyer Act (1839), 315

Gibault, Fr. Pierre, 31

Gibson, Charles, 342–43

Giddings, Salmon, 95

Gieszen Immigration Society, 143

Gilded Age, The (Twain and Warner), 216

Gillespie, David, 285

Gilligan's Coffeehouse, 167

Gilpin, William, 139–40, 273

Glasgow, William, 259

Glasgow, William K., 226, 341, 344

Glasgow family, 347

Glen Echo Country Club, 344–45

Glennon, John (Archbishop), 413

Globe-Democrat. See St. Louis Globe (Globe-Democrat)

Glover, Samuel, 232, 237, 244, 263, 265, 306

Godoy, Manuel, 64, 68

Goering, Karen M., 545

Goldberger, Paul, 521, 524

"Goldbugs," 352, 362

Goltermann, Charles E., 420

Gompers, Samuel, 360

Gordon, Harry, 11

Gottschalk, Louis, 308

Gould, Jay, 211, 293–94

Graham, Richard, 344, 476

Granby Mining and Smelting Company, 192

Grand Army of the Republic, 264, 413

Grandel Square, 471

"Grand Pacific Railroad March," 208

Grand Prairie, 15–17, 38

Grange de Terre, La (Barn of Earth), 1, 18, 555

Granite Mountain silver mines, 345

Grant, Ulysses S., 140, 179; military career of, 246, 254, 264, 282; political career of, 268–70, 301–3, 371

Gratiot, Charles, 47, 50–52, 58, 85, 95, 111, 113; and the Louisiana Purchase, 69–70, 72–73

Gratiot, Charles Jr., 52, 73, 149

Gratiot, Emilie Anne, 52

Gratiot, Henri (Henry), 52, 81

Gratiot, Isabella, 52

Gratiot, Julia, 52

Gratiot, Marie Thérèse, 52

Gratiot, Victoire, 52

Gratiot family, 52

Gratiot League Square, 51, 306, 417

Gratiot Street Prison, 248, 258

"Graveyard Stretch." *See* Mississippi River

Gray, Asa, 186

Gray, Mel, 491

Great Basin, 201

Great Depression, 439–45

Great Fire of 1849, 167–68, 182, 203, 453

Great Lakes, 1–3, 40, 45, 110, 160, 193

Great Plains, 328

Great Salt Lake, 127

Great West and Its Commercial Metropolis (Edwards and Hopewell), 178

Greeley, Carlos, 225, 251, 255, 279, 285, 341

Greeley, Horace, 230, 270

Greenback Labor Party, 314

Greene, Colton, 233–35

Green River, 126, 128

Greenwich Village (Manhattan), 524

Gregg, Josiah, 187

Gregg, Norris B., 382

Griesedieck, Henry, 346

Griesedieck family, 347

Griffith, D. W., 411

Grimsley, Thornton W., 140

Grobman, Arnold, 547

Grocery trade, 134, 142, 333–34

Grosvenor, William, 269–70

Gros Ventres Indians, 59, 125, 129

Guilfoil, Thomas J., 535

Guion, Amable, 19, 31, 43

Gulf of Mexico, 4, 110, 275

Gundlach, John, 396, 400–1, 403–4, 409, 421, 448

Guyol, François, 90

Haas, Lieber, and Coste Company, 333

Habb, Victor, 194

Hadley, Herbert S., 372

Hagenbeck Wild Animal Show, 390

Haines, Jesse, 425

Haldimand, Frederick, 40

Hall, Willard P., 240, 260

Halleck, Henry W., 246–48, 250

Hamilton, Alexander, 68

Hamilton-Brown Shoe Company, 437

Hammond, George, 175–76

Hammond, James, 175

Hammond, Samuel, 73, 79, 96, 101, 106

Hancock, W. Scott, 370

Hannibal, Mo., 161, 201, 437

Hannibal and St. Joseph Railroad, 201, 207, 209, 217–18, 272

Harbor: improvements to, 148–50

Harborplace (Baltimore), 523–24

Hardware trade, 332

Hargadine and McKittrick
    Company, 334–36

Harmar, Joseph, 54

Harmony Mission, 95

Harney, William S., 233, 238–39,
    249, 252, 258, 341, 344, 476

Harper, James, 408

Harper's, 395, 468

Harris, Cortlandt, 407

Harris, William Torrey, 216,
    320–26, 343, 485, 493

Harrison, Edward, 352

Harrison, James, 197–99, 205,
    213–15

Harrison, William Henry, 73–74, 76

Harrison family, 349, 352

Harris-Stowe State College, 493

Hart, Jim, 491

Hart, Oliver A., 213–14

Harvard University, 196, 349, 529

Hawes, Harry B., 351, 353–54, 359,
    362, 368–71

Hawken Rifles, 130

"Hawkeye Bill," 174

Hawks, Cicero (Bishop), 264

Hayward, George, 342

Head, Walter W., 459

Hearnes, Warren, 483

Hegel, Georg: and Hegelianism,
    216, 320–22, 324

Hegel's Esthetics (Bryant), 321

Hegel's *Larger Logic* (trans.,
    Brokmeyer), 320

Heinrichshofen, William, 346

Helderbrand, John, 143

Hellmuth, Obata and Kassabaum,
    524–25

Hemp: production of, 28

Hempstead, Charles, 100

Hempstead, Edward, 73, 79, 81–82,
    95–96, 98, 101, 102, 111–13, 124

Hempstead, Mary, 111, 124

Hempstead, Stephen, 95, 126

Hempstead, Susan, 52, 106

Hempstead family, 52, 349

Henderson, John B., 264, 302

Hendrick, George, 515

Hennings, Thomas, 456

Hennings, Thomas C., 353

Henry, Andrew, 125–27

Heritage and Urban Design
    Commission, 504

Hermann, Mo., 200, 209

Hermann, Robert, 511–12

Hernandez, Keith, 515

Herzog, Whitey, 515

Hess, Lydia, 317

Hesse, Emanuel, 40–42

Hickok, James, 457

Hill, David B., 348

"Hill, the," 417–20

Hill, William P., 402

Hill and McGunnegle Company, 133

Hill 2000, 419

Hinkle, Joseph, 97

"Hiroshima Flats" (Mill Creek
    Valley), 468

Historic preservation movement,
    504, 507–8, 510–11, 518–20,
    522–25, 548–50

History Museum, 543–45. *See also*
    Missouri Historical Society

History of Chicago, The (Andress),
    224

History of Education, The
    (Davidson), 321

Histrionic Society, 184

Hoback River, 128

Hocker, Lon V., 447

Hoessle, Charles, 544

Hogan, John, 159, 197–98, 261

Hohenlohe (prince of Germany), 388

Holmes, M. Patricia, 295

Home Guard, 232–33, 235–36, 239,
    256

Homeless, the, 528–30, 538, 542

Homeless Services Network, 528–30

Homer, Truman J., 279

Homer G. Phillips Hospital. *See* Hospitals

Homes of the New World (Bremer), 160

Honoré, Louis (Tesson), 45

Hooverville, 439–40

Hope, Bob, 512, 520

Hope House, 529

Hornsby, Rogers, 425–26

Horrell, Rev. Thomas, 95

Horrigan, Kevin, 546, 548, 550

Horse racing, 183, 186

Hortense Place, 346

Hortez, Joseph, 40

Hosmer, J. K., 321–22

Hospitals: Charter Hospital, 531–32; during Civil War, 251–54; City Hospital Number One, 459, 499–500, 502, 530–32; Homer G. Phillips Hospital (City Hospital Number Two), 423, 499–500, 502–3, 517–18, 530; Regional Medical Center (County Hospital), 531–32; St. Luke's Hospital, 471, 531–532; Sisters of Charity Hospital, 151, 166

House of Delegates, 351, 353, 365–66, 369–70

Houser, Daniel, 302

Houston, Tex., 332; as competitor of St. Louis, 477, 480, 495

How, John, 151, 170–73, 191, 198, 226–27, 229, 232, 237, 279, 349, 492

Howard, Benjamin, 101

Howard, Don Carlos, 67

Howe, Julia Ward, 322

Howison, George, 321, 326

Hoyt, Waite, 425

Hubert, Antoine, 30

Hudson, Thomas B., 140

Hudson's Bay Company, 60, 127–28

Huger, Benjamin, 76

Hughes and Company, 337

Humboldt, Alexander Von, 140

Humphreys, Solon, 292

Hunt, Anne Lucas, 206, 344

Hunt, Charles Lucas, 258–59

Hunt, Theodore, 93, 96, 104

Hunt, Theodosia, 214

Hunt, Wilson Price, 79, 85, 96, 110

Hurd, Carlos, 353, 415

Huttig, Charles, 355

Huxley, Thomas H., 322

Hyatt Regency Hotel, 525–26

Hyland, Robert, 506, 508, 510, 530

Icarian Colony, 417

Iconoclast, 358

Illinois, Indians in, 3, 5, 10–11, 19–20

Illinois and Michigan Canal, 160

Illinois and St. Louis Bridge Company: and James Eads, 285–92; and Lucius Boomer, 280–81, 284–85

Illinois Central Railroad, 207, 224

Illinois Indians, 20, 48

Illinois River: and the fur trade, 3, 12, 20, 45, 67, 110, 135, 159, 161

Illinoistown, 207, 278–79. *See also* East St. Louis

Immigrants, 82–83, 142–43, 155–56, 314–15, 338–39, 416–17, 442; dominant groups, German, 143–44, 155–56, 164, 314–15, 338, 416–17; dominant groups, Irish, 164, 225, 314–15, 338–39, 416; dominant groups, Italian, 417–20

Incorporation of St. Louis: as city, 118; as town, 402–3

Independence, Mo., 130, 135, 140, 273

Indiana: as territorial authority, 72–74, 76–77

Indian attack, 40–43, 405

Indians. *See* specific tribes

Indian Territory, 278, 326

Industry: major, in St. Louis, 437–38; production levels, 327–28, 330–33, 337–38, 528

Initiative, Referendum and Recall, 402, 409, 411

Inland Architect, 524

International Air Races, 427–30

International (Liggett) Building, 508–10

International Shoe Company, 437

Interstate Commerce Commission, 293–94, 398

Iowa Indians, 1

Irish, 140; and anti-British sentiment, 434; and riots, 169–73; and labor strikes, 314; and the vote, 168–69, 350, 410. *See also* Immigrants; Mulligan's Irish Brigade

"Irish Crowd," 93, 164–65, 168

Irish Emigrant Society, 166

Irish Rebellion of 1795, 86

Iron, industry, 199–200, 219

Ironclad gunboats, 282, 288

Ironclad oath, 262–65, 269

Iron Mountain, 199–200, 219

Iron Mountain Company, 200

Iron Mountain Railroad (St. Louis, Iron Mountain, and Southern), 145, 201, 218–20, 278, 292, 376, 437

Iron Rd., 200

Iroquois Indians, 3

Irving, Washington, 85

Island Number 10, 282

Italian Opera Company, 185

Ittner, Anthony, 299

Ives, Halsey C., 383, 493

J. C. Penney Company, 335, 337

J. C. Swon (steamboat), 236

Jaccard, Louis, 134

Jackman, S. D., 258

Jackson, Alphonso, 518

Jackson, Andrew, 103, 111, 137, 169

Jackson, Claiborne F.: and Civil War, 210, 228, 231–32, 234–36, 239–40, 249, 264, 315

Jackson, David, 126–27, 131

Jackson, Hancock, 231

Jackson, Jesse, 539

Jackson's Hole, 126

"Jacobins," 67–68, 264

Jails, 97, 132, 175

James, Frank, 212, 263

James, Harry, 353

James, Jesse, 212, 263

James, Thomas, 130

James, William, 321

Jameson, Smith, and Cotting Company, 285

Jaminet, Alphonse, 286–87

Janin, Fr. Pierre, 91

Jannus, Albert, 427

January, Derrick A., 191, 194, 226, 249, 418

January, Thomas, 344

Jefferson, Thomas, 110; and the Louisiana Purchase, 68–69, 73, 76–78; memorials to, 374, 392–93, 452, 455, 544–45

Jefferson Barracks, 133–34, 144, 155, 218, 253

Jefferson City, Mo., 117–18, 146, 203, 206, 211–12, 214, 233, 239, 243, 260, 299, 318, 502, 547

Jefferson Club, 351, 353, 362, 370

Jefferson County, 218, 478, 481–82, 493

Jefferson Hotel, 376, 452
Jefferson Junior College, 493
Jefferson National Expansion
  Memorial Association, 397,
  452–57, 512
Jennings, Mo., 476
Jews, 261, 338, 413, 416–17,
  475–76
John, Elton, 512
John Adams (steamboat), 164
Johnson, Andrew, 269
Johnson, C. P., 263, 369
Johnson, J. B., 251, 258
Johnson, Kathryn, 413
Johnson, Reverdy, 228
Johnson, Robert, 532
Johnson, Walter, 425
Jolliet, Louis, 2–3
Jones, Breckenridge, 346, 382
Jones, John Rice, 77
Jones, Joseph W., 136
Jones, Virvus, 539–41
Journal of Speculative Philosophy,
  320–21, 325
Joy, James F., 223–24, 293
Joyce, John A., 301–2
Judson, Frederick, 350, 353, 400
"Junto," "Little Junto," 111–12, 115

Kaiser Wilhelm II, 385
Kansas City, Kan., 327
Kansas City, Mo., 6, 140, 210, 215,
  220–21, 273, 280, 302, 340, 366,
  371, 393, 396, 440–41, 477, 480,
  536
Kansas City and Cameron Railroad,
  221
Kansas City Star, 371, 467, 516
Kansas City Times, 540
Kansas Indians, 1–2, 6, 30, 44, 102
Kansas (Kaw) River, 61
Kansas-Nebraska Act, 227
Kansas Pacific Railroad, 222

Kansas (territory and state), 214,
  223, 234, 252, 256, 277, 293,
  370, 387, 440
Kant, Immanuel, 320–22
Karsten, Frank, 456
Kaskaskia, Ill., 3, 5, 9, 11, 16, 25,
  31, 37, 40, 47–48, 50, 62, 77, 86,
  129, 135
Kaskaskia Indians, 3, 129
Kaskaskia River, 488
Kaufmann, Aloys, 459–60, 464–65
Kavanaugh, Bishop Henry, 264
Kayser, Alexander, 168, 186, 247
Kayser, Henry, 150, 154, 165, 168,
  186, 226
"Kayser's Lake," 154, 157
Kean, Charles, 184
Kean, Jefferson R., 452
Kearney, Stephen W., 247
Keckley, Elizabeth, 317
Keemle, Charles, 184
Keller, Helen, 393
Kelly, Charles, 367–69
Kelly, Margaret, 541
Kelly, Robert, 516
Kemble, Fanny, 185
Kemper, William, T., 452
Kennard, Samuel, 296, 346, 355
Kennerly, James, 96
Kennett, Ferdinand, 174
Kennett, Luther M., 151, 154, 157,
  165, 167–69, 174, 185, 206,
  208–9, 218, 221, 226
Kennett family, 344, 349, 368
Kenrick, Archbishop Peter, 264
Kentucky Derby, 186
Keokuk and Northern Packet
  Company, 287
Kerr, Matthew, 132, 136
Kerry Patch, 339, 353
Kessler, George, 393, 406–7
Kettle River Creosote Company,
  438

Keystone Bridge Company, 384, 387

Kiel, Henry, 408, 412, 422–23, 538, 540

Kiener Plaza, 510–11

Kiercereau, René, 19

Kiercereau family, 52

King, Thomas Starr, 255

King, Washington, 172–73

Kingsbury Place, 356

Kinloch Country Club, 344

Kinloch Telephone Company, 355

Kinney, Michael, 363, 408, 413, 445

Kinsey, E. R., 420

Kirksville, Mo., 440

Kirkwood, Mo., 208, 416, 445, 478, 480

Kling, S. Lee, 507

KMOX Radio (CBS), 506

KMOX–TV, 462–63

Knapp, C. W., 346, 376, 382

Knapp, George, 226, 285, 341

Knapp, John, 285, 310

Knapp-Monarch Company, 436

Knight, Charles, 535

Knight, Harry H., 428

Knights Templar, 290

Know-Nothing Party, 170, 172–73, 230, 261, 264

Knox, Samuel, 257

Kobusch, George, 368

Koch, Robert, 155

Koerner, Gustavus, 280

Kolkschneider, Henry, 410

Kosciusko Redevelopment, 469

Kossuth, Louis, 181

Kratz, Charles, 365–67

Kraus-Bolte, Maria, 324

Kreismann, F. H., 402

Krekel, Arnold, 261

Kreyling, David, 351

Krieckhaus, August, 304

Krum, Chester K., 369

Krum, John M., 154, 165, 180, 192, 226, 279, 294

Kuang Hsu (emperor of China), 288

Kuhn, Loeb and Company, 352

Ku Klux Klan, 314, 418

Labbadie, Sylvestre, 24, 30, 72, 102

Labbadie, Sylvestre Jr., 52, 89, 90

Labbadie family, 52, 63, 72, 89

Labeaume, Charles E., 228

Labeaume, Louis A., 98, 183, 188, 205–6, 225, 241

Labor organizations, 309–13, 351, 358–59, 442–43, 508–9, 517; American Federation of Labor, 360; building trades, 442–43, 463; construction unions, 508, 517, 527; Operating Engineers, 508; Carpenters, 508; Pipefitters, 508; Public Employees, 532; Steamfitters, 463; Street Railway Employees, 358–59; *See also* Strikes.

Labusciere, Joseph, 15, 21, 23, 33, 45, 48

Lackland, Rufus, 267, 342

Lackland family, 341

Laclède, Jean de, 12

Laclède, Pierre de, 7–14, 19–20, 23, 26, 28–30, 35, 48–50, 52, 93, 130, 404

Laclede Gaslight (Gas) Company, 267, 355–56, 450, 530

Laclède's Landing, 332, 512, 516, 519, 542

Laclède's Landing Redevelopment Corporation, 519

Laclède's stone house, 9, 15

Laclède Town, 468

Ladies' Union Refugee Aid Society, 246–47

Ladue, Mo., 478

Lafayette, Marquis de, 133

Lafayette County, 263
Lafayette Park, 16, 182, 268, 342–43
Lafayette Square, 343, 350
Laflin, Sylvester, 289
Laidlaw, Donna, 525
Lake Michigan, 2, 11, 45, 160, 202, 204, 223
Lake Peoria, 3
Lake Superior, 2
LaLande, Jean Baptiste, 129
Lamb, Robert, 213
Lambert, Albert Bond, 346, 427–28, 483
Lambert, J. D. W., 428
Lambert, Louis, 30, 33, 36
Lambert Field (St. Louis International), 429, 482–84, 489, 522, 533, 549; planning of, and the FAA, 482
Lamy, Marie Thérèse, 49
Lancastrian Seminary, 90
Land Clearance for Redevelopment Authority, 460, 468–72, 505–6, 520, 522, 529
Land grants: under Spanish system, 70, 73–74, 76–77, 79–82, 101, 104–5, 114–16
Landmark Banks, 507
Landmark Redevelopment Plan Corporation, 506, 508–11
Lane, Anne, 253
Lane, Hardage, 155–56
Lane, William Carr, 120–23, 133, 140, 145, 151, 154, 201, 226, 253, 447
Langenswalbach, 300
Langhorst, Ollie, 508
Larkin, David, 448
LaSalle, Robert Cavelier, Sieur de, 3, 404
Lasalle Park renewal project, 471
Lasater, Donald (Mercantile Bank), 502, 511, 518
Lassallean Socialism, 314

Laugel, Auguste, 182–83
Laveille and Morton Company, 134
La Vigilante, 64
Law, John, 4
Lawler, John, 509
Lawless, Luke E., 114, 176–78, 228
Laws of the Territory of Louisiana, The, 89
Lazzeri, Tony, 425
League of Cities, 406
League of Women Voters, 466, 477, 532
Le Bourget Field (France), 430
Le Dée, Jean François, 8
Leduc, Maria P., 93
Lee, Patrick, 68
Lee, Robert E., 149–50
Leffingwell, Hiram, 306
Legal Aid Society, 529
Leggett, Ronald, 541
Lehmann, Frederick W., 402
Leighton, C. R., 395
Leighton, George E., 321, 381
Lemp, William, 195
Lemp Brewing Company, 195, 330
Lemp family, 347
Lenox Place, 346
Leonard, Abiel, 198
Leopold (king of Belgium), 385
Letourneau, Amable, 33
Levee: extensions of, 119–21, 153, 158, 167–68, 266–67, 467; flood plain of Missouri River, 535
Levi, James, 522
Lewis, Meriwether, 81–82, 100, 110, 405
Lewis and Clark College, 493
Lewis and Clark expedition, 60, 81, 110, 124, 405
Lexington, Battle of. See Battles (Civil War)
Liberal Republican Party, 268–71, 299–301

Liberman, Lee, 530

Liberty Bonds, 435–36

Libraries: in the territory, 89

Liggett, John H., 332

Liggett and Myers Tobacco Company, 332, 436–38

Lightner, John H., 279, 304

Limits of Evolution, The (Howison), 321

Limpach, Fr. Bernard de, 32, 90, 93, 186

Lincoln, Abraham, 225, 230, 233–34, 239–41, 244–45, 249–50, 256–57, 260, 264, 268; assassination, effect of, in Missouri, 264

Lincoln, Mary Todd, 250

Lincoln Institute, 318

Lincoln Memorial (Washington, D.C.), 455

Lincoln Trust Company, 366, 376

Lind, Jenny, 157, 184–85

Lindbergh, Charles A., 395, 428–30

Lindell, John, 119

Lindell, Peter, 109, 136, 206

Lindell Grove, 236

Lindell Hotel, 181, 267

Lindenwood College, 493

"Linear mall," 505–9

Link, Theodore C., 294–96

Linn, Lewis F., 201

Linville, J. H., 284, 287

Lionberger, Isaac, 342, 345, 353, 373, 420, 445

Lionberger, John R., 282, 285

Lionberger family, 341

Lipton, Donald (Donn), 506–10

Lisa, Manuel, 60–61, 79, 83, 93, 102, 111, 123–25

Little, James D., 537

"Little Italy," 417

Livingstone, Robert R., 68, 452

Livres Terriens (land books), 14

Lock and Dam 26, 488

Loewenstein Jewelry Company, 338

Lofgreen, Peter, 310, 312–13

Log Cabin Club, 465

Loisel, Regis, 60

Lomax, Neil, 534, 536

Long, John, 97

Loretto-Hilton Repertory Theater, 495

Lorillard Tobacco Company, 331

Loth Jeans Company, 337

Loubet, Emile, 385

Louis IX (Saint Louis), 10

Louis XIV, 3

Louis XV, 10, 18

Louisiana: district of, 72, 77

Louisiana Purchase and Treaty (1803), 68–71, 116, 445

Louisiana Purchase Exposition (1904 World's Fair), 348, 363, 372, 374–77, 378–95, 402, 407, 427, 479, 512; "Battle Abbey", 389; "Boer War" exhibit, 389; Inside Inn, 377; Jim Key, "the educated horse," 389; "Ten-Million-Dollar Pike," 389–90; Tyrolean Alps, 390–91

Louisiana (state), 204, 254, 256, 274, 334, 437

Louisiana (steamboat), 150

Louisiana Territory: defenses in, 18–19, 22–27, 38–45, 64–68. *See also* France: empire of; Spain: empire of

Louisville Times, 467

Lovejoy, Elijah, 175–78, 180

Love's Labours Lost (Shakespeare), 89

Lucas, Charles, 112–14

Lucas, J. B. C. II, 356, 424

Lucas, James H.: and development of St. Louis, 182–83, 191, 199; and railroads, 203, 205–6, 213–18, 225, 236, 249, 258–59, 279, 341

Lucas, John (Jean) B. C., 76, 78–80, 82, 89, 106, 112, 114, 116–18, 132, 144, 179, 366
Lucas and Simonds Company, 197–99, 206
Lucas family, 186, 344, 347, 349, 357
Lucas Market, 311–13
Lucas Place, 182, 341–43, 493
Ludlow, N. M., 184
Lutheran Church, 144, 350, 433
Lynch, James C., 195
Lynch, W. A., 134
Lyon, Nathaniel, 226, 234–37, 239–40, 247, 433

McAfee, J. Wesley, 459, 465
McBlenis (O'Blenis), Robert, 189–90
McCall, Mrs. Louis M., 380–81
McClellan, George B., 257–58, 260–61
McClure's, 357, 367–68, 388–89
McClurg, Joseph, 269
McConachie, Scot, 256, 358
McCullagh, Joseph, 302, 319, 357
McCulloch, Benjamin, 240, 246
McColloch, George, 157
McCune, John S., 226, 287
McDonald, John, 301–2
McDonnell, James S., 487, 492
McDonnell, William, 465
McDonnell Charitable Trust, 477
McDonnell Douglas Corporation (McDonnell Aircraft), 465, 486, 488, 492, 550
McGee, Willie, 515
McGuire, Dan, 509
McGuire, Fr. John, 413
McGunnegle, Andrew, 221
McHaney, Powell B., 459
McHose, Isaac, 195
McIntosh, Francis (McIntosh affair), 175–78

McKay, A. J., 219
McKee, William, 245, 266, 269–72, 301–2
McKelvey, J. N., 128
McKinley, Andrew, 306
McKinstry, Justus, 242–44, 266
McKittrick, High, 399
McKittrick, Walter, 346
McKnight, John, 130
McKnight, Thomas, 83, 122
McLeod, Nelson, 371
McLure, Charles, 344
McNair, Alexander, 82, 93, 97, 111–12, 116–17, 119, 130
McNary, Eugene, 481, 498, 503, 512–13, 516, 531–38, 541
McNeil, Frank, 367
McPheeters, Sallie, 248
McPheeters, William B., 247–48
McPherson, William, 285
McQuillin, Eugene, 362
Mackay, James, 60–61, 63, 73, 79
MacKaye, Percy, 403–6
Macon County, 217, 220
Madison, James, 101–2
Madison County, 432, 475, 478, 481–82, 493
Madisonian, The, 206
Madison Iron Company, 218
Maestre, Sidney, 465–66
Maffitt, C. C., 352–53, 358
Maffitt, Julia C., 306, 341
Maffitt, Pierre Chouteau, 191, 346
Maffitt, William, 341
Magrath, C. Peter, 547
Maguire, George, 154, 165
Maguire, Thomas, 93
Maha (Omaha) Indians, 1, 25, 59, 123
Maid of Orleans (steamboat), 134
Malaria, 119, 340
Mallet, Paul, 6

Mallet, Pierre, 6

Mallinckrodt, Edward, 345

Mallinckrodt Chemical Company, 437

Mamas and the Papas, The, 512

Mandan Indians, 59, 64, 123–24

Mansion House: apartments, 474; hotel, 108, 116

Mantia, Richard, 509, 516

Manufacturers' Railroad, 450

Maplewood, Mo., 445

Maramec Iron Works, 199, 201

Marechal family, 62

Marest, Fr. Gabriel, 3

Marguerite v. Chouteau, 24

Maritz, William, 511, 516, 518–19, 553

Marmaduke, John S., 310, 313

Maroney, Andrew, 370

Marquard, Henry C., 219

Marquette, Fr. Jacques, 2–3

Marriott Pavilion Hotel, 471, 516

Martigny, Jean Baptiste, 22–23, 30, 35, 40

Martin, J. L. (Pepper), 432

Martineau, Harriet, 178

Martorelli, Jack, 508

Marx, Karl, 322

Marx and Haas Jeans Company, 337

Mary Institute, 341

Maryville College, 493

Mason, William P., 179

Massey, Samuel, 201

Matchekewis, Chief, 40

Mathewson, Christy, 425

Matlock, White, 108

Matthews, Lawrence, 189–90

Maxent, Gilbert Antoine, 8, 35–36, 51, 55

Maxent, Laclède and Company, 8, 20, 35

Maxwell, Fr. James, 91

May, Morton D., 465, 490

May Company, 335–36, 458, 465, 473, 520, 554

Meachum, John Berry, 146, 317

Meatpacking industry, 192, 328, 438; and slaughter, 146, 196, 328, 437–38

Mechanics' Bank, 198, 355

Medill, Joseph, 274

Medwick, Joseph, 432

Meehan, Eugene, 463–64

Meet Me in St. Louis, 395

Meier, Adolphus, 167, 205, 226, 277

Meigs, Montgomery, 244

Menard, Pierre, 59

Menominee Indians, 40

Meramec River, 5, 24, 48, 51, 64, 69, 199, 207, 378

Mercantile Library, 186, 233, 261, 274

Mercantile Trust, 314, 355, 465; Mercantile Bank, 474, 502, 511; Mercantile Bancorporation, 517–18; Mercantile Tower Building, 474, 477

Mercantilism, 4, 20, 27–28, 33–34, 36

Merchants' Bank, 198, 233, 247

Merchants' Bridge, 294

Merchants' Exchange, 193, 215, 249, 274, 280, 290, 294, 302, 304, 399; Union Merchants' Exchange, 249, 277

Meredith, James, 485

Meriwether, Lee, 351–52, 362–63, 399

Mermod-Jaccard Company, 338

Merriam, Charles E., 452

Merry, Samuel, 154, 200–201

Metcalf, Terry, 491

Methodism, 95, 264

MetroLink Light Rail System, 549–50. *See also* Transportation and street railways

Metropolitan Church Federation, 477

Metropolitan Life Insurance Company, 525

Metropolitan Medical Society, 532

Metropolitan St. Louis Survey, 477

Metropolitan Sewer District, 477, 545

Metropolitan Square Building, 525–26

Meurin, Fr. Sebastian, 31

Meusel, Robert, 425

Mexican silver, 139

Mexican War, 172, 201–2, 405

Mexico, 3, 33, 52–53, 57, 64–69, 80–81, 111, 129–30, 169, 201–2, 329, 367, 386

Meyer, Ferdinand, 249

Meysenburg, Emil, 365, 367, 369

M'Gunnegle, George, 137

Miami Indians, 20

Michilimackinac, 40, 52

Militia: Creole, 40–42, 44–46; War of 1812, 102; in 1816, 102; in 1854 riots, 170–72; in Pacific Railroad construction, 208; in 1861, 235–38; in general strike, 312–13

Mill Creek Valley, 193, 207, 277, 288–89, 380, 421, 436, 458–59, 462–63, 468–70, 529

Miller, Henry B., 169

Miller, Steve, 523

Miller, Victor, 443, 449

Miller's Exchange, 193

Milles, Carl, 424

Mills, A. L., 205

Milwaukee Brewers, 515

Mincke's Grove, 207

Minneapolis Tribune, 467

Minnesota, 124, 159–60, 221, 226, 228, 277, 375, 437

Minnesota Vikings, 491

"Minoma" (Jefferson Clark estate), 344

Minor, Virginia L., 305

"Minute Men," 233–34

Miró, Don Esteban de, 24, 54–55, 64

Mirror, The (Reedy's *Mirror*), 353, 369, 400

Miseré, Misera (Ste. Genevieve), 21

"Miss Jim" (elephant), 408–9

Mission San Gabriel, 127

Mississippian culture, 1, 16

Mississippi and Missouri Railroad, 224

Mississippi Bridge Company, 279

"Mississippi Bubble," 4

Mississippi Glass Company, 437

Mississippi River and valley, settlement of, 1–88, 108, 133, 135, 151, 155, 158–61, 163–64; travel on, growth along, 177, 188, 200, 205, 208, 221–24, 238, 246, 266–67, 275–88, 291–94, 378–80, 398–400, 405, 423–24, 437, 481, 488; confederate blockade, 255; channel improvements, 149–51; "graveyard stretch," 138, 149

Mississippi (state), 254, 332

Mississippi Valley Agricultural and Mechanical Fair (1856), 185–86, 277, 372, 393–94, 511–12

Mississippi Valley Fuel Company, 450

Mississippi Valley Sanitary Fair, 255

Mississippi Valley Trust Company, 297, 355, 366

Missouri: and drive for statehood, 114–18, 122

Missouri: territory, 100–102; state, 334, 473–76, 488, 513, 536

Missourian, 242

Missouri Argus, 139–40, 176

Missouri Botanical Gardens
(Shaw's Gardens), 187, 306,
323, 380, 449, 542–44

Missouri Compromise, 233–34;
debates on, 115–16; enabling
act, 116; in antebellum politics,
169; Second Missouri
Compromise, 118–19; ruled
unconstitutional, 228–30

Missouri Democrat, 170, 173, 211,
215, 243, 245, 266, 269–70, 272,
281, 301–2, 425

Missouri Department of Natural
Resources, 507

Missouri Fur Company, 123–24

*Missouri Gazette (Louisiana
Gazette)*, 86–89, 97, 103–6, 108,
112–14, 116–17, 122, 164

Missouri Health Services Review
Committee, 532

Missouri Historical Society, 374,
391–93, 402, 544–46; zoo-
museum district campaign,
544–46; Board of Trustees,
545–46; education department,
545; new library, archives, 546

Missouri Hotel, 102, 108, 117,
317

"Missouri Idea," 370–71

Missouri Indians, 1–3, 5, 10, 25–28,
30, 55, 106

Missouri, Kansas and Texas
Railroad, 293, 437

Missouri legislature, legislators,
116–19, 146, 172, 198, 201,
211–13, 216, 237, 266, 269–70,
297–300, 309, 321–22, 371–72,
464–65, 473, 514–15, 536–37,
542, 547–48

Missouri News and Editorial
Service, 538

Missouri Nurse's Association, 532

Missouri Pacific (Pacific) Railroad,
153, 190, 201, 206–12, 214–18,
220–21, 224

Missouri Park, 341

Missouri Public Service
Commission, 378

Missouri Railway Company, 190

Missouri Reporter, 169

Missouri Republican, 122, 135,
139–40, 142–43, 148, 150, 154,
164, 167–68, 170, 173, 175–78,
183, 196–97, 199, 205, 226,
230–31, 234, 238, 242–43, 248,
264, 266–68, 270–72, 274, 277,
281, 288, 298, 300, 308, 310–11,
321, 357, 425, 436, 447;
Republic, 357, 371, 413, 435

Missouri River and valley, 1–2,
4–7, 10–12, 18–20, 25–28,
37–40, 52–53, 67–73, 82–84,
110–12, 117, 122–30, 133,
135–36, 143, 158–60, 161, 163,
199–200, 206–8, 218, 220–23,
239, 275, 378–80, 423–24,
488–89, 534; Spanish
fortifications on, 18–20

Missouri River Railroad, 214

Missouri State Militia, 242–43, 246

Missouri Statesman, 209

Missouri Supreme Court, 228,
262–65, 473, 541–42

Missouri Volunteer Fire Company,
167

Missouri Wine Company, 226

Mitain (consort of Manuel Lisa),
124

Moberly, Mo., 220–21

Mobile, Ala., Mobile Bay, 4, 38,
184, 219, 277

Mobile and Ohio Railroad, 219

Moll Company, 333

Moloney Electric Company, 436

Monroe, James, 69, 452

Monroe County, 481, 483

Monsanto Company, 437, 465,
486–87, 517

Montardy, Pierre, 23, 40

Montez, Lola, 185

Montgomery, John, 44

Montgomery Ward and Company, 335

Montreal, Bank of, 523

Montreal, Canada, 47–51, 89–90

Moore, George H., 449

Moore, H. C., 214

Morales, Don Juan, 68, 80

Morgan, E. D., 220

Morgan, H. H., 321

Morgan, J. P., 392–93

Morgan, Junius S., 285

Morgan's Raiders, 23

Morning Herald, 242

Morrison, W. R., 285

Morrison, William, 129

Morton D. May Amphitheater, 510

Motard, Joseph, 26, 28, 58

"Mound City" (nickname), 1, 154, 339, 404

Mound City Paint Company, 382

"Mountain Men," 126–32

Mua (Des Moines) River, 38

"Muckraking," 357–58

Mueller, Alan G., 514

Muench, Frederick, 143

Muench, Hugo, 346

Mull, William, 175

Mullanphy, Bryan, 106, 154, 165–66

Mullanphy, John, 89, 119, 136, 164, 166, 194–95, 238, 341, 376

Mullanphy family, 344, 349

Mullanphy Hospital, 166

Mulligan's Irish Brigade, 241

Municipal Assembly (post 1876), 351, 354, 362–70, 378, 399–400, 402, 409–10

Municipal Bridge and Terminal Commission, 399

Municipal debt, 150–51, 153–54, 188, 192, 352, 380, 420, 424, 443

Municipal Free Bridge, 399–402, 424, 432, 443

Municipal Opera, 406, 423–24, 432, 495, 525

Municipal Reform Association, 298

Municipal Theatre, 406

Muraskin, Jack, 401

Murphy's Boarding House, 167

Murray, Francis W., 572–73

Murrell, Edward, 367

Murrell, John K., 366–67, 370

Museum of Westward Expansion, 456

Museums (St. Louis area). *See also* Art Museum; History Museum; Missouri Historical Society

Musial, Stan, 458

Music: German influence, 186; blues, 553; symphony, 186, 435, 494–95, 516, 543–44

Musick, Abram, 143

Musick, David, 143

Mutual Insurance Company, 138

Myers, George H., 331

N. and J. Friedman's Company, 337

Nagel, Charles, 455

Napoleon Bonaparte, 60, 68–69, 92, 375, 397

Napton, William B., 214

Narrative of the Founding of St. Louis (Chouteau), 8

Natchitoches, district and Spanish administration, 20, 25, 55

National Association for the Advancement of Colored People (NAACP), 411–12, 413–14, 468

National Bank of Commerce, 355

National Baseball League, 425, 512, 515

National Education Association, 326, 391

National Federation of Women's Clubs, 391

National Football League (NFL), 534–37

National Guard Armory, 313

"National Guards" (militia company), 172

National Labor Union, 309

National Lead Company, 438

National League of Cities, 529

National Magazine, 348

National Medical Enterprises, 531

National Nut Grower's Association, 391

National Park Service, 456, 512–13

National Recovery Act (NRA), 442

National Register of Historic Places, 507, 522

National Union (Republican) Party, 260

Native Americans. *See* Specific tribes

Nativism, 164–73, 175, 237, 435–36

NCAA basketball, 537, 546

Negro Civic League, 409

Nelson, William, 282

Nelson-Eads shipyard, 282

Neutrality League, 434

New Deal, 442–45

New England: similarities with, 197; influence of, 143, 178, 215–16, 223, 225–26, 375

New Life Evangelical Center, 530

New Madrid, Mo.: district of, 17, 72; representation, 101; earthquake at, and land values, 102, 112

New Mexico (territory and state): and Louisiana Purchase, 70; and silver trade, 136; struggle for control of, 5–6, 18–19, 25, 129–32, 187; as trade route, 332, 334

New Orleans: battle of, 103; as beginning of trade route, 8–9, 13, 25, 30–31, 64, 108, 134–35, 161–63, 202, 333; and the Catholic Church, 92–94; as competitor of St. Louis, 372, 375; and capital removal, 273–74; French rule of, 60, 68; and Louisiana Purchase, 69–71, 80–81, 405; Spanish rule of, 17–21, 26–27, 34–35, 37, 53–55;

"New St. Louis," 363, 377, 380–81, 394, 422

New York News, 243

New York Sun, 257

New York Times, 429, 521

New York World's Fair (1965), 471

New York Yankees, 425–26, 458

NFL Partnership (NFL Enterprises), 536–37

Nicholson, David, 226

Nicolaus, Henry, 355, 366, 369

Niedringhaus, Frederick, 375

Niedringhaus, Thomas K., 345

Niedringhaus family, 347, 398

Niel, Fr. François, 90, 94

NIT basketball, 546

Noble, John W., 310, 347

Nolte, Louis, 460

Noonan, Edward, 352

Nooney, Gregory (Nooney Company), 447, 525

Normandie Golf Club, 344

Normandy area, 344–45, 478, 492–93; Lucas estate, 113, 186

Normandy Board of Education, 493

North American Company, 355–56

North Broadway Industrial District, 437

Northcliffe Prize, 428

North Elementary School, 315

North Missouri Railroad, 217, 219–23, 266, 281–82, 291–93

North St. Louis, 145, 152; in politics, 499, 513–14, 518, 539–40, 545, 547

Northwest Confederacy, 267

Northwest Fur Company, 57, 59–60

Northwest Ordinance Territory, 46, 72

Norvell-Shapleigh Company (formerly A. F. Shapleigh Company), 332

Norwood Court, 48

Note brokers, in private banking, 137–39, 197

Number One Busch Place, 330

Nungesser, Charles, 429

O'Blenis. *See* McBlenis

O'Brien's Coffeehouse, 166–67

O'Fallon, John, 111, 133, 136–37, 144, 183, 186, 188, 198, 200, 203–7, 218, 220–21, 225, 242, 249, 278–79, 344, 476

O'Fallon, John J., 346

O'Fallon family, 347, 349

O'Fallon Park, 307, 376, 380

O'Farrell, Bob, 426

O'Neil, Hugh, 137, 164

O'Reilly, Count Alejandro, 20–24, 31

O'Sullivan, Thomas, 209

Ober, S. R., 119

Observer (St. Louis, Alton), 177

Ockerson, J. A., 420

Odd Fellows, 290

Ogden, William B., 223–24

Ogilvey, Richard, 482

Ohio and Mississippi Railroad, 198, 206, 208, 215, 218, 221–25, 278–79, 281, 291, 294

Ohio River, 4, 22, 26, 52, 55, 108, 135, 154, 161, 192–93

Old Cathedral, 454

Old Courthouse, 180, 182, 452, 505–6, 510

"Old Crow" (bourbon), 332

Old Post Office, 542

"Old Stonewall" (bourbon), 332

Old Warson Country Club, 465

Olympic Games (1904), 386

Omnibuses, 189–92, 209

Omni International Hotel, 524, 526

One Bell Center, 506, 525, 527

One Centerre Plaza, 520

One Million Population Club, 396, 402

Operating Engineers Union, 508

Operation Breakthrough, 468

"Operation Brightside," 503, 517, 530

"Operation Safestreet," 503, 517

Opinion in the Case of Charles Lyons, Free Negro, 180

Oppenheimer Properties (of New York), 522

Order of American Knights, 258–59

Ordinance of 1785, 46

Oregon Trail, 453

Orleans, Territory of, 72, 101

Ormsby, Earl, 448

Orr, Sample, 231

Orteig, Raymond, 428

Osage Indians, 1–2, 6, 25–28, 29–31, 55–58, 60–62, 67, 81–82, 95, 102, 123, 130, 326, 404

Osage River, 2, 117

Oster, Donald, 403

Otoe Indians, 1, 6, 25, 60

"Ousting Ordinance," 262–63

Overland, Mo., 445, 478

Overstolz, Henry, 300–301, 309–10, 312

Owens, Robert, 62

Ozark Airlines, 489

Ozark (ferryboat), 149

P. and J. Powell Company, 141

Pacific Hotel, 174

Pacific (Missouri Pacific) Railroad, 153, 191, 201, 203–18, 220, 222, 224, 226, 239, 281, 285, 291–93, 332, 368, 376, 417

Pacific Ocean: and trade routes, 58, 110–11, 131

Paddock, Gaius, 180

Page, Daniel D., 193, 201, 203, 205–7

Page and Bacon Company, 167, 193, 197–98, 221

Pageant and Masque, 403–6, 409

Pain Court, village of, 11. *See also* St. Louis

Palm and Robertson Company, 208

Palm Court (Plaza Hotel, N.Y.), 525

Palmer, John N., 280

Palmyra Missouri Whig, 203

Panét, Pierre, 49

Panimaha Indians, 20

Papin (Pepin), Jean Marie, 67

Papin, Joseph, 24, 58

Papin, Sylvestre, 83

Papin family, 52, 72, 93, 349

Papin land grant, 306

Paragon Corporation, 510

Paramore, J. W., 277

Parker, G. W., 363

Parks: and playgrounds, 305–7, 397–98, 406–8, 459, 467

Parkview Realty Company, 376

Partnerships for Progress (UMSL), 547

Partridge, George, 225, 251, 255

Pasadena Hills, 480

Paschall, Nathaniel, 86, 231

Passage to India: as theme, 2, 57–58, 110, 201

Patronage system: in "county" offices, 308, 464, 497–98, 538–40, 542

Patterson, Deborah, 527

Patterson, Henry, 211, 213

Paul, Teresa, 215

Paul Chouteau and Brothers Fur Company, 124

Paxton, John, 108

Payne, Nathaniel, 119

Peach, George, 541–42

Pearce, James, 341

Pea Ridge, Battle of. *See* Battles (Civil War)

Pease, J. S., 141

Peck, Charles H., 213–14

Peck, John Mason, 91, 95–96, 105, 146, 317

Peirce, C. S., 320–21

Pekitanoui (Missouri River), 3

Pendleton Act, 270

Penn, Shadrach, 169

Pennock, Herb, 425

Pennsylvania Railroad, 211, 214

Penrose, Clement Biddle, 79, 95, 98

People for Jobs and Growth, 514

People's Finance Company, 443

People's League, 402

People's Theatre, 184

Peoria Indians, 17

Pepin, Jean Marie. *See* Papin, Jean Marie

Percich, Mrs. Raymond, 499

Percich, Peter, 540

Percich, Raymond, 498–99, 540

Perez, Don Manuel, 66

Perkins, Marlin, 484

Perpetual Insurance Company, 138

Perrault, Louis, 30, 48

Persons, Wallace, 483

Petite Prairie, La, 17

Petite Rivière, La (Mill Creek), 16, 31, 35, 96, 124, 147, 149

Pettis, Spencer, 136

Pfeifer, Charles, 284, 290

Phelan, Michael, 304

Philipson, John, 194

Phillips, Homer G., 412, 423

Phillips, Wendell, 269

Pickering, Loring, 174

Pierce, Henry Clay, 345, 373

Pierce, Lawrence, 365
Piernas, Don Pedro, 19–28, 30–32, 44, 51, 402, 405
Pierre's Hole, 126–27, 129
Piggott and O'Dwyer Company, 141
Pike, Zebulon, 129
Pilcher, Joshua, 106, 124
Pile, William, 280
Pilot Knob, 199, 218, 259
Pilot Knob, Battle of. *See* Battles (Civil War)
Pinet, Fr. François, 3
Pinkerton Detective Agency, 310
Pioneer Corps, 172
Pipefitter's Hall, 508
Pisney, Raymond F., 545
Pitman, Charles, 412–14
Pitzman, Julius, 346
Pius XII Memorial Library (Saint Louis University), 492
Place d'Armes (la Place), 13
Planetarium, 467
Planter's House (Planter's Hotel), 108, 181, 233, 240
Platte River, 127
Playground Association of America, 397
Plaza Square, 460–73
Poelker, John, 471, 488, 497, 505
Police Board, 171–73, 233, 235, 242, 265, 312–13, 351, 353, 359, 370, 415–16, 498, 502
Polizzi, Fr. Salvatore, 419
Polk, James K., 150
Polk, Mrs. Trusten, 247
Polk, Trusten, 226–28, 247
Polyhymnia Society, 186
Ponca Indians, 25, 59–60, 123
Population. *See* Censuses; Immigrants
Poro Beauty College, 443
Portell, Marie, 472

Portland Place, 346–48, 478
Port of St. Louis: authority of, 487–89
Post, S. S., 281, 284
Post-Dispatch. See St. Louis Post-Dispatch
Pottawatomie Indians, 45
Pouré, Eugene (Beausoliel), 23, 30, 40, 45, 62
Powder River, 488
Powell Symphony Hall, 495
Powerhouse Restaurant, 524
Prairie des Noyers, 17, 51
Pratte, Bernard, 93, 98, 110–11, 115–16, 118, 128, 278
Pratte, Bernard Jr., 152, 165, 183
Pratte and Vasquez Fur Company, 124
Pratte family, 183, 349
Preetorius, Edward, 410
Preetorius, Emil, 263, 266, 351, 359, 388
Presbyterians, 95, 349
Price, Sterling, 210, 219–20, 233, 238, 241, 246, 249, 258–60
Pride of St. Louis Redevelopment Corporation, 508–10, 549
Priest, Henry F., 368
Primm, Wilson, 165
Princeton University, 349
Progressives: and reform, 357–58, 363–72, 396–407, 420–24
Prohibition, 418, 436, 445
Prostitution, 167, 174, 265
Provident Association, 443
Provost, Étienne, 126
Pruitt-Igoe, 461–64, 512
Public Employee's Union, 532
Public housing, 458–64, 473, 485–86, 499, 512, 529–30, 542. *See also* individual projects
Public library, 467
Public markets, 13, 99, 132

Public Ownership Party, 362, 399
Public Recreation Committee, 397
Public Works Administration, 444
Pulitzer, Joseph, 269, 272, 299, 303, 356–57
Pulitzer Prize, 449
Pu Lun (prince of China), 388

Quakers, 418
Quality Row, 132
Quantress (Quantrill), William C., 258
Quarantine Island, 156
Queeny, Edgar M., 465
Queeny Park, 494
Quincy, Ill., 135, 280, 380
Quincy College, 491

Radical Republicans, 211, 216, 219–20, 250–51, 256–63, 265–71, 281, 298–302, 309, 315–19, 412–13, 435–36
Radisson Hotel, 516
Radisson–St. Louis Hotel, 472
Raiche, Stephen, 395
Railroads, 200–225, 327–28, 488, 522, 536; and Gasconade bridge disaster, 209, 239, 281; strikes on, 310. *See also* individual railroads
Ralston-Purina Company, 465, 471
Rand, Edgar, 465
Rankin, David, 210
Rankin, Robert, 134
Rassieur, Leo, 413
Raton Pass, 130
Raven, Peter, 542–43
Ray, E. Lansing, 428
Rea, George H., 212–16
Read, Joseph C., 219
Real Estate: ownership, restrictions on, 342, 412–14
Real Estate Exchange, 411
Real Estate Row, 507, 510, 549

Reavis, Logan U., 273–75
Rebstock and Company, 332
Rector, William, 83, 96, 116
Reed, Hiram, 243
Reed, James A., 371
Reedy, William M., 353, 358, 363, 368, 371, 381, 394, 400, 410
Regional Commerce and Growth Association (RCGA), 482, 487, 492, 495
Regional Development Assocation, 510, 482
Regional Health Care Corporation (RHCC), 531–32
Regional Medical Center. *See* Hospitals
Reilhe, Antoine, 58
Reily, J. I., 165
Renault, Philippe, 5
Report of a Journey to the Western States of North America (Duden), 143
Republican Party, 227, 230–32, 249, 260, 265, 268–71, 274, 305, 314, 349–50, 353–54, 362, 371, 402, 409–10, 413, 444–45, 477, 501–2, 518, 538, 540–41
Revels, Hiram H., 317
Reynolds, Thomas C., 226, 228, 231, 233, 240
Rice, Rev. Larry, 530, 538
Rice-Stix Company, 335–36
Richardson, H. H., 295
Richmond Heights, Mo., 445
Riddick, Thomas Fiveash, 95, 100, 104, 107, 116, 315
Ridgeley, Stephen, 212
Rigauche, Marie, 90
Riley, James, 286
Riots, 166–67, 169–73, 175–76; and Riot Act of 1855, 172–73
Riú, Don Francisco, 18–19
Roberts, John C., 371
Roberts, Michael, 539–40

Roberts, Johnson and Rand (International) Shoe Company, 371

Robertson, Frank, 454

Robertson, George, 368

Robertson, William, 454

Robertson Aircraft Company, 454

Robidoux, Antoine, 128

Robidoux, Joseph, 58, 60, 66

Robidoux, Papin, Chouteau, and Berthold Fur Company, 124

Robidoux family, 93

Robinson, John, 289

Rock Island Railroad, 224, 280, 297, 347

Rocky Mountain Fur Company, 127–28

Rocky Mountains, 58–60, 69, 103, 110, 126–32, 201, 222

Roddy, Clara, 515

Roddy, Joseph E., 499, 515

Rogers, Will, 551

Rollins, James S., 198, 265

Rombauer, R. E., 213, 299, 319

Roos, Lawrence, 482

Roosevelt, Franklin D., 436, 445, 452–53

Roosevelt, James, 255

Roosevelt, Theodore, 357, 369–71, 385–86, 407

Roosevelt Field (N.Y.), 429

Rosati, Fr. Joseph, 93–94

Rosecrans, W. S., 258

Rotchford, Professor, 90

Rothchild, House of, 200

Rouse Corporation, 523–24

Rowe, Thomas J., 369

Roy, Antoine, 96

Royce, Josiah, 320

Rumbold, Charlotte, 397, 403–4

Russell, Ann C., 206

Russell, Ernest J., 420

Russell, William, 112, 206

Ruth, G. H. "Babe," 425–26

Ryan Aircraft Company, 428

S. B. Lowe and Company, 208

S. Grobinsky Company, 337

Saarinen, Eero: and the Gateway Arch, 455, 457, 505

Sacred Heart Order, 93

Saengerbund (choral club), 186

Sage, Russell, 293

St. Ambrose Catholic Church, 417–18

St. Andrews, 63

St. Ange de Bellerive, Louis, 11, 15, 19–25, 30, 41

St. Ann, Mo., 478

St. Charles, Mo., 62–64, 67, 86, 94, 105; district of, 72, 74, 82; temporary capital, 117; county of, 101, 103, 220, 416, 478, 480–81

St. Charles Democrat, 261

St. Clair, Arthur, 54

Ste. Genevieve, Mo., 5, 8, 11, 17, 21–22, 25, 27, 31, 40–41, 48, 51, 72, 86, 91, 101, 111

St. Grasse, Hyacinthe, 58

St. Joseph, Mo., 198, 238, 328

St. Joseph River, 20, 45

St. Lawrence River, 2

St. Louis (steamboat), 156

St. Louis Academy, 90–91

St. Louis Academy of Science, 187

St. Louis and Cedar Rapids Railroad, 220

St. Louis and Illinois Bridge Company, 279, 281, 285

St. Louis and Pacific Fast Freight Company, 215–16; White Line of, 214–16

St. Louis and San Francisco Railroad, 376, 437, 450

St. Louis and Suburban Railroad, 355, 359–60, 365, 367, 369

St. Louis and Vincennes Railroad, 221

St. Louis Blues, 491, 548–49

St. Louis Brewer's Association, 355, 365

St. Louis Brewery, 194

St. Louis Bridge Company, 292

St. Louis Browns, 425, 458, 489; as Brown Stockings, 425

St. Louis Business Journal, 508

St. Louis Car Company, 428, 437

St. Louis Cardinals (baseball), 425–27, 430–32, 457–58, 485, 489–91, 515–16, 519–20, 549

St. Louis Cardinals "Big Red" (football), 458, 490–92, 534–36

St. Louis Centre, 518–22, 525, 527–28, 542, 549

St. Louis Club, 363, 465

St. Louis Community College, 491, 493

St. Louis Community Development Agency (CDA), 474, 508, 527

St. Louis Compress Company, 277

St. Louis Corset Company, 337

St. Louis Country Club, 347, 375, 465, 478

St. Louis County: and city-county consolidation, 299–300, 303, 447, 477; and city-county separation, 299–300, 303–4, 306–9, 477–78, 480–81, 542; conflict with city, 297–301, 476–78, 481–84, 533–34; cooperation with city, 512, 516, 531–33, 541; population growth of, 476–78, 551

St. Louis Daily Press, 273

St. Louis Directory, 94, 108, 124, 135

St. Louis Dispatch, 266, 268, 298, 307

St. Louis Enquirer, 108, 110, 125, 127

St. Louis Flying Club, 428

St. Louis Gas Light Company, 138–39, 153, 188, 267

St. Louis Globe (Globe-Democrat), 301–2, 308, 310, 357, 371, 399, 402, 412, 428–29, 437, 449, 465, 489, 500, 510, 532, 550

St. Louis Grays, 172, 207, 234–35

St. Louis Hills, 447

St. Louis Industrial District, 432, 437

St. Louis Landmarks Association, 507, 509–10, 548

St. Louis Normal School, 324

St. Louis Observer, 176–77

St. Louis Philharmonic Society, 186

St. Louis Post-Dispatch, 272, 353, 356–58, 367–69, 371, 374, 389, 394, 399, 402, 421, 428, 448–49, 455, 466–67, 471, 482–83, 499, 502, 507, 509–10, 514, 518, 522, 532, 535–36, 539, 546, 550

St. Louis Provident Society, 251

St. Louis Railway Company, 191

St. Louis Regional Convention and Sports Complex Authority, 536–37

St. Louis Register, 108

St. Louis Republic, 357–58, 371, 376, 400, 413–14, 434–35

St. Louis Research Council, 482

St. Louis Reveille, 167

St. Louis Sanitary Company, 364

St. Louis School of Fine Arts, 382

St. Louis Smelting and Refining Company, 418

St. Louis Star (Star-Times), 365, 371, 421, 434, 449

St. Louis Station Associates, 523, 525

St. Louis Steamers, 491

St. Louis Sun, 550

St. Louis Symphony Orchestra, 435, 494, 516, 543–44

St. Louis the Crusader, 393, 544

St. Louis Theatre, 182, 184

St. Louis, The Future Great City of the World (Reavis), 273, 275

St. Louis Times, 266, 268, 303, 310, 371

St. Louis Transit Company, 356, 358–59, 365–66, 377

St. Louis Union, 174, 245, 248

St. Louis Union Trust Company, 355, 465

Saint Louis University, 165, 349, 468, 477, 491–93, 502, 546, 547; medical school of, 165, 172, 186, 502, 530

St. Luke's Hospital. *See* Hospitals

St. Martin, Pierre, 90

St. Mary's of the Barrens (Perryville), 91

St. Vincent DePaul Society, 443

St. Vrain, Ceran, 130

St. Vrain, Jacques, 67, 70, 77, 79, 98, 194

Salcedo, Don Manuel de, 61, 68

Salisbury, Mary, 315

Salt River, 104

Salvation Army, 443, 529

Samuel, August A., 355

San Diego Zoo, 484

Sanford, John F. A., 228

Sanguinet, Charles, 58, 61

Santa Fe, N.M.: and trade route, 5, 102, 128–30, 186–87

Sanwa Bank (Toyko), 537

Sarpy, Gregoire, 61, 98

Sarpy, John B., 205

Sarpy family, 52, 72, 93, 183, 349

Saugrain, Antoine, 89, 92, 104

Sauk and Fox Indians, 2, 20, 41–45, 55, 74, 82, 102

Saukenuk village, 44

Savine, Fr. Francis, 91

Sawyer, Samuel, 317

Scammon, J. Young, 223–24

Scanlan, Mary, 297, 344

Scanlan, Philip, 397–98, 406–7

Scharf, J. Thomas, 272

Schewe, Christopher, 143

Schewe, Frederich, 90

Schiele, Charles, 332

Schoemehl, Vincent C., 499–503, 539–42; and civic improvements, 507–10, 513–18, 520, 528–29, 548–49; and health care, 530–33; and football team, 536–38

Schofield, John M., 246, 249–50

Schoolcraft, Henry Rowe, 110

Schools. *See* Education

Schuettner, Nicholas, 236

Schuler's Hall, 313–14

Schultz, Christian, 82, 83

Schurz, Carl, 266, 269–71, 371, 388

Schwab Clothing Company, 337

Schwarz, Frank, 407

Scientific Design, 549

Scott, Dred, 228–30

Scott, Jesup W., 273

Scott, John, 111, 115, 118

Scott, Thomas, 211, 214, 291, 293

Scott, William, 228

Scott and Rule Company, 133, 136, 141

Scullin, John, 358, 369, 376, 382, 400, 438

Scullin Steel, 438

Scully, Vincent, 507

Sealsfield, Charles, 133

Sears-Roebuck Company, 335

Seminole Wars, 176

Senter, W. M., 277

Seward, William H., 230

Sewers, 148, 153–57, 267, 477

Seymour, Horatio, 268

Shanahan, Michael, 548

Shannon's Coffeehouse, 167

Shaw, Henry, 141, 187, 226, 306

Shaw and Cross Company, 141

Shawnee Indians, 66, 102

Shaw's Gardens. *See* Missouri
    Botanical Gardens

Shelby, Joseph, 210, 219

Shepherd of the Valley, 177

Shepherdess (steamboat), 149

Shepley, Ethan A. H., 465, 492

Shepley, J. H., 308

Sheraton–St. Louis Hotel, 474, 516

Sherman, William Tecumseh, 191,
    236–37, 246, 254, 257–58, 261,
    264

Sherman Anti-Trust Act, 332

Shields, George H., 304

Shiloh, Battle of. *See* Battles (Civil
    War)

Shoes: manufacturing of, 370,
    436–38

Shoshone Indians, 59

Shryock, Lee R., 274

Sierra Nevada Mountains, 127

Sigel, Franz, 236

Signaigo, James, 501

Simmons, Hezekiah, 133

Simmons, Samuel, 219

Simon, Herman, 520

Simon, Melvin, 518

Simon Associates, 518, 520

Simpson, Robert, 88, 100

Sinclair, Patrick, 40

Singer Brothers Company, 337

Sioux Indians: Santee group, 20,
    40, 42–43, 124; Teton group,
    124–26; Yankton group, 123

Sisler, George, 425

Sisters of Charity Hospital. *See*
    Hospitals

Sisters of St. Joseph of Carondelet,
    317

Six Flags Over Mid-America, 458

Skiff, Frederick J. V., 382

Skinker, Thomas, 306

Slatkin, Leonard, 543

Slaughter, Enos, 458

Slavery: abolition of, 116, 169–70,
    175–78, 228–30, 234, 236, 250,
    256, 261–62; of Africans,
    introduced, 4; and auctions,
    180, 233; during Civil War,
    232–34, 243, 262; emancipation
    proclamations, 243–44, 256;
    and freeing of slaves, 179,
    229–30, 245, 256; of Indians,
    23–24, 48; in Missouri, 17, 21,
    24, 28, 35, 43, 46–48, 62, 72,
    115–16, 133, 147, 169–70,
    178–79, 226, 227–34, 261–62,
    317; and treatment of slaves,
    180, 233

Slavery As It Is (Weld), 175

Slayback, Alonso, 357, 372

Slayback, Charles, 372–73

Slums, 339, 396–98, 445–47,
    461–64, 467–71, 529

Smith, A. J., 310, 313

Smith, H. Shaler, 221

Smith, Jackie, 491

Smith, Jedediah, 126–27, 131

Smith, John, 137

Smith, John B. N., 106

Smith, Kirby, 258

Smith, Luther Ely, 396, 400, 403,
    452, 454

Smith, Sol, 184

Smith, Tom K., 465

Smith, William, 83

Smith and Schroder Company, 337

"Smith T.," John, 79, 81, 85

Smythe, C. R., 212

Snake Indians, 58

Snake River, 128

Snead, Thomas L., 240, 243

Snider, Denton J., 321, 324

"Snowflakes," 245

Snyder, Robert M., 366, 368, 370

Social Gospel, 360, 400

Social Justice movement, 400–4

Sociales Saengerchor (choral club), 186

Socialists, 310–14, 402, 413

"Solar Walkers," 351, 353, 400

Soldiers' Homes, 254

Soldiers' Memorial, 424, 460

Soldiers' Orphans Home, 354

Sommer, Bruce, 474

Soulard, Antoine, 50, 63, 67, 72, 77, 79

Soulard, Julia (Cerré), 50, 144

Soulard district, 420, 458

Soulard Market, 169

Sousa, John Philip, 372

South Elementary School, 315

Southern Bank, 198

Southern Guard, 235

Southern Illinois University at Edwardsville, 491, 493

South Pass, 127

South St. Louis: addition to, 145, 188

Southwest: and trade route, 6, 129–30, 223, 226, 272, 334–35, 425

Southwest Branch Railroad, 222

Southwestern Bell Telephone, 465, 477, 506, 527

Southwestern Railroad system, 293–94

Spain: empire of, 2–7, 17–70, 75–76, 80, 129; fleet of, 64–68

"Spanish Mines": lead district of, 74

Spanish Pavilion, 471, 474

Spaunhorst, H. C., 212, 303

Spencer, C. H., 383

Spencer, Selden P., 413

Spirit of St. Louis (plane named), 429–30

"Spirit of St. Louis" (slogan), 422–23

Sports. *See* St. Louis Blues; St. Louis Browns; St. Louis Cardinals (baseball and football); St. Louis Steamers; Saint Louis University Billikens

Sportsman's Park, 457–58

Springfield, Mo., 240, 536

Stanard, E. O., 277, 279, 341

Standard Metropolitan Statistical Area (SMSA), 478–81, 497, 504, 528

Standard Oil Company, 309–10, 373

Stapleton, Jack, 538

Star Mill, 193

Starkloff, Max, 408

Stay Law, 107

Steamboats, 108, 134–35, 141–42, 149–50, 160, 173, 216; accommodations aboard, 161–63; risks of, 139, 149, 163–64. *See also* specific boats

Steffens, Lincoln, 303, 367–68, 370

Steines, Frederick, 154–55

Steines, Hermann, 144

Stengel, Casey, 458

Stephan, Martin, 144

Sternweger-Stoffregen Company, 333

Stevens, Thomas Wood, 404

Stevens, Walter B., 382

Stevenson, John D., 313

Stewart, Robert M., 209, 297

Stickney, A. S., 331

Stickney, Benjamin S., 213–14, 341

Stiefer, William, 435

Stifel, Charles, 341

Stifel, Otto, 355

Stix, Charles A., 403

Stix, Baer, and Fuller Company, 335, 465, 473

Stix family, 347

Stock, Philip, 365

Stockton, J. Roy, 425

Stoddard, Amos, 51, 54, 69, 72, 77

Stoddard addition, 188, 345

Stolz, Robert, 511

Stone, Edward D., 458

Stone, William J. "Gumshoe Bill," 370

Stony Creek, 147

Stouffer's Riverfront Towers, 470, 474

Stowe Teacher's College, 493

Stracke and Caesar Company, 332

Strauss, Leon, 525, 529

Strauss, Mary, 525

Streets: condition of, 121–22, 154, 157–58, 167–68, 352–53, 381–82, 467–68, 503, 517; naming of, 13–16, 48, 121–22; plan for, 145

Strikes: general strike of 1877, 310–14; transit strike of 1900, 358–60, 362. *See also* Labor organizations

Sturgeon, Isaac, 220, 226, 281

Sublette, Milton, 128

Sublette, William, 126–27, 130, 137, 139, 418, 488

Sublette and Campbell, 167

Suffrage, 269, 305

Sullivan, John C., 116

Sullivan, Leonor, 456

Sullivan, Louis, 296, 507, 524

Sumner High School, 319

Swasey, W. Albert, 507

Sweetwater River, 128

Swift and Company, 438

Switzler, William F., 262

Symington, Stuart, 456, 483

System of Shakespeare's Dramas, The (Snider), 321

Taft, William Howard, 386, 413

Taillon, Charles, 40, 45, 62

Taillon, Joseph, 23, 31, 35

Tallmadge, James, 115–16

Tallmadge Amendment, 115–16

Talon, Jean, 2

Tamaroa Indians, 3

Taney, Roger B., 228

Taussig, William, 282, 285, 288, 290–91, 294, 296

Tawney, James, 375

Taxes: abatement of, 464, 468–70, 473–75, 519, 527; after Civil War, 299–304, 308, 317–19; and federal restoration credits, 523–24; income tax, 464–65; during settlement, 70, 99–100, 151–53; and single-tax movement, 398, 409; at turn of the century, 375, 380; and zoo-museum district, 409, 484–88, 513, 543–44

Taxpayer's League, 304, 410

Taylor, George R., 191, 211, 214, 225, 230, 234, 246, 344, 349

Taylor, Isaac, 382, 393

Taylor, Stephen J., 495

Tebbetts, L. B., 355

Tecumseh (Shawnee chief), 102

Terminal Hotel, 522, 524

Terminal Railroad Association, 294, 327–28, 355, 377, 398–99, 401–2, 437–39, 449–50, 454, 456

Terrence Brady's Coffeehouse, 167

Teuscher, Louis, 303

Texas and Pacific Railroad, 293

"Thespian Society," 100

Third National Bank, 355

Thirty Years' View (Benton), 227

Thomas, A. J., 292

Thomas, James S., 175, 261, 265, 268, 299, 343

Thompson, Earl, 428

Thompson, M. Jeff, 219, 244

Thompson, William H., 382

Thoreau, Henry D., 319

Thumb, Tom, 185

Thurston, Lloyd, 452

Tice, John, 315

Tillman, Benjamin, 375

Title Guaranty (Lincoln Trust) Building, 507–10

Tobacco, 55, 62, 331–32

Todd, Albert, 304–5, 307

Toft, Carolyn Hewes, 510, 548

Tony Faust's Oyster House, 311, 330

Tornadoes: striking St. Louis (in years following), 1896, 343, 346, 350–51; 1957, 462

Tourism, 456–58, 484, 513, 519–20; and conventions, 391, 472–73, 487, 495, 526–27, 536–37, 550

Tower Grove Park, 268

Tracy, Charles, 292

Tracy and Wahrendorff Company, 141

Trade: and northern route, 159–61, 226; during Civil War, 255–56; and foreign markets, 291, 347, 349

Transportation: of goods, 135, 488–89, 550; public, lack of, 515, 549; of passengers, by railway, 190–92, 343, 345, 351, 358–60, 362, 522, 533, 549

Trans-World Airlines, 489

Treaty of Paris: in 1763, 8; in 1783, 45

Treaty of San Ildefonso, 68

Tree, Ellen, 184

Trinity Lutheran Church, 144

Troupe, Charles "Quincy," 499

Trudeau, Don Zenon, 51, 57, 60, 66, 79, 94

Truman Sports Complex, 536

Trusheim, H. Edwin, 506, 509–10

Truteau (Trudeau), Jean B., 59–60, 90

Tucker, Raymond, 449–50, 462, 464–65, 477–78, 538, 540

Tufts University, 529

Turco Development Company, 510

Turley, Clarence, 465

Turnbull, B. L., 137

Turner, Charles, 352, 355, 358, 365–66, 368–70

Turner, Harry, 345, 366, 400

Turner family, 341, 344, 347

Turnverein (Turner's Hall), 232, 290, 310–11, 433–34

Tuttle, David, 119

Twain, Mark, 151, 216

Twain (Serra), 511, 516

Typhoid fever: epidemics of, 267, 378

Uhrig's Cave, 183

Ulloa, don Antonio, 17–21

Ulrici, Rudolph, 303

Unemployment, 309–14, 439–45, 528–29, 532. *See also* Homeless, the

Union Addition, 188

Union Army, 210, 236–37, 246, 259–60, 264, 274

Union College, 206

Union Depot Company, 291, 294, 310

Union Electric Company, 355–56, 438–39, 465, 548

Unionists, 173, 180, 226, 233, 237, 244, 248, 250, 254, 317, 413; conditional, 232, 234, 243–44, 250; and loyalty (test) oath, 245–47, 262–64; provisional government of, 240, 244–46; refugees, 246–47, 250–55; state convention of, 240, 245; unconditional, 232–34. *See also* Conservatives

Union Pacific Railroad, 210–13, 293
Union Station, 294–97, 365, 424, 505, 510, 518, 521–25, 527, 542, 548–50
Unitarians, 249
United Drug Company, 438
United Hebrew Temple, 545
United Methodist Metro Ministry, 529
United Railways Company, 356, 378, 402
United Welfare Association (UWA), 411
Universalists, 95
University City, Mo., growth of, 416–17, 427, 445, 468, 475–76, 478, 480, 485
University of California, 321
University of Missouri System, 492–93, 546–47; curators, 216, 547; intramural rivalry, 546–47; Columbia campus (UMC), 246, 546; School of Journalism, 385; Rolla campus (UMR), 493, 547–48; St. Louis campus (UMSL), 463, 490–92, 499, 546–48
University of Notre Dame, 492
Unzaga, Don Luis de, 22–23, 26, 39, 51
Upper Louisiana: Spanish Illinois, Americans in, 69–70; defenses in, 18–19, 22–27, 38–45, 64–68
Urban Development Action Grant (UDAG): development with, 506, 517, 520, 523
Urban League, 442–43, 532
U.S. Army, 133–34, 144–45, 201, 238–39, 244, 256–57, 259–60; Army Corps of Engineers, 90, 279, 288, 292, 488; Army of the Tennes*see*, 254; Seventeenth Army Corps, 257; Topographical Survey, 201

U.S. Department of Housing and Urban Development (HUD), 506, 517, 530
U.S. Department of Human Services, 529
U.S. Department of the Interior, 522
U.S. Sanitary Commission, 255
U.S. Supreme Court: on segregation, 413–14, 484; on tobacco trust, 332; on transportation tax, 378
Uthoff, Frederick, 366, 367, 368

Valentine, Fr., 32
Vallandigham, Clement L., 258
Vallé, François, 22–23, 28
Vallé, Jules, 200, 218, 225
Vallé family, 183, 341
Vandenbenden, Louis, 66–67
Vandeventer Place, 345–46
Van Dorn, Earl, 246
Van Horn, Robert T., 273
Van Nuys, Frederick, 452
Van Wagoner, G. C., 212
Varieties Theatre, 184
Vashon Center, 459
Vasquez, Benito, 26, 28, 30, 32, 40, 58, 93
Vastola, Edward, 531
Vatterott, Charles, 477
Vaughn, George L., 412
Vaughn Apartments, 461, 463
Veiled Prophet (VP), 372–73, 394, 403, 511–12
Velda Village, 480
Verandah Row, 182
Vest, George G., 375
Veuve Pescay's Young Ladies' Academy, 90
Vicksburg, Battle of. *See* Battles (Civil War)
Vide Poche. *See* Carondelet

Vierheller, George, 409, 484
Views of Louisiana (Brackenridge), 88
Villa, Thomas, 513, 541–42, 548
Ville, the (Elleardsville), 468
Vinita Terrace, 480
Vinton, Alfred, 186
Vivalla, Signor, 184
Vogel, John C., 219, 226
Voltaire, 13, 91
Von Phul, Henry, 96, 122, 143
Von Phul family, 341
Von Rippert, Kurt, 434
Von Starkloff, H. M., 346
VP Fair, 512–13, 515–16
Vulcan Iron Works, 312, 344

W. T. Grant Company, 335
Wabash Railroad, 278, 292, 294, 347–48, 368, 376, 413, 437
Wabasha, 40, 42
Wabash River, 4, 20
Waddle and Blanchard Company, 119
Wade, Festus, 297, 400
Wagner Electric, 355, 436
Wahrendorff, Charles, 143
Wainwright, Ellis, 195
Wainwright, Ellis Jr., 365
Wainwright Building, 507, 522
Walbridge, Cyrus, 350, 376
Waldo, William, 131
Waldorf Hotel (N.Y.), 330
Walker, George, 527
Wall, Robert, 268
Wallace, Charles, 511
Walsh, Edward, 137, 192, 198, 205–6, 226, 272, 355
Walsh, Isabella De Mun, 355
Walsh, James, 193
Walsh, Julius, 192, 292, 355, 358, 366, 400, 407

Walsh family, 341, 347, 349, 355
Walsh's Row, 341
Walther, C. F. W., 144
Walther, Otto, 144
Walton, Elbert E. Jr., 499
Wamser, Jerry, 501–2
War Bulletin, 242
Ward, Samuel, 200
Warner, C. G., 382
Warner, Charles Dudley, 216
Warner, William, 371
Warren, G. K., 288
War of 1812, 102–4
Warwick, Dionne, 512
Wash, Robert, 96
Washington, D. C., 72, 76, 202, 235, 240, 275, 419, 444, 455, 502
Washington, George, 64, 452, 455, 534
Washington County, 218
Washington Guards, 172, 235
Washington Monument, 452, 455
Washington University, 284, 321, 334, 346, 349, 377, 382, 286, 391, 393, 400, 448–49, 465, 477, 487–88, 492–93, 495, 502, 532, 546–47, 550
Water: supply of, and waterworks, 151–54, 168, 266–68, 378–80, 423–24
Waters-Pierce Oil Company, 345, 372
Waverly Place, 343
Webbe, Sorkis Jr., 508, 518
Webbe, Sorkis Sr., 508
Weber, Frederick, 143
Weber, William, 176
Webster, Daniel, 181
Webster College, 493, 495
Webster Groves, Mo., 446, 478, 480, 493
Wedding (Meeting) of the Rivers (Milles), 424

Wehrli, Roger, 491

Weidemann, Wayne, 489

Weidenbaum, Murray, 495

Weinsberg, Charles, 435

Welch, James E., 95

Weld, Theodore, 175, 178

Wells, Erastus, 189–92, 247–48, 267–69, 274, 280, 298, 344, 368

Wells, Robert W., 228

Wells, Rolla, 346, 349, 352–53, 361–65, 368–69, 371, 377–82, 391, 394, 397–402, 443, 465

Wellston, Mo., 416–17, 468, 485

Welsbach Lighting Company, 356

Wendel, George, 532

Wendel, Mary Collins, 532

Wentz, Arthur, 485

Wentzville, Mo., 483, 486, 528

West: and orientation of St. Louis, 5, 178, 186, 201–2

West, Thomas, 358

West-End Narrow Gauge Railway, 344–45

Western Journal, 273–74

Western Sanitary Commission, 251, 254–55, 314, 318

Westliche Post, 263, 266, 269, 299, 351, 359, 410, 432, 434–35

Westminster Place, 346, 350

Westmoreland Place, 346–48, 420, 478

West Point (U.S. Military Academy), 52, 246

Westport, Battle of. *See* Battles (Civil War)

Westport Industrial/Business Center, 474, 510

Westwood Country Club, 466

Wetmore, Claude, 367–68

Wherry, Mackey, 68, 98

Whig Party, 140, 146, 151, 164–65, 167–70, 198, 231–32, 261, 265, 270

Whiskey: distilling of, 108, 194, 301–3, 332; and Whiskey Ring scandal, 301–3, 332, 413

Whitaker, Edwards, 358, 360, 400

White, William A., 452

White Cloud (steamboat), 167

White Hair (Osage chief), 61

Whitney, Asa, 202

Wholesale trade: beginnings of, 108–9; in 1800s, 134, 141–43, 159, 180, 190–94, 255, 277, 332–39; in 1900s, 436–37, 440–41; and Folk campaign, 370–71

"Wide Awakes," 226, 231–32

Wiggins, Samuel, 278

Wiggins Ferry, 278–79, 281, 291–94, 297, 344

"Wildcat Chute," 182

Wilkinson, James, 54, 69, 77, 79–82, 97, 129

William Barr Company, 335

William Schotten and Company, 333

Williams, Fred E., 499, 541

Williams, Larry, 514

Williams, Walter, 385

Williams, William S. "Old Bill," 95, 128

Willing, James, 37

Wilson, J. C., 151

Wilson, Larry, 491

Wilson, Woodrow, 434

Wilson's Creek, Battle of. *See* Battles (Civil War)

Wilt, Christian, 83, 88–89, 100, 103, 106, 119, 143

Wimer, John, 165, 230

Wind River Mountains, 201

"Wings of Lead" (Crane), 430

Winnebago Indians, 40, 42, 44

"Wire Road," 200

Wisconsin River, 40

Wise, John, 427

Wishart, James, 157

Withnell, John, 144, 226

Wizlizenus, Friedrich, 186

Woerheide, A. A. B., 366, 376

Woerner, W. F., 346

Woesselhoeft, John, 186

Woodson, Silas, 270, 290

Woodward, Calvin, 325

Workingmen's Party, 165, 309, 311–14

Works Progress Administration (WPA), 443–44, 453

World Series, 425–27, 457–58, 515

World's Fair. *See* Louisiana Purchase Exposition

World War I, 432–36, 505

World War II, 418, 459

Wright, Frank Lloyd, 522

Wright, John S., 272

Wright, Uriel, 226

Wyeth, Nathaniel, 128

Wyman's Hall, 185

Yale University, 320, 349

Yeatman, James, 186, 205, 226, 239, 251–55, 317, 321

Yellowstone River, 59, 124–26, 135

Yellowstone (steamboat), 128

Yosti, E. C., 209

Young, Bob, 491

Young, Phyllis, 518

Young, Thomas C., 507

Zagonyi, Charles, 240

Zebulon M. Pike (steamboat), 108, 134

Ziegenhein, Henry, 352–53, 362–63, 367

Zoo, 307, 393, 407–9, 432, 459, 467, 484, 516, 544; zoo-museum tax district, 409–10, 484–85, 543–44, 545

Zych, Thomas, 498, 500–501, 509

About the Author

Born in Edina, Missouri, James Neal Primm received his B.S. from Northeast Missouri State, and both his M.A. and Ph.D. from the University of Missouri–Columbia. He is the author of *Economic Policy in Missouri 1820–1860*, *The Haywood Case* (with Abe Rautz), *The American Experience*, and *Foregone Conclusion: Founding of the St. Louis Federal Reserve Bank*. Primm was the curator's professor emeritus of history at the University of Missouri–St. Louis from 1987 until his death in 2009.